ENCYCLOPEDIA OF
TELEMARKETING

Edited by

Richard L. Bencin

Donald J. Jonovic

PRENTICE HALL, INC.
Englewood Cliffs, New Jersey 07632

Prentice-Hall International (UK) Limited, *London*
Prentice-Hall of Australia Pty. Limited, *Sydney*
Prentice-Hall Canada Inc., *Toronto*
Prentice-Hall Hispanoamericana, S.A., *Mexico*
Prentice-Hall of India Private Limited, *New Delhi*
Prentice-Hall of Japan, Inc., *Tokyo*
Simon & Schuster Asia Pte. Ltd., *Singapore*
Editora Prentice-Hall do Brasil, Ltda., *Rio de Janeiro*

10 9 8 7 6 5 4 3

10 9 8 7 6 5 4 3 2 1 PBK

Chapter 12, "Handling Objections," and Chapter 22, "Catalog Telemarketing," have been reprinted with permission from *Strategic Telemarketing*, by Richard L. Bencin, ISBN 0-915601-02-8, © 1987, available direct from Cresheim Publications, P.O. Box 27785, Philadelphia, PA 19118, 1/800-792-6732.

Library of Congress Cataloging-in-Publication Data

Bencin, Richard L., 1935-
    Encyclopedia of telemarketing / Richard L. Bencin, Donald J.
Jonovic.

    p. cm.
    Bibliography: p.
    Includes index.
    ISBN 0-13-275918-7
    1. Telemarketing. I. Jonovic, Donald J., 1943- . II. Title.
HF5415.1263.B46 1989   88–32110
658.8'5—dc19   CIP

ISBN 0-13-275918-7

ISBN 0-13-277062-8 PBK

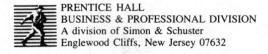

PRENTICE HALL
BUSINESS & PROFESSIONAL DIVISION
A division of Simon & Schuster
Englewood Cliffs, New Jersey 07632

Printed in the United States of America

To Tracy Bencin--wife, love, friend, and confidant

Richard L. Bencin

To Léon A. Danco, master communicator, who understood before many
why a marketer must also be a revolutionary

Donald J. Jonovic

Meet the World's Experts

(In Alphabetical Order)

ENCYCLOPEDIA OF TELEMARKETING

Richard L. Bencin
President
Richard L. Bencin & Associates
Cleveland, Ohio

(Editor/Author)

Richard L. Bencin is President of Richard L. Bencin & Associates in Cleveland, and an international consultant for direct marketing and telemarketing who has assisted many corporations in the U.S., Canada, the United Kingdom and France.

The firm's consulting work includes telemarketing start-ups, operations reviews and executive recruiting. Complete direct marketing program integration with telemarketing (including video brochure emphasis) is also a specialty.

His major clients have included the Xerox Corporation, Apple Computer, Maxwell Communications, Control Data, Combustion Engineering, Blue Cross/Blue Shield, B.F. Goodrich Company, Ohio Bell, Mountain Bell, NYNEX, AT&T, American Automobile Association, Armco, MCI, McGraw-Hill, American Greetings, BBDO, Inmac, BP America, Crain's Communications and many others. Some of his international clients have included Xerox of Canada, Rank Xerox, and Christian Brann (NYNEX).

Mr. Bencin is also Senior Vice President of Cresheim Management Consultants, one of America's 100 largest consulting companies. He is a former National Telemarketing Manager for the Xerox Corporation and Telemarketing Manager for Ohio Bell.

Mr. Bencin is the author of two other books: *The Marketing Revolution* and *Strategic Telemarketing*, both published by Swansea Press, Inc., Philadelphia. He is also a contributing author of *How To Create Successful Catalogs* (Maxwell Sroge Publishing, Inc., Colorado Springs), *Telemarketing: The Corporate-Caller Skills Program* (MacMillan Publishing Co., New York), *Telemarketing Start-Up Information Kit* (Direct Marketing Association, New York) and *Industrial Marketing Management: Cases and Readings* (Random House, New York). He assisted in writing, "Telecommunicating: its Potential Effect on Profits and Productivity," a comprehensive study of the emerging remote work force and its impact on markets and organizations (Electronic Services Unlimited, Inc.).

Mr. Bencin is also one of the most prolific marketing writers in the world today, with more than 300 published articles in more than 80 books, magazines and newsletters. He is the featured telemarketing columnist for *Direct Marketing* magazine and has served as a Contributing Editor with *Marketing Communications*. His contributions have appeared in such magazines as *Business Marketing*, *Marketing News* (American Marketing Association), *Marketing Times* (Sales Executives' International), *Advanced Management Journal* (American Management Association), *International Management*, *Direct Marketing*, *DM News*, *Telemarketing*, *TeleProfessional* and many others.

He holds a BBA in business administration from Western Reserve University, Cleveland.

Warren Blanding
Chairman of the Board
Marketing Publications Incorporated/Customer Service Institute
Silver Spring, Maryland

(Chapter 23: Customer Service Telemarketing)

Warren Blanding is the Founder and Editor of *Customer Service Newsletter, The Customer Communicator* and *Customer Care Calendar*.

Mr. Blanding is the author of 11 books on customer service, including the definitive *Practical Handbook of Distribution Customer Service* (Traffic Service Corporation, 1984), *101 Ways To Improve Customer Service* and *133 Ways To Handle Customer Service Complaints, Inside Selling and Telemarketing for Customer Service Representatives,* all published by Marketing Publications, Inc.

He is Founder of the International Customer Service Association and has developed and chaired seminars on customer service for the American Management Association, Canadian Management Association, Japan Management Association and 45 colleges and universities. Mr. Blanding is considered one of the world's leading authorities on customer service management.

In the late 1970's, Mr. Blanding developed his Advanced Customer Service Seminars, which have been attended by more than 4,500 managers from organizations of all types and sizes. He has also developed programs and has conducted training sessions for customer service personnel at 150 companies, including GTE, Johnson & Johnson, *Reader's Digest*, Abbott Laboratories, Sony, Mobil Chemical, W.R. Grace and many others.

Mr. Blanding is an honors graduate of Harvard and a veteran of the Ski Troops and intelligence work in World War II.

Richard T. Brock
Chairman
Brock Control Systems, Inc.
Atlanta, Georgia

(Chapter 17: Computers)

Richard T. Brock is Founder and Chairman of Brock Control Systems, Inc., which develops multi-user software and systems for sales, marketing and telemarketing.

Mr. Brock has more than 15 years' experience in the development of telemarketing of vertical market systems for the IBM, AT&T and DEC environments. He was the Founder of Management Control Systems (now a subsidiary of Prentice Hall Professional Software), a leading publisher of micro- and minicomputer software for public accounting professionals.

His major clients include American Express, AT&T Information Systems, Bell Atlantic, Cincinnati Bell Telephone, General Electric Credit, Hewlett Packard, Eastman Kodak, McDonnel Douglas, Monsanto Company, Northern Telcom, Polaroid Corporation, Rubbermaid, Weyerhaeuser and many others.

Mr. Brock is a Certified Public Accountant, and holds an MBA from Louisiana State University.

Ed Burnett
President
Ed Burnett Consultants, Inc.
Englewood, New Jersey

(Chapter 13: Databases and Data Banks [Lists])

Ed Burnett, during the course of his 30-year career in the direct mail business, has helped mailers select more than 2 billion names.

He is President of Ed Burnett Consultants, Inc., a firm specializing in direct mail consultation, compilation and management. He is widely recognized as the pioneer of many of the list marketing concepts and techniques used today throughout industry.

He was one of the creators of the business of list management more than 20 years ago. Today, well over 70% of all mailing lists are in the hands of list managers, many of the most successful originally trained by the Burnett organization. Mr. Burnett designed and implemented the 5th-digit SIC, now prominently featured in the directories of every major compiled business list marketer in the field. He originated the use of 5th-digit ZIP for sample selection, and he wrote (in 1963) the first commercial computer letter (upper case only).

Mr. Burnett is the author of the *Handbook of Direct Mail Lists & How To Profit from Their Use* (Prentice Hall). He was named MASA "Man of the Year" in 1978, and was honored with their L.U. "Luke" Kaiser Educational Award in 1983. The Direct Marketing Association's List Council also honored him in 1983 with an official presentation of the "List Leader" Award at List Day in New York, the first time such an award was presented by the DMA.

Mr. Burnett presents 10 seminars a year on the art of mailing list selection and use, and counsels such Fortune 500 clients as Xerox, IBM and AT&T on direct response marketing. He is a prolific writer for major trade journals, a frequent keynote speaker at industry functions, and has served for three years as a representative on the Technical Advisory Committee to the Postmaster General.

For five years prior to starting his own business, Mr. Burnett was a management consultant with EBASCO Services, the Management Engineering Arm of Electric Bond & Share.

ENCYCLOPEDIA OF TELEMARKETING

Dwaine L. Canova
Chairman & CEO
Canova Saunders International, Inc.
Pleasanton, California

(Chapter 16: The Bottom Line)

Dwaine L. Canova is Chairman and CEO of Canova Saunders International, Inc., a marketing consulting firm specializing in guiding companies that are incorporating telemarketing into their sales and marketing functions.

Mr. Canova has consulted for such companies as Sears, Citicorp, J.C. Penney, Centel, Bank of America and many others. He has been working in all aspects of telemarketing since 1969.

He is Chairman and CEO of Zacson Corporation, a full-service telemarketing agency with eight offices around the U.S. Zacson conducts business telemarketing and consumer telemarketing for major companies such as General Motors, Texas Instruments, Sears, Citicorp and General Electric.

For nine years, he was the Executive Director of the Center for Professional Studies (CPS) in Pennsylvania. His area of emphasis was teaching and consulting in the area of designing and using financial reports.

Mr. Canova co-authored the working notes that were used for five years in the Fortran classes for the MBA programs at the Wharton School. Also, he rewrote the operations training manual that was used at the Academic Computer Center at West Point.

He has conducted hundreds of accounting and finance seminars for managers. He was an instructor at West Point and was also a teaching fellow at the Wharton School, teaching Fortran to the students and administrator of the Wharton Game, a computer-based training model.

Mr. Canova has an MBA from the Wharton School, with an emphasis in the area of information needs of top managers. He is married with three children.

MEET THE WORLD'S EXPERTS

Connie Caroli
President
Telemarketing Recruiters, Inc.
New York, New York

(Chapter 6: Organization and Staffing)

Connie Caroli is President of Telemarketing Recruiters, Inc., New York, New York, a national executive search firm that specializes in the recruiting of telemarketing management personnel.

Ms. Caroli's experience includes extensive recruiting in telemarketing, direct marketing and circulation for clients including NYNEX, *USA Today*, Citicorp and Montgomery Ward. She has advised corporations on the development of corporate structure and organization, especially as they relate to integration of telemarketing into the total marketing mix.

She is the author of the *Telemarketing National Salary Guide*, and has written extensively on the telemarketing industry for national trade publications. She has also been a guest speaker at national telemarketing conferences, including the American Telemarketing Association.

Ms. Caroli graduated *magna cum laude* from the State University of New York at Binghamton with a BA in psychology.

H.B. Crandall
President
Crandall Associates, Inc.
New York, New York

(Chapter 6: Organization and Staffing)

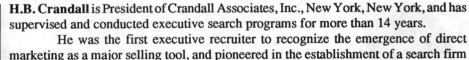

H.B. Crandall is President of Crandall Associates, Inc., New York, New York, and has supervised and conducted executive search programs for more than 14 years.

He was the first executive recruiter to recognize the emergence of direct marketing as a major selling tool, and pioneered in the establishment of a search firm specializing in the fields of direct marketing, circulation and telemarketing.

His articles on direct marketing, telemarketing and personnel recruitment have appeared in *Telemarketing, TeleProfessional, Direct Marketing, DM News* and *Zip Target Marketing*, among others, and he has been quoted frequently in *Advertising Age, Boardroom Reports, Friday Reports* and *Folio.*

A forerunner in the recruitment of telemarketing personnel, his monograph, "How To Evaluate a Professional Telemarketing Manager," is considered the definitive guide for companies faced with the problem of evaluating candidates in a field in which they have very little or no experience.

He has served as a speaker on telemarketing throughout the country and has been guest lecturer at Hofstra University and Hunter College. He was featured on the inaugural cover of *Zip* magazine as one of 27 national figures "who cares about the future of mail communications."

A graduate of Queens College, Flushing, New York, he served as a newspaperman before opening a direct mail agency. Prior to becoming a recruiter, he was president of a Wall Street stock brokerage firm.

MEET THE WORLD'S EXPERTS

Thomas A. DePrizio
President
U.S. Telemarketing, Inc. (UST)
Atlanta, Georgia

(Chapter 29: Step-by-Step for Startups [A Review])

Thomas A. DePrizio is Co-Founder and President of U.S. Telemarketing, Inc., Atlanta, a national business-to-business teleconsulting and teleselling firm specializing in the development and implementation of integrated telemarketing programs.

A former National Sales Manager for the Marketing Services Division of Dun & Bradstreet, Mr. DePrizio was instrumental in increasing the growth of his division to more than 500 employees nationwide, producing a sales volume in excess of $20 million.

During the 1970's, he was associated as Senior Vice President of Sales and Marketing with AMR International, Inc., a management education firm. As one of the telemarketing pioneers in the seminar industry, he was the first to introduce the concept of a four-level telephone sales department. Through his efforts, AMR was able successfully to build a telemarketing department in excess of 50 TSR's, producing more than $20 million in educational services, making AMR the second-largest management education company in the U.S.

As Vice President of Consulting Services for National Data Corporation, he was instrumental in the development and design of a new 250-position, automated telemarketing center.

Mr. DePrizio has lectured extensively in Europe, Asia, Australia, New Zealand and Mexico, and has been responsible for the development and implementation of telemarketing installations all over the world. He is also the principal lecturer on telemarketing for the American Management Association. He has been a contributor to *DM News, Telemarketing* magazine, *Target Marketing* and *The DeLay Letter*.

In 1986, convinced of the need for a network of highly personalized and tightly controlled regional telemarketing centers, Mr. DePrizio founded U.S. Telemarketing, Inc., to provide clients with closer company/client contact, geographic/demographic similarity and synchronized coordination. The firm now has operational offices in Washington, Philadelphia, Chicago and Atlanta.

Holder of an MBA from City University of New York, Mr. DePrizio is currently writing a book on the rising need for telemarketing integration with other marketing media.

William P. Fawns
Vice President, Information Systems
Zacson Corporation
Pleasanton, California

(Chapter 15: Reporting Systems)

William P. Fawns is Vice President, Information Systems, at Zacson Corporation, which provides management information systems for corporate needs, as well as order entry, surveys and closed-loop lead management systems. Client systems have been developed for a variety of clients, including General Electric, Pacific Bell and various high-tech companies.

Mr. Fawns has served as a telemarketing automation systems consultant to J.C. Penney and Pacific Bell, and is a former manager in the Computer Center at California State University, Hayward, where he worked with large financial and student information systems. From 1980 to 1983 he was an independent consultant on system design. During this period he designed and implemented numerous custom information systems. He has been with Zacson Corporation since 1983, where he is responsible for in-house and customer information systems.

He has taught programming for seven years at Ohlone College in Fremont, California, and quantitative methods and computer simulation for graduate students at California State University, Hayward, California.

Mr. Fawns, who is married with one daughter, holds a BS degree in chemistry from California State University, Hayward, and has done graduate work in geography.

Peg Fisher
President
Peg Fisher & Associates, Inc.
Racine, Wisconsin

(Chapter 24: Distribution Channel Telemarketing)

 **Peg Fisher** is President of Peg Fisher & Associates of Racine, Wisconsin, sales and marketing consultants specializing in the design and development of telephone sales operations. PF&A also carries out industry-sponsored research studies.

The firm's consulting work encompasses development of marketing strategy, design of support systems and training materials required to effect implementation, training personnel and periodic monitoring. PF&A also provides evaluation services for existing operations, recruiting services and packaged programs designed to teach management the ''how to's'' of self-implementing telephone sales functions.

Ms. Fisher is the author of two books: *Successful Telemarketing: A Step-by-Step Guide to Increased Sales at Lower Cost* (Dartnell Corporation, 1985) and *Planning Your Telephone Sales Operation* (Peg Fisher & Associates, Inc., 1987). She regularly appears on trade association convention programs, representing the merchant wholesale-distribution industry. More than 50 of her articles have appeared in industry trade publications.

She has served on various company boards, including the Editorial Advisory Board of *TeleProfessional*. She is former Director, Customer Service/Telemarketing Division, Universal Training Systems Company, a consulting and training program development firm in Northbrook, Illinois. She is also former Director of Training & Management Development, North American Operations, Manpower Temporary Services, Milwaukee, Wisconsin, where she was responsible for developing sales, marketing, branch and franchise management training courses.

Ms. Fisher holds BS and MS degrees from the University of Wisconsin - Milwaukee, and is an instructor at the School of Business Management Institute, University of Wisconsin - Madison.

Jonah Gitlitz
President and CEO
Direct Marketing Association
New York, New York

(Appendix B: DMA/Telephone Marketing Council)

Jonah Gitlitz was named President and Chief Executive Officer of the 70-year-old, New York-based Direct Marketing Association in 1985.

Mr. Gitlitz joined DMA in 1981 as Senior Vice President, Public Affairs, with responsibility for the Association's extensive government relations programs and public affairs activities. His work has been instrumental in increasing the stature and visibility of DMA with government and regulatory agencies.

Before joining DMA, Mr. Gitlitz spent 12 years as Executive Vice President, American Advertising Federation, in Washington, DC. At AAF, he contributed to the development of the National Advertising Review Board, the respected self-regulatory arm for national advertising complaints.

During his time at AAF, Mr. Gitlitz was also instrumental in initiating the AAF College Chapter Program, establishing nearly 125 AAF college and university affiliates across the country. In addition, he served as President of AAF's Advertising Education Foundation.

Mr. Gitlitz is also former Manager of the Washington Office, Code Authority, National Association of Broadcasters, as well as former Managing Editor of *Television Digest* and reporter for *Broadcasting Magazine*, both Washington-based.

He holds a BS degree from the American University, Washington, DC, and currently serves as Chairman of the American Advertising Federation's Inter-Association Council. He is also on the Board of Directors of the AAF, the Council of Better Business Bureaus and the Advertising Councils.

Away from his office, Mr. Gitlitz is an able and enthusiastic runner, and has, to date, participated in three marathons.

MEET THE WORLD'S EXPERTS

Gary S. Goodman, Ph.D., J.D.
President, Goodman Communications Corporation
Editor/Publisher, *Telephone Effectiveness Newsletter*
Glendale, California

(Epilogue)

 **Dr. Gary S. Goodman** is Founder and President of Goodman Communications Corporation of Glendale, California, a firm specializing in conducting sales and management training, and in developing customized telephone effectiveness and telemarketing programs. Blending practical experience with specialized knowledge of the behavioral sciences and law, Dr. Goodman has developed unique methods for enhancing telephonic persuasion within prevailing social, legal and transactional constraints.

He is a pioneer in telemarketing education through scores of universities and trade/professional associations. His "Telephone Effectiveness Library," consisting of four complete audiotaped instructional programs, has been used by business and the professions since 1979, and is updated frequently.

He is Editor and Publisher of the *Telephone Effectiveness Newsletter*, as well as the author of a number of books, including: *Winning by Telephone, Reach Out and Sell Someone, Selling Skills for the Non-Salesperson, You Can Sell Anything by Telephone!, Gary Goodman's 60-Second Salesperson,* and *Gary Goodman's Breakthroughs in Telemarketing.* He has also contributed original articles to publications such as *Marketing Times* and *Business Digest.*

Dr. Goodman has appeared on hundreds of radio and television programs, and was awarded a five-star rating for interviewing excellence by the Copley News Network. He was identified by the U.S. Navy as one of the 60 most qualified management consultants in America. He has also served as a consultant to major firms such as Beatrice, DuPont, General Foods, Polaroid, Upjohn, Wang and Xerox.

After embarking on a full-time career in telemarketing and management with *Time/Life*, he earned three degrees in communications, including a Ph.D. from the University of Southern California. Thereafter, he earned his Juris Doctor degree from Loyola Law School, Los Angeles, and is a member of the State Bar in Califiornia.

Dr. Goodman is a popular personal and professional communicator. His presentations are spiced with humor and are augmented by 40 celebrity impressions that he has perfected through 15 years of professional platform speaking.

Richard Herzog
Senior Vice President, Corporate Communications
Zacson Corporation
Pleasanton, California

(Chapter 4: Consumer Programs)

 **Richard Herzog** is currently Senior Vice President, Corporate Communications, for Zacson Corporation in Pleasanton, California. He has 18 years of marketing experience, and for the last 15 years, he has concentrated on direct marketing as a consultant, service agency executive and head of in-house telemarketing operations.

Zacson Telemarketing operates a leading telemarketing service agency fielding more than 800 telemarketers in six regional centers. Other Zacson divisions include consulting, computer systems, personnel services, fulfillment and research. Clients include more than 50 of the Fortune 500 companies, plus a wide variety of automotive, financial, industrial, high technology and retail organizations.

Mr. Herzog holds an MBA in international marketing and a Graduate Degree in management. He speaks frequently throughout the nation and holds leadership positions in several direct marketing organizations.

He serves on the Board of Directors of the American Telemarketing Association, and on the Operating Committee of the Direct Marketing Association's Telephone Marketing Council. His articles have been published in a variety of magazines and newspapers.

Steven A. Idelman
Chairman and CEO
Idelman Telemarketing, Inc.
Omaha, Nebraska

(Chapter 30: Telemarketing: Yesterday, Today and Tomorrow)

Steven A. Idelman is Chairman and Chief Executive Officer of Idelman Telemarketing, Inc., an Omaha-based outbound telemarketing company. ITI operates more than 900 phones, employs more than 1,800 people and is the second-largest, fastest-growing outbound telemarketing company of its kind in the world.

Prior to Idelman Telemarketing, he was Co-Founder and President of WATS Marketing Outbound, a company he built from its inception to more than 600 phones in four and a half years.

He serves on the education committee of the Mid-America Direct Marketing Association and sits on the Board of Directors of Continental Communications Group.

Mr. Idelman is co-author (with business consultant, Grady Dobbs) of *Managing Growth in Outbound Telemarketing* (Prentice Hall, 1988). He has authored articles on telemarketing management for several publications, including *Telemarketing* magazine, *Zip* magazine, *Financial Footnotes* and others.

He has spoken at many marketing conferences, having addressed such groups as the Chicago Association of Direct Marketing, the New York Direct Marketing Club, the American Direct Telemarketing Association, the Mid-America Direct Marketing Association, the Iowa Telemarketing Association and the Telemarketing and Business Telecommunicators Conference. Mr. Idelman also lectures at the University of Nebraska.

With more than 14 years experience in the telemarketing industry, Mr. Idelman has been involved with successful programs for many major U.S. companies, including Amoco Oil Company, American Leisure Industries, SafeCard Services, Comp-U-Card International, AT&T, MCI, McDonald's, U.S. Borax, General Mills, *Sports Illustrated* magazine, Bantam Books, *Inc.* magazine and Sears Discount Travel Club.

Mr. Idelman has been a leading proponent of strong backend performance, and a forerunner in the development of systems and techniques to enhance backend results. His system for tape recorded verification of all confirmation closes has been duplicated by several other firms and, as a general statement, his approach to the "back end" has become the industry standard.

Mr. Idelman is a native of Chicago, and presently resides in Omaha with his wife and business partner, Sheri, and their daughter, Alison, 11.

ENCYCLOPEDIA OF TELEMARKETING

Donald J. Jonovic, Ph.D.
President
Family Business Management Services
Cleveland, Ohio

(Editor/Author)

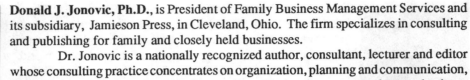 **Donald J. Jonovic, Ph.D.**, is President of Family Business Management Services and its subsidiary, Jamieson Press, in Cleveland, Ohio. The firm specializes in consulting and publishing for family and closely held businesses.

Dr. Jonovic is a nationally recognized author, consultant, lecturer and editor whose consulting practice concentrates on organization, planning and communication, particularly within the closely held company. He has been a consultant to business owners throughout North America since 1973. His research interests include advertising and marketing, as well as issues of persuasion and influence, particularly as they apply to marketing.

Dr. Jonovic is the author of five books: *Someday It'll All Be Yours...Or Will It? How To Survive--and Enjoy--Succession in a Family Business; Passing Down the Farm: America's OTHER Farm Crisis* (with Wayne D. Messick); *Iron, Industry and Independence: A Biographical Portrait of Courtney Burton, Jr.; The Second-Generation Boss: A Successor's Guide to Becoming the Next Owner-Manager of a Successful Family Business*; and *Outside Directors in the Family-Owned Business: Why, When, Who, and How.''* (with Léon A. Danco, Ph.D.). He also designed and produced (with Janet L. Halliday) *The Micro-Director*, a PC-based software program written to assist business owners with financial performance and market share change analysis.

He has served as Executive Editor of Cresheim Publications (published by The Cresheim Company, one of America's 100 largest consulting companies). He was Senior Editor for *The Marketing Revolution* and *Strategic Telemarketing*, by Richard L. Bencin, as well as *Technology to Payoff*, by Frederick J. Buttrell, Ph.D., all Cresheim Publications (an imprint of Swansea Press, Inc.).

Dr. Jonovic holds an undergraduate degree in mathematics from Marquette University, and received his M.A. and Ph.D. in communication at the University of Wisconsin - Madison. He is an adjunct professor of communication at Cleveland State University.

He lives in Shaker Heights, Ohio with his wife, Pamela.

Eugene B. Kordahl
Vice President, Marketing
International 800 Telecom Corporation, Service 800
Randolph, New Jersey

(Chapter 26: International Telemarketing)

Eugene B. Kordahl is Vice President of Marketing for International 800 Telecom Corporation, Service 800, an important competitor to AT&T in international toll-free services. Responsible for development of markets through promotion advertising, direct mail, telemarketing, seminars and direct sales, he is a director of all phases of telemarketing strategic planning, as well as human resource and database management.

Mr. Kordahl, who spends approximately 65% of his telemarketing consulting and seminar activities in the international arena, has been published extensively, and is an internationally recognized authority on telemarketing. His work has appeared in such professional publications as *Target Marketing, Direct Marketing, Fortune, Forbes, Wall Street Journal* and the *New York Times*.

He is Co-Founder and first President of the American Telemarketing Association (ATA), which consists of more than 900 members internationally. He is former President of National Telemarketing, Inc., of Randolph, New Jersey, and was involved in telemarketing management with AT&T and New Jersey Bell.

Mr. Kordahl is author of *Telephone Sales Training Systems* (1983) and *Telemarketing for Business* (Prentice Hall, 1984). He is also co-author and researcher for *The Annual Guide to Telemarketing*, an industry resource for statistics that has been published annually since 1980. He is a contributor to the *Handbook of Small Business Management* (Van Nostrand and Reinhold, 1987).

He frequently participates as speaker, lecturer, panelist, judge or committee member in marketing, direct marketing, business and telemarketing trade shows, and served as adjunct professor in the first American postgraduate course on telemarketing management at New York University.

Mr. Kordahl is an industrial engineering graduate of the University of Minnesota, and has attended Rutgers University and Fairleigh Dickinson University.

Peg Kuman
President
The Power Line
Port Washington, New York

(Chapter 5: Business-to-Business Programs)

Peg Kuman joined Publishers Clearing House Telephone Marketing Services in 1983, bringing with her more than 17 years of business experience, 15 of which were exclusively dedicated to telephone marketing. The agency changed its name to The Power Line in early 1987.

Ms. Kuman is one of America's leading authorities on telephone sales and marketing, possessing experience in both consumer and industrial telephone marketing, including outbound and 800 applications. She has successfully implemented telephone marketing campaigns and sales programs for companies ranging from large corporations such as Kayser-Roth, Panasonic, Bell & Howell and Chase Manhattan to medium-size manufacturing companies and non-profit organizations.

She lectures widely on the subject of telephone marketing, and is the author of numerous articles in professional and trade journals. She is past Chairman of the Telephone Marketing Council of the Direct Marketing Association, and is a member of the faculty for the Direct Marketing Educational Foundation Collegiate Institute.

Prior to joining The Power Line, Ms. Kuman pioneered telemarketing programs for Fingerhut Corporation, a Minneapolis-based direct mail and marketing subsidiary of Primerica. Before joining Fingerhut, she worked for Garden Way Manufacturing Company, a leading direct marketing company, and manufacturer of outdoor power equipment. Her seven years at Garden Way included managing their Canadian Mail Order Division, International Marketing and General Sales Management, in addition to successfully launching their 800 and outbound telemarketing programs.

Ms. Kuman holds a BA from Hartwick College and did her graduate work in business administration at Syracuse University.

Judy F. Lanier
President
SofTel Systems
San Jose, California

(Chapter 17: Computers)

Judy F. Lanier is a senior consultant who specializes in business-to-business tele-marketing. She has set up operations and designed training programs for a number of large corporations and many small to mid-sized companies. Her clients include Electronic Data Systems, Alcon Laboratories, Datapro Research Corporation, Ginnie Johansen Designs, American Automobile Association and Carlton Greeting Cards.

Co-author of *Step Up To Automation*, a book on the subject of computer-assisted telemarketing, Ms. Lanier also wrote and co-produced a video-based tele-marketing training series entitled, "Telemarketing Technologies," that is distributed by the American Telemarketing Association (ATA).

Regarded as a leading expert in micro and mini-based computer-assisted telemarketing systems, she has assisted numerous clients in selecting the correct system. A specialist in translating strategic goals into proper tactics, Ms. Lanier focuses her consulting activity on system implementation and training.

Ms. Lanier is a respected speaker at industry events and conventions, and writes for numerous publications, including a software review column for *Telemarketing Management.*

She designed and conducted a series of telemarketing management and sales techniques workshops sponsored by the University of Texas at Arlington. She has continued to lead workshops at major university business extension centers. Today, much of her work is involved with the set up and implementation of operations and systems, but she still enjoys delivering skills and motivational training to those she considers to be the keys to a program's success--the sales and service representatives on the front line.

Ms. Lanier is a graduate of the University of Texas at Arlington, with a degree in Russian language and education. She has taught at both the secondary and college level, and has done graduate work in political science at North Texas State University.

Michael J. Marx, Ph.D.
President
Selection Sciences, Inc.
San Francisco, California

(Chapter 7: Profiles of Telephone Sales Reps)

Michael J. Marx, Ph.D., is the President of Selection Sciences, Inc., in San Francisco, a group of organizational psychologists who design systems to help major corporations recruit, screen and promote top performers. Companies who have been served by Selection Sciences, Inc., include Pacific Bell, Fireman's Fund, Memorex, Hewlett-Packard, Hillhaven, Bank of America, Adds, Nice and Telemarketing Services Corporation.

Dr. Marx is the author of *Adaptive Leadership: A Manager's Resource Book* and *Adaptive Leadership: A Sales Manager's Resource Book*, and he has published articles in such areas as stereotyping in advertising, employee role negotiations, employee selection in multicultural environments and management training for employee screening.

Dr. Marx is currently involved in a nationwide project to develop screening and management tools for the telemarketing industry, including automated applicant screening, structured phone and face-to-face interviewing, TSR job simulations, automated employee attitude surveys and exit surveys, videotaped supervisor training in screening and performance management skills.

He was formerly President of the National Forensics Institute, an organization which provided training in speaking and research skills. He has also taught communication skills and organizational behavior courses at the University of Oregon, University of Wisconsin, University of San Francisco and Golden Gate University.

Dr. Marx received his undergraduate BA from Gonzaga University in Spokane, Washington, in speech and communication. He received his MS from the University of Oregon in rhetoric and communication. He received his Ph.D. in organizational communication from the University of Wisconsin.

Aldyn McKean
President, Actel Marketing
Editor/Publisher, *The Telemarketer*
New York, New York

(Chapter 20: Inbound Telemarketing)

Aldyn McKean is President of Actel Marketing, a telephone marketing consulting and training agency, and Publisher of *The Telemarketer*, an industry newsletter and the oldest periodical in the industry (published in English and French).

Actel Marketing specializes in the design and implementation of customized telemarketing programs, the training of telemarketing personnel and the creation of persuasive telephone presentations.

Mr. McKean is a highly respected speaker at industry events and conventions, and is one of the leading telemarketing authorities, inbound telemarketing in particular. He is author of the *Directory of Telemarketing Centers*, which is updated annually.

He started his career as Manager of Telemarketing for Treves & Company, a brokerage firm in New York City. At Wunderman, Ricotta & Kline, he created print and broadcast ads designed for productive telephone response. As Creative Director of Direct Marketing Services, an inbound/outbound telephone service angency and subsidiary of Young & Rubicam, Mr. McKean created telemarketing campaigns for Spiegel, General Foods, Lincoln-Mercury and others.

He is Chairman of the Telephone Program Board for the annual Direct Marketing Symposium, held in Montreux, Switzerland, and has often been quoted in such publications as *Fortune, Wall Street Journal, Los Angeles Times, Venture* and *USA Today*.

His consulting clients have included General Foods, Citicorp Diners Club, IBM, Dun & Bradstreet, J.C. Penney, National Liberty Life Insurance, the Telecommunications Administration of the Republic of France, Telephone Marketing Services, U.S. Telecom, Doyle Dane Bernbach and Spoleto Festival USA.

Mr. McKean's training sessions have been delivered for such companies as Polaroid, American Airlines, McGraw-Hill, the WATS Marketing affiliate of American Express and the Salesnet subsidiary of Dun & Bradstreet.

He graduated *magna cum laude* from Harvard University and received his master's degree from New York University.

Paul R. Mohr
President
Direct Marketing Systems, Inc.
Wynnewood, Pennsylvania

(Chapter 21: Service Bureaus)

Paul R. Mohr is the President of Direct Marketing Systems, Inc., of Wynnewood, Pennsylvania, a computer systems consulting firm that specializes in telemarketing applications. DMS helps direct marketing clients to use contemporary computer and telecommunication systems to reduce costs, increase competitive position and satisfy customer expectations.

Mr. Mohr has written several articles which discuss both automated telemarketing concepts and the industry's future for *Target Marketing* magazine, *Direct Marketing* and the *AT&T Business Report.*

He is a former Management Information Systems Consultant with Coopers & Lybrand's Philadelphia office. In this capacity, he performed information system engagements for a broad national client base. He is also a founding member of the American Telemarketing Association (ATA) and has actively worked to professionalize the telemarketing industry through the Association, as an ATA Board Member, Treasurer and President. He also served as an Advanced Telecommunication Instructor for the U.S. Air Force, Tactical Air Command.

Mr. Mohr holds a BS degree in electrical engineering from Drexel University, and a MS degree in industrial engineering from Lehigh University.

MEET THE WORLD'S EXPERTS

Gere Picasso
Principal Owner and Partner
Engel Associates
Chatham, New Jersey

(Chapter 14: Habitat)

Gere Picasso is a principal owner and partner in Engel Associates, a consulting firm in Chatham, New Jersey, that provides planning, design and construction consulting for high-technology, high-stress work environments on an international basis. She is an environmental researcher and office planning consultant specializing in telemarketing center planning and management. She has designed centers for the Office of the President of the United States, as well as for many corporations in the U.S. and abroad.

Ms. Picasso's firm offers a range of specialized project management services, such as communications and automation system evaluation; workplace design, vendor evaluations and project management; market research programs; real estate analysis, negotiations and site implementation; and center audits and evaluations.

Prior to forming Engel Associates in 1984, Ms. Picasso was AT&T's Senior Technical Consultant for National/Major Accounts, with applications in telemarketing, teleconferencing, intelligent-building technology and teletraining. While at AT&T, she also developed and managed a major research-oriented database on telemarketing applications. With her special focus on the environmental impact on worker performance for these centers, Ms. Picasso spearheaded AT&T's technical consulting force, providing design expertise for 150 major corporations throughout the country. In the U.S. and Australia, she developed several experimental model telemarketing environments, which demonstrated the relationship between work place satisfaction and job performance.

She is co-author and developer of the *Bell System Technical Education Course* for telemarketing center management, and the *Australian Telecom* course for Phonepower consultants. Her articles have appeared in such journals and publications as the *Journal of the American Psychological Association*, *Journal of the Environmental Design Research Association*, *Journal of the American Acoustical Society*, *Interiors Magazine* and *Facility Design and Management Magazine*.

One of her major contributions to the design of telemarketing centers has been her direction of a research project co-funded principally by AT&T and the New York State Center for Advanced Telecommunications & Technology. This study, done in conjunction with Polytechnic Institute of New York, looked primarily at the impact of both technology (automation and communication) and the environment on the performance, morale, job satisfaction, motivation and environmental satisfaction in some newly designed telemarketing centers.

On the basis of this research project and using its findings, several companies, including NYNEX, General Electric and *The New York Times* have developed new telemarketing centers.

Ms. Picasso obtained her education at Parsons School of Design, where she earned a BFA. She did continuing graduate work in environmental psychology at Polytechnic Institute of New York, with special programs in management at the University of Wisconsin and the Harvard Graduate School of Design.

John A. Pollpeter
Vice President and General Manager
Rockwell International, Switching Systems Division
Downers Grove, Illinois

(Chapter 18: Telecommunications [ACD])

John A. Pollpeter is Vice President and General Manager of Rockwell International, Switching Systems Division at Downers Grove, Illinois.

He joined Rockwell International in 1962 in Cedar Rapids, Iowa, and began a steady climb through its electronics organizations. From Systems Test Engineer, he became a Programmer/Analyst, and then a Supervisor of Software Engineering. In the latter capacity, he served in the field of navigational computer systems and avionics software.

Mr. Pollpeter began his active involvement with the design and engineering of automatic call distributors (ACD's) in 1973. He was a key member of the team that brought the first digital ACD to the business world: the Galaxy ACD. He soon progressed from Supervisor to Manager of Voice Systems Software, and then to Business Manager of ACD products.

In 1983, he transferred to Downers Grove as Director of Business Development for Rockwell's Switching Systems Division. Shortly afterward he was named General Manager of Business Communication Systems for the division. He was appointed to his present position in 1986.

Mr. Pollpeter holds a BA in business administration from the University of Iowa. He is a member of the Executive Advisory Council, National Communications Forum and was a keynote speaker at the TBT Convention in Atlanta in 1988.

He is married with four children.

MEET THE WORLD'S EXPERTS

Barry Schlenker
President
Schlenker Research Services
Morganville, New Jersey

(General Research)

 **Barry Schlenker** is President of Schlenker Research Services located in Morganville, New Jersey, a firm he founded in 1986 to provide custom and multi-client market research services.

His firm conducted the research study *Telemarketing Intelligence: The Current Use and Anticipated Growth of Telemarketing in American Business*. This in-depth study developed information on a series of topical areas covering both in-house (captive) telemarketing operations and service agency organizations. A national survey with a representative sample of adults to assess consumer attitudes toward telemarketing sales calls is also included.

Client companies include the two leading industry trade associations (Direct Marketing Association and American Telemarketing Association), telecommunications equipment and service companies (such as AT&T, various Bell Companies, Rockwell Telecommunications, ITT, Northern Telecom), computer hardware and software companies (such as IBM, Tandem, Texas Instruments), in-house telemarketing organizations in a variety of industries, consulting companies and many of the leading telemarketing service agencies.

Mr. Schlenker is a frequent speaker at industry meetings, and most recently presented the keynote address at the Annual Conference of the American Telemarketing Association.

He has held management positions with market research firms and manufacturing companies in his more than 25 years of market research experience. At the Dun's Marketing Services Division of Dun & Bradstreet, he held the position of Director of Research Operations, providing market research studies in the industrial/commercial area to many of the country's leading corporations. At Schering-Plough Corporation, his responsibilities included management positions in market research, marketing and corporate planning.

Mr. Schlenker received his education at City College of New York and Columbia University Graduate School of Business.

ENCYCLOPEDIA OF TELEMARKETING

Neal H. Shact
President
CommuniTech, Inc.
Elmhurst, Illinois

(Appendix D: Telecommunications [Peripheral Equipment])

 **Neal H. Shact** is the Founder and President of CommuniTech, Inc., the largest independent distributor of telephone headsets and the largest telecommunications peripherals dealer in the country.

He is a noted author in the field of telephone peripheral equipment. He is New Products Editor and a featured columnist in *Telemarketing Management.* He is also author of the first "Telephone Headset Round-Up," published in *Telemarketing* magazine.

CommuniTech was founded to fill the need for a distributor dedicated to working with the increasingly complex telephone headset market. They provide telephone headsets to many *Fortune* 500 companies, airlines, public utilities, Bell Operating Companies, airlines and financial institutions.

CommuniTech has its own customer service and repair staff working closely with accounts to provide assistance for all after-sale aspects of headset use.

Mr. Shact's previous industry experience includes managerial positions with General Tele-Distributors and Illinois Bell Telephone. He holds an MBA from Northwestern University's Kellogg Graduate School of Management, and he graduated *magna cum laude* and Phi Beta Kappa from Clark University.

Art Sobczak
President, TeleMarketing Design, Inc.
Editor/Publisher, *Telephone Selling Report*
Omaha, Nebraska

(Chapter 10: The Sales Call and the Selling Skills Required)

Art Sobczak is President of TeleMarketing Design, Inc., Omaha, Nebraska, a telephone selling skills training, consulting and resource company. He is also the Editor and Publisher of the company's international training newsletter, *Telephone Selling Report*.

TeleMarketing Design, Inc., provides telephone selling skills training in the form of seminars, customized on-site training, audio and video tapes, company and industry-specific training newsletters.

Mr. Sobczak has spoken before numerous associations, groups, conventions and professional meetings on the topics of telephone selling skills and techniques. His firm has developed audio cassette training programs on developing a complete business-to-business telesales call and effective speech and voice techniques for the phone.

He began his career in telemarketing and telesales with AT&T Long Lines at the Bell System's Telemarketing Center in Kansas City, and later founded and managed the Outbound Telemarketing Division of TelMark, Inc., a service agency in Shawnee Mission, Kansas. He also served as a National Sales Manager for the Outbound Division of WATS Marketing of America, one of the nation's largest total telemarketing service agencies and a subsidiary of American Express. While working for another subsidiary of American Express, CharShare Services, Inc., Mr. Sobczak ran direct marketing programs that involved large volumes of telemarketing calls.

Mr. Sobczak holds a bachelor's degree in business administration from Creighton University in Omaha. His graduate work includes study at the Center for Direct Marketing Education at the University of Missouri/Kansas City. He is married with two children.

Eugene D. Sollo
President
Carlyle Marketing Corporation
Chicago, Illinois

(Chapter 5: Business-to-Business Programs)

Eugene D. Sollo is President of Carlyle Marketing Corporation in Chicago, a full-service telemarketing agency. He was one of the first to recognize the incremental benefits of coordinating direct mail with the telephone, and created numerous successful multi-media campaigns for major companies in the United States. As a pioneer in the telephone marketing industry, Mr. Sollo worked with Murray Roman in the early years to help promote and sell the idea of telemarketing throughout the country.

Mr. Sollo has contributed material to and assisted in the editing of *How To Sell to Women* by Lawrence Dunton and *How To Build Your Business by Telephone* by Murray Roman, both published by McGraw-Hill.

As a former Executive Vice President of Encyclopedia Britannica in Chicago, Mr. Sollo directed a $100 million sales division, with a national sales force of 5,000. He was responsible for developing third-party lead programs and, in doing so, became a pioneer in the development of such programs.

In 1987, Mr. Sollo was elected to the position of Vice Chairman of the Direct Marketing Association's Telephone Marketing Council. He has been honored by the Direct Marketing Association in recognition of his pioneering efforts in the telephone marketing industry, and has been the recipient of awards from several direct marketing associations.

Mr. Sollo is also listed in *Who's Who in the United States*.

As a member of the Board and Executive Committee of the Direct Selling Association, Mr. Sollo participated in setting up the ethics code for that Association. While President of the Chicago Association of Direct Marketing in 1980, he guided the direction and development of their code of ethics.

He has actively counseled students and educators, and helped direct them in their search for marketing careers. He is listed in the Chicago Association of Direct Marketing, Master of Science in Marketing Communications program of Roosevelt University's "Direct Marketing Education Honor Roll," in recognition of his leadership in marketing education. He has also taught numerous basic direct marketing and telemarketing seminars for the American Management Association, Direct Selling Association, Bank Marketing Association and the Chicago Association of Direct Marketing.

Mr. Sollo holds a BS degree in advertising from Northwestern University and is a member of Pi Sigma Epsilon National Fraternity of Sales and Marketing Executives.

Lee R. Van Vechten
President, F.G.I.
Publisher, *The Van Vechten Report*
Freehold, New Jersey

(Chapter 9: Compensation/Motivation)

Lee R. Van Vechten is President of F.G.I., of Freehold, New Jersey, a management consulting firm that specializes in turnkey telephone marketing installations for businesses, specifically the creation of telephone selling resources for clients.

In 1985, Mr. Van Vechten was one of the recipients of the DMA's Telemarketing Council's Pioner Awards. He is also the Co-Founder of the American Telemarketing Association and has served on its Board of Directors as Secretary.

He is the publisher of *The Van Vechten Report*, a pro-active telephone sales skills newsletter. He is also the publisher of *TSR Hotline*, a weekly training reinforcement for telephone sales representatives, and *CSR Hotline*, a biweekly skills publication for customer service representatives.

Mr. Van Vechten has performed consulting services for more than 85 companies, including Digital Equipment Company, Dun & Bradstreet (U.S. and Canada), Honeywell, Inc., General Electric, Champion Paper, Westvaco, Peterbilt, AT&T Corporate, General Foods, Smith Corona and Rayovac Corporation.

He has written many articles for industry publications and is a frequent speaker at conferences sponsored by the Direct Marketing Association and the American Telemarketing Association. He has presented skills seminars for the Dartnell Corporation, Direct Media, Inc., Marketing Publications and the Universities of Alabama, Minnesota, Georgia and Syracuse.

Mr. Van Vechten is a former Vice President of Sales and Marketing with AMR International, where he developed and implemented a successful telephone marketing sales organization. He was also Vice President of Marketing and Sales at Arthur W. Weisenberger & Company, a major institutional brokerage firm.

He spent 14 years with Dun & Bradstreet in various sales and management assignments with Duns Marketing Services. He was instrumental in the management of 250 sales representatives, selling primary and secondary research services. His final position with D & B was as Senior Manager of Research Fulfillment and Sales.

Mr. Van Vechten majored in labor management at the College of Business, Pennsylvania State University, and served as a communications officer in the U.S. Army.

Ron Weber
President, American Telemarketing Association
President, Ron Weber and Associates, Inc.
Orange, Connecticut

Appendix A: (The American Telemarketing Association)

Ron Weber, with more than 25 years of experience in telemarketing and direct marketing, is President of Ron Weber and Associates, Inc., an eight-year-old telemarketing service and consulting agency headquartered in Orange, Connecticut. The firm operates out of three facilities, two in Connecticut and one in Iowa, employing more than 200 people.

Mr. Weber's firm has been listed for the last four years as one of the top 50 service agencies by *Telemarketing* magazine. The firm is comfortable serving small companies as well as those in the Fortune 500, and boasts a track record that includes an average client relationship of more than four years. From pharmaceuticals to financial services, from publishing to credit card acquisition, including business-to-business and business-to-consumer programs, its product and client lists have been diverse.

Mr. Weber is one of the original founding members of the American Telemarketing Association, and is currently National President. He served on the Board of Directors for three years prior to being elected President, with past responsibilities including Chairman of the Legislative Committee, Chairman of the Education Committee and member of the Strategic Planning Committee. Prior to his election to the Board of Directors, he was Outbound Consumer Subcommittee Chairman.

A graduate of New York University with a BA in marketing, Mr. Weber has spoken before many groups, has been published widely in the telemarketing field and has been very active in combating negative telemarketing legislation and regulation. He is a leader in the move to educate legislators and upgrade the telemarketing profession.

Jeffrey C. Wooden
President
ComTel Group
Malvern, Pennsylvania

(Chapter 8: Training)

Jeffrey C. Wooden is President of ComTel Group, a Malvern, Pennsylvania, firm he founded in 1982. A significant aspect of ComTel's consulting involves the recommendation and development of telemarketing training.

Mr. Wooden has more than 15 years of financial services and marketing experience. For the past six years, he has been totally involved in the telemarketing industry as a management consultant specializing in developing and implementing telemarketing strategies for businesses.

He was the primary designer and producer of *Telemarketing for Better Business Results*, ComTel's seven-part video-based telemarketing training program. He has written articles for such publications as *Telemarketing* magazine, *Training News, Bank Marketing* and *Telemarketing Management*.

Mr. Wooden has made presentations before the ATA National Convention and the Telemarketing Foundation. He has served as a full-time assistant professor of marketing management at several New Jersey state colleges.

He holds a BA from Hillsdale College, and an MBA from Fordham University in New York.

Charles E. Yates
Vice President-Market Planning, Business Markets Group
AT&T
Basking Ridge, New Jersey

(Chapter 19: Telecommunications [General])

Charles E. Yates is Vice President-Market Planning, Business Markets Group for AT&T in the company's headquarters in Basking Ridge, New Jersey. He is responsible for marketing strategy planning, market definition, market analysis and forecasting, data networking and network management.

Mr. Yates began his career with AT&T in 1961 as a student engineer in Kansas City. He moved quickly through a number of engineering and engineering management positions before being named Director of AT&T's Rate and Tariff Planning Department in 1977.

He then held positions as Director of Administrative Practices, Director of Marketing Sciences and Director of Service Development. In 1983, Mr. Yates was appointed Assistant Vice President of Marketing Planning, and assumed his current position in 1986.

Mr. Yates received a degree in civil engineering from the University of Arkansas, and is an MIT Sloan Fellow, class of 1972. He serves as a Trustee of the Marketing Sciences Institute and as a member of the Board of Directors of American Transtech, a major user of telemarketing to serve its customers.

Mr. Yates lives with his wife, Gayle, and their two children in Chatham, New Jersey.

Seldon O. Young
President and Chairman of the Board
NICE Corporation
Ogden, Utah

(Chapter 21: Service Bureaus)

Seldon O. Young is President and Chairman of the Board of the NICE Corporation in Ogden, Utah, one of the largest U.S. telemarketing service agencies.

NICE Corporation provides direct marketing clients with a full range of support services, from inbound and outbound call processing to fulfillment and creative consulting services. With three U.S. sites, 650 telephone lines, and 2,200 telephone service representatives, NICE processed more than 20 million domestic and Canadian inbound and outbound client telephone calls in 1987.

NICE also processes international telephone calls through affiliate sites in France, Spain, England and Australia.

Mr. Young is a leading specialist in the direct response industry, providing extensive consulting services to European direct marketers. An American Telemarketing Association (ATA) founding member, Mr. Young has actively worked to professionalize the telemarketing industry through the Association and as an ATA Board member.

He is also a partner in Living Scriptures, a multi-million dollar firm which produces and distributes religious audio and video cassettes.

Mr. Young is a member of the Board of Directors of Ogden's United Way Chapter, an active member of Weber State College's Centennial Planning Committee and the Local Economic Development Committee's Board of Trustees.

CONTENTS

Introduction

Richard L. Bencin

Donald J. Jonovic, Ph.D.

Marketing, like nostalgia, is not what it used to be.

This exciting, if somewhat uncomfortable fact has come home to stay for most marketing professionals. Changes in markets, technology, distribution and communication have worked like earthquakes to fold and shift hallowed assumptions--burying some, elevating others, and exposing entirely new approaches.

Telemarketing has experienced all of these changes. Old approaches are no longer acceptable, tested and proven wisdoms have become even more important, and new demands have forced the evolution of unprecedented new capabilities and powers.

Clearly, the time has come to survey and chart this new telemarketing landscape.

Such a project is not a simple one, however, because too much has happened and too much is happening for any single individual to understand fully. Telemarketing, as a whole, is too broad a subject for even experienced, qualified specialists like the contributors to this book to deal with fully. Instead, we have had to create a telemarketing "genius" by combining the best minds in the business in a collaborative effort to bring the full impact of telemarketing's evolution to professionals and novices alike.

This is a "*how to*" book, to be sure. But it is also a "*why to*" book, a "*how not to*" book, a "*when to*" book, and a "*when not to*" book. It's a *handbook*, in essence, within which are covered virtually every important facet of telemarketing and its key related disciplines. Each topic area is an "expert system" in print--a data processing specialist deals with computers and telemarketing, a specialist in database marketing writes the chapter on list management, etc. To help make the book even more useful as a handbook, we have developed a glossary of terms and a detailed index geared to the user and student of telemarketing.

The specialists chosen to contribute to this book are *the best*. Each is recognized as an authority in his or her field, not only in knowledge, but also in practice. Each is a specialist who has wrestled with the theory and applied that theory in the field.

Although our contributors share a level of expertise, they vary greatly in background, experience, and interest. Represented here are publishers, editors, authors, leading consultants, and managing executives of telemarketing specialty services. On these pages, you will find founders, presidents and chairmen of the American Telemarketing Association, the International Customer Service Association, and the Telephone Marketing Council of the Direct Marketing Association. These are not only telemarketing leaders, they are also telemarketing pioneers who represent hundreds of years of experience, and have been present at the creation of thousands of telemarketing operations.

1

In short, the *Encyclopedia of Telemarketing* is a functional treasure chest of telemarketing knowledge, based widely enough and with enough detail to qualify as an "encyclopedia."

HOW TO USE THE ENCYCLOPEDIA

Each reader will use this book in his or her own way, of course, but we have a few suggestions based on our experience with the subject and the content of these chapters.

The first step, something most readers do quite naturally, is the quick overview. But as you flip through the pages (front to back, back to front, as you will) give particular attention to the figures and tables. These will provide what is perhaps the quickest introduction to the chapter's subject and the author's point of view. This book has been designed primarily to be used for reference, and this preliminary grounding will give you a sense of the wealth of material available to you on your bookshelf.

You may, however, be coming to this encyclopedia with a particular objective. It's possible that you are thinking of starting up a telemarketing operation. You may be facing the challenge of turning a troubled operation around. You might be involved in an existing, successful center, looking to expand and become even more successful. You could simply be looking to add to your skill and understanding as a telemarketing manager.

Allow us to be a little presumptive, here, and suggest some "guided tours" that we think make the most sense for specific reader requirements. Throughout these "guided tours," we assume the introductory and background chapters (**Chapters 1, 2, 4, 5, 17-19, 27,** and **30**) will be read by everyone. For each "tour," we'll suggest specific chapters to read in a specific order.

Tour #1: The Telemarketing Start Up. The challenge of starting a new telemarketing operation is also a great opportunity. It's a chance to begin *right*, to avoid many of the common mistakes made in setting up an operation--and to take advantage of many years of experience of hundreds of people who've gone through the experience.

Here are the chapters we recommend for startups:

1) **CHAPTER 29:** *Step-by-Step for Startups (A Review).*

2) **CHAPTER 14:** *Habitat.*

3) **CHAPTER 6:** *Organization and Staffing.*

4) **CHAPTER 10:** *The Sales Call and the Selling Skills Required.*

5) **CHAPTER 7:** *Profiles of Telephone Sales Reps.*

6) **CHAPTER 8:** *Training.*

7) **CHAPTER 9:** *Compensation/Motivation.*

8) **CHAPTER 11:** *Scripts and the Offer.*

2

9)   *CHAPTER 12: Handling Objections.*

10) *CHAPTER 15: Reporting Systems.*

11) *CHAPTER 16: The Bottom Line.*

12) *APPENDIX D: Telecommunications (Peripheral Equipment).*

Tour #2: The Troubled Center Turnaround. If you're faced with taking some uncomfortable, but necessary steps to make an existing, ineffective center viable, you should consider reading chapters in the following order:

1)   *CHAPTER 28: Taking the Reins of a Troubled Telemarketing Center.*

2)   *CHAPTER 21: Service Bureaus.*

3)   *CHAPTER 13: Databases and Data Banks (Lists).*

4)   *CHAPTER 14: Habitat.*

5)   *CHAPTER 16: The Bottom Line.*

6)   *CHAPTER 15: Reporting Systems.*

7)   *CHAPTER 7: Profiles of Telephone Sales Reps.*

8)   *CHAPTER 10: The Sales Call and the Selling Skills Required.*

9)   *CHAPTER 8: Training.*

10) *CHAPTER 9: Compensation/Motivation.*

11) *CHAPTER 11: Scripts and the Offer.*

12) *CHAPTER 12: Handling Objections.*

13) *APPENDIX C: Telemarketing Books/Magazines in Print.*

14) *APPENDIX D: Telecommunications (Peripheral Equipment).*

Tour #3: Improving an Already Effective Center. If your most significant problem happens to be finding ways to build on success--a fortunate situation to be in--here are the chapters that might be most helpful to you:

1)   *CHAPTER 16: The Bottom Line.*

ENCYCLOPEDIA OF TELEMARKETING

Nothing in these "tours" is meant to exclude the specialty chapters, such as chapters on fundraising, inbound or customer service programs, etc. We assume you will customize your own program to fit the unique challenges you face. The fact is, the more involvement you have with telemarketing, the more worn and dog-eared this book will become.

One final comment before you begin your exploration of this powerful marketing tool. No living discipline stands still. Change is constant and to be expected. So, too, this encyclopedia will change over the coming years as it keeps up with telemarketing developments. We, the editors, as well as all the contributors, encourage you, the reader, to become involved in this continuing process.

Please help us uncover new topics, add new contributors, and generally make the *Encyclopedia of Telemarketing* a living document that grows and develops with this exciting discipline. Please write or call with *any* thoughts you might have concerning this edition or the next.

In the final analysis, telemarketing is *people.* Your contribution is extremely important to us and to all readers of future editions.

RLB
DJJ
Cleveland
November, 1988

CHAPTER 1

Why Telemarketing?

Richard L. Bencin
Donald J. Jonovic, Ph.D.

In a frustrated moment, internationally known consultant, W. Edwards Deming, wrote the following words:

> *"Management does not know, today in America, what they must do. . ..*
> *Improvement is what we need, not rigor mortis, not management in a state of*
> *paralysis."*

Hyperbole for the sake of rhetoric is no sin. Deming's point is sound, and he certainly isn't the first or the last to make it. We hear the same thing from many pundits--complaints about America's preoccupation with the bottom line and the immediate return on investment. We seem in the thrall of short-term thinking and planning. Research and development funding has declined seriously, and we've been very slow to implement factory automation technology.

Couldn't we also make the same complaints about the state of marketing today? The fact is, much of the problem with American industry could be placed in the laps of America's marketers, the people whose job it is to create the markets, to sell the products and services, and to bring in the vital cash flow. Innovative, courageous marketing strategy can help companies build market share and, thus, justify and finance development for the future, yet our marketers have not always kept up with the challenge.

According to Lester Wunderman, Chairman of Wunderman, Ricotta & Kline, the world's largest direct marketing agency:

> *"Right in the midst of the greatest technological revolution in the history*
> *of man, many businesses are failing to use the incredible power of the new*
> *marketing techniques available to them."*

Further, as reported by *Business Marketing*, Mr. Wunderman conducted a survey of the top 100 companies in the U.S. to determine their level of sophistication in marketing. The report showed, in part:

* *About 50% of the companies studied could not estimate their cost of sales.*

* *About 50% frankly admitted they didn't know what was happening in the field.*

* *And only 18% of the respondents described telemarketing as a systematic procedure.*

5

Most of us would agree that there is much that needs correcting in our economy, but there are two essential failures for which we have very little excuse: insufficient innovation and a lack of management courage.

Fortunately, the necessary innovations exist in marketing, primarily in the various direct marketing channels: direct mail, catalogs, print/broadcast direct response, video brochures and telemarketing. Courage, however, is more problematic.

These new channels offer the potential of reducing overall marketing costs while pinpointing results. In short, with direct marketing channels, advertising and marketing programs become *accountable*, often for the first time in the organization's history. Voluntary exposure to that kind of accountability requires a commitment to cost-effective marketing and the guts to stand behind that commitment.

A UNIQUE MARKETING TOOL

Telemarketing has emerged as a significant marketing tool over the past quarter century or so, principally because it is a cost-effective solution to expanding marketing problems.

The cost of a typical sales call has mushroomed dramatically. This isn't due solely to the obvious cost increases in travel and rising compensation. They have played their part, to be sure, but almost more important is the increasing complexity of the marketplace coupled with the multiplicity of products and their features.

There was a time in most industries when it was sufficient to invest in advertising and promotion campaigns designed to create awareness, preferences and, of course, sales leads. The sales force would then simply follow up on the generated leads or "knock on doors" when so inclined.

Simple enough. . . until the impact of the "Marketing Revolution":

* *Markets began to fragment, vertically and horizontally.*

* *Competition intensified on a global scale.*

* *Sales costs exploded.*

* *Marketing productivity of the field sales force diminished.*

* *The increasing efficiency of lead generation led to growing mountains of inquiries.*

* *The expanding range of product/service features meant each new lead was a miniature database in itself, turning the simple process of keeping track of information into a major organizational challenge.*

The entire process of targeting markets, reaching them, handling the resulting information, and turning leads into sales has become so complex that new technologies are required. What marketing requires today is a *systems* approach, the use of direct response media and the telephone to generate, track, and identify real prospects for cost-effective closing by the telephone or the field sales force.

The key is *cost-effectiveness*. Costs in all areas of marketing have grown enormously. No matter where the marketer turns, the world has changed. Advertising expenditures are increasingly under scrutiny.

> *"The long-term trend of sales costs rising faster than advertising costs continues, according to McGraw-Hill's Laboratory of Advertising (LAP) which conducts the survey."*[1]

The average cost of a business-to-business sales call with a field sales force increased 160% between 1977 and 1987, a trend that has hardly slowed down in the years since.[2] Total average cost to close an order rose to more than $1,400.

There have been two major cost changes behind this startling rise. First, the average cost of an industrial sales call direct to industry increased to $251.63 in 1987 from $96.79 in 1977, according to McGraw-Hill Research. Second, and probably more important, is the fact that within the two-year period of a 1981 study, a virtual extra field sales call became necessary to close the typical order, resulting in the requirement of 5.6 calls per sale.

There are a lot of reasons that could be given to explain that increased sales requirement. It could be the changing economy, or changing times and attitudes, or perhaps it's just that the sales force isn't doing what's necessary to properly qualify their prospects. Or maybe salespeople, despite all of the rising costs, are still just knocking on every door.

Maybe the "cold call" is the old war-horse of selling, but the rising costs of making that call has been staggering. The cost of sale of new business initiated by salespeople--that portion of the cost-of-sale average that excludes both the regular customer and the prospect-initiated business--in some companies now *exceeds the list price of the product*! If this isn't yet widely recognized, it's because the true numbers are buried in the averages. Some Fortune 500 companies have determined that about half of their business comes from the direct initiative of prospects and customers and that only about 25% of the sales reps' time is required to close that business. The other half, the *sales rep-initiated business*, however, takes 75% of the sales reps' time-- certainly not profitable.

The increasing expense can't be ignored forever. A fact of modern business life is that companies cannot continue to ask their field salespeople to "hit the bricks," to always keep making more sales calls at random. If cold calling continues unabated, these organizations won't have to worry long about all of the other problems relating to their businesses. The numbers now work against this time-tested sales strategy. The more indiscriminate cold calls the field sales force makes, the further behind the company falls. Sales may increase with this effort, but so will costs--and profits will dwindle.

The problem is not only the cost of maintaining a sales force or even a system of sales representatives. Sales reps and manufacturers bring with them a whole range of costs not directly related to their individual support. They *travel*. They buy airline tickets, stay in hotels, eat in restaurants. When they're not on the road (and not selling?) they must support offices and office staffs, pay rent--all the accouterments supporting a field selling organization.

There's also a personnel cost. Legions of reps leave their companies each year because of cold-call frustration. That only adds to corporate selling expense.

There is, in short, a major need in industry today to reduce the level of human involvement in sales, and telemarketing is a big factor in filling that need.

7

WHAT IS TELEMARKETING?

Telemarketing, quite simply, is the use of telecommunications, combined with a database, to promote a business's products and services--using the telephone as a direct marketing medium through which a variety of sales and market research activities can be carried out. Selling is only part of the process.

Telemarketing can also be a key source of information on a company's prospect and current customer base, markets, inventory, distribution channels, advertising and promotional efforts. When combined with information and management systems, it can bring trained personnel into computerized contact with potential customers--and maintain that contact profitably.

There are many definitions of telemarketing, many of them educations in themselves. Here are a few examples:

> *"Simply stated, telemarketing combines the telephone and a database as an integral system for such marketing functions as direct response marketing, account handling, customer service and field sales support. Its primary purpose is to establish or increase sales in a measurable, cost-effective manner. On the other hand, telemarketing's use for customer service plays an important part in retaining loyal customers by offering quick solutions to questions and problems that the customer may encounter."[3]*

> *"Telemarketing is an on-going process by which buyers and sellers are linked in a personal dialogue on a 'real time' basis. It allows a company to have more contact with the marketplace--and allows the marketplace to have more contact with the company."[4]*

> *"Part of a marketing medium rather than a single sales tool."[5]*

A more detailed definition appeared in an AT&T telemarketing manual:

> *"Telemarketing--a new marketing system--is a synthesis of telecommunications technology with management systems for a planned, controlled sales and service program.*

> *"Telemarketing is a component of the marketing communications mix. It can be used solely or in combination with media advertising, direct mail, catalog selling, face-to-face selling and other communication modes--efficiently and cost-effectively.*

> *Telemarketing can be applied to any and all functions in the marketing spectrum--from order taking to full account management. It can be used to respond to inquiries, supplement (and sometimes replace) personal selling, qualify leads, sell to marketing accounts profitably, trade-up orders, increase advertising effectiveness, replace traditional retail shopping and render instant and cost-effective personal service to customers when they need it most. . .*

WHY TELEMARKETING?

"By conducting conventional marketing and service activities in innovative ways, telemarketing is a new communications channel, delivering high impact at low cost, for critical marketing service roles. That is why it must be integrated into the total marketing mix."

The major strengths of a meaningful telephone marketing program are the personal contact it generates and the give-and-take interaction it allows--precisely the qualities being sacrificed to economic pressures in marketing today.[6] It is potentially useful to marketers in five ways:

* *As a less costly substitute for personal selling.*

* *As a supplement to personal selling.*

* *As a higher impact substitute for direct mail and media advertising.*

* *As a supplement to direct mail and other media.*

* *As a replacement for other slower, less convenient techniques.*[7]

WHY TELEMARKETING IS GROWING

The growth of telemarketing has not been an accident. There is too much built-in momentum to continue business as usual.

"Basic selling methods haven't really changed much since the days of the Dead Sea Scrolls. We've had face-to-face selling and written purchase orders since that day. In fact, if you were to examine the scrolls, you would find they actually contain a buy/sell agreement for olives![8]

"Today's salespeople still rely on face-to-face contacts to persuade the buyers on the merits of their products. I don't know how many prospects were seen in the ancient world in a given day, but salespeople today call on fewer than seven potential customers and at a cost considerably over $100 - $200 a visit. As the cost of the sales call has gone up, we must ask 'Has productivity gone up as well?'"

Telemarketing is a conscious response to a reality. Companies are pushed by inflation, which cuts spending and makes competition more intense. They are pushed by soaring energy costs, which reduce travel. Profits go down as the cost of making the sale skyrockets. Productivity lags. Competition grows.

Companies are also pulled by changes in consumer and business life-styles. Whatever their market, be it industrial or retail, all companies are affected. Today, people don't have time. They're busy, demanding, in a hurry. Less and less do consumers find it fun to go shopping. And more and more do business people seek faster and more convenient ways to get their work done.

AT&T once listed these reasons as causes for the growth of telemarketing:

9

*   *High inflation is driving up costs, eroding the buying power of consumers.*

*   *Capital for expansion and modernization is difficult to find--the alternative, of course, is stagnating productivity.*

*   *High interest rates are boosting the cost of maintaining inventories and slowing down collections.*

*   *Competition is getting stiffer and more difficult to meet, threatening the very existence of companies.*

*   *Consumerism is establishing its own set of demands. Meeting them is costly, but they must be reckoned with.*

*   *Energy prices are rising, inflating operating and selling costs, and affecting retail shopping patterns.*

*   *Changing lifestyles--two-income families, more single-person households-- leave less time for shopping and are altering consumer buying habits.*

*   *Travel and hotel costs are rising, increasing the expense of visiting prospects and customers.*

*   *Productivity in sales and service resists improvement, resulting in escalating marketing costs.*

These aren't the only factors. Network TV advertising costs have gone far beyond the point where television advertising could be used as a matter of course. Everywhere the marketer turns, the world has changed--toward the more costly and expensive end of the spectrum. To use John Wyman's words: "...the need for productivity will no longer permit marketing-as-usual."[9]

Telemarketing is an answer to many of these concerns. It's true that the telephone is an expensive medium. But when compared to the cost of a sales call or even the cost of direct mail using bulk or first-class postage (and its relatively low response rate), telemarketing is a bargain.

The acceptance of the 800 number has had a lot to do with telemarketing's growth. We've seen a generation of Americans conditioned by television, newspapers and magazines to call "toll free" to order. Good evidence of this acceptability is the fact that advertisers are now feeling comfortable enough to eliminate the "toll free" reference, assuming that consumers have become educated to that fact already.[10]

MARKETING BENEFITS OF TELEMARKETING

Compared to face-to-face selling, telemarketing has a number of real advantages that have brought it to the top of so many marketing managers' wish lists.

10

WHY TELEMARKETING?

Cost Efficiency. A properly managed telemarketing operation can be much more cost-effective than a comparative field sales operation. The whole problem of physical logistics is greatly reduced with telemarketing. With telemarketing, there is no downtime involved with travel between calls, missed appointments, weather or traffic disasters and waiting room neglect. Consequently, more customers can be contacted at much lower cost.

While the typical field sales call can absorb anything from 15 minutes to a full day, not counting the time spent in travel, the typical telemarketing call is usually less than 10 minutes in length. Much of the time spent on a person-to-person sales call is often spent on required social conversation and small talk designed to build a rapport between the salesperson and the customer. Social conventions and habit ensure that this sort of time-consuming rapport building can be greatly abbreviated during a phone call.

Telephone marketing, because of its lower cost, can be used effectively with marginal accounts that normally wouldn't rate a field sales call. Such customers can frequently be turned into profitable accounts with telemarketing. It can also be used with almost equal efficiency no matter what the customer's geographical location might be. Thus, penetration of new markets and major shifts in market geography can be accomplished quickly with telemarketing.

Finally, the telephone can be a more flexible device than the field salesperson. By this we don't mean to demean the salesperson's significant skills, only to point out that the telephone can be used to bring more than sales skills to bear on the marketing situation. It is often easier and more efficient, for example, to do customer surveys by phone, to set up appointments, to announce significant changes in price or products, to upgrade orders and to check details.

Time Management. In business-to-business marketing, telemarketing can be used in an appointment-setting program that can significantly increase the total field selling time available. It stands to reason that if field sales reps can be provided with specific daily appointments, especially at the beginning and end of the day, management can be reasonably assured that the field sales organization is likely to be out doing what it is supposed to be doing: making sales presentations to qualified prospects. Telemarketing, when used this way, effectively extends the field selling day, thus increasing sales productivity and reducing sales costs. Personal experience with clients has shown that appointment setting through telemarketing can result in a 25% gain in qualified field time.

Control. Since before the time of Marco Polo, marketers have complained about the difficulty of controlling field sales efforts. Salespeople are notoriously resistant to paperwork, yet such feedback as call reports are essential to effective marketing. Furthermore, every individual evolves an individual sales style and approach. Sales and marketing managers have only limited influence on the conduct and content of the sales call in the field.

Telemarketing, however, allows much closer control of personnel, training, and performance since the managers and supervisors are usually in the same physical location as the telemarketing representatives. Handled properly, this proximity allows for immediate evaluation and correction of sales performance, while, at the same time, helps to avoid the classic psychological separation of the sales force from the ''home office.''

Market intelligence gathering is also more immediate with a telemarketing operation. The sales

11

representatives, dealing as they do with greater numbers of customers in a shorter time, can detect changes in the marketplace much more quickly than field sales reps. They can notify management much more quickly of these changes, and management can react much more quickly.

Improved Cash Flow. Telemarketing programs can have more immediate results than field sales programs, and they can often begin to generate orders almost instantly. Such immediate results, of course, can allow cash flow to cover marketing costs, as well as permitting much tighter inventory control.

Market Expansion. Expanding an organization's market has historically been a dauntingly expensive and time-consuming process, usually involving expansion of the sales force. Telemarketing can relieve a great deal of this pressure by more readily targeting new customers, efficiently making initial qualification contacts, and, in many cases, closing the sale--all essentially independent of geographical considerations. Where field sales calls are required, the prequalification process makes it much more likely that expansion can be accomplished with the existing sales force.

Prospecting over Long Time Periods. Combined with careful tracking of a computerized prospect database, well-scheduled telemarketing follow-up calls can continue to maintain and reinforce long-term relationships with prospects. Big ticket purchases can often be tracked and managed for one or two years. Telemarketing enables the seller to more often be in the right place at the right time.

Customer Relations. One of telemarketing's primary benefits is the fact that it allows high levels of responsiveness. In the first place, a phone call takes much less of the customer's time than a face-to-face sales call. Secondly, phone calls can be more regular and frequent than sales calls. Thirdly, since telemarketing can be either inbound or outbound, the customer familiar with an organization's telemarketing operation can get much quicker response to ongoing problems or questions. It would be difficult to overestimate the importance of these conveniences to customers. They, after all, are experiencing the same problems of effectiveness and efficiency as the seller.

Seasonality. Telemarketing allows the marketer to get around the restrictions of seasonal selling periods. Because of mailing times and delays, telemarketing allows the marketer actually to extend the buying period by speeding up receipt of the order.

Greater Order Volume. Trained telephone people can, during the sales call, introduce new products, sell related products, upgrade orders and do follow-up selling. Again, the results are reduced inventory, improved turnover, increased sales volume and greater profitability. Sales volume can be increased with the expert use of such techniques as upgrade selling, cross-selling and turning service calls into sales.

Lower Personnel Costs. A telemarketing staff, despite all the training and experience required, is much less costly to maintain than high-priced field sales personnel. Fewer people are needed, and there are no bodies to transport, shelter, feed and entertain.

WHY TELEMARKETING?

High Volume. Given that a trained and experienced telephone rep can complete up to 20 or more calls per hour, the volume benefits of telemarketing over field sales is obvious. Even in the more complex environment of industrial marketing, the telephone rep has an eightfold advantage over his field sales colleague.

Versatility. Once a functioning telemarketing operation is in place, it can be easily adapted to a wide range of functions. The same reps and the same equipment can be used, among other things, to sell, to conduct surveys, to announce changes or special offers, to make appointments, to qualify leads, to cross-sell, to up-sell and to check credit.

Ease of Start-Up. Since the equipment used in telemarketing is readily available, and since telemarketing operations can often be set up using existing space and personnel, a telemarketing operation is relatively easy to start up. This very benefit, however, can turn quickly into a disadvantage without the proper preparation and planning (See Chapter 27: Anatomy of a Boiler Room).

SOME SUCCESS STORIES

Who's taking advantage of these benefits? Many companies. Here are a few examples:

IBM was determined to replace expensive selling time by less expensive methods of reaching the increased numbers of potential computer users. In the past few years, therefore, IBM has expanded its selling into other direct marketing channels beside personal selling.

IBM uses telemarketing as its primary source for generating qualified sales prospects for both the Freedom Fairs and their field sales force. At the heart of the IBM telemarketing effort is a computer database which is kept current by "tele-prospecting." Media advertising generates leads through 800 numbers. Lists are also purchased. All names are verified and updated by continuing telephone prospecting, and then matched to sales territory grids for territory analysis and marketing research. Hot leads are sent directly to the nearest IBM branch for follow-up.

If the TM-generated prospect is not ready to buy, he or she is placed in a "conditioning program," which is a six-month series of direct mail packages containing "bounce back" cards the prospects can use to let IBM know when they are ready to purchase.

Grolier. This encyclopedia giant got into telemarketing in 1978. By 1980, telephone sales had exceeded the door-to-door operation. Within three years, Grolier went from nothing to $40 million in telephone sales--1.5 million encyclopedia orders per year.

Xerox. Inside salespeople can work independently to sell goods and services completely by phone. This sales tactic is a good fit for such sales situations as repetitive supply purchases or selling readily identifiable products. But telephone selling is not limited to low ticket items. Xerox has had major success with their direct-response operation in Henrietta, New York. Using direct mail with both a coupon and an

13

800 number, Xerox sold thousands of office copiers, worth thousands of dollars apiece, outright--without ever having to send a field sales rep out to close the sale.

MCI Telecommunications. MCI was able to double sales revenue in one fiscal year through the use of telemarketing. A major competitor to AT&T, MCI makes the most of its sales of long distance usage through the practical and cost efficient use of telemarketing.

Chrysler. Chrysler used telemarketing to out-flank both GM and Ford on business fleet sales in 1982. Fleet owners were targeted for massive telephone qualification programs that determined near-term purchases of auto fleets. Local new car dealers were then advised and expected to follow up within 10 days of the prospect's notification. Delinquent dealers were eventually bypassed in favor of their nearest competitor. Chrysler had stunning success--a 32% sales increase in fleet sales in 1982.

General Electric. GE has been responsive to increased competition and spiraling sales costs. Telemarketing has been an important factor in the success of their industrial sales process. Inbound telemarketing is used as an alternative to more conventional means of handling inquiry responses from the various advertising promotions. With telemarketing, GE is able to handle lead qualification and literature fulfillment concurrently.

To provide their dealers and direct sales forces with well-qualified and pre-screened leads, GE uses outbound telemarketing, allowing sales reps to spend their valuable field selling time with the prospects who show the highest potential.

Visualon, Inc. This smaller company in Cleveland has been able to go up against the giants, Xerox and 3M, by using scientific market segmentation and an outbound WATS program to take its business national. In spite of a recent recession, excessive discounting and extraordinary selling costs in the industry, Visualon has created enormous sales growth.

Instead of merely qualifying leads for a field sales force, Visualon determined it could sell graphic arts supplies (overhead projectors, acetates, markers, etc.) directly over the telephone. The result has been greatly increased sales, lowered selling costs and increased profitability.

DEC. Digital not too long ago placed full page ads in *MIS Week* with headlines asking "When was the last time you saved $25,000 on a phone call?" The ads sold $86,000 computers and a 30% discount by telemarketing--using an 800 number.

McDonell Douglas. This aircraft manufacturer successfully marketed fighter aircraft by telephone! If you find it ludicrous to think that somebody would advertise fighters on television, you'd better consider McDonell Douglas's cable ad run during an Army/Air Force football game. The ad offered a 50-page booklet and received only 50 telephone replies. But, according to Buck Buchanan of J. Walter Thompson, all of these responses were serious requests from people who could influence purchasing.

Ellett Brothers. Chilton Ellett took over his family shooting goods distributorship in 1970, when sales totaled $1 million. By 1981, using a massive in-house telemarketing program, Ellett Brothers' sales had grown to $52 million. Ellett put the first sales rep on the phone in 1969, and by 1971 began a total phase-out of his field sales force. According to Ellett, every time he put a sales rep on the phone, she "beat every man on the road" (Ellett used an entirely female telemarketing sales force). Ellett exclaimed:

"I knew I had a bear by the tail."

3M. This corporate giant uses a telemarketing center to assist customers with equipment troubles. After calling the 800 number, the customer describes the problem to a skilled analytical technician who has access to the latest equipment and an on-line computer system. On more than 30% of the calls, 3M has found the difficulty can be solved in minutes without having to send a service technician--resulting in a tremendous saving in service costs.

Ralston Purina. This company recently launched a "Great American Dog" public relations campaign that used "900" numbers as an integral part of the program. The company selected five finalists from more than 22,000 pet entries, and included photos of the dogs and their owners in newspaper ads reaching more than 40 million people. The ads contained five "900" telephone numbers, one for each finalist, for people to use in voting for their favorite pet. Over a one-week period, the Ralston Purina numbers received more than 60,000 calls.

TELER$_x$ Marketing. This computer-managed telemarketer serving the healthcare industry has had phenomenal success with computerized telemarketing. The Spring House, Pennsylvania, company uses computer power in all phases of pharmaceutical telemarketing for clients.

One client, for, example, was a manufacturer of "biologicals" that wanted to replace costly sales force coverage of pediatricians' offices with a program that was much more cost-effective. Direct field selling was not profitable.

Teler$_x$ telephone representatives spent 4,790 hours on the phone in 1983 for this client, a program representing a marketing investment of approximately $286,000. For this investment, the program was able to achieve a close rate of 30%, generating direct sales of more than $2.5 million--a return on investment of 8.7 to 1, a rate superior to that achieved by many conventional field sales forces.

PITFALLS TO AVOID

We would be doing the reader a disservice, however, not to mention the downsides of telemarketing. Much can be said about the successes of telemarketing, but care must be taken to make sure that the listing of benefits--increased sales, cost reduction and market share enhancement--doesn't imply the benefits are, somehow, automatic.

For every success in telemarketing, there are probably several failures. Of the telemarketing operations that don't fail, many achieve only marginal results.

According to Lee Van Vechten, Publisher of the *Van Vechten Report*, 65% of all telemarketing start-ups fail in the first year. Within another two years, another 15% stumble off into oblivion.

Specific reasons for failure or poor results vary infinitely with the individual operations involved, but we can safely generalize from experience that there are five major reasons why so many new telemarketing operations are stillborn:

1) *Telemarketing looks too easy.*

2) *There is an insufficient investment in people, facilities and time.*

3) *The telemarketing consultant has insufficient or inappropriate experience.*

4) *Myths and old wives' tales are believed in the process of selecting telemarketing managers.*

5) *Management fails to give telemarketing the support it requires.*

Here is how these misunderstandings and mistakes operate:

Telemarketing Looks Easy--Too Easy. Because we are all familiar with the ubiquitous telephone, many of us believe that telemarketing is simple, requiring just a little instruction and practice. In fact, with proper leadership, program creation and appropriate execution, telemarketing can look easy.

Looks, however, can be deceiving.

We have had a national sales manager tell us that he could create and implement a telephone selling operation with no problem because, in his words, "it's got to be simpler than running a field sales force." At another client, a company president had tried to implement his own telemarketing program. It failed. He went out and had the local telephone company provide an off-the-shelf telemarketing program with "individual customization." That program failed, too.

The hidden problem here is related to measurement and control. In other words, the success of telemarketing can be closely tied to how well the effort is analyzed, and how that analysis is used to enhance telemarketing productivity. But this measurability is of a different nature from the measurability of a field selling operation. The typical national sales manager has a difficult time knowing whether his sales reps got out of bed on any given day, much less what they are saying to the prospects or what the prospects are saying to the reps.

Field sales managers are generally used to this kind of built-in ignorance, and the good ones have learned to manage around it. But because telemarketing is inherently more measurable and controllable, its management requires greater technical sophistication. Adding database management and the required precise interrelationships with other direct marketing disciplines such as direct mail, catalog selling, broadcast media, print, etc., the required level of management sophistication diverges greatly from that required for managing an army of field sales reps. Not that either skill is more or less important; we only should realize that the requirements are vastly different. This means that a great deal of attention needs to be given to selection of telemarketing managers.

The company president who failed with his own strategy eventually hired a consultant, and had a professional telemarketing program implemented with management personnel meeting the consultant's specifications--one success after two failures, all because telemarketing initially "looked so easy."

16

WHY TELEMARKETING?

Minimal Investment in Time, People and Facilities. Very often, organizations decide to go into telemarketing but are unwilling or unable to make the necessary investment, particularly in the proper selection of the senior telemarketing executive.

Perhaps a classic example of a situation like this is a midwestern company that decided to go into outbound telemarketing, but at the least possible effort and cost. This company selected a telephone customer sales rep from their *inbound* customer service department to become their new outbound, business-to-business telephone sales manager! The only training given to the new manager was a short telemarketing seminar conducted by the local phone company.

This person's job was to conceive the telemarketing program, develop the tel-sales center, staff it with *existing* inbound customer service personnel, and manage it successfully. She was expected to use the same customer service facilities as the *inbound* operation to launch her new outbound telemarketing venture. As we could easily have predicted, the new operation "didn't work." But it didn't fail because outbound telemarketing was a bad idea for this company. It failed because:

1) *Customer service personnel generally do not have the specific expertise, patience and resistance to rejection required of outbound telephone sales reps.*

2) *The mix and match of inbound and outbound calling by the same personnel is often very difficult to manage, at best, and most of the time is impossible.*

3) *The former inbound customer sales rep did not have the necessary experience, training and managerial skills to create and execute a finely honed telemarketing program.*

The senior management of this company had simply not made the proper telemarketing management selection in the first place. They went the easiest and cheapest way and expected their new manager to do the same.

Because they set up their outbound operation on the cheap, they paid the price of failure.

Ineffective Consulting Advice. Ever since telemarketing started to blossom as a bona fide marketing strategy, the number of telemarketing "experts" has multiplied. While some of the so-called "experts" are virtual scoundrels, some of these people have telephone experience of some sort and some are qualified for various forms of consulting. Few, however, have the wide range of experience to qualify them as across-the-board telemarketing consultants.

Many limited-experience consultants come from the ranks of telecommunication (hardware) consultants or field sales trainers. These are often competent people in their fields of expertise, but lack the more generalized telephone marketing knowledge and experience of the qualified telemarketing consultant. Telemarketing is no different from any other consulting field. Finding a qualified consultant is often a difficult task compounded by the client's basic ignorance of the qualifications required.

A good way to determine the experience and qualifications required in a competent telemarketing consultant would be to read the biographies of contributors to this book (see: *Meet the World's Experts*).

17

Myths and Old Wives' Tales. Much is wrong with the entire field of marketing management selection and employment, but when it comes to hiring senior telemarketing management, things are in an almost disastrous state.

Many organizations still seem to believe the old saw that claims "a good manager is a good manager," no matter what or where the job. Granted, this might be true for some industries and certain fields, but it certainly isn't true in telemarketing. Telemarketing management must understand database management, telecommunications, computers, the interrelationship with all of the direct marketing disciplines as well as the intricacies of the creation of a telemarketing plan and its sophisticated execution, analysis and *guarantee* of program success.

Recently, a Fortune 200 company asked one of their product managers to create and launch a major telemarketing effort. There was no budget for a consultant. The corporation merely expected this competent manager to switch fields, learn all about telemarketing and create a premier telemarketing program. Predictably, it failed.

Often, salary offers to outside people are too low to substantiate any successful, experienced management personnel. Management fails to factor into their compensation equation the tremendous leverage potential of a superior telemarketing manager. In many industries, a competent manager with 20 full-time telephone sales reps could potentially produce as much as a 200-person national field sales force-- with significantly lower sales costs. On the other hand, a underqualified manager or an inappropriate company transplant could spoil the entire operation. In these situations, millions in sales could be foregone in order to save $10,000 in salary.

An international bank recently went searching for a vice president of telemarketing. They attached a long list of requirements to the search, including a minimum requirement of 10 years' experience in telemarketing. So far, so good (although less than a handful of premier candidates were gleaned by the executive search firm--10 years of experience eliminated many potential candidates).

But the requirements didn't stop with telemarketing experience. The group vice president of the bank also wanted the management candidate to have experience in banking. That additional requirement effectively eliminated all of the top candidates and the selection process slipped several notches down in order to surface a telemarketing management candidate with the required banking experience. Needless to say, the bank filled its telemarketing management position with a significantly less qualified candidate than it could have had without the stipulation of experience within the banking field.

It is important to understand that telemarketing savvy far outweighs specific product experience in judging the qualifications of a telemarketing manager. This is particularly true since there are so few qualified and experienced telemarketers. The product capabilities and the market can be and should be learned. It is the validated telemarketing management expertise and experience that's in short supply--and the most critically needed.

Failures of Management Support. It is critical for any direct marketing program to have the full support of top management. Telemarketing has special support needs, however, since it tends to involve itself with many areas of the organization. Experience has shown that until each level of management involved in the program has been completely sold, it makes little sense to begin implementing the program. This might sound obvious, but agreement isn't always what it seems--superficial support is not enough.

18

WHY TELEMARKETING?

The objectives of the telemarketing program must be understood in detail, and the process of reaching those objectives, in stages and in detail, must also be agreed to. There must be agreement, further, on how long the program will take, how much it will cost and what the measures of success will be. Only an aware management can be counted on to provide the full support, the patience and the resources necessary to make the program work.

Consider, too, the political issues that tend to arise around new telemarketing programs. For example:

* *The sales manager may fear loss of control as he shifts the responsibility of prospecting from an outside sales force to a group of telephone reps.*

* *The direct mail promotion manager may feel threatened when leads are followed up by phone rather than by mail.*

* *The data processing manager may be confused by the new demands being made on his database, and by the complex follow-up procedures that telephone marketing requires.*

Everyone affected by the telemarketing program must understand, accept and support the new effort if it is to be successful. Telemarketing is *very* vulnerable to unrestrained and uncontrolled intra-organizational snipers.

SHOULD YOUR COMPANY USE TELEMARKETING?

Telemarketing is not necessarily a sensible sales strategy for every business. While many different kinds of businesses in many different industries are using telemarketing effectively--e.g., retailers, brokers, cable franchises, publications, distributors and even major manufacturers--only a careful analysis of a given organization's business, customer base, prospect universe, marketing organization and underlying costs can lead to a comfortable answer to the telemarketing question.

While much of the information in this Encyclopedia has been designed to help in the decision of whether or not telemarketing makes sense, it would be helpful to run through some of the basic questions right here to get a feel for the scope of the problem:

* *Does the product/service lend itself to telemarketing?* While organizations have marketed everything from magazine subscriptions, to stock brokerage services, to office supplies, even to major equipment costing $10,000 or more, there are some products or services that just might not be effectively sold through telemarketing.

* *Are most sales one-time-only or do customers rebuy?* One time sales tend, in general, to require more sales effort per sales dollar, and may be more appropriate targets for a telemarketing effort. On the other hand, telemarketing could also be useful in managing rebuying activity.

19

* *Who are the customers?* Customer bases differ, and some are more appropriately reached by telephone than others. For example, customers in rural areas are often too spread out to justify in-person sales calls, while truck drivers would be almost impossible to reach, reliably, by phone. Certain customer groups are used to being solicited by phone (e.g., purchasing agents), while others are not (e.g., CEO's, research scientists).

* *How technical and engineered are the products to be sold?* The simpler the product or the concept, the easier it is to sell direct over the phone. Very sophisticated and highly engineered products are more difficult (but not impossible) to sell via telephone. Should video brochures and/or field sales reps complement the telemarketing effort? Could direct mail and highly illustrated catalogs make the telemarketing effort viable?

* *What is the size of the customer and potential customer database?* Businesses with very few customers/prospects lose much of telemarketing's selling power. "Limited universe" usually means a lower telemarketing profile. Are there other growth or service opportunities that should be undertaken (via telemarketing) to help spread the risk? Conversely, a huge customer/prospect universe indicates a significant telemarketing opportunity.

* *At what level of integration would telemarketing make the most sense?* Would the entire marketing and sales operation be converted to telemarketing? Should telemarketing be combined with a field sales force? Should telemarketing be an integral part of customer service? Would/should it be combined with other forms of direct marketing (e.g., direct mail)? Should telemarketing be done in-house or by a service agency?

* *Would the increase in sales justify the cost of the telemarketing operation?* It is by no means certain that telemarketing would be more cost effective than present sales/marketing methods. What would be the start-up costs? Would other selling costs decrease? By how much?

TELEMARKETING'S FUTURE

Telemarketing is changing forever the way business is being conducted in the United States. The future will see even greater changes brought about by this relatively new marketing medium.

Growth Trends. Consider a recent study by Arthur Andersen. The accounting firm had clients rank "capable inside people"--telephone sales reps and others--as well as outside sales reps in overall importance. Inside salespeople ranked fifth as the most important criterion for doing business in 1970. By

1980, that criterion moved up to fourth, and Arthur Anderson expects it to be *the* most important criterion by 2000.

Conversely, contact with field sales reps is declining in importance. Ranking number one in 1970, it slipped to third in 1980 and is expected to drop to eighth rank by 1990.

Perhaps even more startling is Arthur Andersen's recent study for the National Association of Wholesalers that indicates that almost two-thirds of *all* sales reps will be "inside" (telemarketers) by 1995.

Arthur Andersen isn't alone in predicting the major growth for telemarketing:

* *As far back as 1983,* U.S. News & World Report *predicted that telemarketing would be the fastest growing occupation in America, generating eight million new jobs by the year 2000--four times more new jobs than the combined runners-up, computer-aided design, computer-aided manufacturing and software development.*

* *Technology Marketing Corporation, in 1985, predicted a 235% growth in telemarketing sales between 1985 and 1990, from $130 billion to $435 billion.*

* *Schlenker Research Services, in their recently copyrighted* Telemarketing Intelligence,[11] *reports that the outlook for continued telemarketing growth is very encouraging. More than 60% of the companies surveyed expect to add work stations during 1988, and more than 80% expect to expand within three years.*

In 1981, telemarketing expenditures exceeded those of direct mail, and by 1987, telemarketing expenditures ($41.2 billion) were almost triple the $17.2 billion spent on direct mail, and were greater than advertising spending in newspapers ($26.9 billion), broadcast ($29.3 billion), and magazines ($8.0 billion).[12]

This kind of double-digit growth is expected to continue. Eugene B. Kordahl, President of National Telemarketing, Inc., and past Co-Chairman/President of the American Telemarketing Association, and Arnold L. Fishman of Marketing Logistics, Inc., provided these statistics: In 1986, the average business-to-business telemarketing sale was worth $1,500. In that same year, consumer telemarketing sales averaged $61. Kordahl and Fishman believe that by 1990, the average value of a business-to-business sale should be at least $1,700 and maybe closer to 2,000.[13]

Increasing Legislative Attention. There has been growing pressure in many state legislatures to restrict or regulate the activity of telemarketers. There has been concern about who telemarketers call, when they call, the sales methods they use and the use of automatic dialers. Issues have been raised about "invasion of privacy" and even harassment. There have been flim-flams and con games. All industries have them, of course, but it seems they've been particularly visible in telemarketing of late.

Legislators have reacted. California, for example, passed a 1985 law (Article 1.4, California Business and Professions Code, Telephone Sellers) which among other provisions, requires telemarketer registration with full ownership and management disclosure, regulates prizes and gifts and even requires filing of all scripts and sales information used in telemarketing with the state. According to Steven A.

Meyerowitz, Legal Contributing Editor of *Business Marketing*, the National Association of Attorneys General is preparing an example telemarketing statute for all 50 states to use as a legislative model.

The state of Florida became the first to pass the so-called "asterisk bill." Telephone subscribers are allowed to specify "no soliciting calls" within their directory listings. Telemarketers from other states calling into Florida are exempt. Florida businesses, however, will be required to check their calling lists against hundreds of local directories before making solicitation calls to individual consumers. The fine for each violation is $10,000. Only newspapers managed to secure exemptions to the Florida law (First Amendment right or power of the press?). Calls to previous customers, inbound calls and all business-to-business firms are not affected.

The common, and important, monitoring of outgoing telemarketing calls is coming under attack also, with states regularly introducing bills requiring either a beep-tone warning, or overt consent by the telephone sales rep and the called party to the monitoring. Monitoring is done principally for quality control and training purposes, and such requirements obviously decrease its effectiveness and practicality. There is also a possibility of a Federal law requiring the beep tone.

Two other major issues are the demands for legislation designed to regulate so-called auto-dialed recorded message players (ADRMPs), and the potential that states will impose sales and use tax collection responsibility on out-of-state marketers.

The industry hasn't been idle, however. The Direct Marketing Association provides a Telephone Preference Service, which offers consumers the chance to have their names taken off many calling lists simply by notifying DMA. These names are compiled by the Association and made available to telemarketers for purging their own lists. Julie S. Crocker, Director, State Government Affairs for DMA has noted an increasing willingness among telemarketers to do more to help fight restrictive legislation, mostly through cooperation to reduce the need for such legislation. Both the DMA and the American Telemarketing Association are assisting this necessary effort.

In particular, the American Telemarketing Association has made a significant effort to police its own industry by urging its members to maintain appropriate standards. After 18 months of compiling and editing, the ATA recently released their *Telemarketing Standards & Ethics Guidelines* [14] whereby the telemarketing industry can measure its own performance (see: *Appendix A: The American Telemarketing Association*). Hopefully, adherence to these guidelines will reassure lawmakers.

Like any valuable tool, telemarketing brings a great deal of potential benefit to marketers, but it must be used carefully, ethically, with great attention and with consummate skill.

----

[1]News editorial, *Business Marketing*, July 1988, p. 23.
[2]McGraw-Hill Research, "Average Cost To Close an Industrial Sale," *Laboratory of Advertising Performance [LAP] Reports*.
[3]James M. Mahood, "Telemarketing: Increase Sales in Cost-Effective Manner," *Direct Marketing*, July 1982, p. 46.
[4]Dr. Steven E. Permut, Associate Professor of Organization and Management at Yale, "Managing Your Markets in the 80's," in a report produced for Mountain Bell.
[5]Rudolph J. Oetting, "Telemarketing: An Answer to Rising Sales Costs," *Direct Marketing*, August 1982, p. 73.

WHY TELEMARKETING?

[6]Louis A. Kislik, "Telephone Marketing: At Last, An Integral Part of the Multimedia Mix," *ZIP Target Marketing*, January 1982, p. 32.

[7]John Wyman, quoted in "Wyman Discusses Future of Telemarketing Services," *Telephony*, February 21, 1983, p. 158.

[8]*Ibid.*

[9]*Ibid.*

[10]Oetting, *op cit.*, p. 72.

[11]*Telemarketing Intelligence*, A Report from Schlenker Research Services, 47 Calgary Circle, P.O. Box 358, Morganville, New Jersey 07751, June 1987.

[12]*Direct Marketing*, December 1987, p. 25.

[13]*Guide to Telemarketing: 1986*, Marketing Logistics, 175 Olde Half Day Road, Suite 145, Lincolnshire, Illinois 60069.

[14]*Telemarketing Standards & Ethics Guidelines*, 1987, The American Telemarketing Association, 5000 Van Nuys Builevard, Suite 400, Sherman Oaks, California 91403.

CHAPTER 2

Integrating Telemarketing with Other Direct Marketing Disciplines and Field Sales

Richard L. Bencin
Donald J. Jonovic, Ph.D.

When used in concert with other direct marketing channels, telemarketing yields much greater response effectiveness than the traditional channels--or even telemarketing itself--can by themselves alone. Achieving this synergy is vital for an organization to take full advantage of telemarketing's potential.

Why is synergy so important? Most obviously because there are more than 180 million telephones in use today. That's a penetration of about 98+% that surely will have importance to other marketing channels. Consider the potential benefits of combining this ubiquitous medium with other marketing approaches:

* *Telemarketing can be used to screen and generate sales leads for the sales force.*

* *Phone plus mail provides a 2 1/2 to 10 times leverage over direct mail alone.*

* *Catalogs combined with aggressive inbound and outbound telemarketing can significantly increase conventional catalog response.*

* *Response TV/radio with 800 number emphasis can generate huge responses if properly implemented.*

* *Telemarketing, direct mail and video brochures--telefocus marketing--can provide a powerful, new selling synergy.*

* *Telemarketers can follow up on inquiries from print or other media, closing the advertising loop via telephone and computer tracking.*

* *Telemarketing can open the ''store'' 24 hours a day, allowing the placing of orders at night and on weekends.*

In many cases of consumer telemarketing, and almost every case of successful business-to-business telemarketing, other direct marketing channels usually work in concert with telemarketing. Very seldom does one find successful, stand-alone telemarketing operations.

Integration doesn't occur naturally, however. In order to accomplish it, the telemarketing operation must

1) *Be given an organizational status equivalent with all other directly related sales and marketing functions, and*

2) *Have equivalent reporting access to the senior sales and/or marketing manager.*

Although titles may change, the field sales, marketing and direct marketing management should be responsible to *one* sales and marketing executive. This is necessary so that one corporate individual is charged with all sales/marketing strategies and the profitability of the complete selling effort.

Without such dedicated corporate leadership, infighting, competition and empire-building can often erode all possibility of cross-fertilization among the marketing channels. Telemarketing must serve and be served within the context of the other marketing channels in order to be most effective, and this is likely to happen only if a single individual is responsible for orchestrating telemarketing and the other channels.

Managing this "orchestra" requires a fine understanding of the various "instruments," however, particularly an understanding of how they can work together. In this chapter, we'll discuss each of the important direct marketing channels and attempt to give a clearer idea of how telemarketing can function effectively with them.

PRINT

Many companies have used direct response print advertising for obtaining sales leads, most often depending upon "bingo cards" (or reader service cards) to carry the response. Because bingo cards from the publisher can often take up to six weeks to be forwarded to the advertiser (from McGraw-Hill studies), many potential sales can be lost due to these inordinate delays.

In a recent study of inquiry handling, George E. Steinbrenner, a Cleveland-based inquiry handling specialist, found that only a minority (44%) of Northeast Ohio manufacturers were able to respond to advertising and publicity inquiries within a 60-day period, and more than 25% of the advertisers studied took more than two months, an average, in fact, of 93.4 days![1]

It doesn't seem the advertisers or publications can blame their old scapegoat, the Postal Service. "*Despite being the brunt of many complaints,*" Steinbrenner reported, "*the Post Office delivered 95.5% of the responses within two days.*"

Steinbrenner's most important conclusion, and one that reinforces what we're trying to say here, was that:

"*. . . there is a general lack of respect for the sales inquiry and a lack of commitment to professional processing.*"

The debate about the relative value of bingo cards and how efficiently they're moved by prospect, publication, Postal Service and vendor will probably go on for a long time to come. The point to bringing it up here is to suggest that there might be more effective ways to use a tried and proven response vehicle.

Also, as the sales leads are distributed to field sales (direct or distributor), management has no assurance that the leads will ever be followed up by the field sales personnel (only 28% of the inquiries sent in by business publication readers are ever followed up by a sales call, per the Center for Marketing Communications).

And, finally, without a "closed loop" feedback and analysis system, marketing executives simply have no idea whatsoever of the bottom-line sales value of their print advertising. And they often wonder why their advertising budgets are cut back during recessionary periods.

A combination of print ads, telemarketing and a computer provide a better solution. Ideally, a dedicated telemarketing qualification center assisted by appropriate computer programs should be implemented to provide the following to gain an improved sales and analysis response:

* *Provide a central incoming and outgoing telemarketing operation with literature fulfillment.*

* *Utilize both bingo cards and an incoming toll-free 800 number for inquiry responses (let the prospect determine the immediacy of his or her own needs).*

* *Qualify all incoming sales inquiries to determine which should be followed up by field sales personnel or telephone sales reps, which should receive "mail conditioning" and which should be suppressed (e.g., duplicates, competitors, bad credit risks, etc.).*

* *Qualify all bingo card inquiries after receipt from the publisher via outbound telephone calling.*

* *Track all inquiries to be handled by field and sales management personnel to determine individual and group sales effectiveness.*

* *Analyze the complete cycle of events to accurately determine the ultimate dollars sold per dollars spent on various print advertising.*

Consider, for example, the synergy possible when bingo cards are teamed with toll-free 800 numbers. The combination is far faster than just using bingo cards themselves.

With an 800 number available, respondents in a hurry, ready to buy, call for a required immediate response. Those with a casual interest, or a legitimate future need, can go the easier route of annotating and mailing the readers' service card. Both methods, therefore, complement the needs of the inquirer and the advertiser.

This type of well-managed computer/telemarketing operation should be ideal in assisting with all sales inquiry tracking, sales results and media analyses. Overall benefits include: faster mailing fulfillment, better utilization of the field sales force, increased sales, improved customer service, and media results documentation.

But is the combination used? To quote George Steinbrenner again:

INTEGRATING TELEMARKETING

"Modern telephone marketing techniques have not penetrated the industrial market as deeply as expected with only 15.2% of the surveyed firms utilizing '800' toll-free numbers." [2]

For a further discussion of how telemarketing can be used to manage leads, no matter what their origin, see the section on "Closing the Advertising Loop."

DIRECT MAIL

By using telemarketing follow-up to direct mail, response rates can be increased significantly. Most experts believe that response rates can be increased by a factor of 2.5 to 10 times.

A telemarketing/direct mail combination can be used in several ways. Direct response programs can be triggered by mass mailings and 800 numbers. Some organizations follow up inbound responses with outbound calls to increase overall close rates.

A variation on the above technique is the more limited and specific targeting of direct mail lists to allow outbound telephone follow up to non-respondents as well. The extent of the mailing wouldn't exceed the intent of the telephone calling, i.e., all mailers would be followed up by outbound calls. The practicality of this depends on outbound phone sales productivity and cost/performance ratios.

Targeted mailings can also be used between a qualification survey call and an appointment request or "close" call. Here, the distinguishing feature is the prequalification of the mailing list, thus mailing only to fully qualified prospects. Telephone calls both precede the initial mailing and the follow up.

Mail responses also can be generated during telephone sales calls, usually determined by the individual prospect's needs and requests. Responses sent after the telephone call are generally specific literature packages, proposals, order acknowledgements, or "thank you" letters.

Within a few years, direct mail techniques are very likely to become as sophisticated and flexible as custom tailoring. Computers will examine prospect files for information, compose laser-printed letters tailored exclusively to each prospect's need and buying situation, and automatically select brochures and other items for the mail package. Electronic mail responses *direct from the computer* will also be possible.

Then, after "softening" the prospects with the appropriate mail contact, telemarketing can follow up to close the actual order.

CATALOG

Closely allied to telemarketing/direct mail programs is the telemarketing/catalog synergy. Generally, both the number of catalog orders and the size of the orders are increased by the use of an 800 telephone number. Also, there is a greater opportunity for cross-selling (selling related items) and up-selling (selling more expensive and profitable items).

Clearly, use of an 800 number provides a competitive edge.

Utilization of appropriately trained telephone sales personnel rather than just plain order takers also helps. Using minimally qualified personnel simply to record orders is a waste of sales opportunity.

Also, in business-to-business catalog marketing, outbound calling to determine appropriate contacts and develop initial interest can precede the mailing of catalogs to targeted prospects. Follow-up telephone calling to close for orders completes this cycle of "rifle cataloging."

Special telephone-only discounts help to maintain the controlled outbound catalog selling effort after new customers are developed, an excellent way to get around the problem of "catalog glut."

Closure rates for this kind of targeted catalog marketing can be very high. Of course, list selection and list enhancement remain critical elements in this type of target-marketing process.

BROADCAST/CABLE

Sophisticated and efficient telemarketers can provide significant assistance to direct response network or cable TV. Even with the relatively low cost of cable advertising, the overall costs of response TV advertising (which, if we include the production costs, the media time and telemarketing will probably *begin* at $50,000), make profitability on single sales of single products very difficult to achieve. The key to profitability is often a matter of follow up--which happens to be one of telemarketing's key strengths--and quick, accurate measurement (which happens to be another).

Properly trained, CRT-guided telephone sales representatives (not order takers) can generate *significant* incremental business in broadcast/cable response. Here, they can have the same function as catalog telemarketing reps, always watching for opportunities to cross-sell and up-sell. Clearly, by increasing average order size, telemarketing can help increase profitability of the response TV effort.

Measurement is a bit more problematic. As with other forms of direct response advertising, there are two types of analysis possible: *front-end* and *back-end*. The former represents immediate feedback on the response performance of a given outlet, which, in the case of broadcast, would be on a daily basis. Back-end analysis is a relatively more leisurely measurement of the details of response. Consider for a moment where telemarketing can help with both of these measurements.

Front-End Analysis. As we indicated above, response TV advertising is expensive. It is critical to concentrate advertising dollars on the stations or outlets that are performing well. Telemarketing reps are able to provide a daily estimate of where spots are running and how they are performing, by station.

Knowing *where* spots are running is important because much response TV time is bought on PI (per inquiry) or ROS (run of station; preemptible) to lessen risk or save costs. This means the stations decide when and where the spots are run. Once the marketer knows how many spots clear on which outlets, it is possible to quickly calculate the cost, per lead, per station and immediately cancel spots on stations that aren't performing.

Back-End Analysis. A more careful study of response after the station affidavits are in makes it possible to better target future advertising. Some of the important variables here are:

* *Response percentage.*

* *Size of audience.*

28

INTEGRATING TELEMARKETING

* *Type of audience.*

* *Day of the week.*

* *Time of day.*

* *Time of response.*

* *Linkage of response to spot.*

* *Length of spot.*

While not all of these variables are collected by telemarketing (Arbitron audience ratings, for example), many could not be collected without the person-to-person interaction telemarketing allows. Also, the use of unique 800 numbers can help to quickly differentiate response by station within specific markets.

As cable TV becomes increasingly a "target casting" vehicle, reaching an estimated 50 million households by 1990, the value of efficient telemarketing to measure response, to handle the responses, to convert them to orders and *fulfill quickly* will become a critical factor in response TV marketing success.

From Tony Everett, Vice President, Doner Direct, W.B. Doner and Company, here are a few key points for success in creating a TV response using telemarketing:[3]

* *Test both 60 and 120-second spots, keeping in mind the purpose of your ad (generating sales or soliciting inquiries).*

* *Use unique 800 numbers for each station within a market to pinpoint response.*

* *Leave the 800 number up at least 20 seconds on camera. And here's a money-saving tip: Have the actor off camera--or use a voice-over--when you announce the 800 number since it costs a lot to have to reshoot when you want to change numbers.*

* *Seize the audience quickly. Like the cover of your catalog, the opening of your TV spot must talk directly to the prospect. It must stand out from all other commercials so he or she recognizes, "This is meant for me."*

* *Tell prospects to call NOW. If you do not, they tend not to call at all, and you lose them. Saying "Call now" tells viewers your store is "open." Responses on Sundays, for instance, when those words are not used, are low. On Monday morning, however, responses are up.*

* *Give a specific reason for viewers to make the call. And, if you want them to buy over the telephone, tell them to get their credit card ready so you do not pay the telemarketer to wait while they go to find it.*

* *Fulfill quickly. There is a relationship between the immediacy of TV and prospects' expectations of fast fulfillment--particularly in lead development. If you do not get back to these prospects quickly, they will never become customers.*

FIELD SALES

Probably one of the most popular and fastest growing telemarketing applications is using telemarketing reps to handle the 80% of the company accounts that provide only 20% of the business. Field sales reps, then, concentrate on the 20% of the accounts that provide 80% of the business. Overall sales costs are drastically reduced.

Also, this sort of program frees the account executives to better protect the heartland of the profit base, enhance major account revenues and open up new major accounts by concentrating on high-level sales prospecting. Other telemarketing/field sales rep tie-ins include assisting with handling invitations to seminars, demo vans, product showings and other events sponsoring mass presentations/demonstrations by field sales reps to groups of prospects. Lead generation by calling cold "suspects" to determine prospect qualifications, decision-makers and buying status is also another major application.

Often, a two-pass telephone call routine is used within this context. The first telephone call is made to establish appropriately qualified prospects. After an introductory mailer is sent, a second telephone call is initiated to set up an appointment for the field sales rep. Sales programs such as these have often increased sales by over 150%.

The essential point is this: with the current average sales call cost at more than $200, and the ever-greater profit squeeze from competitors, companies can no longer afford to send field sales reps out to visit those smaller accounts. Therefore, many companies are now marrying both a telemarketing operation for marginal and inactive accounts (and smaller prospects), while concentrating the field selling organization on the larger major accounts and prospects.

Account Selection. Individual management organizations must determine which accounts should stay with the field sales force, and, of course, which should be delegated to the telemarketing operation. Many organizations have initially experimented with using telemarketing to handle only the smaller of accounts (as well as the inactive ones). Then, gradually, they have increased the size of the accounts to be handled by the telemarketing unit.

Once the field sales force/telemarketing parameters of account size are ultimately established, however, it is important to track account changes to make sure the appropriate reps are handling the right accounts.

Benefits. There are many benefits to this type of field sales and telemarketing integration. First and foremost is the fact that sales will, in all probability, increase while sales costs will drop.

Why? Because prior to the implementation of telemarketing, the bulk of the smaller accounts probably did not receive nearly the attention they should have, simply because many of the field sales reps knew it wasn't cost (or commission) effective to make field sales calls on these accounts.

Other benefits from telemarketing/field sales integration are account protection, prevention of competitive inroads and the ability to position field sales reps strategically to handle only the largest and most lucrative customers and prospects.

The other side of the telemarketing coin, therefore, is that major accounts will significantly grow and provide increased revenues because of the increased executive sales support given to those high-potential customers and prospects. Both large and smaller company accounts can now receive better service, more responsive customer handling and, of course, improved account development as a result of a synergistic field sales/telemarketing operation.

This is why the vice president of sales should oversee both complementary operations so that the best balance can be provided to get maximum efficiency from the field sales/telemarketing effort. Separate management heads would invariably cause friction, empire-building and the lack of balance.

Compensation/Organization. Compensation is frequently a problem for organizations setting up a field sales/telemarketing operation. Here are a few suggestions gleaned from experience:

* *Pay the telephone sales reps on a salary/commission basis, or on a guaranteed draw against commission.*

* *Upon the establishment of the telemarketing operation, and the original distribution of accounts to the telephone sales reps, pay a "double commission" for an overlap period of three to six months so that the "I had been working on that account" problem can be nullified or at least decreased. Do not continue to double comp indefinitely.*

* *Upgrade the current field sales reps to executive sales reps and expect more from them in major account and prospect development (this and the prior comment should help to assuage the feeling of the field sales reps as the telemarketing operation is implemented).*

* *Use normal attrition as an opportunity to reduce the size of the field sales force so that further economies of the telemarketing operation can accrue.*

The Payoff. Bottom line, if the appropriate integration of field sales and telemarketing is accomplished, an organization should be able to improve its overall profitability. After all, increased sales, lower selling costs, account protection, and effective new business development should go a long way toward improving overall sales/cost performance.

CLOSING THE ADVERTISING LOOP

Because advertisers and their direct-response advertising agencies want to do a better job targeting

31

inquiry response programs and qualifying responses, various specialists have designed systems for handling inquiries. Many of these are just too cumbersome or incomplete to really work, however.

The ultimate goal should be to "close the advertising loop," making the response truly *measurable*. It's one thing to have a *statistical count of actual inquiries* to broadcast, print and direct mail advertising. The real dream, and another thing entirely, is to develop a clear report of *actual qualified leads* and a *projected revenue-to-advertising ratio* based on empirical data.

Responsiveness. First and foremost, the ideal inquiry handling system must be *responsive*. Here, again, many programs still rely totally on the ubiquitous "bingo cards" (reader service cards). This seems logical, until one realizes that many of these cards can take up to six weeks to arrive from various magazine publishers, according to McGraw-Hill studies.

Couple this delayed responsiveness with the fact that 43% of all inquiries are processed too late, according to the Center of Marketing Communications (now a part of the Advertising Research Foundation). In other words, the client's advertising dollar is wasted 43% of the time because the advertiser was not able to respond on a timely basis.

Efficient Lead Qualification. Qualification of the sales lead, however it is received, is another critical area of concern.

Some advocate the use of bounce-back cards, along with the mailing of the literature to the inquirer. Bounce-back cards are basically self-addressed printed questionnaires that ask the prospects to qualify themselves for the eventual benefit of the vendor. Noncompliance is usually met by mailing bounce-back card number two, and, probably, bounce back card number three if there's still no reply.

The logic goes something like this: If the prospect is *really* interested in our product or service, he/she will let us know!

Think for a moment about what's going on. The prospective buyer with perhaps an immediate need has dutifully circled his reader service card, mailed it to the magazine publisher, waited for the eventual processing of the magazine and advertiser's paperwork/literature mills and is now faced with a mailed questionnaire (the "bounce-back" card) asking what his level of interest is in buying the vendor's product or service!

The results? Experience has shown a 10%-30% eventual response to the multiple mailing of bounce-back cards. But remember, by this time we've probably already lost a large segment of our potential new market share. It may already be too late to follow up on the qualified leads of those who did respond.

What about the other 70%-90% of the original respondents who didn't return their bounce-back cards? Could they have already made their purchase from a competitor? Or were they not real leads?

What good does it do to concentrate on definitively analyzing bounce-back card respondents only, even if they represent a 10%-30% response? The most complicated computer software and the most expensive hardware can be used, and a great deal can be learned--but only about those who responded. Lost forever is 70%-90% of the analysis base and, perhaps, a major slice of the potential buyers as well. We need to learn, too, from the customers who don't respond.

Are the sales reps the answer to lead qualification/follow up? No. Surveys done by the Center for Marketing Communications have shown that only 28% of the inquiries sent in by business publication readers are ever followed up by a sales call. Further, studies by the Center also have found that less than half of those

32

surveyed reported receiving requested literature on a timely basis (18% of the requests were *never* received, and 43% of the inquirers received the material too late to be of any value). This is a *total* front-end waste of 61% of the advertiser's investment!

The evidence is strong, in short, that the sales force just isn't doing the job. It's not all their fault. It's simply an inappropriate use of their time.

Consider this list of reasons why field sales reps shouldn't be expected to qualify their own response leads:

* *Leads are often processed by field sales reps too late (they have other priorities, vacations, sickness, changes of territory, procrastination . . .).*

* *Some leads may not be worthy of follow-up by sales reps (not enough potential business, too expensive, too isolated, etc.).*

* *Sales reps are not automatically expert at interviewing or evaluating prospects by telephone.*

* *Without at least some preliminary contact--"mail conditioning," proposals, etc.--there's no way for sales management to know which leads are even worth qualifying.*

* *Management will have to relinquish control over the prospect inquiry database to the sales reps (exposing the database to data loss through turnover, loss to competitors, error, etc.).*

And if these reasons aren't enough to persuade you to avoid this misuse of the field sales force, consider this one final reason:

* *The time of a sales person is almost always better spent selling than anything else, including qualifying.*

Well, if the sales force shouldn't be used to qualify leads, who should? What about the follow-up to qualification, the work that's supposed to lead to the ultimate sale?

The "Premier" System. The answer comes in many specific forms, depending, to a great extent, upon the specialist to whom you're talking. But there is generally a common agreement that an *inquiry tracking system* is essential.

The precise form of a system is extremely variable--anywhere from a three-part card system (one for the field sales rep--after qualification is completed, one for the sales manager, and one for control), to very exotic computer processing and analysis. But the form the system takes is not as important as making sure *all of the necessary prospect information* is processed.

Here is what a premier inquiry-handling system should be doing to help make sure the system can "close the advertising loop."

The initial response to the inquirer should be .a combination of a toll-free 800 number *and* bingo cards (if available). It makes sense to let the potential customer determine the immediacy of his or her needs.

33

For low-volume or occasional needs, an outside service agency can provide the initial response. Higher-volume applications, and those with very technically oriented products or services, need to be looked at carefully to determine whether an in-house direct telephone response or a service agency approach is best.

It's important, however, at this juncture, for the advertiser to be in a position to review and prescribe the necessary evaluation procedure for answering the incoming respondents' telephone calls. Not only is it essential to provide for an immediate response, but it's necessary to evaluate the inquirer's needs and prospect potential, one-on-one, over the telephone. Compare this to the serial effect of the classic solo bingo card response with the subsequent series of three bounce-back cards.

In fact, with an appropriate computer software program and video display terminals (VDT's), it is quite possible for the response to the inquirer to be guided through some fairly complicated branching so that the inquiry can be handled adroitly. The information can be gathered over the telephone for qualification purposes, but the computer program can be designed to weight the caller's responses so that the telephone sales rep can suggest the necessary follow-up.

Nonprospects (e.g., competitors and brochure collectors) can also be handled *most discreetly*.

Those respondents who have chosen the route of replying with bingo cards can be handled in the same manner via *outbound telephone qualifying*. Again, the decision whether to go in-house or use a telephone service agency has to be evaluated.

The computerized terminal helps the telephone sales rep decide whether to close immediately (if closing is an option), or to send literature. He or she can suggest that a product manager call back, or hint that the lead will be directed immediately to a field sales rep. (This becomes a "hot lead" that truly *is* hot.) If this latter option is taken, the system calls for either an immediate call to the field sales rep, or an automatic transmission of the lead electronically.

With the response in and analyzed, literature can be sent, proposals created, follow-on mail conditioning established, and orders processed. Here, again, a computer should be used.

Follow-up activities also are made much easier with a computerized inquiry system. Territory determinations and lead follow-ups on a 30-, 60- and 90-day basis can be generated for sales reps/distributors at the appropriate time intervals.

A Total Tracking System. Once the initial response to the inquirer has happened, and the initial prospect data is captured, information is available for tracking all necessary data, to ensure the most responsive follow-up possible.

Sales managers still must attend to the reporting system, of course, to help ensure that the necessary sales follow-up and field sales rep status responses are, in fact, completed on a timely basis. But at least now the advertiser has responded to and evaluated the prospects quickly. Very importantly, the advertiser and agency now are dealing with a full deck of information.

Best of all, management, not field sales , is now in full control of the overall inquiry response system.

Documentation of the overall advertising and sales effort can be made much easier because the response has been made in the most propitious manner and efforts have been chronicled in detail. The premier inquiry handling system is now:

* *Responsive.*

* *Current.*

* *Complete.*

And the advertiser and the agency can now "close the advertising loop" by not only increasing the value of the response, but also by knowing the exact return from each advertising dollar spent.

The result? The advertiser's dream: the ability to develop a realistic, empirically based, *projected revenue-to-advertising ratio.*

CONCLUSION

Although there are some examples of exclusive telemarketing, most applications require a symbiosis with other direct marketing disciplines. It is mandatory that the multichannel marketing effort be strategically handled with special care, effort, and coordination.

If all this sounds too logical, think for a moment about a major division of a large company that set up a (supposedly) integrated field sales, catalog and telemarketing operation. Each of the separate three entities reported to a different sales or service executive with no one taking sales/marketing responsibility for coordinating the overall program effort.

In fact, the telemarketing manager was rebuffed by the catalog manager when the suggestion was made to integrate the efforts of catalog and telemarketing. The catalog manager, who had only nominal direct mail experience--not catalog experience--told the telemarketing manager that she did not want to "confuse" the nature of "her" business-to-business catalog with the telemarketing operation.

This particular division has been losing money for some time. Unfortunately, with this kind of misguided direct marketing leadership, it will almost certainly get worse.

The moral of this story, and too many others like it, is that when companies are repositioning within the "new marketing" framework, they should appropriately structure the direct marketing leadership in the first place, hire the best creative direct marketing specialist(s) possible, and integrate all associated multichannels into one synergistic selling operation.

Telemarketing is not an entity onto itself. It should be part of an overall, strategic marketing plan, a plan that can be very successful when properly integrated with the other direct marketing disciplines.

Changing marketing and selling styles for the future is quite right, but the coordinated creative plan and follow-up execution is absolutely critical--the difference between success or failure.

----

[1]Steinbrenner, George E., *A Study of Northeast Ohio Industrial Advertisers' Response to Advertising and Publicity Inquiries*, Cleveland: 1985, E.S. Advertising Services, Inc., 1890 E. 40th Street, Cleveland, Ohio 44103.

[2]*Ibid.*, p. 2.

[3]*Catalog Age*, November 1987, p. 148.

CHAPTER 3

Telefocus Marketing

Richard L. Bencin
Donald J. Jonovic, Ph.D.

At the Direct Marketing Association's 1987 Spring Conference in Honolulu, Stan Rapp, Chairman of the Rapp & Collins Group, climbed out of a "DeLorean time machine" prop on stage and identified for the audience five signposts that he said will shape the future of marketing. The co-author of *Maximarketing* proceeded to unveil video brochures as one of the key tools of tomorrow's marketers.

Video brochures? A key element in future direct response advertising? Was Rapp indulging in some unsupported fantasy? Many people in his audience had never heard of video brochures.

If he was fantasizing, he isn't alone.

"Video brochures are definitely a new, valid medium for direct response selling," John Carter, Director of Marketing for The Alderman Company in High Point, North Carolina, has said, *". . .a vehicle that will maximize product sales simply because it can visually describe merchandise (products or services) better than print media. Entertaining, high-quality productions will yield tremendously high buying responses."*

Carter's company, one of the world's largest photographic service firms, plans to move quickly in this new video brochure marketplace. And this is no small move, bringing to bear The Alderman Company's 500,000 sq. ft. studio, a 10,000 sq. ft. carpentry shop for set production and a Dallas fashion office.

THE VIDEO BROCHURE/TELEMARKETING CONNECTION

Stan Rapp's positive prognosis for video brochures is based on their major advantage--they make it possible to carry a *visual message* into the home or business that is *specifically tailored* to each prospect. But the emergence of this new marketing channel is also the result of a number of important factors, he believes, all coming together at the same time:

* *The ability to target specific audiences.*

* *The decreasing costs of video brochure production and reproduction.*

* *Increasing entry of competitors to the field, thus providing a more competitive environment.*

36

* *Video's inherent selling power.*

* *The growth of cable and the video rental industry.*

* *The consumer's increasing dependence on video for information.*

In short, the American consumer, whether adult or juvenile, is very comfortable with the process of slipping a tape into the VCR. Clearly, video has become a pervasive medium, and just as clearly, it has great marketing potential.

But how can marketers use it effectively?

With a process called *telefocus marketing.*

This isn't simply a new buzzword invented by overzealous consultants. The process--and it *is* a working process--combines video brochures with direct mail and telemarketing. It is a totally integrated marketing program that uses the inherent strengths of each discipline, while leveraging each against the other for maximum marketing efficiency.

HOW TELEFOCUS MARKETING WORKS

The idea is best described through the use of an example.

Assume that Porsche Motor Cars has decided to use telefocus marketing in the U.S. to market their new Model 924S sports car. Their major goals for the campaign would be to greatly increase sales, expand market share and achieve swift distribution of their new, low-cost (relatively, for Porsche, at $24,000) automobile.

Their campaign would probably work something like this:

* *A direct mail piece would be sent to current owners of Corvettes, Datsun 280ZX's, Nissan 300 ZX's and Mazda RX 7's, using lists readily available from state motor vehicle registrations.*

* *The copy in the mailing piece would list the most exciting features of the new Porsche model and would offer a demonstration ride via an action video tape.*

* *An 800 number would provide the response vehicle for prospects to order their demonstration video tape. During the call, the prospect would agree to return the video tape within 30 days, leaving a credit card number as a deposit.*

* *Prospects who respond would be sent a video tape through the mail.*

* *Telemarketing would be used to follow up by phone with nonrespondents to the mailing.*

*   *All recipients of the video brochure would be encouraged by the brochure
program to visit a local Porsche dealer for an actual demonstration ride.
Incentives, such as a factory rebate or a special option package in exchange
for the tape, would help support the promotion.*

This example clearly shows the potential video brochures could have in marketing programs for high-ticket items. Highly involving products imply highly involved information-seeking on the part of the potential consumer. The video brochure answers this need very well.

Videologs--a Close Cousin. Full-motion video catalogs, as either a complement to print catalogs or, better yet, an *extension* of print catalogs, are potentially powerful relatives of the video brochure. Video can help make a product or products (e.g., high-fashion clothing) come vigorously alive, while slow motion and appropriate freeze frame photography can focus the consumer/prospect on important product details and features.

Royal Silk, for example, produced a video catalog in Hawaii at a cost of only $40,000, a videolog that was very successful according to producers Jerry DeSantis and Apo Oguz of the Video Marketplace. It wouldn't be surprising if this new company were only one of the first to enter into this new video production business.

Desktop Videos. As a complement to full-motion video brochures, desktop videos combine the technologies of both the personal computer and video, creating low-cost, high-resolution graphic productions.

"Computer-motion video," prepared on IBM-compatible PC's, can provide significantly lower cost video brochure presentations. A regular VCR-equipped television set or large screen TV monitor can be used for the prospect's viewing.

It now appears that IBM's Personal System/2 line of computers, with its high-resolution visual graphics array (VGA) circuitry, will help speed the advent of desktop videos. These machines provide a palette of over 256,000 colors.

Excited by the prospect of creating low-cost, quality marketing visuals, Robert P. Colgan left his Senior Vice President/Group Director position at Young & Rubicam in 1985 to form his own desktop video marketing and consulting firm. As president of Colgan & Associates in Detroit, Colgan's creative desktop video concepts are getting some very good reviews, indeed.

According to Colgan, "*High-resolution graphics with virtually an endless color spectrum can be prepared via special software and an IBM-compatible-based microcomputer.*" Colgan uses a Targa desktop video program called the System 3000 (Targa Systems Corporation, Hartford, CT).

Clearly, virtually anyone with an initial investment of less than $20,000 for both the software and a computer could prepare their own homemade desktop video presentations. However, it does take an experienced marketing professional with creative ability to produce a professional product.

Colgan believes that high-quality animated presentations using graphics that seem to dance around the screen can result in exciting marketing presentations. "*Computer-motion video that moves left to right, up and down, and with the ability to fade and dissolve back onto the screen with superimpositions provides a completely integrated, information-rich presentation.*"

Automobiles or human models, for example, can fade or dissolve while other visuals gambol across the screen. Also, a number of images can be capsulated within each frame. Add highlighted information with strobe-like effects, music and professionally recorded voice over and you have an excellent basis for a video brochure.

The Targa 3000 software, for example, can take virtually any video source, such as photos, video tape or video disk and integrate them with business graphics, 13 fonts of type and models. Captured video can be modified by cropping and scaling, and original artwork can be created from scratch.

Another inherent flexibility of such presentations is that, because the master copy is stored on a computer, customization of the presentation is relatively easy. Content can be selected for various audiences right at the computer keyboard and virtually an infinite number of presentations can be developed. This is target marketing to the nth power.

Asked about the costs of a professionally prepared desktop video (creative and production costs), Colgan estimated costs at about $500 to $1,000 per edited minute--less than half the cost of a relatively inexpensive full-motion video. Of course, photographic material and copy sources should be provided by the client. Research and photography significantly increase the cost, should the producer be asked to do so.

THE ADVANTAGES OF TELEFOCUS MARKETING

In addition to being able to market high-ticket items relatively easily through a fairly sophisticated selling process, there are other major advantages of telefocus marketing:

1) *Sales cost reduction.* Mail, phone and video can, in many cases, replace or complement the very costly process of using field sales representatives to search out prospects, to develop sales audiences, to demonstrate products and services and to build rapport and credibility.

2) *Targeting sales effort.* Telefocus marketing, using its process of graduated involvement and qualification, can help to target the most intensive (and expensive) sales effort to those most likely to buy.

3) *Leveraging direct response promotion.* The use of video in coordination with direct mail and telemarketing allows for a highly sophisticated, concerted promotional message.

4) *Measurability.* The use of direct response media, particularly telemarketing, allows for much greater precision in measurement of the success of a particular sales approach. This precision is difficult, if not impossible, to achieve through the use of a field sales force alone.

5) *Speed.* Telefocus marketing allows for a swift, controllable blanketing of the target market, thus preempting effective response by the competition.

Other advantages to telefocus marketing, as opposed to broadcast TV, have been noted by John Carter. Telefocus marketing is significantly less expensive, allows for presentation of a more complete sales message, offering both entertainment and information, relatively unlimited message length, convenience for the prospective customer and an interactive, direct response marketing channel.

Given the ubiquitous nature of charge cards and VCR's (more than 70 million in the hands of consumers and businesses), along with the growing acceptance of 800 numbers, the market seems well poised to accept this new medium.

KEY ISSUES TO BE RESOLVED

Our Porsche example might seem a bit contrived, or, at least, ready-made for telefocus marketing. Can this approach be used effectively in the variety of product and market situations that exist in the real world? To answer this question, we need to take a harder look at the strategic value of the various direct response elements.

First, some strategic questions need to be answered:

*   *What are we trying to accomplish with our program? Do we want orders?*
     Appointments for demonstrations? Information requests?

*   *Would an 800 number response-oriented campaign be more productive than*
     an outbound campaign?

*   *Should the direct mail piece precede a video brochure, or is our market*
     targeted enough to send them together?

*   *Are orders closeable over the phone, or is it more appropriate to attempt to*
     set up qualified appointments with a salesperson?

There are many other issues to resolve. Which list to use, for example, what kind of offer, what sort of direct mail package, which pricing points for the product and the video brochure will be the most productive? These questions are very familiar to direct marketers. What may be unfamiliar, however, is how to answer them in the combined context of direct mail, telemarketing, and video.

PRODUCTION/COSTS

According to John Carter, the rule of thumb for producing a relatively inexpensive, but professional-quality full-motion video brochure is about $2,000 to $2,500 per edited minute. Other qualified sources agree. Thus, a finished 20-minute videotape presentation could be produced for $40,000 to $50,000. Included would be the script preparation, local professional actors, filming, editing and the final preparation of a master tape. Not included, however, are multiple-location shoots, elaborate set designs, well-known personalities, or cassette duplication. Elaborate productions certainly cost $100,000 or more to produce.

TELEFOCUS MARKETING

Cassette duplication is relatively inexpensive. Thirty-minute tapes can easily be duplicated for a cost of about $3.50 per cassette. Program lengths and quantities produced would, of course, determine the actual tape duplication cost.

Bill Drummy, Marketing Director of New York Television, Inc. (NYTV), located in Lebanon, New Jersey, has some different thoughts on the entire matter of production costs.

"Costs per minute quotes are bogus," he claims. *"It really depends upon the number of visual elements. Consider a simple shoot of the President of the United States using one camera, a couple of lights and one half hour of uninterrupted filming time. Now compare that with doing a 30-second commercial for MasterCard on eight locations using Don Johnson."*

So, cost estimating is complex, and guidelines only useful as a beginning approximation. Some of the major considerations that impact on production costs are:

* *Elaborateness of the production.*

* *Involvement of major personalities.*

* *Number of required shooting days.*

* *Requirement for special effects or animation.*

* *Locations and the number of them required.*

* *Amount of travel required.*

Although the various visual elements are sometimes more important in budgeting than the actual length of the video, there are some rules of thumb for cost estimates.

Simple shoots, according to Drummy, using one location, local professional talent, simple staging and *"one high-production day,"* could be done for as little as $25,000. It would be a professional presentation with concept, script writing, shooting and editing included (both the shooting and post-production editing). Competent actors can be hired for about $400 to $500 per day, and it appears that there are many professionals available "between engagements."

From the point of view of strategic design of a video brochure, Drummy feels that rather than a client creating one design and getting three production companies to bid competitively, it's better for the client to disclose budget requirements and ask for three separate *original* designs. That way, he believes, the client would probably get the best strategic video production plan for the money.

According to NYTV's Executive Producer, Michael DeFabrizio:

"The most essential element to a program's success is also the most difficult area to price: the video firm's ability to design and package your message creatively while effectively managing your money. A creative team with an overall vision is needed to design exciting and cohesive TV. It's up to you to find the right group of people to work with, and to weigh the value of effectively communicating your message. Remember: your audience

is extremely TV literate and will undoubtedly compare your program to the network TV shows they watch every night at home."

TELEFOCUS MARKETING--ALREADY A CORPORATE REALITY

TCC Limited, one of the largest telemarketing organizations in Canada, has recently entered into telefocus marketing in a big way. In fact, they were the first to create a special major division called TeleFocus Marketing.

Nadine Lucki, President, seeing the enormous potential of telefocus marketing, teamed up with Ken Mallett to reshape the direction of their telemarketing service agency. Mallett, now Vice President, was formerly Director of News and Information Programming for the Global Television Network, and founder of Flightime Television, a production and marketing company specializing in targeted advertising videos for the air travel industry.

Not only the marketing head of TeleFocus Marketing, Mallett puts his technical skills to use as the Executive Producer of the video element of the service.

Both Lucki and Mallett see telefocus marketing as the way of selling in the future. Their view of the new marketing process is that the combination and synergy of telemarketing, direct mail and video brochures, as well as computerized analysis, creates a premier selling matrix--either as a stand-alone selling process or one that readies the potential prospect for a face-to-face closing.

Toronto, they believe, has many advantages for the creation and production of video brochures. At the center of one of the three major video production areas in North America, Toronto boasts many competent actors as well as excellent production facilities. Further, a favorable currency exchange between the U.S. and Canada also offers American companies some special cost benefits.

It looks very much as though TeleFocus Marketing in Canada will be the first of many telemarketing service agencies to become similarly oriented.

POTENTIAL CANDIDATES FOR TELEFOCUS MARKETING

According to Lucki and Mallett, there are certain marketing situations that lend themselves well to the powerful combination of direct mail, telemarketing and video brochures. Here is their profile of client situations that lend themselves to telefocus marketing:

* *High-ticket products and services.*

* *Upscale buyers.*

* *VCR owners (or those with convenient access to VCR's).*

* *Complicated selling processes (generally a long sales cycle, previous use of face-to-face selling).*

TELEFOCUS MARKETING

* *Demonstrations generally required.*

* *Products not easily portable.*

* *Prospects not easily accessible (e.g., physicians, senior executives).*

* *Quality presentations essential for image enhancement (i.e., need for credibility support through studies, reports and testimonials).*

* *Tight control of the selling process required.*

Examples of products or services that generally meet these criteria would be expensive furniture, designer clothing, luxury automobiles, yachts, condominiums, mainframe computers, financial services, franchises, corporate promotions to dealer networks and medical supplies or equipment.

Both Nadine Lucki and Ken Mallett see telefocus marketing as the selling of the future. They view the synergy inherent in combining direct mail, telemarketing and video brochures/catalogs as a powerful marketing process, either on a stand-alone basis, or in support of a field sales program.

SOME TELEFOCUS MARKETING PIONEERS

Several luxury automobile manufacturers have already started marketing via this new medium.

Cadillac, for example, has used video brochures to help introduce their top-of-the-line Allante. Carefully selected prospects were targeted for a video tape presentation. The objective of the brochure was two-fold: product positioning and selling. *Mercedes-Benz* has used a similar campaign in the U.K., with such success that a similar campaign was rolled out in Canada.

Air France illustrated in a video brochure just what it would be like to dine in the luxury restaurants of Paris. Well-known scenes of the city were combined with video visits to fine hotels. Print photos or brochures could never have matched the immediacy and sense of "being there." This particular campaign combined the power of print media, 800 telemarketing, direct mail and video brochures.

In one of Stan Rapp's campaigns, *International Gold* placed a full-page ad in the *Wall Street Journal*, offering a video brochure via an 800 number. The informative tape told the story of gold and how one could invest in that precious, but volatile, commodity. Response, according to Rapp, was excellent.

Soloflex, Inc., selling a relatively high-ticket item at $850, also leveraged the power of well-produced video. Their 22-minute tape showed an attractive, clearly well-exercised couple demonstrating the company's new exercise station. In still photographs, the Soloflex equipment can look like little more than a couple of bars of steel arranged in various positions. The video brochure allowed the company to show the consumer exactly what can be done with the equipment, how it works and (subliminally, to be sure) how one might begin to look after faithful use of the product. Video added the necessary dimension, clearly, since nearly 50% of the prospects who received a video brochure placed orders! This was a response rate five times Soloflex's previous direct mail experience.

The *Bauer Corporation*, manufacturers of industrial ladders, created an 18-minute safety video brochure for targeted production executives in major corporations throughout the U.S. Addressing the problem of their dealers' great difficulty in cracking new major accounts, the company used telefocus marketing to help them sell direct.

A major prospect database was created using Dun & Bradstreet sourcing to select the top 1,000 U.S. businesses. Also, to help complement the major user prospects, 30,000 readers of related industry publications *Occupational Hazard* and *Industrial Safety & Hygiene* were added. Safety engineers, production managers and others interested in industrial and construction safety were targeted as likely prospects for telefocus marketing, 31,000 in all.

Once the database was created, the direct mail program was implemented. In the case of the major companies, an individually typed and stamped letter from Bauer President, Norman Miller, was sent, first class, to senior safety executives. A telemarketing canvass, to determine the identity of these executives and their titles had preceded this step to ensure accurate mail targeting.

The broader 30,000 prospect list, on the other hand, received "Overnight Safetygrams," which were graphically designed around the familiar telegram format. In these Safetygrams, specific names and titles were used.

Both messages were built around the following themes:

* *That 95% of all ladder accidents are caused by people, not ladders.*

* *The Bauer Corporation had created and produced an 18-minute safety video and a companion 28-page booklet designed to promote the safe and efficient use of ladders and other work access equipment.*

* *The video could be used for safety meetings to help promote internal plant and/or construction safety.*

* *The video was not a sales film, but an interesting parody on the Dragnet TV series titled, "The Case of the Wrong Ladder."*

Bauer provided the film for a nominal rental charge of $25, and the rental fee was refundable in full if and when the videotape was returned. An 800 telephone number was used as a response vehicle to handle requests for both the video brochure and the 28-page report. Although the Bauer-sponsored film was not directly a sales video, it did include visual references within the context of the program to the Bauer logo and product labeling.

After thousands of responses to the no-risk video tape offer had been received, and the respondents had had time to use the video for internal safety training purposes, outbound telemarketing took over. Multiple telephone scripts were implemented by trained Bauer telemarketing personnel. Three follow-on scripts had been designed for serial presentations to all safety and plant executives who had taken advantage of the Bauer safety video offer.

Script one was a follow-up call to determine the magnitude of the response to the safety videotape and to determine who were the appropriate personnel to talk to for Bauer product evaluation. Referrals and permission to use the original executive's name were adroitly solicited.

Armed with specific buyer references and referrals, major prospects were then called for a telephone product introduction and a request for the prospect to review a ladder/work access equipment product catalog.

Because, in most cases, the buyers were already familiar with the Bauer name and the company's concern for safety, quality and reliability, a very large percentage welcomed the product literature and agreed to a follow-up telephone call.

This "targeted cataloging" approach was finally followed by a third telephone call. In this call, telemarketers suggested a purchase of several ladder products to the buyers for overall Bauer product evaluation. Bauer re-emphasized its commitment to both quality and safety.

Bauer's direct sales approach was then followed up by the involvement of the appropriate multi-line agents/distributors to ship and bill the ladder products. It was now that the local agents were asked to follow up the initial product evaluation order with field sales visits to the now-qualified, pre-disposed Bauer customers.

Telefocus marketing had created the initial customer interest, need and purchase of ladders within a total direct marketing strategy. Telemarketing, direct mail (including catalogs) and video brochures had combined to make it happen.

This successful pull-through program for distributors at the major account level, as well as the broader safety market, has helped the Bauer Corporation to manage the strength and direction of its nationwide distributor program.

GETTING STARTED

Telefocus marketing, in the right place, situation and company, can be an effective extension of telemarketing's ability to communicate, service and sell. Marketers have, of course, been able to market by telephone well enough with direct mail and sometimes with print, broadcast TV, radio and cable advertising. They have not, until now, been able to demonstrate and illustrate products effectively on a one-on-one basis. Usually, marketers have had to depend on a field sales rep or a retail store clerk to close the sale.

Video brochures are now emerging as an alternative to the personal sales call.

While this begins a new ball game in direct marketing, some marketers will be tempted to jump into telefocus marketing without the necessary strategic planning. This new tool depends upon a synergy among channels, and that synergy is fragile. The video must be targeted and designed for direct response. The direct mail must be targeted and "databased." The telemarketing program must be sophisticated--both inbound and outbound.

The tool must be used, in short, in the way it was intended to be used.

CHAPTER 4

Consumer Programs

Richard Herzog
Senior Vice President, Corporate Communications
Zacson Corporation
Pleasanton, California

Outbound consumer telemarketing is an important component of contemporary sales and marketing efforts. Whether it is being used for marketing, sales, servicing or research, it is providing a competitive edge for the companies that successfully use it. By providing a way for penetrating the clutter of the marketplace, as well as a technique for establishing and then cultivating relationships, outbound telemarketing is playing a leading role in successful relationship marketing.

This chapter will overview a selection of applications that successfully use outbound consumer telemarketing. No aspect of commerce has been unresponsive to this powerful tool! By reviewing product launching, appointment setting, affinity marketing, fund raising, political marketing and subscriptions, we will provide an indication of the flexibility that telemarketing can provide in meeting today's business challenges.

We will also point out the importance of the following basic principles in the strategy, development, execution and analysis of outbound consumer programs:

* *Executing a customer-creation process that is responsive to the needs of each individual.*

* *Integrating the appropriate media, sales techniques and distribution methods.*

* *Using people with the most appropriate skills for telemarketing.*

* *The importance of good targeting, excellent lists and disciplined database management.*

* *The need to handle sensitively the relationship based on high standards and ethics.*

* *The effectiveness of cross selling, up selling and add-on selling.*

* *The importance of scheduling the frequency of calling into your lists.*

*   *The advantage of presenting your message many times using a variety of media until overall response rates fall to uneconomical levels.*

CUSTOMER-CREATION PROCESS

In all of these programs, outbound telemarketing has been linked together with other marketing and distribution techniques to create successful partnerships. The purpose of the partnership is to develop a media mix that executes a *customer-creation process*. The components of the media mix (partnership) are first used to target and identify *suspects*. Next, these suspects are qualified into *prospects*. By interacting with the prospects and building the relationship, many decide to place an initial purchase, thus becoming *customers*. Ongoing communication and sourcing helps to build the relationship so that repeat orders are placed, thus creating *clients*. The partnership of media continues so that some become *advocates*, saying great things, sending business and acting as references!

Telemarketing links together and drives the variety of media that build the relationship. Depending on your application, the mix could include: telemarketing, direct mail, response advertising, radio, TV, personal selling, seminar selling, trade shows, premiums, public relations, newspapers, point-of-sale, inserts, outdoor, events and magazines--whatever traditional techniques have proven successful. Outbound telemarketing is a key to success because it enhances other programs by providing a very cost-effective, personalized delivery system.

Successful programs occur when these techniques are combined into an effective *"customer-creation process."* Regardless of what mix is used, the result is a carefully orchestrated effort to *target the audience*. The mix then *creates awareness*. It next builds and *generates interest*. In less complex cases, a decision to buy can often be made at this point. However, with more complex or technical products and services, an *education cycle* is often needed. Whether or not the education cycle has been needed, a *qualification process* can be applied to those who have reached the point in the cycle where they are knowledgeable enough.

Qualification is based on whatever criteria the seller finds appropriate. The important thing is that it establishes a method that enables differentiation of prospects. By this segmenting of our prospects we can direct more resources, treat with higher priority, etc., those who have a greater probability of buying.

A key to the success of well-developed, integrated outbound telemarketing programs is that they permit us also to courteously and effectively handle the other groups of prospects. The groups not yet ready to buy are simply nurtured so that their relationship is continued until they reach a more active qualification level. At that point, they are redirected into the mainstream of the process.

To continue with the overall process, when our prospects are qualified as buyers, we *ask for the order*. In many cases, we will more than likely have to ask for the order many times and in many different ways. Next we use the mix of techniques to *close the order*. Here again there will more than likely be more than one attempted close.

Now we *fulfill or implement* our product or service. And, finally, we have what differentiates the excellent program from the commonplace, the *follow-on* or the ongoing relationship-building that makes for long-term customers!

Let's now take a brief look at a variety of programs that illustrate the power of integrating outbound telemarketing together with other media and techniques.

PRODUCT LAUNCH

The AT&T Equal Access Long Distance Service campaign serves as an excellent example of the integration of a variety of media, setting the stage for outbound telemarketing. Nearly every traditional marketing technique was used to position this product and create brand awareness. Then the phone was used to reinforce the messages, respond to questions and concerns, clarify competitive claims and make the sale-- to close those individuals who had not yet been closed.

Not only is this case history significant because it illustrates excellent integration and telephone closing, it is also notable since it is, perhaps, one of the largest campaigns ever. The breakup of the Bell System set off a great race, as millions of customers were asked to choose a long-distance company.

The challenges were considerable: There was a huge number of prospects in a nationwide market. Communication had to be timed and coordinated to take place in each area of the country at the optimum moment in the decision-making cycle. And a multitude of competing long-distance providers were spending heavily and using major campaigns to win the consumer's long-distance business.

Bringing considerable resources to the effort, AT&T mounted a major campaign that integrated every type of advertising and marketing technique. *Over the two years of the campaign, more than 250 million outbound calls were made, 350 million mail pieces sent out, countless pages of print advertising released and hours of mass media aired!*

Keeping track of so many customers and ballots was a major effort that resulted in more than three-fourths of the prospects selecting AT&T as their long-distance carrier during the campaign, which ended in 1987.

This campaign is particularly interesting because the 70.5 million affected households were asked to make an active decision about their long-distance service, a product which, prior to the campaign, had a very low customer recognition. Some have aptly called this campaign the largest nonpolitical election in the history of the country.

APPOINTMENT SETTING

Using telemarketing to set appointments is an application that is being updated. As one of the first widespread uses of telemarketing, appointment-setting campaigns have been used throughout the nation by local home-improvement and insurance companies for a long time.

Today, companies selling products requiring demonstrations are turning to telemarketing as a method of developing business. Often the sales cycle requires the physical interaction of the customer and the field salesperson.

Fred Tregaskis perfected appointment setting on a national scale during his 35 years with Olan Mills, the nation's largest photo studio chain. Over the years, using the telephone to set appointments became the primary source of business at Olan Mills.

Tregaskis says that today's appointment setting is not being left to the demonstrator, but is being completed by dedicated telemarketers. These highly trained communicators are using the phone in structured campaigns to generate leads and set appointments for others whose job it is to fulfill the appointments. The procedure has now become a true two-step process, which is executed by separate professionals.

This has happened because leading organizations have found that effective telemarketing requires different skills and, often, different people. They have discovered that the field closers and demonstrators don't like to do the telemarketing--or can't.

And, it's not the best use of their time, anyway.

In fact, exit interviews at one of the nation's largest insurance companies found appointment setting was the most disliked responsibility of the departing agents. Combining this information with the fact that agents were being hired to sell, not generate appointments, has caused this company to restructure its procedures accordingly.

At Olan Mills, Tregaskis took care to explain to his telemarketers the two-step approach to the successful procedure. The telemarketers' job was not to sell pictures, simply appointments. People at the studios were the team members who sold the photographs.

This two-step team approach is that strategy that will grow and succeed in businesses that require on-site service or selling. By presenting a special offer and scheduling the appointment, the burden of selling products or services that can't be shown or demonstrated over the phone is removed from the TSR and correctly placed with the field sales rep.

FUNDRAISING AND POLITICAL MARKETING

Mike Gordon, of Gordon and Schwenkmeyer, Culver City, California, chronicles the following successful outbound consumer telemarketing application. It shows the importance of good targeting, excellent list selection and disciplined database management.

Our relationship with Senator Alan Cranston began in March of 1985. At that time, Senator Cranston had just begun his bid for re-election to the U.S. Senate. The consensus among most political insiders was that Cranston was going to be especially vulnerable as a result of his defeat in his race for the Presidency. In addition to that loss, Senator Cranston had become the target of the Moral Majority, led by Senator Jesse Helms and Rev. Jerry Falwell.

The concern of the Cranston campaign was the need to raise funds to offset the tremendous financial base his Republican opponent would receive from Helms and the conservative movement. The plan assembled by the Cranston campaign was a multifaceted approach that would draw from every potential fundraising source. These sources, or lists, would be carefully selected, tested and analyzed. One of those potential sources was the small donor telephone solicitation.

Prior to Senator Cranston's campaign, small donor telephone solicitation had not really been tested in a Senate campaign. The prevailing viewpoint was that telephone solicitation could be used to re-activate nonresponding direct mail donors or to enhance a direct mail return as a direct response mechanism. A stand-alone program was not thought feasible.

ENCYCLOPEDIA OF TELEMARKETING

My partner, Kris Schwenkmeyer, and I had direct experience with free-standing telephone solicitation while we were with the California Democratic Party. We watched the Party raise considerable amounts of money from people whom we historically had never asked to contribute. It was our feeling then that Senator Cranston had a tremendous amount of support within the voter file, and would do extremely well with Democratic voters if we could simply make the outreach effort. We were able to convince the Cranston campaign staff to test the viability of telephone solicitation in the Senator's campaign.

The program began in March 1985. We developed a three-tier approach to the solicitation effort. The first tier was composed of individuals who had previously contributed to Cranston. The second was made up of people who had contributed to like causes. The third consisted of a direct solicitation into the Democratic voter file. Each tier was, in effect, a different list segment.

Soliciting Cranston's own donors was the most logical place to start. These individuals had already demonstrated their willingness to support the Senator financially and, therefore, would probably be inclined to contribute again. We were able to reactivate approximately 6,000 of his former donors.

The second tier effort was directed toward like causes. These groups included national Democratic organizations, contributors to other legislative donors and Democratic activists and nonfinancial supporters of Cranston. This solicitation generated an additional 12,000 contributors and returned a profit.

With the first two tiers of solicitation completed, we considered whom we would solicit next. Historically, no one had ever conducted telephone solicitation to the level our program had already reached, so we had no programs to use as models. We concluded that the next move should be to look closely at the Democratic voter file to determine if we could ask rank-and-file Democrats for a contribution. Our theory was that there were probably hundreds of Democrats who would be willing to help Cranston if we would only ask. Nobody had attempted to raise money from the voter file in the past, so we didn't know what to expect.

The voter file solicitation program began in September 1985. The program was set up to contact loyal Democratic voters whom we believed would be in a position to make a contribution. Surprising us beyond our conservative expectations, the effort was a *tremendous success*. Not only did the program generate new donors, but it also was able to raise enough money to cover the cost of the prospecting solicitation. Through the campaign, we developed over 25,000 contributors from voter file solicitation.

By the time we had concluded our three tiers of prospecting, Cranston had acquired a telephone contributor file of more than 52,000 people. Additionally, in the process of conducting the voter file solicitation, more than 775,000 Democratic households in California received the Cranston political message. Lastly, the campaign was able to develop more than 5,000 volunteers to participate in a get-out-the-vote program. All of this was a result of the telephone solicitation project.

In total, Senator Cranston raised more than $1.7 million, with the campaign showing a profit of more than $1 million. It was the most successful telemarketing effort ever conducted by a Senate campaign. Senator Cranston now has a donor file that he will be able to solicit for years to come, with annual returns greater than $250,000.

We believe the facts speak for themselves. Telemarketing in the political arena is clearly going to become a major component of campaigns throughout the country. For the first time, presidential campaigns are now using telemarketing as a way to raise funds. Previously, this had been exclusively a direct mail area.

We are confident that future campaigns will employ the voter identification, voter persuasion and fundraising components demonstrated in Cranston's campaign.

It's hard not to share Mike Gordon's confidence.

AFFINITY MARKETING

Affinity marketing to a customer base is another flourishing area of outbound consumer telemarketing. Maintaining a good relationship with the customer base is the critical factor in affinity marketing. The telemarketing call must not change positive feelings to negative ones!

Let's take a look at the affinity marketing program of Citicorp's U.S. Card Products Group, the world's largest credit card marketer of MasterCard and Visa. This case illustrates good standards and ethics. It underscores the need to handle the relationship with customers very carefully, and the extraordinary success that can result when customers are dealt with in a win-win fashion. It highlights the effectiveness of cross selling, up selling and add-on selling. Finally, it underscores the importance of carefully scheduling the frequency of calling into your lists. In short, don't call too often!

Leslie Tolf, Vice President, Citicorp Telemarketing Service in Baltimore, indicates that telemarketing is becoming the most cost-effective method of generating new products sales among its customers. Citicorp has developed a telemarketing ethics policy for all programs within the bank card business. These guidelines ensure that the quality of telemarketing is consistent with Citicorp's standards of service quality. Tolf says that the key points are:

* *Only quality service and products are offered and Citicorp stands fully behind them.*

* *Every call is handled courteously, professionally and with sensitivity to the customer's time constraints.*

* *Every telemarketing sales representative is knowledgeable about the subject of the call and able to respond to all probable questions immediately or after investigation.*

* *Customers who indicate that they don't wish to be contacted by telephone are not called. Card members are able to remove their names permanently from the telemarketing list if they so desire.*

* *The customer is always given a clear choice to accept or reject any telemarketing offer, and pressure tactics are never used to close a sale.*

Citicorp does not call customers too frequently. When they do call, it is with an offer that is likely to be relevant to that customer's needs. With 20 million calls being made annually, this is of more than casual concern.

Tolf explains that the way to accomplish this is through effective list management. Citicorp has built list management controls into the system to assure that customers are not called repeatedly for a variety of programs. These controls help them conserve the most valuable resource in affinity sales: customer goodwill.

Outbound affinity marketing programs at Citicorp include:

* *Alternate brand.* MasterCard customers are offered a Visa as a second card, and vice versa.

* *Conversion.* Bank card customers with good credit histories are offered a Preferred MasterCard or Preferred Visa to supplement their present account with a higher credit limit.

* *Citishopper.* A computerized long-distance discount shopping service that guarantees the lowest available prices on 250,000 name-brand items.

* *Cititravel.* A toll-free agency service that guarantees lowest available fares plus opportunities for special last-minute travel bargains.

* *Protection Plus.* A card-registration program that acts as a safeguard against lost or stolen cards.

* *Hospital Income Protection.* A daily hospitalization cash payment plan.

* *Graded Benefit Life.* A senior citizen's low-benefit life insurance program.

Offering these enhancements and services as additional card membership benefits has been very successful. Telemarketing is the dominant sales vehicle on a number of these programs, among them Citishopper, Protection Plus and Cititravel. Telemarketing sales accounted for a significant percentage of the income from fee-based bank card products in 1987. Successful programs generally maintain conversion rates above 20%. And, while telemarketing is not used for acquiring new customers, it accounted for 24% of conversion revenues and 28% of alternate brand sales in 1987.

Affinity telemarketing successes are one of the reasons that Citibank is developing an even more sophisticated database. Relationship marketing and even more targeted programs will continue to be prevalent in financial marketing.

Based on their successes with affinity telemarketing, Citibank, American Express, Sears and other leading marketers are developing even more sophisticated databases. Higher levels of customer satisfaction and even more cost-effective telemarketing should result. We look forward to even better relationship marketing and consumer full-account management programs in the future.

SUBSCRIPTION CALLING

A discussion of outbound consumer telemarketing is incomplete unless one mentions subscription calls, one of the first and still one of the most widespread uses of outbound calling in the consumer environment. Whether used for new subscriptions, renewals, or reinstatements, the outbound call has proven successful in case after case.

Subscription programs illustrate the success that results when the message is repeated. Regardless of whether it is used for newspapers, *TV Guide,* Time-Life books, record clubs, season-ticket subscriptions or the latest video cassette clubs, the outbound phone call has worked, even after multiple mailings and termination of delivery have proven unsuccessful. Success dictates using a quality approach, combined with a variety of media. Getting to the target at the right time and in the right manner is key.

CONSUMER PROGRAMS

ADRMP'S

Though widely different, the outbound consumer telemarketing programs reviewed have had one thing in common--the message has been presented by a live telemarketer.

Automatic dialing and recorded message players (ADRMP's) are an alternative to using live telemarketers. Unfortunately, these machines have generated a great deal of negative press and have caused quite a bit of consumer and legislative activity due to their *misuse*. But there are a considerable number of consumer ADRMP programs that have been successful.

When the Sears machine called me to let me know that my order had arrived, and was now available for pick-up at my local store, I was very pleased with the effective manner in which the computer handled the transaction.

Though not as relieved as I was to receive his ADRMP call, a Midwestern friend reacted quickly after being called by his child's school on a recent day. The school was checking on the absent child, and my friend was able to call back with the report that his child was ill.

Joe Pannullo of Valor Telecom, Ltd., West Orange, New Jersey, points out two basic reasons why these applications are successful in contrast to those causing the consumer relations problems.

According to Pannullo, automated phone calls should be placed *only to parties who already have a relationship with the calling organization.* His second principle is the "theory of mutual interest." When two parties in a relationship have a vested interest in the objective or success of a given program, each party is necessarily motivated to ensure its success. In any fully automated communication, it is essential that the message transmitted or information gathered serve a purpose to each party.

Once again, in the case of school call-backs, it is in a parent's best interest to know as soon as possible that a child is not in school, as presumed, and in the school's best interest to make the parent aware of this fact as soon as practicable. In the Sears example, it's in the consumer's best interest to know a product is ready for pickup, just as it's in Sears' best interest to deliver stock immediately.

Ensuring that all called parties have a mutual interest in the contact and have already been involved in some exchange of business with the calling organization helps to direct the course and goals of the communication expected of the system. This also dramatically lowers the potential of angering the respondents as would random contact. In positive, beneficial applications of ADRMP, the respondent, the message and the form of contact have been selected very carefully.

Using technology that enables one to contact a great deal of people in a short period of time must be done with a great sense of responsibility. There are many easy ways to misuse fully automatic dialing systems. The user must always be aware of the potential for abuse. Subjecting all applications to the basic rules outlined above will ensure the proper perspective when considering new applications.

Correctly used by live telemarketers or by automated systems, outbound consumer telemarketing can be a very effective tool for marketing, sales, servicing and research. This chapter illustrates the flexibility of this technique.

In summation: Use telemarketing to complement your other media, sales techniques and distribution systems. Also, search for ways to use telemarketing more cost-effectively to get your sales/marketing objectives accomplished.

53

CHAPTER 5

Business-To-Business Programs

Peg Kuman
President, The Power Line
A Publishers Clearing House Company
Port Washington, New York

Eugene D. Sollo
President, Carlyle Marketing Corporation
Chicago, Illinois

The term business-to-business is an idiomatic expression meaning to do or conduct business between business operations. Specifically, business-to-business telemarketing refers to marketing products or services by phone from one business to another, as opposed to consumer telemarketing, which is business-to-consumer.

HISTORY

While the use of the telephone in business goes back almost to the invention of the instrument in the late nineteenth century, its primary usage in the beginning was almost solely as a means of *communicating* between businesses. There is very little evidence of any conscious measurement of the cost/profit impact at that time of using the telephone to achieve any given objective, including sales.

It wasn't until the late 1930s that R. H. Donneley pioneered telemarketing by using the telephone to entice potential advertisers to buy ad space for the Business Yellow Pages in local telephone directories. The door was opened, permanently. From that time on the telephone has been used, almost as a matter of course, by businesses to market products and services.

Even so, prior to the late 1960s, the telephone was typically not a measured variable in the selling or service transaction. Rather it was typically seen as little more than a part of general overhead and administration expenses. While there were many companies using the telephone for business marketing purposes prior to the early 1970s, the principles of business marketing by telephone were first formalized by Murray Roman, a telephone agency entrepreneur working in the New York City area at that time.

Roman is generally credited with creating the first business-to-business telemarketing *program*, with his successful use of a live sales rep, combined with a prerecorded message made by Norman Cousins,

54

to sell *Saturday Review* subscriptions to professional people.

Roman was joined by other professional marketing and sales executives such as Rudy Oetting and Gene Sollo, who helped pioneer the unification of telephone operating procedures and direct marketing/sales principles.

AT&T began promoting telemarketing in the late 1970s and early 1980s, and with its considerable promotional impact helped to establish this "new" marketing tool.

The growth has been and will continue to be impressive. An estimated 1,500 companies were using the telephone to make outbound or proactive calls in 1975. Current projections are that, by 1990, 30,000 companies will be engaging in business-to-business telemarketing.

PHILOSOPHY

Simply using the telephone to sell, however, whether the program is outbound or inbound, does not guarantee that sound marketing principles are being applied or that telemarketing success is anything but certain. It should be clearly understood that without careful business planning, clear business objectives and the mechanisms in place to measure performance in reaching those objectives, the impact of telemarketing cannot be predicted with any accuracy.

In fact, a poorly planned program could actually be detrimental to the overall organization. Remember always that the telephone, by its very nature, can be perceived to be intrusive or interruptive. While this issue is far more sensitive on the consumer side, it is by no means exclusive to consumer marketing. Business-to-business telemarketers should not only consider economic issues, but corporate goodwill, too.

Consider this: every time a telephone sales rep makes a contact on your organization's behalf, your name, product or brand identification is being communicated to the marketplace. And, regardless of the outcome of the call, an *impression* is made.

How you manage the program, how you direct that "impression," will determine if it's largely positive or negative. Long-term positive impressions are vital, particularly considering that long-term relationships--not just the immediate outcomes of transactions--make up the future of any organization.

Perhaps AT&T and the Bell Companies could have done business a greater service if they would have termed the use of the telephone for marketing purposes something like "marketingtele." What this alternative term would have lost in euphony, it would have gained by putting the marketing horse where it belongs, before the telephone cart. It would have recognized the absolute need for doing a sound marketing plan *first*, and only when that is done, using the telephone to execute that plan.

GROWING REALIZATION OF THE NEED FOR CHANGE

The rapid growth in outbound telephone marketing in the business community, particularly during the last five years, has resulted primarily from the ever-increasing costs of conducting a field sales call. Ten years ago, the cost of a field sales call ran between $125 and $150. Today, those costs can average $250 to $300, double the sales expense of the prior ten years.

As the cost of doing business has increased, so has competition--both from abroad and here at home. Improvements in manufacturing technologies that maintain or even reduce product costs over time can't always offset the dramatic increases in marketing and sales costs.

These changes set the stage for business-to-business telemarketing. Managers began looking for logical ways to reduce costs, while at the same time increasing business, and meeting the competition head-on. Regardless of the particular business situation, the allure of getting more for less seemed irresitible. Telemarketing seemed worth a probe, maybe a test, and eventually a large-scale implementation.

As you would expect, however, many of these managers soon learned that while telemarketing can indeed serve as a viable sales and marketing tool, it too comes with a price tag. Though telemarketing is, in most instances, more cost-effective than the field sales call, the telephone should only be applied to sales and marketing where it makes financial and productive sense.

For example, it usually makes sense for field sales reps to concentrate on key accounts, large volume customers and major prospects. Where this is true, business-to-business telemarketing makes the most sense in the following areas:

* *Opening new accounts (small and medium-sized prospects).*

* *Reactivating/revitalizing old accounts.*

* *New product introductions.*

* *Managing marginal accounts.*

* *Existing account maintenance.*

* *Existing account customer service.*

Generating leads, qualifying leads, setting appointments for the sales force, opening new accounts, reselling existing accounts and other legitimate applications can all be done more efficiently by telephone or in a combined effort with the field and the telephone.

Many large manufacturing companies whose primary sales channel is field sales have begun using telephones to support that effort. From a financial perspective, telemarketing can often be justified because of its greater potential to achieve two goals:

* *To reduce the cost of a field sales call to smaller, marginal accounts.*

* *To penetrate market areas where the field sales reps typically do not call.*

This is particularly true where field sales reps are compensated on commission.

LISTS

Just about every marketing program must begin with a list. That list may be an existing customer list, it may be an existing inquiry list or it may be a cold list of prospective customers based on demographic or psychographic data secured from a list broker or compiler. It might also be a list secured from fellow manufacturers who sells ancillary or affinity products in similar marketplaces.

Once the list is secured, a number of activities must take place prior to implementing the program. The first and most important is to make sure that the list is "clean." This simply means that the contact name, title, company name, address and telephone number are accurate. Often, when working with older lists, you will find that the contact names are no longer valid, or that the company or organization has moved its decision-making office to another location.

The simplest way to clean a cold or new list is to call the individuals on that list, gather the appropriate information and then prepare the list for actual telephone sales follow up. This can be done by using a trained group of people who specialize in securing this kind of information.

In addition to "cleaning" the list, it should also be "de-duped"--a process of removing existing customers from the prospect list. Many telemarketing programs have appeared to have poor results because the program designers overlooked the simple matter of eliminating duplicates on a new list.

TARGETING PROSPECTS AND CUSTOMERS

New lists, however, are not necessarily the most fertile ground for telemarketing. Since the list is such a critical factor in program success, it's important to be very careful in deciding who is actually going to be called.

It's often natural to think first about telemarketing to new prospects, but consider this: new prospects are often the least qualified, most difficult and least rewarding groups that can be called.

Typically, other name categories that are better qualified as prospects:

* *Current customers.*

* *Past customers.*

* *Prospects requesting product/service information.*

Many specialists have said in many ways that your customers are your best prospects. Certainly, current customers hold the greatest promise of sales success. They know you. They like your product(s)/ service(s). They also have a known credit history. But then the question must occur to you: Why use the current customer list to *test* telemarketing when we know they'll buy? How can that prove anything?

It will prove the most important theory of all--that telemarketing can be productive and profitable. The secret to successful testing is to limit each test to one variable. In the case of testing a telemarketing program, the most critical variable is the *telephone*, not the list. If you test new prospects, you have two variables--new prospects and the telephone. If the test doesn't work, which variable is at fault? You'll never be sure.

Assuming, then, that the list we will be using will be made up of existing customers, we have some further refinement to do if we want to increase the chances of success. Question: Do we want to call all current customers or only those customers who:

57

* *Buy specific products/services?*

* *Don't buy specific products/services?*

* *Buy more than a specific dollar volume?*

* *Buy less than a specific dollar volume?*

* *Buy every week? Month? Year?*

* *Buy in specific geographic areas?*

Let's assume you wish to target current customers who buy only a part of your product line and under a certain dollar volume on your primary product. The objective is to sell new products and increase dollar volume. These may be current customers, but the job is far from easy. After all, the reason telemarketing is even being considered is that nobody in the organization has been able to do it to date.

By implementing a professional telemarketing program, it can soon be determined whether an aggressive effort can accomplish great results. The power of telephone sales can be both determined and documented.

BUSINESS-TO-BUSINESS TELEMARKETING: CUSTOMERS

There are a number of ways telemarketing can be used to work more effectively and profitably with customers.

Small Account Management. A popular application for telephone marketing in business today is handling small accounts. Often, when selling via manufacturers' representatives or a field sales force, the small, or inactive accounts are often overlooked. This is a good opportunity area for telephone selling to increase an organization's revenue stream.

Typically, the field handles the A and B markets (the larger accounts). But, often, the C, and certainly the D, markets (the smaller accounts) are overlooked. By developing lists for telephone marketing follow up, the small accounts can be opened, managed, and resold on a regular basis, all by telephone. And, as accounts grow, they can be turned over to the field upon reaching a certain size.

Add-On Sales. Many organizations will automatically call a customer after receiving an order by mail or a field salesperson. Generally, verification of information on the signed order is the reason for the call back. Also, at the time of a phoned-in order an attempt to upgrade the order can be made by suggesting companion, or telephone "sale" items, which can be shipped along with the original order.

Proactive Customer Service. Many customer service units also handle inbound sales calls, and in a growing number of organizations, the customer service units are turning proactive. They're making outbound calls, too, rather than waiting for problems or orders to be called in by the customer.

The premise is really rather basic. Consider calling your customers often enough to establish awareness, to keep tabs on what is happening to your customer market competitively and to anticipate service problems when possible--and, yes, sell additional products or obtain referral leads. But this selling activity is secondary to your preliminary objective which is to say "thank you" for doing business with us.

Catalog Marketing. A rapidly growing further use of proactive telemarketing is in catalog marketing. Most catalog telemarketing has used inbound 800 numbers to facilitate call-in orders. However, proactive outbound calling to increase the frequency of customer orders and the average dollar volume of orders written is generating additional business. Also, telephone reactivation of past customers is being used successfully by more marketers every year.

Another approach that can be successful for the catalog telemarketer is the use of a *selectivity matrix.* This matrix composed of the cataloged products (possibly by major and minor subclasses) along one dimension. The other dimensions can be the previous buying habits of customers, and, possibly, the nature of the customer's business. For example, if a company sells chemical products to gasoline service stations, a matrix could show if and where there are certain stations that would not buy a given product because they have no service bays and only sell gasoline.

These are the kinds of variables that could be factored into a selectivity matrix to make telephone selling more rational, more efficient and more successful.

BUSINESS-TO-BUSINESS TELEMARKETING APPLICATIONS: PROSPECTS

We don't mean to imply, however, that telemarketing can only be effective with customer lists. There are also many effective ways to use the telephone in working with new lists and prospects.

Executive Surveys. Telemarketers can use surveys as a method of *prospect profiling* or *market research*. These two uses should not be confused with each other, however, despite their similarities.

Market research, when properly done by a competent agency, includes sophisticated research techniques such as statistical sampling and scientific interviewing procedures, to develop results that can safely be generalized to the sample's "universe."

Prospect profiling is less ambitious, but just as important. Profiling is simply obtaining the answers to a number of questions that will help determine a prospect's current or future need for an organization's products and/or services.

Lead Qualification. Once a list is cleaned and you have identified your specific program objectives, a lead qualification program can begin.

The first step is to develop a script or call guide that helps achieve your program objectives. For example, begin by contacting the company, identifying the decision-maker, conducting an exchange series of questions and information about your product or service and then determining the prospect's interest level.

Typically, one will qualify the lead by grading responses in varying degrees. A "hot" lead is one who requires immediate follow-up. A "warm" lead is one who may require further attention, but is not

59

interested in buying now. A "cold" lead is one you can let sit for awhile. This is a simplistic classification system, to be sure, but it's a beginning of a lead grading system and everyone must start somewhere.

A key point to remember: without the support of the selling organization, the program will probably be destined for failure or, at best, continued negative "press" within the selling organization. Typically, problems arise when a marketing organization develops telephone sales as a new marketing medium, and the sales organization is only informed about that fact long after the program's strategies have been set.

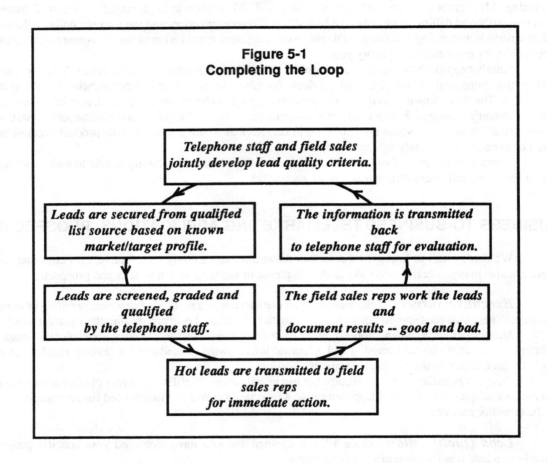

Figure 5-1
Completing the Loop

Telephone staff and field sales jointly develop lead quality criteria.

Leads are secured from qualified list source based on known market/target profile.

The information is transmitted back to telephone staff for evaluation.

Leads are screened, graded and qualified by the telephone staff.

The field sales reps work the leads and document results -- good and bad.

Hot leads are transmitted to field sales reps for immediate action.

Instead, a company must first involve the selling organization at the front end. Ownership is critical to the success of the program, particularly if the field is going to be handling the leads generated by telephone. To avoid the common complaint: *"Telephone leads are worthless,"* one must develop the criteria for grading and qualifying the leads by working directly with the people whose job it is to turn the lead into a sale.

We refer to this involvement as a *complete-the-loop* effort.

Systems and often compensation must be structured in such a way that the field is motivated not only to follow up on the leads presented to them, but to do it in a timely manner--*and* to report the results of the calls to program management.

Confirming that someone from the field will be following up with the prospect by telephone is a great way of further screening the leads for quality. It also ensures that the field sales force will be talking to someone who is indeed interested in discussing the product.

Appointment Setting. From here, we can move on to a somewhat more complex use of telemarketing, one that has its beginnings in lead qualification--using the telemarketing sales force to set appointments for field sales follow-up.

Here, again, it is absolutely critical that the field sales force be brought into the picture early on to participate in the development of the program. Participation simply means that the field sales force identifies those criteria that they feel "profile" a qualified lead for a visit or appointment.

When setting an actual appointment, it is important to have systems in place to coordinate time schedules and dates. While there are many options, one is to preplan schedules and have the field commit to blocks of available time so that the telephone force has some degree of flexibility in setting appointments.

Very often, however, the field (particularly if it is a large sales force) does not have the flexibility in appointment setting to schedule blocks of time, *general* appointments can be made. This saves time and energy in attempting to coordinate schedules. In this instance, the TSR will say something like:

> *"We'd like to have* (name of field rep) *call you to set up a specific appointment to meet. When is the best time to call you back?"*

One of the most commonly overlooked yet most critical components of the appointment-setting process is the appointment confirmation call. Even though the field salesperson may personally confirm his appointment, another option is to use the telephone sales rep to contact the prospect prior to the appointment, confirming the date and time. This effort should help to eliminate "no shows."

Opening New Accounts. Another objective when supporting the field is to open new accounts. Often, field sales reps will, for all of the appropriate reasons, follow up with large national firms. However, there are many smaller business opportunities that companies tend to overlook for reasons of economics or geographic considerations.

With the development of a telephone sales force, either internally or by utilizing an outside service agency, opening new accounts can be done successfully by phone. Typically for most industrial or retail products, this is a two- and sometimes three-step process.

For example, the prospect first must be qualified. At the point of qualification, the telephone sales rep can send a descriptive brochure, catalog, video, or even product samples to the prospective buyer. This information should be dispatched within 24 hours of the telephone call and typically includes a letter confirming the recent telephone conversation.

During the initial call, the telephone sales rep should also confirm the best time and day to reach the buyer. This will insure a much higher contact rate for the second and subsequent calls and serve to reaffirm the fact that this is indeed a selling transaction; that the buyer will expect to make some kind of a decision regarding the product or service being sold.

Depending on how the follow-up sales material or product samples are sent, the next telephone sales call should be scheduled. Typically, if one uses first-class mail, the fulfillment package will be received within two to five working days of the initial call. At that point, one should schedule the second call to be made approximately one week after the information has been dispatched. If lower classes of mail are being used, a minimum of ten days should be allowed.

The second call can be a follow-up sales call or a go-for-order effort. Often, the sales cycle may have to be a multiple effort, giving the time for the buyer to review the material sent or to test the product sample. While this process may take a bit more time, it should be worth the effort and delay.

Dealer/Distributor Support Programs. The telephone has been used for many years to support dealer/distributor networks. By the 1970s, after 800 numbers had been tariffed for use nationally, experiments with 800 numbers in addition to the bingo cards brought early success. The biggest problem with bingo cards in trade journals and magazines was the inordinate amount of time it took for the card request to reach its final destination.

With ''Bingo 800,'' the sense of urgency or immediacy could be conveyed--and maintained.

In addition, advertisers began to run 800 numbers in other types of advertisements such as print, radio, television and direct mail. The old phrase *''Send for more information''* became *''Call today, for valuable information now!''*

This presents an opportunity for the marketer to tele-market at point of inquiry. *''Can you tell me where the nearest dealer is located?''* is a customer-initiated lead that can be qualified for subsequent dealer and/or distributor follow-up.

Some distributors/dealers are using telemarketing internally. Other manufacturers are arranging for telemarketing services through an independent telemarketing agency that allows the distributor/dealer to simply order his telemarketing program and avoid the overhead and supervision responsibilities.

Regardless of which way the distributor/dealer does his telemarketing, it should be done with the greatest of professionalism.

New Business Development. One should not get the idea that business-to-business telemarketing requires co-existence with a field sales force. It doesn't.

Many businesses are currently using telemarketing, along with other related direct marketing procedures (direct mail, catalog, video brochures, etc.), to sell and service accounts *without* any field sales force whatsoever!

In fact, as the newer, more innovative businesses come on line, managed by savvy entrepreneurs, consultants and telemarketing service agencies alike are being asked, *''How can we market our products and services without field sales reps or store clerks?''* Because of the escalating costs of supporting a field sales organization and its virtual unmanageability, the telephone is now being chosen more and more as the one-on-one, interactive selling medium.

Today, in America and around the globe, products/services of all shapes, sizes and price tags are being sold *completely* by telephone.

Here are just a few examples:

*   *Office and computer supplies.*

BUSINESS-TO-BUSINESS PROGRAMS

* *Copiers, facsimilie devices and typewriters.*

* *Word processors, electronic typewriters.*

* *Franchises.*

* *Medical/disability group health plans.*

* *Auto fleets (Including Rolls Royces and Mercedes Benz's).*

* *Service agreements.*

* *Consulting services.*

* *Business systems (accounting, marketing, production, etc.).*

* *Computers (personal and minis).*

* *Advertising space ads.*

* *Newsletters, seminars, training aids.*

* *Long distance services.*

* *Telecommunications systems.*

* *Overhead projectors and supplies.*

* *Industrial ladders and work access equipment.*

* *Car, hotel rentals.*

* *Greeting cards to retailers.*

* *Business and computer forms.*

* *Express mail and package services.*

This list is just the tip of an enormous iceberg. As time goes on, we'll see greater sophistication in the synergies of direct mail (and catalog), video brochures and telemarketing. Larger, higher value and more sophisticated products will, therefore, be sold (and supported) over the telephone.

In fact, a better question than, "*What can be sold over the telephone to businesses?*" is the question: "*What can't be sold if you provide voice (telephone), video (video brochures or videologs), and documentation (direct mail, catalogs, agreements)?*"

FUTURE TRENDS

The issues surrounding American business today aren't different from those that surrounded us in the 1920s. In fact, reading a 1926 issue of *Fortune*, we noted familiar concerns being expressed about time, productivity, profitability and competition.

The telephone should continue to play a major marketing role in helping American business as it has in the past. If telemarketing was "the" new marketing tool of the 1980s, then the realization of its full potential should continue on into the next decade.

In comparison to most traditional marketing methodology, telemarketing has indeed proven itself to be more productive and cost-efficient. It also serves to enhance business marketing where face-to-face contact is still required.

The real impact of telemarketing in American business is just beginning. Many applications that were once considered "esoteric" in certain industries are today being "rolled out" successfully by companies all over the world.

The keys to success in American business have always been the level of service and the quality of the product that one delivers in the marketplace. So it is with business-to-business telephone marketing. Using the telephone to provide a greater level of service by making that phone call to find out if things are going well, or to ensure that the customer understands that the organization is there whenever he or she needs help, can help that customer perceive that your brand, product, company or organization is the best in business today.

CHAPTER 6

Organization and Staffing

Connie Caroli
President, Telemarketing Recruiters, Inc.
New York, New York

Hal Crandall
President, Crandall Associates, Inc.
New York, New York

In any labor-intensive organization, your employees can make or break the bottom line. This is especially true of telemarketing.

The key component in a successful telemarketing operation is management's ability to run the department. Even if your strategic concept is on target, and your prospect list is highly qualified, telemarketing is doomed to failure without a richly sophisticated and experienced management team to guide the telemarketing effort.

While the telemarketing industry continues to grow at a phenomenally high rate, many telemarketing operations fail to meet expectations and are jettisoned after a substantial investment of money and time, but *in almost every case, the failure can be traced to an ineffective and inexperienced telemarketing "chief."*

Ironically, this leader often was a highly productive salesperson who was promoted to the new responsibility and wound up facing a demotion or, more frequently, dismissal because of the failure.

To capitalize on the sales potential that telemarketing offers, a company must have a professional telemarketing staff with a comprehensive grasp of the complexities of this type of management.

We will begin examining the structure of the telemarketing management staff with job descriptions for each level, and then discussing differences in management responsibility by department function.

GENERAL JOB DESCRIPTIONS

Telemarketing Vice President/Director. This position represents the highest position within the telemarketing department. This person has complete marketing, strategic and operations responsibility for the telemarketing division and generally reports to an executive concerned with other areas of the company's operation.

The major responsibility for the Vice President/Director is integrating telemarketing into the company's total marketing mix. This requires coordinating the telemarketing department's function with

65

other channels of distribution that the company employs. This entails integrating telemarketing with the field sales effort, direct marketing or advertising efforts, or a system of dealers and distributors.

Figure 6-1
Job Description:
Telemarketing Vice President/Director

1) Integrate telemarketing into the organization's total marketing mix.

2) Direct the sales and service activities toward established goals, monitor the effectiveness of the division and report performance to upper-level management.

3) Establish an overall budget for the department.

4) Oversee operations, including facility planning, equipment selection, line service selection, systems design and cost control.

5) Establish personnel policies and recruit other management-level personnel for the division.

A sound strategic plan and clearly defined goals for the department is key in this integration. The Vice President/Director directs the sales and service activities toward these established goals, monitoring the effectiveness of the division, and reporting performance to upper-level management.

The Vice President/Director also has profit and loss responsibility for the division and is charged with establishing an overall budget for the department.

Aside from strategic and marketing responsibilities, the Vice President/Director also oversees operations, including facility planning, equipment selection, line service selection, systems design and cost control.

The Vice President/Director also establishes personnel policies and recruits other management-level personnel for the division. This may include the Telemarketing Manager, Telemarketing Supervisor, Training Manager and/or Program Managers.

Telemarketing Manager. This next level in the telemarketing department's chain of command carries responsibilities that are generally more operational than those of the Vice President/Director's.

The Manager plans, implements and manages the department and its programs to meet the goals set by upper-level management. The Manager develops the operational procedures for the department and directs all necessary administrative functions, including drawing up the fiscal budget for the department.

Of great importance is the Manager's responsibility for hiring and training the Telephone Sales Representatives (TSR's). The staff must be trained in telephone sales techniques and instructed about product benefits and features. Another important component is determining and monitoring productivity standards and individual sales quotas for the sales staff.

The Manager also structures the compensation plans for the telemarketing staff, including devising

---

Figure 6-2
Job Description:
Telemarketing Manager

1) Implement and manage the department and its programs to meet the goals set by upper-level management.

2) Develop operational procedures for the department and direct all necessary administrative functions.

3) Hire and train Telephone Sales Representatives (TSR's).

4) Determine and monitor productivity standards and individual sales quotas for the sales staff.

5) Structure compensation plans for the telemarketing staff.

6) Make list selections and analyses.

7) Develop direct mail or other advertising campaigns.

8) Structure the product offer, including pricing.

9) Write scripts and call guides used by TSR's.

---

incentive and motivation plans to keep productivity high and turnover low.

The marketing responsibilities of the Manager include list selection and analysis as well as the development of direct mail or other advertising campaigns in support of the telemarketing sales effort.

The Manager may also have responsibility for structuring the product offer, including pricing, and writing the scripts and call guides used by the TSR's.

Although much of the Manager's day is consumed with administrative tasks, a good Manager should spend at least 60% of his or her time training and developing the staff rather than handling administration.

Telemarketing Supervisor. The Telemarketing Manager may have one or more Supervisors reporting to him. These supervisors have first line responsibility for a group of TSR's. The Supervisor determines the schedule for the TSR staff and administers the payroll. In many organizations, the Supervisor may also interview and recruit additions to the TSR staff.

67

The Supervisor should spend the greater portion of his or her time monitoring, training, motivating and evaluating the TSR staff. This includes preparing progress and productivity reports for review by upper-level management.

Figure 6-3
Job Description:
Telemarketing Supervisor

1) Determine the schedule for the TSR staff.

2) Administer the payroll.

3) Monitor, train, motivate and evaluate the TSR staff.

4) Interview and recruit additions to the TSR staff.

5) Prepare progress and productivity reports for review by upper-level management.

Training Manager. In general, large telemarketing organizations have a separate Training Manager function. In recent years, these companies have come to the conclusion that this function is a necessity for the proper initial and continued training of TSR's to reduce turnover and maintain standards.

The Training Manager often has responsibility for researching and creating a telephone sales training manual as well as delivering the training sessions for both initial training and ongoing training.

The Training Manager also has responsibility for maintaining complete personnel records. He or she may also be involved in the screening and hiring process for TSR's.

The Training Manager is also involved in establishing performance standards and implementing tracking programs to maintain call quality. He or she also has responsibility for monitoring and critiquing TSR's as well as assigning personnel to various telemarketing programs through an assessment of the various TSR's strengths.

Program/Product Manager. Some telemarketing organizations running multiple programs or projects find it effective to have a separate Program or Project Manager function. This is particularly true of telemarketing service agencies.

As the title implies, Program/Project Managers develop programs and procedures to ensure the success of a particular telemarketing project. In a service agency, they act as liaison with the client on a regular basis.

68

ORGANIZATION AND STAFFING

The Program/Project Manager also gathers product information and translates the project goals into a working format for the TSR staff. This includes developing a workable and effective script, testing and monitoring effectiveness and analyzing results. The Program/Project Manager then makes specific product and project recommendations to management and keeps the client abreast of the program's progress.

Figure 6-4
Job Description:
Telemarketing Training Manager

1) Research and create a telephone sales training manual.

2) Deliver training sessions for both initial training and ongoing training.

3) Maintain complete personnel records.

4) Assist with the screening and hiring process for TSR's.

5) Establish performance standards and implement tracking programs to maintain call quality.

6) Monitor and critique TSR's.

7) Assign personnel to various telemarketing programs.

Sales Director. Telemarketing service agencies employ a separate sales staff for development of new business presentations and sales of telemarketing services. Generally, a Sales Director has the responsibility of hiring and administering the sales executives (Account Executives) who sell services to other corporations.

The Sales Director's marketing responsibilities include evaluating the marketplace and developing effective sales and marketing strategies. The Sales Director supervises the development of lead generation programs, trade advertising and promotional literature for the support of the sales force.

The Sales Director prepares marketing plans for current and prospective clients and designs customized programs for client companies. He or she also often works with the service agency's major clients, and sometimes assists the Account Executives in closing new accounts.

Account (Sales) Executive. In service agencies, the Account or Sales Executives make new business presentations. This includes prospecting, making cold calls (qualified with appointments) and following up leads.

The Account Executive transmits the client company's needs to the service agency's management

69

Figure 6-5
Job Description:
Telemarketing Program/Product Manager (Service Agency)

1) Develop programs and procedures for individual projects.

2) Act as liaison with clients on a regular basis.

3) Gather product information and translate the project goals into a working format for the TSR staff.

4) Develop workable and effective scripts.

5) Test and monitor effectiveness.

6) Analyze results.

7) Make specific product and project recommendations to management.

8) Keep the client abreast of the program's progress.

Figure 6-6
Job Description:
Telemarketing Sales Director (Service Agency)

1) Develop new business presentations.

2) Sell telemarketing services.

3) Hire and administer the sales executives (account executives).

4) Evaluate the marketplace and develop effective sales and marketing strategies.

5) Supervise the development of lead-generation programs, trade advertising and promotional literature.

6) Prepare marketing plans for current and prospective clients.

7) Design customized programs for client companies.

8) Assist the account executives in closing new accounts.

staff for evaluation of feasibility and eventual implementation.

Once the client makes a commitment to a program, the Account Executive develops the client's marketing plans, does direct mail analysis if applicable to the program, and makes recommendations for the telemarketing component of the program. The Account Executive then manages the project implementation at the service agency and the administrative needs of the account. This may include billing and maintaining all corresponding records.

A successful Account Executive has an eye toward maximizing client billings by initiating new projects for the client and suggesting expansion of ongoing programs.

Figure 6-7
Job Description:
Telemarketing Account (Sales) Executive (Service Agency)

1) Make new business presentations.

2) Prospect, make cold calls (qualified with appointments) and follow up leads.

3) Transmit client company needs to the service agency's management staff.

4) Develop client marketing plans.

5) Analyze client direct mail programs.

6) Make recommendations for the telemarketing component of client programs.

7) Manage project implementation at the service agency.

8) Bill and maintain all corresponding records.

9) Initiate new projects for clients and suggest expansion of ongoing programs.

DIFFERENCES IN RESPONSIBILITY BY DEPARTMENT FUNCTION

There may be vast differences in responsibilities between the telemarketing management staff from one company to another. This will depend on the focus and goals of the telemarketing department and to whom they are selling.

Corporate Telemarketing Departments vs. Service Agencies. One major difference lies between the in-house telemarketing department and the telemarketing department at a service agency.

71

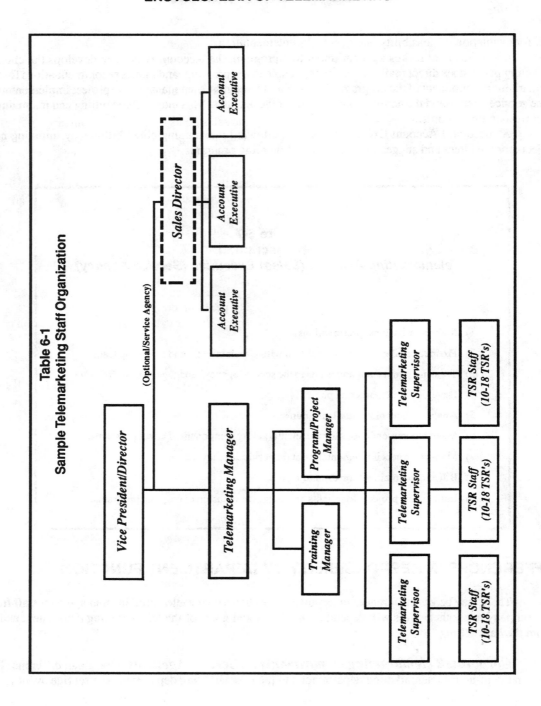

Table 6-1
Sample Telemarketing Staff Organization

ORGANIZATION AND STAFFING

A corporate telemarketing department is one in which a product or service is sold on behalf of the company by the company's internal personnel. By contrast, the service agency sells products or services for other outside corporations on a project or contractual basis.

Although a corporate telemarketing department may run several types of programs and sell many different products, the department always sells the company's own products. Thus, the focus of the department and its management staff is toward achieving the sales goals of their own company.

In a service agency, the client company's sales goals are of paramount importance. The service agency also tends to be more project oriented, and may not always be privy to the entire marketing goal of the client company.

Because of the emphasis on client program goals and the necessity for communication between the service agency and the client, service agencies often employ Program/Project Managers. These are the individuals who act as liaison between the telemarketing department and the client.

The service agency also employs a Sales Director and staff of Account Executives to sell the telemarketing services to the outside client companies.

The Sales Director is often concerned with both the service agency's sales goals in new account development and the client company's program goals.

The telemarketing department in a service agency tends to be highly production oriented. An emphasis is put on telemarketing production measured in calls per hour, contacts per hour and sales per hour on behalf of the client, since the service agency is generally paid by the client on an hourly basis and must attain certain standards in order to keep the client satisfied.

Outbound vs. Inbound Telemarketing Departments. Another major distinction in management responsibility occurs in those departments that make outbound phone calls compared to inbound operations.

One major dimension for distinguishing the two is how they respond to the marketplace. Outbound departments could be classified as *pro-active*, while inbound departments tend to be *reactive*. Further, the telemarketing management staff in an outbound department must have a targeted list of prospective customers, while the inbound department receives calls from prospects generated by other means (e.g., space advertising, broadcast advertising, direct mail, catalogs).

Inbound telemarketing departments generally serve two functions: order capture and customer service.

Inbound Order Capture. In an order capture department, the Telemarketing Manager is responsible for implementing and monitoring the order entry system. This responsibility includes developing policies pertaining to fulfillment of orders placed by phone and notification of back-ordered merchandise and cancellations.

The inbound order capture department can be very sales oriented, even though it operates in a reactive mode. This sales orientation is achieved by training the TSR's to upsell the customer in both quantity and quality of product ordered. The department may also try to sell other products to the prospect during the same call. These products may be related, or accessories for the initial product ordered, or a totally different product line on sale or at a special discounted rate. The Telemarketing Manager is responsible for all of these upsell and cross-sell programs.

Inbound Customer Service. The manager of an inbound customer service telemarketing department

73

must be aware of consumer service regulations. He or she must make sure that customer service inquiries are handled on a basis that is satisfactory both to the consumer and the corporation. It is also the responsibility of this manager to make sure that the caller with a complaint is retained as a customer of the company.

Consumer vs. Business-to-Business Telemarketing. Another major distinction in responsibilities of management staff becomes apparent when comparing companies that sell to other businesses with organizations selling to the consumer at home.

Business-to-Business. When selling to businesses, the telemarketing staff may work with a field sales force or on a full account management basis.

When working with a *field sales force*, the telemarketing department may generate leads for the people in the field, or they might qualify leads that have already been generated. They can also set appointments for the field sales representative.

Telemarketing staffs working on an *account management* basis usually have complete responsibility for the sale of the product or service. Thus the entire sales cycle is completed on the telephone during one or more phone calls. These departments may receive incoming calls from customers, as well as make outbound calls on a regular basis to establish a reorder business. Each TSR is generally assigned to a specific group of accounts and has responsibility for maintaining those accounts, in addition to expanding his or her account base.

In a business-to-business environment, because the sale of the product or service is generally more complex, a series of phone calls may be required before a sale is made. In contrast, sales in a consumer telemarketing operation are often closed in one phone contact.

SELECTING THE RIGHT MANAGEMENT FOR YOUR DEPARTMENT'S NEEDS

Sound hiring is a methodical process, principally a method that allows a thorough analysis of the weaknesses as well as the strengths of each candidate. Most hiring mistakes result from a failure to detect weaknesses during the selection process. When the right *process* is used, however, the selection will most often result in a choice of the "right" candidate (the one with the greatest strengths and the minimum of flaws) over all the others.

Managers who hire effectively treat hiring as a skill that must be applied in a well-organized, orchestrated series of steps. The chances of reaching a sound decision are greatly increased if the proper steps are recognized and followed--and if the pitfalls are effectively avoided.

The proper steps are five:

1) *Define the goals of the telemarketing department and develop a job description based on attaining those goals.*

2) *Attract a sufficient pool of quality candidates, even though talent is sparse.*

3) *Insist that candidates present a resume or letter of employment history.*

4)   *Interview carefully and listen for both what is and what isn't said, while scrutinizing the candidate's track record.*

5)   *Check references as though your organization's fate depended on finding the right person, not just your department.*

STEP 1: *Defining the Position.* To properly define a Telemarketing Manager's position, for example, it is essential to first define the goals of the telemarketing department he or she is to manage. This is particularly crucial if the department is new. While it may be unrealistic or impossible to set exact goals in sales dollars, a basic definition must be developed before beginning the hiring process.

Here are the kinds of definitional questions that need to be asked:

*   *Will the department work in conjunction with a field sales force, or on a full account management basis?*

*   *Is the department expected to do account maintenance or break new accounts by cold calling?*

*   *Are there (or will there be) leads, or a targeted list of prospects available for the department to use?*

Answers to each of these and other functional questions will help to develop a job description that includes all of the responsibilities the successful candidate will have to shoulder. This *process* is exactly opposite of the approach we've seen many organizations take, in which the job description is developed from the resumes received or through the results of the interview process. The manager is being hired to manage a specific department, not his or her own career, and thus the job description must fit the department first. Developing this definition may entail using the services of a telemarketing consultant, who can help provide an objective, informed viewpoint.

But allowing the candidates to define their own job isn't the only typical mistake made. It's also very tempting to try to limit financial exposure with the new telemarketing venture by paying an unrealistically low salary. The result, predictably, will be the hiring of unqualified people. This mistake has led to the failure of many new operations--and, often, when these operations are re-tried with qualified people hired at competitive salaries, they work. Telemarketing professionals are in great demand, so you will not attract qualified people unless you pay a competitive salary.

If the person you're seeking is a replacement, it is possible to gain a great deal of insight about the position by speaking to the person who held it most recently. But remember, here, that people tend to mold their work to their skills and interests, not necessarily to what you would like the department to accomplish.

To protect against this problem, you can also speak with other employees who worked with the last person in the position to be filled. Pay close attention to how the job was done, but also to how it could be done better. Once you have developed insight, write the job description, focusing on what you should be looking for in an applicant.

For example, if the position is in a start-up department, concentrate on applicants who have been involved in the start-up or major expansion of a department. Similarly, if you are filling an established position, but now wish to automate your department, focus on candidates who have either worked in an

75

automated environment, or who have been responsible for automating a department.

>   ***STEP 2: Finding the Talent.*** It is important to explore many options in order to identify a large
enough pool of qualified candidates. Even though the number of experienced telemarketing managers is still
limited, it is possible to attract enough of a pool to make an informed selection.

>   The first option to try, clearly, is the pool of internal candidates. Caution: this should only be
considered if you have an established telemarketing department in place. Avoid the major pitfall of
considering a field sales manager or other internal candidate with product knowledge but no telemarketing
experience. Candidates you consider, all of them, *must* have previous telemarketing experience.

>   You could also call your supplier of telemarketing equipment and ask him who he knows and
respects. Suppliers of telemarketing equipment or line services may be able to put you in touch with some
very qualified individuals who may be unhappy in their present position.

>   Other avenues:

>   *   *Contact your local telemarketing association and the American Telemarket-*
        ing Association (ATA).

>   *   *Advertise locally and nationally in general interest newspapers (but remem-*
        ber that you'll only attract those who are actively job hunting).

>   *   *Advertise in trade magazines and publications (which can be excellent*
        sources of extraordinary candidates who may not have thought of changing
        jobs, but who typically read through the entire trade "book").

>   *   *Call an executive recruiter (but make sure the firm you choose has extensive*
        experience recruiting telemarketing professionals). Avoid the pitfall of
        choosing a recruiting firm that you have to educate on telemarketing, or that
        relies on employment ads you could have run yourself. You may be surprised
        at the quality of candidates that recruiters can identify--it's their job.

>   ***STEP 3: Require a Resume.*** Many employers, in their anxiety to hire a "leader" overlook
this step. The position you are trying to fill should be worth some effort, even to the most harried executive.
Besides, do you really want someone aboard who can't find the time to satisfy such a simple request, even
if you called him or her?

>   Interestingly, employers who insist on resumes find few "shoppers" wasting their time. Equally
important, they find that the person who will write a resume is more prone to accept a good offer.

>   Finally, the appearance of the resume will also be the first clue to a candidate's organizational
abilities and should be viewed as a reflection of the candidate's professionalism.

>   ***STEP 4: Interview Carefully.*** The interview is your opportunity to take an in-depth look at
the candidate, never forgetting for a moment that he or she must add significantly to your organization's
success and growth. Prepare yourself carefully for each interview with questions, both technical and
managerial. Under no circumstances can you afford to make assumptions. You must ask.

For example, it's not sufficient to simply ask a prospective candidate if he or she has ever recruited TSR's. The answer will almost always be "yes," but this doesn't tell you how much of the actual recruiting came under the candidate's responsibility. Nor does it tell you whether he or she actually wrote and placed the ads and did the initial screening. That could have been done by a personnel department. To get these answers, and others, you have to probe with carefully prepared questions.

Find out what approaches to finding qualified TSR's the candidate manager has used. Has he or she recruited from local universities, tried to tap the senior citizen market, or even tried recruiting spouses at local military bases? The more innovative candidates will be much more likely to keep your department fully staffed with quality TSR's.

You will want the interview to keep rolling smoothly, so you have to speak. But, as much as you can, let the candidate do the talking. Even the most sophisticated professional will reveal his or her weaknesses if you ask the right questions and give them the time to answer completely.

This implies another important key to successful interviewing: listen carefully. Try to determine if the candidate's answers are rationalization or astute deductions. Make sure statements of "fact" are not simply assumptions. Do not allow the charismatic candidate to overwhelm the scales with presence instead of substance. And, most importantly in judging a candidate, remember the difference between job skills that can be acquired on the job, than those that the candidate must have on his or her first day on the job.

Caution: *Do not require that candidates have knowledge of your product or service.* This is learnable knowledge, and requiring its preexistence will severely limit your selection pool.

For example, a computer software publisher interviewed, in person or by phone, more than 100 candidates for the telemarketing manager's job, but wound up rejecting all of the candidates because none of them had ever sold software productivity tools! *"No one was qualified,"* they lamented.

On the other hand, a major financial services firm hired a director of telemarketing who had strong management experience, but no financial services background. In just a few months, the new director cut turnover dramatically, restructured a previously ineffective TSR incentive plan and started to generate substantial profits for the corporation.

Remember that what you need is someone with extensive *telemarketing* experience, not knowledge of your product or service. Your organization is the expert in product or service knowledge, and should be able to overlay that knowledge onto any reasonably intelligent candidate, no matter how complex the situation is.

One other area to examine in the interview is personality. Personal traits are elusive and difficult to determine in an interview, but we have found that only about 25% of dismissed employees were fired because of incompetence. Presumably many of the other 75% had social or personality problems of some sort.

For example, if a key component of the position you want to fill is motivation of TSR's, explore the candidate's enthusiasm and ability to communicate that excitement. If those skills aren't there in something as intense and important as a job interview, how can you expect them to be there when it's time to motivate the telemarketing staff?

STEP 5: Scrutinize the Candidate's Track Record. Examine work history in terms of longevity in specific jobs and general turnover, job-to-job. Did the candidate stay long enough in previous positions to launch the operations and have them functioning effectively? Did the candidate groom a successor, an important mark of a good manager?

Find out if the candidate has ever run a program that failed, and, if so, what was wrong with it. The candidate who claims to have had only successes probably doesn't have enough experience.

Find out the candidate's most significant accomplishments in each previous position and how each was accomplished. Be wary of the candidate who has to think long and hard before coming up with accomplishments, unless the ones finally remembered are significant.

Determine if the candidate has ever run a phone operation "hands on," if that experience is what your position requires. Make sure you understand what experience the candidate has had in creating telephone presentations, and whether he has previously had line responsibility for a department.

Professionalism is important, too. Find out how well-informed the candidate is on the telemarketing industry. Is the candidate a member of the American Telemarketing Association or the Telemarketing Council of the Direct Marketing Association? Is the candidate familiar with the legislative and regulative challenges now facing the industry? What telemarketing seminars or conventions did he or she attend in the previous year? What professional publications or books has he or she read? Candidates who actively seek to improve their skills and industry knowledge are likely to be professional on the job.

Beware of the candidate who has little to learn.

STEP 6: Check References Thoroughly. The fate of the telemarketing department may depend on the quality of the individual you choose, so don't ignore references simply because you like the candidate.

When checking references, prepare your questions carefully and in advance. Plan to check the candidate's range of knowledge, scope of experience, working habits, accomplishments discussed in the interview, as well as his or her relationships with the employer, the staff, and the suppliers. Assume little.

You will get better and more revealing answers if you phone. Few past employers will put anything pejorative about a candidate on paper, particularly in these litigious days. Make sure the person has time to talk when you call. Tell him or her that you have questions that may take a while, and inform the listener that the position you are filling is an important one for your organization.

If you discover a pattern of evasion on the part of the previous employer, probe. Usually, people don't want to stand in the way of a person getting a new position, so negative appraisals are seldom offered. It's your responsibility to examine the hesitations and explore the pauses.

Also, while practically all employers who check references in depth consult with the candidate's previous supervisors, there's also a lot to be learned by speaking to the people who reported to the candidate.

Caution: References should be checked only after employment has been offered, conditionally, to the candidate.

COMPENSATION AT THE MANAGEMENT LEVEL

Once you have found the right candidate for your telemarketing department, you will have to offer a competitive salary and incentive plan to get the person on board. But the role compensation plays in developing successful telemarketing department does not end with initial salary levels.

The salary and compensation structure should be reviewed on a regular basis, approximately every six months, to make sure you are offering competitive wages. Salary considerations are the main reason why telemarketing management professionals jump to another company or organization. Particularly in today's market, when there are more vacant positions than truly qualified telemarketing professionals, compensation is a critically important factor in the success of an operation.

Base Salaries. Although most telemarketing management professionals are very incentive-oriented, paying an adequate base salary is just as important as structuring a motivating incentive plan. You will not be able to attract a top candidate unless the initial salary offered is considered attractive. This means that you will have to offer a base that is 20% to 30% above a candidate's current base salary.

The national average base salaries paid to various key telemarketing positions (1988 statistics) are shown in **Figure 6-8**. Here are some key factors to consider for each position:

Vice President/Director of Telemarketing. In general, those departments that sell business-to-business on an account management basis pay salaries at the higher end. In addition, those Vice President/Directors who are responsible for multiple location telemarketing departments with large numbers of TSR's are also compensated at the higher end.

**Figure 6-8
Job Description:
Typical Salary Ranges*, by Position
(1988 Statistics)**

1) Vice President/Director of Telemarketing .... $60,000-$80,000

2) Telemarketing Manager .... $35,000-$45,000

3) Telemarketing Supervisor .... $20,000-$25,000

4) Telemarketing Training Manager .... $32,000-$38,000

5) Telemarketing Program/Product Manager .... $28,000-$35,000

6) Sales Director (Telemarketing Service Agencies) .... $50,000-$60,000

7) Account Executive (Telemarketing Service Agencies) .... $35,000-$40,000

*Please note that salary levels have been increasing at the rate of approximately 10-15% each year for the past several years.

Telemarketing Managers. Managers of an outbound business-to-business department are compensated at the higher end of the range while managers of consumer departments are compensated at the lower end of the range. Further, managers in corporate telemarketing departments tend to earn a higher base salary than managers in service agency telemarketing departments.

Telemarketing Supervisors. Supervisors in corporate, outbound, business-to-business departments earn at the higher end. Those in inbound, consumer, service agency departments earn at the lower end.

Telemarketing Training Managers. Training Managers who have line responsibility for a staff of telemarketing trainers earn salaries at the upper end of the range. Also, Training Managers who are responsible for the development of a staff selling a complex or technical product or service tend to earn higher salaries.

Telemarketing Program/Product Manager. Program/Project Managers who handle larger, complex programs for key clients tend to earn base salaries at the higher end of the range. Additionally, those managers who are required to travel to client locations to give presentations also tend to earn higher salaries.

Sales Directors of Telemarketing Service Agencies. Total compensation for these managers is usually heavily influenced by incentives, although base salaries tend to be significant. Sales Directors with line responsibility for a large staff of account executives tend to earn base salaries at the higher end of the range, as do those Sales Directors whose agencies cater to business-to-business accounts.

Account Executives at Telemarketing Service Agencies. In addition to their typical base salaries, Account Executives are generally paid a commission for business that they bring to the agency.

Additional Compensation.
Most organizations wouldn't dream of paying a field sales person or field sales manager a straight salary, yet some of these same organizations see nothing wrong with paying their telemarketing management staff on a salary-only basis.

Since telemarketing is a revenue-generating sales function, all telemarketing management professionals should be paid some type of incentive in addition to their base salaries. This additional incentive can be awarded in many different forms, but whatever the formula, it should be motivating and realistic, not frustrating and impossible to attain.

It's important to involve the telemarketing management professional in structuring his or her own incentive plan. Let the manager provide input in the design of the plan, and allow for feedback once the plan has been structured.

There are almost as many ways to structure an incentive plan as there are companies utilizing telemarketing. Of course, you will want an incentive plan that will keep total compensation in line with the rest of the salary structure, always keeping in mind that telemarketing is a revenue-generating function.

One of the most common incentive plans for Telemarketing Managers or Supervisors is an "override plan." With an *override*, the Manager or Supervisor receives a dollar percentage of each sale made by the department, or a set dollar figure for each sale made.

There are many ways to structure a bonus plan. In some cases, the management professional earns a bonus if sales meet a preset target or goal level. In other cases, the management professional earns a bonus or percentage of sales made over the preset target level. The bonus is sometimes structured in a step fashion, where the management professionals earn an escalating dollar amount for sales meeting each preset step. In still other cases, a discretionary bonus is awarded if upper management is pleased with performance of the telemarketing department as a whole.

Other perks or incentives can include a corporate profit sharing plan, stock purchase plans or options, company car, club memberships, or paid vacation travel benefits.

Salary Projections for the Future. Several trends are emerging in the compensation of telemarketing management professionals. One of the most interesting trends is the diminishing of regional salary differences. In other words, corporations located in lower cost-of-living areas must pay salaries competitive with those found in major metropolitan centers in order to attract top candidates. Candidates will not take a pay cut, or accept less of a pay increase because a company is located in a lower cost-of-living area. As a matter of fact, corporations located in lower cost-of-living areas that may be considered geographically undesirable sometimes have to pay a higher salary than those located in metropolitan areas in order to attract top candidates.

Base salary averages for telemarketing management professionals will continue to increase at a rate higher than the inflation rate. Salary levels have increased at the rate of approximately 10% to 15% each year over the preceding few years.

At the same time, incentive plans will continue to play an ever-increasing role in the total compensation of telemarketing management professionals.

Corporate telemarketing positions will continue to pay more than management positions at telemarketing service agencies. Additionally, positions in business-to-business departments will continue to pay more than positions in consumer departments, and management positions in outbound departments will continue to pay more than those in inbound departments.

SOME MISCELLANEOUS CONSIDERATIONS

Excessive turnover of telemarketing management staff can stifle your organization's growth, especially since experienced telemarketers are an organization's greatest asset.

Excessive turnover is also very costly. Attracting a new executive can cost as much as 50% over and above the candidate's compensation if recruitment fees and relocation expenses are included along with the loss of high-priced time for interviewing, screening, briefing and training by other executives once the individual is on board.

Paying a competitive base salary and having an adequate incentive plan are essential for keeping turnover at the management level low, but just as important is the commitment of upper-level management to the telemarketing effort.

Few experiences are more frustrating to the telemarketing professional than working in an organization where telemarketing is not supported by upper-level management. The telemarketing function should be respected as an income-generating sales and marketing tool, not an ancillary support mechanism.

Whenever possible, promote from within the organization and let it be known that this is the policy. For example: Telemarketing Supervisors should be trained to become Managers, and internal Managers should be considered for a vacant Director's position. You will be able to keep turnover and its associated expenses low if you develop staff from within.

Another way to keep turnover and frustration low is to develop communication among all the department heads. These dialogues can be developed by inaugurating in-house training programs with different department chiefs giving seminars on their specialties. In this way, telemarketing will be respected by all as a cost-effective, income-generating function, rather than the proverbial disturbing call at dinner time.

OPPORTUNITIES AND PROBLEMS: ASSESSING THE FUTURE

If telemarketing continues to grow at the rates predicted, there will be many opportunities in the coming decade for organizations and telemarketing management professionals--but, unfortunately, there will be almost as many problems.

The available opportunities will increase dramatically for experienced and qualified telemarketing management professionals at all levels. This includes an increased number of opportunities in large Fortune 500 corporations, as well as small blue-chip quality companies. Telemarketing will be utilized for a wider variety of applications including an increase in full account management applications.

The major problem associated with the growth of telemarketing will be the dearth of qualified experienced professionals. Thus it will be even more important for organizations to develop management from within.

And to keep their management staffs challenged and content.

CHAPTER 7

Profiles of Telephone Sales Reps

Michael J. Marx, Ph.D.
President
Selection Sciences, Inc.
San Francisco, California

As the telemarketing industry matures, it faces a number of significant challenges. Maximizing the use of human resources to increase profitability is one of the most difficult.

Some of the most profitable firms in the industry have successfully addressed this challenge, but the vast majority have not. If those who haven't are to survive the intense sales competition that is forecasted for the coming years, they will have to find more effective ways to recruit, screen, motivate and retain top producers.

This chapter is intended to encourage and assist them in this process.

Before most companies utilizing telemarketing modify their hiring procedures, they need to see the relative advantages of doing so. They need to appreciate just how much a poor hiring decision costs in terms of low performance, absenteeism and turnover. They need to believe that these problems are not inherent in the telemarketing industry and can be solved. Once companies realize that poor hiring is unprofitable and avoidable, they need to more clearly define what type of employees "fit" their organizations and the jobs they do; otherwise, they will continue to hire the wrong people. They must then design their recruitment, screening, and motivational programs to attract and keep these people. These are difficult tasks that must be addressed.

THE COSTS OF POOR HIRING DECISIONS

Turnover and lost production are serious problems in the telemarketing industry, and they cost individual companies millions of dollars each year. In a recent survey of American Telemarketing Association (ATA) members, we found that turnover ranged from 0% to nearly 1,000% annually. The larger the company was, the greater the tendency for turnover. Companies with over 100 TSR's rarely had turnover under 50% a year and were generally in the 75-100% range.

Most respondents to our survey were not able or willing to estimate accurately the costs of turnover and lost production, although the managers we interviewed estimated that they spent from five to 30 hours recruiting, screening, training and supervising each new TSR until each was sufficiently productive. Managers who had cost figures estimated between $2,000 and $3,000 per candidate for hiring expenses alone.

These costs are reason for concern, but if we examine the range of expenses involved in a hiring decision, they are probably underestimated. The costs of placing an advertisement for a week, conducting telephone screening interviews, processing applications, conducting face-to-face interviews, checking references, training, compensation and benefits until the person is productive, usually raise the total cost of hiring dramatically.

Consider also the average number of sales that are lost while the hiring process proceeds, and the lower level of sales productivity of a new hire coming up to speed. Also consider that a poor performer produces, on average, less than half of what a good performer produces in sales. Finally, add to the total costs the negative effects of a dissatisfied employee on the morale and productivity of others, and the expenses involved in termination (including administrative time, and occasionally, legal fees).

These costs are undoubtedly much higher than most companies realize, and, worse, every time an employee leaves the organization, these costs are nearly doubled. *Someone must be hired as a replacement.* In this context, the cost figures of one West Coast insurance company that relies exclusively on telemarketing to sell personal insurance policies seem realistic. After carefully computing all the expenses and lost sales involved in a poor hiring decision, senior management estimated that each poor hiring decision cost them in excess of $20,000.

Companies that sell even more expensive products and rely on even more experienced TSR's than this insurance firm should not find these figures exaggerated.

THE MYTH THAT PERPETUATES THE PROBLEM

In light of the high turnover rates and costs associated with them, one would expect more companies to be dissatisfied with their hiring processes. Surprisingly, most of them are not. When we asked a sample of ATA members to rate their satisfaction with their companies' current hiring procedures, over 80% were moderately to highly satisfied. They did not feel that poor hiring decisions were a major contributor to turnover. Nor did they tend to feel that low pay, working conditions or low motivation were major factors. Most of them felt that turnover was primarily due to the kind of work telemarketers do. In other words, "*It's just the nature of the business.*"

This is a *myth*. There are many other industries and even companies within the telemarketing industry where turnover is low.

The statistical correlations between perceived job characteristics and job satisfaction for tele-marketers make the above belief even more suspicious. Our research suggests that when telemarketers perceive their jobs to provide fair pay that increases as their performance improves, job security and promotional opportunities, they tend to be more satisfied. Likewise, when they enjoy their co-workers, feel like part of a team, believe other employees set high performance standards for themselves, and have a chance to influence decisions made by their supervisors, they also tend to be more satisfied. Our research also demonstrates that *the greater TSR's job satisfaction is, the longer their job tenure will be.*

Fortunately, all of these factors can be influenced by organizations to a greater or lesser degree. They are not "*Just the nature of the business.*"

Job satisfaction tends to be an "additive" construct. This means that when a company cannot provide one factor adequately, it can usually compensate by providing or adding another. Lower pay, in some cases, can be compensated by job security, good employee relations and recognition. Successful companies know this. They provide at least some of the factors which affect employee satisfaction, and they select people who value these factors enough to commit themselves to the company.

In short, successful telemarketing firms tend to be more systematic about the selection and management of their human resources. More than anything else, they tend to know the requirements of their jobs and the attributes of the TSR's who succeed and stay with them.

How do they identify the critical job requirements (knowledge, skills, abilities)? How do they select employees who meet these requirements and screen out those who do not? How do they keep top performers for long periods?

These are the questions we will try to answer here.

HOW TO IDENTIFY CRITICAL JOB REQUIREMENTS

There are several methods used to discover what *knowledge, skills* and *abilities* (KSA's) are essential to job success. Observations, interviews and critical incidents are but a few of them.

One simple way is to conduct a set of interviews with job experts: managers, supervisors, consultants, top performers. They are asked to divide the job into major areas of responsibility and to list specific tasks under each. They are asked to identify the KSA's that are critical to perform each of those tasks. It is then possible to obtain relative importance ratings of tasks and KSA's and to design selection systems that emphasize the KSA's ranked as most important for success.

We interviewed a broad cross section of job experts representing various aspects of the telemarketing industry. From those interviews we were able to identify a list of KSA's or characteristics that seemed relevant to most telemarketing jobs. We then invited companies to participate in a National TSR Selection Project in which their job experts would describe the nature of their particular telemarketing jobs and rank order the KSA's according to how critical they were for successful performance and long tenure.

Once the KSA's were ranked, we were able to test the consensus among independent raters from each company to ensure that their perceptions of the job were indeed similar. In some of the companies sampled, we also asked high- and low-production TSR's to rank the list of KSA's according to how characteristic they were of them as individuals. This allowed us to compare their rankings to the rankings of the job experts (or what we called the *ideal profile*) in order to further test for validity. We also obtained high and low production TSR's perceptions of their work situation (supervision, compensation, work environment, etc.) and compared these with their intention to stay with the organization.

What we have found in the initial stages of the study is that while the critical KSA's do vary from company to company and job to job, there are some interesting consistencies.

THE RESULTS OF THE PROJECT

The first outcome of the study is a list of 72 KSA's that job experts consider to be important for successful performance in telemarketing positions. Some of those KSA's referred to in our discussion of findings are listed below:

* *Good Listener.* Ability to maintain attention when others are talking and to understand and remember what they said when important.

* *Believes in the Product.* Having the belief that many people need or could benefit from the kind of product(s) or services offered by this company.

* *A Sale Closer.* Ability not to let people off the hook. To tactfully put them in a position where saying "no" is somewhat uncomfortable for them. Asking for the sale and not accepting "no" the first time.

* *Cool Under Fire.* The ability to respond to the angry outbursts of others in a cool, calm, controlled manner; to receive negative feedback or criticism without becoming defensive.

* *Extroverted.* Strong preference for opportunities to communicate and deal directly with people; being energized by the chance to talk and be with others. Usually preferring social situations over being alone.

* *Reliable.* Ability to be dependable, punctual, reliable. Emotionally consistent from day to day. Keeping promises, following plans, not easily frustrated by things others do.

* *Goal Oriented.* Sets challenging personal goals for the year, month, week and individual situations. Feels a strong personal commitment to meet goals once they are set.

* *Genuine.* Ability and desire to be honest and straightforward when dealing with others. Being seen as genuine and authentic.

* *Intelligent.* Ability to quickly grasp difficult ideas, concepts, and procedures, and apply them in actual situations; the ability to learn quickly.

* *Rapport Builder.* Ability to build rapport with people quickly by putting them at ease and talking of mutual interests. Getting them to open up about themselves.

* *Self-Confident.* Strong belief in own ability to achieve challenging objectives, overcome problems, and be successful in a variety of situations. Can stand criticism and uses it to improve.

* *Clear Communicator.* The ability to talk to others in a clear, concise,

organized and grammatical manner. To speak in a way that is easily under-stood by others and is pleasing.

The second major outcome of the study is a set of dimensions that emerges to summarize the large number of KSA's associated with the telemarketing sales job. Some of the *critical KSA dimensions* are as follows:

* *Service Oriented.* Good listener, helpful to others, sensitive to others, empathetic, opens up others.

* *People Oriented.* Extroverted, genuine, reads people well, likeable, clear communicator.

* *Achievement Oriented.* Career oriented, competitive, goal oriented, high energy, intolerant of failure.

* *Detail Oriented.* Attentive to detail, focused, accurate, thorough, record keeper.

* *Influence Oriented.* Sale closer, commitment builder, confronting, good leader, persuasive.

* *Good Self-Esteem.* Cool under fire, internally motivated, values recognition, assertive.

* *Mentally Tough.* Disciplined, reliable, patient, steady, committed, consistent.

* *Analytical.* Intelligent, logical thinker, mathematical, strategic thinker.

* *Production Oriented.* Procedural, internally motivated, organized, meets deadlines, sets priorities.

* *Growth Oriented.* Multiple focus, likes variety, career opportunity.

* *Financially Oriented.* Values financial rewards, financially responsible.

There are a variety of other KSA's that cross the boundaries of more than one dimension, but the above list illustrates the range we are examining in the study. How do the KSA's under each dimension vary in their importance for the different telemarketing jobs?

INBOUND VS. OUTBOUND

Job experts on both the inbound and outbound side ranked several KSA's in the same order in terms of their importance for successful job performance. Being a clear communicator, self confident and reliable seem to be important regardless of the nature of the sales activity. Being intolerant of failure, needing variety, and exhibiting financial responsibility were commonly rated as least important for success on the job.

The two job areas tend to differ in some obvious ways. Outbound TSR's need to believe in the product, to listen closely, to be able to close sales, and to be mentally tough. Inbound TSR's need to be cool under fire, accurate, and thorough.

Figure 7-1
Most Important KSA's for Successful Job Performance

Outbound Telemarketing

Clear communicator
Self-confident
Reliable
Belief in product
Mentally tough
Good listener

Inbound Telemarketing

Clear communicator
Self-confident
Reliable
Cool under fire
Accurate
Thorough

Overall, the findings suggest that *outbound TSR's need to be much more able to communicate information clearly to people while maintaining enough emotional distance to ask for the sale and withstand rejection. Inbound TSR's need to be able to make sure the information that is communicated to them is complete and accurate while maintaining enough emotional distance not to take criticism personally.*

For outbound or inbound TSR's, the factors that most influence their job satisfaction tend to be the extent to which they receive immediate feedback about their performance, have good relations with co-workers, feel their salaries increase with performance, and have the proper equipment to do the job well. Outbound TSR's job satisfaction is also influenced by a sense of teamwork and cooperation among co-workers. Inbound TSR's job satisfaction is influenced by job security, working conditions, opportunities for advancement, and praise for good performance.

Outbound TSR's need to feel like part of a team, while inbound TSR's need to feel like a part of an organization. Both need to feel financially and personally rewarded for their efforts.

PROFILES OF TELEPHONE SALES REPS

Our study also confirms most managers' suspicions that many success factors are unique to their corporate climate, work force and sales jobs. KSA's such as the need for financial rewards, extroversion, high energy, and tolerance for stress fluctuate greatly in their importance across companies, although they may contribute significantly to the profile of successful employees. This suggests the need for companies to tailor profiles to their individual setting.

BUSINESS TO BUSINESS VS. BUSINESS TO CONSUMER

Job experts in the business and consumer areas tend to see many of the same KSA's as critical to successful performance. This should not be surprising. It is often asserted that business TSR's must develop more of a long-term relationship with a client, sell bigger-ticket items, and present themselves more professionally and intelligently.

While this is partially confirmed in our results, it appears that consumer TSR's may often establish a similar selling relationship. An insurance company that sells property and casualty coverage to individuals is an example of a long-term, high-ticket, consultative sale to consumers.

Figure 7-2
Most Important KSA's for Successful Job Performance

Business-to-Business

Clear communicator
Good listener
Reliable
Self-confident
Thorough

Business-to-Consumer

Clear communicator
Reliable
Good listener
Cool under fire
Flexible style

The ideal TSR's in these areas are perceived to be clear communicators who are good listeners and reliable. On the business side *they tend to be more self-confident, thorough, genuine, and good at building rapport.* On the consumer side *they tend to be cool under fire, flexible, and persuasive.* The business profile describes a person who is capable of developing a long-term relationship with a client and being more consultative. The consumer profile describes persons who are capable of quickly adapting to prospects, getting them to act as they desire, and withstanding emotional outbursts from prospects.

For both business and consumer TSR's, several job factors contribute to their satisfaction: feelings of job security, a spirit of teamwork and co-workers they enjoy, immediate feedback, and salary increases based on performance. Consumer TSR's job satisfaction was also influenced by the need to exercise judgement and the authority to make important decisions. Business TSR's job satisfaction was influenced by other unique factors such as fair pay, good working conditions, opportunities for advancement, recognition, work that requires technical training, equipment that is up to date, co-workers who set high standards for themselves and status as a professional.

The above factors combined with the critical KSA's suggest that business TSR's *are more concerned about operating in a professional environment for a long period,* while consumer TSR's *have more immediate concerns about the rewards and the people with which they work.*

LARGE-TICKET VS. SMALL-TICKET SALES

Small-ticket sales (under $100) and large-ticket sales (over $250) TSR's share the same need to be clear communicators and present themselves professionally, but those selling higher-priced products need to be more self-confident, better listeners, more thorough in pursuing solutions, and flexible. Those selling the lower-priced products need to be more intelligent and learn quickly, to be able to ask for the sale, and to persuade people to purchase the product.

The long sales cycle versus short sales cycle difference emerges here. TSR's selling bigger ticket items often need to make more than one contact. They need to take action prior to the close of the sale, to probe more into the prospect's needs and to change strategies when necessary. TSR's selling smaller ticket items often make a single contact. They deliver a scripted message and usually have fewer chances to select the persuasive tactic that will result in a sale. They must think quickly, for there is rarely a second opportunity with the same consumer.

IMPLICATIONS FOR SELECTING TOP PERFORMERS

There are several important implications of these findings for the recruitment and selection process.

1) Job advertisements should be tailored to the type of candidates being sought. When the job requires someone with high self-confidence and professional style, the advertisement needs to suggest that the company and position are very professional in nature. This may mean more lines in the advertisement, more description of the job's potential, more emphasis on the training provided, or placement of the advertisement under sales instead of telephone sales.

For inbound positions the emphasis may be on the company's merits, whereas for outbound positions it may be on the job's merit. When the job requires less extroversion (as is the case for in-bound, order-taking positions), the company may want to describe the job in less extroverted ways. For example, when the ideal candidate is described as aggressive, outgoing, friendly, with good selling skills, introverts tend to pass over the opportunity. They may be the best people for the job, however.

2) Every company needs to establish its own success profile. While we found a good deal of consistency in the job requirements across positions and companies, there is a great deal of variation that occurs due to the local economic environment, corporate climate, product(s) being sold and sales process. The company that relies solely on its intuition or industry-wide standards may be losing precision in its selection tools.

Figure 7-3
Most Important KSA's for Successful Job Performance

Large-Ticket Sales

Clear communicator
Professional style
Self-confident
Good listener
Thorough

Small-Ticket Sales

Clear communicator
Professional style
Intelligent
Closing ability
Persuasive

---

3) Multiple methods for screening applicants are necessary. Some of the critical KSA's are clearly skills, such as being a clear communicator. They can be tested best through a structured phone screen or job simulation. Other critical KSA's are clearly personality traits, such as self confidence. They can be best evaluated through personality questionnaires that measure behavioral tendencies and preferences. Other critical KSA's are more clearly aptitudes, such as intelligence. They are best measured through

91

aptitude tests. Once a company knows what KSA's are critical to success, it can select the appropriate mix of selection tools to evaluate them.

4) *Candidates need to be given a realistic preview of the job they will be performing.*
The need to hire employees with high self-confidence, professional style, and reliability suggests the need to let candidates "self-select" into the job. Not everyone will be self-confident, professional, or reliable in all situations. Even the most self-confident individuals can approach situations for which they have little aptitude and experience a subsequent decline in their confidence.

By letting final candidates observe TSR's on the job, ask TSR's questions in confidence, and even "test" their own selling skills before accepting the position, companies can avoid eventual problems. When candidates see exactly what is expected of them, they can better estimate their own ability to perform. They will also accept more responsibility for their employment decision which, in the case of some dissatisfied new hires, may be enough to keep them on board through a difficult learning period.

Finally, candidates who are truly high in self-confidence, professionalism and communication skills are most able to find another job quickly if this one is not to their liking, so they may as well be given the opportunity to decide for themselves whether this is their preference.

5) *Interviews need to be structured for consistency and validity.* Managers and supervisors clearly differ in their perceptions of what KSA's are most important for success. In nearly every company we studied, two or three job experts were dramatically out of line with the consensus of other experts. Assuming their perceptions are incorrect, their misconceptions could account for a significant portion of their companies' turnover. When interviews are properly structured in advance, these managers are forced to concentrate on the critical KSA's in their interviews and to rely less on their incorrect "gut reactions" or irrelevant questions.

Managers and supervisors also vary in their ability to evaluate important KSA's in an interview. *Most studies find little relationship between interviewers' predictions of candidates' success and actual success.* Questions that are non-leading and require very specific behavioral evidence of the critical KSA's will help interviewers to more accurately judge the suitability of their candidates. For example, it is not enough to ask candidates to name their five greatest accomplishments, as many interviewers do. They must also be asked to describe the behaviors they performed and obstacles they overcame for each achievement. Only then does evidence of self-confidence, reliability and tough-mindedness begin to emerge.

The findings further suggest that greater weight should be given to the phone screen since it is the best tool for evaluating professional style, clear communication, flexibility and the projection of self confidence.

6) *Thorough exit questionnaires are needed, as well as the tracking of attributes of departing employees.* Companies rarely have anything more than a cursory exit interview with employees who voluntarily depart. By tracking employees' perceptions of the characteristics of the job and company (e.g., fair pay, working conditions, co-workers, decision involvement), *it is possible statistically to determine which perceptions are contributing most to turnover.*

Likewise, by obtaining profiles of applicants when they arrive, it is possible to compare those who leave with those who stay to identify the characteristics that best predict job success and tenure. In one study we found that TSR's who left tended to be much more extraverted and sensitive to others' feeling than those who stayed. The company modified screening procedures to account for this finding and turnover was significantly reduced while sales increased slightly over the next year.

IMPLICATIONS FOR KEEPING TOP PERFORMERS

Our findings also carried implications about keeping good employees within the organization.

1) Compensation packages must be perceived as fair and increase as performance improves. When TSR's perceive their pay to be significantly below other jobs within the company or comparable jobs outside of the company, they are more likely to be dissatisfied and to leave the organization voluntarily. Furthermore, when their pay does not increase as their productivity increases, they are likely to feel dissatisfaction. When these two perceptions exist, *employees are likely to take steps to restore feelings of equity by lowering their effort, being dishonest, shifting work to others, or looking for alternative employment.*

2) The working environment must exemplify professionalism and respect for employees. The most satisfied TSR's reported good working conditions (heating, lighting, ventilation, adequate work space and room to move around in, the proper amount of equipment and supplies, and up-to-date equipment). Poor physical surroundings and equipment suggest to employees that they are not valued resources. This message can dramatically affect their self-confidence and commitment to the corporation, especially if they see themselves as professional.

3) Supervisors need to be good people managers. In order to ensure high confidence, professionalism, reliability, and effective selling practices, supervisors need to know how to properly manage performance. They need to be able to define expectations clearly, to train new employees thoroughly, to provide constructive feedback after monitoring initial sales activities and to recognize good performance with praise and other rewards. Our results suggest the need for supervisors to involve TSR's in decisions that may affect their work and to create a team atmosphere in which co-workers cooperate and benefit from each other's success.

Supervisors are often selected from the ranks of successful TSR's. While job knowledge is important, *supervisory skills may be more important and companies need to take steps to train their leaders in basic performance management, decision-making and interpersonal problem solving skills.*

4) New employees should be quickly and thoroughly oriented. New employees need to become integrated into the social fabric of the sales unit. TSR's may be slightly less extroverted than most sales professionals, but they still have a need to feel a part of the group, to get along with their co-workers, and to feel a part of the social mainstream of the work unit. New employees may be assigned a mentor. They may be invited to lunch with a couple of experienced employees and advised about the informal norms of the work unit.

5) Employee attitudes should be monitored regularly. This should be done in a systematic manner, perhaps by questionnaire once every six months. Surveying employees allows the company to monitor overall levels of satisfaction, commitment and self-reported effort. It also allows the company a means by which to diagnose the causes of problems in these areas. Employees should be asked to score, anonymously, their perceptions and evaluations of various aspects of the job and company. These can then be correlated with satisfaction, commitment and effort to determine if procedural changes need to be implemented in order to solve current problems or avoid future ones.

THE FUTURE OF THE NATIONAL TSR SELECTION PROJECT

We will continue to gather data on employees nationwide in order to determine the critical KSA's in various telemarketing positions. As the sample increases, our ability to make progressively finer distinctions between the different TSR positions should increase. We should also be able to improve our ability to identify the factors that contribute most to employee dissatisfaction and turnover.

Our findings thus far convince us that 72 KSA's, the most important of which were discussed here, consistently predict success. Companies need to identify which of these KSA's are most important for them and to take clear steps to more systematically manage their human resources. This involves designing recruitment strategies that attract the right people, designing selection procedures that identify the right people, providing orientation procedures that integrate these people into the organization and, finally, designing management and compensation practices that keep these people.

Every poor hiring decision a company makes can cost a great deal in lost sales and turnover. This does not have to be the case. Telemarketing companies can significantly improve their ability to recognize top performers. They can recruit, screen and manage their human resources in order to better attract and retain dedicated and skillful TSR's who fit their organization. This requires a commitment to invest in these processes.

Our evidence and experience suggest that the investment is very likely to be returned in multiples. The "nature of the business" is what we make it.

AUTHOR'S NOTE:

The author gratefully acknowledges the contribution of Terry da Luz for her compilation of the results cited in this chapter, as well as for her valued editorial suggestions.

94

CHAPTER 8

Training

Jeffrey C. Wooden
President
The ComTel Group
Malvern, Pennsylvania

The issue of telemarketing training is one that must be addressed early in the strategic planning process. This is due to the lead time required to evaluate existing generic training programs, to establish a training plan and design and to develop the final course components.

This process is more involved and challenging than most individuals ever perceive. It is an intricate task that requires insight, imagination, intuition and creativity. Such an investment, however, is well worth the work involved, since the results of your training program will be totally dependent on the time and effort put into developing it.

At first, the process may seem intimidating, but it should not be discouraging. Avoid getting overwhelmed by building your training design steadily, in a step-by-step fashion--one module, concept, exercise, etc., at a time. Before you know it, you will have designed all the components of a fully integrated training package which can be refined and expanded as you develop ongoing training for your telemarketing sales and service representatives.

BENEFITS OF AN EFFECTIVE TRAINING PROGRAM

Here are the benefits a sound, professional training program can provide:

Job Satisfaction/Self-Esteem. Training leads to greater satisfaction and self-confidence, which translates into reduced turnover. There have been studies that indicate turnover can be reduced as much as 50% per year when employees have received good initial and ongoing training. If you know your average firing cost per telemarketing sales rep (TSR), then you can quickly see the annual dollar benefits arising from just this one benefit.

Better Candidates. You can expect to attract more and better job candidates when you can announce the existence of a complete training program. The telemarketing industry for years has been publicly guilty of providing inadequate training. For this reason, many qualified and potentially successful job seekers have either left the telemarketing field or avoided it completely. If your company provides

95

professional training, you want to emphasize this in your recruitment process. The word will spread and your company image will be greatly enhanced.

Increased Probability of Success. This benefit, of course, can be measured *quantitatively* through increased revenues and profits, but also *qualitatively* through improving your telemarketing rep's self-esteem and attitude and building a feeling of team spirit. So you should view your training as a real investment, one that provides a win-win situation for all.

This chapter will give you an outline and specific guidelines to follow in creating and implementing a telemarketing training plan. The most difficult part is taking the first step--that is, setting aside blocks of time in your schedule to research and develop the first piece of your training puzzle. Once you use the materials and exercises you've created with your staff and have seen how well your reps respond to the information, input and attention you provide, it will be a lot easier to discipline yourself to continue developing your training design.

NEEDS ANALYSIS

There are several facets to conducting a needs analysis and your training objectives will evolve from the findings made in each facet.

Determining Call Objectives. You must thoroughly understand your telemarketing call objectives (applications) before they can be related to specific training objectives. Is your telemarketing training program designed to qualify leads, set appointments, handle inbound calls, sell a one-time offer or build repeat business through full account management?

Selling Skills Required. Depending on the application(s), you will need to determine how much emphasis to place on *selling* skills in structuring that portion of the training module. For example, the appointment-setting application requires the same level of sales skill as needed in direct sales because the rep is, in fact, "selling"--not "setting"--the appointment. Since this process involves all of the same selling steps and needs-discovery skills required in more complex sales presentations, all you may need to adapt the telesales training to fit this application is to change the wording to fit your situation. Other sales applications may call for more extensive changes. Certainly, all of the other training components will be necessary for this kind of training program.

Defining Presentation Approach. Another important consideration when defining your training needs relates to the type of sales presentation approach used by your reps. Do you use tight verbatim scripts or more loosely structured call guides? If the latter, the training emphasis should be on communications skills, especially voice and listening training. This might include prepared audio tapes to serve as positive models and also extensive taped role plays, practicing and critiquing script delivery.

Fully scripted sales presentations are often effective in getting less skilled sales reps up to speed and on the phone quickly. If possible, try to wean these reps off strictly reading scripts and allow them to use their own style, personality, and abilities to interact with the prospect. As the sales calls become more natural, they will most likely need additional training in needs discovery and handling objections skills, as well as much more in-depth product/service knowledge training.

Assessing Product/Service Sophistication. How complex or technical is the product or service being sold? The greater the complexity, the higher training skill level the rep needs in order to take the conversation in any one of a number of different directions based on the prospect's responses. In such situations, you may want to place greater emphasis on product/service knowledge, interpersonal and communication skills and role playing.

Integrating with Automation. If your telemarketing group is automated, you will have to concentrate, at least initially, on getting reps familiar and comfortable with the system. This could include a typing course and computer training augmented with group and one-on-one instruction.

Many times there may be only one rep to train at a time. It would be very costly to assign a supervisor or trainer to train a person one-on-one. Whenever possible try to utilize interactive training methods. For computer systems, training could be either a computer-generated training tutorial or an audio tape training tutorial.

When developing or buying a software package include the capability of having a computerized training tutorial designed as part of the package. If not possible, you can easily produce your own self-paced audio program combined with a study guide to lead the rep through all the system screens and entry commands. These audio tutorials can be played back on a Dictaphone-type machine equipped with earphones and foot control pedal.

Make sure, however, that you don't overemphasize computer procedures to the detriment of communications, sales, listening skills and other forms of instruction that will have more of an impact on the rep's on-phone performance.

Clarifying Goals and Expectations. Lastly, you must not only understand senior management's training goals and expectations, but also elicit input and feedback from your telemarketing representatives in designing training appropriate to your staff. Surely, management must help you to set the direction and focus for your program in determining: which products or services to emphasize, price and competitive positioning of products, growth expectations, revenue projections and many other strategic issues.

It is important not to forget the people on the front lines who are the ones who are supposed to benefit from this training.

Remember to pinpoint the sophistication level of your training by also examining the profile of your "average" rep for education level, age, past work experience, and level of sales or product knowledge.

THE COMPONENTS OF A TELEMARKETING TRAINING PROGRAM

The following section will illustrate a model for a possible telemarketing curriculum including an inbound telemarketing function. Included are some suggestions for collateral materials and audio-visual training aids that would be appropriate to each specific learning module.

Module 1: Product Knowledge. Product training should be broken down into the major product or service groups, if appropriate. Within these groups, break out individual product/service offerings and provide learning modules on each. Designed in concert with your marketing department, these modules should include:

1. Product description. Include detailed write-ups of specific product characteristics including benefits, features and competitive positioning. The purpose of this section is to provide the trainee with a firm understanding of how this product is used by the customer and what needs it meets.

Learning exercises will help the rep to better process this information. Such "learning by doing" also provides you with feedback to evaluate how well each individual has grasped the information and what further product training is required. An objective product knowledge test is the best way to ensure competency in each area.

2. Marketing strategy. The well-informed, professional telemarketing rep should have a sound understanding of your company's approach to reaching each product's target market. This training should include a thorough review of:

* *Direct response strategy.*

* *Mail piece design and copy.*

* *Competitive (pricing) positioning.*

* *Potential market population size.*

3. Customer Profile. The telemarketing rep must also be familiar with the general profile of each potential customer for a specific product/service. Reps should be provided with demographic and psychographic information about prospects as well as how they will use the product or service. If at all possible, reps should have the opportunity to use the products themselves--or at least observe how they are used, if only in a laboratory setting.

Suggested training aids:

* *Slides for group presentations should cover the key points and summarize handout materials.*

* *Trainee workbooks should include all training course texts, exercises, product information and handouts.*

* *Support materials should include a complete glossary of industry terms and any specific company "jargon" the trainee should be familiar with.*

* *No matter what your position on scripting, consider creating a "product profile job aid" for initial training purposes. Especially effective within on-*

*line computer training programs, the job aid should help reps become
familiar with the features and benefits of particular products and learn how
to use them in a "sales-focused" conversation.*

Module 2: Effective Communications Skills. This training module has applications beyond the telemarketing department and can be used to improve the communications skills of employees throughout the entire company. This argument can be used in justifying the costs of the time and financial investment in developing this module. It should include:

1. *Understanding communications.*

    A. Develop a definition of good communications through interaction and participant feedback.

    B. Review how the components of good communications can affect the two-way sales or service conversation. Exercises should illustrate the difference between one-way and two-way communication and why reps must elicit feedback in order to uncover needs and offer solutions.

    C. Discuss the barriers to good communications and how they can be overcome.

2. *Professional telephone techniques.*

    A. Describe and discuss the key conditions of telephone communications:

    i)   *The voice, through words and inflections, is the only tool you
have to convey attitudes on the phone.*

    ii)   *Pay attention to both the spoken and unspoken communication
from your prospect.*

    iii)   *Use the prospect's name frequently to build rapport.*

    iv)   *Help the prospect form a mental image by using word pictures.*

    v)   *Ask leading questions to elicit feedback in a two-way conversa-
tion.*

    vi)   *Be prepared to answer any type of objection without hesitation.*

    B. This section should also cover how a good telephone voice is the pre-requisite of an effective tele-personality. Use voice exercises to practice techniques taught in this session.

    C. Include an overview of the general rules of common telephone courtesy and your company's call-handling policies.

3. *Listening skills.*

    A. Start with a listening test to show how everyone's listening habits could stand improvement.

B. Add a review of the keys to good listening, as well as why and when to listen.

C. Include concentration and retention techniques for processing information.

D. Examine the factors that can hamper the ability to listen--and how to avoid and overcome distractions.

Suggested training aids:

* *Interactive audio tapes.*
* *Trainee workbooks containing developmental exercises (relating generic learning to your specific application and products) and pre-and post-training tests.*
* *Facilitator's guide.*

Module 3: Customer Service. The customer service module is almost as important to the telemarketing rep who must occasionally handle incoming calls as it is for the customer service rep in an exclusively inbound customer service or order-handling environment. The customer service module should be closely aligned with the communications module.

1. *Customer service functions.*

A. Review customer service responsibilities and functions and how they relate to corporate objectives. Focus on the importance of good customer service habits within every job function including telemarketing.

B. Emphasize customer problem-handling techniques and their positive impact on the rapport and relationship building process.

2. *Call flow logic.*

A. Analyze the eight steps of a reactive call:

i) *Identify self and company.*
ii) *Control the call.*
iii) *Clarify customer needs.*
iv) *Use judgment to determine what action should be taken.*
v) *Respond to request.*
vi) *Bridge to sales mode (if applicable).*
vii) *Offer additional help.*
viii) *Express thanks and close the call.*

3. *Computer system interface.* Based on the call flow logic, review how information gained at each stage of the call should be input into the computer to develop a total picture of the call handling process. Suggested training aids:

* *Videotape vignettes illustrating various call handling scenarios.*

* *Trainee and facilitator workbooks.*

* *Case studies, roleplay exercise.*

Module 4: Telemarketing Sales Skills. This module is segmented into a seven-part course covering all the essential activities and skills required for an effective and proactive telephone sales call. The emphasis throughout is on discovering needs and selling product benefits to those needs. The components of this module include:

1. *Pre-call planning.*

    A. This module provides hands on follow-through to the product knowledge gained in Module 1. The trainee should learn to develop the features and benefits for each product/service into characteristic, application and benefit statements. The objective at this point is to teach the trainee to think and communicate in "sales focused" language.

    B. Information about competitive products and market positioning should be covered briefly to help prepare the rep to handle objections about the competition.

    C. Call objectives. Develop a pre-call planning exercise to help the rep set primary and secondary goals for the call and think ahead in the sales presentation process.

    D. Time management. Give the rep guidelines on organizing first calls and callbacks to meet sales objectives and make the most of each day.

2. *Call introduction and opening.*

    A. Introduction. Help reps to develop their own opening statements as you review the importance of getting the prospect's interest and attention early on in the conversation. Discuss why the prospect is distracted from the sales message until the following questions have been answered:

        i)   *Who are you?*
        ii)   *Where are you calling from?*
        iii)   *How long is this going to take?*
        iv)   *Why are you calling me?*
        v)   *What are you selling?*

3. Fact-finding.

    A. Help rep to develop general and specific questions into detail questions (that provide background information about the prospect's situation), dissatisfaction questions (to identify the prospect's current problems) and decision questions (to develop the prospect's need for a solution).

B. Through transfer exercises (in which reps relate generic techniques to your particular product/market applications), develop specific needs discovery questions for various products/services.

4. *Sales message.*

A. Based on the needs identified in Step 3, develop a sales recommendation offering the prospect a specific solution via your products/services.

B. Help the rep develop a sales vocabulary to use features and benefits within your sales message.

C. Instruct reps on using trial closes to "test the waters" and gain agreement throughout the sales conversation.

D. Include feature/benefit differentiation exercises and help reps develop their own feature/benefit statements.

5. *Dealing with objections.*

A. Show reps how to apply their newly learned listening skills in handling objections. Teach them to acknowledge the objection through paraphrasing it to verify the rep's understanding of the objection, then "turn the corner" via "feel, felt and found" and other objection-handling techniques.

B. Give reps an overview of the four major types of objections--no need, no money, no confidence (in your company) and no hurry--and how to overcome them.

C. Use transfer exercises to develop a list of the most likely objections reps will encounter and their responses.

6. *Securing commitment/closing the sale.*

A. Review the four most effective closing strategies and how to use them:

i) *The direct close:* "With your permission, Mr. Brown, I'll write up this order right away."
ii) *The alternate choice close:* "Two dozen or three?"
iii) *The if/suppose hypothetical close:* "If we went ahead on this today, how soon would you need delivery?"
iv) *The assumptive close:* "I know you'll want to get your reps trained on this system as soon as possible--would you prefer a group training session or one-on-one training?"

7. *Sales call summary.*

A. Show reps how to summarize the details of the commitment the prospect has just agreed to.

B. Help reps develop an explanation of the actions to follow, and how they will follow through on their end of the commitment.

Suggested training aids:
* *Narrator-led interactive videos with vignette examples of the various scenarios.*
* *Trainee and facilitator workbooks.*
* *Case studies and roleplaying exercises.*

Module 5: Role Plays. Role playing is a training technique in which trainees have the opportunity to take turns playing the telemarketing rep and the prospect. By actually talking with "a customer," reps learn what to say and how to say it, getting experience communicating with your market before they actually have to get on the phone with your customers. We have found that dividing your staff into triads (sub-groups of three) greatly enhances the learning experience.
Some basic guidelines.

* *Select a different triad for each role-play scenario you design.* Members of the triad should elect one person to play the role of the rep. The other triad members will serve as support and counsel to the person in the rep role.

* *After distributing role-play scenarios, allow the participants several minutes to plan and review their strategy.* Encourage them to refer to the guidelines and make notes during the role play for discussion afterward.

* *Designate that "the customer" be played by the trainer or telemarketing manager.* Rarely do telemarketing reps have the experience or market knowledge to play the customer role effectively.

* *Conduct "blind" role plays.* Participants should not see each other so they can learn to deal with callers without using visual clues. Ideally, the "rep" and "customer" players should be in separate rooms communicating via a teletrainer unit or interoffice call connection--with a speaker phone in the classroom with the rep player and the trainees.

* *Instruct observing trainees to watch how posture, gestures and facial expressions convey attitudes to the prospect.* Trainees should critique each call for telephone courtesy, communication and selling skills.

* *Establish the role play to be about the same length as that of actual calls.*

* *Use all the same call guides, paperwork and reference materials the rep is expected to use on the job.*

* *Tape record role-play exercises so they may be reviewed, evaluated and used in future training sessions.*

Role Playing Procedures:

1. *First, explain the purpose of the exercise (e.g., to aid the telemarketing rep in learning how to overcome customer objections).*
Some of the participants may be a little nervous about role playing and using a tape recorder, so try to put them at ease. The more they role play and try out various techniques, the better prepared they'll be to handle real prospects.
Make sure everyone understands that the kind of feedback they'll receive will be constructive. Remember, it is your responsibility to make sure it is constructive.

2. *Ask for a volunteer group for the first role play.* You could say *"We'll take the volunteer now and the draftees next."*

3. *Distribute the role play case studies.* The telemarketing rep should initiate the role play with the cues provided in the case study.

4. *Request that as you record the role play, the other group members should note observations and comments.*

5. *When each role-playing situation is finished, you should play back the recording, especially for the benefit of the participating telemarketing rep.* During this playback, participants should again note their comments for feedback.

Role-Play Discussion:

1. *Ask participants to evaluate themselves.* (It's the best learning experience when someone can catch his own mistakes.) Ask them to include both the good points and constructive criticism, if possible.

2. *Ask other participants for their input, encouraging both praise and constructive criticism.*

3. *Finally, it is up to you to comment on the role play.* Include both your comments and an evaluation of the other participants' comments. Be careful to make the kinds of comments you want the others to make. You set the tone.
If the role play was successful, reinforce the techniques used. Here are some examples of the kinds of comments you and the observers should make:

* *"The telemarketing rep listened very carefully to the customer's concerns and answered the objections very well."*

* *"The telemarketing rep sounded professional and gave knowledgeable answers to customer's questions."* (Give specifics.)

* *"The telemarketing rep's tone of voice was calm, interested and courteous."*

* *"The telemarketing rep expressed genuine concern and interest in the customer's situation."*

4. *All role plays should be taped and played back during the evaluation and review sessions.* The tape can produce startling results (telemarketing reps hear themselves as monotonous robots in the beginning) and can also help reps see how much they change and improve during the training program. Play earliest tapes

back at the very end of the training program. The results will be so surprising to the reps that it will generate great excitement and self-confidence.

5. *Ad-libbing during role play--start out quite tightly, restricting telemarketing reps rigidly to call sequence and content guidelines*. Let ad-libbing and paraphrasing develop during program development. Never let telemarketing reps skip or deviate from call sequencing--show them that this results in repetition and vagueness and is devastating to their control of the call.

6. *Another training technique that has been found extremely effective is to use pre-training role play tapes*. Although a time consuming exercise, you may want to conduct impromptu role plays with each participant prior to the beginning of the training course. This usually provides each participant with dramatic evidence of how their skills and abilities have improved through training. By comparing the pre-and post-training role plays, the results of their training efforts can be readily seen and the entire learning process is greatly enhanced.

TRAINING MEDIA TO ENHANCE THE LEARNING PROCESS

The use of various training and audio-visual media in training will have a positive impact on the level of learning comprehension and retention. Without varying your delivery modes, you are sure to lose the attention of many of your participants and diminished learning can be certain. It is rare to find a training facilitator who can maintain the audience without the use of video tapes, slides, audio tapes, overheads, flipcharts, workbooks, handouts, etc.

You need to determine the appropriate media mix based on such factors as budget, number of training locations, the kind of product/service you are marketing. On the lower-cost end are professionally designed and prepared slides, overheads, charts or handouts. These methods are essential for most any presentation you would want to make during your course. They are most effective when used to provide an overview of what will be said or covered, and also for a summary of what was presented. They are passive in nature so they don't necessarily elicit feedback or interaction, but rather serve as additional reinforcement.

When evaluating the use of an audio-visual medium, the process becomes much more complicated because of the costs involved and the ranges in production qualities. We will discuss the purchase of generic, off-the-shelf audio-visual training programs in the next section. Our discussion here will focus on producing custom, in-house video tape presentations.

Production of a Custom In-House Video. Many managers are faced with the choice of whether or not to produce a video for their telemarketing training. From strictly a training viewpoint, well-produced video training modules teach more subject matter in less time than conventional classroom instruction through a concept called "time compression" or "speed learning."

There have been several studies on the subject by the American Society for Training and Development and private consultants. They found that by comparison to conventional stand-up, classroom instruction, well-designed video tape presentations yield measurably better results in one-fourth to one-sixth the time.

A typical training session that could have lasted five days can now be completed in three days with appropriate video presentation. That represents a decrease in salary expense of 40% and allows new employees to begin selling and generating revenues 40% sooner. There are also significant savings in salary, travel and lodging expenses for training staff and for company personnel traveling to various locations for training sessions.

The decision to produce a custom in-house video to complement your training program is an excellent one, provided you have the budget to produce an effective presentation. Can you afford to produce a training video with the production values and credibility that won't be laughed at by our sophisticated TV viewers in your training audience? Before you can decide if you can afford to produce a training video tape that meets your trainee's expectations, you must have a fairly accurate cost estimation.

Production Costs. Without any personal expertise or the help of a video-literate associate, trying to establish a cost estimate is extremely difficult. Instead, begin by contacting independent video producers to obtain prices. Unfortunately, it is extremely difficult even for an experienced video professional to give an accurate price without a script. The script is like a blueprint that will allow the producer to identify the required time, manpower, equipment and numerous other variables that will affect the production budget. There is a "Catch-22" situation here because no one wants to go to the time and expense of creating a script if the cost is going to be impossible to justify.

Therefore, as a benchmark you should expect to spend a minimum of $1,000 to a maximum of $4,000 per finished minute of video produced for a corporate-quality video. The width of this range is due to the many production and post-production variables. Some of the production aspects which will affect your final costs are the number and location of production sites, amount of studio production time, use of professional actors, type of equipment and video format used and amount of computer animation or digital effects required.

Off-the-Shelf Video Programs. Part of your decision process to produce your own video will involve previewing existing off-the-shelf video programs. If they can fill your need (even on an interim basis), this will save you both time and money. There is little doubt that video has the ability to communicate more economically and effectively with your audience. It is not a panacea, but can serve as a very effective contribution to the achievement of corporate objectives.

EVALUATING TRAINING PROGRAM ALTERNATIVES

There are basically two options available for acquiring a telemarketing training program:

* *Purchase an "off-the-shelf" generic program* or

* *Develop a customized training course.*

When the topic of generic training programs comes up, the typical objection always arises: *"This doesn't talk to my product or service, my reps won't relate to this."* Although a valid concern, there are ways to minimize the problem to make the most of professionally developed training packages. The real question to ask is whether the programs you are considering possess sound learning and instructional design methodology.

TRAINING

The use of "talking head" video tape lectures have minimal instructional value. If your telemarketing trainee can't relate or has "tuned out" two minutes after the tape began, very little learning will take place. Therefore, it is important that you evaluate many aspects of each training program. You should assess the following criteria before deciding on a particular training acquisition direction:

1. *How complete is the training program in terms of delivery methods?* Does it contain well-designed and produced workbooks, leader's guides, video tapes, interactive video discs, audio tapes, slides, transparencies, role plays, exercises and tests? The use of only one or two delivery methods will probably give you poor results.

2. *Are the program objectives clearly stated for the overall program and each program section or module?*

3. *Is the program modular?* Can each module stand on its own and be taught individually by itself? This relates to the flexibility of the program, as it is not always possible to spend a full day or two to train your reps. Training time might have to be broken up in shorter periods. If the program is not designed by modules, breaking up the training may be ineffective.

4. *What are the capabilities of transferring techniques, concepts, skills from the generic to the specific?* This is crucial and provides the ability to semi-customize a generic program to the nomenclature and marketing environment that your reps are familiar with.

5. *How quickly will the material become outdated due to the audio/video aspects of the program?*

6. *How is the course facilitated?* Must the program be administered by an instructor in a group or is it self-paced with the participant completing it individually? It would be ideal to have an option for both methods.

7. *If there are workbooks, can they be copied or reused or is there a licensing agreement requiring each participant to have a workbook?*

8. *What is the ability for follow-up training or other reinforcement after the initial training?*

9. *Are you comfortable with all or most of the techniques, skills, methods and other course material presented?* Is the subject matter credible, while remaining simple enough for good comprehension?

The following matrixes developed by Dann Bergman and Dr. Maynard Howe[1] should help greatly in the course evaluation process. Not only do you want to assess the course material itself, but also as important is the background of the program designers and distributors. They may have produced the greatest course, but offer little support or may not even be around in six months to provide additional course material.

So, to simplify the selection process, we have included a specially created checklist in which to organize the criteria for comparing telemarketing training programs (See **Figure 8-1**). Included are the criteria that we believe are critical to training within a telemarketing operation. In addition, you will want to add criteria specific to your needs. We grouped the criteria under two major headings: *Instructional Criteria* and *Vendor Credentials*.

To use the checklist, list all relevant, decision-making criteria resulting from your training needs assessment in the column provided on the left. In the spaces provided across the top margin of the matrix, note the names of the vendors (or programs) under consideration.

While you should examine each criterion carefully, you may find that some criteria will be more important to training within your organization than others. (For example, easy customization may be extremely important while the length of the program is only somewhat important.)

As you work through the list of criteria, decide how important each item is to your particular need.

107

Figure 8-1
Training Assessment Matrix

ITEM	All	Vendor 1		Vendor 2		Vendor 3	
PART 1: Instructional Criteria	A Import. 0-5	B Effect. 0-5	C Desire. AXB	B Effect. 0-5	C Desire. AXB	B Effect. 0-5	C Desire. AXB
Overall Goals/Objectives							
Delivery Method							
Role Plays							
Discussions							
Audio/Video Production Value							
Audio/Video Scenarios							
Other Media Included							
Program Administration							
Instructor Guide							
Customizable							
Meets Needs							
Other							
TOTAL PART 1							
PART 2: Vendor Credentials	A Import. 0-5	B Effect. 0-5	C Desire. AXB	B Effect. 0-5	C Desire. AXB	B Effect. 0-5	C Desire. AXB
Reputation							
Previous Training Experience							
Previous Telemarketing Experience							
Instructional Design Experience							
Vendor Support							
Availability of Support							
Discount Policy							
Training the Trainer Offered							
Trainers Available							
References Available							
Other							
TOTAL PART II							
TOTAL PART I							
OVERALL TOTAL							

Matrix developed by Dann Bergman and Dr. Maynard Howe. Used by Permission.

Assign each criterion a numerical value of 0 to 5, with 0 as the least important and 5 as the most important. List the values for each in column A: *"Importance."*

Now review each of the programs on your list. Indicate the degree (from 0 to 5) to which each vendor's program addresses or satisfies each criterion in column B: *"Effectiveness."*

Multiplying the *"Importance"* rating by the *"Effectiveness"* rating will give you a *"Desirability"* number in column C for each vendor to help determine which offers the program best-suited to your needs.

Once you have purchased your training package you will likely want to add some customized touches to it. The following will give some simple suggestions for enhancements to make the course more company/market specific:

1. *Skill exercises.* Wherever there are general skill exercises, be sure to develop exercises using your products/services, company terms and policies. Discuss your unique features and benefits, and have the class develop specific ones for their product. Also, have prepared handouts to distribute at the end of each discussion.

2. *Tape recordings.* Use tape recordings of actual calls to illustrate positive models for various skills or techniques discussed during each module.

3. *Handouts.* Use as many prepared handouts as possible that further explain a skill in relation to your product/service.

4. *Case Studies.* Design custom case studies and role plays that involve your products/services and selling environment. A case study is a well thought out and realistic selling scenario that requires the participant to write out solutions to various problems presented in the study. The second part is to discuss the case in class. Then the scenario is finally acted out as a role play. See **Figures 8-2** and **8-3** for examples of a simple case study format.

5. *Trainer's responsibility.* Responsibility for transferring skills from generic to specific should fall directly on the shoulders of the trainer. He or she should continually relate concepts into the organization's environment.

TRAINING FACILITATION GUIDELINES

Effective training and presentation skills are not learned overnight. It is recommended that anyone involved in training be exposed to public speaking or some kind of presentation skills course. There is much more to effective presentation than just your voice and not using "umm's" and "ah's." Trainers should learn such skills as how to use flipcharts and overheads, and develop an understanding of presentation approaches, such as how much movement is acceptable when in front of a class. Such organizations as Dale Carnegie and Toastmasters offer excellent programs for developing presentation and public speaking skills.

Group Size. The ideal group should not exceed 12 in order to ensure maximum interaction. You may also want to divide the class into triads (smaller groups of three), so they may practice techniques and exercises together, while sharing ideas and opinions. If your program has been designed for one participant to take the course independently, you'll want to be sure there is a mechanism for feedback and evaluation. The trainer or supervisor must meet with the participant at intervals to discuss the training material.

109

Trainer's Responsibilities. It is essential that the trainer preview all training program material thoroughly and be prepared for questions or other challenges. The trainer should collect and have enough copies of all relevant company materials for discussion at various points during the training. Stock materials might be:

* *Product and service information, including description, specifications, applications, customer testimonials and pricing.*

* *Competitive product and service information, as complete as possible.*

* *Company organization and responsibilities relevant to telemarketing.*

Figure 8-2
Case Study Example 1

Call Scenario: You are calling Ms. Marion Collins in New York City, who is a professional meeting planner. She used the Hershey Hotel for an Eastern Regional Sales Conference, doing the planning for Sun Oil Refineries back in September, 1987. You have not had any business from her since, and don't know how things went previously.

Call Objective: To uncover any possible needs for future business, and to sell her on your facility.

1) *Plan carefully for your call opening and write one here:*

2) *What kind of fact-finding questions will you want to ask?*

3) *How will you close this call if you uncover a need or needs?*

---

* *Information about your organization's marketing campaigns, such as direct mail and advertising through other media, that affect telemarketing efforts.*

* *Copies of any forms and reports required to complete.*

* *Outlines of any scripts your company provides telemarketing reps.*

* *References that contain basic information about business and market segments.*

110

* *Any other reference information that's a useful and helpful adjunct to selling and handling incoming calls in your company.*

ESTABLISHING A COACHING/COUNSELING PROGRAM

Coaching takes the interpersonal skills discussed and applies them to a step-by-step process designed to assist you in developing your people. The responsibility for developing your team and the individuals that make it up rests with the management team. You are responsible for providing guidance, strategy, advice and opportunities to improve individual and team performance.

Figure 8-3
Case Study Example 2

Call Scenario: Paul Jones, Vice President, Administration, of Kahn Industries has your Lynk Station 802 on trial for two weeks. You are calling to find out how he is doing. During the call, you discover several problems that could impede closing a sale.

Call Objective: To clarify the problems and overcome his objections (describe how you would handle each of these example scenarios).

   1)   *Mr. Jones feels the workstation is more than adequate, but does not want to replace his ASCII printers.*

   2)   *Mr. Jones has received a lot of resistence from his operators, who have been "uncomfortable" with larger keyboards.*

   3)   *He says that he is more comfortable with his 3180 workstations and doesn't see any reason to change.*

Thus, coaching should be viewed from both an individual and team perspective, encouraging individuals to apply their skills and abilities in harmony with the whole department.

The objectives of a coaching program are three-fold:

1. *To maintain or improve the TSR's performance in demonstrated areas of strength.*

2. *To improve and strengthen areas of performance that are found to need improvement.*

111

3.   *To coordinate the skills of the team to meet objectives and goals.*

As a coach, you will need to apply your skills as a communicator and manager in order to meet these objectives. Coaching is a process of observation, feedback and reinforcement. Observation is in the form of monitoring the telemarketing rep's call activities and identifying their strengths and weaknesses; feedback refers to the interaction and discussion with each rep concerning the skills, abilities, strengths and/or

---

Figure 8-4
Coaching Steps

A. Pre-Call Briefing
1. Review calls to be made.
   * Objectives.
   * Background.
   * Review coaching objective.

B. Monitoring
1. Listen.
2. Identify the steps of the call (transition).
3. Record noteworthy interaction.
4. Identify skill utilization.
   * Listening.
   * Sales skills.
   * Telephone techniques.
5. Objective identification (did the TSR reach stated objectives?).
6. Determine problem areas (following call).

C. Post-Call Review
1. Solicit feedback from TSR (self-analysis).
2. Review call.
3. Give information/feedback (identify problem areas).
4. Ask for feedback.

D. Development Program
1. Identify problems.
   * Communication skills.
   * Sales skills.
   * Knowledge.
     - Product.
     - Market/industry/competition.
   * Preparation.
2. Ask for suggested improvement steps: additional training, remedial help.
3. Confirm action steps (get agreement).

---

weaknesses that you have observed during the monitoring session.

The focus is always on the improvement of performance through the enhancement of skills and or behavior modification.

Lastly, a good coaching program should always involve the telemarketing rep in a planned action for improvement or positive reinforcement to correct any deficiencies.

A well-planned and implemented coaching program will offer the following benefits:

*   *Firsthand, objective analysis of each telemarketer's strengths and weaknesses.*

* *The opportunity to work with individuals to improve strengths and eliminate weaknesses.*

* *Development of self-analysis skills that will assist your people in self-improvement.*

Coaching the Individual. It should be remembered that even in a team environment no one ever outgrows the need to be treated as an individual. As coaches we should also understand that most people tend to either overlook their shortcomings or to justify their position. It is natural for people to also feel defensive when being monitored and coached, especially if they are made to feel that they are being watched for mistakes.

To ensure that your coaching program will be effective, use coaching routinely as a method of helpfulness. Little will be accomplished if every time you announce a monitoring session your people resort to unnatural styles (due to anxiety and stress) and thus move away from a true performance level.

Keeping the following points in mind will help you to focus on your coaching objectives:

* *Coaching is an on-going development process.*

* *The call is an observed call, not a joint call.*

* *Coaching is the gathering of information which is fed back to the TSR, in a positive, constructive manner.*

* *Coaching should be tailored to the individual.*

* *Coaching should be focused, yet remain flexible and open.*

* *Coaching should result in an action plan for improvement.*

* *Coaching is not a disparaging disciplinary tool.*

Implementing a Coaching Program. Coaching should begin right after the training of your telemarketing reps. This will ensure:

* *Continuity of training.*

* *Sustained momentum.*

* *Identification of individual strengths and weaknesses.*

In order to reduce any misunderstanding and lessen the anxiety in your people, the coaching process, its objectives and purposes should be presented to your team. By reviewing the following steps at a team meeting or with each individual, you will prepare and inform them of your objectives. Look for and expect questions and openly address the issues. Presenting the following in positive terms will lay a foundation for mutual trust:

1. *Coaching overview.* Explain the mission and objectives of coaching.

Figure 8-5
Call Quality Evaluation

Name: _____ Date: _____
Time On: _____ Time Off: _____ Length: _____

Category	Notes	Needs Improvement	Satisfactory	Good	Superior
Preparation:					
Approach:					
Fact Finding:					
Recommendation:					
Close:					
Implementation:					
Listening Skills:					
Call Control:					

Developmental Plan

Strong Areas: _____

Areas To Improve: _____

Suggested Improvement Measures: _____

SUPERIOR: Demonstrated outstanding quality on many aspects of the call.
GOOD: Demonstrated above average quality throughout the call.
SATISFACTORY: Demonstrated moderate call quality.
NEEDS IMPROVEMENT: Improvement required in areas denoted above.

2. *Pre-call briefing.* Review pre-call planning steps (for both inbound and outbound calls).

3. *Call monitoring.* Observe the call and record the call information.

4. *Post call review.* Feedback on call, review call information.

5. *Development program.* Identify the observed problem areas and establish a course of action for improvement.

A detail of *Coaching Steps* are outlined in **Figure 8-4**, along with a *Call Quality Evaluation*, **Figure 8-5** and a *Performance Appraisal Action Plan*, **Figure 8-6**. These tools and their appropriate use should greatly assist one's coaching efforts.

Figure 8-6
Performance Appraisal Action Plan

Based on calls observed on _____ the following PAAP was designed for:

Employee Name: _____

Identified Problem Areas:

_____

_____

_____

_____

Improvements Needed:

_____

_____

_____

_____

Progress Made:

_____

_____

_____

_____

115

TRAINING VALIDATION

Now that so much time, energy and money have been expended putting your training program together, how do you measure its success or effectiveness? Building a validation mechanism is very important, but is not always an easy task. There are, certainly, quantitative measurements such as increased sales, higher closure rates, more call presentations, etc., that can be tracked pre- and post-training. This is an evaluation activity that should be performed with all existing telemarketing reps where performance and productivity have been recorded for at least six months.

Another mandatory requirement for a legitimate validation process is that a monitoring program be in place and appropriate coaching and counseling be offered on an ongoing basis. For any permanent behavioral changes to take place as a result of training, there must be continual reinforcement throughout the coaching process and remedial and follow-up training.

Pre- and Post-Objective Test. It is recommended that all training participants be required to take a pre- and post-objective test. The test should measure the participant's skill and sales knowledge level prior to going through the training. There should be a predetermined score increase that would indicate an acceptable level of progress. Certainly, where participants don't show any significant improvement after training, they should not go on the phones until the trainer or manager is totally comfortable that the individual is sales skills competent.

Control Group. Another effective training validation method is to establish control groups. From your telemarketing team, randomly choose the first group to complete the training; this will be your control group. Be sure that there is a true cross section of individuals in terms of experience, skills and talents. Then don't attempt to train your other people for at least two to three months. During that period, make a concentrated effort to monitor and coach the people in your control group. Careful tracking of all sales statistics must be established if not already being done, with an individual performance evaluation of each rep. If your training program was designed and facilitated properly, there should be a marked difference in the team and individual performance of the control group versus the other reps.

What can be assumed if the control group does not show superior results? It would be highly unlikely that such a situation would occur if all training design, observation and coaching procedures were followed.

First, be sure that there is truly a cross section of individuals in each group. Once satisfied, you can assume that some important aspect of the selling process has not taken hold. More intense monitoring should take place by several qualified observers. It is likely that certain negative trends and skills deficiencies will soon surface. At this point, the training curriculum should be reviewed and enhanced to produce an increased awareness of these areas. The remaining telemarketing reps can now proceed with their official training.

Ongoing Training. Training is a continual process. Make sure everyone has the basics as part of their everyday selling behavior. Ongoing training in the basics must be committed. For those selling situations that are more sophisticated, advanced sales skills training may be implemented in such areas as negotiations skills, neurolinguistic programming, interpersonal skills or supervisory and management training.

116

TRAINING

If you have a training program in place now, make it a point to take a hard look at it and evaluate ways to update or enhance it soon. If you still don't have a formalized, structured telemarketing training program, commit to making it a primary goal. That commitment will pay you back with increased sales, reduced turnover and more successful and fulfilled telemarketing reps.

----

[1]Dann Bergman and Maynard Howe, Ph.D., *Telemarketing Management,* January 1988, *pp. 17-18.*

CHAPTER 9

Compensation/Motivation

Lee Van Vechten
Publisher, *The Van Vechten Report*
CEO, FGI
Freehold, New Jersey

Compensation planning really doesn't vary from industry to industry, or profession to profession, but it does vary according to time periods and the maturity of the industry and/or profession involved. Compensation plans are also affected by the employee's perception of his or her worth and the value of his or her effort.

Telemarketing is a good example of this phenomenon. A perception reigned in the 1970's that the telephone was simple to use and, therefore, the skills required to use it were simple. And, of course, given that the task and skills required were "simple," it was logical to conclude that the jobs only warranted minimum wage.

What business managers and owners have learned since those early, less "complicated" days is that the resource called telemarketing is not quite as simple as it once appeared. As a matter of fact, it is getting more complicated each day.

A definition of telemarketing would be useful here:

Telemarketing is the intensive use of the telephone in a business environment.[1]

CALL OBJECTIVE IMPACTS COMPENSATION

This definition suggests a question about a given telemarketing task: "intensive use" to accomplish what? The objective(s) of the call can, in fact, have an impact upon compensation logic. Would you, for example, hire the same type of individual for an inbound 800 order-entry desk for men's shoes as you would for a physicians' referral service located in a major city hospital? Or, do you need the same type of individual to sell complicated computer software as to sell subscriptions to the local Sunday paper? Hardly.

Clearly, the degree of difficulty can vary greatly from job to job. And just as clearly, different telephone assignments can require different personalities and behavior patterns. These differences in call objectives--and, therefore, requirements of the TSR (see **Figure 9-1**)--are what create differences in compensation.

As noted in **Figure 9-1**, not all telemarketing assignments are created equal. The degree of difficulty

118

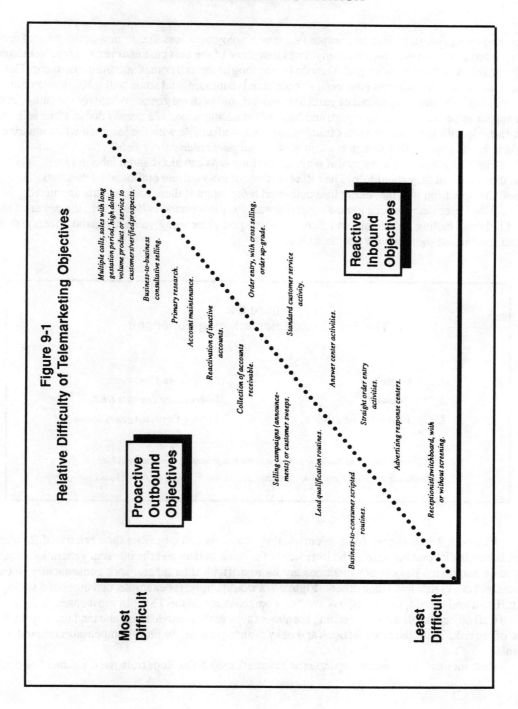

Figure 9-1
Relative Difficulty of Telemarketing Objectives

Most Difficult

Multiple calls, sales with long gestation period, high dollar volume product or service to customers/verified prospects.

Business-to-business consultative selling.

Primary research.

Account maintenance.

Reactivation of inactive accounts.

Order entry, with cross selling, order up-grade.

Standard customer service activity.

Collection of accounts receivable.

Answer center activities.

Selling campaigns (announcements) or customer sweeps.

Straight order entry activities.

Lead qualification routines.

Advertising response centers.

Business-to-consumer scripted routines.

Receptionist/switchboard, with or without screening.

Least Difficult

Proactive Outbound Objectives

Reactive Inbound Objectives

and the degree of risk (e.g., risk of compensation or employment loss due to non-performance) can vary greatly. It has also been documented many times that some of the best customer service representatives are literally unable to behave proactively. They do fine as long as the call comes *into* the department. However, ask them to make 100 outbound *cold calls* to people or businesses, and some will rebel or even quit.

Adult behavior is a product of past environment, and perhaps genes. Whatever the cause, behavior styles appear to be set, for the most part, and basically unchangeable. If a person doesn't like selling, or is uncomfortable with the task even after training, or is uncomfortable with the job even when measured and thought to be successful, that person is *misplaced in that particular career field.*

Time after time, we are asked if outbound selling reps can also handle inbound calls. The answer is, yes, they can--but they shouldn't. The call objectives of inbound and outbound telemarketing just do not mix, and the operation will inevitably lose outbound momentum if these assignments are mixed.

Why? Because the reps almost naturally wait for the inbound call--to them, the easier of the two tasks. Outbound calling is difficult, and there's nothing particularly enjoyable about the rejection that goes with the assignment (not for sane people, at least!).

Figure 9-2
The Six Basic Telemarketing Functions

1. **Outbound**	*4.* **Business-to-Consumer**
2. **Inbound**	*5.* **In-House or On-Site Units**
3. **Business-to-Business**	*6.* **Service Bureau Agency Units**

Most Difficult: Outbound, business-to-business, on-site, proactive, consultative selling.

Least Difficult: Inbound, business-to-consumer, service agency, reactive, fully scripted selling.

Figure 9-2 lists the six basic telemarketing functions and describes their relative difficulty. All telemarketing is difficult because of the intensity of the environment and the inherent generation of tension, pressure or boredom. But certain functions are more difficult than others, and, consequently, should be compensated at a higher level than others. **Figure 9-2** would imply, for example, that outbound selling is the most difficult and should, therefore, pay the best compensation to the TSR. In most cases, it does.

Call objectives that involve selling are almost always the most difficult and tend to carry the highest degree of job risk. Thus, the more difficult and risky the assignment, the more compensation should be made available.

Risk, incidentally, tends to separate the Telemarketing Sales Reps from the Customer Service Reps.

Therefore, when other telemarketing personnel wonder why they don't earn as much pay or recognition as their sales-oriented brethren, they should be made to understand that their positions do not carry the same amount of *job risk*.

TELEMARKETING COMPENSATION IN HISTORY

The history of telemarketing compensation is interesting. About 50 years ago, marketers perceived the need to find ways to contact large numbers of organizations or people quickly and inexpensively. The first shell into the breech of the direct marketing cannon was direct mail. The Postal Service provided an answer, and lobbyists did the rest.

During the 1940's and 1950's, hundreds of millions of *tons* of consumer direct mail did what direct selling organizations and retailers had found so difficult to do--they reached massive numbers of prospects/ customers at low costs, with fairly simple offers. Thus were selling expenses reduced and market shares increased.

These pioneers were mainly the consumer marketers, however. Business-to-business marketers didn't jump on the bandwagon immediately. It took them another decade or so to see the value of direct mail.

A similar evolution occurred in telemarketing. Business-to-consumer came first (e.g., Murray Roman and Olan Mills, the portrait people), followed by business-to-business telemarketing.

Just as perception of telemarketing usefulness took time to develop, the perceived value of telemarketing sales reps took time to evolve. Telemarketing assignments in the earlier years were generally perceived as low-pay, low-talent positions. Transient labor and part-timers made up the bulk of the TSR ranks, all inhabiting low perches in the organizational pecking order.

Compensation was often lower than minimum wage, or 100% commission "off the books." All sorts of fascinating but unprofessional compensation schemes were employed.

TELEMARKETING COMPENSATION TODAY

The "present" of telemarketing compensation came into being, for all practical purposes, in the early to mid-1970's. At that time, the industry/profession started to take on an aura of legitimacy, primarily because of the arrival of business-to-business telemarketing. Curiously enough, the biggest credit for this evolution (or, perhaps, *revolution*) goes to the creation of OPEC in 1965. Given the stranglehold the oil exporting countries had on energy, American businesses and organizations found themselves hard-pressed to afford traditional, energy-consuming selling and promoting methods.

Telemarketing went from poor relation to honored guest. Then the recession of the early 1980's bestowed knighthood.

There is another factor keeping the upward pressure on telemarketing compensation levels: a shortage of people. A majority of experienced TSR's (60%) are women, who, for various reasons, aren't excited about the idea of transferring around the country. Thus, the pool of available people is both at a low level and difficult to tap. In some areas of the country, organizations are forced to hire people independent

121

of qualifications. In some areas of the East, for example, where unemployment levels are lower than 4% (1988), it is extremely difficult to attract qualified people.

For all these reasons, telemarketing today is a career that approaches appropriate levels of compensation, and the future looks even better. From my position as an industry specialist, I see an interesting phenomenon occurring. It was once thought (even assumed) that telemarketing and field sales were "twains" that never would meet.

We have been asked, however, by the training community to train field-selling organizations in the skills and techniques of telemarketing. Conversely, telemarketing organizations are asking for training in the skills of field selling.

Draw your own conclusions about the effect this merging of functions will have on the status of telemarketing within organizations--and, hence, on compensation levels in the future.

RISK/REWARD

Various commission plans that have been popular in field sales organizations over the past 35 years have centered around the playoff of risk versus reward concepts. These approaches can be effective if designed and implemented properly. They can also de-motivate the sales employees involved.

Negative Plans/Motivators. Many organizations absolutely hate to pay sales reps or others for selling products or services. It's almost as if they expect products or services to sell themselves.

While most of us know that products don't sell themselves, it's still possible to act subconsciously on the premise that commissions are an evil. How else can we explain the negative compensation plans that rose in popularity during the early 1980's, than through this "we hate it but have to do it" thinking?

Here are some examples of negative "motivators":

* *Do the job and you get a chance to keep yours.*

* *Sell $100,000 and you get 2%. Sell another $100,000 and you get 1%, or maybe no commission because the plan is capped.*

* *Sell $10,000 at no incentive, then we will give you 1% on all sales over $10,000, etc.*

These "plans" remind me of a civil engineering supply company where I once worked in sales. They made oak stakes for surveyors to stake out property and center lines for road construction. The employment ad read: *$1.45 per hour and all the stakes you can eat.* I fell for it . . . once.

Positive Motivators. A risk-reward program that combines salary (which is the reward) with a commission on each sale for *every* dollar sold (the risk) is much more likely to motivate people than the above plans. This concept can also apply to non-sales, defined telemarketing task assignments. Simply, the more the TSR sells, or the more tasks he or she completes, the more the TSR earns.

Clearly, plans like this tend to reward the achiever and eliminate the underachiever. Coupled with increasing commission steps (i.e., the more product/service sold, the greater the reward), positive risk-reward plans provide a framework that keeps compensation variable and rewarding to the employee. A full explanation of these concepts, and examples of the plans, follow.

TELEMARKETING/FIELD SALES PAY PLAN PARITY

It is not unusual for organizations to have different pay plans for different departments and divisions. Many times, such differences are even necessary. But if these various plans are intended to serve as positive motivators, one rule of thumb is important to follow: *similar kinds of assignments should receive similar compensation.*

Selling to the organization's account structure is simply that--selling to the account structure. It shouldn't matter whether the sales person works out of a car or over the telephone. Nor, ultimately, should the size of "territory" make a difference. Certainly relative sales volume would have an impact, but most often the larger sale carries a lower profit or margin percentage. Specifically, a $1 million field sales territory can often produce less profit than a $200,000 telemarketing territory. Most organizations target profitability, not volume, and the compensation program should always keep this in sight.

Further, we suggest that you look at compensation as a form of recognition. The dollar isn't everything (although it's a big part of it), and recognizing achievement can lead to a great deal of creativity in compensation planning. It can also solve problems money alone can't help. I have seen TSR's who were earning $60,000 annually walk up to management and state, *"That's it! I can't do it anymore. Good-bye!"*

Recognition "compensation" can take many forms--career pathing, a simple "thank you," a plaque--and, balanced with dollar compensation, recognition can be a powerful motivator, indeed.

Don't get the idea that there's anything wrong with designing innovative plans for the telemarketing unit. The fact that compensation plans don't look like other plans and policies in the organization doesn't automatically make them unacceptable. The objective is to motivate a specialized staff working in a difficult environment, a fact often overlooked (or not understood) by the people in Finance or Accounting. Tension and pressure can often alternate with boredom in these units, and often it's the compensation plan that banishes these devils from a telemarketing operation. Remember always that you are looking for ways to reward and motivate effort and success, not simply to pay for four or eight hours of work daily.

This is an idea you may have to reinforce periodically with your financial people. Don't let them dictate poor business judgment in compensation planning.

SELLING COMPENSATION PLANS TO MANAGEMENT

I have often heard TSR managers complain after presentations on compensation, *"I wish my manager would've been here to hear this."* Unfortunately, they weren't--and weren't likely to be in the future. Clearly, the TSR manager was going to have to sell effective plans to management and didn't know how to do it.

Selling management on innovative compensation plans for the telemarketing operation is often one of the major challenges the TSR manager faces. To be successful at it, it's necessary to understand management's "internal" language.

First, consider some key points:

* *Management is motivated by profits and revenues (whether they are for-profit or non-profit "revenue-neutral").*

* *Management always thinks about the budget primarily in percentages, secondarily in numbers. (For example*: "We are talking about a more than 23% profit improvement, amounting to over $100,000.")

* *Management is often concerned, even fearful, about disturbing existing compensation practices.* ("If it ain't broke, don't fix it.")

* *Management often perceives the TSR's job as a simple one.* ("So why such a complicated compensation plan?")

Given these inclinations and preconceptions, it's important to prepare justification, evidence and proof of a compensation plan's worth *before* approaching upper management for approval. Specifically:

1) *Collect case examples of organizations that reduced their sales expenses by using the telephone.*

2) *Know the necessary "numbers"--profit percentage your company is seeking, margin contributions, etc.*

3) *Know your existing sales expenses, and their percentage of net revenue.*

4) *Prepare a model compensation program with plenty of "What-ifs."*

5) *Offer to test the compensation plan against the previous year's actual sales.*

6) *Compare your sales costs to field sales costs by percentages to contribution (e.g., $20 million in sales at a 9% sales cost and 4% contribution for field sales, versus $2 million in sales at 8.2% sales cost and 23% contribution for telemarketing).*

7) *Compare new accounts or reactivated account results to the same contribution by other marketing methods.*

8) *Get management involved (e.g.,* "I need your advice, Boss. If we could reduce our overall compensation percentage against revenue while increasing both top line and enhancing our bottom line by 30% with a compensation plan change, would management be interested?").

9)   *Use testing to prove plan effectiveness.*

Testing can help, by the way, both in plan design *and* justification to management. Because of the large volume of calls that can be made in a short period, statistically sound samples can be developed, often in periods as short as six months. In that time, testing a subset of your people, you should be able to determine how a given compensation plan will produce and pay out for both the organization and the TSR.

Over the past nine years, I have personally demonstrated in well over 75 telemarketing units, that compensation plans with fixed and variable expenses can be used to motivate. In other words, as soon as base salary, FICA and insurance contributions, which are fixed expenses, have been covered, then the variable expense would consist of additional compensation for surpassing goals and exceeding objectives.

In practice, the variable expenses, as a percentage increase over fixed costs, turns out to be very small. In mathematical terms, the more that the TSR sells, the more cost of sales (as a percentage of sales) will drop. This can be pointed out to management in many ways, including graphically, and it can help change their entrenched opinions about compensating the telemarketing staff.

In summary, sell your compensation plan! Nobody else will do it for you.[2]

A CASE EXAMPLE

Good compensation planning radically improved the sales and profits of Advanced Management Research, Inc., New York, an education company selling seminar registrations, business-to-business. The company marketed through direct mail (20 million pieces) and had no field sales organization. They began telemarketing with seven TSR's.

Here's what happened:

Initially, the new telemarketing unit was viewed as an organizational pariah. The average order was $324. The starting compensation for TSR's was $12,000 annually, with 3% commission on all sales *over* a $12,000 per month quota. All underages were carried forward, and TSR's lost their jobs if under quota three months in a row. TSR's were, for the most part, rejects from other industries or out-of-work actors.

Fixed bonuses of $1,000 to $3,000 were awarded on net sales over $120,000 per year. Average income was $16,000. Top income was $32,000. The cost-of-sales, fully burdened (i.e., including rent, utilities, overhead, etc.), was 43% of revenue. Combined sales volume of the seven TSR's, three managers and three fulfillment people was $1.65 million.

Dissatisfied with these results, AMR hired a new vice president of sales to determine the problem. He took action immediately by terminating all non-sales personnel (essentially the entire management team), retrained fulfillment people and fired four non-producing TSR's.

He further redesigned compensation packages, developing professional sales programs similar to those presented in this chapter. As the basis for his redesign, he used 50% of compensation, in base, for both managers and TSR's, and 90% base for support staff. The remainder of compensation was to be earned by reaching assigned sales objectives, with open-ended compensation for exceeding objectives.

He then changed call objectives, concentrating on consultative selling techniques and the benefits of business education and AMR service. No more *"Do you need any seminars today?"*

Here are the results he achieved:

* *Direct mail revenue was unchanged.*

* *The average sale rose from $324 to $465.*

* *Telemarketing revenues increased from $1.65 million to $8.25 million in 30 months.*

* *Cost-of-sales dropped from 43% to 26.8%, and the company paid dividends to its stockholders for the first time in its 16-year history.*

The results on existing telemarketing staff compensation were just as dramatic. Average income moved from $16,000 to $28,500. Top TSR incomes went from $32,000 to $60,000-plus. Management incomes went from $40,000 to $129,000 (don't forget that sales costs dropped dramatically). Turnover rates shrunk to 12% terminations and 13% "quits."

The credibility this telemarketing operation achieved with these results was impressive. From the chairman of the board on down, upper management perceived this unprecedented success to be attributable to the new compensation plan.

It took courage for Anthony Whyte to install his compensation plan at AMR, but he clearly recognized it was the most effective way to achieve the organization's objectives: increased top-line revenue, lower selling costs and the installation of a profitable operation. His plan ignored the old concept of paying an exact amount for a specified job. Instead, he chose to reward contribution directly related to achieving those objectives.

THE LOGIC OF COMPENSATION

We've already discussed why any compensation plan that has a penalty of some sort built in is a negative motivator. Similarly, compensation "caps" or limitations are also demotivators. Both approaches lose sight of the fundamental compensation logic: find ways *to pay*, not ways *not to pay*!

The potential benefits of telemarketing have been proven. Armed with, and supported by, a marketing plan, telemarketers in either transactional or reactive environments can have definite and positive impacts on success and profitability.

Companies and organizations who fail to recognize this contribution often are outdistanced by companies that do. It's not uncommon for a neighbor organization, just a few miles down the road, to increase base salary and additional compensation to attract experienced TSR's--*yours*. What do you think goes through a TSR's mind in an organization where compensation is capped? Here is what they hear the organization saying to them:

"You've exceeded your sales budget, so stop selling!"

In fact, they're hearing correctly. Anyone who has been in field sales or telemarketing knows that people will not make contributions over and above what the compensation plan will pay for. Instead, they're more likely to hold out sales in case they run into a "dry spell" during the upcoming period.

If it makes financial sense to concentrate on reducing expenses while increasing profits--and when has that not made sense?--*it makes sense to motivate people to exceed their objectives.* A compensation plan that limits what a TSR can earn is a loaded revolver playing Russian roulette with the success of the telemarketing unit.

Simply:

1) *TSR's seek out jobs that recognize and reward their contribution.*

2) *The objective of the compensation plan is to motivate.*

3) *If your plan rewards, but doesn't motivate, it's only half a plan.*

In emotional terms, the TSR should feel that the organization wants him or her to achieve and is willing to share the victory (and profits) with the producer. In this kind of environment, the rep has no problem justifying working harder, longer and often smarter. I see many telemarketing operations "enjoying" various degrees of TSR burnout and turnover, and I know if they took a close look at their compensation plans, they would see a direct cause-to-effect relationship.

Any organization that sees no problem with, say, paying $5.00 per hour for people to make 170 calls a day, five days a week, four weeks per month, for as long as they can stand it, has a "death wish." The likely outcome is a continual search for warm bodies to serve as telephone fodder until the wish inevitably comes true.

The compensation environment is changing very fast, quickly destroying what minimal justification bad compensation plans might have had. Over the past nine years, I've watched TSR incomes go from levels like $9,000 up to $35,000 (total compensation, business-to-business, outbound selling environments). It's not uncommon these days for telemarketing managers to leave $21,000 positions for new jobs paying $35,000, with the possibility of an additional $15,000 if objectives are reached.

A TSR COMPENSATION PLAN (EXAMPLE)

Enough theory for the moment. It would be helpful to look at an actual plan, one we designed for a client. If the base salary seems low, it's because this company is located in a rural farm area with a high percentage of unemployment. Feel free copying the plan, but make sure to tailor the dollar amounts to your industry and your area.

This plan addresses:

A. *Base salary.*

B. *Merit increase to base salary.*

C. *Commission.*

D. *Bonus.*

A) Base Salary. Per company policy, base salary is determined by the telemarketing manager,

127

and reviewed once per year. This review can be on a calendar year basis or on the anniversary of employment, a decision made with the employee when employment is accepted.

B) Merit Increases to Base Salary. Merit increases are awarded for continued high performance, and are an adjustment to base salary. Merit reviews are held with any salesperson exceeding goal (accountability) by 10% or more. An increase may be granted of up to 10% of the amount sold over accountability, not to exceed 10% of the existing base salary. The actual amount of the merit increase is determined by the telemarketing manager, per company policy.

For example:

Accountability (goal):	$1,032,000
Net Sales:	1,050,000
Increase over Accountability:	18,000
10% of Increase:	1,800
Existing Base Salary:	15,000
Salary Increase:	1,500
New Base Salary:	16,500

C) Commissions. Commissions are payable monthly. The schedule of commission rates has five "step-through" levels which reward productivity (see **Figure 9-3**). Each ascending level is earned

Figure 9-3
Sample Five-Level Commission Rate Schedule

Level	Sales	Commission % Rate	Commission	Cumulative Commission	Cumulative Sales
First	$200,000	.5%	$1,000	$1,000	$200,000
Next	225,000	.75%	1,687	2,687	425,000
Next	250,000	1.00%	2,500	5,187	675,000
Next	300,000	1.25%	3,750	8,937	975,000
All Over	975,000	1.50%	------	------	------

by individual sales performance and relates solely to achievement. Commissions are accumulated over the compensation year, and any business sold, but not shipped, at the end of the year is commissioned at the first level.

D) Accountability Bonus. This bonus is awarded to each TSR who exceeds accountability. It works as follows:

*   *Every salesperson will be assigned a monthly NET accountability of $86,000.*

* *Cancelled sales or returns are subtracted from the total.*

* *A bonus of 2% will be paid on all net sales over accountability.*

* *All sales shipped in a given month will count toward this accountability.*

New sales staff hired after the original start date always begin at the lowest step commission. At the end of the compensation year, everybody reverts to the lowest commission on the scale.

A MANAGER'S COMPENSATION PLAN (EXAMPLE)

Here is an example of a compensation plan for telemarketing managers. It worked, in that all managers hit their quotas and received approximately $50,000 each in total compensation. Again, pay more attention to the concepts than the numbers.:

This plan addresses:

A) *Monthly quota.*

B) *Quarterly quota.*

C) *Yearly quota.*

D) *Product line bonus.*

A) Monthly Quota. In order for telemarketing managers to qualify for any bonus, they must achieve 100% of their total budget objectives. A bonus is paid each month for achieving the projected net sales objective for a month. Any overage for the month can be carried over into the next month within a quarter. Monthly overage cannot be carried from one quarter to the next. If a monthly objective is missed, it cannot be recovered. The monthly incentive is $300 per month, or $3,600 on an annual basis.

B) Quarterly Quota. A bonus is paid each quarter for achieving the quarterly sales objective. In any quarter where sales exceed the objective, the overage may be carried forward or backward *one* quarter.

Here is an example of a manager's plan:

Base	$23,000
First Quarter:	3,000
Second Quarter:	4,000
Third Quarter:	5,000
Fourth Quarter:	6,000
	$18,000

If a quarterly objective is missed, then the succeeding quarterly bonus award will be reduced one step. For example:

First Quarter Bonus:	Missed
Second Quarter Bonus:	$3,000

Third Quarter Bonus:	4,000
Fourth Quarter Bonus:	5,000

As you can see, the first quarter objective was not met, yet the second quarter objective was. Thus, the payout for meeting the second quarter dropped back to $3,000. We call this a Sliding Scale Bonus Plan. Missed bonuses can be made up. As I've said before--*try to find ways to pay, as opposed to ways not to pay.*

If the objective is missed in any quarter, that quarter's bonus can be recaptured *if* the deficit is picked up in the *next* quarter. However, that current quarter must have its target met. If the overall objective is then on target, the bonus scale advances according to the original plan.

In our last example, the *deficit* for the first quarter was not made up in the second quarter. However, the second quarter's target was met.

C) *Yearly Quota.* A year-end bonus of $3,000 will be paid if the total annual objective is achieved. The bonus is payable in the first quarter of the succeeding year (or fiscal year) after reconciliation of the unit's sales.

D) *Product Line Bonus.* A product line bonus will be awarded and will be based on percent of margin and other factors decided by management. This bonus will be in the $3,000 range.

COMPENSATING SUPPORT STAFF

It makes sense to put the entire telemarketing department--that is, including clerical and support staff--on some sort of a compensation plan. This fosters a team spirit and encourages everyone to work together to reach the department's goals.

A simple way to compensate support and fulfillment people is through a *fixed bonus* arrangement, with bonuses paid quarterly and increased throughout the year. This kind of a plan can be very new to people not used to anything other than straight salary or hourly wages. If they have the following traits, however, the chances are good that they can be pulled together as a team:

* *They can be motivated by recognition and more dollars.*

* *They show potential for working with others.*

* *They are interested in moving up to a more advanced selling assignment.*

As with the two plans described above, the following plan was designed for one of our client companies. Again, don't pay too much attention to the numbers. You can fill in your own amounts, depending on your type of business, your location and the economic environment.

This compensation plan addresses:

A) *Base salary.*

B) *Merit increase to base salary.*

C) *Bonus.*

COMPENSATION/MOTIVATION

A) Base Salary. Base is determined by the telemarketing manager, per company policy. It is reviewed annually, either on a calendar year or employment anniversary basis as decided on acceptance of employment.

B) Merit Increases to Base Salary. Merit increases to base salary are awarded for continued and sustained high performance. Actual amounts are determined by the telemarketing sales manager, per company policies.

C) Bonus. Bonuses are earned whenever the entire telemarketing department meets its quarterly objectives. For example:

Base:	$16,000

If the unit meets sales objectives:

Bonus

First Quarter:	$100
Second Quarter:	125
Third Quarter:	150
Fourth Quarter:	<u>175</u>
Bonus Total:	$550

The logic behind this plan is as follows:

* *Every sales clerical person starts even, no predetermined prejudice.*

* *Sales clerical people enjoy bonus growth based on the success of the tele-sales department, with no artificial waiting period.*

* *Sales clerical people will earn a quarterly bonus if the sales unit meets its revenue goals.*

* *No complicated tracking system is required for the payout.*

ALTERNATIVE METHODS OF COMPENSATION: CONTESTS

Most sales departments have contests of one type or another, although the reasoning behind them aren't generally well understood. Here are the basic justifications for sales contests:

* *Contest, by definition, suggests competition. It is a well established fact that salespeople like to compete for recognition and money (another form of recognition).*

* *Organizations can get a "second effort" through a well-designed contest with clear objectives for both the sales representatives and the company.*

131

* *Contests can neutralize, if not temporarily eradicate, the negative impact of boredom, pressure and tension.*

There are negative sides to contests. They can be run too often and sales units can become addicted to them. Sales people may hold back production if a contest is anticipated. The way to control for these problems is to announce "sprint" (short duration) contests only on the day the contest starts.

Further, a contest should have a budget and a reward that's worth shooting for. Forget the Stetson hat or free Cadillac for a week. Offer the sales staff what *they* think is interesting.

Here are some examples of "sprint" or short-term contest designs:

Example 1--The "Balloon" Contest. This contest was run in an organization that wanted to add service contracts to product sales. The specific objective was to generate 200 new service contracts at $250 each.

To qualify to "break" a balloon at the end of the day, the TSR's had, first of all, to maintain daily production objectives. After four service contracts were sold, each contract thereafter was worth two throws at the balloons. After 15 contracts were sold, three throws were won for each contract sold.

The game was played at the end of each day. The balloons, stuffed with slips of paper indicating a bonus value from $.50 to $100, were pinned to dartboard-like material and reps were allowed to throw the number of darts they had "won" during the day. Value slips were distributed in the balloons as follows:

BALLOONS	AMOUNT
1	$100
4	50
10	20
24	10
5	1
10	.50
54	$750

With $250 budgeted for replacement balloons, the total budget for this contest was $1,000. The contest provided a lot of fun, some excitement and the required competition. It ran for one week and then was discontinued. If service contracts were subsequently cancelled, the awards were charged back to regular commissions.

With contests like this, it's important to keep careful pay-out records and to post blurbs as to who won what. Cash awards should be paid immediately, in cash, with deductions worked out later.

Example 2--The "Wheel of Fortune" Contest. This contest is similar to the "Balloon" contest, except that a 36-inch Wheel of Fortune is rented and each "win" gets a spin of the wheel. Awards can be dollar values, trips, tickets, etc.

Long-term contests are possible, but they can be a problem. The primary difficulty is the short attention span of the people you're trying to motivate. Contests running a month or more in duration can suffer a significant decline in interest. The option to terminate the contest should be left to the manager's discretion.

COMPENSATION/MOTIVATION

A LEGAL ISSUE: EXEMPT OR NONEXEMPT?

The Federal Wage and Hour Guidelines specify minimum salary and hourly wages. These must be met for any positions not exempt from the law. Sales people on commission are exempt as long as they meet the guidelines, specifically that they spend 80% of their time *outside the office environment* performing their assignment.

Clearly, the Federal Government doesn't believe that selling can be done by telephone!

The American Telemarketing Association and the Telephone Marketing Council of the Direct Marketing Association are working on correcting this improper situation. Meanwhile, the best advice is to consult with your accountant or attorney before finalizing your compensation plan.

A FINAL WORD

Compensation, by itself, is not the key to success. Recognition is important, too. When designing compensation plans, find *ways to pay* or *recognize*, not ways not to pay or not to recognize.

Do not, I repeat, *do not* change plans frequently or without at least three months' advance notice. Frequent changes can play havoc with the morale of your unit.

----

[1]L.R. Van Vechten, *The Van Vechten Report*, Volume No. 1, March 1982.
[2]*Ibid.*, Volume No. 4, December 1986.

133

CHAPTER 10

The Sales Call and Selling Skills Required

Art Sobczak
President, TeleMarketing Design, Inc.
Editor/Publisher, *Telephone Selling Report*
Omaha, Nebraska

Nothing happens until something is sold.

Sure, it's a cliche, but it has deep impact--particularly on the readers of this encyclopedia.

Sales, the cliche says, puts the bricks in the bottom line. In short, any investment we make in marketing strategies, computers, lists, ergonomic environments will return very little if the *person* placing the telephone calls isn't adept at what to say and how to say it.

I don't mean to minimize the importance of any of the operational, support, or strategic areas of telemarketing. On the contrary, too many companies fail miserably because they lack the commitment to these important aspects. But, bottom line, selling by phone is a *people* business. Machines and organization only support those people.

This chapter will focus on the skills used in placing a consultative, professional telephone sales call. We won't discuss telemarketing. We'll talk about tele-*sales*. That's because the word "marketing" implies a whole range of functions, like selecting products, pricing, packaging, strategy, etc. Instead, in this chapter we'll cover ideas, tips, techniques, and skills that will help people to *sell* more by phone.

Although everyone who is involved in *telemarketing* should benefit from this chapter, there are many others who cringe at the thought of being dubbed a "telemarketer," yet will find this information especially profitable. For every company that has made the commitment to a full-fledged telemarketing program, there are scores of others who might have one or two people on the phone, beating away at the keypad daily...placing calls, setting appointments, qualifying leads and closing sales. Not to mention the thousands of securities brokers, insurance reps, real estate agents, and others who rely on the phone for their livelihood.

It's important to get rid of any prejudice you might have against "telemarketing," particularly if a major portion of your business is done over the phone. Why? Because tele-selling is a lot tougher than outside selling, and requires a very special sophistication.

There are two primary factors making tele-selling a special management and marketing challenge. First, since there is no channel for nonverbal communication on the telephone, many of the important sales "clues" are missing. A salesperson can be severely handicapped by not seeing a prospect's eyes, observing his or her body language, or sensing hidden emotions and agendas. Secondly, because the telephone allows contact with many more people in a given time period than face-to-face selling, its very efficiency increases the daily rejection rate. This, in turn, increases the personal stress level of the salesperson.

Fewer sales cues. Greater rejection rate. Yet it's far from unusual to hear of companies that spend tens or hundreds of thousands of dollars for computers, contoured chairs, and wiz-bang phone systems, but scrimp when it comes to the training--both initial and ongoing--of the *people* who actually close the sales.

Sadder still is the business owner, sales manager, or supervisor who believe this little self-delusion:

"I'm a good salesperson, therefore I can teach selling to my people."

Talk about confusing success with talent! In most cases, the sales reps hired are "green," and are starved for high-quality, professional sales training, whether it is in the form of seminars, tapes, books, newsletters, or whatever. But because their over-confident superiors suffer from an *"I've seen all of this stuff before, we don't need it"* syndrome, the many excellent outside training sources aren't used and the sales reps suffer. Few of us would automatically assume good teachers are good salespeople. What, then, justifies this assumption in the other direction?

Small wonder new salespeople suffer. In order to become truly adept at selling, a sales rep must be exposed to the basics of selling, and then have the opportunity to practice, to review, to practice more, and then to have the benefit of continuing education. Effective sales behavior isn't so much a skill as it is a *habit*. And developing habit requires repetition, as well as a continuing exposure to new sales skills and ideas. To the extent that supervisors avoid creating formal, professional sales training programs, sales reps will be limited to learning sales "history," or *"Here's how we've always done it."*

Consider the personal characteristics needed for success at telephone selling:

1) *The desire to learn.*

2) *The self-motivation to practice.*

3) *The discipline to stay with it.*

4) *Confidence in abilities.*

5) *Good communication skills.*

6) *Product/service knowledge.*

Quite a list--and few of these skills are in the genes. Even fewer are fully developed in the womb.

PREPARING EMOTIONALLY

Probably the most important characteristic necessary for successful tele-selling is persistence. By this, I don't mean doggedness or stubbornness, although sometimes these are necessary. Persistence in tele-selling is the ability to retain confidence, a positive attitude and creativity in the face of some of the unique difficulties faced by telephone sellers.

Let's look at these difficulties in turn:

135

Handling Rejection. Telephone selling is not a natural human activity. Just as most of us couldn't naturally execute a "split Cuban 8" maneuver in an F-14 at mach .7, most people could not endure at telephone selling. Humans are just not conditioned by evolution or society to continually withstand the perceived head-bashing that is associated with the inevitable "no's" tele-sales reps hear, day in, day out.

Yet, those who continue to prosper in telephone selling have found ways to insulate themselves from the seemingly endless barrage of "no's." Here are some of the most important methods they use:

1) *Accept the fact that you will get "no's."* Many of them. And then more.

2) *Don't take it personally.* It's not YOU that the prospect is rejecting. The prospect doesn't even know you. It's the product or service you're offering. People who say "no" simply do not have an immediate perceived need for what's being offered.

3) *The last call made has absolutely no bearing on the next call.* Each call is an entirely new situation. The fact that you didn't meet your objective on the previous call shouldn't affect your attitude or presentation on the ensuing call. Your largest sale ever could be on the very next dial. Be prepared for it.

4) *Learn from each "no."* Analyze exactly why the objective was not accomplished. Could you have done anything differently? Were you ready for the objections? How should the situation be handled the next time it arises? Understanding what happened, and learning from a call that had a negative result also helps to diffuse the feeling of rejection.

5) *Place the next call.* It's like falling from a horse. After you dissect the last call, move on. Don't dwell on it. There are people who can't remember their best friend's phone number, yet can graphically recall every single "no" of the day. Try to wipe any negative thoughts from memory. Force yourself toward the next call. We best overcome fear by tackling the problem head on. Remember what fun it can be to ride, and get back on that horse!

6) *Smile, and laugh!* Laugh at yourself, and at rejection. Remember, it's nothing personal. So why take yourself or rejection so seriously? One tele-sales team gathers monthly at a local watering hole to try and top each other with the most outrageous "Rejection of the Month." It's a fun way to blow off steam, and to put rejection in its proper light.

7) *Remember your successes.* The thrill of victory lasts a lot longer than the temporary sting of rejection. Visualize and feel a period or situation where

everything was going right for you. Then think back to your most outstanding sales accomplishment. Dwell on the part of the call where you particularly excelled. Seize the feeling and attitude you possessed during that time.

8) *Even if prospects are discourteous to you--and some will be--be nice to them.* Behavior has a lot to do with attitude. Scientists have proven that. So be friendly. It will help you maintain your positive attitude.

9) *Visualize the next call.* Picture yourself making the presentation. See and hear yourself placing a successful call. watch yourself confidently handling the tough objections. After you experience this pleasant event in your mind, your subconscious will "believe" it as if it were real. Then, your mind becomes conditioned to think in terms of positives and successes, and this puts your goals within closer reach. It also helps eliminate thoughts of rejection.

10) *Don't be afraid to waste a few calls.* So what if you got a "no"? You have an effectively infinite number of calls available to you. Go ahead. Try again.

11) *Phone your most satisfied customer.* He or she will probably tell you how good you are and how pleasant it is to buy from you. A little stroke now and then, richly deserved, never hurts.

12) *Finally, re-emphasize to yourself that you are calling to HELP people, not to SELL them something.* Often, a telephone sales rep's fear of phoning and rejection arises from a sour experience he or she had with a pushy peddler who tried to unload an unneeded product. You're not trying to "unload." You're trying to help, and striving to create a win-win situation.

Be At Your Best. Because of the sheer number of calls often associated with tele-selling, it is very easy to grow stale. If your heart is not in the calls, you are just going through the motions and your prospects will know it. Staleness in a tele-seller can grow like a malignant cancer and destroys effectiveness just as surely. This is, in fact, the root cause of failure of many once-successful sales reps.

There was an old vaudeville comedian who once estimated that he'd done the same routine 15,000 times. Someone asked him how he could possibly do that, and his answer was something we all should remember:

"Every time I go out on that stage, I remember that no matter how many times I've heard the jokes, this is THEIR first time."

Even though you might have placed the same type of call many times earlier that day, or even hundreds of times that week, this is probably the first time you will speak with that next prospect. He or she might be the one who could account for a good percentage of your future commissions. You don't know for sure. Therefore, it's essential that you create that enthusiastic, favorable impression. Prospects, like a comedian's audience, will be forming a mental picture of you as you introduce yourself, and will listen to the extent that you, yourself, seem to be paying attention.

Do 100-Yard Dashes. If you place a sizeable number of calls on a regular basis, you've probably had an instance or two at the beginning of the day or week where you looked at the task before you and likened it to scaling Mt. Everest.

Facing any laborious project can be a bit discouraging for anybody, particularly if the job is considered as a whole. Yet, not many people are discouraged by the sight of a big steak sizzling on a platter. They know how to eat it. Like the steak, if you can slice the job into swallowable pieces, the job will begin to seem what it is, easy and enjoyable.

For example, it's safe to presume that relatively few people can, or would want to, run a marathon. But a high percentage could easily handle a 100-yard dash--particularly if there's a sizeable reward just for finishing.

Telemarketing consultant, Bernie Palmatier, originally coined the term "Telemarketing 100-Yard Dash." His suggestion is to divide the day into a series of short "races." For example, plan two dashes, one in the morning and one in the afternoon. The key to success in "dashing" is in doing nothing but phoning during those spans of time. The paperwork should be minimized, and you should be fully prepared to make the calls without having to search around for materials, scripts, forms, pencils, etc.

Select a precise starting and ending time for your calling. Start exactly at, say, 8:20 a.m. BANG! The gun goes off, and you blast out of the blocks. If your dash is scheduled to end at 11:20 a.m., be sure to stop then. Don't run into the chain link fence at the end of the track.

By breaking your day into smaller segments of activity, you will be better off emotionally, and your results will likely be enhanced.[1]

TELEPHONE COMMUNICATION

A *Wall Street Journal* radio commercial made this thought-provoking statement about money: "*Although there's plenty of it to go around, unfortunately it doesn't come with instructions.*" Essentially the same can be said about telephone communication.

Everyone has been using the phone, almost as far back as most of us can remember. But few people have ever been shown how to use the phone effectively, or even correctly. This explains, at least in part, some of the horrid, ear-wrenching misuses of the phone we've all heard from receptionists, prospects, and, unfortunately, other sales reps.

As mentioned earlier, selling by phone is much more difficult than face-to-face sales. The primary communication reason for this is the fact that, communicating by phone, you are using less than 40% of your available communication tools. Absent are the nonverbal, visual modes of transmitting your message and receiving feedback from the prospect.

Therefore, to become a successful tele-seller, you must become a master at effective telephone speaking and, more importantly, listening.

THE SALES CALL AND SELLING SKILLS REQUIRED

Listening. Listening, not speaking, is the most vital strength to master as a tele-sales rep. Very simply, listening allows you to identify and understand your prospect's needs, concerns, emotions, wants and desires. Only then are you able to present an effective presentation that meets those needs.

Many sources report that people, on the average, listen with less than 50% efficiency, and the typical attention span is around 5-10 seconds.

These are frightening statistics, considering that a tele-seller's livelihood depends on how well he or she is listened to on the phone. Equally important, though, is how well the rep listens. Only through effective listening is a tele-seller able to understand the prospect's feelings, needs, desires and concerns.

One of the best ways to improve and maintain listening efficiency is described in the "Keys to Listening Effectiveness." This list has surfaced in numerous books, publications and seminars (we use it in ours). Although many sources take credit for it, we first encountered it from AT&T.

Here is our refined version:

KEYS TO LISTENING EFFECTIVENESS

1) *Prepare in advance.* You are able to listen best when your mind is not cluttered, and you are not preoccupied by worrying about what you will say next. Have all of your essential material in front of you.

2) *Limit distractions.* Clear your work area of magazines, newspapers or other items that potentially could divert your attention.

3) *Increase your attention span.* React, in your own mind, to everything the prospect says. Cling to each word.

4) *Think like the prospect.* By placing yourself in the prospect's shoes, you are better suited to be able to understand what he is saying. Therefore, try to listen from his point of view.

5) *Limit your own talking.* The best conversationalists are people who are the best listeners. Obviously, you can't be listening when you are speaking. The purpose of your call is to determine what the prospect needs. The less you speak, the better. Everyone has two ears and one mouth, and they should be used in that same ratio.

6) *Listen for feelings and ideas.* Words communicate only about 10% of a message. *How* something is said accounts for the *real* meaning. You need to listen for the emotion behind the words. To illustrate, take the simple word, "Oh." Think about all the various ways you can say it to convey different signals such as a question, surprise, disappointment, confusion, and so forth.

7) *Don't jump to conclusions.* Too often, we think we know what a prospect is

139

going to say, so we tune out and begin formulating our response. It is necessary to focus on everything the prospect utters, even if we believe we know what he or she is about to say. After all, what if we're *wrong*?

8) *Don't dismiss their ideas.* Sometimes prospects may jump off on a tangent, or otherwise speak about something that conflicts with your line of reasoning. Instead of disagreeing with them in your mind, listen, and try to understand why they say what they do. Remember, tangents always have a connection to the circle they come from.

9) *Concentrate.* Listening is hard work. You need to internalize everything the prospect says, so that your response can be sensible and effective. Often, people don't hear the last few words of what someone is saying because they are too involved with deciding what they'll be saying next, themselves. To avoid this "amputation" trap, make it a practice to pause for at least one or two seconds after the other person has finished speaking. This will give you an opportunity to frame your response, and it will assure you the person has finished. Also, it will help signify to the prospect the fact that you are truly interested in what he is saying.

10) *Never interrupt.* Never. Ever. It is rude, and it also deprives you of information you might need to close the sale. More, it subtly tells the prospect that what you have to say is more important to you than what he is saying-- the opposite of the impression you want to give.

11) *Take notes.* When a prospect touches on an area you want to dwell on, don't bust in. Jot down a few key words. Then, you can come back to the point after the prospect is finished. This way, you'll keep listening, won't have to interrupt and won't miss any vital information.

12) *Ask questions.* If you don't understand (something that often happens more to good listeners than bad), ask. Get more information. Probe. Understand. Most people are so pleasantly surprised at having the chance to explain themselves that they open up readily to intelligent questioning.

13) *Listen "reflectively."* This is "reflective" in the sense of a mirror. Respond frequently to let the prospect "see" that you are listening by encouraging him with words and phrases like "Yes," and "I understand." Remember, the prospect has no visual cues. For all he knows, he might be talking to a tape machine.

14) *Look for nonverbal cues.* "Read" between the lines of what's being said--or not being said. For example, silence at various points in the conversation can

be very meaningful, if you're alert enough to notice.

15) *Listen for changes in voice pitch.* This is particularly important when you encounter an objection. Research has shown that people raise the pitch of their voices when they are intentionally trying to deceive others. This can be an important clue to the truthfulness of the objection.

16) *Visualize the prospect.* Close your eyes during the call. Picture the other person as you think he appears. Visualize him sitting across the desk, speaking with you, looking at you, and gesturing. This will help to block out distraction, and it will allow you to devote total attention to listening and reacting to your prospect.

17) *Practice.* The only way to become a better listener is to practice, and you can do it all the time. Practice with friends, relatives, even the radio and TV. Also, tape some of your calls and listen to them. Just as when you read a book or watch a movie for the second time, determine how much you missed the first time you listened and work on improving yourself.

There is a major difference between hearing and listening. Hearing is simply being aware of sound, while listening is giving meaning to what is said.

Practice these keys to effective listening--and notice how your overall performance improves.

Telephone Speaking. The manner in which a product, service or idea is presented can make the difference in getting the sale. An irresistible offer can be smothered by a slurred, monotonic delivery, while an ordinary product can be made more alluring with a clear, motivated explanation of the benefits.

Not everyone is blessed with the looks and build of the models from the pages of *GQ* and *Vogue*. In face-to-face selling, sales reps need to go to great lengths to compensate for whatever physical shortcomings they might have, plus they need always to be prepared with crisp, clean, well-pressed shirts, suits, blouses, etc. There is no second chance to make a first impression and face-to-face reps know that well.

This isn't to imply that tele-sellers should neglect their appearance. The point is that the telephone seller has almost full control over how the person at the other end of the line sees him. Within the first 30 seconds of the call, the prospect if forming a mental image of the caller. What that impression becomes is almost totally in the control of the caller.

Few of us begin life with the melodic, polished tones of a radio announcer. Fortunately (for us), most radio announcers didn't either. Good sound comes through practice, and if deficiencies are present, most can be cleared up or minimized through awareness and practice.

The two key speaking deficiencies are *articulation* and *inflection*. Let's look at each more closely, as well as the function of vocabulary and a positive projection:

Articulation. Poor articulation can cause a prospect to believe that the tele-rep is unprepared and unintelligent. These assumptions do *not* assist the sales process.

Symptoms of articulation problems are primarily the slurring of words and omission of the final

141

consonants of words so that they appear to melt together. Here is how poor articulation can sound:

"Worsappeartobemeltintagether."

Demosthenes, the ancient Greek orator, had this problem as a young man and to cure it, he spent many hours speaking with a mouthful of marble spheres. Prof. Henry Higgins cured Eliza Doolittle of dropping her "aitches" (e.g., 'enry 'iggens) in much the same way.

Most of us can improve without the danger of swallowing ball bearings, however. Articulation can be improved by increasing your awareness of the problem, then working on problem areas. First, use a recorder to tape some of your typical calls. Listen for articulation problems. Then practice, practice, practice clearing them up. You can even try recording tongue twisters like "rubber baby buggy bumpers," slowly at first until you get it right, then with increasing speed.

Also, an articulation warm up can be useful just before you begin calling. Try this one: "The tip of the tongue, the lips and the teeth."

Be sure to pronounce every consonant of each word. Exaggerate the pronunciation at first, and then relax when it becomes habit.

Inflection. In English, meaning is communicated through emphasis, as well as through words. Inflection is putting emphasis at various places in a sentence. For example, in the sentence *"Why, Mr. Finster, what an unexpected call,"* putting your emphasis on the word, "call," would indicate happiness at the interruption. Emphasizing "unexpected," however, would give the impression that the call came at an inconvenient time.

Proper inflection might seem like a natural skill, but it's not. Just remember all the people you've spoken to over the phone who seem to sound impatient or angry, when actually they're only trying to be serious. They have poor inflection. Think, too, of the lecturers or speakers who put you to sleep with their monotonic drone. They have *no* inflection at all.

Poor inflection responds as well as poor articulation to self-critical listening. Tape some of your calls and see if your inflection isn't what it should be. If it needs word, try this simple exercise:

Invent a nonsense language, and imagine you are speaking with someone. Your task is to explain how your product or service is used. Don't use words. Just sounds. Through the tone and pace of your voice, try to get your point across. Begin by using some gibberish like *"zigga momba jimbo gowieboop, abba dabba doobie doo."* If you are asking a question, your voice should inflect upward. If you are excited, show it!

As you become proficient at this exercise, next take something boring, like a product description, or a technical brochure, and read it into a tape recorder. Focus on your inflection. Be dramatic! After a while, you should easily be able to apply the same principles to your everyday conversations.

As telephone salespeople, our message is only as powerful as the way it is presented. By improving articulation and inflection, we can greatly enhance the meaning and effectiveness of almost any presentation.

Vocabulary. Again, because the prospect is unable to see you, you must do everything in your power to help him visualize your offer. This is done through the effective choice of words.

As a communicator, you should consider yourself an artist. Words are your painting materials. Your job is to select, blend, and mix them to create a word portrait.

For example, the sentence, *"This copier has a sorting feature, and also reduces and enlarges,"* simply states the facts. The sentence is clear, but hardly vivid or inspiring. On the other hand, the following sentences maintain clarity, while adding vivid pictures. They also "inspire" by showing how the copier can save time and work. *"This state-of-the-art deluxe model collates your documents for you, saving you the problem of spreading oceans of paper all over a desk. Also, it enlarges or reduces originals that are too clumsy to fit in anything, or so small, you get a headache trying to read them.*

Better vocabulary and word use comes from attention, reading, regular use of your thesaurus and dictionary, and practice.

Adapting Your Language. People tend to speak in different ways depending upon their education, locale, industry, and many other factors. There is a theory dedicated to explaining the communication process: neuro-Linguistic Programming (NLP). This theory has important implications for the tele-sales rep.

Briefly, NLP theory describes three modes in which people operate: sight (seeing), touch (feeling), sound (hearing). The mode a person is operating in can be determined from what they say. For example, a person in the "sight" mode might say something like, *"I see what you're saying,"* or: *"I get the picture."*

Similarly, "feeling" people will make statements like: *"This just doesn't feel like a good deal,"* or *"I need to reach a better comfort level with this."* Sound oriented folks will say things like: *"That sounds like a winner!"* and: *"I hear what you're saying."*

An understanding of NLP principles can become an extremely powerful sales tool. If you can learn to recognize what mode your prospect or customer tends to favor, you can use language that fits the same mode. It takes practice, but the payoff is worth the effort. If you want a more advanced discussion of this theory and its application, you can check your library or book store for books on the topic.

Similar to the NLP approach is learning to pay attention to the pet phrases an individual tends to use. For example, sports terminology often provides pet phrases. *"He dropped the ball on that one."* *"We're all on the same team."* Clearly, it could be to your advantage to use similar phrases in return. This can help you communicate on the same "channel" with your prospect, which can help drive the message across.

Avoid Negativisms. Using words and phrases with negative connotations can quickly self-destruct your presentation. Try to avoid such words as *"can't"* and *"won't."* Instead of saying, *"This order won't be ready by Tuesday,"* it's better to turn the negative into a positive by stating *"We can have this delivered first thing Thursday."*

It is also good to shy away from such phrases as *"Do you understand what I'm saying?"*, *"To be honest with you. . .."* and *"Now, I might be wrong, but. . .."* Phrases like these are negative and carry unfavorable connotations.

Effective telephone communication is a learned skill. Become an expert telecommunicator and you will mightily enhance your message.

PRE-CALL PLANNING

Are you beginning to get the feeling that there is much more to tele-selling than picking up the phone and dialing? Good. As you probably have already detected, for a caller to be effective and successful, much preparation and forethought is required. Here are some specific areas that require preparation:

Features and Benefits. Buying is an emotional decision as well as a logical one. People decide to purchase when they feel that purchase will meet a need, real or perceived. Furthermore, people base their decisions on their understanding of what the benefits of a product or service will be.

Benefits are personal, and they evoke emotion. Simply stated, the better job a tele-sales rep does at identifying needs, and crafting a sales message that presents benefits in an emotional way, the better the chances are of winning this sale.

By definition, a feature is a fact; a physical aspect of a product, service, company, individual or whatever it is that one is trying to sell. People do not buy features. They buy because of what the feature will do for them. That is the "benefit."

For example, a computer might have a 20-megabyte hard disk drive. That is a feature. While that feature might imply a benefit for some people, it wouldn't for most prospects. To put this feature in benefit terms for a prospect who has a need to store vast quantities of data, you could say "*. . .which gives you the capability to store and sort your large mailing lists easily, without swapping disks. Thus, you save time and headaches.*"

People do not by grass seed or lawn services. They buy a lush, green, beautiful yard. In business, people essentially buy because they see your offering as a way to make money, save money or save time.

Before you get close to a phone again, you should analyze the features and benefits of what you are selling. Take some time, and actually write down all of the features you can think of. Then, for each feature, explain a benefit in terms of what it will do for your prospects.

An easy way to do this is to insert the words "*which means,*" or "*What this means to you is. . .*" after each feature. For example:

"*Our widgets are made with a special polymer formula which means that they will hold up during your overload levels, assuring you'll have no down time.*"

As a self-check to determine if your benefits truly are "benefits," use the "*so what*" test. After writing out a benefit, put yourself in the position of a prospect. If you can honestly say "*so what?*" after reading the benefit, it isn't strong enough. Try again.

People buy benefits. Sure some benefits can be implied from the features, but why make your prospects think about them? Be prepared to explain your product or service in very beneficial terms.

Setting Objectives. Every call a telephone seller places should have an objective. Not having a precise plan is a primary cause for callers to ramble aimlessly about irrelevant features.

Developing a specific objective prior to a call gives you a road map to the desired result, whether it's a sale, an appointment or simply a request for more information. If the caller doesn't know where he or she is going, the likelihood of getting there is fairly small.

Since, in sales, your primary objective will generally not be achieved in a majority of the calls you make, it is a good idea to use the so-called "Three Objective Plan." On any given call, you should have a Primary, a Secondary and an Ultimate objective.

For example, your Primary Objective is the objective for which you're making the call. Let's say you want to call your regular customer, Joe Smith at ABC Co. Based upon his purchase history, you have a hunch it is time for him to replenish his supply of widgets. Therefore, you want to supply him with a case to ensure that he doesn't run short.

Let's say, further, that your timing, luck and preparation are so impeccable that you're able to waltz in and achieve your Primary Objective almost effortlessly. Is that it? Should you quit?

Not if you've also set an Ultimate Objective. This is a goal you've set for those rare situations when you have a chance to "bag the elephant," or make that big sale. Since this call worked so well, your Ultimate Objective might be to cross-sell (or up-sell) this prospect into the new, automatic Bezabs (or whatever).

Most often, however, you will not be able to reach your Primary Objective. Is that it? Should you quit here? Not if you've got a Secondary Objective to help keep you from wasting a prospect. There might be some future potential here, so you want to plant a seed (if you're prospecting) or go for a smaller order (if you're selling to a current customer). A Secondary Objective would be a positive outcome that can be attained in most situations, but not all. It serves as a method of salvaging any potential the prospect holds and, very importantly, it provides a sense of achievement on calls that otherwise might leave a rep feeling dejected.

Every call needs a direction. Follow your own Three Objectives, and give yourself options for handling various tele-selling situations.

Tele-Time Management. Here are several tips to help you prepare for your call, and to maximize your selling time and effectiveness once you are placing your calls:

1) *Prepare your work area with the sales materials you will need during your calling.* Have them organized in the order they are likely to be used. One advantage of prospects not being able to see you is that you can use sales aids such as price lists and fact sheets the way actors or news anchormen use cue cards and teleprompters. Use your own prompts to advantage.

2) *Don't clutter your area with needless items.* These will only distract you. Remove everything except what you need to sell effectively.

3) *Search for early birds.* Start phoning earlier in the morning. Keep a list of prospects and customers you know are early risers. Many executives answer their own phones before their secretaries come in.

4) *Call during lunch.* Many busy decision-makers lunch at their desk. Also, the regular secretary is likely to be gone to lunch, allowing you a better chance at getting through.

5) *Don't stop at 5:00 p.m.* Call after others around you have quit for the day. Many executives work and even answer their own phone after hours. It also happens to be a good time to call the West Coast (if you are calling from the East or Midwest).

6) *Don't hang up between calls.* If you use a handset, and place a great number

of calls, it's more efficient to simply depress the button with your finger. While you're waiting for the prospect to answer, complete your paperwork from previous calls. This strategy can help to greatly increase your connect time.

WORKING WITH "SCREENS"

Most cold calls that attempt to qualify and sell a prospect require two important steps prior to actual conversation with the customer. First, you must identify and locate the person you need to speak with, and then you must convince his or her "screener" that what you have to say is worth the decision-maker's time. (Depending on the size of the organization you're calling, it's conceivable that you might speak first with a switchboard operator and then an administrative assistant or executive secretary. In smaller companies, one person might perform both functions.)

Let's first cover how to locate the decision-maker. Then we'll look at how to effectively communicate with "screeners."

Using Operators as a Resource. Switchboard operators can be a valuable source of information. It's important to understand that their duty is *not* to screen calls, but rather to provide information and to direct calls quickly and accurately. Here are some tips for talking with switchboard operators:

1) *Ask for their help.* They are often treated with disrespect. Everyone enjoys feeling important and needed. By asking the operator for help, you'll help that person feel his or her job is significant. The operator will also, then, be more likely to share information with you. For example:

> Operator: "*Good morning, ACE Company.*"
> Caller: "*Good morning. I'm Bill Davis with Terrell Supply. I hope you can help me...*"

2) *Ask for names.* When searching for decision makers, be sure to ask for the *name* of that person, rather than simply "the person who makes the decision regarding. . .." The reason for this is the fact that a busy operator might simply honor your request and dump your call as quickly as possible, before you have a chance to say anything else. The problem, here, is that you might be transferred directly to the correct person, but you won't know the person's name! This creates an awkward situation, and causes an atmosphere of unfamiliarity.

3) *Go to the higher level.* If the operator isn't sure who you should speak with, always ask for the person at the highest level in the organization who could conceivably be involved in the buying decision. Your hunch might be right.

146

Even if it isn't, the person you are connected with is likely to know the person you should deal with. This will also arm you with the name of the first person you talked to, to use in your introduction to the prospect:

> *"I was just talking to your sales manager, Joe Blake, and he suggested I speak with you, since you're the person who's responsible for. . .."*

4) *Qualify, using the operator.* Since it is the operator's duty to be helpful, that person can be a fountain of information. You can save valuable selling time by asking general questions about the company's operations, structure, and so forth. Also, by gathering data from the operator, you'll appear to be less of a stranger to the prospect, and he will feel that you know something about the company--which you do!

Communicating with "Screeners." Operators are only the first barrier, however. It's also essential to understand the functions of *screeners*. Despite the experiences of many callers, it is *not* generally their duty to block all sales calls. Their job is to protect the executives' time. Screeners will only permit polished, professional representatives to speak with "the boss." Callers, therefore, must present themselves skillfully, and they must demonstrate why the decision-maker would be interested in speaking with him or her.

Here are some tips to help you in your conversations with screeners:

1) *Treat them with respect.* Too often, screeners are treated as adversaries, someone to go through, around or under. Actually, most executive secretaries have worked their way to this level through intelligence and competence. They make the decision whether or not your call is important enough to be put through. By treating them as the professionals they are, you greatly increase your chances of talking with more buyers.

2) *Get the screener's name.* Each of us likes to be recognized and called by name. If you get the person's name on the first call, if you ever need to call back, you can use the person's name. This way, you'll seem less of a stranger, which builds rapport. One caution, though. Be genuine. Experienced screeners are used to the "smoothies," and can quickly see through insincerity.

3) *Be an "important person."* You want to convey the image of the busy, important person that you are. This impression shows the screener that you shouldn't be pigeon-holed with other, mediocre, unskilled peddlers who inevitably call. For example, if a screener says, *"Mr. Alexson is in a meeting,"* instead of limply replying, *"Oh, darn. When can I call back?"* try: *"Ann, I'm also on a tight schedule today, and really need to speak with him. I can call back at 2:30 or 3:45. Which would be better?"*

147

4) *Explain why you are important.* Some exceptionally tough screeners will force you to plead a strong and detailed case before you are allowed through. Amateur reps often become irritated and indignant under this sort of treatment from someone they consider "just a secretary." When asked to explain the reason for their call, they sigh a quick, one-breath burst of: *"It'sabout-Widgets. IsHeIn?"* The skilled user of the telephone, on the other hand, will respect the wishes of the screener, and realize that only the good offers ever get to "the boss." Instead of a frustration, the screener represents an opportunity. A more appropriate response would be:

> *"I'm calling because we recently introduced a new widget that is 15% less expensive, and twice as efficient as the ones you are probably now using. That's why I want to speak with Mr. Jones, to find out exactly what you are using, and to determine how much money we could save you. Is he in, please?"*

Further, it's very important never to deceive screeners. Some shady characters will make statements such as, *"I'm returning his call,"* when in fact this isn't true. Another big lie is *"It's a personal matter,"* when it isn't. These techniques might get a caller through once, but he's not likely to get that far again after the decision-maker realizes he used deception to get through.

Other Ideas for Working With Screeners. Sometimes, even despite your best efforts, you'll have some trouble getting through. You then need to resort to some contingency techniques. For example, if the screener says, *"Send Ms. Peterson any information you have, and I'll be sure that she gets it,"* you should be ready to counter with: *"(chuckling) If it were that easy, I wouldn't be wasting my time and hers with a phone call. You see, there are a few critical pieces of technical information I need from Ms. Peterson to determine if your business would qualify. Could you connect me please?"*

Another idea for handling the "send info" response: *"I plan on doing that. But I was calling to determine exactly what to send. We have volumes of literature, but I want to provide him with information on the precise system that best suits his needs. A little time spent with me now will save him a lot later. Could you connect me please?"*

Successful tele-sales reps realize that screeners are an integral element of the sales process. Screeners have the power to slam the "door" in the rep's face, or to graciously welcome him into "the boss's" office. Treating that screener with respect and professionalism will gain you access to many more selling opportunities.

OPENING STATEMENTS

Once you've gotten through the operator and past the screener, it's "show time." You now have roughly 30 seconds, during which the fate of your call will be decided, or, at the very least, the tone of the remainder of the call will be set.

Your opening statement is the most pivotal part of your call. It's the "key" that opens up the prospect and persuades him or her to share information with you. It's the "headline" that generates interest and pulls the prospect into your story.

Given the weakness of most opening statements--and the opening's importance--it's little wonder that many folks are reduced to tears at the thought of placing another cold call. Chances are that in their last call they were blown off the phone before they were two paragraphs into their presentation.

Stated as simply as possible, your opening statement must *earn* the prospect's time so that he will listen to you and be willing to share information. The formula for success with openers is simple, but not easy. It requires work and practice. But I have yet to find an instance where this three-step process didn't work.

The Three-Step Process for Opening Statements. The three steps involve identification, purpose and involvement.

Step 1: *Identify yourself and your affiliation.* This can be simply and clearly done: "*Good morning, Ms. Rosen, I'm Bill Gordan with Whoozat Industries.*" At this point, depending on whether or not it's a cold call, or depending on what you feel comfortable with, you might want to engage in some small talk and build rapport. This can be done by saying things like "*How are you this morning,*" but there is nothing more transparent and phony as the "*How are you?*" that humans are conditioned to utter at the first contact with another.

Small talk is an effective ice-breaker. Why else is it such an important part of human conversation? Still, if you must use such a phrase, PLEASE make it sound sincere. Or, use variations such as "*I understand the snow is really piling up in your part of the country.*" Some people, particularly in certain geographic regions, are used to a little small talk before the "meat" of a conversation. If you detect that, and you are comfortable with it, by all means use it.

Step 2: *State the reason for the call.* Here, use an interest-arousing benefit: "*Ms. Rosen, the reason I'm calling is that our company is a specialist in factory labor productivity improvement. We regularly take companies in industries like yours and help increase their output by 40%, with no increase in labor costs. There's a likelihood that we could do the same for you.*"

Step 3: *Get the prospect involved.* Remember, you really can't meet the prospect's needs until you find out what they are. Therefore, you need to compel the prospect to share information with you. Since you have already prompted interest in the "purpose" statement, here's where you persuade the prospect to talk about himself:

> "*In order to determine if and how we could help you to show similar savings, I'd like to ask you a few quick questions. First, please tell me about the size of your factories.*"

Notice the last sentence is an instructional statement, not a question. People normally do what they are told. Plus, it's designed to elicit paragraphs of information--not one or two words only.

Although the Three-Step Opener is my personal favorite, there are several others that can be equally effective.

The "Hypothetical Question" Opener. The premise here is that you present an hypothetical question that will be of interest to the prospect, using the question to draw him into the presentation. For example:

"Mr. Sanders, I'm Bradley Lambert with D.C. Castings. A question that many companies in your industry have is 'How do we reduce overage, but increase profitability?' Well, I'd like to share with you how we've answered that problem for many organizations. First, please tell me a little about your overage ratios."

The "Related" Opening. This technique is related to the "Hypothetical Question":

"Mr. Cunningham, I'm Gerald Illner with Isell Industries. The reason I'm calling is this: A major company in your industry, Computer Controls, had a problem collecting their accounts receivables. Using our Strong R.M. collections process, they've improved their recovery by 80% and have retained goodwill in the process. I'd like to determine if you could show similar results. How are you handling this situation now?"

The "Idea" Opening. Many people are resistant to salespeople. Still, most business people are receptive by nature to good ideas. Their success and their business have generally been based on good ideas, and ideas are, therefore, less threatening to many prospects than are typical "sales pitches." Thus, it's sometimes easier to take this approach:

"Cindy, I'm Ann Stevens with First American Bank. I'm calling today because I have an idea that just might help you cut down on your monthly lease payments. If you don't mind, I'd like to ask you a few questions to see if the idea makes sense, OK?"

A fine way to emphasize the importance of interest-creating opening statements is to show an actual example of a terrible one, and then how it should have been stated. Here is a call I actually received:

"Hi, I'm Joe Jones with Better Advertising. I was wondering if you ever considered advertising with us?"

My response, of course, was "no." It went downhill from there. This opener left the rep tripping over himself as he tried to dig his way out of the hole he dug. He did nothing to generate my interest, to get me to share information, or to listen to anything he had to say. A better alternative would have been:

"Hi, I'm Joe Jones with Better Advertising. We're a direct marketing card-deck company that specializes in helping marketers lower their cost per order while increasing sales. The reason I'm calling is that I received your direct mail piece, and I've an idea that could help you generate more orders with virtually no risk on your part. What types of promotion do you use besides direct mail?"

Notice that in the second, revised opener, the caller mentions some benefits, alludes to a track record, which helps establish credibility, and ease the prospect into the conversation.

When you call a prospect, you are interrupting. Therefore, your opening must as quickly as possible answer these questions in the prospect's impatient mind:

1) *Who is this?*

2) *Why is he calling me?*

150

3)   *What's in it for me or my company?*

Be sure your opening statement answers these three questions. Write it out and see if it does. If not, start over. Work with it. Test it out until it's just right. Memorize it so you can recite it smoothly. Most important, adapt it as you use it. Sometimes a word change here or there can make a major difference.

QUESTIONING

Once you've stimulated interest with your opening statement, your next job is to begin collecting information. It's during this fact-finding phase that you learn about the prospect, qualify him and uncover his needs.

Skillful questioning is an art. Your purpose, as the caller, is to get certain information that you must have. You also hope to get other data that's not essential, but important. You acquire this information through a delicate blending of different types of questions. And while you're doing this conscious blending, you must maintain a conversational tone, so that the prospect doesn't feel as if he or she is on the witness stand or taking part in a survey.

Here are some guidelines to follow in questioning:

1)   *Set Objectives.* Prior to each call, determine exactly what types and amounts of information you want and need. For example, to qualify the prospect, an auto fleet sales rep might need to know how many people drive company cars. Then, if the prospect qualifies, he would like to find out about the current lease or purchase arrangements, what types of vehicles they are, the mileage and use information, and so forth.

2)   *Using your objectives, prepare a list of topics.* List out the broad topics, such as those mentioned above. Then, beneath each topic, list key words or questions which will help you to gather the information you need.

3)   *Mix types of questions.* Use open-ended questions to get the prospect talking, questions beginning with words like *"How do you. . .?"* or *"Why have you been. . .?"* Use closed-ended questions to determine specific facts. The answers to closed-ended questions are usually brief. Sometimes one word is enough: *"How many cars do you have in your fleet?"*

4)   *Explain your reason(s) for asking questions.* This is usually accomplished at the end of your opening statement, but it could take place elsewhere in your questioning, particularly if you are seeking sensitive information. For example, *"Sue, so that I can determine if we could save you money, I'll need to know what your current payments are."*

5)   *Build on previous answers.* After you get a response, pause. Then layer your

151

questions. Get the prospect to expand. Use such words as *"Oh?"*, *"Interesting,"* and *"Tell me more about. . ."* Often, repeating what the prospect just said, in the form of a question, can get them to add information to a previous statement. Example:

> Prospect: *"We don't have an absenteeism problem ."*
> Caller: *"You don't have a problem with absenteeism?"*
> Prospect: *"Well, at least it's not as bad as it used to be."*

6) *Don't use manipulative questions.* Stay away from such inane questions as *"Of course, you would like to be 50% more profitable next year, wouldn't you?"* Questions like this are straight from the old school of high-pressure peddling--and they're an insult to everyone's intelligence.

7) *Use FEELING questions.* If you ask a prospect what he thinks, you might get a useful answer. You might also get an "I'm not sure," or "I don't know." On the other hand, asking someone how he *feels* about an idea will likely elicit an insightful response. It's easier to have a feeling about something than to have a relatively well-formulated thought about it.

8) *Know when to quit.* Ask only enough to get the information you need. Follow your plan. Prospects can get annoyed if they keep answering questions, but can't see a direction to the call.

9) *Ask key questions.* These are powerful information-getters:

> *"What is it that you like best about your present supplier?"*
> *"If you could change anything about your situation, what would it be?"*
> *"Is there anything else I should know before I tell you about how we could help you?"*

THE SALES MESSAGE

Once you've completed fact-finding to your satisfaction, you should have a gold mine of valuable information. If your questioning objectives were set properly, and achieved, it's likely that you will know exactly what you need to say to sell your product or service.

Through your probing, you qualified the prospect, while learning his or her needs, concerns and desires. The next step is to assemble a sales message that addresses each of those needs, using the benefits of what you are offering.

At this point in the call, it is critical that you focus *only* on what the prospect is interested in. We've all been subjected to salespeople who drone on incessantly about features we couldn't care less about. By zeroing in on the areas you have identified as important to the prospect, you're likely to have his undivided attention.

Your sales message doesn't need to be long--and shouldn't be, for that matter. You should soon make the transition from your fact-finding with a "bridge" phrase similar to this:

"Susan, based upon what you've told me, I'm confident we could help you (save money, make money, save time. . .)."

Your next step, then, should be a summary and review of the needs the prospect related. For example:

"If I understand your situation correctly, you told me you've used sales incentives other than cash for your sales reps, but felt that they weren't effective because not everyone cared for the gold pen sets you gave. And now, since sales are down, you are looking for an incentive that will appeal to a broader group. Plus, you're looking for something that can be used year-around, but doesn't require a lot of storage space. Is that all correct?"

At this point, the prospect will either agree--which, of course, is great, since that in effect confirms what you need to say to close the sale--or she will correct your facts. A correction is also good, since the prospect will, in the process, provide more information that you might have missed otherwise.

Reviewing or paraphrasing the prospect's needs accomplishes a couple of very important objectives:

First, it ensures that you have a thorough understanding of the prospect's situation. Secondly, it allows the prospect to hear, in *your* words, his needs repeated and understood. Your restatement of the facts, even if the prospect doesn't perceive his situation as a problem, might just open his mind to the way things really are. This turn of events should make him more receptive to your *solution*, which, coincidentally, is your actual sales message.

Consider this:

"Susan, we have an exciting sales incentive that has worked well for many companies that were in the same situation you are. It's called the Super Shopper program. We've negotiated an arrangement with a major catalog retailer that carries a wide variety of merchandise--over 10,000 items, assuring there's something for everyone. Plus, there are seasonal catalogs, meaning that the program goes year around. Your salespeople can earn gift certificates that they apply towards the merchandise. We handle all details of sending the certificates to you for the reps as they are earned, so you don't have the headache of worrying about inventory, storage, pilferage and so forth. Finally, you decide how much you want to spend, which means you control your budget. The bottom line is that your salespeople can be more productive, because they are truly motivated by something they perceive has real value."

NAVIGATING THE GIVE AND TAKE

By now, you might be saying to yourself, *"But every call doesn't necessarily follow a nice, neat, predetermined format."*

True. You will encounter prospects who try to control the call, or don't want to answer questions, or who might throw an objection in your path right away, before you've even had a chance to talk about your offer. On the good side, you might find a prospect who wants to buy before you're half way through your sales message. How do you handle these situations? Do you complain about the "unfair" objection? Do you tell the willing prospect, "Wait! It's too early to order"?

Of course not. Clearly, on any sales call you have to be able to think on your feet. The parts of the call we are covering here are in the recommended order that you would follow on the IDEAL call.

But most, as you recognize through experience or just plain common sense, just aren't "ideal." The outline is only meant as a road map. If, for example, you were to journey by car from Kansas City to St. Louis, the map would tell you that Interstate 70 is the most efficient path. But that doesn't mean you won't have to veer off momentarily, perhaps at Columbia to have lunch, or somewhere else to take in sights along the way. Still, it's likely that you'll be spending most of your time on the logical path to reach your end destination.

The same is true with your calls. If the prospect interrupts you during your sales message, by all means, let him, and encourage him to talk. What he has to say is most important, since he is giving you an indication of his particular mindset at that point in time. At the same time, you should have evolved the skills to redirect the conversation at the right time to the logical path you're trying to follow.

RESISTANCE AND TRIAL CLOSES

Once you've voiced your sales message, several possibilities exist. Of course, the preferred outcome is that the prospect will say, "*Sounds good. Sign me up.*" But we all know that's not usually the case.

During and after the sales message, you will encounter some type of reaction from the prospect. The particular reaction can be interpreted as either buying signals or resistance signals. *Buying signals* are favorable and are your cue to begin the closing process. We'll look at these more in depth later during the discussion on "closing."

Resistance signals are the prospect's way of signifying that he or she is not quite yet convinced. *Don't confuse resistance with rejection.*

Again: *Don't confuse resistance with rejection.*

Many salespeople *do* confuse the two--and when they do, they let the prospect off the phone when a little persistence could easily have closed the sale. Remember that most people are resistant to sales. This is quite natural and to be expected. We are conditioned to be resistant. After all, we are bombarded by sales messages every day in many forms: direct mail, newspaper ads, radio and TV commercials, billboards...you name it. They all ask us to buy something. We resist all but a few.

Countering the "Silent Treatment." If the prospect is silent all during your sales message, he might be resisting. In this case, you need to coax him back into the presentation so you can get an idea as to why he feels the way he does. Resistance is a symptom of a lack of information, and we need to understand the nature of that "ignorance."

To get the silent prospect reinvolved, you can say something to the effect of, "*Well, what do you think so far?*", or "*How does that sound to you?*" These "trial closes" will extract answers that will allow you to redirect your efforts, if necessary. On the other hand, you might find out that you're doing just fine!

Countering the "Negative Counter." Resistance can also take the form of negative statements such as disagreements or vague statements. For example, if the prospect says, *"I don't think we need any widgets now,"* that needn't be accepted as a rejection. It may simply be resistance, which could be handled with statements such as, *"Oh? Why do you say that?"*, or *"That's interesting. Why do you feel that way?"* These responses sound direct, and they should. They are. But used in a sincere, almost surprised tone of voice, they can prompt the prospect to open up and give you the real reason he or she is resisting. There might be a valid objection--something we'll be covering very soon.

Don't let resistance shake you. You should approach every call *expecting* some resistance. Your mission is to get the prospect to explain his reason for resistance, because only then are you able to answer his questions or concerns.

CLOSING

A lot of talented people have attempted telephone selling, and many of them failed. They're now in other careers.

Was it their bad voices? Were they bad at building rapport? Maybe they were failures at generating interest-creating opening statements, or they were unable to probe properly. Possibly. But I have learned from experience that the greatest cause of failure is the lack of one, vital skill: the ability to close.

Closing is asking for the sale. Success at it requires exquisite timing and persistence. Let's look at each of these more closely:

Timing. Good closers know the appropriate times to ask for the sale. They sense their timing using the buying signals we discussed above. When the good closer perceives that the prospect is leaning in his direction, he immediately gives the prospect a closing nudge.

Remember, few prospects will "volunteer" to buy. Even if you have just completed a sparkling job of uncovering needs, and presented a bevy of hard-hitting benefits, and successfully melted away resistance, you probably still won't hang up with the sale in your pocket. . .*unless you ask for it.*

Pick when the fruit is ripe. Listen for the signals that indicate the prospect is pleased with what you are saying. This is much easier in a face-to-face encounter, since you can analyze body language, but because that advantage is nonexistent in phone selling, you must concentrate on the prospect's every verbal reaction.

Here are some examples of buying signals you can expect from prospects:

1) *Specific questions about delivery time, installation etc.*

2) *Questions about the product or service become more specific and frequent.*

3) *Positive statements of agreement, such as* "That sounds like something we could use," *or* "That's not a bad price."

155

4)   *The prospect becomes more at ease in the conversation.*

5)   *The prospect begins speaking in terms of how he would use your product or service:* "I would imagine that system would fit in nicely with our existing equipment. Plus, Sherry is a whiz at learning this stuff."

6)   *The prospect becomes very interested in negotiating price. At this point, he is probably sold. Otherwise, if he didn't have a need, he wouldn't care about the price, would he? Your quest in this situation is to convince the prospect that the value outweighs the price.*

Persistence.   So, let's say you have detected some buying signals. Now what do you do?
You ask for their money.
Simple as that.
Many salespeople are afraid to close because they feel they are being pushy. Their attitude is that if the prospect was truly interested in buying, he'd say so.
Nonsense!
When faced with a buying decision, a natural tendency for people is to "clutch." This last-minute hesitancy is normal, especially on a purchase involving a large amount of money. At this point, buyers need that gentle push that will help them make the positive decision they know they really want to make.
At this point in the call, leave no doubt that you want the prospect's business. You have an *obligation* to close. Actually, it would be *rude* not to. Consider that you have just taken up a portion of the decision-maker's valuable time by asking questions and explaining benefits. Unless you ask him to accept your solution, you are doing him, and yourself, a great disservice. Not closing is like inviting someone to your house for dinner, but not giving them food unless they ask for it--assuming, presumably, that if they're hungry, they'll say so.
Closing is just like munching potato chips. One is seldom enough. You'll need to try several times before you can maximize your results. How many times? Well, it depends on the situation, of course, but figure on at least three and, often, it'll take five.
That may sound like a lot, maybe even a little pushy. But consider a study done by the Marketing Department at the University of Notre Dame. According to the *Hot Buttoneer* newsletter, Notre Dame's study of closing attempts disclosed that 46% of the tele-reps observed asked for the order and then quit. Another 245 tried twice before throwing it in. Further, 145 asked for the sale three times, and 12% persisted four times. That might sound ambitious, until you find out that the survey showed that 60% of the acceptances came on the fifth attempt.[2]
You will be the ultimate judge of when you are bordering on too many closes, and the judgment is important--you don't want to hard-sell the prospect by badgering him. However, the major danger is going the route of the hesitant closers and underestimating the closing attempts needed. If your sincere desire is to truly help the prospect, and you thoroughly understand the prospect's needs, *and* you are convinced that what you have will better his situation, don't worry about closing too often. If the prospect remarks on your persistence, simply respond, "*Yes, I am persistent, because I firmly believe what I have can help. Wouldn't you expect the same effort from your own sales reps?*"

THE SALES CALL AND SELLING SKILLS REQUIRED

Closing can be done almost an infinite number of ways. Here are a few among the hundreds of more common ways to ask for the sale:

1) *The Direct Close*. With this close, there's nothing fancy. You simply ask for the order. By asking, *"May I go ahead and write this up for you?"* you expose yourself to a "no." But that's okay, since you'll then be able to uncover real objections if any exist.

2) *The Alternate Choice*. With this close, the question assumes the prospect will buy. You present two alternatives, either of which means a sale for you. *"Jane, do you want to start with six cases or four?"*

3) *The Assumptive Close*. This technique is most effective when strong buying signals have been expressed. Since the prospect is indicating he is sold, there's no need to ask for the sale. You assume it. This is done by asking questions, and discussing terms related to the sale, delivery, and so forth. *"Mr. Stone, when did you want to schedule the first training session?"*

4) *The Pause Close*. Using this close, you simply present the facts, which strongly support the purchase of your offer, and then pause, putting the burden of a response on the prospect. *"Cindy, we seem to be in agreement that this is exactly what you need, at the best price available. . . ."*

5) *The "OK?" Close*. People have a natural tendency to say "okay" themselves when they hear "okay" stated as a question. This automatic reaction can be a very powerful tool in closing. For example: *"Bill, I can go ahead and enter your order today, meaning you'll have delivery by next Friday, Okay?"*

6) *The Payback Close*. Using this close, you demonstrate the payback a purchase will bring the prospect. For example, assume that a prospect's company sells service contracts and each sale is worth $65.00 of gross profit. Here's your close: *"Mr. Fishman, as you mentioned, you have 12 sale- speople who would likely read our sales training newsletter each month. I'm sure, based upon the experience of other readers, that they will find ideas they can use in every issue. But, let's say they each use an idea that helps them close only one additional sale for the year. Using your figure of $65 profit per sale, times 12 reps...that's $780 in profit for only a $99 investment. And that's being conservative. Why don't we go ahead and sign you up right now? Would your name be on that subscription?"*

7) *The Elimination Process Close*. This close takes advantage of the prospect's indecision. What you do is present several choices. One is a real dog that

157

you'll throw out immediately, another is a middle-of-the-road alternative, and the last is the option you really think he should take. Your close, then, is as simple as tossing out the choices until only the best one remains. It's a process you've seen operate at a restaurant. Everyone frets about which of the selections to choose. Then the waiter explains the specials...and describes his favorite. With sighs of relief, some of the diners snap their menus shut, their decision made for them by the waiter. Prospects are no different.

The number of closes available to you are limited only by your imagination and creativity. Go to your local book store, and you'll find volumes devoted to sales closing. Knowing about a lot of closes isn't important, however. What is crucial is becoming proficient with a few, and using them often.

OBJECTIONS

After you try a close, you'll often hear objections. Since the ability to handle objections is so important, an entire chapter is devoted to the subject. For our purposes, a few key examples are sufficient:

Overcoming Buyer Loyalty. Some prospects are reluctant to try a new supplier because they feel a loyalty or even an obligation to their present vendor. Often this is true even when they are not getting the best possible value or service for their money. Here are a few suggestions for handling this problem:

> *"I can respect your feelings. At the same time, you have a greater obligation to your business and shareholders to operate as efficiently and profitably as possible. And by working with us, you'll save. . ."*

> *"Your loyalty is commendable. However, it's actually COSTING you money to be loyal to your present vendor. Here's why. . ."* (Proceed to show figures substantiating the savings you can provide.)

The Friend/Relative Objection. Many of us prefer doing business with friends. But, as profit-minded business people, we're always on the lookout for the best opportunities. Keep this in mind as you encounter an objection like, *"I buy all of my widgets from my brother-in-law who owns ACME Widget Supply."*
Here, an appropriate response could be:

> *"I understand. I like to support my friends and relatives, too. Still, you'd probably agree that no one has a monopoly on ideas. What I'd like to do is give you some ideas that could make you more profitable. After all, you're an important relative, too."*

> *"I can appreciate that, and I'm not trying to steal your loyalty from your brother-in-law. What I'll do for you instead is be on the lookout for you when new opportunities develop, opportunities that other sources aren't always aware of. Okay?"*

Don't ever put down the prospect's present supplier, especially if it's a friend or relative. The above responses allow you, in a non-threatening way, to imply that there are some opportunities he might not be taking advantage of now.

Reduce Price to the Ridiculous. If your higher price is a roadblock, position it so the objection seems ridiculous. For example:

> *"I understand your concern, but how long do you think you would use this machine? And how much, too much, do you feel it costs? Okay, let's try something that one of my most astute and successful clients showed me a few months ago. Divide that $2000 by the life span of five years. What do you get? Now, divide that $400 by 12 months? How much is that? All right, now take that $33, and stretch it over 20 monthly working days. Good grief! What we're talking about is a grand total of $1.65 a day to have the most modern machine, with the latest technology at your fingertips. I think you can see why your competitors are willing to spend an extra $1.65 a day for the best. Did you want to issue a purchase order, or is it easier for you to issue a check?"[3]*

Silly Objections. Sometimes a prospect will bring up objections that are entirely without basis and are simply an attempt to stall or get you off the phone. One way to handle such a situation is to ignore the objection. Another is to ask the prospect to repeat the statement.

There are several reasons for responding this way. First, you might not have completely understood the objection or question. Asking the prospect to repeat it may cause him to present the question in a more logical context. However, if the objection is ludicrous, and you both know it, asking that it be repeated is likely to expose how ridiculous it really is. The prospect might still repeat it, but he also might now say, *"Well, as I said... But what I actually meant was..."* This will give you a clearer picture of the *true* objection.

Turn Objections into Questions. Another way to handle an objection is to rephrase the "resistant" statement into a question--which *you* can immediately answer. For example, if a prospect states that high price is a reason for not buying, you can respond: *"You've raised a good question. Would the added cost of our product be worth the expense? Is that the question?"*

If the prospect answers "yes," then you can present your evidence as to why your product is worth the higher price. If the prospect says, *"No. That isn't my question,"* then you are moving closer to uncovering the real objection. Once you've answered the objection, you can move toward your close by saying, *"Does that answer your question?"*

This technique effectively treats an objection as what it really is, a request for more information, not a refusal. It helps you ensure that you are dealing with a real objection, and then it prepares the prospect to listen. Finally, this technique provides you with an opportunity to answer the prospect's question/objection and then shift smoothly into your next attempt at closing.

THE "WRAP-UP"

Finally, the conclusion of your tele-sales call is the wrap up. it's important not to drop the ball here.

159

Here are some tips for the final moments of your conversation:

1) *Always end every call on a positive note.* No matter how irritated you might feel after some thick-headed yo-yo has told you he won't listen to you, resist the temptation to tell him where he can place his phone. Regardless of how gratifying it would feel, you never know when you might want or need to recontact a prospect. Situations and needs change. Plus, ending calls negatively makes you feel that way yourself.

2) *Whatever the outcome of the call, review what is to happen next, in specific terms.* If you'll be sending information, let the prospect know when to expect it. If you're going to place a follow-up call, set a phone appointment. A phone appointment, you say? Sure. You'd make an appointment to visit the prospect in his or her office. Why should a phone visit be any different?

3) *If you have a sale, finalize the details and terms to be sure everyone is of the same understanding.* This done, thank the prospect and exit. Don't hang around with small talk or more explanations of why he made a good choice. In addition to taking up time unnecessarily, you might make the prospect suspicious and give him second thoughts.

4) *Conduct a call "Post Mortem."* This is very important to your future success, and should not be overlooked. After each call, pick it to shreds. Analyze what went right, and what went not so well. If you didn't get the sale, ask yourself why? If you aren't sure, you didn't do a good job on the call. If the prospect had an objection you couldn't overcome, bend your mind until you arrive at a suitable response. This exercise will only take you a few minutes after each call, but the return on your investment will be substantial.

FOLLOW-UP CALLS

After a smooth first call, there is a tendency for tele-reps to think that things are going well, so they can ease up on the prospect. The opposite approach is the one to take, however.

You have to do as much, or more selling on follow-up calls as you did on the initial approach. Your prospect receives many calls every day. He or she might not even remember you or your offer when you call back. That's why opening statements such as *"Well, I was just calling back to find out what you think,"* and *"I was calling back to see if you had any questions,"* are so ineffective. Here are some guidelines to keep in mind for your follow-up calls:

1) *Just as for any other call, be sure you set an objective.* Are you now going for a trial order? An appointment? Write it out.

2) *Be sure you once again have an interest-creating opening.* For example:

> *"Mr. Thomas, this is Jack Miller with Good Chemicals calling back. I'm following up on our conversation last week where we discussed how you could save money with our solvents. I sent you the comparisons you requested, and would like specifically to go over the one that shows how you could decrease your expense by $3,000 yearly. Is that information handy, or should I wait while you get it?"*

3) *Bring up key facts and personal information you uncovered on the first call.* These notes should be on your call record. If the prospect went on a trip, ask about it. Of, if he spoke about his kid's soccer game, find out how it went. You'll seem less of a stranger, which is a great advantage.

4) *As the call progresses, review all of the important needs you uncovered on the first conversation, and all of the benefit you can provide.* The prospect probably didn't take notes on the first call, and won't remember the detailed discussion that covered exactly what you could do for him.

5) *Continue to qualify the prospect, and ask yourself, "Does he have the potential to be a buyer?"* Test your assumptions about the prospect's interest, authority to buy and budget. Be careful to avoid getting trapped wasting time with prospects who can't or won't make decisions. It's better to get a "no" now, rather than seven or eight "maybe's" later.

6) *If you are calling on regular customers, be sure to have something new to say on each call.* Don't get lackadaisical, and routinely call, expecting to get your regular order. Don't take your customer for granted. Search your mind for new ways your customer can benefit from your relationship. He will appreciate you more and look forward to your call.

SUMMARY

These pages have covered the basics, as well as some advanced techniques for placing an effective telephone sales call.

Taken alone, these ideas will help you to develop a good presentation, or refine an existing one.

However, to maximize your sales ability, use this chapter as a foundation. Take each individual area covered, and work with it, seeking new ideas, and creating your own. Strive to sculpt the absolute best presentation you can. Practice your new skills and techniques until they become second-nature. Repeat the process with each area of the call, and you are destined for tele-selling greatness!

----

[1]*Secrets of Telemarketing*, Tape Program, AT&S Publishing, Bernie Palmatier, P.O. Box 541, Newcomerstown, Ohio 43832.

[2]*The Hot Buttoneer*, The Lacy Institute, 15 Paine Rd., South Yarmouth, New Jersey 02664.

[3]*Double Your Income Selling on the Phone*, Stan Billue, Double Five, Inc., P.O. Box 267, Debary, Florida 32713.

CHAPTER 11

Scripts and the Offer

Richard L. Bencin

Donald J. Jonovic, Ph.D.

There's probably no area of telemarketing that specialists disagree about more than scripting. The disagreements aren't only about what kind or how to do it. Sometimes, specialists even disagree about scripting's value.

From our point of view, the value of scripting in a telemarketing operation depends on how it's done. Scripting, to stretch a simile, is like marriage: It's what you make of it--great if you go about it correctly, and downright awful if done badly.

Almost everyone, by now, is familiar with bad scripting. Usually, it's consumer telemarketing that interrupts us during the dinner hour at home.

"Hi. I'm Bob Jones...how are you today?"

Usually the call goes downhill from there. The patter from the other end of the line sounds canned, is read poorly, is terribly paced and often reeks of boredom or is charged with aggression. Often, our first objection throws the poorly trained and supervised telephone sales rep (TSR) off his or her stride.

To drag out our last simile, telemarketing scripts are like hairpieces. We only notice the bad ones, not the good ones. When a script is properly developed and presented, it shouldn't sound like canned telemarketing. It should become a pleasant, interactive dialogue that's designed for the mutual benefit of marketer and customer. A professional script doesn't have to (in fact, shouldn't) sound like a reading. It should sound the way a professional actor would perform in a well-written dialogue. The script should be transparent.

PURPOSE

A script is exactly what the name implies: A carefully pre-written sequence of statements for use by a telephone sales representative when speaking with prospects or customers. A script is a must for any telephone sales campaign, because it's the key factor in assuring one of telemarketing's major benefits--complete control of the progress and content of the telephone calls. Telephone sales representatives should never be allowed to "wing it," to indulge in *ad lib* dialogue without structure. Duplications, omissions and improper sequencing can absolutely destroy a professional telephone selling effort.

Imagine a motion picture director telling his cast, *"Just say whatever comes into your heads."*

163

It's always good to recall that a TSR faces the same problem a direct mail piece faces. After the initial greeting, he's probably got less than 45 seconds to get the listener's attention. And, even with the attention, there's little more than a few minutes available to present the offer or proposal and complete the call. Scripting can help make sure the best effort is given toward getting the prospect's interest, then it can help guarantee that the few minutes available are used in the best way possible.

Stripting has other important purposes:

* *Scripting assures the accuracy and efficiency of testing. Because of the consistency and degree of control scripting allows, the telemarketer is much more able to measure front-end response. Further, the consistency of scripting makes accurate testing possible with many fewer calls.*

* *Scripting can greatly improve productivity by assuring that carefully tested, efficient communications are repeated consistently by all TSR's.*

* *Scripting allows the telemarketer to make full use of the experience and knowledge of telemarketing researchers.*

* *Scripting helps assure a consistency of presentation over the inevitable range of individual differences.*

THE SCRIPTING TEAM

Few telemarketing operations exist in a vacuum. There are often several departments involved in the sales and marketing function, and each of these departments has an important effect on success. Thus, the telemarketing specialist would do well to avoid solitary scriptwriting. Much more effective scripts can be written by *teams* of people.

A key member of the scripting team or committee, of course, is the telemarketing specialist. This person brings the experience and technical knowledge. With luck, he also brings the leadership to help develop full support of the telemarketing program throughout the various departments involved.

The other members of the scripting team would be a function of the operation involved. Often, such teams include people from advertising, accounts receivable, order entry and management--anybody whose input can help assure that the script is designed both to sell and to make the overall operation as efficient as possible.

The primary involvement of this team would be at the script prototype development stage, but their input should also be sought during the revision process. Revisions come about due to test results, of course, but they also can be initiated in response to changes in the environment (e.g., competition, market shifts, public opinion). The various department specialists on the team are often more likely to be aware of these environmental changes than the telemarketing specialist, and can call them to his attention.

Steven A. Idelman, of Idelman Telemarketing, Inc., describes a scripting team and its *modus operandi* as follows:

164

SCRIPTS AND THE OFFER

> *"A script-creation committee should consist of a chief creative writer, one or two sales managers, one or two experienced telephone reps and a 'lay person,' who will represent a typical prospect. First, the group lists in order of importance the product or service benefits and features, from which the approach to use on the phone is determined. This might take anywhere from four to ten hours. Approximately another ten hours are devoted to fashioning the basic presentation of the offer. Using real names from the prospect list, each team member makes phone calls for about an hour, trying out the first raw script. The committee reconvenes, compares notes and further refines the script and 'phone tests' it again. The process of trial, error and polishing is repeated until the script is 'phone-rep ready.'"*

Scripts are developed the way good plays and books are developed. They are written, tested, rewritten, evaluated, re-evaluated and rewritten. The scripting team, because it brings a number of different outlooks, experience bases and styles to bear on script development, can greatly assist in this trial and refinement process.

WRITING A SCRIPT

A number of important variables control the content of a telemarketing script. They should be defined as a first step, before the first word of the proposed script is written. Here are the most important of the variables:

Objective. The "objective" of a telemarketing program is a purpose that can be tracked. In science, this is called "operationalizing" a variable--redefining a qualitative item into a quantitative item that can be measured. Perhaps some examples might help here.

There are many purposes telemarketing programs can be designed for--to arrange sales call appointments, to invite people to a presentation, to get information, to develop referrals, or to announce trial offers. Are the calls being made to sell a product, for example? The objective would then be a set *number* of units sold or a level of sales volume achieved. "Sell more product" is a *purpose*. "Sell 500 units in seven days" is an *objective*. If the purpose is to generate leads, then the objective could be a lead generation rate of .3 leads per call. To use an inbound telemarketing example, if the purpose is order taking, then the objective could be to close a specific percentage of incoming calls.

A clearly defined objective is an important guide to script development. It keeps the script from drifting off target and maintains focus on the ultimate goal.

Data Collection Requirements. Most telemarketing programs require the TSR to obtain information from customers. Planning the script should include consideration of what information will be needed and how it will be recorded. Recording method is important for two principal reasons.

First, since the time available on the call is so limited, the TSR must have the ability to record quickly. This implies from the outset that only *essential* information should be collected. The temptation is often very strong to get as much information as possible--product surveys, customer demographics, competitive product use, etc.--but such detail can compromise the program. Where possible, it's best to use samples for surveys and preserve most of the list for the principal offer. Also, it's often more efficient to make the order form an integral part of the script, and always more efficient not to collect information you already have (e.g., name and address of repeat customers).

Second, the recording method should fit as closely as possible with the organization's method of using the information. For example, if order-processing is automated, written information from the TSR will require re-keying into the computer. It would be more efficient to have the TSR record the information directly into a terminal.

TSR Reference Material Requirements. Depending on the program objective and the product/service being sold, TSR's often are required to answer questions or supply specifications/prices. Time constraints are, again, important to consider. Reference material requirements (spec sheets, price lists, etc.) should be considered in script design. For example, if the TSR is to gather information on a customer's product use, the questions he asks should be designed to follow the overall organization of the specification sheets/manuals.

Prospect/Customer Profile. Knowing the customer is, of course, a central requirement of successful marketing. Nevertheless, even though you may know who the customer is, there are some factors that are particularly important to script design. For example, will the TSR be likely to connect directly with the customer (e.g., a consumer called at home), or will there be a "screen" involved (e.g., a secretary or receptionist at a business office answering the phone for the customer)? Clearly, if a screen is involved, provision will have to be made for handling him or her. Another example: if the prospect is a repeat customer, it might be important for the TSR to have information on that customer's past purchases.

TSR Profile. Since the TSR is the company's representative to the customer, it's important to consider how much that TSR knows about the customer, the product and the offer. Important factors here include reference material availability, information collection, training and the help/input of outside sales people. Understanding of TSR sophistication and knowledge will also help in the decision of which script type to use.

Script Types. With many of the above questions explored, the scripting team must next decide upon the type of script to use. There are three basic script formats in general use, each most appropriate in specific circumstances:

Closed Scripts. Sometimes called "full" scripts, closed scripts specify everything about the call and allow the TSR the minimum latitude for flexibility.

Word-for-word closed scripts are written exactly as they should be presented over the phone. These scripts are generally ideal for consumer calls, simple business-to-business propositions and survey calls. *Logical-flow* closed scripts allow for branching, depending upon customer responses to key questions. *Computerized closed scripts* are particularly useful in catalog telemarketing and other situations where the branching of logical-flow scripts is exceptionally complex.

166

SCRIPTS AND THE OFFER

Extensive branching of script presentations can render the usual 3-by-5-inch manual card overlay systems useless. With a computer, as prospects respond to introductory statements, questions and selling points, the most appropriate positive responses can appear on the screen to guide the TSR. Virtually all the gatekeeper's remarks, questions and objections can be anticipated, with the best responses having been built into the software. Trial close and re-close statements can appear on the caller's screen at the precise moment required during a presentation.

CRT scripting can, thus, be used to electronically "clone" the organization's best representatives by embedding their most effective responses to the most frequently asked questions or objections with the sales script.

Consumer telemarketing often involves a large volume of calls to the mass market. Generally, the offers are relatively uncomplicated and can be scripted easily for a word-for-word presentation. Also, close control is often necessary to keep telephone sales personnel within legal bounds.

One type of call must necessarily be tightly scripted, often right down to the inflections: the survey. Survey calling demands that each and every query be phrased precisely the same way every time. Without rigid continuity, responses can vary simply because of subtle variations in the way questions are asked.

Closed scripting is most useful in situations where:

* *Time is a major constraint and the maximum information must be presented/ collected in a very short time,*

* *The TSR's are relatively inexperienced or unfamiliar with the product, the marketplace and/or the customer, and*

* *Certain information (e.g., legal disclaimers) must be presented exactly.*

Prompt Scripts. Often called "dialogue" or "guided," prompt scripts generally have some word-by-word components (e.g., in the introduction, the benefits statement(s) and the close), but much of the call is guided through suggested questions and responses. Suggestions are also usually provided for handling typical objections. Prompt scripts generally are most effective when:

* *TSR's are experienced or well-supported with automated order or inquiry-handling systems,*

* *TSR's have had training in objection-handling, and*

* *It's important to establish rapport or a personal relationship with the customer.*

167

Outline Scripts. These scripts are essentially carefully designed checklists, often combined with detailed customer information and fill-in-the-blank forms for the TSR to complete. This script form often is used where TSR's are required to probe for customer needs, or otherwise face problems/opportunities similar to those faced by the sales force. Since this form of script allows great flexibility for the TSR, it is most appropriate when:

*   *The TSR's are exceptionally well-trained and professional,*

*   *Customer rapport is exceptionally important,*

*   *Time is not a major consideration or call volume is not high, and*

*   *The offer is complex or designed to fit particular accounts, or*

*   *The call is following up on established customers.*

Conversation Style. The question of style is not often enough considered in scripting. There are three basic styles for telemarketing. A *controlled* style ("*Just the facts, Ma'am*") is appropriate when information collection is far more important than social niceties (e.g., collecting emergency services information, or basic demographics). A *conversational* style becomes more appropriate as good manners become more important in the call (e.g., billing inquiries, simple fund raising). Finally, a *rapport-building* style becomes most appropriate in those situations where time is not critical and establishing a dialogue with the customer is important to the success of the call and/or the person being called is a long-established customer (or contributor, or member, etc.).

Call Length. While most telemarketing calls should be limited to five to seven minutes in length, the scripting team should try to determine whether it's appropriate to have *fixed-length* or *flexible-length* calls. The former is an important management control in "production line," or high-productivity environments. The latter is most appropriate in complex situations requiring a high level of TSR creativity.

Medium. Scripts are physical entities. They must be presented to the TSR on some form of medium. Medium selection is primarily a function of the script type. *Paper* is workable for relatively brief, closed scripts and simple prompts requiring little information retrieval. *Cards/overlays* (usually 3" X 5") can work well for logical-flow scripts, or scripts with several versions or components. Often cards are differentiated by specific colors for individual components (e.g., opening, information-gathering, close). *Computers* are especially useful in situations where the product line is exceptionally deep, the logical branching of a script is very complex, or when the organization's order processing and fulfillment functions are automated.

CONTENT

There are, of course, an infinite number of possible scripts. No two scripts are alike, nor should they be. Nevertheless, the good scripts tend to share certain key elements in common.

An excellent typology has been developed by Steven Idelman, of Idelman Telemarketing, Inc. He believes that there are 12 key elements to a successful telemarketing script: *greeting*, *statement of empathy*, *product or service information*, the *offer*, the *trial close*, the *probe*, *responses and answers*, *first trial close*, *second effort*, *final close*, *confirmation close* and *farewell*. There are, of course, others, and some excellent scripts could work very well without covering each of these elements, but Idelman's classification can nevertheless be very useful for the telemarketing scriptwriter.

Let's look at each one in turn:

The Greeting. The primary function of the greeting, other than getting the conversation started, is to assure the right person is on the other end. The secondary function, almost equally important, is to involve the customer/prospect in the call. Generally, the greeting should ascertain the customer's name by asking a question (*"Is this Mr. John Martin?"*), and should inform the prospect of the caller's name and affiliation (*"This is Marilyn Chalmers of Acreson Realty Co."*). There is a specific advantage to the question format. Interrogative sentences tend to end on an up-note, giving the impression of energy and interest.

The Statement of Empathy. Early in the conversation, it is essential for the TSR to establish some realistic rapport with the customer/prospect. The objective is to keep the prospect involved and interested as much as possible by demonstrating that the TSR shares his or her feelings. A fund-raiser, for example, could empathize with a prospect's typical annoyance at getting calls at home in the evening (*"I know, Mr. Martin, that your evenings, like mine, are a time to relax, but there is no other time we can be sure to reach couples interested in Shangri Lodge's new condominium expansion. . ."*). This can help to diffuse the natural annoyance or mistrust people feel during calls from strangers.

Product or Service Information. Once the prospect has been qualified and put somewhat at ease, it is time to present the concept of the call and/or the benefits being offered. Time is at a premium for everybody and most people will appreciate the caller's getting right to the point (*"Let me tell you right away why I'm calling. You expressed an interest in Shangri Lodge some months ago, and you asked to know when our model condominium was finished. . ."*).

The Offer. This is a clear statement of what the caller is offering to the prospect (*"If you can make it out to the Lodge in the next two weeks to tour the model, we will offer to buy you and Mrs. Martin a dinner on us in the Main Lodge Brasserie. . ."*).

The Trial Close. As soon as possible after the offer has been presented, the TSR should attempt to get a "yes" answer from the prospect on an important question (*"We felt it would be convenient for the two of you to be able to relax after the model tour to discuss your reactions in private over a quiet dinner. Don't you agree?"*) A "yes" answer at this point would allow the TSR to move directly to the close.

The Probe. If there is a "no" answer, however, some more work needs to be done. The TSR will now have to probe for the reasons behind the negative answer (*"Could you tell me why?"*). The question should be involving--requiring an answer from the prospect--and the TSR should be respectful of the answer

169

(*"My wife is ill,"* shouldn't result in the TSR's saying: *"Well, she'll probably feel better by next week."* Better: *"I'm sorry to hear that, Mr. Martin. Would you like me to give you a rain check on the dinner and call you back in a few weeks?"*).

Responses and Answers. If the prospect's negative answer requires further discussion, or if he asks a question, the TSR should be ready to oblige. Many objections, for example, can be foreseen during script presentation, and appropriate answers made ready (*"I realize it's a one-hour drive to Shangri Lodge, but the fall colors should be at their peak over the next two weeks. Why not leave a little early to enjoy the colorful drive, have an early dinner and plan to be home by 9:00 p.m.? We'll make sure you aren't delayed."*).

The First Trial Close. If all the questions have been answered and the objections dealt with as completely and honestly as possible, it's time for the TSR to ask, in a very positive way, for the order (*"I can fit you in for an early dinner any evening but the 23rd, 25th and Sunday, the 26th. Which date would be convenient for you?"*). The prospect can still say no to a positive question, of course, but it is much easier to say yes and set up an appointment.

The Second Effort. Hesitation at the first trial close should always be anticipated, and the TSR should be ready to break the block and continue toward the goal (*"It's really worth seeing the model, Mr. Martin, if only for the beautiful pine paneling in the library and the wonderful masonry work in the den fireplace. Please let me set an evening aside for you. . ."*). Here, you can begin to see the major advantages of scripting to handle objections. Also, TSR training shows its greatest benefits during these second efforts. This TSR, for example, was given a tour of the model before beginning his outbound calls. Her product knowledge shows.

The Final Close. This isn't a final second effort. It's a graceful exit. If the prospect continues to resist over a reasonable number of second efforts, the likelihood that he's not interested is high. For the sake of continued positive relationships, the image of the telemarketing organization and the prospect, it's time to gracefully let the customer get back to whatever he was doing (*"I'm sorry the timing's not right, Mr. Martin, but thank you so much for giving me your time. All of us at Shangri Lodge thank you for your continued interest. Hope to see you up here again soon. . ."*).

The Confirmation Close. This could also be called "taking the order," and how the confirmation is done can be extremely important for getting the best back-end (actual purchase, appearance, payment, etc.) results. The TSR should confirm the order, usually by restating what has been agreed. If more information is needed, she should ask the customer's permission to record a few important items of information. After making sure there are no more questions she can answer, the TSR now need do little more than thank the customer and say "good bye."

These basic elements can also apply in business-to-business situations, although the selling situations are usually very different. In business-to-business telemarketing, the offer is usually more complex and the TSR more highly trained in objection and question handling. Also, the structure of the conversation tends to be more flexible. See the example scripts on the following pages to get a sense of the differences between business-to-business and consumer telemarketing scripts.

EVALUATION/UPDATING/REVISION

No telemarketing script is static. After the TSR's have had some experience using the script in actual calls, the telemarketing manager should take the time to discuss script performance with them. What parts work? What parts don't? Why? What can be changed? Added? It's also possible after the first flight of calls are completed to look at the level of success meeting the objective. If performance is below expectations, a review of the script is probably in order.

As the script gets more and more refined, revisions will tend to become increasingly minimum. But evaluation should continue throughout the life of the script, if for no other reason than the fact that changes in the environment can render a good script nearly useless almost overnight. Regular evaluation can detect these changes and allow alteration of the script before too much damage is done.

SOME EXAMPLE TELEMARKETING SCRIPTS

The following are everyday examples of word-for-word and combination word-for-word/prompt scripts. They vary greatly in length, but each is an example of good script design.

Business Office Equipment. This first example is a copier sales script. It is meant to be used by an outside sales representative who is attempting to schedule appointments. We can assume that some preliminary qualification has already been done. (Please note the alternate choice method of getting agreement for the appointment and the emphasis on the importance of the prospect's actually being in at the time the interview is scheduled.)

* Hello, Mr./Ms. _____, I'm _____ from Chicago Business Systems, Inc. I'm calling today because we have some ideas on how a _____ can increase your office productivity and reduce your operating costs.

* Mr./Ms. _____, I'd be happy to drop by and share these ideas with you at your convenience. Would a morning or afternoon be best for you?

* Fine, I'll see you (day) at (time). The spelling of my name is _____. Please call me at _____ if there is a change of time, because I'm setting that hour aside for you.

Advertising Sales. This is an example of an advertising space sales script. Notice the interjection of three questions during the script presentation to determine the level of knowledge and interest on the part of the prospect. Also note the mixture of prompts within the body of a word-for-word script. For example, "Review size/color/insertions. Emphasize size/color/repetitive significance. Discuss quantity discounts. Review costs. Review closing."

* Hello, I'm _____, from *RUBBER PRODUCTS MAGAZINE*, calling long distance from New York. I'd like to speak to your sales executive who

171

handles your national advertising and public relations.

*   Hello, I'm _____, from *RUBBER PRODUCTS MAGAZINE*. I represent our publication as account executive for your area.

*   How familiar are you with *RPM*, Mr./Ms. _____?

IF FAMILIARITY IS LIMITED:

*   *RUBBER PRODUCTS MAGAZINE* is the most widely read publication devoted exclusively to the rubber product manufacturing industry. We provide the highest circulation within the industry at more than 15,000--with a 45,000-plus pass-along readership--and the lowest cost-per-thousand-circulation of all competitive publications.

    Because of these advantages, we're the most valued advertising vehicle in the industry, with 66 percent of all print advertising in the rubber product manufacturing industry.

*   Our publisher, Mr. Walter Jones, has asked me to call you regarding a special emphasis issue on _____, scheduled for _____. Because you are a _____ supplier, we felt you and your company would greatly benefit from advertising in that issue.

*   Sound interesting?

*   Also, by coupling a print ad in our _____ issue with an ad card from our Card Pack, your company would have a special opportunity to not only increase your product/service awareness, but also to develop immediate prospect leads!

    The Card Pack goes out separately to all 15,000+ subscribers. Because the industry average of response is one-half of one percent, this would give us a target of 77 sales leads for your company.

    Of course, excellent copy and an outstanding offer could possibly generate an even greater response. We have generated a high of 460 leads for one of our advertisers.

*   Our combination of print ad and Card Pack should help you and your company increase product awareness, build sales volume and improve net profit.

*   Sound like a good idea, Mr./Ms. _____?

* Good. Let's first choose a size layout for you and then I'll explain how we go about placing your ad for both our news publication and the Card Pack.

REVIEW SIZE/COLOR/INSERTIONS

* Emphasize size/color/repetitive significance.

* Discuss quantity discounts.

REVIEW APPROPRIATE COSTS OF PRINT AND CARD PACK

REVIEW CLOSING/MAIL DATES

EXPLAIN METHOD(S) OF AUTHORIZATION OF ADS

* (If ad layout is a problem, suggest free assistance from our creative personnel at *RPM*.)

* Thank you, Mr./Ms. _____ for your insertion order. I'm sure you and your company will be quite pleased with the positive response.

* Goodbye.

Visual Products Sales. This next script is an excellent example of how to determine who is the person with buying authority. Also, it includes a complete survey of buying needs so that an appropriate recommendation can be made. As with the previous script, the prompt technique is embedded within a word-for-word script. Please note, also, the "I recommend:" portion of the script.

* (Operator answers.) Hello, I'd like to speak with the person who buys your transparencies for overhead projection. Who would the person be, please? (Get spelling of name and title.)

  (Note: Usually purchasing, the office manager, duplicating department manager, graphic arts manager, copier key operator or supplies manager.)

* (Buyer answers.) Hello, Mr./Ms. _____, I'm _____, from Visual Products, Inc. We're the company that specializes in overhead projection supplies and equipment. Mr./Ms. _____, are you the person who determines which kind of overhead transparencies your company uses?

* (If "no" response, determine who is responsible. Also get title and department. If possible, try to get yearly volume and method of preparation.)

* (If "yes" response.) Fine. Mr./Ms. _____, our company, Visual Products, Inc., is a one-stop shopping center for overhead supplies and equipment.

173

Many of the largest and most cost-efficient companies in the _____ area use our products--and that's why we're the fastest-growing visual products company in the U.S.

* We offer three basic benefits to our customers: better products, faster service and lower prices. Sound interesting? (Get prospect response.)

* (If appropriate.) Fine. My call is also very timely because we're offering not one, but two special incentives:

* First, a special 15% telephone discount. . .and

* Second, a free executive telescoping pointer or a calling-card sized calculator for first-time buyers.

* Now, Mr./Ms. _____, if I can ask you a few questions about your current needs, I'll be able to serve you and save your company money. OK? (Get prospect acceptance.)

* Good. First:

-- How many boxes of transparencies does your company use annually?

-- How are they prepared? (thermal, xerography, PPC or diazo)

-- What type do you use? (manufacturer, number, weight and colors)

-- Current source?

-- Current price?

-- What is the current level of satisfaction with your current supplier? (Very satisfied, slightly satisfied, slightly dissatisfied, very dissatisfied)

-- Current stock?

-- Would you be interested in more dramatic color and bold imaging in your presentations?

-- Accessories/supplies needed at this time? (frames, markers, tape, thermal paper, other)

* We also have a special promotion on a budget-priced overhead projector. Do you need a replacement or an extra one?

174

* Now, let me determine the best overhead transparency/product value for you, Mr./Ms. _____. May I have a minute to figure this all out for you or should I call you right back? (Get preference.)

* Mr./Ms. _____, thank you for waiting. My recommendation for your company will increase the quality of your transparencies and reduce your costs at the same time.

* I recommend:

-- Product(s)

-- Benefits (from benefit sheet)

-- Applicable free gift

-- Special telephone discount of 15%, gives us a price of _____ for _____ boxes.

* How does that sound, Mr./Ms. _____? (Get response.)

* Excellent. And we usually can provide a quick one- to two-day delivery. Also, we are always available by telephone to respond to your questions.

* So that you can get our special telephone transparency value and free executive gift (specify), can I place your order for you?

* Fine. How do you want me to set up the account information? (Bill to. . ., Ship to. . ., etc.)

* (Take data and reconfirm order.)

* Thank you, Mr./Ms. _____. I know you'll be pleased with both our products and our service.

* Goodbye.

A Two-Pass Script. This final example portrays a two-pass telephone script. The first call (first pass) explains the reason for the call and gets the prospect to agree to review an office supply catalog, as well as a follow-up telephone call. The second telephone call (second pass) establishes that the prospect has reviewed the catalog, specific prospect needs have been determined and an order has been placed. This is a very specific example of "rifle cataloging."

Also, after an order has been taken within the second-pass telephone call, the caller is scripted to set up the new customer for follow-on account calls.

175

ENCYCLOPEDIA OF TELEMARKETING

FIRST PASS

* Hello, Mr./Ms. _____, I'm _____, from the ABC Company.

* (If letter sent.) Have you received a letter from our president, Mr. Dee?

* (Letter sent or not.) Well, as our president, Mr. Dee, has stated, ABC Company will provide to all of our new and regular customers the very best in office supply products, the lowest overall prices, fast delivery and an unconditional guarantee of customer satisfaction.

* And, in addition to our regular low prices, Mr./Ms. _____, ABC Company will offer a monthly selection of office supplies at very special discounts available to our customers only by telephone.

* For example, this month's specials are:

* (Review telephone specials.)

* Also, Mr./Ms. _____, as an incentive to consolidate your office supply purchases, we are providing free gifts for orders of _____, _____ and _____.

* (Review free gifts and order levels.)

* So that we can review your current office supply needs and determine your free gift, may I personally send you our office supply catalog?

* Fine. I'll send one out today and give you a telephone call in a few days. Sound OK?

* Excellent. Have a good day, Mr./Ms. _____. Goodbye.

SECOND PASS

* Hello, Mr./Ms. _____, this is _____, calling back from ABC Company.

* Have you received our catalog?

* Good. As I mentioned last week, in addition to the items listed there, we're offering the special telephone discounts on (items).

* Also, remember, for consolidated office supply purchases of (levels), we are offering free gifts. And this month they are (gifts).

SCRIPTS AND THE OFFER

* Which items in our catalog and telephone specials do you think you would like to order for your company?

* (Take order, determine gift and review.)

* Fine, Mr./Ms. _____. We'll send this order out within ___ days. I believe you will find our merchandise excellent, our delivery service quick and our overall prices to be the lowest for the value received.

* And remember, if for any reason you are not completely satisfied, we provide an unconditional satisfaction guarantee.

* (Explain guarantee and provide telephone number.)

* Sound good? Fine. I thank you for your order today. I'll call you next month to advise you of the new telephone discounts. OK?

* Thank you. Talk to you next month.

CHAPTER 12

Handling Objections

Richard L. Bencin

"Sorry. We're not interested."

Telephone sales representatives have a significant occupational hazard, but it's not back pain or numb ear lobes. It's prospect objections. Depending, of course, on what's being sold or encouraged over the phone, objections can vary from reasoned and cogent to downright vicious. Without the proper preparation and training, the phone rep can quickly become discouraged by these manifestations of the prospect's natural defenses.

Such discouragement is not only unnecessary, however, it's actually inappropriate. The prospect's objections can actually serve as tools to help in reaching the objective. Once the telephone sales rep has learned to understand and handle buyer objections, he/she will begin to welcome them because they help.

The first reaction to this statement is naturally a profound skepticism, but it *is* true. Objections can tell a telephone sales representative a number of crucial things.

* *An objection indicates the prospect's attention is being held.* Prospects don't have to listen at all. They always have the option of saying they're not interested and hanging up. But when they enter into a dialog with the sales rep, they may be indicating that there is something in what's being offered that has piqued their interest. This interest, of course, is the classic "foot in the door."

* *Specific objections are "mile markers" indicating how far the conversation has progressed.* As the prospect begins to consider and question issues of greater detail and complexity, he/she also is beginning to absorb the sales message. Selling is communication, and communication requires that we know what is being heard. Objections will tell us that directly.

* *Specific objections indicate what remains to be covered to reach a sale.* Often, a prospect will understand issues that the rep would expect to be the most difficult, yet will get hung up on questions originally thought to be peripheral. By carefully listening to objections, the sales rep can get a valuable sense of what the prospect still doesn't understand.

With this sort of conversational chart, the telephone sales rep can avoid wasting time covering questions that aren't at issue, and get right to the core of the sales problem.

HANDLING OBJECTIONS

There is, therefore, no reason to fear objections. With the proper training and understanding, a telephone sales rep can use them effectively and creatively in making the sales presentation. They help plot the course of the sale by indicating the direction of the prospect's thought processes. In fact, the only time the sales rep should be truly concerned about objections is when they're not being raised, or when they can't be answered adequately and completely.

Objections aren't handled naturally, however. Objection-handling isn't an inbred skill. Objections must be anticipated and thought through. Replies to them must be developed, and the ability to deliver those replies must be learned.

We'll look first at the various classes of objections, then at the specific techniques for handling them.

AN OBJECTION "TAXONOMY"

1) The Unspoken Objection. This kind of objection is one that is unexpressed by the prospect.

In many ways, it's probably the most dangerous type for the telephone sales rep to handle because of the nature of the medium he/she is using. With the telephone, it's difficult to be aware that an unspoken objection exists. Because of this, the telephone sales rep may not adequately provide a logical and constructive reply to the potential customer.

Clearly, it's impossible to answer an objection when one doesn't know it exists. So the answer to this objection is to find a means to counter its hidden nature. A very simple means of meeting this particular type of objection is merely to ask questions and encourage the prospect to talk. If the telephone sales rep can bring out the inward thoughts of the prospect into a discussion, it becomes much more likely that the salesperson will be able to know exactly what the objections are and intelligently phrase the response.

2) The Legitimate Objection. The legitimate objection is one which the salesperson is powerless to overcome.

It's as simple as that. Legitimate objections are bona fide objections, usually taking the form of reasons why the prospect doesn't have the time to listen, the authority to buy, or the need for the product. The following are some examples of "legitimate objections":

> *"I'm too busy to talk to you right now."* (Assuming the telephone sales rep perceives the prospect is, in fact, busy.)

> *"I'm sorry, but we've just entered into Chapter 11 and aren't about to buy a $10,000 copier."*

> *"Thanks for calling, but they don't let me make those kinds of decisions. You'll have to talk to our vice president."*

When confronted with an objection that appears to be legitimate, the telephone sales rep will have to determine with as much certainty as possible that it is, in fact, legitimate. It could, after all, be a stall. But if it is legitimate, the obvious course is to acknowledge it and counter with an alternative proposal.

For example, the answer to the first statement above might be:

"Oh, that's okay. Believe me, I understand what it's like to be hassled. When would be a better time for me to call you back?"

A response to the lack of authority objection could be:

"I'm sorry to have taken your time. Could you give me the name of the person I should talk to?"

One other form of legitimate objection is a complaint about a minor, but real, product disadvantage. In the face of this sort of objection, the sales rep would do best to point out, as tactfully as possible, the *overall advantages* of the product and how they fully outweigh the rather small disadvantage.

3) The False Objection.
A false objection is an argument or excuse offered by the prospect in an effort to seek a delay in the closing of a sale, or to avoid the closing entirely--all in a way that will avoid the unpleasant task of saying "no" to the telephone sales rep.

Objections like this are defense mechanisms that are used quite automatically by prospects. It's a basically natural inclination to protect one's funds, and most people don't get much pleasure saying "no" to others.

The problem with the false objection is that it can't really be answered. It's not, after all, a true objection, so the prospect doesn't really want a reply. An authority on salesmanship, Frank Bettger, has written that a large percentage of the objections first expressed by sales prospects were not real reasons for not buying.

Bettger did a careful analysis of more than 5,000 interviews in an effort to find out why people bought or failed to buy. In 62% of the cases studied, the original objection raised was not a true objection. Only 38% of the time did the prospect give his or her real reasons! This study points out the importance of knowing how to recognize and handle a false objection.

Here are some examples:

"Your product just isn't any good." (This generally indicates a hidden objection. Just what is it that makes the prospect say that?)

"I'm not interested." (Maybe so, but that's usually because the prospect needs more information to become interested.)

"Your prices are too high." (The real meaning here is that the desire for the product is too low.)

Basically, the false objection usually means that the prospect's interest has not been aroused or that the telephone sales rep is going to have to probe deeper to find out what the hidden reason for the objection is.

Probing usually involves questioning the prospect until the real objection is brought out. This can often be accomplished simply by asking "why," to get the prospect talking. For example, a telephone sales rep selling telephone services might hear a prospect object that accepting collect telephone calls from potential customers is not worth the expense. True enough, the sales rep might reply, but only for single orders. What about accepting collect calls from customers who order in quantity?

Another useful tool for pinpointing the real objection is a sentence like:

"Isn't there some other reason why you feel that way?"

If the false objection is an obvious excuse for avoiding making a decision on the telephone sales rep's proposal, there is no hidden reason. The prospect simply isn't interested enough. This is the time for the telephone sales rep to fully explore further benefits to the customer. Instead of shadowboxing with a sham objection advanced purely as a stall, the sales rep should continue selling. His or her job at this point is relatively clear cut--to build up the buying benefits enough to overwhelm the excuse-type objection.

4) The True Objection A true objection is an argument offered in good faith by an as-yet-undecided, but still interested prospect. This class of objection demands a complete and adequate answer, because the potential customer wants and has a right to such a reply. The true objection should never be "glossed" over.

PREPARING FOR--AND HEARING--OBJECTIONS

One of the most useful and productive techniques for handling objections is the careful, advance planning of replies.

Some objections recur frequently, and by simply making a list of common objections about the product or service, the organization can begin to prepare well-organized, effective replies before the first call is made.

These replies can be incorporated right into the sales presentation itself, thereby preventing many objections from entering into the sales discussion at all. Others would be left to the chance of conversation. If a prospect should express a common objection, the telephone sales rep would be prepared to handle it.

A word of caution, however. The more verbose the phrasing of the reply, the greater the chance that somewhere along the line the prospect may become confused. A good, concise reply is usually safest.

The following are excellent examples of brief, but effective replies:

OBJECTION: *"I'm trying to cut costs and keep my expenses down."*

REPLY: *"But this product isn't an expense if it brings in more business and helps you keep the customers you already have. It's an investment."*

OBJECTION: *"A combination lock is useless to me because I can't open it in the dark like I can a key lock."*

REPLY: *"True, you can't open it in the dark. But then neither can a burglar. To pick it, he has to do something very dangerous to him, use a light."*

There are a number of objections that telephone sales reps, in general, can expect to hear. They are

181

generic in the telemarketing business and almost totally independent of the product or service involved. Here are a few of the more common:

> OBJECTION: *"You're just trying to sell me something!"*

> REPLY: *"No, it's too early to say that. First we need to discuss your company's needs to see if there are any benefits we can offer. A short discussion should allow us to find that out."*

> OBJECTION: *"You'll be wasting your time giving me a sales pitch."*

> REPLY: *"I'm calling because I believe we can help increase your productivity, lower your operating costs and improve your sales. I don't look upon that as a waste of time."*

> OBJECTION: *"Well, I don't know if an appointment is worthwhile. Just drop a brochure in the mail. That's more efficient."*

> REPLY: *"I'd be happy to do that, but a brochure won't be able to answer your questions, nor will it be able to explain benefits unique to you. This product really requires a demonstration geared to your situation. Can we get together sometime next week?"*

> OBJECTION: *"I already own another product just like it."*

> REPLY: *"Well, how old is it? There's always a point when it's an advantage to change--when the repair frequency gets too high, for example, or your needs change, or the technology is significantly better. I think it's worth your time to find out if a change might be due in your case."*

> OBJECTION: *"Look, just give me a quick description and tell me what it costs."*

> REPLY: *"I can do that, but it wouldn't be fair to you. We offer a wide range of services, and I can't recommend the right one for you until I fully understand your requirements. What we offer isn't for everyone, but where*

applicable, our products/services can bring significant benefits.

"Now, what I need to know, quickly, is. . .."

OBJECTION: *"Your product's too expensive; we can't afford it."*

REPLY: *"If we can determine the product will save you money, cost shouldn't be a problem. Cost savings--which I know this product offers--are certainly worth some time. Could we get together, just briefly, sometime next week?"*

A great danger in handling objections is handling the wrong objection. One rule should be engraved above the doors of telemarketing operations, and followed to the letter:

LISTEN AND LET THE PROSPECT TALK!

Listening closely to what the prospect has to say is critical to telephone sales success. Most telephone sales reps overlook this technique, however, and often begin formulating (even speaking!) their replies before the prospect has finished talking.

The sales rep should bite his/her tongue and carefully scrutinize what the prospect is saying. This approach is particularly useful when the prospect is abusive, complaining, critical or just plain grouchy. When this happens, it's interesting to watch the difference in reaction between the experienced and inexperienced telephone sales rep. The inexperienced sales rep experiences an adrenaline rush and leaps into combat. The experienced sales rep sits back in his chair and simply *listens*.

Objecting, arguing, or interrupting on the part of the telephone salesperson is likely to lead only to a more heated argument. When a prospect or customer wants to let off emotional steam, it's wise to let the prospect go ahead and deflate. In doing so, the sales rep will get all of the information about the expressed objection and, in addition, will defuse the hostility in the prospect. Sheer expression can soften a prospect, but so too can the experience of having one's objections given a respectful hearing.

SOME BASIC OBJECTION-HANDLING TECHNIQUES

Experienced salespeople evolve many methods for handling resistance and objections. Many of them apply as well to telephone selling as to face-to-face sales. Here are a few of the more common techniques, proven to work well in telephone sales:

Concede before Continuing. Before a telephone sales representative starts rebutting a sales objection, he/she should concede that the prospect has raised an important point. This both bolsters the prospect's ego and demonstrates that the sales rep sees what the prospect sees: a keenness of observation.

A telephone sales rep who is reluctant to concede anything at all is certainly in direct opposition to the prospect, which is anything but a healthy sales situation.

It pays every telephone sales rep to heed the advice of Benjamin Franklin:

> *"First give a little water to the pump. You may thereafter get from it all the water you wish."*

Rephrase the Objection into a Question. Closely related to the concession technique above is the principle of converting objections into questions. Using this method, the telephone sales rep can rebut without getting into the uncomfortable position of having to prove the prospect wrong. For example:

> OBJECTION: *"My neighbor says she's had a bad experience with your company."*

> REPLY: *"Well, that really raises the question whether or not my company cares about its customers. You know, we've recently done a survey which showed that 98% of our customers are repeat buyers. There must have been something uniquely wrong in the case of your neighbor--and I'm sorry about that. Still, most people think we're good enough to order from more than once. That's really quite an endorsement."*

Reduce Broad Objections to Specifics. When faced by a sweeping general objection, the telephone salesperson must realize that only specifics can be effectively answered. The broad objection simply must be reduced to its specifics. Unless this is done, the overall question is likely to prove too complex and cumbersome to handle adequately.

Here are some sample questions to use in narrowing broad objections:

> *"How often would you say this happens?"*

> *"Can you give me a few examples of the problem you just mentioned?"*

> *"Could you explain exactly what you mean?"*

> *"What particular parts of the equipment are causing the problem?"*

Use Third-Party Testimonials. Answering objections generally demands a lot of skill on the part of the telephone sales rep, particularly since the response has to be given in such a way that it doesn't clash with the prospect's point of view.

The testimonial of another person is an excellent and valuable tool to use in these situations. If the third-party is perceived as neutral and respected, it can provide a focus for fusing the opposing opinions of the prospect and the salesperson.

Take the "I" Out of the Interview. If a telephone sales rep has a predilection for using the pronoun "I," it won't take long to see that using "I" in replies to objections causes some real problems.

Every time the first person pronoun is used in a conversation with a prospect (particularly one about objections), the risk increases that the prospect may interpret disdain in the sales rep's words. A telephone sales rep should not be fighting for "first fiddle." Instead, his or her objective should be to play "second fiddle" as skillfully as possible, to win the point by modestly letting the prospect have his or her way.

Consider Carefully before Answering. Eagerness in answering questions may be a virtue in a job interview, but in a telephone sales call it can be a mortal sin. Sales have been lost through overly eager responses to objections.

Experienced telephone sales reps purposely slow up, and sometimes delay their replies in order to give the impression that the objection has been given considerable thought.

And, if the program is properly planned and executed, it has. But just because the reply was formulated and rehearsed long before the specific call is no reason that the prospect should be led to believe the objection is not considered important.

Hold on to Your Temper. The most effective way to throw a prospective sale away is for the telephone sales rep to respond angrily to a harsh objection. All such a response will do is increase the prospect's defensiveness.

It's worth remembering that people are seldom argued out of their opinions, but they can easily be argued into a negative attitude toward their antagonist. If the heat starts rising under the telephone rep's collar, it needs to be radiated, to be sure. But the worst direction in which to let it out is toward the prospect. Every one of us has a personal way to "count to 10," and every telephone sales rep should keep his or hers close at hand.

The seller-buyer relationship only works only when it is kept on a cooperative and congenial level. Even when discussing a very strong objection, the prospect needs to feel that he and the telephone sales rep share a desire to solve the problem as effectively and objectively as possible.

To summarize everything in this chapter in a few words: the prospect's objections should be used to help the sale, not hinder it.

This Chapter has been reprinted with permission, from *Strategic Telemarketing*, by Richard L. Bencin, ISBN 0-915601-02-8, © 1987, available direct from Cresheim Publications, Post Office Box 27785, Philadelphia, PA 19118, 1/800-792-6732.

CHAPTER 13

Databases and Data Banks (Lists)

Ed Burnett
President
Ed Burnett Consultants, Inc.
Englewood, New Jersey

There are a number of myths in this field that have had the effect of impeding the development of database marketing. Here are seven of the most important:

MYTH #1: DATABASE AND DATA BANK ARE INTERCHANGEABLE TERMS

There is actually a distinctive difference that can be sorted out by the relation of the user to the data.

Those data which belong to one company or institution (for one, or more than one establishment) make up the "*database*" for that entity. In general:

1) *All the data on the base are self-generated by the owner.*

2) *All added transactions come from the owner's activities.*

3) *All data added to records already on the base come from activities of the owner.*

Overlays (additions) to the major information on the database (e.g., U.S. census data, ZIP codes, carrier routes, telephone numbers) generally originate with outside vendors, and often the application of the overlays may be done by outside services. Frequently, a database is not available for outside rental or sale, because it incorporates the single most important set of records for its owner--namely the customer (or donor, or subscriber) file.

A *data bank*, on the other hand, embraces multiple sources, often both compiled and response-oriented, and is generally available for rental. A data bank offers a large number of records already pre-merge/purged and unduplicated. Data banks for rental almost always have been overlaid to produce appropriate U.S. census data, ZIP codes, carrier routes and telephone numbers. While some data banks are proprietary and thus include the proprietor's customer records, it is more usual for a data bank to include outside sources only. (A number of multiple magazine publishers make available an unduplicated merged list of subscribers and recipients--in effect a hybrid--a database for internal use, a data bank for outside use.)

186

MYTH # 2: ANY LIST OWNED BY A CUSTOMER IS PART OF THE CUSTOMER'S DATABASE

Not quite! Most marketers have a list of customers, a list of sales by classification, a list of inquirers, a list of requests, and possibly several lists of prospects. But these various lists do not talk to each other. They do not interrelate. They, therefore, are not part of the database.

MYTH #3: THE IMPORTANT ASPECT OF A DATABASE APPROACH IS TO ORGANIZE THE DATA—THE OPERATING OR MANAGEMENT SYSTEM THEN FOLLOWS

In fact, the management operating system is just as important as the data itself. Data, no matter how carefully defined, collected and organized, is meaningless without the system to control, unduplicate and manage it.

MYTH #4: ITEM ORIENTATION IS THE ESSENCE OF DATA BASE MANAGEMENT—TRANSACTIONS ARE THE KEY

The essence of database management is a move to customer orientation, not item or transaction. Until and unless this is done, there is no database to manage.

MYTH #5: DATABASE MANAGEMENT IS TOO MUCH TROUBLE, TOO COSTLY, AND ONLY FOR THE BIG BOYS

True, database management is a lot of trouble. A file of customers is not a homogeneous entity. It includes excellent customers, poor customers, customers who buy often and customers who will never buy again. But unless and until a business can identify one type of customer from another, it will simply drift. There will be no control of growth. So the toil and trouble and time to build a database management system is one of the best investments a marketer can make.

MYTH #6: A DATABASE MANAGEMENT SYSTEM MUST BE RUN IN-HOUSE

It may be *preferable* to control such a system in-house, but there is no law that makes this *mandatory*. Both inside and outside options should be carefully considered.

187

MYTH #7: ONCE BUILT, IN PLACE AND RUNNING, A DATABASE SYSTEM SHOULD NOT CHANGE

Au Contraire! A database management system is a dynamic entity. There is an exceedingly small possibility that all needs and demands on the system will be anticipated in the original design.

TELEPHONE NUMBERS

Myths "dispelled," we can now backtrack a bit to look at the telemarketer's key data item in each record--the telephone number. It's very useful to review the way telephone numbers get on to data banks--and from data banks on to databases--and from databases to telephonic communication.

Virtually all telephone numbers used by direct marketers originate in one of four ways:

1) *Registered telephones at household addresses found in the alphabetic telephone directories published annually by some 1,500 phone companies.*

2) *Registered telephones at non-household addresses found in the classified sections (the Yellow Pages) of some 4,700 telephone directories published annually in the United States.*

3) *Reported phones in connection with some mail order response to a mail order merchant.*

4) *Actual canvas at the door for data published in some 1,500 city directories.*

Note that we are discussing *listed* phones only. There are 87 million households in America. Some 85 million of them have TV sets and 83 million have connected phones. But only 57 million of those connected phones are listed in directories. And of that number, only 52 million are published with mailable addresses. So a remarkably large minority of phones (over 40%) are not listed or not published. It is, for example, a little known fact that households on welfare in New York City are not permitted a listed phone, so those deprived householders pay extra to New York Telephone Company for an unlisted number.

At the present time, R.H. Donnelly is the only company compiling all listed phones in America. Donnelly sells a copy of this list to Metromail. Metromail, until very recently, sold phone data in selected states (where car registrations were unavailable) to R.L. Polk. Polk canvasses and publishes data including phones in city directories covering some 26 million families. Then Polk proceeds, partly via purchase and partly through its own efforts, to add phone data for almost all states. The Polk file in 1987 included 55 million families with listed phones.

A fourth file, called Data Bank America, incorporates phone numbers from all listings, plus unduplicated coverage from the city directories, plus that phone data available in one of the largest age-base lists in America, plus those phones that have been compiled by Life Style Selector. This file is now the dominant file in America used to tag telephone names to alphabetic (household and householder) lists. It is this list, for example, which is the essence of the "Focus Master" overlay service provided to major consumer mailers by CCX, the huge computer service directory for the direct response field.

On the business side, there are also four lists commercially available with virtually every business phone number. One is Dun & Bradstreet (which claims to have no name on its file from classified that is not confirmed by another source). The other three, all of which include every listing of every classified directory in America, are:

1) *Data Base America.*

2) *Compilers Plus.*

3) *American Business List.*

Of these, Data Base America now has 6.1 million records (of a total of 8.3 million) that are confirmed by at least a second source, and more than 4.5 million of its phone numbers have been verified through phoning within the previous six months. Data Bank America-Business for overlays is available through Pagex, Inc., and MAGI. In addition it is the file selected by CCX for its "Focus Master" overlay service for business mailers and telemarketers.

There are other entrants--primarily individual telephone companies, which offer an overlay service to tag customer files with phone numbers--but each of these is limited to one area or one state. For example, it is possible to obtain a phone matching source for the State of Illinois through its list manager, Qualified Lists--and for the State of Maryland through its list manager, Ed Burnett Consultants, Inc. But as yet, most phone data--which is more current than the data compiled from published directories--is not available, even piecemeal.

One major list, larger by far than any other, and more current than any yet on the market, exists-- but not for rental or sale. This is the vast data bank owned by AT&T, which is, for most of America, the "service of last resort" for long distance. AT&T's list of household phones total over 100 million, while its business list is well above 10 million. As a universal phone service, AT&T has on its files those many millions of phone users who are neither published nor listed. There is, however, little likelihood that this list will come on the market in any form in the foreseeable future.

It should be noted that each of the lists noted above is a data bank. However, at least three of them, D&B, AT&T and Data Base America, are utilized in part as databases. D&B and Data Base America match their tens of thousands of list buyers against their nationwide data files and select those establishments by classification and size most likely to utilize names and addresses for marketing purposes. AT&T does a good portion of its marketing of services to its clients for long distance service.

RESPONSE FACTORS

For both tele-prospecting (cold calling) and direct mail prospecting, the same basic factors influence response:

1) *Copy (script/printed piece).*

2) *Offer.*

3) *Timing.*

4) *Package (vocal and mental picture of telecommunicator; the "dress" and design of mailing piece).*

5) *List or market.*

From a response point of view, by far the most important factor of these five is the list or market. In essence, the influence of the market on response is the one factor which in tele-prospecting can be accurately measured--by comparing results, one list against another.

Response to one list can vary from the response to another by as much as 1,000% (10 to 1!). This vast difference emphasizes the importance of knowing as much about each list utilized as possible.

HOW LISTS VARY

The watchword here is *criteria*--that which distinguishes one list from another, and that which distinguishes one segment of the same list from another.

There are four major types of criteria:

1) *Demographic characteristics.*

2) *Psychographic characteristics.*

3) *Physical characteristics.*

4) *Customer characteristics.*

Demographic characteristics include sex, age, family size, number of children, geographical location, educational level, length of residence, car ownership, type and value of residence, telephone number and, above all, income, both individual and family.

Business demographics include geographical location, city size, number of employees, advertising index, telephone number, and above all, classification by 2-, 3-, 4- or 5-digit *Standard Industrial Classification* (SIC) code.

Psychographic characteristics describe life style--how the individual or the family lives and spends time. The main determinants are what people buy, what they read, what they own, what they belong to, what they support, and what hobbies or interests fill their spare time. *Physical characteristics* relate to the size of the list or segment, its relation to the universe, its accessibility, who controls its use and how this control is exercised--and whether or not a valid phone number is available.

Customer characteristics (other than telephonic aspects) are covered by an acronym: *REF$USISM.*

RE-*ecency.*

F-*requency.*

$US-*dollars (total, highest, periodic).*

I-*tem (or service purchased).*

S-*ource of the order (initial source, which can be direct mail, space or electronic advertising, telephone, friend of a friend, warranties, trade show, etc.).*

M-*ethod of payment.*

DATABASE CONSTRUCTION

This now brings us back to database construction. Databases are collections of data about customers. Thus, the more that is known about the customer, the better the database, and the better the uses that can be made of it. This means measurement of use (promotion) against the lifetime value of each name on the file.

The use of a customer database for telemarketing adds a whole new layer of data to each customer on the file.

1) *Phone number, by source, and date.*

2) *Phone utilization.*

   * At what time(s).

   * With what results.

3) *Special instructions.*

   * Do not call again.

   * Call only at specific time.

   * Speak only with Ms. A or B.

   * Re-call in "X" time.

   * Have a sales representative arrange to visit.

4) *Production.*

   * Sales, by item.

   * Repeat sales by cycle--for re-calls.

   * Call reporting (to lead to penetration analysis).

5)   *Procurement of additional data.*

   * Households.

      Hobbies.

      Interests and tastes.

      Children.

      Birth dates.

      Family members.

      Friends of a friend.

      Product evaluation.

   *   Non-Households.

      Executive by name.

      Size (number of employees or sales

      volume).

      Classification (type of business).

      Sister establishments.

      Effectiveness of direct sales support.

      Product evaluation.

   The act of listing the many types of data that can be captured, customer by customer, on a database, can provide a vivid illustration of why it's important to determine at the outset how this vast assemblage of data is to be handled.

   Also, the determination of exactly which reports are to be generated calls for serious study--by all divisions (accounts receivable, accounts payable, marketing, inventory control, finance, production, for example) who are to have access to the database.

   A good way to begin is to generate a ''wish list,'' a listing of reports that might help answer questions like the following:

1)   *Which Customers buy on a regular, periodic basis?*

   * By mail only.

DATABASES AND DATA BANKS (LISTS)

      * By phone only.

      * By both mail and phone.

2) *Which are the best customers on the file?.*

3) *Which customers are lapsing toward expiration?.*

4) *What promotion to salvage?*

      * Mail.

      * Phone.

5) *Which source or sources provide the best return?*

      * Mail.

      * Phone.

6) *What has been the cost to promote?.*

      * One-time buyers.

      * Multiple buyers.

      * Nonbuyers.

7) *What is the lifetime value of a given customer cell, after including costs for promotion?*

      * By mail.

      * By phone.

If you already have a list, here are some tips on changing it into a living, breathing *database*:

1) *Decide what it is you NEED to know--and what it will cost. (Remember, there are three kinds of knowledge--must know, need to know, nice to know. Forswear the latter!)*

2) *Obtain all data (all items, all transactions) on old, current and new customers. (Don't simply accept what is easily available. Dig! It pays!)*

3) *Obtain all data on efforts (mail and phone and field sales calls) and to whom directed--and when.*

193

4) *Arrange to keep all source data and the original date of the first transaction. (Don't accept the statement that such data is no longer available. Again, dig!)*

5) *Capture and keep all inquiries, friends of friends, catalog or literature requests--with codes for control.*

6) *Chain together all data--so as to link source, promotion, transactions, and add data to each individual customer. (For business files, call in one of the three or four major players who understand the intricacies of business merge-identification.)*

7) *Establish sales bogies, by mail and by phone, for each effort--and test by cell (by age, and dollars, if not by regression analysis) to determine effective and useful cut-off points.*

DATABASES DEFINED

It is probable that there are about as many definitions of what is meant by the word *database* as there are marketers writing about them.

To students in computer courses, a database is an on-line, real-time, disk-oriented group of interrelated files that react to a transaction affecting one or more files. To a software house, a database is a program that controls the workings of interactive, on-line, real-time files. To marketers, a true "direct marketing database" would be such a set of files providing on-line, real-time data on the following:

1) *Customer database.*

2) *Inventory database.*

3) *Inquiry request database.*

4) *Prospect and suspect database.*

5) *Agency, dealer, wholesaler, branch database.*

6) *Order file database.*

7) *Catalog item database.*

8) *Promotion use and response database.*

On such a set of interrelated files, if a mailing is made to a customer, it shows on the promotional file and on the customer file. When a purchase is made, this affects the order file, the customer file, the

194

inventory file and the response file. With maximums and minimums set on the inventory file (as well as location and on-order status), that order may trigger a new order for inventory, or move inventory from back-up to picking bin status.

The order automatically increases accounts receivable, creates a bill with an audit trail, updates the sales tax due, and updates the catalog item file.

A direct mailer and/or telemarketer who adds recency, frequency, and dollars to his customer file has created a database if it satisfies the following conditions:

1) *It is owned exclusively by one firm.*

2) *It is dynamic--thus it is and can change.*

3) *It is on-line in real time so individual records can be reviewed and changed or updated at will.*

4) *The owner uses the data derived to improve customer sales and customer responsiveness.*

Of these four points, the most important is the last. There is no reason to build *REF$USISM* into a database system if the analytic data this can provide is not used as a tool to manage the customer file. Many firms become enamored of the mechanics of the database and forget the reason for building it. The correct term is really not "database," but database *management*. "Management" should be the operative word, here. The interrelationship of the data elements is designed to help management make more intelligent decisions.

John Stevenson of *Experts in Direct Marketing* notes:

> *"The feedback in direct response is a continuous stream of facts and certainties. They come out of the real world from real people, and real markets, about real products and services. In this feedback, everything is done--any single piece of the process--becomes a variable that can be individually identified and thus can be measured. And the relationships between variables can be observed. There is far more to the direct marketing process and in the feedback than sales alone."*

The database of customers provides a means for a mailer and/or a telemarketer to locate and reach and have a dialogue with each cell of customers on the file. With database management, a manager can reach his prime customers more often, shorten intervals between catalog request conversion mailings, identify segments of customers who should not be mailed or called more than once or twice a year, and at the same time identify cells of customers that should be mailed 12 times per year.

Once prime customers have been identified, steps can be taken to take extra efforts to locate and promote others. If, for example, there is no way to determine which sources provide customers who buy more than once, prospecting is relegated simply to renting those names which produce the highest number of sales per thousand. If two lists are sampled, and it's found that one can bring in first-time customers, 30% of whom will buy again in the following year, while the other shows just 10% re-buyers, then the most responsive list will continue to be used while the other is discontinued.

Every name on the database arrives there through some source, through some offer. Every inquiry, every request has its own history. The source may have been space, or mail, or telephone, or a premium offer, or a card deck, or a response to a general advertisement--each of these inquiries ''voted'' to respond. This history tells what they did, what they bought, how much was spent, how often they purchased, how and when the purchases were paid. This history of promotion and response indicates, in fact, the value of each separate cell on the file.

Once this history of promotion and response is updated on an ongoing basis, the variables (the cells of customers and inquiries based on the ''REF$USISM'' function) will tend to cluster in one of three layers:

1)   *Cells that correlate to a high degree with response.*

2)   *Cells that correlate to a lesser degree with response.*

3)   *Cells that always appear to be highly correlated with nonresponse.*

To repeat, and the reason now may be more clear, in database management, the emphasis changes dramatically from ''item'' to the ''customer.'' It is the historical record of the customer that is important; not just what is bought, but who buys what, when, how often, and at what influence on the profitability of the company or effectiveness of the organization.

DATABASE SELECTION ITEMS

Perhaps the most important computer acronym in database management is ''NINO''--which says, succinctly, ''Not In--Not Out.'' What is not put on the file in a codable way can just never be pulled out or selected for use.

The database selection options, keeping NINO in mind, could embrace some or all of the following:

1)   *File Source*--Who owns or maintains the file.

2)   *List Profile*--The essence of the data on the file--businesses, executives, consumers, buyers, inquirers.

3)   *Prefix Title*--To permit proper salutation for Doctors, Reverends, Captains, etc.

4)   *List Source*--The source of the individual list (or lists) from which the individual record comes.

5)   *Employee Size*--Exact number of employees at a given location, or for a company as a whole, or ranges of same.

6)   *Title Select*--Access to the entire gamut of business titles found in the database.

7) *Field of Interest or Function*--A VP may be in sales, finance, production, or research.

8) *Recency*--The date of the last transaction by the database operator with a given record.

9) *SIC and Industry Group*--A two- to five-digit SIC coding.

10) *Multi-Buyer*--Selection of those who have purchased two or more times.

11) *Cell Count*--Access to count data by different segmentation; also on a one-for-10 basis, the number of records in a given cross-section for research purposes.

12) *Record Selects*--By 5th-digit ZIP, or Nth name, or first letter of last name.

13) *Add Titles*--Option to add titles where title is not available, also the ability to add extra records for a given establishment.

14) *Max Per Record*--To limit the number of names selected from a given firm to a predetermined maximum.

15) *Flights*--A means to isolate multiple prospects at one location and arrange to mail them a few each day in separate "flights" and, thus, reduce a glut of identical third-class mail pieces at the company mail receiving room.

16) *Split Outputs*--The capacity to split out any key, any segment, any list source for individualized attention--and then tag such a cell for future capture of source.

DATABASE MANAGEMENT SYSTEM

It is axiomatic that simply creating a database does not launch a company into database *management*. The first step is to create a database management *system*. This involves capturing all desired information on a computer large enough to handle the system needs, organizing that data for use, arranging methodology for updating and maintaining it, and establishing channels to be able to readily retrieve and manipulate the data for marketing use.

Sad but true, this is a very complex, very difficult, very time consuming and very expensive task. It is not for the faint of heart! Data collection involves a need for highly disciplined keying standards, which must incorporate name data, address data, background data, and all interactions between the data and the business.

And, finally, database marketing puts extra emphasis on the back end, on what happens when a phone call comes into the WATS line, what happens when a request comes in for information, what happens when a new order hits the telephone order desk. Everything that has gone before can be reduced to rubble if the fulfillment is not in place to match the marketing.

So database management is more than data on a computer. *It is a system for controlling the manpower to see the system works.* It provides raw data that must be targeted, planned, and created and implemented.

Last, but not least, the fulfillment must match the marketing needs created.

Since direct marketing is becoming more and more a continuous, ongoing process, the database, which links together all of the interrelated factors involving marketing, becomes more and more important in the planning, the execution and the evaluation of marketing.

Database marketing using predictive weighting is long-term, not short-term, in orientation. It makes possible careful targeting of each effort, even one effort piled on another, and it offers a means for measuring results in hard dollars and cents. By quantifying all aspects, both long and short-term, of marketing, it provides a means for building a direct mail and telemarketing business on a solid mathematical base.

One master builder of databases for customers puts it this way:

> *"Knowledge is power--the power to define, the power to identify, the power to predict, the power to sell, the power to fill a need."*

Databases define, identify and provide the facts for realistic prediction and sales. Telemarketers *must*, therefore, understand and apply both database technology and management.

They are essential ingredients of success.

198

CHAPTER 14

Habitat

Gere Picasso
Principal Owner/Partner
Engel Associates
Chatham, New Jersey

The drive to increase worker productivity has a long history. From ancient times to today, managers have been faced with the task of measuring, counting or weighing the value of human output. This task has been complicated in recent times by the emergence of the office as the primary place of work, a development that has created a crisis for many industries.

For example, where traditional sales jobs were done in the field, the change to telemarketing--selling at a desk operating a video display terminal (VDT) and telecommunication equipment--has been traumatic.

According to a recent study by the U.S. Bureau of Labor Statistics, American office workers represent more than 54% of the total work force, and earn wages and benefits that have doubled during the past decade. Office costs have also increased and now account for more than 50% of the annual business expense. These costs are growing at a rate of 12-15% annually.

For telemarketing executives trying to navigate these changes safely, cost of work is just one of the many issues that need to be faced. Telemarketing representatives, too, are concerned about the kinds of places they work in, the nature of their work tasks and their ability to participate in decision-making processes. They are also confronted by increasing amounts of work-related stress that can take its toll on their health and overall productivity. Problems such as illness, absenteeism, burnout and employee turnover have reached to all levels of organizational life.

In telemarketing centers, for example, where computer work applications are common, local governments and Federal agencies are considering legislation to relieve and regulate the impact of machines and offending office environments.

It is inevitable that new management and planning strategies have to emerge to deal with these issues. As the business environment becomes more dynamic, the need to accommodate change will increase as well. The process of planning a telemarketing environment is, however, generally out of the hands of employees who meet and deal with its outcome and to whom the impact is greatest.

This was brought home to me during a recent project, when I had the opportunity to tour a state-of-the-art telemarketing center. No expense was spared in implementing the new technologies, staff selection, training or compensation programs. The employees had the tools and the training to accomplish more work, faster and more efficiently than before, but something went wrong in this center.

Eight weeks after move-in, productivity began to lag, absenteeism increased, complaints of

199

headaches and eye strain were commonplace and there was a lot of talk among the workers about finding other assignments. The center in question was located in a glass-enclosed atrium in a large corporate headquarters. The rationale in locating the center in this space was the need to use all unoccupied space within the building.

This was a cost-saving decision based on the building's efficiency rather than what was appropriate for the telemarketing center or its occupants. Our evaluation of the center clearly showed that some of the problems were caused by the type of work space in which the representatives worked. The first and most remarkable clue to the causes of the problem was the fact that the telemarketing service representatives were *wearing hats on the job*.

In order to reduce the solar glare in their eyes and on the machines, the workers had to cope with the problem in the only way available to them. The hats did not interfere with their ability to see the screen as sunglasses would have. They also used cardboard visors over the terminals as well.

In addition, the hats gave them some personal privacy in their "fish bowl" environment by sheltering them from the people who *looked down on them* from the floors above.

The post-occupancy evaluation (POE) of the center confirmed that not only were there physical (e.g., hat, light and noise) problems with the space, but social or behavioral (e.g., sense of insecurity, lack of group affiliation, low self-esteem) problems as well. The methods that are used by some facilities planners to design space for people leads us to wonder how they establish their priorities.

People are the ultimate answer to increasing performance, but only when all components (management style, people, technology and facilities) function together as a whole, are real gains in worker satisfaction and productivity made.

THE TELEMARKETING CENTER TODAY

Around the world, office space in general is still in many cases the office of yesterday--the creation of the late 19th Century. By 1913, all the principles on which the organization of office space and personnel are now based had been clearly articulated and put into practice.

Factory Design. The planning concepts employed in factory design become the models for these work centers. Offices were created by the development and growth of businesses, which required as many people to process their paperwork as earlier tool-based industries had required to run their machines. With hardly any variation, these same patterns are repeated over and over again in offices today. Each element of the physical design of space, from the building exterior down to the workplaces themselves, are based on principles and methods that are rarely questioned or evaluated.

This *laissez-faire* attitude toward buildings and office space has been manifested in the problems created by a lack of information or data to support change. Until recently, little was documented about the impact of office environments on people or the work process. Technology, telecommunications and telemarketing strategies are changing some of these notions about space and facilities usage.

Current Notions of Design. The manager, in planning a telemarketing work environment has to consider that there are two basic notions by which many facilities planners develop center designs.

One notion is that since work is compartmentalized and people departmentalized, *planning techniques could follow the traditional lines of the organizational chart*:

* *President.*

* *Vice president(s).*

* *Managers.*

* *Supervisors.*

* *Technical/professional workers.*

* *Clerical support.*

As a result, people and desks are distributed either in very quiet, isolated offices or in neat public rows in open spaces. The choice is dictated by the organizational hierarchy.

The second notion is that *buildings are status symbols.* Many buildings bear the stamp either of the organization that gave rise to them, or the architect who created them. Even in leasing building spaces, organizations are looking for sites favorable to the company's image or presence in the marketplace.

I saw an example of this on a recent trip to Australia. While there, I had the chance to visit one of the world's newest architectural masterpieces: the Sydney Opera House. It looks wonderful from the harbor, but, inside, it's another story. Some seats in the house cannot be sold, because their occupants could neither see nor hear the performance. Some of the seats are so high up that the very young and the very old have a hard time getting to them.

There's a fundamental point here that we should always keep in mind: good buildings and office environments should not be judged on the basis of appearance, but on the basis of *what they do to their occupants and the work process.* Cost, profit and status motives for planning and design are, by themselves, inadequate without the consideration of people and what those people are supposed to be doing with the space or building.

In developing the strategies for creation of a telemarketing center, decision-makers should consider not only the cost of the space, but also the effect of space in all its ramifications (technological, physical, social and behavioral).

RESEARCH RELATING TO PHYSICAL ENVIRONMENT

Although the volume of research on the physical environment of telemarketing centers has been relatively small, it has consistently shown that individual attitudes, perceptions and behaviors are directly influenced and guided by the spaces in which people work.

Office Attitude Study. In a study of the attitudes of office workers conducted by Louis Harris (for Steelcase, Inc.), office workers were asked to list elements in their work place which they thought might lead to better job satisfaction and performance. The study was conducted among a national cross-section of 1,047 office workers and managers in major corporations. The answers were a little surprising to the pollsters. An overwhelming 92% of the office workers perceived a *connection between their personal satisfaction with their office surroundings and their job performance.*

Fully 85% of the respondents mentioned good lighting as a factor, and almost that many said a more comfortable chair was important. Heating and air conditioning changes were cited by 70% of the responding workers. About two-thirds mentioned the need for more privacy, and 90% said that they would feel better about their work place if they had been consulted about design elements.

By contrast with the *environmental* factors, only 67% mentioned pay raises as a contributing factor, and 25% even went so far as to say that they would be willing to accept a *lower pay raise in exchange for a better environment.*

Effect on Office Workers. Clearly, this study implies strongly that facilities planning has both a direct and an indirect effect on workers. The physical setting appears to have a *direct* effect on individual task performance and the work process as a whole *when that work environment hinders the successful completion of tasks* (e.g., disruptive noise when a worker is trying to concentrate).

The *indirect* effect works through the environment's impact on such factors as personal control, status and participation, factors perceived by employees as symbolizing individual rank and worth within the organization.

GETTING THE TELEMARKETING CENTER TO WORK

To get the physical plan of a center to work for people, an organization must support a program of research and analysis of the impact of facilities design on users. Further, the organization should involve the people who will be affected by the new space in the planning process. In supporting a program of this nature, companies can achieve the following benefits for the telemarketing center:

* *Increase the opportunities for enhancing job performance and satisfaction.*

* *Control or reduce the costs of facilities changes.*

* *Provide better service to the organization.*

* *Enhance internal management efficiency.*

* *Improve corporate and public image.*

The root of the problem in centers today, as we have seen, is that space is not planned, designed or measured in humanistic terms. Some of the major factors that need to be reconsidered by planners of telemarketing centers are the hazards that exist in many offices today.

Employee Health. As we have evolved from the paper-intensive office environment to the

202

electronic work station, the role of the machine in the work place has become an increasingly significant issue. Today, man/machine environments are being forced to operate in offices and buildings not designed for those functions.

The failure to adjust environments to new office technologies is only one problem, however. Other problems stem from the building systems themselves, which can actually *cause* illness.

Studies have shown that rates of illness are at least twice as high in multiple-floor, air-conditioned office buildings than in naturally ventilated, low-rise facilities. In addition to microbiological contaminants, there are many chemical substances in offices that can cause health problems (e.g., petrochemicals in heating, ventilating and air-conditioning systems; formaldehyde in carpets, screens and office furniture; carcinogens such as tobacco smoke).

Employee Performance. During World War II, human factors engineering became an important consideration in pilot performance. Engineers learned during the war that the design of the work module (in this case, the cockpit of an aircraft) influenced the person's ability to perform a task. This discovery led to widespread changes in industrial design.

In the last decade, human factors criteria have finally worked their way into the office environment. Stimulated by the computer industry, office furniture manufacturers began to consider design changes or new products that could accommodate the human needs arising from adding more machines to the office.

We aren't concerned here solely with the design of lighting systems, work surfaces, chairs and the like. These present important design challenges, to be sure. But other, often more important issues are raised by the need employees have to locate each other and communicate effectively. Designers also have to consider carefully the effects of office layout and signage systems on employee performance.

Even legislators are getting into the act. Once only concerned about the effect of environment on the physically disabled, lawmakers are today considering setting standards for machine-intensive environments. These regulations will have an effect on facilities design.

Employee Rights. According to office folklore, if you ask people what they need, they're sure to ask for what you can't provide. This myth, plus the common assumption that you can't please all the people all of the time, has restricted development of feedback channels on the office environment. People may be unhappy, but we don't ask them--and they don't talk.

Even a cursory glance at many of today's offices, however, will make obvious the potential that exists for improving performance through better facilities design. Today's office standards seem more oriented to making life easier and less complex for managers of the space than for the workers occupying that space. A good example of this misdirection of attention is the common practice of centralizing the control of everything from ambient building conditions to the height of the work surface. Such centralization strips each worker of all but a modest capacity for fine-tuning the environment to the job.

Sharing the responsibility for developing design performance criteria with employees will enable organizations to create high-performance work environments. With employee input, organizations are far more likely to respond properly to individual needs, to change creatively and to instill higher degrees of technology successfully in the work place.

203

A CASE IN POINT

AT&T, with some of its major business customers, undertook a research study of automation and worker performance. Over the last three years, the research looked at the impact that facilities have on worker effectiveness and job satisfaction in telemarketing centers. The findings and conclusions presented here were drawn from a database of 1,590 respondents from a cross-section of 70 companies in seven major industry segments. The participants responded to a questionnaire that surveyed their work climate, job satisfaction, physical environment and level of technology.

One of the study objectives was to determine which job factors most frequently influenced worker satisfaction in these centers. The data was also bundled by industry segment and work center type (e.g., order processing, customer service center), to look at the results more specifically. In each case, the physical environment was shown to be a significant factor (among such other factors as supervision, the work itself, advancement potential, responsibility, other workers, security, company policies and pay) in contributing to job satisfaction.

Data analysis also determined which factors contributed most significantly to environmental satisfaction. Of those surveyed, *91% reported that the physical environment affected their performance*. Half of the respondents reported that their current environment affected them positively, while 41% reported that it had a negative effect. Only 9% of those surveyed felt that their work space had no effect on their attitudes toward their jobs.

Of special concern to many workers participating in this program were several characteristics of an office environment which they cited as important to job satisfaction and performance. Foremost among these were:

* *The need to interact and communicate effectively in the environment.*

* *Air quality and temperature conditions.*

* *A space that allowed people to concentrate without noise and other distrac-tions.*

* *Personal safety.*

* *Personal security.*

* *Work space and equipment that are adjustable by individuals to the job tasks.*

* *Comfort.*

Forty-seven percent of the respondents in one study reported that they had difficulties locating and communicating with peers and supervisors in the office. Thirty-nine percent also said that locating individuals and departments was so difficult that they avoided trying, *even when the work depended on it.*

Participants were also asked how important it was for them to have input into various discussions regarding the design and planning of the work space. They expressed a strong desire for this, especially with respect to their specific work space. Sixty-eight percent considered it important to job satisfaction to participate in decisions and to be allowed some form of self-expression about their work place.

The conflicting messages that are being sent out by organizations to employees who, on one hand, cannot adjust their work space to their job needs and, on the other hand, are told that they are the organization's most valuable resource cannot help but have a negative effect on employee morale. In fact, when poor relationships exist between supervisors and subordinates, subordinates viewed an open office design as a managerial ploy to reduce their personal freedom and control.

Clearly, the mission of the facilities planner should be to achieve the best fit possible between the people and their work place, consistent, of course, with the organization's mission.

TOMORROW'S CENTER TODAY

Combining state-of-the-art office and building technology with humanistic design considerations is the way to begin designing the telemarketing center of the future. But introducing change in an organization is almost always disruptive, time-consuming and costly. Changes in office design can frequently collide with established behavior patterns and the social relationships among employees. Thus, behavioral considerations have to be added to technical and people factors in developing performance criteria for the telemarketing center.

The telemarketing manager should make sure that the planner is aware of the following factors:

* *The changing nature of the organization and its business goals and objectives.*

* *The expanding skills and rising levels of expectations of people working in centers.*

* *Changes and trends in telemarketing technology.*

The planner has a responsibility, in turn, to keep the telemarketing manager informed about changes in office facility design, products and services.

Together, the planner and the manager have a responsibility to ensure that every center design project has measurable performance criteria, goals and objectives. Through programs such as audits, pre/post occupancy evaluations or center performance surveys, they should further collect historical data to help them make better informed decisions about office planning.

In addition to provisions for obtaining the support of top management and allowing for user input and evaluation, environmental planning strategies should include a realistic transition time frame and a program for employee orientation. Built-in design features such as chair adjustability or acoustical control are of little use to the worker who has not been told how to use them.

The focus should be on the specific changes which will yield the greatest degree of user acceptance and productivity improvement.

Such programs can evaluate building performance in terms of people, technology and building systems, and, coupled with management objectives, can support and stimulate productive work while allowing quick, cost-effective response to changing conditions inside the organization.

Keep in mind, too, that planning for a telemarketing center should be a team effort. The team should consist of knowledgeable individuals from management, work groups, architects and other professionals. Technical resource people, both internal and external to the organization, are crucial to a project's success. Their selection should be based on both the content of their knowledge about telemarketing and the process (or style) of their work.

NYNEX Telemarketing Center. We recently completed a project for the NYNEX Information-tion Resources Co., in which we used data gathered from a major research study as a basis for a telemarketing center design. The research indicated that management and design strategies should be focused on the development of work groups and team-building activities as a means of enhancing organizational productivity. The design of individual work stations concentrated on the tasks performed--both manual and automated.

In the meantime, the overall design of the center focused on creating a setting that facilitated group tasks and communication needs. In this task/team approach to design, supervisors and representatives were grouped together in work clusters. These clusters were based on the supervisor/subordinate ratio and management-guided group activities.

Another unique feature of the design was the easy accessibility of workers to break and conference areas within each work cluster arrangement. This allowed workers some "free" space in close proximity to their work station. It also increased the number of informal meeting areas without significantly adding space to the floor plan area.

The design solution for the telemarketing center (**Figure 14-1**) supported NYNEX's concerns about worker motivational issues as well. Specifically, the physical design helped to demonstrate, to the workers and visitors alike, the company's commitment to:

* *Maintaining career opportunities within the center.*

* *Ensuring a cooperative work effort.*

* *Enhancing worker status.*

* *Maintaining excellent working conditions.*

Within each work "cluster," team spirit and worker recognition can be bolstered by management through the use of physical design features and furniture elements. Consequently, management objectives are enhanced by the physical environment. The environment can no longer act as an obstacle to enlightened management.

LOCATING THE CENTER

In selecting a site for the telemarketing center, three points of view should be considered:

* *The concerns of the organization as a whole.*

HABITAT

* *The concerns of the employees.*

* *The concerns of the community.*

These concerns are manifold: financial, social, physical and strategic. They include the corporate image and goals, community relationships, the nature of the local labor market, growth projections for the center, and even the accessibility to such amenities as restaurants and stores for shopping during "off time." Other considerations include the availability of parking and the adequacy of mass transportation.

In planning, the team should consider the average commuting time required, the desirability and/or affordability of adjacent residential areas, distance to the airport, etc. Also important are the advantages and disadvantages of city versus suburban location and, of course, the specific needs of the organization itself.

Too often, the investment in a new telemarketing facility has been viewed simply as an unavoidable overhead expense. Proper planning, however, can turn such an investment into a proposition yielding a handsome return. The following factors should be used in evaluating a facility's potential as a telemarketing center, regardless of the size of the proposed facility:

The Building System. Can the physical requirements of people, notably the disabled, be met? Can the required equipment be accommodated? Does the facility meet personnel environmental needs such as humidity control, heating, ventilating and air conditioning? Can ambient sound (acoustics) be controlled? Is the lighting system adequate? Does it minimize glare? Are all systems efficient?

Architectural/Interior Design Elements. If the facility is open-plan, is the minimum distance between columns 25 feet? Are narrow spaces avoided (to maintain quality of acoustics)? Is there an adequate number of restrooms for men and women? Is there adequate provision for building and parking lot security for centers operating beyond normal working hours and on weekends? Is the finished ceiling height at least 8' 2"? If a raised floor is required for managing wiring and cabling, is there a full 8' of clear ceiling height above the finished raised floor?

Investment in Facility/Furnishings. Specific considerations in this area are unique to the particular facility. But it is worthwhile keeping in mind that, of the total cost of the center operation during its life cycle, approximately 92% of the cost will go for operations, 6% for maintenance and only 2% for the initial investment in the facility and its furnishings. Hence, this is not an area where the benefits of skimping and economizing will outweigh the negative effects of inadequate facilities on operations.

SIZING THE CENTER

The amount of space that will be required for a telemarketing operation depends on several variables, each affected by individual corporate norms and culture. Generally, for initial planning purposes, some minimums have been established which can get the planning ball rolling.

At the outset, a preliminary space occupancy program should be completed with the help of department heads and other key individuals. A good rule of thumb is to allocate a minimum of 100 to 130

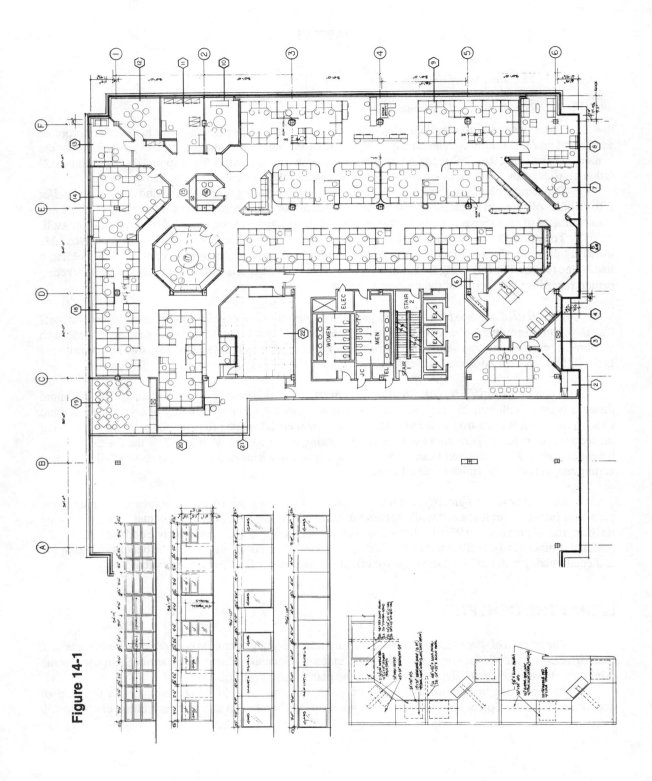

Figure 14-1

Figure 14-1L

NYNEX Telemarketing Center (Plan Legend)

1. **Main Entry.** Angled walls were constructed to focus attention of visitors and employees arriving at the telemarketing center. Signage indicating the company's identification is strategically placed here. This is a key area where people get their first impression of the center.

2. **Employee Training/Conference Area.** This conference area has many functions. It will be used primarily as an orientation/training center for employees and visitors. This dual function is accomplished by the placement of the room off the main entry, as well as by using modular tables that can be easily reconfigured to conform to the room's intended use.

3. **Kitchen/Serving Area.** This area is separated from the Training/Conference room with sliding screens. Its function is to support group breaks or luncheons when called for, or coffee service to waiting visitors.

4. **Main Reception Room.** The seating area, reception desk, art/sculpture display and Japanese "Shoji" screens establish the design theme for visitors, as well as focusing them on corporate image of a high tech company that is concerned about traditional values.

5. **Closet.**

6. **Storage Area & Coat Room.** Promotional material and training support material is stored here.

7. **Personnel Interview and Staff Conference Room.** Non-threatening conference atmosphere for new-employee interviewing, outside of the main work area. Also sound-insulated conference space for staff meetings and personnel discussions.

8. **Employee "Soft" Lounge.** Informal break area for employees with soft seating to encourage one-on-one conversations, studying or reading. The room also has exterior views and medium/low level lighting. This area is intentionally separated from the lunch room with its more noisy atmosphere.

9/18. **Telemarketing Center Work Area.** The concept of "Task/Team Clusters" was developed to support the work of the individual while fostering the attitude of a team effort. Each cluster contains 8-12 (depending on the application) telemarketers' primary places of work, the team supervisor's work space with monitoring equipment, a small, informal conference and break area (*see illustration at the side of the drawing*) and a communication center for group information or motivational messages. Visitors and others can see the work occurring in each cluster without disturbing the employees. Beyond creating a sense of group effort, these clusters also help to delineate the work itself and employee career paths within the center.

10. **Management/Application Planning Office.** Variable-use office for application work-planning, scripting conferences and visiting company management.

11. **Administrative Support Area.** Clerical support area with copy, central file facsimile transmission, word processing and supply/storage facilities.

12. **Management Conference Room.** Private conference room with sound-isolation for higher privacy needs. Can be used by supervisors and by the center's management.

13. **Center Manager's Office.** Both formal desk and informal "soft" seating areas furnish the manager's office. This office is centrally located, but out of the mainstream of agent activity.

14. **Telemarketer Training Room.** Free-standing furniture allows this room to be rearranged to fit a variety of applications. Set-ups match the different cluster work stations for hands-on training. Also serves as an overflow work area for the center during periods of high activity or peak-load emergencies.

15. **Refreshment Station.** Situated adjacent to windowed training room for both employee orientation and control, this coffee area is also adjacent to the visitor/customer areas for easy access.

16. **Monitoring Room & Report Area.** The policies of many telemarketing centers to use straightforward monitoring practices is supported by this design solution. The room is strategically placed in the general office area. It is in the center of the main circulation aisle, in a glass-enclosed environment. This provides employees with visual and spatial clues to the candid "open" nature of the company's monitoring policy.

17. **Customer Presentation Center.** Main customer presentation, observation and closing room. This puts customers inside the space, surrounded by the center. This was done to encourage the concept that the workspace belongs to the employees. Some companies that also use a center to "sell" telemarketing mistakenly create a back-office effect, which also diminishes the importance of the telemarketing representative. Glass walls, fitted with electric blinds, allow the company to program viewing of three different application areas, training room and computer/communications room. Electronic support includes active and slave monitors, ACD telephone connections, hard-copy printers and both slide and VCR presentations. Central conference table and ring counter allow for a wide variety of customer/company focusing.

19. **Lunch Room.** "Hard" break area -- with tables and chairs for employees. Fitted with refrigerator, microwave oven, sink, several vending machines and quality exterior views.

20/21. **Fulfillment Area.** Paper handling of telemarketing applications (direct mail, coupon receipts, orders and correspondence) are handled in this area with direct access to the building corridor for delivery and receipt. The space is outfitted with high-speed printers, mail counters, supplies storage and sorting areas.

22. **Computer/Communications Room.** Combined facility with raised access floor. Halon fire suppression, separate air conditioning and uninterrupted power supply (UPS) systems. Controlled access. Window visibility for MIS manager from outside.

NOTE: Room numbers referred to on this page are contained within octagonals on the print (Figure 14-1).

square feet for each person who will be located in the center.

During the programming phase of the project, requirements for space allocation will be refined to determine more specific facilities specifications. These refinements will take into consideration such common or group facilities such as lounges, a cafeteria, conference rooms, monitoring and training facilities, mail and fulfillment rooms, copy and coffee centers, shared storage areas, as well as reference/information areas, individual work spaces and circulation factors.

THE BUILDING ENVIRONMENT

Lighting. Proper lighting is a balance of quantity, type, source and balance, and depends upon a variety of factors including:

* *Use and type of video display terminals.*

* *Written reference materials and reading tasks required.*

* *Writing or typing requirements.*

* *Anticipated color/texture/reflectivity of furniture and equipment.*

* *Objective "mood" of the center.*

A lighting plan should combine these requirements into a system that is functional and efficient. Functionality in a telemarketing center is the ability to help people do their jobs while maintaining a sense of physical well-being. In short, the lighting system should provide a comfortable, pleasant, reassuring, interesting and functional space for the people who work in the center, in the most cost-effective way possible. Lighting level codes should, of course, be considered, but they should be used mainly as guides.

Lighting in telemarketing centers (and offices in general) has undergone a number of changes over the past few years. During the late 1970's, when energy costs were soaring, conservation programs began to reduce the amount of lighting used in offices. These lower levels (70-80 footcandles) have been further reduced by the influx of video display terminals in the agent or representative areas. Automated telemarketing centers, which depend heavily on VDT's, are experiencing new concerns about existing lighting systems because screen glare and contrast problems can cause eye strain and other ailments.

Avoidance of these problems often involves special kinds of lighting equipment--ambient fixtures with parabolic lenses or indirect lighting systems--located strategically throughout the work environment. Generally, the old practice of having uniformly bright light everywhere simply will not work well in an automated telemarketing center.

Heating, Ventilation and Air Conditioning. The HVAC plan for the telemarketing center should be an integrated system (i.e., automated heating/cooling as required, plus continual ventilation appropriate to staffing levels). Special consideration should be given to the following factors in planning:

* *Hours of operation ("normal" building hours or longer as required).*

210

* *Duration of each shift (exposure of any single employee).*

* *Heat sources (equipment, solar, lighting, occupants, etc.).*

* *Allowable noise (frequencies and intensities).*

* *Allowable static discharge levels (terminals, printers, etc.).*

* *Particular requirements for meetings, smokers, etc.*

* *Requirements of regulatory agencies or union contracts.*

Consideration of these and other related factors will help to ensure that all occupants will be free from drafts, cold surfaces and odors. Proper warmth and humidity ensures comfort and aids productivity, particularly for the sedentary individual.

The American Society of Heating, Refrigeration and Air Conditioning Engineers (ASHRAE) has set standards for environmental comfort and energy conservation. The fundamental "comfort zones" recommended by ASHRAE are as follows:

* *Temperature:*   *68-78 degrees F.*

* *Humidity:*   *20%-60% RH (Relative Humidity)*

* *Air Flow:*   *0.15 cfm/ft² (cubic feet per minute per square foot)*

* *Air Velocity:*   *70 fpm (feet per minute)*

However, these criteria do not take into consideration the general physical activity levels of space occupants, the amount and type of office equipment, or general design of the building structure. This information should be provided by a specialist in the field.

Consideration should also be given in design to ensuring flexibility in the system for future changes or growth--particularly if changes in occupant density or equipment usage are projected as part of the long-term expansion/development plan.

It is also important to pay careful attention to the maintenance of the system once the center is occupied. Regular programs for cleaning and air filter changes are important in the upkeep of these systems. A well-designed system, for example, with dirty filters cannot perform the function for which it was intended.

SPECIAL CONSIDERATIONS

Cigarette Smoking. In recent years, several states have enacted legislation regulating environmental quality. Organizations in these states are required to provide smoke-free work space for non-smoking employees, a trend that appears to be gaining momentum throughout the country. The provision of non-smoking areas which resist infiltration by cigarette smoke is a function primarily of the HVAC system's design and implementation. This problem should be considered early in the design process, particularly since many modern buildings have been designed primarily for energy efficiency, which usually makes smoke isolation provisions very costly.

Equipment/Automation. One of the benefits of automation is the increased computer processing power available at the personal work station level. A drawback of all this new-found power, however, is the increased amount of heat, noise and dust dumped into the environment.

Printers and other paper processors generate large volumes of paper dust, which can be a severe irritant to humans. Personal computers and other office equipment release heat into the space, often directly into confined work station areas. With the advent of acoustically resistant panels separating work areas, this heat and dust is trapped in the worker's area, causing significant deterioration in the environment.

It is, therefore, important to consider all potential heat, noise and dust sources and identify these to the HVAC engineer, so that each can be considered in the overall design. It is important, too, to consider potential extensions, enhancements, growth and change in equipment over the anticipated life of the facility. Once a system is in place, it can be extremely disruptive and expensive to modify.

Acoustics. The acoustic system for a telemarketing center should provide normal "speech privacy." This will enable the average person to escape from the intrusive nature of conversations or equipment in adjoining work stations (telephone or person-to-person). This requirement will place extra demands on the facility as well as on the furnishings used in the space, and must be carefully planned.

Speech privacy criteria must be established early in the planning process. Most experts in the field propose that to achieve this degree of privacy, the listener should not be able to overhear more than 20% of a conversation from approximately 10 feet away.

Some sound-absorbing ceiling, carpeting, acoustical partitions and (potentially) a sound-masking system are required to achieve this degree of privacy. There should also be some policy within the telemarketing organization controlling impromptu meetings in aisleways.

WORK PLACE DESIGN

Sizing the Individual Work Space. The general concept of appropriate space for a particular work area within the telemarketing center must be derived from a clear image of:

* *Worker tasks.*

* *Attitudes and behaviors management wants to encourage.*

* *Work styles of the people who will be using the facility.*

* *Image, identity, strategic positioning and other corporate objectives for the facility that may be demonstrated through physical work space design.*

These factors can be used to design the individual work places or for shared group areas. For example, the size and amount of desktop office equipment in part determines the size of the work surface and the number of people/shifts and their duration help to determine their allocation for lunch and/or break areas.

Establishing the size of the center as a whole is a tricky task for planners because improper sizing or arrangement can create hidden costs in the future. For example, in some centers, employees report that they sometimes avoid contact with others upon whom their work depends (supervisors and coworkers) if it is difficult to locate them quickly.

Specific Determinants. The determination of how much and what kinds of space need to be built (or created with furniture components) within the center requires an analysis of the following factors:

* *Size and configuration of the total space available for use.*

* *Size of individual work spaces and their relationships.*

* *The quantity, size and type of private spaces (floor-to-ceiling walls with doors) versus open-area common areas.*

* *Objective density of the facility.*

* *Required circulation space (aisles, corridors, hallways, etc.).*

* *Regulatory code requirements.*

* *Short and long-term planning considerations.*

* *Other related factors.*

Many centers use a lot of open-plan furniture (panels and components) to configure the space as opposed to constructed-in-place partitions (gypsum drywall or other material). This is primarily due to the flexibility provided by open-plan furniture.

The chart and questionnaire that follow will help define more specific information about the nature of the work task and required space. Note that these forms are meant as guidelines only, and in no way should they be used to replace the analytical and programming processes.

ERGONOMIC FURNITURE SYSTEMS AND EQUIPMENT

Telemarketing application workers, whose duties require them to spend the largest portion of their workday seated at a desk and terminal, require furniture and equipment that are ergonomically designed. This means that the products people use, the way they use them and the places where they are used should be safe, comfortable and physically easy to operate and/or adjust.

For most telemarketers, the products that will frequently influence their ability to perform their jobs are primarily their work surface (desk or work counter), their chair and their terminal (if any).

It's important to recognize those characteristics which enhance or inhibit productivity and working

Figure 14-2
Facility Strategic Planning
for
Telemarketing Centers

Application	Work Task							Minimum Required Square Feet
	Telephone	VDT	Reading or Writing	Collating or Filing	Planning	Meetings	Interactive Job Function	
ORDER ENTRY	●	●						25 to 30
CUSTOMER SERVICE	●	●	●	●				30 to 60
SALES SUPPORT	●	●		●	●	●	●	60 to 80
ACCOUNT MANAGEMENT	●	●	●	●	●		●	80 to 100

Legend: 75% and over · 50% · 25% · 10% and under

HABITAT

Figure 14-3
Sample Employee Data Questionnaire

Please complete the following information. It will be used to determine your workspace needs. If you have any questions, please call the facility planning representative at _____.	Name _____ Building _____ Room _____ Phone _____ Job Level _____ Supervisor _____ Dept. _____ Responsibility Code _____

Summary of Job Responsibilities

_____
_____
_____

Communication

List the individuals in your department that you communicate with most often. Include how often, how long and by what means.

Person contacted	Frequency	Duration	Means

Conferences

At a conference location:

How many conferences do you attend per week? _____

What is the average number of people? _____

What is the average length of time? _____

At your work station:

Do you have conferences in your work station (yes or no)? _____

If so, what is the average number of people involved? _____

How many confidential conversations do you have per day? _____

How often in a day will a co-worker(s) be in your work station? _____

What is the average length of time of such visits? _____

Travel

How many hours during an average work week to you occupy your work station? _____

Office Equipment

Do you have a typewriter? _____

Do you have a CRT or other terminal at your work station? _____

Do you have your own assigned telephone? _____

What is the total time you spend on your telephone each day? _____

Do you have any special equipment that requires floorspace? _____

Do you share any equipment with your co-workers? _____

Do you use a calculator? _____

How many times a day do you use a copy machine? _____

How many times a day do you use a central reproduction facility? _____

Are you right or left handed? ( ) right ( ) left

List the product names and model numbers of your equipment:

_____
_____
_____

215

Figure 14-3
Sample Employee Data Questionnaire (Continued)

During an average work week, you spend how many:

Hours reading, writing or dictating (total)? _____

Hours attending scheduled/unscheduled meetings? _____

Hours using a computer, CRT or other terminal? _____

Hours filing, collating, copying papers (total)? _____

Work surfaces

How many work surfaces? _____

What is the size of each work surface? _____

How much time do you spend on a typical day:

At your work space alone? _____

At your work space with someone? _____

At special task areas (copy room, library)? _____

In aisles, lunchroom, lounges? _____

Do you have any medical problems or handicaps we should be aware of?

Filing and Storage

How many files do you have in your work area? _____

How many linear feet of filing do you require? _____

What percentage of these files are referred to at least once per week? _____

How many linear feet of book storage do you require? _____

What percentage of these books are referred to at least once per week? _____

Do you store the following forms (yes or no)?

    Stationary _____

    Slides _____

    Other _____

Do you share working files with another member of your department? _____

Explain storage requirements unique to your work station and not included above

    (e.g., computer printouts). _____

_____

Display

Are you required to display maps, charts, memos, etc.? _____

Do you require a drafting board? _____

What is the largest standard sheet size used (in inches)? _____

Is a reference table required? _____

Comments

What do you think about your work area? _____

_____

_____

What do you like the least about your work area? _____

_____

_____

Please feel free to attach any additional comments. Thank you for your cooperation.

conditions when considering what products to select for furnishing a center.

Work Surfaces. Traditional desks in many centers are obsolete because of their inability to be adjusted to meet changing tasks and equipment needs. The following is a checklist of worksurface characteristics which influence functionality and appropriateness:

1) *Size.* The size of the work surface is dependent on the types of tasks that agents will be required to perform. On average, reading and writing tasks require a minimum of 36 inches in width and 20 inches in depth. Although VDT's come in many sizes and shapes, usually most can be accommodated in an area 30 inches wide by 26 inches deep. Personal computers, which are located on a work surface, will usually require not more than space suggested for a VDT. However, the disk drives may require additional space. While many VDT's and PC's are smaller than the area indicated above, due to the heat-release factor and the need to accommodate the terminal (or PC), plus accessories and paper, the areas suggested are a minimum.

2) *Adjustability.* The traditional writing and reading height of a work surface was 30 to 31 inches before the advent of ergonomic designs. Desks of more recent vintage and component work surfaces are usually 28 to 29 inches above the floor. This height is acceptable for these tasks. However, a computer terminal or personal computer will require special consideration.

    The keyboard, in particular, should be two inches below the level of the terminal screen base. The work surface should be split into two levels--the main surface supporting the VDT or PC, and the secondary surface to hold the keyboard at the lower level.

    PC's that contain disk drives as part of the component system may be four to eight inches higher (to the center of the screen) than an equivalent size VDT, and require additional consideration for space. The terminal support surface should have the ability to be lowered so that the screen center can be maintained at the proper level of comfort. It is vital to good design and productivity that the individual be able to control these factors.

    To solve the keyboard height problem with existing furniture, many manufacturers offer an option of a keyboard shelf or drawer that slides or rotates under the primary work surface. Care should be taken in specifying these products, since the resulting leg room can be reduced below the minimum necessary for individual comfort.

    In shift operations, adjustability is a very important factor as the work surface not only supports a variety of tasks, but is complicated by the need to fit a

217

variety of potential users. In this type of condition, it is critical that adjustments to the work surface(s) be made simply and conveniently by the workers.

There should be sufficient room on the work surface to allow the individual to move the equipment to conform to particular work habits (e.g., right or left-handedness) or environmental conditions (e.g., glare).

3) *Sturdiness.* Work surfaces that support computer equipment should be able to withstand approximately 600 pounds of pressure and have a minimum thickness of 1.5 inches. Designers and specifiers should consider both the weight of any potential equipment, paper, reference manuals, books, etc., as well as the potential for an individual to sit on the surface. Further, consideration of the transmission of typing vibrations from one worksurface to another is quite important. Care should also be taken to ensure that these surfaces are free from sharp edges, protruding connectors, screws or other structural elements.

Seating. For workers in a telemarketing environment, *the chair is the single most important piece of office furniture.* An attractive, well-designed center does not compensate the worker for an uncomfortable, non-supporting chair. The two characteristics that managers should look for in selecting seating for their centers are *proper back support* and *adjustability.* These are best tested by a variety of people who work in the center before making a final selection.

1) *Back Support.* The chair in which the telemarketing representative sits should support the lumbar (lower) region of the back. The chair back should allow, at minimum, for vertical adjustability of 4 - 10 inches. The chair should be equipped with a tilt capability and a locking mechanism so that the back rest (and seat) can be firmly fixed in place when needed. The back rest should be contoured to the shape of the back. The chair seat itself should be large enough to allow the person to shift seated position and to support the leg area. The chair should also swivel and be equipped with wheels or casters (depending on the floor covering). The base of the chair should have five supports rather than four (typical for older chairs), since the highest number increases stability and resists overturning better. Lastly, the base of the chair should not be smaller in diameter than the seat, since a smaller base requires additional torsional exertion to move the chair within the work station.

2) *Adjustability.* The most important criterion in chair adjustability is the convenience and ease of the adjustment. Workers should be able to make most adjustments *while in a seated position.* It should be noted, however, that providing chairs with these adjustments without an employee orientation

218

and training program that tells workers how to make the adjustments is of little benefit.

Initial training should be followed up periodically with reminders and demonstrations so that workers are reinforced in their ability to make adjustments to the environment to meet their work needs. In shift operations or in companies where workspaces are not permanently assigned to individuals it is very important to provide chairs with pneumatic (gas) lifts, which allow the person to simply depress a button or handle and raise or lower the seat instantly. The alternative to such a lift mechanism is a screw-thread device, which usually requires the person to turn the chair over and manually crank or spin the base. Our research shows that if people are required to exert this much effort to make the chair fit their size or activity, the adjustments are almost never made and, consequently, the person endures the discomfort (with its attendant productivity and attitude deterioration) rather than making the adjustment each shift.

Terminals. In 1984, the National Institute of Occupational Safety and Health (NIOSH) found that people doing jobs such as data entry could be more productive when the terminal was ergonomically designed. In selecting these pieces of equipment, it is, therefore, important to look for specific characteristics when selecting hardware.

Screen displays are generally a matter of user preference. However, specialists recommend that the darker the background, the more the user will be subjected to glare. Multicolored and amber colored screens are considered most preferable. The screen itself should have a matte finish glass (nonreflective, dull), or be retrofitted with a surface filter to cut the surface reflectivity. These are readily available from both computer hardware vendors or computer supplies vendors. To assist in the reduction of phosphorescent halos around alpha-numeric characters, polarizing filters are recommended as an applied material. These are available from similar sources, and can be attached either permanently or temporarily to the screen.

The screen should have the ability to be tilted and rotated easily, so that the user may change the viewing angle up or down by about 20 degrees.

The keyboard should be independent of the terminal so it can be positioned in the most comfortable arrangement by the user. If tasks such as numeric input are an integral part of the job, a numeric keypad, preferably separated from the keyboard, is a good feature. In addition, major function keys such as "insert," "cancel" and "execute" should be highlighted, either with color or lights.

Sources of glare on VDT's can be controlled by the proper relative placement of the terminal in the workplace. If possible, *the terminals should be placed parallel to any windows (rather than perpendicular to them) as well as parallel to and between lighting fixtures* (See **Figure 14-4**).

Routine Breaks. According to NIOSH guidelines, continuous work with VDT's should be interrupted periodically with rest breaks or other work activities that do not produce unusual fatigue or muscular tension. At a minimum, it is suggested that a break should be given to telemarketers after two hours of continuous VDT work. However, breaks should be more frequent as visual, muscular and mental burdens

219

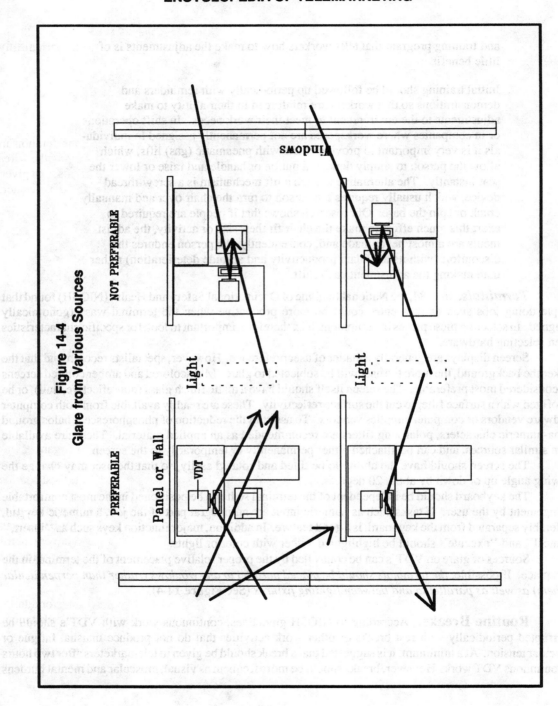

Figure 14-4
Glare from Various Sources

increase. It is also a good idea to have worker's vision checked before beginning VDT work, and periodically thereafter, to ensure that they have adequately corrected vision to handle the job tasks.

OTHER FACILITIES CONSIDERATIONS

Cabling. Telephone, electrical and terminal cabling distribution is a major consideration in bringing a new or retro-fit telemarketing center on-line. There are many alternatives in managing the wires that are the nerve center of the telecommunications, data and power systems. Consideration must be given not only to these alternatives, but to future costs as they affect the growth and long-term viability of the center. The following alternatives should be evaluated by the planning team:

* *Building under-floor wiring systems (in-slab troughs or ducts).*

* *Suspended ceilings with wiring drops to each work station (power poles).*

* *Below-floor wiring runs, with slab penetrations as required.*

* *Raised flooring systems (computer-room type pedestal floors).*

* *Flat wiring, under-carpet systems.*

* *Furniture system wireways combined with either power poles or core drilling.*

* *Pre-wired furniture systems coupled with wireways for communication and data cabling.*

Special Space Needs. If the telemarketing center is not co-located with other organization-owned or leased space, provisions may be required for building service areas such as storage rooms, janitor closets, mechanical equipment (HVAC) and electrical equipment rooms, telephone closets, food service areas and other related backup support spaces.

Special rooms that are required for the center itself may include monitoring rooms, report printing areas, call processing equipment spaces, on-site computer areas and mail processing areas (for both direct mail co-applications, as well as administrative mail). These should be located where they are convenient for access, but at sufficient distance from the telemarketing work areas so as not to interfere with the representative's primary tasks.

Administrative and Clerical Support Areas. The work areas and workstations for administrative and support personnel functions should also be designed for their specific jobs. These workstations should be designed in an integrated fashion with the balance of the center.

They should be separated from the main agent/representative work area. Administrative functions tend to generate a significant amount of noise from equipment such as copiers and printers, as well as conversations and conferences. This noise can distract or interrupt the telemarketing personnel in their general work area.

Lounges. Every center should have an area where people can get away from their primary place of work. As mentioned before, informal break spaces can be designed into the agent group task areas where it is possible to assemble representatives when sudden volume surges or emergencies occur. This does not, however, preclude the need for separate "break-away" space where people can separate themselves from the high-stress work process while on their own time.

Figure 14-5
Furniture Budgets

Application	Basic Workstation	Seating
Order entry	$3K - $5K	$600 - $800
Customer service	$5K - $7K	$600 - $800
Sales support	$8K - $10K	$600 - $800
Account management	$10K - $12K	$600 - $800

List Prices in U.S. dollars. Based upon 1988 published list prices for medium-grade furniture products. *The prices do not reflect negotiated discounts, taxes, delivery or installation costs.* Discounts can average between 40% to 70%, depending upon the size of the order.

The lounge areas should represent approximately 7-10% of the total usable space within the center. The lounge should offer beverages and snacks, as well as a small refrigerator, microwave oven and sink if there is no building cafeteria or if breaks are limited. The furniture should be durable and relatively portable so that people can create their own groupings within the space.

For those centers where shifts are greater than four or five hours in length, and where personnel are provided a formal meal break, consideration should be given to a small recreational area such as a TV space or table game (cards, checkers, chess, etc.) area. Small concessions to employee morale can go a long way toward maintaining and even restoring worker enthusiasm for their jobs.

Figure 14-5 is a guide to developing furniture budgets for telemarketing centers of various types.

MOVE-IN AND POST-CENTER DESIGN EVALUATION

The move into a new center should be conducted as a part of the planning process. This will ensure a smooth transition for telemarketing representatives and minimize the stress associated with the change. A

222

pre-move meeting informing everyone of what to expect in the new space is vital. Documents that inform workers about adjusting their personal space, as well as any guidelines on how the facility will be managed (e.g., smoking/non-smoking areas) should be discussed at this time. The planning team should conduct a detailed pre-move evaluation to avoid any last-minute delays caused by the improper arrangement of workplaces or equipment malfunction.

Once the move is completed, the planning team should be expected to provide the center manager with a detailed punch-list of open items to be completed or replaced. This evaluation will also involve the various specialists who should measure and adjust the lighting, HVAC, acoustic, power, communications and data/automation systems to ensure that they are performing as planned.

User evaluation usually occurs after everyone has had time to settle into their workplaces and into the overall facility in general. About six weeks after move-in has been completed, an employee attitude survey should be conducted by interview and/or questionnaire. The objective should be to gather user opinions on all aspects of the environment, including:

* *Workplace size and layout.*

* *Communications and information access.*

* *Comfort.*

* *Furniture and equipment design.*

* *Technology assessment.*

* *Work climate study.*

The survey should not ask just close-ended questions, but should allow for a range of responses. Depending on the nature of the questions, confidentiality may also be important. The survey, once completed, should assist the manager in identifying worker concerns and/or provide a guideline for future fine-tuning of the environment, future change or center enlargement.

CONCLUSIONS

I have found that there is no single "best" design for a telemarketing center. What is appropriate depends on the marketing strategy, the mix of people, the tasks being done and the resources available.

Many companies want to "pilot" or try out the concept of telemarketing before they allocate major resources to centers. In some instances, however, *this attitude of "making do" with what is available can effectively sabotage the telemarketing pilot effort from the outset.*

I have tried consistently in my work to have a positive influence on telemarketing center design thinking. The major objective is to have a positive impact on the prospects of telemarketing success, and the morale and working conditions of telemarketing workers.

Workplace design *does* make a difference, and every organization intending to start or upgrade a telemarketing center needs to keep this fact in the forefront of the planning process.

CHAPTER 15

Reporting Systems

William P. Fawns
Vice President, Information Systems
Zacson Corporation
Pleasanton, California

This chapter will provide information system suggestions, guidelines and actual samples of the reports necessary for managing a telemarketing operation.

The information is applicable to all types of telemarketing operations such as the following:

* *In-house.*

* *Off site.*

* *Inbound only.*

* *Outbound only.*

* *Combination of inbound and outbound.*

Various management reports will be explored and explained. They will deal with:

* *Profitability.*

* *Payroll.*

* *Accounts receivable.*

* *Telecommunications.*

Remote office management will also be addressed by campaign and employee.

MANAGEMENT REPORTS

Profitability. To determine and maintain a constant knowledge of company profitability, it is necessary to track activity for all work locations. Of course, if there is only one location, this matter is automatically simplified. However, straightforward tracking of the profitability of multiple work locations

224

is possible, and the design of such a system can be simplified by developing it one step at a time.

Among the items to be considered is the *total hour capability* of a particular office. This will depend on the following:

* *Time zone of office.*

* *Time zone of all lists.*

* *Percent of employee coverage.*

* *Pricing for each campaign hour or unit of production.*

* *Fixed and variable costs.*

All other tracking can be combined to provide the data necessary to develop a summary report, which may be divided by:

* *Office.*

* *Business or residential.*

* *Telemarketing/other applications.*

* *Expenses for each office.*

Once this summary report is developed and refined to reflect all costs and revenue, monthly updates can and should include cumulative information for the fiscal year of the company or organization.

This *Profitability Report* will encompass all phases of company business and cannot be put into place until all other management systems are developed. It must reflect all overhead costs, including those attributable to headquarters, including marketing expenses.

Profitability Report examples include two *Company Summary Reports* (**Figures 15-1 and 15-2**).

Payroll. A definitive *Payroll Report* is one of the most critical for a company. At a glance, it should provide the organization's executives with the following information:

* *Fixed payroll costs including salaries and hourly wages.*

* *Variable payroll costs, including all commissions, bonuses and other incentives.*

* *An average payroll cost by office as well as by employee.*

This report can be very simple or can be designed to include several ''nice to know'' items, such as the average payroll cost by type of telemarketing or support application. For the purposes of corporate headquarters, this report need not be so detailed as to include each employee by name and/or employee number. However, support documentation will be necessary for each work location and, for that documentation, these individual statistics will be necessary.

Figure 15-1
Company Summary Report I

MANAGEMENT REPORT -- OUTBOUND ANALYSIS
PROGRAMS USED ON FEB 16 1988

PROGRAM	TOTAL	*** DAY ***		***EVENING***		**RC: YES**		****REVENUE***		***PAYROLL***		**PHONE COST**	
CODE	HOURS	% TOT HOURS	HOURS	% TOT HOURS	HOURS	# OF YES	HRLY AVG	REVENUE EARNED	REV/ HOUR	TOTAL PAYROLL	% OF REV.	EST. COST	% OF REV
COMPANY TOTAL:	XXX.XX	XX.X	XX.XX	XX.X	XXX.XX	XXX	XX.X	$XX,XXX.XX	$XX.X	$X,XXX.XX	XX.X	$.XX	.X

REPORTING SYSTEMS

Figure 15-2
Company Summary Report II

MANAGEMENT REPORT -- OUTBOUND PROGRAM ANALYSIS
PROGRAMS USED ON FEB 16 1988

RUN DATE: 02/18/88
RUN TIME: 12:38:48

===

	HOURS	% OF TELEMARKETER	PAY	% OF REVENUE
OUTBOUND TELEMARKETER	XXXX	XXXXX	XXXXX	XXXX
INBOUND TELEMARKETER	XXXX	XXXXX	XXXXX	XXXX
BILLABLE CLERICAL	XXXX	XXXXX	XXXXX	XXXX
GENERAL CLERICAL	XXXX	XXXXX	XXXXX	XXXX
SUPV. & MANAGEMENT	XXXX	XXXXX	XXXXX	XXXX
BILLABLE TRAINING	XXXX	XXXXX	XXXXX	XXXX
NON-BILLABLE	XXXX	XXXXX	XXXXX	XXXX
OTHER	XXXX	XXXXX	XXXXX	XXXX
TOTALS	XXXX		XXXXX	

===

AVERAGE TELEMARKETER PAY	XXXXX	
AVERAGE TELEMARKETER PAY (W/OVERHEAD)	XXXXX	
TOTAL REVENUE	XXXXX	
TOTAL BILLABLE PAYROLL	XXXXX	
BILLABLE PAYROLL AS A % OF REVENUE	XXXXX	
TOTAL NON BILLABLE PAYROLL		XXXXX
NON-BILLABLE PAYROLL AS A % OF REVENUE	XXXXX	
NON-BILLABLE PAYROLL AS A % OF REVENUE	XXXXX	
TOTAL PAYROLL AS A % OF REVENUE	XXXXX	
TOTAL OVERHEAD HOURS	XXXXX	
TOTAL PRODUCTION & TRAINING HOURS	XXXXX	
OVERHEAD TO PRODUCTION / TRAINING RATIO	XXXXX	

An *Employee Hours & Payroll Report* has been included as an example (**Figure 15-3**).

Accounts Receivable. A report detailing client billing or accounts receivable is mandatory for almost every telemarketing operation. An *Accounts Receivable Report*, however simple, will provide executives with crucial information regarding the growth areas of the company or organization. It should include all billing information by campaign, such as:

* Telemarketing time and rate--hourly or by unit.

* Support time and rate--including standard clerical and administrative work as well as data entry, training and creative work.

* Miscellaneous fees for list procurement, telephone number look-up, printing and postage or other forms of delivery (including fax and data transmission).

For telemarketing operations that are only partially automated or totally manual, it is critical to develop a standard method of capturing all billable work done on behalf of a client. This includes all creative or program design done by employees (salespeople) who usually don't fulfill this function.

Another area that easily "falls through the cracks" is the fee for some types of delivery such as fax, data transmission or standard postage. In a partially automated or completely manual operation, this sort of tracking can be accomplished through diligent daily logging of these various activities.

An example *Accounts Receivable Detail Aging Report* is included (**Figure 15-4**).

Telecommunications. In any type of telemarketing application, one of the most important items to keep control of is telecommunications. After all, *people and phones are the two major costs in this profession.* A *Telecommunications Report* should reflect both inbound and outbound WATS lines, as well as local and data lines. It should also take into account equipment and any nonrecurring charges such as installation (although this is not frequent, and may be reflected in a supplemental report as warranted).

For all outbound calling, the following information should be tracked closely:

* Number of calls by destination area code and exchange.

* Length of calls by destination area code and exchange.

* Trunk carrier utilization.

* Least-cost routing and overflow.

When a switch (computer) is used, the utilization reports for this information are tracked automatically and can provide the telecommunications coordinator with daily updates. The importance of this information cannot be overstated, because it gives up-to-the-minute statistics for decisions crucial to profitability and/or efficiency.

For example, the least expensive carrier can easily be determined quickly to adjust trunk carriers

REPORTING SYSTEMS

Figure 15-3
Employee Hours & Payroll Report
02/01/88 TO 02/15/88

RUN DATE:
02/18/88

EMPLOYEE NUMBER: XXXXX   NAME: XXXX

===

DATE	START TIME	STOP TIME	HOURS	PAY CODE	PROGRAM CODE	DEPT #	PAY
02/01/88	XXXX	XXXX	XXX	X	XXXX	XXX	XXX
02/01/88	XXXX	XXXX	XXX	X	XXXX	XXX	XXX
02/01/88	XXXX	XXXX	XXX	X	XXXX	XXX	XXX
DATE TOTAL:			XXX				XXX
02/02/88	XXXX	XXXX	XXX	X	XXXX	XXX	XXX
02/02/88	XXXX	XXXX	XXX	X	XXXX	XXX	XXX
02/02/88	XXXX	XXXX	XXX	X	XXXX	XXX	XXX
DATE TOTAL:			XXX				XXX

229

Figure 15-4
Accounts Receivable
Detail Aging Report

```
DATE: 02/17/88   TIME: 14:45:35

Aged as of 02/17/88 - Includes items past aging date          Cut-off balance due: "All"
Customer range: "First" to "Last"                             Cut-off aging period: CURRENT

Document types:   I = Invoice   P = Payment   C = Cr Memo   D = Dr Memo   B = Balance forward   F = Finance charge
Notes:  Types I, B and f are aged by their due date.  Types P, C and D are aged by due date of the document to which they apply.
        On types I, B, and C and D, Amount-1 is the amount subject to discount.  On type P Amount-1 is cash receipt amt.
        On type F amount-1 is fin charge amt.  On types I, c and D, Amount-2 is the amount not subject to discount.
        On type P Amount-2 is discount plus allowance.  (No Amount-2 for types F & B).
----------------------------------------------------------------------------------------------------------------------------

XXXX  XXXXXXX          OPN-ITM      NET 30 INV DATE                                            XXX       XXX       XXX
                                                             *UNLTD CR*         XXX     XX.XX    XXX     0%        0%        0%
                                                                               29%     71%

DOC-#   DOC-DATE   TYP  APPLY-TO   DUE-DATE   P.O.-#          Amount-1        Amount-2       Doc-balance            Age Reference
XXXX    XX/XX/XX    X    XXX       XX/XX/XX                   XX.XX           XX.XX          XX.XX                  XX
XXXX    XX/XX/XX    X    XXX       XX/XX/XX                   XX.XX           XX.XX          XX.XX                  XX  From O/E Order:XXXX

XXXX  XXXXXXXX         OPN-ITM      NET 30 INV DATE                                            .XX       XXX       XX
                                                             *UNLTD CR*         XXX     XX.XX    0%      0%        0%
                                                                               100%

DOC-#   DOC-DATE   TYP  APPLY-TO   DUE-DATE   P.O.-#          Amount-1        Amount-2       Doc-balance            Age Reference
XXXX    XX/XX/XX    X    XXX       XX/XX/XX                   .XX             XX.XX          XX.XX                  12-From O/E order:XXX
```

selected as warranted. Often, particularly in small or in-house operations, this area is not managed properly, causing losses that are preventable.

In an inbound telemarketing operation, abandoned calls can be tracked, assisting in the determination of the number of lines needed and/or employee coverage required. This area alone can mean profit or loss for an inbound operation. Missed or abandoned calls mean unhappy clients, a consequent loss of business and, possibly, the eventual loss of a program for the telemarketing operation.

Conversely, it is easy to determine whether an excess number of lines has been installed for a particular campaign if telecommunications reports are used effectively. In this case, too, if the excess is undetected, excess costs and program inefficiency can result.

Lastly, through effective use of telecommunications reports, operations providing coverage 24 hours per day, seven days per week, can have the necessary statistics to validate (or disprove) the cost effectiveness of this service.

Examples of telecommunications reports follow, including *Daily Line Group Utilization* (**Figure 15-5**), *Daily Line Utilization* (**Figure 15-6**) and a *Station Message Detail Report* (**Figure 15-7**).

REMOTE OFFICE MANAGEMENT

Profitability. The profitability of a telemarketing company or operation within an organization is totally dependent on the profitability of each individual remote office. This is particularly true in a consumer or residential operation, where the margins are usually smaller than in a business-to-business operation. Clearly, an unprofitable or poorly managed remote facility can rapidly eat away profitability and efficiency.

It is crucial for responsible management and support personnel of a remote operation to understand what is required in the way of tracking and, equally important, *why* that tracking is required. Since they manage the day-to-day operation, they need to know in a timely way what signs mean "danger." Then, assuming the information is clearly understood, necessary adjustment measures can be taken in time to salvage a campaign or, worst case, abandon a project that cannot be carried on profitably.

Of course, corporate management should be watching daily statistics, but local management should always have up-to-the-minute information for decision making.

Profitability at the local level includes maintaining accurate statistics regarding expenses and billing.

Expenses include payroll by employee, as well as production by both employee and campaign. This information, if kept accurately and up to date, provides an added advantage--the ability to manage bonuses for effective personnel management.

A competent telemarketing manager carefully watches both low producers and high producers--the former for obvious reasons, the latter for commendations and potential future management. By carefully analyzing production by employee and payroll expenses, only the best will be retained.

Marginal producers can be provided with additional training, and if this doesn't work, replacements can be made. Overtime and attendance can also be analyzed effectively.

The *Remote Office Management Report* (profitability) statistics will be incorporated into the company's *Profitability Summary*. Included as examples are both the *Remote Office Management Report*

231

ENCYCLOPEDIA OF TELEMARKETING

Figure 15-5
Daily Line Group Utilization

Period Covered: Wed 02-17-88 01:00 Through Thu 02-18-88 00:01

| | Number of Calls | | Hour:Min | | | | Min:Sec | |
Grp No.	In Bound	Out Bound	In Usage	Out Usage	Total Usage	All Busy	Times All Busy	Avg. All Busy	Co Lines
01	XXX	XXX	XXX	XXX	XXX				XX
02		XXX		XXX	XXX	XXX	XXX	XXX	XX
03		XXX		XXX	XXX				XX
04	XXX		XXX		XXX	XXX	XXX	XXX	XX
TOTL	XXX	XXX	XXX	XXX	XXX	XXX	XXX	XXX	XX

Figure 15-6
Daily Line Utilization

PERIOD COVERED: WED 02-17-88 01:05 THROUGH THU 02-18-88 00:01

LINE	LINE NAME	INCOM.	IN USG	OUTGO	OUTUSG	ABNDND	B. CALS	SYSDRP	OUTSRV	GRP
001	XXX-XXXX	XXX	X:XX	X	:XX	X		X	:XX	XX
002	XXX-XXXX	XX	X:XX	XX	:XX				:XX	XX
003	XXX-XXXX	XX	X:XX	XX	:XX	X			:XX	XX
004	XXX-XXXX	X	X:XX	XX	X:XX	X			:XX	XX
TOTAL		XX	XX	XX	XX	X		X	X	

Figure 15-7
Station Message Detail Report

TIME	TYPE	EXT	LINE	DUR	ACCOUNT #	NBR DIALED	ANS	R. DUR	SRV	COST
X:XX	$OUT	XXX	XXX	XX:XX		XXX-XXXX			XXX	XX.XX
X:XX	$OUT	XXX	XXX	XX:XX		XXX-XXXX			XXX	XX.XX
X:XX	IN	XXX	XXX	XX:XX		XXX-XXXX	XXX	XX:XX		
X:XX	$OUT	XXX	XXX	XX:XX		XXX-XXXX			XXX	XX.XX
X:XX	IN	XXX	XXX	XX:XX		XXX-XXXX	XXX	XX:XX		

232

(Figure 15-8) and the *Management Report--Office Summary Statistics* **(Figure 15-9)**.

> ***Daily Production Reports.*** Again, company or telemarketing operational profitability is directly related to the overall success of each office. Thus, *Daily Production Reports* are a must for each office. They should be maintained by campaign and by employee.
> *Campaign Production Reports* should include:

* *Hours worked.*

* *Dials.*

* *Completed calls.*

* *Sales or acceptances (depending on campaign).*

* *Bad numbers (wrong numbers, disconnects).*

* *"Already has" (product/service).*

> They can also include supplemental information such as requests for information. These statistics should be tracked by employee for the added benefit of the client and the telemarketing operation. Campaign averages and quotas can be determined. This information can be tracked by list segment to project success ratios and list quality.
> On inbound programs, average call length will provide added information. Also, "inquiries only" will give the client valuable insight regarding the marketing of the product or service, and it will provide telemarketing management with information regarding training.
> Examples provided are the *Employee Production Report* **(Figure 15-10)** and the *Program Status Report* **(Figure 15-11)**.

CAMPAIGN MANAGEMENT

> ***Cumulative Status-to-Date Report.*** When a telemarketing campaign is designed, projections are made regarding productivity. Some projections are based on accepted statistics of the profession, which include the following:

* *Use of telemarketing in conjunction with direct mail will increase response rates two to 11 times over the response rates of direct mail alone (McGraw Hill/American Management Association).*

* *For residential or consumer programs, an average of eight to 12 contacts with a decision maker will be made each hour of outbound calling. This is for a manual operation and increases up to 70% for a fully automated operation.*

233

Figure 15-8
Remote Office Management

PROGRAM CODE	PROGRAM DESCRIPTION	TOTAL HOURS	*DAY*		*EVENING*		*RC:YES*		*REVENUE*			*PAYROLL*		*PHONE COST*	
			HOURS	% TOT HOURS	HOURS	% TOT HOURS	# OF YES	HRL AVG	REV EARNED	REV/ HOUR	REV % OF REV	TOTAL PAYROLL	% OF REV	EST. COST	% OF REV
XXXXXX	XXXXXXXXXX	XXX	XXX	XXX	XXX	XXX	XX	XX	XXX	XXX	XXX	XXX	XXX	XXX	XXX
XXXXXX	XXXXXXXXXX	XXX	XXX	XXX	XXX	XXX	XX	XX	XXX	XXX	XXX	XXX	XXX	XXX	XXX
OFFICE SUBTOTAL:		XXX	XXX	XXX	XXX	XXX	XX	XX	XXX	XXX	XXX	XXX	XXX	XXX	XXX

REPORTING SYSTEMS

Figure 15-9
Management Report – Office Summary Statistics
PROGRAMS USED ON FEB 16 1988

===

	HOURS	% OF TELEMARKETER	PAY	% OF REVENUE
OUTBOUND TELEMARKETER	XX.XX	XX.XX	XX.XX	XX.XX
INBOUND TELEMARKETER	XX.XX	XX.XX	XX.XX	XX.XX
BILLLABLE CLERICAL	XX.XX	XX.XX	XX.XX	XX.XX
GENERAL CLERICAL	XX.XX	XX.XX	XX.XX	XX.XX
SUPERVISION AND MANAGEMENT	XX.XX	XX.XX	XX.XX	XX.XX
BILLABLE TRAINING	XX.XX	XX.XX	XX.XX	XX.XX
NON-BILLABLE TRAINING	XX.XX	XX.XX	XX.XX	XX.XX
OTHER	XX.XX	XX.XX	XX.XX	XX.XX
	_____		_____	
TOTALS	XXX.XX		XXX.XX	

===

AVERAGE TELEMARKETER PAY	$X.XX
AVERAGE TELEMARKETER PAY (W/ OVERHEAD)	$X.XX
TOTAL REVENUE	$X,XXX.XX
TOTAL BILLABLE PAYROLL	$XXX.XX
BILLABLE PAYROLL AS A % OF REVENUE	XX.XX %
TOTAL NON-BILLABLE PAYROLL	$XXX.XX
NON-BILLABLE PAYROLL AS A % OF REVENUE	XX.XX % (INCLUDING NON-BILLABLE TRAINNG)
NON-BILLABLE PAYROLL AS A % OF REVENUE	XX.XX % (NOT INCLUD NON-BILLABLE TRAINING)
TOTAL PAYROLL AS A % OF REVENUE	XX.XX %
TOTAL OVERHEAD HOURS	XX.XX
TOTAL PRODUCTION & TRAINING HOURS	XXX.XX
OVERHEAD TO PRODUCTION / TRAINING RATIO	X TO X.X

235

Report Date 2/09/88

Figure 15-10
Employee Production Report
01/16/88 TO 1/31/88

EMPLOYEE NUMBER	NAME	PROGRAM CODE	DESCRIPTION	TOTAL HOURS	APPS	APPS /HOURS	DIALS	DIALS /HOUR	CONTACTS	CONTACTS /HOUR	CONVERS %
XXXXX	XXXX	XXXXXXX	XXXXXXXXXXXXXXX	X.XX	XX	.XX	XX	XX.XX	XX	XX.XX	.XX
		XXXXXXX	XXXXXXXXXXXXXXX	X.XX	XX	.XX	XX	XX.XX	XX	XX.XX	.XI
		XXXXXXX	XXXXXXXXXXXXXXX	X.XX	XX	.XX	XX	XX.XX	XX	XX.XX	.XX
XXXX'S TOTAL & AVERAGE PRODUCTION:				XX.XX	XX	.XX	XX	XX.XX	XXX	X.XX	X.XX

REPORTING SYSTEMS

Figure 15-11
Program Status Report
0 2 / 0 4 / 8 8

RUN DATE: OFFICE:
02/18/88   XXXXX

PROGRAM CODE: XXXX   TOTAL HRS: XXXX
==

RESPONSE CODE DESCRIPTIONS	TOTAL RESPONSES	RESPONSES PER HOUR	% OF TOTAL RESPONSES
1. TOTAL DIALS	XXXXX	XX.X	XX.X
2. TOTAL COMPLETED CALLS	XXXXX	XX.X	XX.X
3. BAD NUMBERS	XXXXX	XX.X	XX.X
4. CALL BACKS	XXXXX	XX.X	XX.X
5. NO ANSWER	XXXXX	XX.X	XX.X
6. SALES		.X	.X
7. SALES		.X	.X
8. SALES		.X	.X
9. SEND LITERATURE	XXXXX	XX.X	X.X
10. NOT INTERESTED	XXXXX	X.X	X.X
TOTAL DIALS:	XXXXX	XX.X	XXX.X

==

237

Figure 15-12
Campaign Daily Outbound Success Report

PROGRAM CODE: PROGRAM NAME: XXXXXXXXX   DEPARTMENT CODE: XXXXX

EMP. NUMBER	HOURS WKED	DIALS /HOUR	**TOTAL** DIALS	ANS	ANSWS /HOUR	******* YES ******* TOTAL YES'S	TOTAL HOURS	% OF ANS	**** NO **** TOTAL NO'S	% OF ANS	** HAVE ** TOTAL HAVES	% OF ANS	*WRONG NUM* TOTAL DIALS	% OF TOT DIALS	*NO ANS* TOT DIALS	% OF TOTAL OTHER
XXX	XX.XX	X.XX	XX	XX	X.XX	XX	XX.XX	XXX.X	XX	XXX.X	.XX	.XX	.XX	.XX	.XX	.XX
XXX	XX.XX	X.XX	XX	XX	X.XX	XX	XX.XX	XXX.X	XX	XXX.X	.XX	.XX	.XX	.XX	.XX	.XX
PROGRAM SUBTOTAL	XXX.XX	X.XX	XX	XX	X.XX	XX	XX.XX	XXX.X	XX	XXX.X	.XX	.XX	.XX	.XX	.XX	

REPORTING SYSTEMS

Figure 15-13
Cumulative Program Status Report

02/01/88   to   02/17/88

RUN DATE:
02/18/88

PROGRAM CODE: XXXX   TOTAL HOURS: XX.XX

===

RESPONSE CODE DESCRIPTIONS	TOTAL RESPONSES	RESPONSES PER HOUR	TOTAL RESPONSES
1. TOTAL DIALS	XXX	XX.X	XX.X
2. TOTAL COMPLETED CALLS	XXX	X.X	XX.X
3. BAD NUMBERS	XX	X.X	X.X
4. CALL BACKS	XXX	X.X	XX.X
5. NO ANSWER	XXX	X.X	XX.X
6. SALES/FINANCIAL PLANNERS		.0	.0
7. SALES/CPA FIRMS		.0	.0
8. SALES/OTHER		.0	.0
9. SEND LITERATURE	XX	X.X	X.X
10. NOT INTERESTED	XX	X.X	X.X

| TOTAL DIALS: | X,XXX | XX.X | XXX.X |

===

ENCYCLOPEDIA OF TELEMARKETING

Figure 15-14
Inbound Activity Report

17 FEBRUARY 88

RUNDATE: 02/18/88
RUNTIME: 10:54:18

PROGRAM CODE: XXX   PROGRAM NAME: XXX   DEPT. CODE: XX
· ·

EMPLOYEE NUMBER	NAME	HOURS WORKED	INBOUND MINUTES	INBOUND CALLS	AVG. MINS PER CALL
XXX	XXXXXXXXX	.XX	XX	X	XX.X
PROGRAM SUBTOTAL:		.XX	XX	X	XX.X

PROGRAM CODE: XXX   PROGRAM NAME: XXX   DEPT. CODE: XX
· ·

EMPLOYEE NUMBER	NAME	HOURS WORKED	INBOUND MINUTES	INBOUND CALLS	AVG. MINS PER CALL
XXX	XXXXXXXXX	.XX	XX	X	XX.X
XXX	XXXXXXXXX	.XX	XX	X	XX.X
PROGRAM SUBTOTAL:		.XX	XX	X	XX.X

240

> * *For business-to-business applications, for each hour of outbound telemarketing, it is anticipated that between five and nine decision-makers will be contacted.*

By maintaining a *Cumulative Status-to-Date Report*, the project can be evaluated against the standards of the profession. This, of course, provides the telemarketing operation with vital information to share with the client.

These statistics are dependent upon a number of factors, including:

* *Company/organization name recognition.*

* *Product competition.*

* *Markets promoted (lists).*

This report also will show fluctuations in production based on seasons, days or even hours.

To obtain the necessary information for a *Cumulative Status-to-Date Report*, it is necessary to track each employee's production for a particular campaign.

Report examples, here, include *Campaign Daily Outbound Success Report* (**Figure 15-12**), *Cumulative Program Status Report* (**Figure 15-13**) and *Inbound Activity Report* (**Figure 15-14**).

Production by Employee. The *Daily Production Report* described in the Remote Office Management section of this chapter will be an integral and important component of the *Cumulative Status-to-Date Report*. It, too, is a valuable management tool for the evaluation of individual employees against specific campaign standards and averages.

EMPLOYEE MANAGEMENT

Production Summary by Employee. Thus far, we have discussed various methods of tracking remote office production, campaign results and summary reports. Because the telemarketing profession is a people business, it is imperative that significant attention be given to the individual.

With an *Employee Production Summary*, management has an important key to running a successful operation. This report should include the individual's name and/or employee number, and a detailed summary of his or her production by campaign for a specified time period. This report will show clearly how the employee ranks with others working the same campaign.

It will also show who excels on a particular project or type of project, and will provide management with the necessary statistics to make adjustments in personnel so that the best people work each campaign. The added benefit is higher morale, because employees can see and take pleasure in their accomplishments. Higher morale, of course, usually turns into less turnover, resulting in lower training costs and overall greater success for all concerned.

Attendance Reports. Although attendance can be obtained in a roundabout way from a

241

Production Summary Report by Employee or a *Daily Production Report*, with minimal extra effort, it can be totally separate. A separate *Attendance Report* is recommended for several reasons:

* *It can be maintained by support personnel such as an administrative assistant.*

* *It provides at-a-glance information critical to scheduling.*

* *It also provides a quick look at any "problems" so that effective remedial or other action can be taken.*

This report should include the employee's name and employee number, as well as scheduled and actual worked hours.

MISCELLANEOUS REPORTS

Birthdates. Depending on the operation, an updated list of birthdates may be useful to determine:

* *Eligibility for various employee benefits such as profit sharing or other types of compensation based on age.*

* *Monthly recognition for birthdays.*

It is necessary to explain the reason for requesting this information, since some state laws are very explicit in the area of age discrimination.

Hire Dates. Hire dates may be desired to determine specific employee benefits such as:

* *Eligibility for vacations, holidays, medical, dental and other insurance programs which are available after a predetermined length of employment.*

* *Recognition for length of employment.*

SUMMARY

This chapter has explored reasons for, and the desired content of, various critical reports needed to manage a telemarketing operation, regardless of type or application.

It should be obvious that one major advantage telemarketing has over other marketing media is its almost total measurability--always key to accurate and effective management.

CHAPTER 16

The Bottom Line

Dwaine L. Canova
Chairman
Canova Saunders International, Inc.
Pleasanton, California

The primary purpose of this chapter is to teach the general principles necessary to read, understand and develop the types of financial reports necessary to running a telemarketing operation. A manager who has a fundamental understanding of the traditional accounting reports will be better-equipped to use them properly.

The intended result of this chapter is to help the manager feel more comfortable working with accounting and finance people so that the manager can more effectively contribute to creating better financial reports and, ultimately, to improved performance.

The general style will be to demonstrate how a report is created, itemize the key elements with specific examples and explain what the report is designed to present. The questions *"What does it mean?"* and *"Why have this report?"* will be answered in each case.

This chapter is written exclusively for managers of telemarketing operations. All levels of management will find sections addressed to them, from the sole proprietor of a telemarketing agency to the supervisor of a three-person telemarketing department within an organization.

Readers should be able to learn the following:

* *The process of preparing a budget.*

* *How to understand and use the traditional financial reports.*

* *The planning and budgeting issues that are important to upper management and/or your banker.*

* *The process of determining the amount and schedule of cash needed.*

* *How to calculate the time it takes for a new operation to become self-sufficient from a cash standpoint.*

* *The need for cost centers and the role they should serve.*

* *The standards and ranges of costs in the industry.*

243

*   *Many accounting and finance terms.*

Supplementary materials can easily be found with examples and illustrations for general business. The uniqueness of this presentation is that the illustrations and explanations are all centered around telemarketing examples and the numbers are "real" within the illustrations.

"The Bottom Line" is traditionally a specific reference to the profit or loss number at the bottom of a profit/loss statement. This will also be true in this chapter. However, the reference will be expanded to include the other measures by which an operation or segment of a telemarketing operation is measured for success.

Clear and specific definitions of the desired numerical results will help the management team to be more effective and focused in making their necessary decisions day-to-day and month-to-month. Knowing "the score" and how properly to record and present the numerical results is what "The Bottom Line" is about.

The illustrations will focus on developing budgets. Actual numbers from real operations are (or should be) presented in the same formats as the budgets. This allows for comparisons between budgeted and actual numbers. The calculation of budgeted numbers teaches one the essential processes necessary to analyze the ingredients of the actual numbers.

For example, phone bills come from the phone company and are placed in the actual report. The telemarketing center must take the payroll hours from another source to calculate if the phone bills are reasonable. A simple cross check: If the phone usage hours are greater than the employee hours, there is a problem with the phone bill or the employee records are wrong.

In either case, management needs to know the individual elements and their calculations in order to review the results properly.

I. DEVELOPING A PRO FORMA DIRECT OPERATING EXPENSE BUDGET

This section explains how to create the chart presented in **Figure 16-1**. The purpose is to take the reader through a simple budgeting process to get acquainted with the formats, calculations and locations of the required numbers. It's important to understand how the basic reports are created, in order to be able to read and modify the budget reports you will be preparing for your own operation.

Figure 16-1 is a Direct Operating Expense Budget for a specific program. The case study below will show how this budget was calculated:

Telemarketing Program Case History

This is a one-time campaign designed to sell additional products/services to an existing customer base.

*   *Calls will be made to residences.*

*   *Calling hours will be Monday through Friday, 5:00 to 9:00 p.m., Saturday,*
       9:00 a.m. to 6:00 p.m. (Assume all work done in the same time zone).

Figure 16-1
Outbound Program
Pro Forma Direct Operating Expense Budget

	Month One (Preparation)	Month Two (Start-up)	Month Three	Month Four	Month Five	Month Six	Month Seven (1/3)	Totals
Operating Expenses								
Salaries								
Supervisor	$2,333	$2,333	$2,333	$2,333	$2,333	$2,333	$ 778	$14,776
Asst. Supervisor	1,667	1,667	1,667	1,667	1,667	1,667	556	10,558
Payroll Load	1,200	1,200	1,200	1,200	1,200	1,200	400	7,600
Wages								
Training	1,680	280	280	280	280	280	0	3,080
TSRs	0	5,880	5,880	5,880	5,880	5,880	1,960	31,360
Payroll Load	504	1,848	1,848	1,848	1,848	1,848	588	10,332
Total Payroll	7,384	13,208	13,208	13,208	13,208	13,208	4,282	77,706
Telecommunications								
Installation	389	389	389	389	389	389	115	2,449
Equipment	100	100	100	100	100	100	100	700
Line Charges	191	382	382	382	382	382	127	2,228
Usage Charges	0	4,517	4,517	4,517	4,517	4,517	1,505	24,090
Total Telecommunications	680	5,388	5,388	5,388	5,388	5,388	1,847	29,467
Total Direct Operating Expenses	$8,064	18,596	18,596	18,596	18,596	18,596	6,129	$107,173
Schedule:								
TSR Hours	0	840	840	840	840	840	280	4,480

* *Customer base of 100,000 names with phone numbers.*

Given the information above, one can begin calculating the numbers needed to complete the chart in **Figure 16-1**. There are many other details required and they will be explained as they are encountered in the development process. The four principal items to be calculated are:

* *The personnel hours.*

* *The elapsed time in weeks/months.*

* *The number of people.*

* *The telecommunications expense.*

The result will be the completed Direct Operating Expense Budget in **Figure 16-1**. In this section, each number and relationship to the other numbers will be explained.

A. Personnel Hours. How many telemarketing hours are needed to work the 100,000 residential names properly?

The first consideration is *reachability*--how many of the households will answer their phones and speak to the Telephone Sale Representative (TSR)? At least three attempts should be made to reach each household. The industry standard results range from 55% to 65% of the households (from good lists) with phone numbers that can be reached. The variability is partly a function of the list quality as well as the time of day when the calls are attempted. Some people will not be reached due to wrong numbers, disconnected numbers, or due to the fact that the residents are not home at the time of the call. For this budget, it was assumed that 60% of the households would be reached.

Reachability at 60% is a safe estimate.

The next consideration is *calls per hour*--how many completed calls can be accomplished during each telemarketing hour? The industry standard results range from 12 to 18 per hour for consumer calling. The variability in the standard is partly a function of the length of conversations, and partly due to the relative ability to reach households. (The standards presume manual dialed calls rather than computer dialing. In computer-assisted environments, the completed calls per hour will be higher.) For this budget, it was assumed that 15 calls per hour would be completed.

The total completed conversations for this budget are 60,000, calculated as follows:

100,000 names X 60% = 60,000.

The telemarketing personnel hours required for this program are 4,000, calculated as follows:

60,000 conversations/15 conversations per hour =4,000 hours.

A margin-for-error addition of 480 hours should be included in the projection to allow for variances. This is an adjustment of 12% to allow for less than standard productivity. Some budgeting processes do not allow for an adjustment. Conservative budgets allow for reduced results and, thus, higher costs. Not all managers are allowed the latitude for such "fudge factors."

What is right?

THE BOTTOM LINE

The answer will vary with each organization and department. The author has observed one common ground of agreement between optimists and pessimists: each knows the other is unrealistic.

B. Weeks/Months--Elapsed Time. The next question to be answered is:

How many weeks/months will be needed for a 10 work-station facility to complete the required work? (10 was selected for ease of calculation.)

The individual work-station weekly capacity would be calculated as follows:

Weekdays: 5 days X 4 hours =	20
Saturdays: 1 day X 8 hours =	8
Total Weekly Hours:	28

Recall that the calling is to be done during the evening weekdays from 5 p.m. to 9 p.m., and on Saturdays from 9 a.m. to 6 p.m.

Coverage effectiveness:

Almost no production capacity is ever used to its full extent. Telemarketing stations are often used only 70% to 80% of the available capacity. Some of the reasons are breaks, tardiness, absenteeism and turnover. For the immediate purposes, the coverage effectiveness could be presented as follows:

@ 70%: 28 X .7 = 19.6 hours.
@ 80%: 28 X .8 = 22.4 hours.

C. People. The minimum staff needed properly to manage and work at the 10 work stations would be as follows:

1 *Manager/Supervisor*
($28,000 per year or $2,333 per month).
1 *Assistant Supervisor/Clerical Support*
($20,000 per year or $1,667 per month).
7 *Telephone Sales Representatives (TSR's)*
($7 per hour base rate).

The payroll load for these employees would be 30%. Payroll load is the minimum required payroll taxes, plus company benefits.

Training Expense:

Begin with 12 people, or plan to have initial training for 12 people to staff for the 7 openings. Training could cover 20 hours. Therefore, the training expense would be:

247

12 people X 20 hours X $7/hour = $1,680.

Plan to train two or more people per month to replace those who leave or cannot perform to standards.

2 people X 20 hours X $7/hour = $280.

D. The Telecommunications Expense. The basic minimum telecommunications system would be as follows:

1 Monitor.
10 Single WATS lines.

Installations:

Monitor.	$600
Single Lines.	1,849
6.3 Months' Amortization ($389/Mo.).	$2,449

Equipment Purchases:

Monitor.	$500
Single line sets--$50 each X 10.	500
Headsets--$140 each X 10.	1,400
24 Month amortization--($100/Mo.).	$2,400

Basic monthly line charges.--$382.

The above installation and line charge amounts were obtained from the official rate charts of a long distance carrier, dated January 1, 1988.

Many variations are available to the above. The system presented provides an itemization of the equipment required and the expenses incurred to have the telephone equipment available for use.

E. Usage Charges. Calculation of telephone usage charges is usually done on a monthly basis. Thus, there is a requirement to calculate the number of months needed as well as the number of telemarketing hours.

The telephone line is not in continuous use during each hour the TSR is working. Usage is generally only that time spent speaking with someone. Time spent dialing, listening to rings and "busies" and deciding which prospect/customer to dial reduces the phone usage during the telemarketer hour.

The telemarketing hours available for each work station are calculated as follows:

22 Weekdays X 4 hours =	88
4 Saturdays X 8 hours =	32
Total hours:	120

THE BOTTOM LINE

The total telemarketing hours for the month with seven TSR's working would be calculated as follows:

Evenings 7 X 88 hours =	616
Saturdays 7 X 32 hours =	224
Total hours:	840

The usage percentage standards for efficient calling to residences ranges from 45% to 65% of the telemarketer hour. For illustrative purposes, 55% is used.

Calculating the phone use hours for the month is done as follows:

Evenings: 616 TSR hours X .55 usage = 339 hours connect time.
Saturdays: 224 TSR hours X .55 usage = 123 hours of connect time.

These numbers are not added together at this point since the phone rates are different for Saturday hours.

Calculating the usage charges below for the month is accomplished using actual rates from rate charts of January 1, 1988, of our actual long-distance carrier. For your specific purposes, of course, it will be necessary to obtain the specific rate chart from the carrier and area in which your telemarketing center is established.

Recall from above that the actual evening usage hours figure is a total of 339 hours. Charges would be calculated as follows:

Assumptions:

*   *Home base is Northern California.*

*   *Calling requires using lines that allow access to the entire U.S.*

Evening Hours	
First 25 hours @ $10.83:	$ 270.75
Next 75 hours @ $10.28:	771.00
Next 239 hours @ $9.74:	2,327.86
Total hours (339):	$3,369.61
Saturday hours (123 @ $7.25):	891.75
Total monthly usage charges:	$4,261.36
Estimated taxes @ 6%:	255.68
Total usage charges:	$4,517.04

The $4,517.04 appears in **Figure 16-1** as Telecommunication Usage Charges.

A Review. The following paragraphs should be read while the reader is alternating between the text and **Figure 16-1**. Specific numbers will be identified and their calculations will be illustrated. This review will give you a comprehensive explanation of the prepared budget in **Figure 16-1**.

The headings in the left column are identified as the account name and are referred to by accountants as a "chart of accounts." The process of naming and numbering accounts is an elaborate and specific subject area for accountants and not discussed here, but it's well worth reviewing with your accountant. This illustration provides a basis to begin working with an accountant to develop a more detailed chart of accounts for your own center.

Assumptions. Making assumptions in the budgeting process is essential. Reasonable assumptions are a matter of practice, experience and thoroughness of the person or team making the projections.

The assumptions described below provide further insight into the kinds of considerations necessary:

* *Training wages, Month Seven--"0".*

 Assumption made that no further training will be necessary for replacements during this time as the project will be nearing completion.

* *Usage charges, Month One--"0".*

 Assumption made that the phone lines, even though available, would not be used during the preparatory month.

* *Month One.*

 It was calculated that the projects could be done in 5.3 months. The assumption was made that the management and supervisory team would need some planning time. Also, training should be done before production work began. Thus, Month One was added as preparation time.

* *Line charges Month One--$191.*

 The lines would be installed by mid-month. Even though the lines would not be used, it was felt that they should be available for initial testing and be in readiness for day one of the beginning production month.

* *All items, Month Seven.*

 As soon as the project is over, stop all of the expenses.

There are other explicit and implicit assumptions one can find in review and discussion with various readers. However, space and purpose do not allow for an exhaustive listing. Suffice for the moment that each number included in the projected budget came from a reasoned process.

The reader is now familiar with many expense item calculations and, equally important, familiar with the general format of presenting budgeted numbers.

Figure 16-1 is a simplified operating expense format. Down the left side are the "accounts." The columns are the time periods--in this case a month of activity in each column. The direct operating expense budget itemizes the salaries, wages and telecommunications expenses that will occur in this project.

THE BOTTOM LINE

Operating Expenses. The general category of expenses here are identified as "operating" expenses. These are the fundamental expenses necessary to conduct the work utilizing people and telephones. Expenses such as rent and support services are ignored here for simplification purposes, but will be addressed later on. The focus at this point is on the direct operating expenses. They are used here as the first step in developing an understanding of accounting reports, and are the basic expense areas that will require ongoing management time to create a successful unit--hence the term "operating expenses."

The specific numbers referred to in the following paragraphs appear in the column labeled "Month Three." They were calculated and determined as follows:

Salaries--Prior Reference C (People).

* *Supervisor--$2,333.*

   This is 1/12th of the $28,000 annual rate.

* *Assistant Supervisor--$1,667.*

   This is 1/12th of the $20,000 annual rate.

* *Payroll load--$1,200.*

   This is 30% of $4,000 ($2,333 + $1,667).

Wages--Prior Reference C (People).

* *Training--$280.*

   This is the salaries paid to replacement people while they are in training.
   This is estimated at two per month for 20 hours each at $7 per hour (2 X 20
   X $7 = $280).

* *TSR's--$5,880.*

   Salaries paid to the TSR's working at $7 per hour for the 840 hours required
   to complete the calls ($7 X 840 = $5,880).

* *Payroll load--$1,848.*

   This is 30% of the training and telemarketer wages ($280 + $5,880 = $6,160
   X .3 = $1,848). The 30% includes regular payroll tax requirements plus
   benefits provided by this example company.

   The 30% payroll load may differ between companies, but should be allowed
   for since, obviously, it's a significant cost item.

251

* *Total payroll--$13,208.*

  This is the accumulation of the six account items above ($2,333 + $1,667 +$1,200 + $280 + $5,880 + $1,848 = $13,208).

Telecommunications Expenses and Usage Charges-- Prior References D and E.

* *Telecommunications system installation--$389.*

  This is the monthly allocation of the total $2,449 spread over the full 6.3 months this project will work ($2,449/6.3 = $389).

* *Equipment--$100.*

  The equipment cost is listed as $2,400, and, because the equipment can be used elsewhere for at least a total of 24 months, it is reasonable to assign only a 1/24th expense ($2,400/24 months = $100).

* *Line Charges--$382.*

  This number is obtained from Reference D. This is the expense incurred for having the lines in your facility and available for use.

* *Usage charges--$4,517.*

  The calculation for this number is itemized at the end of Reference E.

* *Total Direct Operating Expenses--$18,596.*

  This summary number is the addition of total payroll and telecommunications ($13, 208 + $5,388 = $18,596).

* *Schedule: TSR Hours--840.*

  These are the total monthly telemarketing hours required to conduct the work. Refer to prior Reference A to review the full calculation.

II. STEPS TO DEVELOP A COMPLETE ONE-YEAR BUDGET FOR A TELE-MARKETING CENTER

This section focuses on the full operating statement budget presented in **Figure 16-2**. This adds significantly to the budget prepared in Section I. However, for clarification purposes, the following point should be emphasized:

THE BOTTOM LINE

The full-year Pro Forma Operating Statement itemizes the:

* *Fees earned by the telemarketing center (+).*

* *Telecommunications expenses incurred (-).*

* *Wages/salaries expenses incurred (-).*

* *Other costs incurred (-).*

* *Administration expenses incurred (-).*

* *And, finally, income before income tax (result)--"The Bottom Line."*

The reader should note that this is a significant expansion from the final comments in Section I. Obviously, one of the purposes of the examples in Section I was to provide a close look at the details of a full-year budget. The purpose of this elaboration is to help the reader grasp the fundamental differences between the simple Direct Operating Expense Budget and the full one-year Pro Forma Operating Statement. Only telecommunications and wages/salaries appeared in the Direct Operating Expense Budget. And to illustrate acceptable flexibility in format, they have been reversed in sequence for the full budget.

Refer to the left-most column in **Figure 16-2**. The headings on the left side of the chart are the "accounts." They label the fees earned by the center, the expenses incurred (telecommunications, wages/salaries) and other administrative expenses. The fees earned are *pluses*, the expenses incurred are *minuses* and the result is the income (*profit*). This simplified statement of the budget format should help the reader understand the reason for creating an operating statement. The operating statement is created to capsulate and present the fees earned, the expenses incurred to create the fees and the net result is: "The Bottom Line."

The author prefers calling this report an *operating statement* rather than an income or profit statement. The reason for this is that the intended reader should be using this report to help run or "operate" his or her telemarketing center better, and should look deeper into the report than simply dwelling on the pluses or minuses of the bottom line (profit/loss). Detailed analysis of the fees earned and the expenses incurred are essential to the proper management of a telemarketing operation. These reports only provide a general framework of presentation within which the analysis can begin.

This section explains how to create the chart presented in **Figure 16-2**. It's a full-year Pro Forma Operating Statement for a stand-alone telemarketing service agency or corporate profit center working on a fee basis. The basis for this operation is described as follows:

* *50 TSR Stations:*

   30 inbound.

   20 outbound.

* *Business-to-business calling only.*

* *Day-time calling.*

253

Figure 16-2
Pro Forma Operating Statement

Month	1	2	3	4	5	6	7	8	9	10	11	12	Total	Sales
Fees														
Inbound	$0	68,800	68,800	103,200	103,200	137,600	137,600	172,000	172,000	172,000	172,000	137,600	1,444,800	64.8
Outbound	0	0	38,700	38,700	77,400	77,400	77,400	77,400	116,100	116,100	77,400	77,400	774,000	35.2
Other Fees	0	0	0	0	0	0	0	0	0	0	0	0	0	0
Total Fees	$0	68,800	107,500	141,900	180,600	215,000	215,000	249,400	288,100	288,100	249,400	215,000	2,218,800	100%
Cost of Fees														
Telecommunications														
Equipment	$2,500	2,500	2,500	2,500	2,500	2,500	2,500	2,500	2,500	2,500	2,500	2,500	30,000	
Monthly Line Charges	0	600	920	1,120	1,400	1,600	1,600	1,800	2,000	2,000	1,800	1,600	16,440	
Usage - IN	0	16,302	16,302	24,409	24,409	32,517	32,517	40,625	40,625	40,625	40,625	32,517	341,473	
Usage - OUT	0	0	6,918	6,918	13,745	13,745	13,745	13,745	20,572	20,572	13,745	13,745	137,450	
Total Telecommunications	$2,500	19,402	26,640	34,947	42,054	50,362	50,362	58,670	65,697	65,697	58,670	50,362	525,363	23.7
Wages/Salaries														
TSRs - IN	$0	17,200	17,200	25,800	25,800	34,400	34,400	43,000	43,000	43,000	43,000	34,400	361,200	
TSRs - OUT	0	0	12,040	12,040	24,080	24,080	24,080	24,080	36,120	36,120	24,080	24,080	240,800	
Clerical	1,200	1,200	2,400	2,400	2,400	3,600	3,600	4,800	4,800	4,800	4,800	3,600	39,600	
Supervisor	2,500	5,000	5,000	7,500	7,500	7,500	7,500	10,000	12,500	12,500	10,000	7,500	95,000	
Training	24,640	20,512	18,448	18,448	18,448	12,256	20,512	18,448	14,320	14,320	8,128	8,128	196,608	
Payroll Load (30%)	8,502	13,174	16,526	19,856	23,468	24,551	27,028	30,098	33,222	33,222	27,002	23,312	279,961	
Total Wages/Salaries	$36,842	57,086	71,614	86,044	101,696	106,387	117,120	130,426	143,962	143,962	117,010	101,020	1,213,169	54.7
Other Costs	$3,934	7,649	9,825	12,099	14,375	15,675	16,748	18,910	20,966	20,966	17,568	15,138	173,853	7.8
Total Costs to Create Fees	$43,276	84,137	108,079	133,090	158,125	172,424	184,230	208,006	230,625	230,625	193,248	166,520	1,912,385	86.2
Gross Margin	$(43,276)	(15,337)	(579)	8,810	22,475	42,576	30,770	41,394	57,475	57,475	56,152	48,480	306,415	13.8
Administrative Exp	$3,462	6,731	8,646	10,647	12,650	13,794	14,738	16,640	18,450	18,450	15,460	13,322	152,990	6.9
Income B.I.T.	$(46,738)	(22,068)	(9,225)	(1,837)	9,825	28,782	16,032	24,754	39,025	39,025	40,692	35,158	153,425	6.9

*   *Starting a new center with an experienced management team.*

Figure 16-3 is a complete, month-by-month itemization of the staffing schedule, work loads and telecommunications requirements. It's called the Pro Forma Staffing Schedule and Telecommunications Requirements. Because it's basically a work schedule, **Figure 16-3** *must* be completed before preparing **Figure 16-2**, the Pro Forma Operating Statement.

Understanding Figure 16-3. The left column of the chart identifies the activity and resource items necessary for the year. It is essential that these items be determined in specific before a budget can be properly established. A brief explanation of each item and how they can be determined follows:

Operating Capacity Percentage. This is the amount of workload anticipated relative to the maximum capacity available. This center has 50 work stations, and in the early months, there is a buildup of 20%, 30%, 40%, etc. This reflects the need to build staff and gradually add more work. In months 9 and 10, the maximum of 80% (40 work stations) is projected. Full utilization is not a practical goal, although it is possible to have 90%. The drop off in Months 11 and 12 reflects the cyclical nature of the work being done. Not all telemarketing centers have a cyclical nature, but many do and this is how it would be charted.

TSR Hours--In. This itemizes the workload in hours expected for the inbound work. It builds rapidly and drops in Month 12 to adjust to the business cycle.

TSR's--In. This is the number of TSR's required for the anticipated inbound hours.

TSR's--Out. This is the number of TSR's required for the anticipated outbound hours.

TSR Hours--Out. This itemizes the workload in hours expected for the outbound work. These are shown to grow and then adjust to a downturn cycle.

TSR's--Training. This is the number of TSR's that would be trained in each of the months. This assumes ongoing training for new and replacement people. If there is a necessity for retraining existing people, the amount here could be different.

Clerical Staff. As the work builds up, there is a need for more clerical support people. This may not be true for some telemarketing centers.

Supervisory Staff. The number of supervisors needed varies dramatically depending upon the complexity of the projects conducted. Generally, a growing situation will require more supervision to allow for the development experience of supervisors as well as the more intense interaction required with newer, inexperienced TSR's. Also, if the projects are changing, there may be more coaching support needed. The supervisory ratios here vary from 3:20 (Month 4) to 5:40 (Month 9). Each set of circumstances will dictate its own needs.

Trainer. This operation is projected to need a full-time trainer continuously. For some circumstances, this may not be enough, while for others, far more than necessary. Determine each on its own merits, but don't forget to consider this expense.

Lines Operating--In. This is a projection of the number of inbound lines needed for this workload and ACD. This is a complex determination and requires significant experience or a highly qualified consultant for startups. A complete discussion is beyond the scope of this chapter.

Lines Operating--Out. This projection of outbound lines is a simpler determination. However, the switch (computer) and workload should also be considered. Again, rely on experience, even if it is not inside your company.

255

Figure 16-3
Pro Forma Staffing Schedule & Telecommunications Requirements

Month	1	2	3	4	5	6	7	8	9	10	11	12	Total
Operating Capacity%	0	20	30	40	50	60	60	70	80	80	70	60	
TSR Hours - IN		1,720	1,720	2,580	2,580	3,440	3,440	4,300	4,300	4,300	4,300	3,440	36,120
TSRs - IN	0	10	10	15	15	20	20	25	25	25	25	20	
TSRs - Out	0	0	5	5	10	10	10	10	15	15	10	10	
TSR Hours - Out	0	0	860	860	1,720	1,720	1,720	1,720	2,580	2,580	1,720	1,720	17,200
TSRs - Training	10	8	7	7	7	4	8	7	5	5	2	2	
Clerical Staff	1	1	2	2	2	3	3	4	4	4	4	3	
Supervisory Staff	1	2	2	3	3	3	3	4	5	5	4	3	
Trainer	1	1	1	1	1	1	1	1	1	1	1	1	
Lines Operating - In	0	15	15	20	20	25	25	30	30	30	30	25	
Lines Operating - Out	0	0	8	8	15	15	15	15	20	20	15	15	
Usage Hours - In	0	1,290	1,290	1,935	1,935	2,580	2,580	3,225	3,225	3,225	3,225	2,580	27,090
Usage Hours - Out	0	0	516	516	1,032	1,032	1,032	1,032	1,548	1,548	1,032	1,032	10,320

Usage Hours--In. These are the actual hours of phone connect time that will be incurred. For inbound, that is projected at 75% of the telemarketer hours in this business center environment. It can be as low as 55%, but rarely is more than 85%. The numbers in this line are calculated by multiplying .75 times the number of TSR Hours--In for each month.

Usage Hours--Out. These are the actual hours of phone connect time that will be incurred. For outbound in a well-run business environment, the average is 60%. It can be as low as 50%, but rarely is more than 70%. The numbers in this line are calculated by multiplying .60 times the number of TSR Hours--Out for each month.

The process of placing one's own numbers in a chart format of this type will vary. Almost every circumstance will require extensive meetings between the operating management team and the sales, marketing or customer service group being served by the center.

These numbers do not always come easily. As the various parties provide their input on the anticipated workloads, there will be considerable "best guessing." Established operations usually have an easier time of this due to experience. However, new operations will probably encounter overwhelming urges to resist putting down specific numbers. Budgets and projections are not one's ultimate bet on the future, but rather a reasoned effort at anticipating the future.

Do not let analysis lead to paralysis, but rather put numbers down, review them, modify them and continually make notes on how the numbers were determined. This documentation serves as the support document called "notes." Each item is explained and so there should be a listing of notes for each item budgeted. This may also be the place to get the proper parties to "sign off" on their commitment to projected numbers to support the budget presentation to upper management, a banker or a board of directors.

With all of the numbers entered in **Figure 16-3**, it is now possible to begin calculating the numbers for **Figure 16-2**. The Pro Forma Operating Statement cannot be completed until the Pro Forma Staffing and Telecommunications Requirements are established.

Explanation of Figure 16-2. A generally accepted method for explaining a Pro Forma Operating Statement is to let the supplemental "notes" do the job. The documentation of the notes (descriptions of assumptions and how the numbers were calculated) will be used here to describe the report in **Figure 16-2**.

The following "notes" are similar to those that would be used in the development and documentation of an actual Pro Forma Operating Statement. The principal difference will be the additional comments made to help the reader understand the range of options and considerations that are appropriate in creating the numbers. All the calculations will use the numbers created for Month 5.

Fees. The word "fees" is used to distinguish these numbers from the sales of services or merchandise. These are the fees earned by the service agency, or corporate profit center working on a fee basis, in selling services or merchandise on behalf of clients, not the actual value of the sale of services or merchandise. The dollar amounts of the sales would be significantly higher. Fees are earned in a number of ways, sometimes as commissions on sales. But for ease of understanding, they are presented here as fees for each professional hour of TSR service. The cost justification of this fee would be determined by the margins on the sales created, a topic worthy of an entire chapter by itself.

Inbound. A rate of $40 per TSR hour was used in developing this statement. Many service agencies with inbound business operations create their fees based on a rate for each transaction (call) they handle.

257

Some create their fees from commissions on the sales or leads they create. Some have a sales schedule based on the hours of service they are set up to provide.

The options are almost limitless. Some telemarketing centers create no revenue fees at all. This will be discussed in a later section on cost versus profit centers.

The actual number for Month 5 is $103,200. This was calculated by multiplying $40 times the 2,580 hours in Month 5 in **Figure 16-3** ($40 X 2,580 hours = $103,200).

Outbound. A rate of $45 per telemarketer hour was used in developing this statement. Again, the basis for fee calculations is broad-based--commissions on sales, fixed fees for leads, hourly budgeted rates, etc. In all cases, however, the fee basis must consider the costs incurred and the $45 rate is a rate that will usually allow a reasonable expression of fees earned versus the costs incurred (profit).

For a real budget, describe the fee basis in as much detail as is available.

The actual number for Month 5 is $77,400. This was calculated by multiplying $45 times the 1,770 hours in Month 5 in **Figure 16-3** ($45 X 1,720 hours = $77,400).

Other Fees. For this example, "0" is used. The other types of fee generators could be:

* *Data processing services.*

* *Administrative/clerical support.*

* *Copying and printing.*

* *Fulfillment of orders.*

* *Telephone number look-up.*

* *Ongoing program consulting.*

It would be necessary to itemize each one and the basis upon which the related fees are calculated. *Total Fees.* Summary total of all fees.

Telecommunications Equipment. The equipment needed is a switch with ACD and outbound features. The original cost for each work station is $2,000, including all the required equipment. The lease schedule is five years, or 60 months.

Lease costs are estimated roughly as follows:

$100,000 + 10% per year or $10,000 per year.

$100,000 + $50,000 = $150,000.

$150,000/60 months = $2,500/month.

The $2,500 amount is used in each month of the statement.

Monthly Line Charges. Both inbound and outbound lines are $40 each. Refer to **Figure 16-3** and multiply $40 times the lines operating in and out. In Month 5, there are 35 lines operating ($40 X 35 lines = $1,400).

Usage--Inbound. Usage is the actual amount of phone connect time. Assume for this example that the connect time for inbound business TSR work is 75% of the TSR hours. The rates are from the same carrier mentioned above with the rates in effect as of January 1, 1988.

The calculation for the inbound usage charges in Month 5 would be done as follows:

First 25 hours @ $13.95:	$ 348.75
Next 75 hours @ $13.26:	994.50
1,835 hours @ $12.57:	23,065.95
Total (1,935 hours):	$24,409.20

From **Figure 16-3**, Month 5--total hours of usage 1,935.

The $24,409 figure is placed on the Usage-In line for Month 5. The numbers for the other months would be calculated in the same way. The $.20 is dropped in the budgeting process, but would be included in the reporting of actual numbers.

Usage--Outbound. Assume the connect time for the outbound business TSR effort is 60% of the TSR hours. The day rates are for California--North (Service Area 5). The calculation for the outbound usage charges in Month 5 would be done as follows:

First 25 hours @ $14.70:	$ 367.50
Next 75 hours @ $13.96:	1,047.00
932 hours @ $13.23:	12,330.36
Total (1,032 hours):	$13,744.86

From **Figure 16-3**, Month 5--total hours of usage 1,032.

The $13,745 (rounded) amount is placed in the Usage-Out line in Month 5. The numbers for the other months would be calculated in the same way.

Total Telecommunications. Summary total of all telecommunications.

TSR's--In. This is the basic payroll for the *inbound* TSR's. The average hourly rate is set at $10 per hour. The calculation for Month 5 would be $10 times the TSR Hours-In from **Figure 16-3** ($10 X 2,580 = $25,800). The numbers for the other months would be calculated in the same way.

TSR's--Out. This is the basic payroll for the *outbound* TSR's. The average hourly rate is set at $14 per hour. The calculation for Month 5 would be $14 times the TSR Hours-Out from **Figure 16-3** ($14 X 1,720 = $24,080). The $24,080 would be placed in Month 5 for the TSR's--Out line.

Clerical. The basic clerical rate is estimated to be $1,200 per month for each clerical person.

Supervisor. The basic rate for supervisors is estimated at $2,500 per month for each supervisor.

Training. Included is a full-time trainer at $4,000 per month. The training period is for one month. The training hours are calculated as follows:

4.3 weeks X 40 hours = 172 hours @ $12/hour = $2,064.

For each person trained, an expense of $2,064 is incurred. **Figure 16-3**, from the TSR's training line, itemizes the number of persons trained. For Month 5, it is seven persons at $2,064 each for a total cost of

259

$14,448. The figure of $18,448 would be placed in Month 5 for the training time ($14,448 + $4,000 for the trainer = $18,448).

Payroll Load. This is estimated at 30% and includes basic payroll taxes as well as benefits. For Month 5, summing $25,800 + $24,080 + $2,400 + $7,500 + $18,448 = $78,228; $78,228 X .3 = $23,468. Payroll load must be calculated on all wages. Companies may differ on benefits they provide for various categories of employees and so that the established percentage will not necessarily be used across the board for all employees.

Total Wages/Salaries. This is a summation of the five wages/salaries categories and the payroll load. (In Month 5, $25,800 + $24,080 + $2,400 + $7,500 + $18,448 = $23,468 = $101,696).

Other Costs. This includes a list of items, and for illustrative purposes, they have been estimated at 10% of the combined totals of telecommunications and wages/salaries. In Month 5, telecommunications is $42,054 and wages/salaries is $101,696; combined, they are $143,750 and the other costs are estimated at $14,375 ($142,750 X .10 = $14,375).

In an actual budgeting process, the individual cost items should be discussed. But, for the purposes of this chapter, listed below are examples of the types of costs that could be included in this general category:

*   *Computer support system.*

*   *Insurance.*

*   *Lists.*

*   *Personnel ads.*

*   *Shipping.*

*   *Postage.*

*   *Copying and printing.*

Total Costs To Create Fees. This is simply an addition down the column of telecommunications, wages/salaries and other costs. In Month 5, they are $42,054 + $101,696 + $14,375; a total of $158,125.

Gross Margin. This is the number that shows how much is being made from operations *before* the administrative overhead is considered. Generally, if there is a negative gross margin, there are serious problems with the telemarketing center. In this center, the projected annual gross margin is 13.8% of sales. Telemarketing service agencies, and corporate profit centers working on a fee basis, range from 10% to 20%.

How a company is structured, the type of work it does, how it allocates costs will all impact the gross margin percentage rate.

For Month 5, gross margin is calculated as follows: total fees ($180,600) minus total costs to create fees ($158,125) equals the gross margin ($22,475).

Administrative Expenses. This has been estimated at 8% of the total costs of fees. This is a reasonable number given the allocation of costs preceding them in the report. Only general overhead expense items remain to be identified. In an actual budgeting process, the individual cost items should be discussed in detail.

THE BOTTOM LINE

Listed below are examples of the types of costs that could be included in this category:

* *Senior management salaries.*

* *Administrative salaries.*

* *Office and computer supplies.*

* *Rent.*

* *Computer payroll services.*

* *Telephone (general office).*

* *Utilities.*

* *Equipment rental.*

* *Maintenance and repair services.*

* *Travel and entertainment.*

* *Dues, subscriptions and contributions.*

* *Taxes and licenses.*

* *Depreciation.*

* *Interest.*

Income B.I.T. (Before Income Taxes). This is the step in calculating profit (income) that precedes the allowance for taxes. After tax considerations, "The Bottom Line" finally emerges. Tax considerations will be ignored for this illustration. The bottom line in this case is 6.9% of telemarketing fees earned. This is respectable. The reported incomes range from 0% to 15%.

It is traditional for all businesses to be penny-, nickle- and dime-focused in terms of making a profit. It seems always to get down to small margins for error. For example, if wages/salaries were all increased by 10% (.1 X 54.7% = 5.4%), it could essentially wipe out the profit.

Summary. Knowing where the costs are, how they are created, how they are presented and how to read and use the accounting reports is essential to be a successful telemarketing center manager. The process of creating a budget (as has been done here) is tedious and laborious. Making it fun for someone with a weak accounting background is certainly a challenge.

Still, by this time, the reader should have an appreciation for the complexity of the development process of budgeting. A reminder and caution: Much detail has been glossed over, necessarily, because of the limits of this chapter. However, enough has been highlighted to give one a greater confidence about the format of the reports and the types of calculations and discussions required to create a budget. Learning this type of material requires repetition, practice and review.

The Pro Forma Operating Statement created could now be used in making decisions to get the telemarketing center underway or for comparing the actual monthly results with the budgeted numbers. Identifying variances between actual and budgeted numbers is an important part of the monthly review of the total results.

The next section will demonstrate how to determine the cash needs for the operation budgeted in this section.

III. CASH FLOW

Cash is necessary to make any business run. All businesses are aware of this as are most telemarketing centers. Only divisions or departments within larger organizations may be insulated from concern about this issue. However, be assured that somewhere in all organizations, someone is concerned about managing cash to cover the checks that are being written. The cash flow statement is a report that shows when and how money comes in and goes out of the business.

This section builds upon the operating budget presented in **Figure 16-2** to show how to plan for the flow of money in and out of the business. The Pro Forma Operating Statement reported only the relationship between fees earned and the expenses incurred within each month and for the year.

The management of cash flow is usually a task left to the controller or chief financial officer of a company. The topic is presented here because many telemarketing centers are small enough to keep top management involved in all dimensions of the business. So, in addition to managing programs, people and the future, many telemarketing center managers will also have to be involved with managing cash.

The following paragraphs describe the Pro Forma Cash Flow Statement presented in Figure 16-4. This is the budgeted cash flow for the same business and time period presented in the Pro Forma Operating Statement in **Figure 16-2**.

Explanation of Figure 16-4. The line headings in the left-most column of **Figure 16-4** presents the major delineation of cash in and cash out. The bottom lines deal with increases or decreases in cash and the use of a line of credit for cash where needed.

The line of credit is a type of loan from a bank used to cover the cash shortfalls for the operating expenses of a business. It assumes the business is making money, but that the business requires cash to pay bills while waiting to collect money that is owed.

The columns are the months corresponding with the same months presented in **Figure 16-2**.

The following notes describe how the numbers were transferred from the Pro Forma Operating Statement in **Figure 16-2**. For consistency's sake, where specific numbers are discussed, the numbers will all be referenced to Month 5.

Cash In--Fees. The cash from fees is assumed to be received 45 days from the date of invoice. In this example, the billing for fees is done at the end of the month in which the work is conducted. Refer to the notes for **Figure 16-2** for a description of how the fees are calculated.

THE BOTTOM LINE

For simplicity's sake, the assumption is made that 100% of fees billed will be paid. In actual situations this may not be true and the history of results will be the basis on which the allowance for uncollectibles will be established.

In Month 5 of **Figure 16-4**, the Cash In--Fees amount is $107,500. This corresponds to the total fees amount in Column 3 of **Figure 16-2**. This is not a calculation for **Figure 16-4**, but a transference only. And, likewise, it would be done for the other months of **Figure 16-4**. A review between the two figures will quickly reveal this.

Cash In--Other. Other, here, is not "other fees," but money from investment such as the $100,000 in Month 1, or money from loans or sale of assets that would bring cash into the business. These are usually one-time decisions that are not operating decisions, but financial decisions. For this illustration, the amount is left at zero for all months except Month 1.

Total Cash In. This is the accumulation of Fees and Other within the month. The addition is down the column, not across the line. The purpose of the report is to have a month-by-month picture of the cash needs. For Month 5, the amount is $107,500.

Cash Out--Cost of Fees/Telecommunications. Telecommunications expenses incurred in Month 3 are to be paid in Month 5. The bill for Month 3 will be received around the middle of Month 4 and actually paid (a check written) sometime early in Month 5. The amount in Month 5 in the Pro Forma Cash Flow Statement of **Figure 16-4** is $26,640. This is the same amount ($26,640) that appears as the total Telecommunications expense in Month 3 of **Figure 16-2**. Transference only--no calculation is involved.

Cash Out--Cost of Fees/Wages, Salaries. Wages are paid on a twice-monthly basis--the 5th and 20th for pay periods of the 1st to the 15th, and the 16th to the last day of the month. Therefore, the first pay period is paid during the month in which it is incurred, but the second pay period is paid during the next month. The wages/salaries amount in **Figure 16-4**, Month 5 is $93,870. This was calculated as follows: The total wages/salaries amount in **Figure 16-2**, Month 5 is $101,696. Half of that amount will be paid in Month 5 ($50,848). Also, the total wages/salaries amount in **Figure 16-2**, Month 4, is $86,044. Half of this ($43,022) will also be paid in Month 5. The actual wages/salaries paid (cash out) is the sum of $50,848 + $43,022, or $93,870. This calculation method was used in all the months for **Figure 16-4** to calculate the pay out of wages/salaries.

Cash Out--Cost of Fees/Other. The description of this item is presented in the notes for **Figure 16-2**. Some of the items may have differing pay-out schedules, but for this illustration, it has been assumed that they will all be paid in the month after they are incurred. In Month 5 of **Figure 16-4**, the Other amount is $12,099. This is the same amount that appears in Month 4 of **Figure 16-2** as "Other Costs."

Total Cost of Fees. This amount in Month 5 is $132,609. The calculation is a summation of the three numbers in the column above ($26,640 + $93,870 + $12,099 = $132,609).

Administrative Expenses. These expenses are assumed to be paid in the month after they are incurred. This is an oversimplification for illustrative purposes. For an actual operation, review of the items listed in the notes to **Figure 16-2** would be necessary with a payment schedule established for each of the Administrative Expense items. The amount in Month 5 of **Figure 16-4** is $10,649. This number was transferred from Month 4 of **Figure 16-2**.

Total Cash Out. Summation of Total Cost of Fees and Administrative Expense. In Month 5, the amount is $143,256; the sum of $132,609 and $10,647.

Increase (Decrease) in Cash. The calculation on this line is to determine if the month's transactions resulted in an increase or a decrease in cash. Decreases would be presented in brackets. There is a *decrease*

Figure 16-4
Pro Forma Cash Flow Statement

Month	1	2	3	4	5	6	7	8	9	10	11	12
Cash In												
Fees	$0	0	0	68,800	107,500	141,900	180,600	215,000	215,000	249,400	288,100	288,100
Other	100,000	0	0	0	0	0	0	0	0	0	0	0
Total Cash In	$100,000	0	0	68,800	107,500	141,900	180,600	215,000	215,000	249,400	288,100	288,100
Cash Out												
Cost of Fees												
Telecomm.	$0	0	2,500	19,402	26,640	34,947	42,054	50,362	50,362	58,670	65,697	65,697
Wages/Salaries	18,421	46,964	64,350	78,829	93,870	104,042	111,754	123,773	137,194	143,962	130,486	109,015
Other	0	3,934	7,649	9,825	12,099	14,375	5,675	16,748	18,910	20,966	20,966	17,568
Total Cost of Fees	$18,421	50,898	74,499	108,056	132,609	153,364	169,483	190,883	206,466	223,598	217,149	192,280
Admin. Expense	$0	3,462	6,731	8,646	10,647	12,650	13,794	14,738	16,640	18,450	18,450	15,460
Total Cash Out	$18,421	54,360	81,230	116,702	143,256	166,014	183,277	205,621	223,106	242,048	235,599	207,740
Increase (Decrease) in cash	$81,579	(54,360)	(81,230)	(47,902)	(35,756)	(24,114)	(2,677)	9,379	(8,106)	7,352	52,501	80,360
Use (payoff) of line of credit	$0	0	54,011	47,902	35,756	24,114	2,677	(9,379)	8,106	(7,352)	(52,501)	(80,360)
Cash Balance	$81,579	27,219	0	0	0	0	0	0	0	0	0	0
Line of Credit (Borrow from Bank)	$0	0	54,011	101,913	137,669	161,783	164,460	155,081	163,187	155,835	103,334	22,974

in cash of $35,756 in Month 5. This resulted from the Total Cash Out amount of $143,256 being greater than the Total Cash In amount of $107,500.

Use (Payoff) of Line of Credit. This line presents the transactions occurring with the line of credit. It shows as a positive amount, and a payment to offset the Decrease in Cash shows as a negative or bracketed amount. The convention, here, arises because the payback takes money out of the company, and the borrowing brings money into the business. In Month 5, there is a need to use $35,756 of the line of credit to keep the cash balance from being negative. This balances with the $35,756 decrease in cash during this month.

Cash Balance. This is the amount of cash in the business. In this statement, it has been kept at "0" due to the draw on the line of credit. However, some banks will require that there be a minimum amount of cash; and in that event, it would be necessary to borrow more from the line of credit to keep a minimum balance in cash.

Line of Credit. The bottom line of this report is the amount of Line of Credit (loans from the bank) outstanding. The peak need amount projected is in Month 7, $164,460. Notice that, as the increases in cash are positive, the line of credit in use is reduced.

How To Use the Cash Flow Statement. The purpose of this statement is to project the peak cash need and to provide a standard against which the actual results will be measured. Management or entrepreneurs can look at this report and determine the entire bankroll (loans and investments) needed to start and continue the business.

As a reminder, note that this measures only the flow of cash through the business and does not report whether the business is doing well or poorly from an operating standpoint.

However, if the cash needs become much greater than anticipated, it becomes obvious that there are potential problems with business operations. The specifics of those problems would be revealed in the Pro Forma Operating Statement.

IV. BALANCE SHEET

A sample format of a balance sheet is presented in **Figure 16-5**.

The purpose of this report is to measure the "book worth" of the business. It answers the question: *"How much is the business worth from an accounting standpoint?"*

The specific presentation of this is at the bottom of the report. The section titled Stockholder's Equity is the section often referred to as Net Worth. If all the assets were converted to cash at the "Book Value" (the amount shown in the accounting records) and all the liabilities were paid off, the amount left would be the Stockholder's Equity or the Net Worth of the Company.

The primary purpose of the balance sheet is to present that amount. It also shows the amounts of the items that, together, create this "worth."

The operations of a business are measured only by inference from this report. The structure of this report is to measure the assets relative to the liabilities and stockholders' equity. The traditional double-entry accounting system assures that these two amounts are the same. The Total Assets line will always be the same amount as the Total Liabilities and Equities line.

A detailed presentation on the balance sheet is not appropriate for this chapter. However, it is proper to highlight some transactions that impact the operating statement and how they find their way into the balance sheet.

Some of the more obvious of these transactions are:

* *Retained earnings are the accumulated years of net profits or income created by the operations of the business.* The profit from operations increases the worth of the business, and an increase in retained earnings is the result. Sometimes, the neophyte is confused by the fact that retained earnings are not presented as an asset, but rather as a liability. One must consider the perspective of the report. The balance sheet presents the perspective of the corporation. The owners of the business are the stockholders, not the corporation. If the corporation retains earnings, it is in effect keeping earnings that belong to the stockholders. Therefore, it is owed and, as such, is a liability to the corporation.

* *Depreciation is an allowance for the using up of an asset.* A simplified example is equipment valued at $60,000 and depreciated over a 5-year period would create a monthly depreciation amount of $1,000. There are many methods for computing depreciation as well as restrictions on the years allowed. The applicable tax law is the source of guidance for depreciation. Consult your accountant or tax advisor.

Specific amounts are not included in **Figure 16-5**. The purpose of this section is to show the structure and comment briefly on how it ties into the bottom line of measuring the success of management.

Two of the key ratios a banker and management look at are:

* *Liquidity or Current Ratio is a comparison of the current assets relative to the current liabilities.* For most industries (each industry has its own), the ratio is generally in the 2:1 range. This means a healthy business should have $2 of current assets for each $1 of current liability. This measures the liquidity or availability of readily usable assets (cash and accounts receivable) that can be turned into cash to pay the current liabilities. This provides a measure of how well a business could handle a near-term slowdown or crisis.

* *Debt-to-Equity Ratio is a comparison of the amount of debt relative to the equity of the owners.* For most industries, lenders like to keep this in the 3:1 or 4:1 range. This means a healthy business should only be borrowing $3 to $4 for each dollar it has in the business. It is a measure of how leveraged or "out on a limb" the business is at the current time. The more debt a company has, the more difficult it becomes for it to survive prolonged periods of slowdown or crisis.

THE BOTTOM LINE

Figure 16-5
Sample Balance Sheet Format

(as of this date)

ASSETS

Current Assets:
Cash   xxx
Accounts receivable   xxx
Prepaid expenses   xxx

     Total Current Assets   XXX

Fixed Assets
Property and Equipment   xxx
Less accumulated depreciation   xxx

     Total Fixed Assets   XXX

Other Assets
Notes Receivable   xxx

     Total Other Assets   XXXX

     Total Assets   XXXXXX

LIABILITIES AND STOCKHOLDER'S EQUITY

Current Liabilities:
Notes payable   xxx
Current portion of long-term debt   xxx
Accounts payable   xxx
Commissions payable   xxx
Other accrued expenses   xxx
Income taxes payable   xxx

     Total Current Liabilities   XXXX

Long Term Liabilities

Long Term Debt   XXXX

Stockholders' Equity:
Common stock   xxx
Retained earnings   xxx

     Total Stockholders' Equity   XXXX

     Total Liabilities and Equities   XXXXXX

V. PROFIT CENTERS VERSUS COST CENTERS

A discussion about cost versus profit centers usually surfaces at the author's seminars on "The Bottom Line." A general recap of those many discussions is presented here from the assumption that there is keen interest in the topic.

It appears that many telemarketing centers within a company begin as a cost center and develop the need to become a profit center. The following points are intended to shed some light on the purpose of cost centers within organizations, and to identify the key differences between a cost center and a profit center.

Cost centers are the segments of the business that can and should be measured for their independent performance.

Examples of cost centers are:

* *Individual departments.*

* *Separate locations.*

* *Individual programs.*

* *Types of programs.*

* *Times of day.*

* *Time periods.*

The principal reasons for cost-center measurement is to perform marginal and comparative analysis of:

* *Individual manager performance.*

* *Seasonal cycles.*

* *Types of work.*

* *Customers.*

* *Industries.*

The general rule in creating a cost or profit center is to be able to consider only the revenues generated and/or costs incurred that are directly related to and/or controlled by the segment of the business being evaluated. This is sometimes difficult where there is a sharing of resources or if the accounting department is not trapping and recording the costs separately.

Some of the key differences between profit and cost centers are listed below:

THE BOTTOM LINE

COST CENTER

* *No revenue control.*

* *Near-term: cost containment.*

* *Units produced/$ cost.*

* *Spend budget or lose it.*

* *Budget basis: call volume.*

* *No outside costs considered.*

PROFIT CENTER

* *Revenue control.*

* *Near-term: sales growth.*

* *Sales produced/$ cost.*

* *Create profit.*

* *Budget basis: sales volume.*

* *Allocation of overhead sales.*

The principal similarities between cost and profit centers are listed below:

* *Management of costs.*

* *Concern about productivity.*

* *Motivation of staff.*

* *Desire to keep management happy.*

Each type of center has its own purpose. *It is only important to make certain that the operating center being managed knows what it is and that the measures of performance are consistent within that.* The management or manager who establishes one or the other should know that each creates its own set of behaviors. Each structure can work well in ideal circumstances.

However, in a soft-sell environment with an established and slowly changing telemarketing application, it could be very frustrating to the TSR's and the managers to be imbedded in an intense profit-center management style. The opportunities to increase revenues, near-term growth and create incentives could be very limited. "Could be" was used in the last sentence, because there are instances where this is not necessarily true.

In situations where there is a need to open new markets, and where there is lots of competition, there may be a need to be more aggressive. The TSR's may need to be given incentives to sell more.

"Aggressive" doesn't necessarily mean "abrasive" or "obnoxious." In fact, it may mean giving the customer more attention, probing for his or her objections, and using creativity in determining how the product or service will fit into the special circumstances of each new customer or prospect.

Cost centers are often required to accomplish support tasks in a cost-contained environment. This usually means these centers are performing a service that cannot be measured relative to the sales generated. This situation can develop in a variety of tasks ranging from customer service work to sales-lead development.

The performance of every center is measured in some way. It is important only that there be

269

consistency between mission and the measurements used to manage the center.

Following are examples of non-dollar units that would be measured in both cost and profit centers. These would be measured to manage costs and identify the levels of productivity being attained.

Non-dollar units measured:

* *Calls completed per hour, day, etc.*

* *Calls received per hour, day, etc.*

* *Average call length.*

* *Staffing hours per day, week, etc.*

* *Staffing ratios.*

Following are three items that would be measured in a cost center to determine overall performance. These *same items* could be measured in a profit center, but they would be used for cost management purposes only:

* *Cost per call completed.*

* *Cost per average call.*

* *Cost per staff hour.*

In a cost center, which concentrates on cost management rather than revenue generation, it's *not appropriate* to measure the following ratios:

* *Staff cost as a percentage of revenue.*

* *Average call cost as a percentage of revenue.*

* *Telecommunications costs per hour as a percentage of hourly revenue.*

A telemarketing cost center's bottom line (primary) focus is on *cost management*. A telemarketing profit center's bottom line (primary) focus is on *creating revenue at a rate in excess of the costs incurred*. Knowing "The Bottom Line" of your center, and creating consistent reporting and management tools, will enhance productivity.

The reader should note that the Pro Forma Direct Operating Expense Budget in **Figure 16-1** applies more to a cost center, while the Pro Forma Operating Statement in **Figure 16-2** applies more to a profit center.

Knowing the kinds of reports that are created by accounting departments will help a management team better report and monitor the performance of their center. Reports containing performance statistics are more fully described and discussed in **Chapter 15** of this Encyclopedia. Review those illustrations in conjunction with the reports presented in this chapter.

THE BOTTOM LINE

VI. SUMMARY AND REVIEW

The standard financial reports have been presented as they can be used within a telemarketing center environment. However, each center will have different requirements, and will need to modify the examples included here to better suit their unique circumstances.

"The Bottom Line" for managers of telemarketing centers is that they are working with accounting professionals to make certain that financial reports are as good as they can be.

Ask questions. Are the reports helpful in managing the center? Are the reports providing as much detail as is really needed?

The illustrations used in this chapter should help both the telemarketing manager and his or her accounting advisor to better understand what is needed. At the very least, they should provide a common ground from which to begin a review of the current reports, and to begin development of new and better financial reports.

271

CHAPTER 17

Computers

Richard T. Brock
Chairman, Brock Control Systems, Inc.
Atlanta, Georgia

Judy Lanier
President, SofTel Systems
San Jose, California

Assuming that "necessity is the mother of invention," it's easy to see why computers and telephones have become an integral part of today's information-intensive, time-critical business environment. If we look at the historical and technical evolution of today's business environment, we can see that the marriage of computers and telephones within the business environment was inevitable from the start.

Telephones, computers and business were made for each other.

THE EVOLUTION THAT BECAME A REVOLUTION

By taking a distant look over our shoulders we can see how the nature of business, computing technology and basic communications have converged to become inextricably linked in telemarketing. If ever there was an example of the overworked word *synergy*, this is it--*the result of the whole being greater than the sum of its parts.* Automated telemarketing today is actually the result of yesterday's need to manage increasing amounts of information and reach new markets.

The Evolution of Business. If we look back far enough, we see that the earliest business transactions were the model of simplicity and efficiency. The local caveman saw what he wanted and took it...perhaps with the aid of a large club. Not exactly a "relationship builder," but an exchange or transaction nonetheless. This type of transaction was more of an *event* than a *process* and tended to alienate repeat business for obvious reasons.

Using this early starting point for our evolutionary time line, we quickly trace through the development of farming, barter and eventually into serious commerce--a monetary system with coinage and currency. At this point things started to get complicated. No longer was the process "*I'll gladly pay you Tuesday for some corn today.*" The basic transaction just became a bit more complicated since *the need to track a calendar- driven process* was now part of the emerging fabric of business.

As we move into the era of durable goods manufacture (not just agricultural products), business immediately runs smack head-on into the industrial revolution. Suddenly, inventory becomes a problem, and the need to reach larger markets to ''get it out of the back room'' becomes critical to a profitable enterprise. Now communications becomes an important element in the business equation. Getting word to the next town that you have a large supply of size-8 sandals can be the difference between success and failure. The obvious migration path is now toward strategic business alliances in those other towns. . . dealers, distributors, wholesalers, value-added firms (sandals with custom tassels).

Assuming that the basic business is successful, the core business eventually branches into multiple product lines, different pricing structures and multiple tiers of distribution. The entire process becomes bound in the elements of time, price, product, delivery and the detailed information necessary to *repeat the process*.

Today's business environment is filled with firms having multiple product lines, selling to many end-users through multiple tiers of distribution. Tracking information and communicating it internally and externally is an absolute necessity if a business is to survive and grow.

The Evolution of Communications. Once again, far enough back in the evolutionary scale, are jungle drums and smoke signals, perhaps the earliest forms of junk mail but no doubt effective for the times. Advances in communication quickly moved through the milestones of mail, telegraph, telephone and radio communications. Among all forms of communications, perhaps one element more than any other is responsible for catapulting the world into the information decade...*the telephone*.

The switched public telephone network has become one of the technological wonders of the modern age. Today, virtually *every business desk in the entire world* is linked by a simple pair of copper wires, and for the first time in the evolution of business and communications, it's possible for even the smallest business to directly access another, anywhere in the world.

The late 20th Century has witnessed the development of global satellite communications and the divestiture of the Bell System, thus creating a free-world market communications economy in which everyone can participate. Mass communications in the form of advertising, direct mail and print media (newspapers and magazines) and broadcast are accessible to the businessman intent on reaching his markets and his allies. Businesses can, for the first time, literally be heard around the world to reach their customers, generate leads and interact with markets in different geographies, time zones, cultures or demographics.

Communications has moved from the general to the specific, with blinding speed. However, this laser-like focus for communications has created new challenges. It's somewhat akin to attending a large party and, after first-time introductions, trying to remember everyone's name, occupation, hobby and special interests on demand. When a business uses the incredible power inherent in mass communications to develop new business, it has the unnerving tendency *to work*.

Companies are learning that mass communications is tremendously effective in *generating interest* in a particular product in the form of *sales leads*, often to the point of becoming an *insurmountable opportunity*. Once again, how does a business separate the suspects from the prospects? How can leads be qualified and turned over to sales in a timely and accurate manner? Historically the process of ''cherry picking'' leads by the sales force took advantage of the obvious hits, with the remainder going into oblivion. A structured approach to information management was the only way a business could track, analyze and act on its information if it were to survive.

273

The Evolution of the Computer. Futurists and historians alike are unsure of the ultimate impact of the computer. Perhaps as did the renaissance of the 13th Century, the computer age is destined to change the nature of human existence for the better. One thing is certain, it has *already* changed the face of business as we know it, and it's clear that those companies that do not embrace, and embrace *quickly*, the power of the computer are doomed to go the way of the dinosaur and buggy whip.

Using our historical model it's easy to trace the dawn of computing from "counting on fingers" to the abacus and onward through the mechanical adding machines and early "electronic brains." The vacuum tube gave way to the transistor and the microprocessor was not far behind. Brainiac and Eniac gave way to the IBM 360; 4-bit processors became 8-bit and 16-bit, with 32-bit processors already in widespread use. Parallel processing and fifth-generation languages are waiting in the wings, while the cost and footprint of today's computer continues to shrink.

Telemarketing--Tying It All Together. Taking a look at the graphic showing the convergence of the three lines (**Figure 17-1**), it's apparent that telemarketing balances the equation for these three elements. Simply put, the complexity of today's business environment requires the leverage of the computer and the telephone to establish and maintain its basic equilibrium.

For continued growth, businesses must be able to reach markets, generate and qualify leads, then close sales and maintain relationships in a timely and efficient manner. Philosophically, little has changed in this "formula for success in business." However, in view of the complexity of information, the pace and the sheer magnitude of the process being handled, automating is the only alternative.

Ground Zero--Where Business, Communications and Computers Meet. The point where the three lines converge in the model is ground zero for the modern telemarketing environment. A successful company will achieve a balance between the development of the business organization, the ability to process information (computer system) and its market development activities (communications and lead generation).

Complex businesses maintaining long-term relationships, managing multiple product lines through multiple channels of communication and distribution, and at the same time engaged in continued growth must establish the right question.

AUTOMATING TELEMARKETING IN THE COMING DECADE

Today, there are as many different ways to implement an automated telemarketing system as there are computers and software programs. The most practical method for automating is by looking at the way you do business. Then, overlay the different software and systems, finding the one that most closely fits your established operating procedures.

An automated system should not change the way you do business; it should enhance a successful business cycle, increasing productivity, results and revenue. However, in today's computing environment, it's becoming more and more difficult to tell the computers apart.

In a very real sense, computers are becoming more alike, and within the coming decade they will,

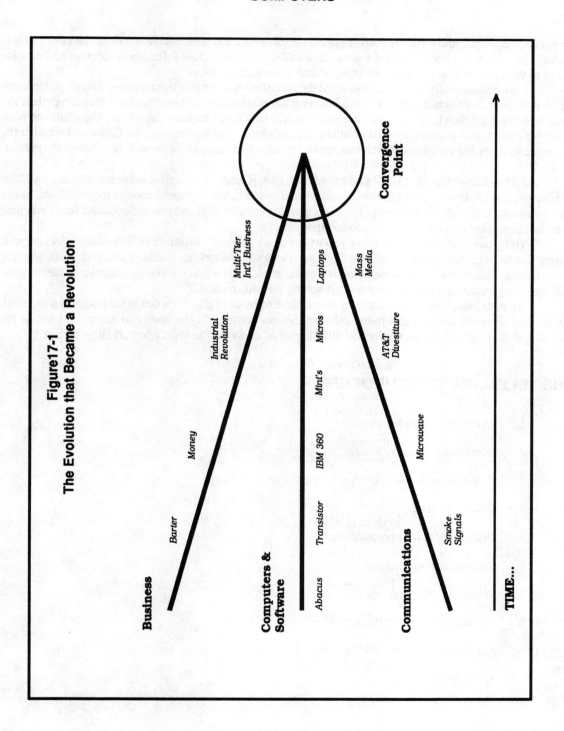

**Figure17-1
The Evolution that Became a Revolution**

Business

Barter

Money

Industrial
Revolution

Multi-Tier
Int'l Business

**Computers &
Software**

Abacus

Transistor

IBM 360

Mini's

Micros

Laptops

Communications

Smoke
Signals

Microwave

AT&T
Divestiture

Mass
Media

**Convergence
Point**

TIME...

for the most part, become virtually indistinguishable. Software and user interface will be the key. For this reason, automation of a telemarketing organization will revolve around the selection of software and the ease of use to the user; not on the selection of a particular piece of hardware.

If a business really wants to understand the role of computers in telemarketing, then an understanding of what runs them is necessary. Once a business has selected the software package that can deliver the "value perceived," then hardware considerations such as how much memory, how many terminals and what type of modem become secondary. It's really a matter of what's on the screen, ease of use and whether the analysis and reporting functions are relevant to the business that determines the overall value of the system.

Software--Where the Rubber Meets the Road. Successful software packages will be flexible enough to allow tailoring for any business environment, yet structured enough to provide the basics for a successful telemarketing process. The telemarketing environment and process contain a set of accepted steps and processes that constitute "a proven approach."

This generic model should apply regardless of a company's business environment or industry. It shows the flow of information and the building blocks necessary to create a credible telemarketing environment. Using this as a starting point, it's easier to evaluate a given software package on meeting the minimum requirements for processing or "crunching the information."

Another important consideration is on the issue of flexibility: Given that the software is structured, can it still be exactly tailored to a particular business environment? The ability to design and define the variables within each of the following activities is part of choosing the right telemarketing system.

THE TELEMARKETING PROCESS:

1. *List sorting/merging/purging.*

2. *Distribution of leads to agents.*

3. *Preparation for the call.*

4. *Dialing contacts.*

5. *Delivery of sales presentation.*

6. *Referencing information.*

7. *Scheduling the next contact.*

8. *Recording contact information.*

9. *Fulfillment process.*

10. *Management reporting.*

The Real World Environment--Making It Work. Telemarketing is just now being recognized for its tremendous potential in today's business environment, although many people continue to use the words *telemarketing* and *telesales* interchangeably. Telemarketing is the planned and systematic use of the telephone in the sales cycle. Telesales is actually concluding a sale over the phone. Automated telemarketing as a critical part of the computer-assistance of the overall business development cycle is still, for a great part, unrealized.

A fuller explanation of telemarketing, and how it fits into the business cycle becomes apparent when viewed in the context of the graphic in **Figure 17-2**. It is clear that the centrally located computer is the "brain" behind the entire process, and telemarketing is a key in sustaining the process.

A CLOSER LOOK AT SOME OF THE PIECES

Computerized Telesales. The use of the computer to automatically load selected names into an autodialer initiates the process. The computer then makes calls by searching and dialing numbers until a connection is made. When someone answers, usually a consumer at home, he or she is greeted with a message similar to *"Hello--please hold for a moment for a message from Hollywood."* At this point, the consumer is presented with a prerecorded sales message in an effort to get him to agree to a follow-up call from a human sales rep.

Automated Telemarketing. Computer-assisted telemarketing, on the other hand is the use of the computer in conjunction with the telephone, to generate and/or close business. This becomes an integral, but not exclusive, step in the marketing and sales process.

Simply having a computer isn't enough. The system has to work within the dynamics of real-life business--generating and qualifying the leads, closing sales, handling customer service problems and complaints, communication with the distribution channels and more. An automated system has the power and intelligence to track, monitor, analyze and report this entire process. Looking at the business cycle, the power of the computer and its pivotal role are apparent.

EVOLUTION OF TELEMARKETING

From initial simple order-taking, telemarketing has evolved into a distinct industry that can be broken into the major categories of in-bound and out-bound, business-to-business and business-to-consumer. The level of automation necessary depends on the different processes to be managed and the specific goals established for the telemarketing program. In typical situations, business-to-business telemarketing develops relationships and is part of a long and sometimes complex, sales cycle. Business-to-consumer telemarketing more often fits into the one-time contact telesales category.

Business-to-Consumer. Business-to-consumer telemarketing developed as a result of other mass marketing mechanisms, such as advertising, direct mail, radio and television. TV advertising in

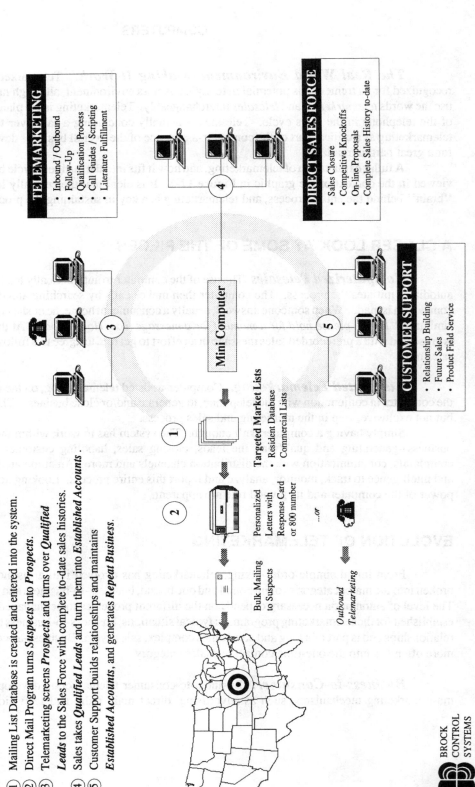

Figure 17-2

Managing the Entire Business Development Cycle

TELEMARKETING
- Inbound / Outbound
- Follow-Up
- Qualification Process
- Call Guides / Scripting
- Literature Fulfillment

DIRECT SALES FORCE
- Sales Closure
- Competitive Knockoffs
- On-line Proposals
- Complete Sales History to-date

CUSTOMER SUPPORT
- Relationship Building
- Future Sales
- Product Field Service

Mini Computer

Targeted Market Lists
- Resident Database
- Commercial Lists

Personalized Letters with Response Card or 800 number

...or...

Bulk Mailing to Suspects

Outbound Telemarketing

① Mailing List Database is created and entered into the system.
② Direct Mail Program turns *Suspects* into *Prospects*.
③ Telemarketing screens *Prospects* and turns over *Qualified Leads* to the Sales Force with complete to-date sales histories.
④ Sales takes *Qualified Leads* and turn them into *Established Accounts*.
⑤ Customer Support builds relationships and maintains *Established Accounts*, and generates *Repeat Business*.

BROCK CONTROL SYSTEMS INCORPORATED • 1600 Parkwood Circle • Atlanta • GA • 30339 • (800) 221-0775 • (404) 956-0081 • FAX (404) 955-5515

BROCK CONTROL SYSTEMS

particular gave rise to inbound business-to-consumer telemarketing with *"special offers not available in stores"* and *"operators standing by now to take your order."*

This business-to-consumer inbound telemarketing program is perfectly suited to automated systems, since the process is really order entry with perhaps credit card validation. The simplest of computerized systems can be used to automate this process as the computer is doing nothing more than receiving data entry. The marketing and pre-sale of the product has already taken place.

Business-to-consumer outbound telemarketing fits next in the hierarchy of automation needs. For example, the margin on magazine subscription sales makes a direct sales force unprofitable. The telephone is the selling vehicle and the computer takes on an important role as information provider. An automated system can contain a database of names meeting certain criteria, thereby delivering more qualified prospect names to the telemarketer than just the general population.

By accessing the database, the telemarketer may get information that will help make the sale, such as buying history, lapsed subscriptions and similar products that the prospect may find interesting.

The automated system provides not only sales information but acts as a "pacer," integrating a power dialing system to assure the maximum number of calls are being made per hour, as well as facilitating the order entry process, and tracking results.

Business-to-Business. The next level for realizing the direct benefits of computer-assisted telemarketing is in business-to-business inbound calling. Here, one business person is calling another in response to a specific marketing message. The call often is the continuation of an already existing relationship. Through the power of automation, previous purchase history, order information and pricing are readily available to support the telemarketing effort.

An example of this type of user is the manufacturer who sells items such as film, floppy disks, cassette tapes and other consumables directly to retailers on a repeat basis. By using targeted direct mail interfaced to the telemarketing master files, vendors can generate a call from the customer through specific marketing campaigns. In fact, many companies frequently plan regular promotions to prompt calls from their customers.

In this situation, the Telemarketing Sales Representative (TSR) can, through computer assistance, find out shipping and order entry information, as well as the customer's previous purchases of all related products. A number of innovative companies are using computer generated follow-up reports to initiate outbound telemarketing to accounts whose purchases of a certain product decline for no discernible reason.

The most aggressive use of computer-assisted telemarketing is in outbound business-to-business calling. Wholesalers/distributors, manufacturers, financial institutions, *Fortune* 1,000 companies, small businesses with a limited direct sales force can all successfully use outbound automated telemarketing to manage the sales cycle from initial contact through account management. An automated system can be adopted as a departmental solution, or as the basis for a company-wide method of managing marketing, sales and post-sale support.

In this environment, knowing "the story so far" becomes a critical element in the sales cycle. A telemarketer has instant access to all previous contacts with a prospect or customer so the complete history of the relationship is in front of the telemarketer when the call is made.

In many outbound business-to-business situations, telemarketing is being used in the truest sense of the word: as a relationship builder until a prospect is ready to be turned over to the sales force. Through automation, competitive information and reference materials are on-line, as well as the best answers in given scenarios. This equips all telemarketers equally well, in essence cloning a company's best rep, making even a novice confident and competent in his efforts.

COMPUTERS IN TELEMARKETING

The marriage of computers and telemarketing is a natural relationship. Telemarketing by its very definition means working with large numbers of names and prospects, and turning over the results as quickly as possible to move on to the next list. Until computer-assisted telemarketing was developed, most telemarketing managers lived under an avalanche of paper covered with various "tic marks" in order to keep track of the process. The telemarketers worked from 3"x5" cards or sheets of paper that had to be hand-tallied for information.

An automated telemarketing system works in a similar way on its most basic level, but by eliminating the manual part of the cycle, the entire process becomes more efficient, more accurate and more productive.

Computer assistance in telemarketing provides the greatest "value received" and is most productive in the specific areas of:

* *Call management.*

* *Information management.*

* *Fulfillment management.*

* *Performance management.*

CALL MANAGEMENT

A computer-assisted telemarketing program manages the calling processing more efficiently, from assigning calls to dialing to facilitating the process of recording the information.

List Conversion. Telemarketing usually begins with a name and a number, most often in the form of lists of thousands. The lists must be turned into manageable chunks to be parceled out to telemarketers. Through computer assistance, a list in the form of magnetic media, such as tape, is "read" into the database of the telemarketing program. The computer can quickly and cost-effectively purge duplicate names--a process impractical on a manual system and a costly waste of resources if not done. The names are then available for further categorization, depending on the campaign and intent of the program.

Call Queuing. The process of assigning lists of names to individual campaigns. An automated system produces a list from the program's resident database, based on key criteria such as region of the country, SIC, follow-up date or campaign. From the list, the telemarketer must be able to directly access the prospect's record, either to begin gathering initial data or for historical reference in a follow-up campaign. At the end of a call, the telemarketer leaves the updated prospect record and returns to the Call Queue for the next name. An automated system marks or retires the names as they are worked, preventing repeat calls (see **Figure 17-3**).

Autodial. An automated telemarketing system takes advantage of autodialing mechanisms through a direct interface. The record or phone number viewed on a terminal screen will be automatically dialed at a keystroke. In large telemarketing operations, the autodialer is also compatible with the various long-distance services to place the call on the least expensive line (least cost routing).

Response. "Automation" implies quick response to commands. In some telemarketing situations, the record is retrieved after the prospect is contacted. The system response time must be compatible with the type of telemarketing operation. A high volume telesales operation will need much faster response than a telemarketing program being used in a qualifying mode where the telemarketer is likely very familiar with the product.

INFORMATION MANAGEMENT

An automated telemarketing system processes and manages information through a central database. The central database provides telemarketers access to all the information necessary to accomplish a successful call. The data gathered through telemarketing can also be retrieved for comprehensive reports on campaigns.

Prospect Tracking Database. The prospect tracking database is the complete record of a prospect; essentially, the heart of any automated system. It is in the prospect record that data is first collected and it is this record which becomes the starting point for all other action. Any activity taken with a prospect becomes a part of this electronic file, building a complete on-line history. A telemarketer looking at the prospect's record for the first time will know as much as the rep who has been working the prospect for a year. The complexity of the arrangement of information in a prospect record depends on the type of telemarketing or telesales operation (see **Figure 17-4**).

Call Guides/Scripting. Scripts are used on many different levels, but in an automated system, the key is instant access to information. "Script" implies a set of questions and answers used by a telemarketer with no variation. From a prepared opening statement, a script-oriented automated system allows the user to key through the question-and-answer format, recording the answers and tallying the results. This method is most useful in high volume, outbound telemarketing. Getting it into the system is obvious but the value comes later when it can be retrieved *on-demand*. Nothing falls through the cracks, and the information can relate to a variety of campaigns, products, accounts or *whatever*.

Figure 17-3
Call Queuing

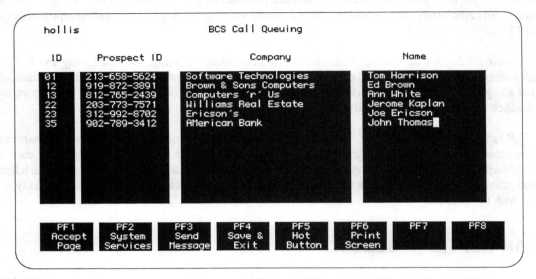

Figure 17-4
Prospect Tracking

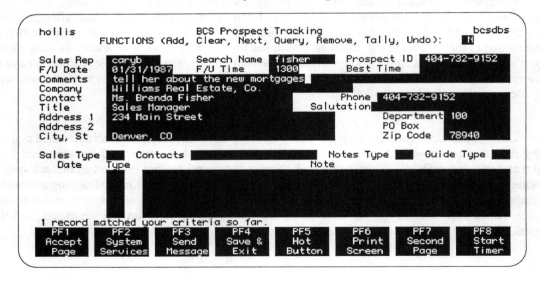

A call guide works as an aide, prompting a telemarketer through the prospect's questions and providing quick access to additional information. This highly flexible system switches to various subsidiary databases, providing telemarketers access to information they could previously only learn with years of training. In business-to-business inbound and outbound calling, competitive information, quick objection handling and extensive product knowledge are essential. An automated system can provide the answers through a keystroke. That's the kind of recall power and delivery that can *only come with a computer*.

FULFILLMENT MANAGEMENT

A critical part of the telemarketing cycle is the fulfillment of the prospect's expectations. An automated system never forgets to send literature or prompt a follow-up call.

End-of-Call Fulfillment. At the end of every telephone call, action is demanded. An automated system maintains the resources for delivering on-the-call commitments in several ways. An interface to a printer produces follow-up letters automatically. The system tracks the materials that become the fulfillment package, recording the activity in the prospect's history. On-line communications send action messages to the appropriate personnel for the fulfillment activity and return verification.

Follow-Up. In telemarketing operations that develop prospect relationships, the follow-up activity is an important element in triggering the next action in the sales cycle. An expectation of a follow-up is created in a call, and an automated system ensures that the expectation is fulfilled. An internal calendar tracks the follow-up dates attached to prospect records and depending on the system, provides lists for calling or prompt mailings, based on any number of additional criteria.

PERFORMANCE MANAGEMENT

Telemarketing management must have a way of analyzing performance of individuals as well as results of specific campaigns. An automated system contains all information in a centrally located database, which is accessed for objective reports based on activity.

Individual Performance Monitoring. Automated systems track telemarketers' performance by capturing a record of their individual calling history. As the telemarketers use the system, their activity is recorded in subsidiary databases that form the basis for management reports. Reports can be as simple as how many calls were attempted and how many connections were made, or as complex as call results analysis (see **Figure 17-5**).

Call Monitoring. An automated system provides call monitoring screen-to-screen and through the phone switch. By accessing the shared database, a manager can view, in real-time, the individual

Figure 17-5
Performance Monitoring

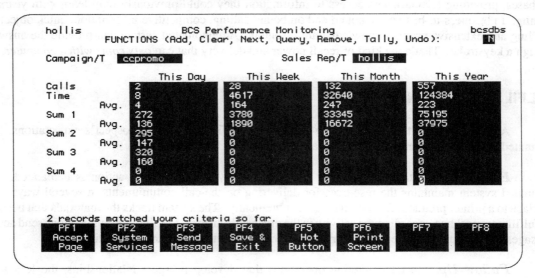

```
hollis                 BCS Performance Monitoring              bcsdbs
              FUNCTIONS (Add, Clear, Next, Query, Remove, Tally, Undo):   N

Campaign/T  ccpromo                    Sales Rep/T  hollis

                  This Day      This Week    This Month     This Year
   Calls            2              28           132          557
   Time             8            4617         32640          124384
          Avg.      4             164           247          223
   Sum 1          272            3780         33345          75195
          Avg.    136            1890         16672          37975
   Sum 2          295               0             0            0
          Avg.    147               0             0            0
   Sum 3          320               0             0            0
          Avg.    160               0             0            0
   Sum 4            0               0             0            0
          Avg.      0               0             0            0


   2 records matched your criteria so far.
  PF1       PF2       PF3       PF4       PF5       PF6       PF7       PF8
 Accept    System    Send     Save &     Hot      Print
 Page    Services   Message    Exit     Button    Screen
```

Figure 17-6
Messaging/Monitoring

```
hollis                 BCS Messaging/Monitoring
 #    Name    Phone #       Comment          Company Name
   Calls  Time  Elapsed  Prospect ID      Contact
  1* bethn
  2* budp
  3* caryb
  4* chrisc
  5* donh                   good prospect   Williams Real Estate Co.
  6   1   0:06     0:06   404-732-9152   Ms. Brenda Fisher
  7* hollis
  8  hp
  9* jimg    404-956-0081
 10* judiv   220
 11* michelel 956-0081     out of town
 12* rdk     240           at the bank




 Name # 05   Message/Comment tell her about the new mortgages
            Sent message to donh at Wed Aug 19 15:39:46 1987
  PF1       PF2       PF3       PF4       PF5       PF6       PF7       PF8
 Send      Send     Update    Exit     Review    Print     Next     Change
Message    Mail    Screen              Record   Screen     Page    Comment
```

284

telemarketer's activity. Through live, screen-based communications, the manager is then available for consultation during a phone call, without interrupting the call.

The phone provides a second link, allowing a manager to listen to a conversation. Then, through screen-based communication, the manager can message additional information or help to the telemarketer (see **Figure 17-6**).

Campaign Performance. As with individual performance monitoring, automated systems dynamically track specific campaigns. The results become part of the database for producing reports on the status and success or failure of the campaign. Not only is a global view available, but individual segments of a telemarketing campaign can be assessed. This gives management enough information to tailor a campaign by fixing specific problem areas without scrapping the entire effort.

THE PROVEN BENEFITS

Benefits to be gained from using a computerized system constitute an impressive and verifiable list. Consider the following areas:

Personnel Productivity. Users state that their systems help minimize and often totally eliminate repetitive and tedious administrative work associated with the job of telemarketing. The elimination of mundane activities helps to prevent burnout and wards off employee turnover. Autodialing increases the potential number of dials and contacts without misdials; this creates a rise in productivity in addition to decreases in telephone costs.

Users report overall improvements in staff productivity by as much as 20% and more, plus significant dollar savings.

Job Satisfaction. Aside from productivity improvements, the telephone sales representative experiences improved job satisfaction. No longer relegated to clerical work, career opportunities for telephone professionals are enhanced in much the same way as typists' careers were with the advent of word processing systems in earlier years.

Sales/Revenues/Profits. In a nonautomated environment, telephone representatives often spend 75% (45 minutes per hour) of their time in pre-call and post-call activities and only 25% (15 minutes per hour) of their selling time with a prospect or customer. Automating can reverse these numbers, which results in increased selling time.

The two largest expenses in a department are labor and telephone. With computers, management can track and measure the cost-per-lead, cost-per-call, advertising costs, effectiveness of lists, programs and people. Both telephone and labor costs, as a result, can be better controlled.

Depending on operating variables, businesses can and are increasing sales by as much as 25%-50%, with no associated increase in the cost of sales.

Management. In a manual operation, managers spend much time collecting and tabulating statistical information and maintaining a number of call and mail lists. With automation, managers have quick access to all information in the database. Some managers report that as much as one hour per day per manager is saved on list maintenance, statistical tabulation and report generation with an automated system.

Fulfillment. In manual environments customer mailings are often selected visually by going through notebooks, then addressed by hand or in some semi-automated manner. Automation allows names to be electronically selected from the database with the generation of personalized letters and labels. Some users report as much as 1,000 plus hours per year savings by automating this activity. In addition, there is a significant savings in postal rates due to the computer's ability to pre-sort in ZIP code order.

Customer Service. Without computer assistance, customer service representatives must place customers on hold while they search for information or advise the customer that a return call will be necessary--a process that results in wasted time, extra telephone expense and poor customer service. A computerized telemarketing system allows direct access to the order system so that representatives can service calls immediately. System users report a time and labor savings of hundreds of hours per year.

Strategic Planning. Because telemarketing is extremely information-intensive, a manual operation cannot effectively capture, maintain and report critical information in a timely manner. Although significant, there is no way to know for sure *how much* information is lost in a manual environment--information that can be crucial for a business to remain competitive.

The information available from a *computerized database* provides a means for management to analyze and react dynamically to the ever-changing market place. Although this category is less measurable than others, automation users say that they could not continue to do an effective job of designing and implementing new programs without computer assistance.

WHEN SHOULD A TELEMARKETING DEPARTMENT AUTOMATE?

Just as telemarketing is not a panacea for all business problems, neither is automation a cure-all for all telemarketing problems. Experts generally recognize the following as specific points where automation should become a major consideration:

* *Multiple campaigns conducted simultaneously.*

* *Information-intensive products/services.*

* *Sales force spends too much time in non-selling activities.*

* *Complex scripts are required.*

* *Large volume of incoming calls requiring capture of customer information.*

286

* *Bottlenecks exist in current system.*

* *Complex statistical reporting required.*

* *Protection of the customer database.*

* *An ongoing requirement for acquiring external prospect lists.*

* *Potential of losing control of the present system.*

* *Some applications, such as catalog sales and sophisticated surveys absolutely demand to be automated.*

Realistic Expectations. When considering purchasing a telemarketing system, prospective users should maintain realistic expectations about what computers can and cannot do for a business. For example, some business members perceive that automation *guarantees* that employees will be better satisfied in their job place. This is simply not the case. Computers will not take the place of thorough training, adequate compensation and effective management.

Horror stories include instances of employees believing that computers would in some way "replace" them, and management not adequately preparing employees for automation. Success stories are those where users have implemented computers *and* new training programs, motivation and leadership techniques.

If a department is completely disorganized, computerizing will not guarantee automatic organization. In fact, *experts generally recommend that a business get its manual system running smoothly before automating, and that start-up telemarketing operations run for six to 12 months in that mode.*

A telemarketing manager would do well to take stock of some very important items when considering automation. Are people patient? When something goes wrong, are they able to work through it before calling the vendor? Are they patient enough to wait for a call-back from the vendor?

Prospective computer users should understand that it will take two to three months to become proficient on the system. It isn't uncommon for a department to actually see a drop in productivity upon initial implementation of a computer system. However, if this continues or improvements are not forthcoming, management should step back and find out what's wrong.

For instance, was training thorough? Was the correct implementation method used? Is there a solid relationship with the vendor?

HOW TO GO ABOUT THE ACTUAL PROCESS OF AUTOMATING

An abundance of literature has been written about the benefits of computer-assisted telemarketing. Vendors, consultants and experts that represent a number of business disciplines speak eloquently about automation. However, not too many experts explain to the prospective user how to proceed through what appears to be an awesome project. This is especially the case for small businesses, where MIS *(management information systems)* and DP *(data processing)* departments either do not exist or are minimal.

287

The telemarketing operations that have achieved the highest levels of success from computer implementations have done so by breaking the project up into a number of distinct parts. By understanding each part and proceeding in a logical order, the project is simplified and success is ensured.

Form a Project Team. Assemble a committee or task force made up of representatives from all relevant parts of the business, i.e., telemarketing, sales, advertising, customer service, product marketing, MIS, etc. Include members who must understand how their departments will be affected by implementation of the telemarketing system.

Develop a Needs Analysis. The purpose here is to understand how the business application flows, identify the pressure points, find solutions to the problems they present and submit these requirements to various vendors in order to find out which one can provide the best solution.

A needs analysis may be developed by the project team alone, with the assistance of a consultant who specializes in this activity, or with help from one or more vendors.

Regardless of who does the analysis, the important thing is that it gets done. Out of this process will come a very important document--the *Request For Proposal* (see example at the end of the chapter). Its purpose is to find a supplier who can best fulfill the telemarketing requirements and determines how much it will cost.

Once proposals are returned by suppliers, the project team should review each and narrow the selection down to the final three vendors/systems.

THE TYPES OF AUTOMATED SYSTEMS

In choosing the best total system for a telemarketing operation, assess the practical limitations of the systems as well as the results you expect. Will each telemarketer work individually or will telemarketers and managers be tied into the same system? Does the telemarketing operation need to interface with a company's mainframe? Are reports to be pulled from the entire system or are simple, individual activity reports enough?

The hardware to power the various systems falls into three categories: the personal computer, the mini-computer and the mainframe. Software is written for each, and each meets a particular need.

The Personal Computer System. PC systems are best utilized in departments where each user will work with a self-contained database, or in the case of networked PC's, when the number of users is 20 or less. The popularity of the PC for business use as reflected in the installed base has resulted in a proliferation of some excellent telemarketing application software. These are usually inexpensive, albeit hard-coded programs that do a good job of gathering data and producing simple reports.

The Mini-Computer System. The mini-computer based automated system is often an excellent solution in typical business-to-business and business-to-consumer telemarketing situations. It provides an ideal processing environment because it is powerful enough to run a relational database to manage the many varied telemarketing processes.

A powerful central processing unit is the heart of the multi-user system. Individual terminals are on each telemarketer's desk, providing direct access to the information stores, while at the same time dynamically collecting incoming data for producing management reports.

A mini-computer system works equally well as a department solution or as the manager of a total environment. As a mid-range computer, its cost is closer to a sophisticated PC than a mainframe, making it a relatively inexpensive solution. It is also expandable, able to grow to accommodate additional users.

The Mainframe System. A mainframe is a large, batch-processing computer that holds tremendous stores of information. It also supports a multi-user environment, but the batch process restricts accessibility because processing time must be shared with other departments.

As a stand-alone telemarketing solution, mainframes are not a realistic option. They are expensive, and the highly technical nature of the machine requires a sophisticated support staff and method of processing information. In situations where vast amounts of information are already contained in the mainframe, such as with banks, tapping into that source is a telemarketing solution. However, that environment is not the typical telemarketing operation.

BASIC RANGE OF SOFTWARE OPTIONS

There are three basic choices for software, each offering various degrees of flexibility and cost-effectiveness.

Developmental Tools Approach. *Development tools* are pieces used to build a system from the beginning. This method offers total flexibility but demands extensive knowledge from the user to construct a working system. This approach makes several assumptions:

* *The buyer has identified all of the problems and system requirements in an automated telemarketing package.*

* *The buyer has determined the solution to his needs, including how the end product should look and operate, as well as how telemarketing reps will interface with the different screens and menus.*

* *The buyer has the time, money, personnel and management commitment to take as long as six months to develop the application.*

Turn-Key, Hard-Coded Approach. *Hard-coded,* canned packages that are "what you see is what you get." There are no options for changing the original package, such as writing additional reports or constructing different screens. This software demands very little knowledge on the user's part beyond simply learning the program.

Fully Developed Systems/Customization Tools Approach. *Fully developed systems* that

289

include tools for *customization*--the optimum solution. The user has the option of using the already constructed systems as well as grafting on their custom solution.

Elements that are common to all telemarketing operations come "built in." The buyer may use this package immediately in any given telemarketing environment. In addition, tools to write new screens, menus, reports and scripts are part of the system and available for building the custom pieces of the program. This allows different telemarketing programs to be run by the same software, while providing a single point of access and management for everyone in the organization.

Through a multi-user system, competitive knock-offs, product background and common objections become part of the shared resources. A multi-user system equips all telemarketers equally with the same broad base of knowledge. From a management standpoint, it also allows a single posting of strategic information that immediately becomes communicated across the entire system. That type of leverage available only with a computer (see **Figure 17-7**).

SELECTING THE SOFTWARE

Software should *always* be selected first because it is the virtual "brains" of the computer.

There are many telemarketing packages on the market, including generic PC-based programs that were developed using popular standard database management systems (DBMS). Also available are the more sophisticated mini-computer based systems developed around proprietary relational data bases and operating systems available through one vendor.

Once the project team has developed the needs analysis, reviewed proposals, and narrowed down the selection, it is time to evaluate the software closely.

SOFTWARE SELECTION CRITERIA

Low-End Systems. For companies without MIS and DP departments, and with users numbering from one to 20, PC-based systems are a good choice because they've been built around standard database management systems. What this means to the user is that should modifications or customized programs be desired, programming expertise can readily be located. Additionally, there is comfort to be found in the fact that the selected software is being used by thousands of other businesses. Mass usage normally indicates a high-quality product that has benefited from sufficient user feedback and a sound developmental evolution.

The following are considerations for selecting a PC-based telemarketing software:

1. *Ease of Use.* How quickly can the average TSR get up and running on the program? A rule of thumb is that any one with minimal computer knowledge should be able to install the program in about 10 minutes and begin to enter, edit and retrieve simple data in a matter of a few hours. Acquiring real proficiency should take no longer than two to three months. Ease of use is a primary consideration due to the turnover rate in most telemarketing centers--a fact that necessitates ongoing training requirements.

Figure 17-7
Options

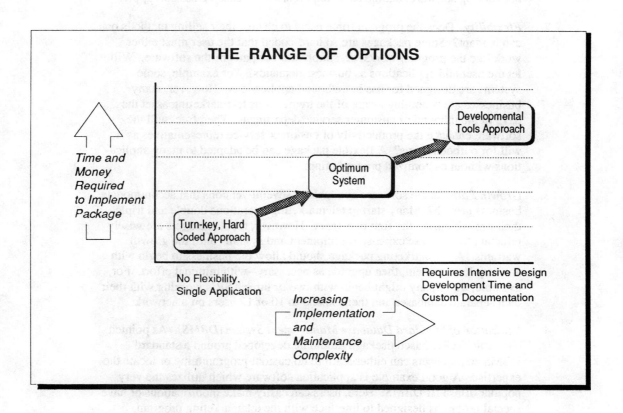

THE RANGE OF OPTIONS

Time and
Money
Required
to Implement
Package

Developmental
Tools Approach

Optimum
System

Turn-key, Hard
Coded Approach

No Flexibility.
Single Application

Increasing
Implementation
and
Maintenance
Complexity

Requires Intensive Design
Development Time and
Custom Documentation

An easy-to-use PC-based package will be "intuitive," that is, designed with friendly user interfaces (moving around in the program). Never should the software force the computer novice to learn foreign commands. For multi-user systems, the technical requirements will be more extensive due to the networking software, but the basic requirements of ease-of-use still apply.

2. *Flexibility.* Does the program force users to change their selling methods or can it adapt? Some packages are so hard-coded that the user must either work like the program works, or, simply not use parts of the software. Will it let the user add applications as business demands? For example, some systems are designed for use in outbound applications. However, many businesses are becoming aware of the tremendous telemarketing asset they have in the inbound or customer service department. Therefore, will the software enhance the productivity of customer service representatives as it will for outbound reps? A flexible package can be adapted to many applications without customized programming.

3. *Growth Path.* Is the software available in several versions that accommodate business growth? Many startup telemarketing operations double and triple their growth during the first two years. However, most managers are wisely reluctant to purchase expensive equipment and systems until the growth warrants. A telemarketing package should allow the business to begin with an entry-level system, then upgrade as necessary--with minimal effort. For example, a company might begin with two or three TSR's working with their own separate databases and then expand to 10 or 12 users on a network.

4. *Utilization of Standard Database Management System (DBMS).* As pointed out earlier, a PC-based package should be developed around a standard DBMS so that users can either learn to do custom programming or locate the expertise. A good example is application software which utilizes the very popular dBase III DBMS. Here, users can easily make modifications or have special programs designed to interface with the telemarketing program.

5. *Minimum Features/Functions.* In addition to the important considerations listed above, a PC-based telemarketing package should include the following basic design features:

    *   *A notepad where contact history and other events can be stored for an indefinite period of time.*
    *   *User-definable data fields and key sort indexes.*
    *   *Ability to flag records for future calls.*
    *   *A simple scripting facility.*

COMPUTERS

* *Ability to generate correspondence directly from the telemarketing program.*
* *An autodialer.*

High-End Systems. Once a telemarketing operation has acquired more sophisticated requirements, i.e., more than 20 users on the system, the need for multi-level branching scripts, simultaneous and multiple campaigns, reports incorporating statistical tabulations, high-volume inbound calls, etc., a minicomputer-based software package might be the solution.

Naturally, the cost of this software will be considerably higher than the PC. Although many of the selection requirements are similar to those of the PC-based products, there are additional considerations:

1. *Relational Database Management System.* The complex, multi-user environment of a large telemarketing operation necessitates data to be gathered and collated into meaningful information from and across multiple databases in a real-time, interactive manner. Therefore, a true relational DBMS should be incorporated into the software. Such a database allows users to modify applications, add applications programs, etc. This is particularly required when multiple campaigns will be run simultaneously and/or where multi-level scripts will be used.

2. *Screen Refresh Time.* Being on-line with customers requires that TSR's locate and disseminate information rapidly; therefore, software must allow the painting of new screens at a time that is reasonable for the specific telemarketing application. For example, for inbound 800 WATS applications, screen refresh time would be more critical, perhaps, than that for outbound account management applications. It is worth noting, however, that screen refresh time is driven not only by software design, but also by the type of computer equipment being used. By most standards, an acceptable average screen refresh time is two seconds or less.

3. *Flexibility.* Although some packages are designed specifically for one application, e.g., lead management, minicomputer-based software should include some type of developmental tools so that users can easily and cost-effectively add, expand or modify telemarketing applications as desired.

4. *Integration with Other Computers/Systems.* Although there is no vendor who is totally addressing integration as yet, a number of software packages and vendors are addressing it on limited levels. For example, a few PC packages have designed interfaces (through "hot" keys or function keys) to let the user switch over to another computer system in order to access order information or other files resident on a mainframe, etc. However, these interfaces are not invisible to the user and typically require quite a few additional keystrokes in order to access the required information.

293

THINGS TO CONSIDER WHILE YOU "SHOP"

Once you have a clear picture of what you need, you are ready to begin considering the alternatives. Jan McCabe, Editor of the *ATA Newsletter*, gives us the following 10 point insight:[1]

1. *Does the System Support Both Inbound and Outbound Applications?* You have to consider your operation both today and for the future. You may only need outbound capability now, but what is the probability of having an inbound application arise? You don't want to be put into the position of making a substantial investment only to find you need to upgrade or replace your equipment.

2. *How Flexible Is the Scripting?* Scripting, whether it is access to a price list, product descriptions, objections or sales benefit statements, must be easily modified and changed. Look for scripting flexibility from both the supervisor's point of view and the TSR's point of view as a user.

    The supervisor needs to be able to make changes in the script quickly. If an offer changes, new benefit statements need to be addressed or objections changed or added, and the changes need to be made quickly and easily. You don't want to have a programmer writing your sales scripts.

    And, unless you insist that all contacts flow exactly the same way, you need to consider how easily the TSR can move within the script. Can they go back a screen or go from one part of the script to another quickly? Can they skip a screen? How many scripts will the system be able to support? And, are there any limitations on the length of the scripts that are used?

3. *Does the System Provide Autodialing?* If you are doing outbound calling, autodialing is essential. You will be amazed at the increased productivity of your TSR's when you eliminate manual calling. In one case, a business who just installed an automated system saw an increase in attempts per hour from 22 calls per hour to 34 attempts per hour the first night of operations! Consider how much more productive they will be when the TSR's have an opportunity to really learn the use of the automated system.

4. *Can the System Support Multiple Applications? Can the System Support Both Inbound and Outbound Programs and Can the TSR Easily Access Any Program?* You will most likely be working on more than one project at a time, particularly if you handle any inbound calls. You need to make sure you can easily access multiple programs and that the system is able to maintain the data capture and analysis integrity of each of the programs within the system.

5. *Callback Scheduling.* Automatic rescheduling of callbacks for busy and don't answer calls for an outbound program is essential for productivity of your staff. You should be able to set system parameters that you can modify for your callback. These parameters not only return the calls for redialing at a preset time interval, they should also determine how many attempts for a number will be made before the system eliminates them from the recall list. You probably will not want to go through the list more than two to three times to attempt the busy/no answers on your list.

    And, your TSR's should be able to schedule individual callbacks to meet the needs of their schedules and their client requests.

6. *Reporting.* The system should provide you with reports on two levels, the *TSR statistics* and *campaign/program statistics.* You should be able to access information such as number of attempts per agent, number of completed calls and length of call on a minimum basis. Additionally, you will want to look at average sales value per TSR.

    On the program basis, you will want statistics that include the number of contacts completed, the number of contacts remaining, the sales values and other statistics you deem necessary for your center.

    Remember, if your TSR handles inbound calls and outbound calls you will be dealing with statistics on at least two programs. Therefore, your individual results and program results will be very different.

7. *System Documentation.* You must carefully assess the written documentation available for the system. Is it easily understood and easy to reference when problems arise? Is support available when you run into problems? How much will the support cost on an annual basis?

    You will also want to assure that training is available both initially as well as after installation. If a user group is available, you have a big plus! Most users will be happy to share the experiences, problems and solutions they have encountered with their system. This type of information can save you weeks of trial and error in establishing new applications and solving problems you may have on a program.

8. *System Management.* What kind of support will you need to maintain your system? Will you need one person, two, or more? How much training will be required? Will you be able to use any of your existing staff--or will you need to hire someone with technical background? Understanding how "user-friendly" the system is will help in determining how much programming

expertise is required to implement your applications.

When you do your daily maintenance, will the system have to be off-line and for how long? You should consider maintenance in conjunction with your center hours to assure all routines can be performed "off-line."

9. *Fulfillment Capabilities*. Can the system generate labels, letters, orders or other specific output requirements for hard-copy correspondence you may have?

What kinds of volumes can be handled, how quickly? Is a letter quality printer available to work with the system? How much more does a letter quality printer cost and what kind of system printer will you need?

10. *How Will You Integrate Your System with the Other Systems in Your Company?* You should consider the communications you have interdepartmentally to discover what outputs you will need to continue to provide, and in what format you will provide them (i.e., hard copy, magnetic tape, floppy disk, etc.).

The vendors you work with need to understand specifically what you need. The more you consider what your specific requirements are, and the more you are able to communicate these requirements clearly to the vendors, the more likely you are to be able to purchase and install a system you will be satisfied with both now and in the future.

WHAT TO DO ABOUT SOFTWARE WHEN YOU FIND YOURSELF "HARDWARE DEPENDENT"

It is worthwhile to re-emphasize that software should always be selected *before* hardware. Additionally, if appropriate software cannot be located that runs on users' existing computer equipment, then a decision must be made to either design software from ground up, or purchase new equipment. The cost of building telemarketing software can range from a quarter of a million dollars and up, plus six to 12 months of developmental time. All the while, the company loses valuable time to begin realizing the increases in sales revenues and profits available from using a computer-assisted telemarketing system.

No doubt about it, for a business which owns a sizeable amount of equipment and insists upon using it, software selection will be a challenge. Today, the majority of software is designed for the PC which take advantage of MS-DOS operating systems because this equipment represents the majority of computer installations. However, for those companies owning minicomputers such as DEC or tandem computers or equipment running on VMS or PIC operating systems, software is available through turnkey vendors-- obviously at a much higher cost (on a per user basis) than PC-based systems.

The availability of ready-made software for mainframe computers is negligible. Vendors have not addressed this market for one primary reason: Due to its real-time requirements, *experts do not recommend that telemarketing compete on a mainframe with other applications such as accounting, inventory, etc.* The recommendation is generally that a dedicated, departmental system be implemented for telemarketing, with the use of distributed processing at remote sites.

With the exception of one vendor, no one is addressing the total integration of all sales and marketing channels, i.e., telemarketing, field sales, headquarters, etc. Those businesses who have integrated their sales and marketing are a handful of forward-thinking *Fortune* 100 corporations. However, due to necessity and demand, users and vendors alike should begin to address sales and marketing integration in the very near future.

SELECTING THE HARDWARE

Actually, the choice of hardware is made fairly simple once software is chosen, as it is the latter that dictates the former. However, for those companies that do not own computer equipment, the following guidelines are offered:

*   *Do not buy based on price alone!* Quality and aftermarket support must be considered. Ask the software vendor for recommendations; they know better than anyone else what works best for their software, and they are often aware of which hardware vendors are the most reliable.

*   *At the PC level, a high-speed AT computer with a color monitor is a luxury package.* An XT with an amber screen gets the job done nicely (there is no research that indicates that a color monitor increases productivity, yet there is some evidence which indicates that an amber screen is easier on the eyes).

*   *Hard disks and floppy drives should be selected on a basis of specific need.* For a single-user system, a hard disk is not a luxury, it is a necessity. For a LAN, floppy drives are acceptable at the workstations, but a hard disk for the file server is a must.

*   *At both the micro- and minicomputer level, processing speed is always a prime consideration for high-volume telemarketing applications.* However, for a single-user stand-alone system, speed is not too critical. Unless manipulating large amounts of data, or connecting to a LAN, users can save money by *not* purchasing high-speed processors when the application does not call for it.

*   *Selection criteria for printers must consider the application, the number of users and the firm's financial resources for this equipment.* Printers currently come in three varieties: high-speed dot matrix, lower speed high-quality

297

impact, and high-quality laser jet; within each of these there is a wide range of selections with varying features and functions. For example, for a small business that can afford only one printer, a high-speed dot matrix printer that has a near letter-quality function and can print envelopes effectively is a good choice. A larger business would, perhaps, select both a high-speed dot matrix and a laser jet printer, depending on output requirements.

CHOOSE A VENDOR

No matter how great software or hardware looks, it is only as good as the vendor who supports it. The true test of a vendor? How fast they get a user up and running after experiencing technical problems. Telemarketing systems vendors usually fall into these categories:

* *A turnkey systems house, which is a firm that sells software, hardware, installation, training and support.*

* *A value-added reseller (VAR/consultant) who can supply a turnkey system (the difference between the systems house and the VAR is that the first usually has only one system to offer, the second offers a number of systems.)*

* *A software-only vendor.*

* *A hardware dealer (after selecting software).*

Buying software direct from the manufacturer poses no real problems, as long as the vendor's customer references have been thoroughly checked and when there is a money-back guarantee offered. Buying hardware mail-order poses many problems and the adage, "*Let the consumer beware,*" is particularly relevant. Purchasing software or hardware from a store-front retailer presents problems only when the buyer must deal with sales people who do not understand telemarketing, and, therefore cannot provide appropriate software solutions. One of the better sources for software especially is a value-added reseller or consultant who can offer telemarketing expertise, knowledge about specific software solutions and about the process of automation.

In the case of minicomputer-based software or turnkey systems, the buyer has no choice but to go to the main source, whether it happens to be located on the East Coast or West Coast.

When software vendors sell through dealers, the quality of support at the local level can be inconsistent. Some do not qualify their dealers based on their ability to support the end user. Therefore, the burden of qualifying the dealer thoroughly falls on the shoulders of the prospective customer.

In the case of hardware, the rule and not the exception should be to *always buy locally from a reliable dealer.* Generally speaking, PC vendors employ less qualified sales people than do minicomputer vendors (the latter can afford to recruit and pay the better people). Since they sell systems that cost a minimum of $30,000 per installation, minicomputer vendors can afford to offer better training to their sales force and after-market support programs to their customers than can PC dealers.

298

It is always wise to check out customer references and to contact the Better Business Bureau to see if there are unresolved complaints against the vendor.

PROFILES OF THE LEADING COMPUTER-ASSISTED TELEMARKETING SYSTEMS' VENDORS

A brief description of a number of the top-selling telemarketing systems is offered here as assistance in the reader's search for a telemarketing system. The authors neither endorse any of the listed products or vendors, nor do assume responsibility for the accuracy of this information.

PC-Based Software

PCAT *(Arlington Systems & Software, 400 Massachusetts Ave., Arlington, MA 02174)*. First installed, 1981. Number companies installed, 1950. MS-DOS 2.0 operating system; Betrieve DBMS. Available in three versions: System 3 single-user $450, System 5 single-user $1,295, System 5 multi-user $4,000 (four users). PCAT is the forerunner of all PC-based telemarketing packages with customer usage in leasing, insurance, services, manufacturing and distribution. Each version is full-bodied with no requirement for purchasing additional modules.

SALEMAKER *(Software of the Future, P.O. Box 531650, Grand Prairie, TX 75050)*. First installed August, 1986. Number company sites installed, 4,000. MS-DOS operating system. Available in two versions; single user $495, network $1,995 (up to five users)--additional five users $995, autodial and scripting modules, $99 each, autodial and script $299 each, unlimited users for network. International versions available in several languages. SaleMaker has installations in a cross-section of industries.

SALESVISION *(System Vision Corporation, P.O. Box 281166, San Francisco, CA 94128)*. First installed, 1982. Number of users installed, 500. MS-DOS operating system; dbaseIII+ DBMS. Two versions available: single-user $494, network $1,995, source code available for both. SalesVision is a versatile telemarketing product which is ideally suited to consultative sales applications, especially those involving high-ticket products and long sales cycles.

TELEMAGIC *(Remote Control, 514 Via de la Valle, Suite 206, Solana Beach, CA 92075)*. First installed, June, 1986. Number users installed, 10,000. MS-DOS operating system; dbaseIII+ DBMS. Three versions available: laptop $95, single-user $295, network--$795 (no restriction on number of users supported). TeleMagic is a general software program with customer usage in lead generation, account management and customer service applications in a cross-section of industries. TeleMagic comes complete with no requirement to purchase additional modules.

Minicomputer-Based Systems

The Close System *(Adelie Corporation, 125 Cambridge Park Drive, Cambridge, MA 02140)*. First installed, 1984 (mainframe), 1987 (mini). Five mainframe installations, one mini. The Close System is installed primarily in *Fortune* 500 corporations with business-to-business applications, both inbound and outbound. Uses VSI, HVS, MVS, Unix and MS-DOS operating systems. Price: contact vendor.

BROCK ACTIVITY MANAGER SERIES (BAM) *(Brock Control Systems, 1600 Parkwood Circle, Suite 100, Atlanta, GA 30339)*. First installed, August, 1985. Number separate sites installed, 150. BAM is installed in banking, manufacturing and distribution with many high-technology industries reflected. Both outbound and inbound applications supported. Unix, Xenix, VMS, HPUX operating system; Informix and Ingress DBMS. Pricing : average $2,000 per workstation for software only.

EDGE *(Coffman Systems, Inc., 13140 Midway Place, Cerritos, CA)*. First installed, 1983. Number installed, 35. EDGE is best suited for corporate outbound and customer service applications as well as service bureau environments. Operating system: PICK unix. Unify and Informix DBMS. Price: contact vendor.

TELATHENA *(CRC Information Systems, 435 Hudson St., New York, NY 10014)*. First installed, 1982. Number separate sites, 35. TeleAthena is ideally suited for environments in which multiple campaigns are conducted, i.e., service bureaus or corporate centers that act as service agencies for a number of divisions. Installations include banking and manufacturing. Operating system: PICK or derivative. Proprietary DBMS. Pricing: contact vendor.

TELEMARKETING CONTROL SYSTEM (TCS) *(Early, Cloud & Company, Aquicneck Industrial Park, Newport, RI 02840)*. First installed, 1983. Number sites, 30. Installations are represented in 22 industries. Applications include inbound, outbound and customer service. Operating system: VM/DOS/VSE, MVS, Guardian, VS. Various DBMS utilized depending on hardware selected. Price: contact vendor.

TELETECH MARKETING SYSTEM (TTMS) *(NPRI, 602 Cameron St., Alexandria, VA 22314)*. First installed, 1981. Number sites, 27. TTMS' installations include five major industries including telecommunications, publishing, banking, service bureaus and fund raising. Applications include high volume inbound and outbound programs. Operating system: VMS. Proprietary DBMS. Price: average cost of TTMS workstation (hardware, software, customization, installation and training) $10,000.

INSTALLATION AND TRAINING

Every system requires time for "debugging" and "check out." Users should allow plenty of time for this important phase, because it is essential to have a telemarketing system that is operating 100% correctly and reliably. Numerous problems can and will occur during the first month of operation--this is known as the "burn in" period--a time to flush out weak links in the new system. This is the time when the customer and the vendor or vendors need to have an especially close and satisfying relationship. Without it, an automation project can be doomed.

To reduce the impact on the existing system (manual or other computer), users should schedule installation during a slow period. Those telemarketing operations which have tried to get a system up and running during peak times know that it tries everyone's patience.

Training is positively the critical element of implementing a successful computer-assisted telemarketing system. It is not as readily available from PC software retailers as it is from value-added resellers and consultants. Minicomputer software vendors generally do an excellent job of offering on-site and remote training, although it is an additional cost that must be factored into the entire cost of the system.

In addition to the telemarketing sales or service representatives, system administrator and telemarketing management who will be actively using the system, there are others in the company who could benefit from system training. These would include managers, administrative staff and others who must interact with the automated department.

Training should be conducted on-site where employees feel most comfortable and where they can learn in a real environment with their own equipment, forms, etc. Courses should be divided into small modules of instruction rather than long continuous classes. People usually learn faster and are less intimidated with a building-block approach to computer training. Users should not stop with a week or so of initial training--it should be available on an ongoing and remedial basis.

Today, most of the minicomputer software suppliers offer comprehensive user manuals, reference books, tutorials and practice databases. A few of the more forward thinking PC-based suppliers also offer good documentation and simulator programs for training purposes. Training and reference materials must be considered in the software evaluation process.

Depending on the complexity of the software, it should take users two to three months to become truly proficient on the system (although if the software was selected for ease of use, users should be able to perform routine activities immediately). However, during the initial period of time, management may see a decrease in telemarketing productivity while everyone is in a learning curve.

One company that experienced poor results after three months of implementation finally realized that they had put their less experienced people on the computer system and kept the seasoned ones on the old manual system--proving once again that automation is not a substitute for experience.

However, once the entire sales force was using the new system, management saw the productivity improvements it had planned for.

IMPLEMENTATION

The process of converting from the old system to the new is implementation. A minimum of 30 days is recommended to carry out this process. Once again, it is during this phase where a good relationship between customer and vendor is needed to help make the translation of strategic objectives into tactical programs.

PC software vendors typically do not get involved in helping the customer convert data, codify, or otherwise implement the system. On the other hand, minicomputer software vendors typically place a sales support specialist on-site with the customer during the initial states of implementation in order to ensure that the customer's strategies are correctly translated into meaningful codes, reports, scripts, etc.

Without a doubt, *experts recommend that telemarketing departments implement computer systems using a parallel method.* This is where the manual and the automated systems are run side by side until the bugs have been worked out of the computerized system and a confidence level in users has been achieved. This method is costly due to the need for running simultaneous systems, however, in the case of severe problems, there is the insurance of a complete backup system.

The job of *system administrator*, is perhaps, one of the most overlooked areas of implementing a computer-assisted telemarketing system, especially in the case of small businesses who do not have much

301

experience with computer systems. After investing $15,000, $30,000 or more in equipment and much time and energy, some companies either forget they need an individual to care for the system, or decide they do not want an extra payroll expense.

Who will routinely back up the database? In order to protect valuable data, it should be backed up daily in most telemarketing departments. Who will update software, update the database, change user ID codes on the LAN? Who will generate the type of reports needed by management? Who will get the system back up and running after some type of failure? The system administrator will perform these duties--*an extremely important job* that must be factored into the total cost of implementing a computer-assisted telemarketing system.

THE CURRENT STATE OF TECHNOLOGY

Technical innovations have advanced quickly in telephony for call management in telemarketing. Switches for tracking calling volume, automatic call distributors, autodialers, and voice activated receivers have long been a part of large telemarketing operations. But, as information gathering has become both a product and a competitive tool in the marketplace, a method to manage, track and utilize the information has taken on even more importance.

The lines between the computer and the telephone are starting to blur.

Today's technology offerings are moving toward bundled systems specifically designed for telemarketing applications. The large computer manufacturers are entering into strategic alliances with the top software producers as are the leading PBX manufacturers. In each case, there is a clear desire to present a package that integrates the generic telemarketing process with advanced telephony features along with a strong processing and reporting capability.

TOMORROW'S TECHNOLOGY

Tomorrow's technology will continue the migration paths that were discussed in the beginning of this chapter. Smaller, faster, more focused and more powerful will be the watchwords for new products. Information management will migrate toward *all forms of information*, and we will see products that seamlessly integrate text, graphics and voice as well as high speed data into the telemarketing environment. Voice mail, image scanning and PC to FAX will become standard product options.

As large field sales organizations begin to automate, we will see the emerging laptop computers become as indispensable to the salesman as his briefcase and automobile. Across the board, these new computers and peripherals will continue to migrate toward faster processors and more intuitive operating systems.

It is widely predicted that by the start of the next decade, the user interfaces among all computers will be virtually indistinguishable. Intuitive use, point and shoot cursor control, multiple windows and plain-English commands with optical mice and touch screens will be as common as today's floppy disk.

INDUSTRY'S COMMITMENTS--TODAY AND INTO THE FUTURE

According to *Telemarketing Intelligence '87*, a report from Schlenker Research Services, major commitments have already been made by captive telemarketing departments.[2]

Of 707 companies interviewed in 1987, all with in-house telemarketing operation, 68 percent reported that they had computer terminals/CRT's in use. Usage was greatest in the larger operations using telemarketing for inbound activities.

Future intentions to purchase computer terminals, hardware and software within the "next 12 months or so" were very strong. About four in ten indicated an intent to purchase.

As we continue on into the future, the level of automation in captive telemarketing operations can be expected to experience significant increases.

ADDENDUM: SAMPLE REQUEST FOR PROPOSAL (RFP)

Purpose of This RPF. There is a twofold purpose for the submission of this RFP. The first is to quickly and clearly apprise you of the functionality required for this installation. The second is to gain a concise reply from you which specifically identifies your system's ability to meet the needs of _____, Inc., Telemarketing Department (see **Figure 17-8**). *Please note that your response, if you are selected as the vendor of choice, will be included as an addendum to the contract for the procurement of this system.*

Response Format

1. The specified system requirements have been listed in outline form. It is imperative that your response address all of the issues in the sequence presented. The final page of this document is a response form which *must* be copied and used to submit your response.

2. Please provide a separate complete materials list of all proposed software and hardware components, including line-item pricing.

3. Include descriptive literature.

4. In the event that the function specified requires additional hardware or software, describe the additions and the price for each line item.

5. Provide samples of all contracts for review by _____, Inc., Legal Department (this is very important to ensure a quick decision process).

Decision Process

1. The submission of this RFP is the first step in determining which vendor will be chosen to implement a turnkey system for _____, Inc.

2.   Responses are due no later than 30 days after receipt of this RFP. Responses submitted in a shorter time frame will indicate your interest in obtaining this business and will demonstrate your ability to react quickly to customer needs.

3.   Demonstrations of the systems of the final two vendor candidates will be held as quickly as possible.

4.   The system will be installed and fully operational within 60 days of the receipt of our purchase order.

Stipulations

1.   _____, Inc., reserves the right to reject any or all responses and to waive any or all formalities in connection with the analysis and selection of a vendor.

2.   Assignment of any contract arising from this RFP or any interest therein, without the prior written consent of _____, Inc., shall be void.

3.   Submission of quotations with the RFP response shall constitute a firm offer for no less than 90 days.

Telemarketing Overview

In 1988, _____, Inc., will activate its first formal Telemarketing Department. The group will initially consist of two telemarketers and will expand to four to 10 telemarketers.

The goal of the Telemarketing Department is to extend the company's market reach and increase sales revenues. A more specific set of goals includes:

1.   *Minimize direct sales expenses.*

2.   *Identify and capitalize on new market opportunities.*

3.   *Maintain and enhance corporate/product awareness.*

4.   *Provide accurate and complete data for strategic planning.*

5.   *Increase revenues from the existing customer base.*

6.   *Improve the sales conversion rate--convert more prospects to customers.*

7.   *Shorten the sales cycle.*

8.   *Increase the sales volume per field sales person.*

9.   *Support field sales personnel to increase their productivity.*

COMPUTERS

The telemarketing group will function as an integral part of the sales team and will support various marketing applications. In effect, telemarketing will act as an internal telemarketing service bureau to meet the telephone marketing needs of the company.

It is important, as a potential vendor of _____, Inc.'s, telemarketing system, that you understand that the implementation of the Telemarketing Department has the full support and commitment of all levels of management. The needs of the department have been given high priority and the success of the department is imperative.

Consequently, the chosen vendor is expected to offer its full commitment to contributing to the success of the program. This means that customer support resources from the chosen vendor must be excellent, due dates must be met and system functions must be delivered as promised.

OVERVIEW

1.0 *Software System Overview*

1.1 Accommodate four telemarketers upon installation.
* *Growth to 10-12 telemarketers.*
* *Includes capacity for a supervisor and one clerical support person.*

1.2 Handle multiple outbound applications/campaigns simultaneously.

1.3 Accommodate incoming calls (simultaneously with outbound calls) which may apply to any application.

1.4 Function as a service bureau-type system separately managing and reporting on various campaigns or applications.

1.5 Function as a full account management system (multi-step sales process).

1.6 Provide the following basic telemarketing functions:
   1.61 *List management.*
   1.62 *Lead management.*
   1.63 *Scripting.*
   1.64 *Literature fulfillment.*
   1.65 *Standard set of reports.*
   1.66 *Ad hoc reporting.*
   1.67 *Autodialing.*
   1.68 *Call scheduling.*
   1.69 *Campaign management.*

1.7 Must be able to have software fully operational within 60 days of receipt of purchase order.

305

ENCYCLOPEDIA OF TELEMARKETING

INFORMATION MANAGEMENT

2.0 *Database (List) Management*

2.1 Capability to interface bi-directionally with a DEC PD11/44 with ability to also interface (bi-directionally) with VAX.

2.2 Capability to concurrently interface with an IBM 4341 mainframe.

2.3 Provide list reformatting to accommodate the loading of commercially purchased lists.

2.4 Capability to merge lists together.

2.5 Capability to match and flag duplicate responses to multiple campaigns, and purge duplicate responses to the same campaign.

2.6 Capability to delete records individually based on specific sort and select criteria.

2.7 Capability to delete records as a group based on specific sort and select criteria.

2.8 Provide list usage reports.

2.9 Capability to print lists as a backup plan for manual use if the computer is unavailable.

2.10 Capability to manage the telemarketing applications by list (campaign) so that each application can be reported on separately.

3.0 *Lead Profile*

3.1 Provide a lead profile (screen) that includes pertinent prospect/customer information. Information for the profiles will be loaded from sources external to the system. They will also be entered by the telemarketers throughout their presentations.

3.2 Provide ability to maintain up to 10 contact names for each lead profile.

3.3 Allow keyboard searches on 15-20 data fields (indexes). Specify recommended number of indexed fields.

3.4 Provide "default" values to be predefined for any data field if no data is input.

3.5 Provide data field editing based on table validation.

3.6 Provide data field editing based on range checks.

306

3.7 Allow specification of optional data entry fields.

3.8 Allow specification of required data entry fields.

3.9 An algorithm is required to rank leads in order of sales priority based on four factors--potential sales volume, immediacy of the sale, the probability of the sale and location by ZIP code. The ranking and weighting factors will be provided. A list must then be able to be generated.

3.10 Provide ability to track how many times a customer or prospect becomes a lead.

4.0 *Ad Hoc Query and Reporting*

4.1 Report writer available to develop specific reports, above and beyond the standard reports, using English commands.

4.2 Provide a storage and retrieval of *ad hoc* report formats for report usage.

4.3 Define report parameters based on keyword sort and select criteria using Boolean Logic.

5.0 *Activity Reports*

5.1 Tabulate types of calls made/received (i.e., inbound, first-call attempts, second-call attempts).

5.2 Tabulate call completions including the number of presentations made, refusals, busies, no answers, disconnects, wrong numbers, duplicates, not available/call back later, left word to call.

5.3 Tabulate presentation results including sales made, sales lost, already bought/ renewed, quote requested, demo requested, call again and literature requested.

6.0 *Resource Utilization Reports*

6.1 Tabulate and report script usage.

6.2 Tabulate and report usage of specific questions within a script as a total and by rep.

6.3 Tabulate and report usage of product information files as a total and by rep.

6.4 Tabulate and report usage of competitive information files as a total and by rep.

6.5 Tabulate and report usage of any other resource files as a total and by rep.

7.0 *Performance Reports--Productivity Measurements*

7.1 Report call attempts/calls received per hour.

7.2 Report completed calls per day.

7.3 Report presentations per hour.

7.4 Report average call length/product.

7.5 Report sales per hour.

7.6 Report quotes generated per hour.

7.7 Report demos qualified per hour.

7.8 Compare all results against predefined goals as a total and by rep.

8.0 *Performance Reports--Effectiveness Measurements*

(Provide the following conversion factor calculations in report format.)

8.1 Presentations per first call attempts.

8.2 Presentations per repeat call attempts.

8.3 Sales per completed or received calls.

8.4 Sales per presentations.

8.5 Sales per completed scripts.

8.6 Sales per non-completed scripts.

8.7 Quotes per completed scripts.

8.8 Quotes per non-completed scripts.

9.0 *General Reports and Report Parameters*

9.1 List validity summary (i.e., wrong numbers, disconnects, etc., by list source).

9.2 List effectiveness (i.e., sales per list used).

9.3 List availability (i.e., number of records used versus number available).

9.4 Script effectiveness (i.e., sales per script used).

9.5 Report number of responses to an advertisement (response to be downloaded directly from outside source).

9.6 Report the percent of responses and rate.

9.7 Report number of responses by media or product.

9.8 Report total cost per response (costs to be stored in a table).

9.9 Report the cost per response/media.

9.10 Report total number of inquiries qualified to leads (by media or product).

9.11 Report total number of leads resulting in orders.

9.12 Report the average order size.

9.13 Report the purchases by type of buyer (industrial, laboratory, veterinary, etc.).

9.14 Report purchases by product and buyer (i.e., number of hospital laboratories who purchased one type of product from telemarketing).

9.15 Report the ratio of new customers to total market place.

9.16 Report the highest potential product market.

9.17 Report the projected annualized billing per customer.

9.18 Target market effectiveness (i.e., sales by target market).

9.19 All reports are to be tabulated separately for each calling campaign.

9.20 All reports must be accumulated and available by hour, day, week and month.

9.21 Report summaries should be retained for at least 13 rolling months.

9.22 All reports are to be available on-screen (real-time access by supervisor/manager).

9.23 Reports are also to be available in hard copy format.

9.24 Summary reports on each telemarketer's productivity as compared to the group's results, must be available, on-line, to each telemarketer (security must limit access to only the individual's results, not their peer's results).

9.25 General lead management report identifying number of outstanding leads in each step of the sales cycle.

ENCYCLOPEDIA OF TELEMARKETING

10.0 Call Scheduling

10.1 Capability to segment call schedules based on calling list (campaign assignment).

10.2 Capability to segment call schedules based on individual telemarketer.

10.3 Ability to prioritize calls within a schedule (queue).

10.4 Allow callback scheduling based on time of day.

10.5 Allow callback scheduling based on date.

10.6 Provide the ability to automatically bypass weekends and holidays.

10.7 Provide the ability to schedule calls based on time zones and ZIP codes.

10.8 Provide default scheduling for same day callback of busies.

10.9 Allow manual override of all automatic call scheduling.

10.10 Ability to assign specific call queues to specific telemarketers.

11.0 Autodialing

11.1 Integrated autodialing will interface _____, Inc.'s, phone system.

11.2 Must be user activated.

11.3 Capability to receive and handle incoming calls.

11.4 Capability to transfer calls to other telephone extensions.

11.5 Interface allows manual indication of call dispositions.

11.6 Interface allows automatic indication of call dispositions based on signals from the autodialer.

11.7 Allow manual dialing in the event the computer is not available.

12.0 Scripting

12.1 Ability for non-technical applications manager to develop, modify and maintain scripts.

12.2 Provide response dependent, user-defined logical branching.

310

12.3 No limitations on script length.

12.4 No limitations on the number of active scripts.

12.5 Allow data entry through scripted presentations.

12.6 Perform on-line calculations based on information gathered.

12.7 Capability to clone (copy) existing scripts at the beginning of creating new scripts.

12.8 Ability to provide hard copy of scripts/screens for review and archiving.

12.9 Provide telemarketer control to move forward/backward through a script.

12.10 Ability to access reference files and return to same place in a script.

12.11 Provide two-second screen change response time.

13.0 *Call Activity Log*

13.1 Maintain call activity information, for each lead profile, in chronological order.

13.2 Automatically log date of each call made or activity performed.

13.3 Automatically log the time of each call made or activity performed.

13.4 Log summary of call result--automatically by function key usage.

13.5 Log a summary of each call result through manual data entry by the telemarketer.

13.6 Automatically log history of literature sent based on fulfillment process (future need).

14.0 *Fulfillment Process*

14.1 Maintain inventory of literature pieces available versus those on order.

14.2 Allow telemarketers to specify literature piece to be sent to a particular lead profile.

14.3 Allow telemarketers to specify the sending of literature kits.

14.4 Generate form letters (personalized by telemarketer).

14.5 Allow telemarketers to specify which form letters are to be sent.

14.6 Allow tailorization of form letters by telemarketers.

14.7 Accommodate the printing of mailing labels.

14.8 Accommodate the printing of envelopes.

14.9 Accommodate forms generation and completion.

14.10 Accommodate the generation of purchase orders.

14.11 Accommodate the printing of sales leads.

15.0 *Reference Resources*

15.1 Provide access to product information files.

15.2 Files must be easily maintained by a non-technical applications manager.

15.3 Allow various information file formats, including full test, bulleted details, matrices or charts.

15.4 Changes to reference files must be non-disruptive to telemarketer operations.

16.0 *Security*

16.1 Provide telemarketer security upon log-in.

16.2 Restrict access to supervisor and system administrator functions.

16.3 Automatically log off if no activity within a set period of time.

17.0 *Training (Optional Feature)*

17.1 Provide training mode to practice scripts with dummy data.

18.0 *Personnel*

18.1 Track lead/sales results and use to calculate commissions for compensation purposes.

18.2 Maintain personnel profiles.

19.0 *Hardware*

19.1 Specify which models are recommended.

19.2 If the systems in 19.1 are not directly supported, must be able to provide an interface to a DEC PDP11/VAX for uploading/downloading of customer records (See 2.1).

COMPUTERS

19.3 Provide *all* hardware components including (specify models).
19.31 *CPU.*
19.32 *Computer terminals.*
19.33 *Printer--high speed printer with near letter quality mode.*
19.34 *Autodialers.*

19.4 Can the proposed hardware be obtained and installed (fully operational) 60 days from receipt of purchase order? (January, 1999).

VENDOR QUALIFICATIONS

20.0 *Vendor Information*

20.1 How long has this software package been in existence?

20.2 How many separate customer sites do you have *installed*?

20.3 How many of your customer sites have the proposed hardware?

20.4 How many of your installed sites have the proposed software version?

20.5 How many telemarketer stations do you have *installed*?

20.6 How many years has your company been in existence?

20.7 How many people does your company employ?

20.8 How many years have you supported telemarketing software?

20.9 List four customer references, including company name, contact name and telephone number.

20.10 Is your company public, privately held or employee owned?

20.11 What services or products does your company provide in addition to telemarketing software?

20.12 Did your company design this software or did you purchase the marketing rights for it?

20.13 What type of corporate environment was the software originally developed for?

21.0 *Installation Support*

21.1 Is a copy of the source code provided?

21.2 If no source code provided, is there an escrow arrangement to assure its availability? If yes--include this arrangement in your proposal.

21.3 What is your installation interval including hardware (minimum or maximum time)?

21.4 What type of installation planning support do you provide?
* *Critical path timelines.*
* *Task checklists.*
* *Peripheral equipment checklists.*
* *On-site meeting.*

21.5 What are your installation requirements?
* *Number of work days.*
* *User involvement.*

21.6 How are system modifications accommodated? Do you perform them or do we? If you make the changes, what is your fee schedule?

21.7 What training is provided? Include length of training and costs.

21.8 When and where is training conducted?

21.9 Do you provide additional training for new personnel? Include the length of training and the cost.

21.10 Describe your system documentation including:
* *User manuals.*
* *System descriptions/charts.*
* *Run procedures.*
* *Report formats/samples.*
* *Control procedures.*

21.11 Do you supply the computer hardware and peripheral equipment?

22.0 *Maintenance Support*

22.1 Do you provide a warranty or guarantee period? Describe.

22.2 What types of maintenance agreements are available? Provide copy and include costs.

22.3 Are software enhancements provided as part of the maintenance agreement?

22.4 Are system documentation updates provided with your enhancements?

22.5 Are education updates provided with your enhancements?

22.6 What is the geographic location of your support office for the New York City area?

22.7 How many technical people are available at this site to support your software?

22.8 Is telephone support available for software and hardware problems? Specify hours and costs.

22.9 Do you service and maintain the computer hardware and peripheral equipment?

22.10 If you do not maintain hardware, will you act as one point of contact (agency) to take responsibility for diagnosing the problem and summoning the appropriate support personnel?

22.11 Is there a user group for your software?

22.12 Do you provide a corporate newsletter or other form of communications that apprises users of changes, enhancements or additions to the product or your company?

22.13 Is your software upgraded in versions (numbered)? How are upgrades handled? (How is it received? How is it documented? How is it loaded?)

23.0 *Technical Issues*

23.1 On what computer hardware was the software originally developed?

23.2 What computer hardware do you currently support?

23.3 What programming language(s) is/are used?

24.4 Do users have the right or option to modify the source code?

23.5 What database management system do you use?

23.6 Describe your security controls.

23.7 What flexibility exists as to changing of screens, documents and reports?

23.8 Is your software menu driven?

23.9 Does your software support function keys? Are they user definable?

23.10 Describe your audit trail controls (reporting).

23.11 Does your software easily accommodate file record expansion? What is the maximum number of fields which can be expanded and how many records are

315

maximum per file?

24.0 *Hardware Issues*

24.1 What hardware configuration is required to support the following:
* *4 telemarketer positions now--growth to 10-12.*
* *1 management position.*
* *1 administrative assistant.*
  Include computer and peripherals. Describe equipment type, manufacturer, model and model features and operating system.

24.2 What type of storage device(s) is/are used? Define equipment type, manufacturer, model and model features, capacity ranges.

24.3 What type of autodial equipment do you support? Will it interface with a Dimension telephone system by AT&T?

24.4 Will the system recover automatically after a power failure?

24.5 Describe your system backup/recovery process.

24.6 What is the migration path for this system? (Expandability of the hardware and portability of the software).

24.7 What type of physical environment does the computer system require?

24.8 What type of hardware training is provided? Include length of training and costs.

24.9 What communications components are required to interface with a DEC PDP11/44 and VAX?

----

[1]Jan McCabe, *ATA Newsletter*, Volume 4, Number 3 (March 1988), pp. 1,8.
[2]Barry Schlenker, *Telemarketing Intelligence '87*, In House Operations Study, Schlenker Research Service, 1987, p. 9.

Figure 17-8
Request for Proposal Response Document

Vendor: _____ Date of Response: _____

Vendor Representative: _____

Telephone Number: _____

	Does your standard software package meet this specification?		
Spec #	No	Yes	Yes -- with customization (specify costs in quotation)

CHAPTER 18

Telecommunications (ACD)

John A. Pollpeter
Vice President & General Manager, Switching Systems Division
Rockwell Telecommunications, Rockwell International Corporation
Downers Grove, Illinois

No telecommunications switching system is playing a bigger part in telemarketing today than the Automatic Call Distributor (ACD).

To define what the all-digital Automatic Call Distributor *is*, and *isn't*, we need to look backward to what life was like before 1973, the year the all-digital ACD was invented.

In those days the world of large volume business communications was the domain of call sequencers and various versions of private branch exchanges (or PBX'S), to name some of the systems at that time. One that was used in numerous business applications was the electromechanical "3A" or "2B" Western Electric ACD.

These types of systems worked fine, but in a limited way. They were fine if businesses didn't care whether all their calls were blocked or not, or whether their agent force was being treated equitably or not. They served their purpose if management didn't care too much about the sparse or incorrect information their systems were giving them. It was apparent that something better was needed.

Unfortunately, at that time most telecommunications suppliers felt that the market for an all-digital ACD was too small, and the time required to develop it took too long to satisfy the needs of the companies that were asking for it.

In the late 1960's, Collins Radio Company, the nation's best-known manufacturer of avionics and transmission equipment, had been experimenting with digital voice technology. Collins had made a commitment to meet the business community's urgent deadline for a switching system that would solve its telecommunications dilemma.

In 1973, Collins Radio was merged with Rockwell International Corporation. Rockwell subsequently became the driving force in the development of the first computer controlled, non-blocking ACD. Rockwell's initial Galaxy[1] ACD system was shipped to Continental Airlines in February, 1974. It was installed in that airline's Houston reservation center and was cut into service in April.

Early Ramification of the Galaxy ACD. Introduction of the Galaxy ACD created an immediate and powerful impact in the airline industry. Airlines reservations managers were delighted with the system. It worked beautifully, saving them much time and money while providing information they urgently needed to show upper management how their call centers were operating at any given time.

Scheduling of reservations agents now became a science, not guesswork, because of the more exact knowledge about trunks that was now available. It was as if a giant light had been turned on, enabling the managements of large groups of agents to see results with *pinpoint precision.*

By 1976, more than 25 Galaxy ACD's were on order, and not just for airlines, but also for hotel reservations departments, car rental companies, credit authorization agencies and other industries in which large volume call handling was a real necessity.

Even more impressive than the hundreds of installed ACD systems were the number of jobs they helped to create in business and industry. Rockwell estimates that hundreds of thousands of agent positions have been established in these installations worldwide, with that number growing every year. In addition, many of those positions are occupied around the clock, using second- and third-shift agents, thus enabling even more people to earn their living as an outcome of the invention of the ACD.

DEFINING TERMS

Before dealing with the ACD as it is applied to telemarketing, we should describe some of the other systems in use today.

Plain Old Telephone Set (POTS). The simple desk set, with rotary dial or touch tone dialing, still suffices for numerous telemarketing operations with relatively small numbers of sales reps or order takers. POTS offers no automatic distribution of the work load, delay queue for callers or management reports.

The Multi-Button Key Set. These are key telephone sets, which have multi-buttons and are used with relay equipment to provide call holding, multi-line pickup, signaling, intercommunication and conference services. Key sets provide more call-handling flexibility than single line telephone sets, however an unequal distribution of the work load still exists. Also, there is no delay queue and there are no management reports offered by this equipment.

The Call Sequencer. Also known as the Universal Call Sequencer or Universal Call Distributor, this is generally an analog system and is used mostly in offices serving from five to 25 telemarketing service representatives (TSR's). It routes the calls to TSR's in a random fashion and has limited reporting capabilities to help management audit agents and trunking activity. Call sequencers can also be seen in larger telemarketing offices. They may, however, block incoming calls even when there are TSR's available, Some of the newer call sequencers offer statistics and can be useful for small telemarketing installations.

The PABX System. These "private automated branch exchanges" generally serve large numbers of telephones. They typically do not have a non-blocking feature, making the system inaccessible during peak calling periods. A PABX might have one trunk serving several phones. PABX's are effective in universal call distribution operations that use key sets and call directors but cannot handle the traffic flow served by a true stand-alone ACD system. Limited operational data is offered to management by PABX's.

319

When a call comes into a PABX, the system identifies the telephone being called, rings it, and connects the two parties when the receiver is lifted. In contrast, a call into an ACD system is taken by the switch, the ACD's computer selects a TSR waiting in queue, signals with a beep or light that a call is coming, and the call is connected. Unlike a PABX, no ringing on the agent's telephone is required with an ACD. The connection time of an ACD call is far faster than one placed through a PABX, or other non-ACD.

Centrex Systems. These "specialized PABX's" operate much the same way as described above. Each agent's phone has its own particular number. Generally, someone calling into an office served by a Centrex wishes to talk to a particular person--a Mr. Jones, for example. With a specific four-digit set of numbers following the company's three-digit exchange (336-9988, for instance), callers who dial through a Centrex system will by-pass the switchboard and connect directly with Mr. Jones at extension 9988.

There's an essential difference between an office that employs a Centrex and one that relies on an ACD. Centrex is designed to bring the caller together with "Mr. Jones," whom he wants to speak with. No one else will do. An ACD system is best suited to help the caller who wants *service*, perhaps to purchase a product seen on a TV advertisement. Here, the caller doesn't care whether Mr. Jones or Miss Smith answers his or her call. Anyone will "do" who can perform the service.

Integrated Systems. Early on, a number of PBX manufacturers saw the benefits of ACD logic and decided to meld the two concepts into a single switch, known generally as an integrated system.

For many installations with reasonably small numbers of agents, the integrated system meets most of the parameters set up for both system concepts. It is a PBX system (routing dialed inbound and outbound calls) but it contains some ACD software (enabling it to route inbound calls to a group of agents whose job is to sell or provide service, or outbound calls made by sales reps). But difficulties begin to surface when one of the two capabilities (PBX or ACD) starts to run out of balance with the other. To make them more cost-effective, PBX-based ACD's are usually *not* non-blocking. Consequently, if a surge comes in, the PBX's ACD software simply cannot handle the load and callers will be blocked.

The ACD capabilities of integrated systems generally have much more limited capacity than do stand-alone ACD systems. One explanation for this involves the manufacturers' view of the market. Since the ACD market is extremely small compared to the PBX market, manufacturers tend to target R&D toward the latter. As a result, integrated systems will usually have less ACD capacity.

A major difference between non-blocking stand-alone systems and integrated systems is that the former will accept and queue all calls presented to it and route all queued calls to the TSR.

The ACD. ACD is a telecommunications switching system designed to switch large volumes of calls to and from teams of sales or service representatives rapidly, accurately and equitably at the most cost-efficient rate possible. Inbound and outbound calls are handled simultaneously and at great speed. Users receive a vast array of operational reports--both in real-time through CRT displays and through printed management information reports.

These reports are provided at predetermined intervals or on demand, and the ACD can generally offer cumulative reports at the end of a shift, the end of workdays, and on a weekly or even a monthly basis.

TWO QUICK DECISION-MAKING QUESTIONS

One quick way to determine if your business is ready for an ACD system is to ask these two questions: Do you have a *sense of urgency* about answering inbound calls or making outbound calls? And, do you handle a *high volume of calls*, either inbound or outbound (or both)?

If you've answered "yes" to these two questions, there's no doubt that your telemarketing operation could benefit from installing an ACD. The ACD, considered by some the "Rolls Royce" of switching systems, is very rapidly finding its way into more and more telemarketing environments--more than anyone would have thought possible just a few years ago. Today, ACD systems are becoming a necessity for the telemarketing community because their functionality is increasing, and telemarketers are understanding the efficiencies and productivity gains.

ACD REPORTING SYSTEM BENEFITS

Perhaps the most visible part of the ACD is its reporting system. To telemarketing managers, the system's *reporting capability* is what places the ACD well ahead of its predecessors.

Some Important Definitions.

*   **Static:** *A non-changing condition, showing on-screen how information or data is entered and/or configured.*

*   **Command entry:** *Data can be entered or changed by your commands to the system.*

*   **Dynamic:** *Data that is constantly changing, i.e., a dynamic CRT display is literally a "snapshot" of information that always is in a state of flux.* In actual fact, "dynamic" information collected by the ACD is accumulated as events occur. To permit the user to grasp real-time data, dynamic information is displayed at nominal intervals, from seconds to minutes, depending on needs.

CRT Reports. On-screen reports generally deal with dynamic system performance that occurs as telemarketing is under way, i.e., during normal business hours. Additionally, supervisors can request "demand reports" which tell them facts about their agent groups, individual agents, trunking, system configuration and much more. Supervisors can make changes with these reports. For example, the supervisor can reassign agents' extension numbers, change trunking requirements and regroup gates of agents using the demand reports. These types of reports are "static," that is, they remain the same when brought up onto the CRT screen--until changed by the supervisor.

CRT screens display vital information informing supervisory personnel about the average call length of an agent group, call-waiting information, length of call waiting queues, and data on the system's trunks, etc.

Printed Reports. The ACD offers the user a variety of printed reports. Telemarketing supervisors have the option of receiving printed reports--automatically--in periodic intervals throughout their workday. Printed reports may be issued every 15 minutes, every half-hour, every hour, or in a merged daily report that contains vital data accumulated through the workday.

The frequency of report issuance depends totally on the needs of the management. Some firms choose to have reports constantly available, while others prefer only a few throughout the workday. Additionally, some ACD's offer weekly, monthly or even yearly reports.

With the reports issued by the ACD, supervisors can make informed, timely decisions on:

* *Overtime requirements.*

* *Rest period scheduling.*

* *Overload-staffing needs.*

* *The performance of its agents, or groups of agents.*

* *General system operation.*

* *Long-and short-term trends affecting service levels.*

* *Trunk utilization.*

* *Overflowing from one gate to another, or from one ACD to another.*

Some ACD's offer literally thousands of data options to supervisors. At the end of the workday or the established cut-off time, data can be accumulated for either total shifts or for the entire day.

The supervisor can also *demand* information at any time from the ACD and get it, through "demand reports." And, in the case of the Galaxy ACD, there is even the software option of creating "Customer-Formatted Reports" that serve the specific needs of a company's management. In these, supervisors can mix data from several of the ACD's reports to create valuable *new* reports.

ACD APPLICATIONS

A number of ACD systems are currently offered in the market. They can be used for telemarketing, credit collections, opinion surveys, order placement and many other applications requiring the *rapid* and *efficient* processing of incoming and/or outgoing calls.

With certain software modifications, as in the case of Rockwell's ACD's, they are used for directory assistance services by many operating telephone companies throughout the nation. In these regulated utility environments, Rockwell refers to Galaxy systems as Integrated Switching Systems (ISS).

ACD's are especially effective for telemarketing companies using agent forces to handle applications for inbound and outbound sales.

TELECOMMUNICATIONS (ACD)

The automatic call distributor can be a most effective tool for producing revenue in a telemarketing call center. It has been said that the ACD can *increase the productivity of an agent force by from 20 to 40 percent*. Modern ACD's are decreasing the average speed of call-answer by 10 to 20 seconds.

All these factors can lead to substantial cost savings for the company that installs an ACD.

BENEFITS

The ACD, with its ability to report on the fundamental, essential elements of a multi-agent call center, has become--in itself--a profit-making tool. The way to view this is by observing the delicate interplay of the call center's basic elements: the *agent force*; the *trunking lines*; the *call volume*.

If call volume suddenly runs high (this is sometimes called "spiking"), callers may find themselves held in-queue for lengthy periods of time. They may become impatient and hang up, thereby causing a loss of revenue to the telemarketer. The most obvious solution to this might be to add more agents, to assure that future spikes can be handled quickly. But what happens during the time the call volume *isn't* spiking, which is most of the time? The call center now has excessive agents on its payroll, and the center's operating costs can begin to skyrocket.

In another scenario, imagine a call center that has 300 trunks, all of which seem to be functioning perfectly. However, a moment may arise in which several trunks are totally out of order (called "hung" trunks). If no ACD system is installed, the call center management may not know their trunks are hung, or may not discover this fact for a long time--all the while paying dearly each month for equipment they assume to be fully functional. Supervisors might think they have 300 fully functional trunks, but actually have only 294. Meanwhile, inbound callers are probably waiting longer to reach an agent, or the sales reps are waiting longer to get dial tone to make outbound calls.

The ACD is designed to inform management about situations like these so that immediate action can be taken. Indeed, some ACD software can even be programmed to automatically correct certain adverse situations.

Balancing the System. The secret behind the ACD is its ability to provide real *balance* between the elements with which every call center must contend. It enables managers to calculate precisely the "right" number of agents, the "right" number of trunks and the "right" queueing of callers, so that the "right" service level is achieved.

Assume that management in a telemarketing service center decides it wants all inbound calls answered within eight seconds by a particular gate of agents in order to maintain its profit potential.

Managers can use the ACD's software to fulfill that objective. They'll know the number of agents required--and the exact number of hours they'll need. They'll know the number of trunks required to serve the agent groups. They can "balance" the ACD's operation to meet their goal of call-answer within eight seconds. In other words, the correct queue length is maintained, trunks and agents are in balance, and agent workload is divided equally.

In a call center, it isn't necessary to have an over-abundance of *any* of these elements. In fact, some centers with relatively few agents can handle thousands of calls per hour if all the elements are "in balance."

323

ENCYCLOPEDIA OF TELEMARKETING

Of course it is important to understand the *type* of call being handled. For example, if a call center has a gate of agents assigned to handle inbound credit card verification calls--which normally run just a brief duration in length--then literally thousands of calls an hour can be processed by a modest number of agents.

In contrast, a telemarketing service center handling inbound calls generated by TV advertising might average 120 seconds per call. The agent needs time to input all the information from the calling party, assuring that names and addresses and credit card numbers are correct. If management were to use the same number of agents as in the former example, the number of calls handled here would be appreciably smaller.

For the call center to remain profitable, the manager would obviously need to recruit more agents to handle these types of calls. The thing to remember is that the ACD, after a very short period of use, will provide managers with the data they need to configure their operation with the "right" number of people and equipment to do the job and make a profit.

Customer Service. Probably the most important benefit of all will be the improvement in customer service achieved by installing an ACD system in a telemarketing center. If customers' calls are answered in a short time--several seconds at most--they'll be satisfied. A lot depends, of course, on the nature of the product or service in question. It obviously takes less time to close a sale on a rock record album than to close a sale on a life insurance policy.

FEATURES

Call Distribution. The ACD distributes calls to agents or groups of agents. How the distribution is arranged is largely the choice of call center management, and this is dependent on the way the particular ACD is configured.

The Galaxy ACD has 32 standard reporting groups. This number can be doubled as an option, with 64-agent and 64-trunk reporting groups, or 64-agent and 128-trunk reporting groups. Managers can therefore divide their operations so that "TV Sales" are at Gate 1, "Radio Sales" at Gate 2, direct-mail catalog sales for the XYZ Corporation at Gate 3, newspaper subscription sales for the *Daily Gazette* at Gate 4 and so on. (Some ACD systems refer to "gates" as "splits.")

Trunk Groups. Trunk groups vary according to the make of the system (Galaxy has 255).

Queueing. This word "queue" became familiar during World War II when people in England "queued up" to board trains and buses, buy food stamps, enter bomb shelters, etc. In the world of the ACD, the word "queue" is key to a company's profitability. If you are selling something, the shorter the customer queue the better; you *want* those callers to reach your agents and you want them to buy.

However, if your center is providing a *service*, you aren't selling a product. Let's assume you're providing owners of tape recorders the names and addresses of authorized repair centers nearest their homes. When it becomes necessary to hold callers in queue for several minutes, you haven't lost any sales. These callers will hang on or they'll hang up and call back later. But an airline reservations sales center might consider a queue wait of more than 12 seconds per caller an anathema. A health insurance company providing information to its subscribers might consider a three-minute-queue wait per caller "average." In a modern ACD, these queues can be managed to fit business needs.

Call Overflow/Network Overflow. One of the many features of the ACD is its ability to handle call spiking efficiently. The Galaxy ACD, as an example, can treat this situation through Overflow and Diversion software. It works in this way: Assume you have a network of ACD systems in various cities. If one node in your network is overloaded while another is handling lighter traffic, loads can be balanced with another ACD in the network. Overflow can be accomplished by sending all or a percentage of your traffic to another ACD, or to a switch of another manufacturer, or to an internal gate in the ACD that is not traffic-heavy at the time.

The ACD's reports will give managers the statistics they need on the number of calls that were overflowed or diverted. They do this by referencing the overflow and diversion information to each gate in the system. Printed reports are made available when a manager has actually implemented the Overflow and Diversion capability of the system.

Generally speaking, Overflow-Out to another switch occurs when a control parameter is set to a delay time. This delay time, in seconds, is chosen by the ACD management. When the longest delayed call exceeds the delay threshold value--let's say it's 120 seconds--calls exceeding 120 seconds will be overflowed to the ACD node selected to receive them.

Diversion is an option that can be applied during abnormal traffic activities. For instance, diversion-out *transfers* all calls, while diversion-in *accepts* all calls.

An example of this use might be when a group of agents is scheduled for an hour-long training session; during that hour, all the calls to that gate are diverted to another gate of agents in the system, or diverted to another ACD node in a different city.

Overflowing is easily implemented in a single call center. Assume a gate of agents is totally occupied and callers have become backed up in queue to an intolerable level. Supervisors observe the condition and arrange overflow of a given percent of the calls to a second or even a third gate. These overflowed calls are sent to agents already trained to handle several assignments.

In call centers handling a variety of business, it is vital that agents be trained for several assignments. Some telemarketing service centers train their agents to handle as many as eight different products. When overflowed calls are sent to them, they can quickly help balance the call load during a spike.

Network Centers. Management of a series of ACD centers, especially ACD's situated in a number of different cities, can become a very difficult job. In recent years, managers have looked for expedient ways to manage dispersed ACD centers in order to optimize, control and administer network operations.

Some of the problems associated with network ACD operations are:

* *Coping with second-hand information which differs from or contradicts what is actually happening at the ACD site.*

* *Coping with gaps in the flow of information--or receiving the information so late that it cannot be handled efficiently.*

325

* *Realizing that there is a problem--but only after the crisis is full-blown and out of control.*

* *Producing incomplete management reports.*

* *Receiving information from all the nodes in the network--but not having the manpower to condense and analyze it in time to make intelligent decisions.*

* *Having infrequent direct contact with supervisors at the sites.*

These are excellent reasons for considering the installation of a network control center--perhaps at the headquarter's location, or at one of the sites that could best accept the equipment and where trained personnel are located. At Rockwell, we call our network control capability a "Resource Management Center" (RMC). A simplified chart (**Figure 18-1**) defines its capabilities for assisting network and customer service managers.

Network control centers can help provide efficient resource management. They can make more effective use of personnel at the various ACD nodes. They also arrange for more productive use of telecommunications resources.

Network centers can improve management's effectiveness by giving them up-to-date reports for their immediate analysis--on the entire network. And, equally important, network centers can centralize the maintenance control of all the ACD's in the network. They do this by monitoring all the ACD equipment in the network all the time, and they can analyze the trunking performance in the network all the time.

Announcements. ACD systems allow the user to operate recorded announcements to the calling party. At one time or another, all of us have heard that familiar phrase, "*All our agents are busy at this time; please remain on the line and a service representative will be with you in a few moments.*"

These messages are critically important in call centers where a selling job is performed. No call manager wants a high percentage of abandoned calls reported, because they represent lost sales. The recorded message reassures the caller that he or she will soon be served. It helps keep the caller on-line. In some cases, two recorded messages are played, at varying intervals. The second message may differ from the first in saying, "*We appreciate your call and hope to have one of our representatives with you very shortly.*" In some cases a single recorded message can be repeated periodically.

Night service at a telemarketing center requires some form of announcement. If a center is closed for the night, or if a specific group of agents at a center is not at work during nighttime hours, the ACD announcement will inform the caller when the center will re-open on the following workday. An emergency telephone number can be part of the announcement. Generally, announcements are controlled by the user of the particular ACD. They can quickly be re-recorded to reflect changing conditions.

Audio Response Units. Many ACD's can accept Audio Response Units (ARU's). This arrangement is often used for highly repetitive types of calls and responses, such as providing quick answers to frequently asked questions. It can be used, for instance, to give information on items in a catalog, or to answer tax preparation questions at a government agency.

The caller generally hears the first announcement, indicating the call has reached the right number

326

Figure 18-1
Resource Management Center (RMC) Information Capabilities

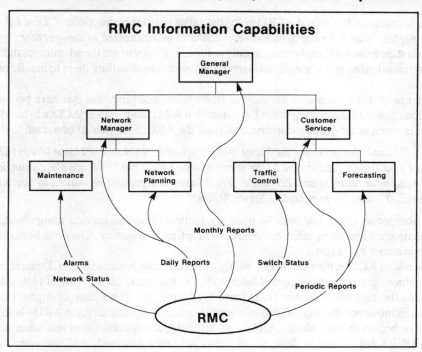

Figure 18-2
Dialed Number Identification System (DNIS) 800 Service

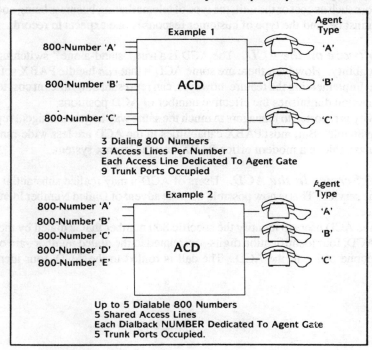

and that an ARU is connected. Then, the ARU gives the caller various instructions: *"Dial 1 for information about incoming flights; dial 2 for departure times; dial 3 to be connected to an operator,"* etc.

In each instance the ARU replaces an agent position. It is easy to see the advantages of having ARU's in certain ACD telemarketing applications, and some companies are installing them to handle basic sales and service calls.

An instance of this is seen with the shop-at-home television programs that have become so popular on cable television. Some of these companies have installed ARU units in their ACD's to handle basic order calls. The caller is given voice-response instruction from the ARU, after being connected to the call center.

> *"Thanks for ordering the Super Widget, as advertised on our Home Widget Show. To speed your order, please give us the name of your credit card. Please state your name. Please read your address and ZIP code. Your Super Widget will be mailed to you within two weeks. Thanks for purchasing Super Widget!"*

Audio Response Units are widely used by banks, financial service companies, universities, transportation companies and many other businesses to save time and money. They can be connected to PBX and other communications systems.

In the world of ACD's, they can play a highly important role, because the ACD can report accurately on each ARU position, giving highly detailed information to managers on the flow of calls into the ARU's. This data includes the call volume over fixed periods of time, the exact time of highest use, and other information that can influence the profitability of the call center. And, naturally, the ARU--being a machine-- doesn't take coffee breaks or need sleep. ARU's are accurate, always courteous and often multi-lingual.

Some ARU's are digital in design. In these, no tapes are used, and the voice quality of the announcements is always undistorted and clear. Others rely on tape cassette cartridges which can jam or wear out. Trade-offs are present; tape recordings generally permit longer messages than digital machines which have specific message lengths. Generally, digital ARU units cost more. Decisions on which to use are dependent upon factors such as cost or the unit, the type of telemarketing business being conducted, how long the announcements must be, and the type of customer responses one expects to record.

PABX Software on the ACD. The ACD is a true "stand-alone" switching system. It is not built with PABX capability. However, there are some ACD's that *can* handle PABX software, should this function be required. Implementing the feature, however, can represent a significant cost to the user, because adding the PABX function diminishes the effective number of ACD positions.

PABX activity is reported to managers in much the same way as gate and agent reports, and detailed printed reports are available. But, most PABX capabilities in the ACD are less wide-ranging in scope and function than those available in a modern office PABX or in a Centrex system.

DNIS 800 Service in the ACD. Users of ACD's may realize substantial cost savings over conventional 800-line service. This is now possible with the advent of Dialed Number Identification Service, or "DNIS 800 service."

DNIS permits ACD users to identify the specific 800 number that is dialed by the caller. When the call is routed to the ACD, four identification digits--correlated to the dialed number--are outpulsed from the serving central telephone office to the ACD. The call is routed to the ACD, four identification digits--

328

correlated to the dialed number--are outpulsed from the serving central telephone office to the ACD. The call is then directed to the proper gate and identified to the agent in one of two manners selected by the center: either by an audible origin announcer or through a brief message on the agent's CRT screen. The call is based on the dialed number, *not* on the particular trunk.

In this way the combination of many trunk groups into *one* group becomes practical. All 800 numbers share all access lines. Because of this, multiple trunk groups can be combined into a single group without losing the ability to identify--and thus route--the call. And, the amount of dialable 800 numbers may equal the amount of access lines in the trunk group. Refer to the two examples in **Figure 18-2**.

Example 1 shows three lightly utilized 800 trunk groups with each number in a three-access-line rotary pickup. *Example 2* demonstrates the possibility of combining the three groups into a single five-line DNIS trunk group. The result is now two additional access paths available to each dialable number, yet the overall number of trunks has been reduced.

The combined DNIS trunk group can concentrate many small and inefficient trunk groups into a single efficient *shared* group, which still provides specialized handling unique to the specific 800 numbers dialed. When the group is properly managed, the user can decrease the overall line requirements, yet allow each client more access paths per dialed number. This can yield better service per number and a lower cost per call.

Currently, AT&T provides this service from its #4 ESS serving offices only. DNIS is compatible with single number service and is a no-cost option.

There are numerous uses for DNIS. They include product sourcing for inbound telemarketing, call type identification for authorization and reporting, locator services, and other applications where the ACD manager wishes to concentrate traffic efficiently, maintain number identity and streamline the management of trunk groups.

Great amounts of call-handling time on each inbound call can be saved with DNIS in a telemarketing service center. If center management elects, its mainframe computer can be connected with the ACD via data links.

Assuming that scripts are available in the mainframe for each of the center's clients, the following scenario is possible: Imagine that a television advertisement for a nostalgic record album is broadcast on a major TV station. The number on the TV screen is advertised as 1-800-555-1234. Assuming that DNIS is used, the final four digits (1 2 3 4) are directly tied to the product--in this case the record album sale. Responding to the TV commercial, a caller dials the advertised number and the call is accepted by the ACD. It is sent to agent Mary. She sees a two-line, 2-second flash on her CRT, indicating that the call coming to her is for the "Lawrence Welk album offer." When she presses the Accept key on her console, she says *"Hello, I'm Mary. Thanks for calling for the Lawrence Welk record. May I have your Master Card or Visa number, please?"*

During the few seconds she uses to say these words, the mainframe has brought up the format and script for the Lawrence Welk sale on her CRT screen and she's ready to handle the remainder of the sales order. More important, she's saved the time it would ordinarily take her to ask the product or service interest of the caller (undoubtedly numbering several seconds) and the time required for the caller to answer (several more seconds).

Telemarketing centers using DNIS estimate savings of seven to 12 seconds per inbound transaction. In a busy call center with DNIS 800 service, savings in WATS time can amount to thousands of seconds per workday. The saving over even a brief period of time can therefore become substantial. Additionally, the accuracy of the data taken by agent Mary is assured.

There is another savings in time and personnel: The agent, Mary, who has now finished taking the order for the record album, returns to the agent queue and awaits another call. Let's say that a radio station has just offered a special one-year subscription to the *Wall Street Journal*, and a listener responds to the 1-800 number. Mary's CRT flashes a 2-second announcement: "*Wall Street Journal* radio annct." She accepts the call and says "*Hello, this is Mary. Thanks for calling the* Wall Street Journal. *How do you wish to charge your subscription?*"

In the time it takes her to say this, the mainframe rolls the script for this transaction onto her CRT and she's ready to bring in this order. Not only has she saved valuable seconds but she's become *double* valuable as an agent. She can handle two different inbound order accounts. It becomes easy to see how a typical agent can handle six, seven, eight or more different accounts with skill, dispatch and accuracy.

Meanwhile, the ACD software tallies each call, so that each client of the telemarketing call center has, at the end of each shift, the exact number of calls taken, the time of day they were taken, the number of orders sold and other vital information geared to its mass-media sales campaigns. Using these techniques, some managers are so expert they can see the precise seconds when the surge was at its *peak!*

Agent scheduling is still another value of DNIS. With the ability of agents to handle so wide a variety of products and services, managers of the center can "spread the load" over a workday, so that serious call spiking ceases to be a problem in all but the most exceptional circumstances. This is because not all products are advertised at the same moment.

Even if there happens to be a great response for a specific product in a telemarketing center, experience proves that response from a TV ad tapers off in about seven minutes. Therefore, with the DNIS 800 capability, a "normal" number of agents can deal with a variety of calls without need for additional agent help. ("Normal" would be the number of agents that experience dictates the center needs to maintain a specific service level.)

Direct Outbound Dialing. ACD's, when configured with an integrated ACD/Data-Base System, can automate direct outbound dialing for sales, collections, opinion surveys, emergency notifications, promotional announcements and other projects. (The Galaxy ACD's have software that permits both agent-controlled and system-controlled outdialing, or both.)

System Interdials. ACD's permit speedy switching from agent to supervisor, or agent to agent, etc., usually via one-digit dialing. Supervisory personnel can organize the dialing code to provide maximum flexibility for interdialing, depending on the nature of the business and the needs of the staff.

An example might be a telemarketing service center that normally receives a percentage of TV direct-response calls from persons who speak Spanish, Italian and German. The firm establishes gates of agents who have these language skills. When a Spanish-speaking caller is connected with an English-speaking inbound agent, the agent merely presses a pre-determined key on the console, for example, a key marked "6." This corresponds to the gate of agents who are Spanish speaking, designated "6" throughout the call center. During the transfer of the call, the caller may hear a brief recorded announcement in Spanish, saying that the call is being transferred to someone who speaks that language. The next available Spanish-speaking agent will then handle the call. Other gates, with other single-digit numbers, correspond to language groups in Italian and German. The ACD speedily makes the transfers, helping the call center retain the calls, make the sales and maintain a competitive edge.

Call Transfer, Hold and Conference Calls. As seen in the preceding description, call transfer via the ACD is handled in a highly efficient manner. The system also can hold calls while the agent looks up information.

During the hold period, some ACD's may play a recorded message saying the agent is busy and requests the caller to remain on-line.

Conference calling is no problem for most ACD's. Conferencing sometimes becomes necessary if a question arises over pricing, sale details or service. The agent can easily bring the supervisor into the conversation. Conferences of three or more persons are possible on several brands of ACD's.

Call-Waiting Indication. Usually agents are informed that a call is waiting by a light on their agent console or a beep in their headset. The ACD may indicate call-waiting to its agents when heavy queueing has begun. This parameter may be set by the management of the call center. If, for example, a queue length of 50 callers takes place in a call center, the call-waiting light will start appearing on the agent consoles. (The ACD has been programmed to indicate call-waiting at the 50 mark.) This indicates to agents that they need to speed up their conversations in order to help keep the customers' queue-time to a minimum. When the call-waiting lights cease appearing, agents know that "normal" talk-time can resume.

Night Service. Many telemarketing service centers operate around the clock and do not require night service recordings. But many centers operate on an eight- or 12-hour schedule, shutting down at the end of the workday. For its after-hours callers, the center's ACD will accept the call but implement a recording telling the caller the center is closed for the night, but will reopen again the following morning (or "next Monday morning") at a given hour.

Some centers may have a small group of agents to handle night calls, while the majority of the center's employees are home for the evening.

Supervisory Alert. Agents can, if required, alert their supervisors if they require assistance with a call. A tap on a special button is all that is needed to bring in the supervisor. At this time, the supervisor can monitor the conversation but remain inaudible to the calling party. (On Rockwell's Galaxy ACD, the supervisor has the ability to "barge in" on a conversation if the situation requires.)

Silent Monitoring. Some ACD systems permit supervisors and training personnel to monitor their agents' conversation. Many telemarketing service companies require that all agents in their employ be monitored periodically to assure high quality service to their customers, and their employees know this.

At least one telemarketing firm invites its client/advertisers to monitor agents' calls in a special "monitoring room" in the center of their calling floor. In this manner clients or prospective clients can hear, first-hand, exactly what transpires during a transaction. The management encourages this type of monitoring because they believe that the better informed their clients are, the more they'll appreciate the sales quality they're getting. Invariably, clients come away from the monitoring room with a greater respect for the work being done and an understanding of the stress often accompanying the agents' jobs.

During training and post-training, most companies will monitor agents to assure that their presentations are acceptable, their voices modulated correctly, their timing right and so forth. Many companies insist on training every agent whenever a new product or service is to be handled. As a part of the training, agents are monitored in their handling of the new item when they return to the call floor, regardless how skilled they have already proven to be.

Emergency Alert. On the Galaxy ACD, an "emergency alert" button is placed on the agent's console. This provision was begun when Galaxy ACD's were first placed in major airline call centers. The airlines were concerned about cranks who called with bomb threats, so the emergency alert provision was conceived. Here, the call would immediately be monitored by supervisors, and a printout of the date, time and agent ID receiving the call would be indicated. The emergency alert remains a feature of the Galaxy ACD, although it is seldom employed.

Supervisor Monitoring. Supervisors need to monitor their agents' performance, and most ACD systems provide this capability. In some, supervisors have the ability to monitor any gate of agents, while in others they are restricted to designated gates only. Generally, supervisors in most installations can monitor everything that takes place in the call center at any time.

REPORTS

Management reports provided by the ACD can be given both on-screen to supervisors' CRT's and on paper in the form of permanent printouts. With these reports, particularly the printed ones, managers can develop a greater sense of what an ACD can do to increase profitability. They'll know when to increase or decrease agent staffing, when to add part-time employees, when agents might require re-training, and when to add or remove trunks.

ACD reports tell management about:

* *Overtime requirements.*

* *Rest period scheduling.*

* *Overload-staffing needs.*

* *Performance of groups of agents.*

* *Individual agent performance.*

* *General system operation.*

* *Long- and short-term trends affecting service levels.*

* *Trunk utilization.*

* *Overflow and diversion of calls, plus much more.*

Some reports are issued at pre-determined intervals (every half-hour, for example). Others are set up to be printed out at the end of the workday or shift. The number and frequency of reports can be determined soon after an ACD is in operation and the management learns how much information it can handle. Some managers require in-depth, frequent data to maintain the service level they've established. Others may require only a final daily report, totaling and/or combining the major data accumulated that day.

It must be kept in mind that reports of ACD data are just that. They are neither "right" nor "wrong." One manager's "good" numbers may be another manager's "poison" numbers. As an example, a business depending on low queueing time, like a hotel reservations center or an airline ticket reservations office, would not like to see data indicating a long delay in call answering. A service industry, like one that answers questions regarding health insurance, would tolerate reports of longer queues.

Regarding the following report descriptions, we have used titles that are given with the Galaxy ACD. In general, they correspond to the titles of similar reports offered by other ACD manufacturers.

*System Status Report (*Figure 18-3*).* System status reports give managers of the call center a summary of their work force as related to *gates of agents*. A broad view of this aspect of the business is therefore provided the management, and these status reports are among the most-often requested by managers.

Looking at system status data, managers can see how a particular line of business is performing. If a line or "gate" of agents happens to handle telemarketing sales for Green Widgets, the supervisor of that line can look at this report and quickly determine how busy the agents were for a given period of time, say a half hour, selling those Green Widgets.

Another supervisor in the same center can examine the system status for a second gate of agents (handling sales for Yellow Widgets) and check on their performance. Over a period of time, management can detect certain traffic patterns that are repeated at specific times of the day or week in each gate of agents. Thus, they can reconfigure agent assignments to gates during those busy times to achieve the optimum matching of agents to their work time. (One interesting fact about some ACD's is their ability to permit managers to reconfigure agents from gate to gate without actually moving them physically. ACD software allows supervisors to check at any time to see where any gate of agents, or any individual agent, is assigned in the workplace.)

Thus, System Status Reports identify trends in order to optimize staffing and increase the service level within the ACD.

Across the top of most reports are the titles of the important fields of information the ACD gathers and assimilates. Here are some typical headings and explanations on the system status reports generated by a typical Galaxy ACD:

* *Time*. Usually listed at the far left of the report, time on a report may be listed for a given period, such as "From 1000 to 1100." On a daily summary, the times are often listed by hours, as "0300, 0400, 0500," etc.

* *Gate*. The name or code number of a gate of agents. It may appear as "GNSLS" for general sales, or as "WDGT B" for widget blue, etc.

333

ENCYCLOPEDIA OF TELEMARKETING

Figure 18-3
System Status Reports

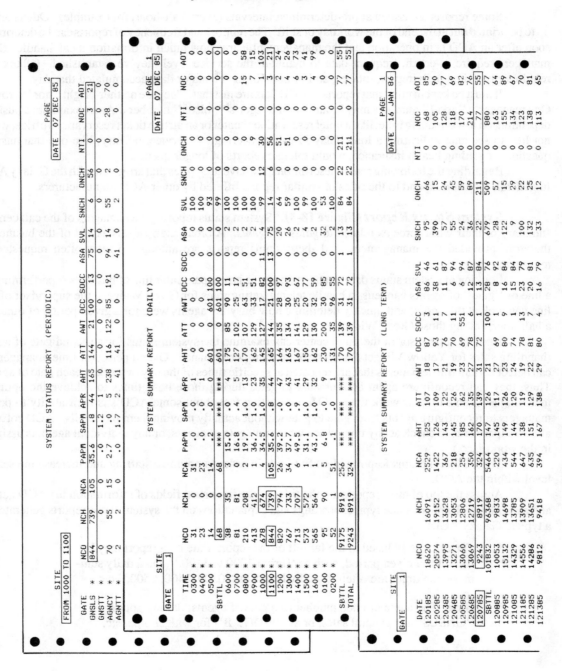

334

TELECOMMUNICATIONS (ACD)

* *Number of Calls Offered.* This data shows the number of external calls and internal gate transfers, internal calls and overflow/diversion calls accepted into the ACD, whether or not they were eventually answered.

* *Number of Calls Handled.* This shows the number of calls, including overflowed calls, which were connected to a position.

* *Number of Calls Abandoned.* These are the number of calls that were accepted into the ACD but that were lost (abandoned) before reaching an agent or ARU. In a sales-oriented environment, supervisors watch this data closely, since every abandoned call equates to a possible lost sale.

* *Primary and Secondary Average Positions Manned.* These data columns indicate the average number of agent positions occupied during the reporting period. Those handling a primary work assignment are listed separately from those handling a secondary assignment for each gate. The data provides clues to whether or not additional agents need to be reconfigured to a particular gate of agents. For example, if secondary assignments in a gate are seen to be climbing rapidly, supervisors know that a surge has begun in the primary agent area and that a temporary shift of agent assignments is required for a period of time, to keep callers from being held in queue too long at the primary gate.

* *Average Positions Required.* This data indicates the average number of primary positions required. With this data, supervisors know if they're maintaining the desired service level for the primary agent assignments in their groups. A glance at this data tells the supervisor if the service level for any group of agents is within established parameters.

* *Average Handling Time.* This indicates the average time, in seconds, the ACD took to handle all internal and external gate transfers connected to a position. It does not refer to the time taken by agents to process a transaction. (See next item.)

* *Average Talk Time.* This indicates the average time, in seconds, a gate of agents (or an individual agent) takes to handle a call. The time is measured from the instant the agent's "IN" lamp lights up to the time the lamp goes off.

* *Average Work Time.* After an agent disconnects from the caller, it may be necessary to deal with paperwork. This indicates the time, in seconds, the agent is plugged-in to the system but not available to take the next call.

335

* *Occupancy.* This data indicates the percent of time agents were plugged in and handling incoming calls. It includes both talk time and call-work time. Some ACD systems offer secondary and tertiary occupancy tables.

* *Average Speed of Answer.* This information tells supervisors the average delay time, in seconds, for calls that have been answered at a gate or by an agent. If the average speed of answer exceeds a predetermined level, supervisors may want to add agents, speed up talk time or make other changes to resume the speed they deem appropriate.

* *Service Level.* This important data tells the supervisor the percentage of incoming calls that have been answered or abandoned in less than "X" seconds. "X" is defined by the supervisor. Some call centers may seek a service level of eight seconds, others may require service levels of 20 seconds, etc.

* *Number of Out Calls.* This indicates the number of out calls made by primary agent positions on outgoing trunks or tie lines.

* *Average Out Time.* In seconds, this shows the average time that trunks or tie lines are used on the ACD for outgoing calls.

There may be other lines of data in System Status Reports, depending on the ACD one is examining. Other elements of printed reports give the date the report was made, the month and year, and the main title of the report (i.e., System Status Report [Periodic], or System Status Report [Daily], or System Status Report [Long Term]). The long term report is a compilation of daily reports, running for each day of a month and totaling all the above columns. The daily report totals the incremental half hour data offered by the ACD.

Agent Status Reports (Figure 18-4). Generally, these reports place agents into the Information Group to which they are assigned. For example, agents may be designated "Group 1," or "Sales Group 7," etc. By grouping agents in this manner, managers can more readily track their performance, based on predetermined criteria. Examples of information groups might be a team that handles critical outbound sales calls, a trainee group, a group handling inbound TV sales calls, etc.

In addition to the usual report headings showing the title of the report and the date and time period, these agent status reports generally show, at the far left, the designated group names or numbers that have been assigned to them by management. In this way, reading across the report, a supervisor can scan a given group of agents for all the criteria listed below:

* *Number of Calls Handled.* All calls that were connected to a position in the assigned information group.

* *Average Handling Time.* Given in seconds, this equates to talk time plus work time, divided by the number of calls handled. If a supervisor sees this number rise above an established "bogie," more agents or trunks may be

TELECOMMUNICATIONS (ACD)

Figure 18-4
Agent Status Reports

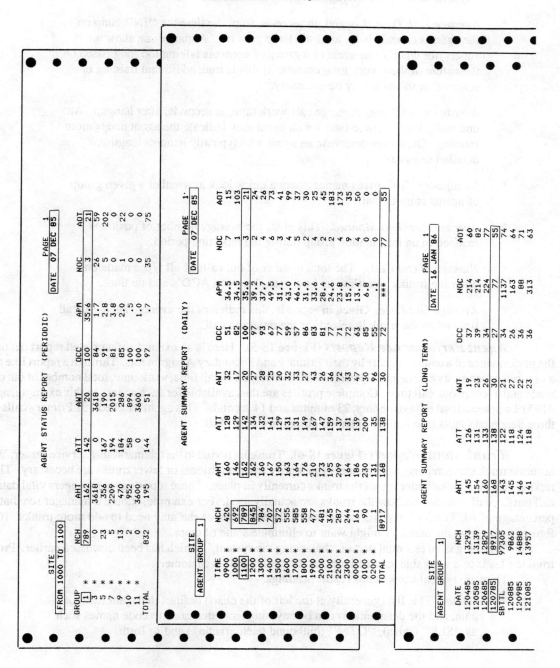

required to bring the average handling time back to "normal."

* *Average Talk Time.* Logged, in seconds, from the time the "IN" lamp on the agent's console is lit, until the lamp goes off. A glance can show a supervisor whether an agent or a group of agents is talking too long based on the nature of their work assignments. If this is true, additional training or some other solution may be necessary.

* *Average Work Time.* Average call-work time, in seconds, after hangup. An unusually long average-time for an agent may indicate the agent needs more training. Or, it may designate an agent who typically handles lengthy, detailed sales calls.

* *Occupancy.* This gives management a quick look at whether a given group of agents is up-to-staff.

* *Average Positions Manned.* This gives the average number of positions manned in an information group during the reporting period.

* *Number of Out Calls.* The total number of out calls of all types made on outgoing trunks, overflow tie lines, etc., between ACD's and tie lines.

* *Average Out Time.* Given in seconds, this indicates the average agent outcall time when the trunk is seized for the outgoing call.

Agent Performance Reports (Figure 18-5). Here is an example of a printed report detailing the performance of a team of agents by their Primary and Secondary Assignments. Through a report like this, a supervisor can study each agent's performance with regard to call time, work time, total number of out calls made and average out-call time. Complete profiles are thus available for each agent. In this example, agent 419513 worked a total of seven hours, 23 minutes and 14 seconds. This agent handled 151 Primary calls and three Secondary calls (see bottom of sheet) during his work shift.

Trunk Status Reports (Figure 18-6). Trunking is vital to the telemarketing service center. With accurate trunk status reports, supervisors can identify when additional or fewer trunks are necessary. These reports also help make better use of the trunks currently in place. These reports give managers vital data on call traffic, call volume and how the trunks are actually used. For example, should a manager see that the percentage of All Trunks Busy is approaching 100 percent, he or she may need to add more trunks. If the figure is very low, the manager might want to eliminate some of them.

Trunking is an essential part of "balancing the system," which has been discussed earlier. Proper trunking leads to a workable service level for the center and its customers.

Here are typical trunk status report headings:

* *Group.* This list (generally at the left of the chart) defines the agent team or gate, and the designations can be anything from numerals to code names such as "SLS" (sales), "OTM" (outbound telemarketing) and so forth.

TELECOMMUNICATIONS (ACD)

Figure 18-5
Agent Performance Reports

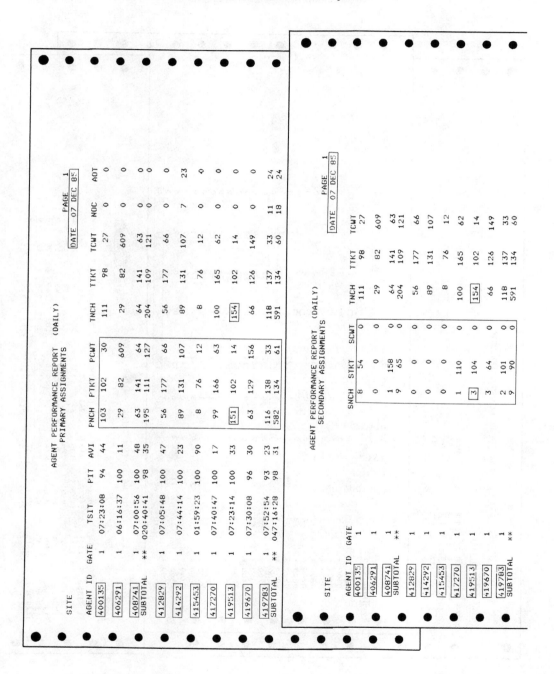

AGENT PERFORMANCE REPORT (DAILY)
PRIMARY ASSIGNMENTS

SITE

PAGE 1
DATE 07 DEC 85

AGENT ID	GATE	TSIT	PIT	AVI	PNCH	PTKT	PCWT	TNCH	TTKT	TCWT	NOC	AOT
400135	1	07:23:08	94	44	103	102	30	111	98	27	0	0
406291	1	06:16:37	100	11	29	82	609	29	82	609	0	0
408741	1	07:00:56	100	48	63	141	64	64	141	63	0	0
SUBTOTAL	**	020:40:41	98	35	195	111	127	204	109	121	0	0
412829	1	07:05:48	100	47	56	177	66	56	177	66	0	0
414292	1	07:44:14	100	23	89	131	107	89	131	107	7	23
415453	1	01:59:23	100	90	8	76	12	8	76	12	0	0
417220	1	07:40:47	100	17	99	166	63	100	165	62	0	0
419513	1	07:23:14	100	33	151	102	14	154	102	14	0	0
419670	1	07:30:08	96	30	63	129	156	66	126	149	0	0
419783	1	07:52:54	93	23	116	138	33	118	137	33	11	24
SUBTOTAL	**	047:16:28	98	31	582	134	61	591	134	60	18	24

AGENT PERFORMANCE REPORT (DAILY)
SECONDARY ASSIGNMENTS

SITE

PAGE 1
DATE 07 DEC 85

AGENT ID	GATE	SNCH	STKT	SCWT	TNCH	TTKT	TCWT
400135	1	8	54	0	111	98	27
406291	1	0	0	0	29	82	609
408741	1	1	158	0	64	141	63
SUBTOTAL	**	9	65	0	204	109	121
412829	1	0	0	0	56	177	66
414292	1	0	0	0	89	131	107
415453	1	0	0	0	8	76	12
417270	1	1	110	0	100	165	62
419513	1	3	104	0	154	102	14
419670	1	3	64	0	66	126	149
419783	1	2	101	0	118	137	33
SUBTOTAL	**	9	90	0	591	134	60

339

ENCYCLOPEDIA OF TELEMARKETING

Figure 18-6
Trunk Status Reports

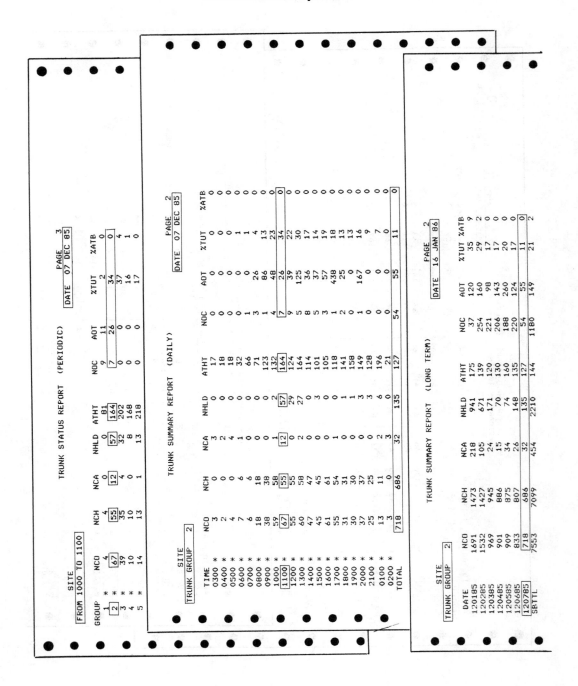

340

TELECOMMUNICATIONS (ACD)

* *Number of Calls Offered.* This gives the number of external and overflow/ diversion calls accepted into the ACD, whether or not they were eventually answered by an agent.

* *Number of Calls Handled.* This indicates the number of external calls that were accepted into the ACD on trunks only--calls that were eventually answered by agents.

* *Number of Calls Abandoned.* Calls accepted into the ACD but later abandoned by the callers. If the number is excessive, it might be advisable to check the Average Trunk Hold time, described below.

* *Number of Calls Held.* This shows the number of external calls delayed "X" seconds or more before being connected to an agent position or abandoned. The "X" time is defined by the user. The limit might be 30 seconds, one minute, or some other length of time.

* *Average Trunk Hold Time.* This data shows the time the trunk is in service, divided by all its activity during the report time period. A high percentage of time in hold could indicate the need for more agents in the gate.

* *Number of Out Calls.* This shows the number of calls made on outgoing trunks, overflow tie lines between ACD's and tie lines. Excessive variance from a "norm" could indicate a hung trunk (a trunk out of order) or the need for more or fewer agents, etc.

* *Average Out Time.* Shown in seconds, the average time that trunks are used for outbound calls.

* *Percent of Trunk Utilization Time.* The percentage of time trunks were assigned and not idle. Unusual deviations from an established normal percentage could indicate a problem with one or more of the trunks.

* *Percent of Time All Trunks Busy.* This data shows the percentage of time during the report interval that all trunks in a Trunk Information Group were simultaneously busy. A constant high percentage might indicate the need for more trunks--or the need to test if any are malfunctioning.

Delayed Call Profile Reports **(Figure 18-7).** This data helps to identify the habits of customers calling into a telemarketing service center. Primarily, the data indicates the callers' tolerance to being held in queue and the level of service being offered. Managers can quickly see how long callers are willing to hold before they'll hang up (abandon) their call.

Armed with this information, managers can optimize their agent force, their trunking and their delay recordings to retain the caller, to prevent the caller from hanging up and to achieve an optimum level of service.

Depending on the nature of the business, the delayed call reports enable management to set the call-answering times that are best suited to their operation. Any revenue-producing telemarketing operation will likely be very sensitive to an excessive number of abandoned calls on this report and take fast action to reduce the number to an "acceptable" level.

Delayed call profiles are graduated by time intervals up to 180 seconds and beyond, beginning with zero seconds to five, 10, 15, 20 and so forth. Then, for each gate, the report lists first the number of calls handled, followed immediately below by the number of calls abandoned. Here is a typical situation: A "General Sales" gate--under the 10-second heading--shows that nine calls were handled and three abandoned. Under the 15-second heading, this same general sales group handled 35 calls and seven calls were abandoned. If this ratio is acceptable to the management, one could say that the company is handling its business within its established parameters.

Taking the general sales group farther along the time-sequence, say to 90 seconds from the time the calls were accepted by the ACD, we see that 197 calls were handled and 12 were abandoned. For most businesses, this might seem a highly acceptable ratio, but perhaps not for the business you run. If this is the case, you might want to reference other reports generated, which could result in your adding more agents to this general sales gate, or reducing the call-handling time by editing the sales script, etc.

In examining delayed call profile reports, one thing becomes evident: there are inevitably some callers who have a higher tolerance for waiting in queue than others.

These delayed profile reports are presented to managers in two different formats. First, the report is generated for a given period of time (a half hour, as an example). It shows the calls handled and abandoned, the increments of time, and naturally the names of the gates of agents. The various summaries of the half-hour reports show a different set of data. These reports take each gate of agents and summarize their performance according to their shift hours. General sales, therefore, might be listed for a shift ending at two a.m. Along the top of the report are headings that give management a detailed picture of that agent group during their shift period.

Here are the headings and what they mean to managers:

* *Percent of Calls Abandoned.* Indicates the percent of calls that were abandoned by callers after being accepted by the ACD. A percentage reading "100" for example, indicates that every call reaching the ACD was abandoned. This obviously indicates that the telemarketing center was closed for business at that time and all inbound callers heard a "center closed" recording. If the percentage reads "3," for example, it means that three percent of the calls reaching the ACD were abandoned in this time-segment.

* *Percent of Calls Held.* This data indicates the percent of calls that were delayed after "X" seconds elapsed. The "X" is determined by the management: it might be 10, 20 or 30 seconds, for instance. Twenty seconds seems to be a normal tolerance level for many call centers.

342

TELECOMMUNICATIONS (ACD)

Figure 18-7
Delayed Call Profile Reports

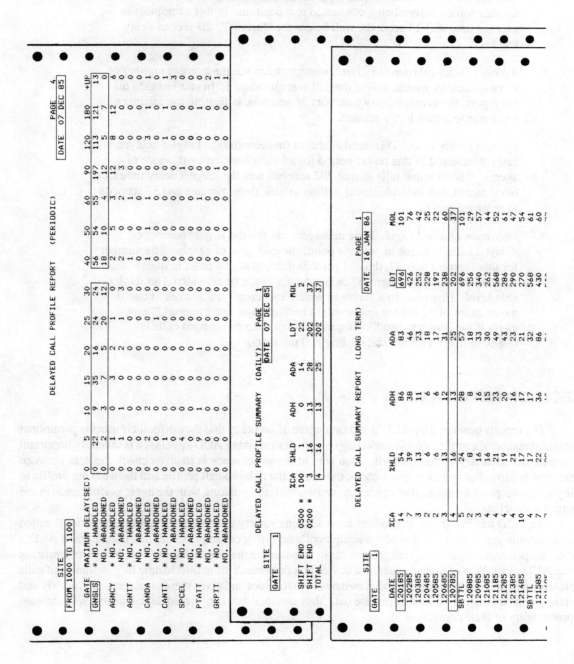

* *Average Delay to Handle.* This figure shows the average number of seconds a caller waited before being connected to a position. In this example, the average time was 13 seconds, well below the "normal" 20-second delay level.

* *Average Delay to Abandon.* Here, managers can see the average number of seconds a caller waited before the call was abandoned. In one instance on the report, the average delay time was 28 seconds, indicating the tolerance level was less than half a minute.

* *Longest Delay Time.* This number shows (in seconds) the longest delayed call encountered in this report period for all calls handled by this gate of agents. The example tells us that 202 seconds was the longest delay time. In other words, one individual was willing to wait three minutes and 36 seconds to reach an agent.

* *Maximum Queue Length.* Here managers can see the largest number of delayed calls in queue at any one point, for each gate of agents. The number for this segment was 37, thus 37 persons delayed at one point in queue. For most telemarketing centers, 37 delayed calls might be considered an intolerable level. However, in a center in which 350 agents are at work at one time, a maximum of 37 held in queue might be "average" or "normal," especially if the center is handling rapid and high volume inbound calls in response to TV commercials listing 800 numbers.

PRECISION REPORTING

The reports generated by ACD's and the degree of accuracy that they offer their users is paramount to the maintenance of a profitable telemarketing center. In examining ACD systems, it is crucially important to examine the *accuracy* of their reports. One way to prove accuracy is to cross check the data between interrelated groups. For instance, cross-check the data in the delayed call profile and the trunking profile to see if you can pinpoint elements that agree. Or, cross-check the trunking with the agent performance to see if there is a matchup.

An ACD has the ability to produce a tremendous variety of reports. The four categories detailed above constitute just a small portion of the equipment's reporting capacity. Other manufacturers of ACD's have developed reports packages that are similar to these, some that are different. The fact to remember is that the ACD, regardless of manufacture, is a device that does much more than handle large volumes of calls efficiently and equitably. It is a device that *measures* what it does and gives these measurements quickly and accurately to its managers. With this precise data, they can then make informed decisions that will increase the profitability of their companies.

To give the reader a view of the scope of the Galaxy's reporting capabilities, here are additional standard and optional reports generated by Galaxy ACD software:

* *Identify All Ports.*

* *Agent Call Count Report.*

* *Trunk Call Count Report.*

* *Agent Information Group Report.*

* *Agent Gate Group Report.*

* *Agent Stroke Count Report.*

* *Trunk Information Group Report.*

* *Trunk Gate Group Report.*

* *Off Net Routing Report.*

* *On Net Routing Report.*

* *Trunk Group Restriction Report.*

Numerous other reporting capabilities are possible with ACD systems. These include listing of agent names in a "profile report" (**Figure 18-8**), which make it easier for supervisors to associate data with names, rather than agent code numbers. Another example would be an agent status display (**Figure 18-9**). In this example, a supervisor's team of agents is listed, identified in this instance by agent code number, and the data shows the current work status of each of them.

In the example given here, two agents are available to answer incoming calls. This screen was obtained from a call center that handles high-volume, short-duration calling. It seems well-staffed at this moment to handle a volume of calls quickly. (The two CRT screens pictured here are typical of CRT "real-time" reports generated by an ACD. Information shown on the screens can often be printed out for permanent reference; however, some ACD data is only available on-screen for instantaneous observation which may require some action by supervisors.)

Shared User Reports. Enable supervisors to partition their ACD by groups or gates and permits them to assign these groups to a *specific* supervisor. In this way, supervisors have autonomy to handle the visibility and control of the call activity and personnel assigned in their gates.

PBX in a Gate. Permits managers to assign PBX lines to a gate in the ACD positions. Because of this, PBX positions can be shifted quickly to operate as ACD positions in an emergency. Also, the PBX positions can be used if the company has remote sites that do not require full ACD agent functionality.

Figure 18-8
Agent Profile Report

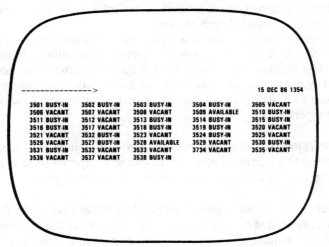

```
---------------------->                          12 FEB 87 1011

                          AGENT PROFILE REPORT
         SITE MIDWEST NDC        DATE 12 FEB 87
AGENT ID 30002
AGENT NAME    PR,SC    SIT     SOT  PIT AVI PCH PTT PWT SCH STT SWT NOC AOT
DINGELS,S      1,2   234655  013114  97  55  56  41   0   8  45   0   0   0
DINGELS,S      1,2   020122  022522  99  53  12  40   1   3  62   0   0   0
DINGELS,S      1,2   022944  034711 100  53  43  40   0   6  76   0   0   0
DINGLES,S      1,2   035851  060004  95  57  61  43   1   1 178   0   1  88
AGENT ID 30005
AGENT NAME    PR,SC    SIT     SOT  PIT AVI PCH PTT PWT SCH STT SWT NOC AOT
SABBIA,R       1,2   052801  070458 100  40  89  39   0   0   0   0   0   0
SABBIA,R       1,2   071104  091507  88  11 140  41   1   0   0   0   0   0
SABBIA,R       1,2   091900  092851 100   9  18  30   0   0   0   0   0   0
AGENT ID 30012
AGENT NAME    PR,SC    SIT     SOT  PIT AVI PCH PTT PWT SCH STT SWT NOC AOT
KALUZNY,R      3,3   060138  062416  99  28  30  31   1   0   0   0   0   0
      ***REPORT IS TOO LONG FOR SCREEN, SEND TO LP FOR COMPLETE REPORT.***  0   0

GATE     SVL  NCO  ADQ  HLD  ASA  AAV  PPM  SPM  NOC  CSL MDE  VIN  VOT  SVC
FMT01    74   71    1    0   13    0   66    0    0   94  -/-   0    0    D
FMT02    67    2    0    0   15    0    0   66    0   89  -/-   0    0    N
FMT03    82   24    0    0    9    3   28    0    0   95  -/-   0    0    D

   ONLINE     LINE   DSR          SYSTEM RDY
```

Agent Profile Report

Figure 18-9
Agent Status Display

```
--------------->                                           15 DEC 86 1354

  3501 BUSY-IN   3502 BUSY-IN   3503 BUSY-IN   3504 BUSY-IN    3505 VACANT
  3506 VACANT    3507 VACANT    3508 VACANT    3509 AVAILABLE  3510 BUSY-IN
  3511 BUSY-IN   3512 VACANT    3513 BUSY-IN   3514 BUSY-IN    3515 BUSY-IN
  3516 BUSY-IN   3517 VACANT    3518 BUSY-IN   3519 BUSY-IN    3520 VACANT
  3521 VACANT    3532 BUSY-IN   3523 VACANT    3524 BUSY-IN    3525 VACANT
  3526 VACANT    3527 BUSY-IN   3528 AVAILABLE 3529 VACANT     3530 BUSY-IN
  3531 BUSY-IN   3532 VACANT    3533 VACANT    3734 VACANT     3535 VACANT
  3536 VACANT    3537 VACANT    3538 BUSY-IN
```

Agent Status Display

Single Trunk Exception Reports **(Figure 18-10).** These money-saving reports are important because they show the user trunks being paid for that are not being used. Highlighted is trunk group 22 which did not handle any calls in the report period. Either the user was over-trunked or these trunks were not functioning properly.

Overflow Reports. Show the flow of traffic between two ACD's or between gates of a single ACD. They also show traffic flow between an ACD and some other type of switch, like a PBX. These reports are printed only when the overflow has been implemented.

Individual Agent Performance Reports **(Figure 18-11).** Detail the performance of each agent. In Galaxy ACD reports, they show both the agent's primary assignment and secondary assignment. Supervisors can therefore study each agent's performance with regard to call time, work time, the total number of calls handled in a time period, the total talk time, the total call-work time, the number of out-calls made and the average out-call time. Complete profiles are thus available to the supervisor for each agent within his or her area of responsibility. The example shown reports the status of agent "Rossiter, T.," showing her sign-in and sign-out times, plus additional information about her performance. With data like this, supervisors can spot exceptional workers, along with those who may require additional help or training.

OTHER ACD REPORT CAPABILITY

Speaking once again for the Galaxy, there are other reports that can be of great use to ACD managers and supervisors. Here are some of them:

Call Record Logging Reports. Answers questions like "*How many times did we call this number?*" or "*Who made that call to that number?*" Supervisors have the data about the out-call activity in a particular trunk group.

Authorization Code Report. This gives a printout of all the valid classes of service and their respective authorization codes for dial access to the network. In this report the codes are assigned to persons, not to phones, and only the managers know the actual codes. Managers can thus control the usage of outbound calling for every person in the telemarketing center.

Gate Reject Count. This is part of the Galaxy's Gate Call Limiting software. A supervisor can compile the quantity of calls rejected by the gate that are over and above a pre-set queue limit. When this happens, the caller gets a busy signal. Gate call limiting allows a busy telemarketing center to *stop* excess calls from reaching the ACD.

It must be remembered that with the Galaxy ACD all calls that actually are *accepted* by the system will be held and will eventually be connected to an agent. If a spiking situation happens and a long queue count materializes, supervisors might want to restrict additional calls from reaching the ACD for a period of

Figure 18-10
Single Trunk Exception Report

```
                SINGLE TRUNK EXCEPTION REPORT
   SITE                                 DATE 16 JAN 86   1148
   TTG   PORT    CCS     NCO     AHT     TYPE EXCEPTION
    18   161      0       0      .0                 ZERO HOLD TIME

                SINGLE TRUNK EXCEPTION REPORT
   SITE                                 DATE 16 JAN 86   1148
   TTG   PORT    CCS     NCO     AHT     TYPE EXCEPTION
    22   465      0       0      .0                 ZERO HOLD TIME
    22   466      0       0      .0                 ZERO HOLD TIME
    22   513      0       0      .0                 ZERO HOLD TIME
    22   514      0       0      .0                 ZERO HOLD TIME
    22   561      0       0      .0                 ZERO HOLD TIME
    22   562      0       0      .0                 ZERO HOLD TIME

                SINGLE TRUNK EXCEPTION REPORT
   SITE                                 DATE 16 JAN 86   1148
   TTG   PORT    CCS     NCO     AHT     TYPE EXCEPTION
    27   546      0       0      .0                 ZERO HOLD TIME
    27   547      0       0      .0                 ZERO HOLD TIME
    27   548      0       0      .0                 ZERO HOLD TIME

                SINGLE TRUNK EXCEPTION REPORT
   SITE                                 DATE 16 JAN 86   1148
   TTG   PORT    CCS     NCO     AHT     TYPE EXCEPTION
    35   340      0       0      .0                 ZERO HOLD TIME
```

Figure 18-11
Individual Agent Performance Display

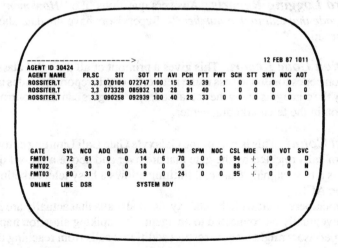

```
--------------------->                              12 FEB 87 1011
AGENT ID 30424
AGENT NAME        PR,SC    SIT    SOT PIT AVI PCH PTT PWT SCH STT SWT NOC AOT
ROSSITER,T        3,3   070104 072747 100  15  35  39   1   0   0   0   0
ROSSITER,T        3,3   073329 085932 100  28  91  40   1   0   0   0   0
ROSSITER,T        3,3   090258 092939 100  40  29  33   0   0   0   0   0


GATE        SVL  NCO  ADQ  HLD  ASA  AAV  PPM  SPM  NOC  CSL  MDE  VIN  VOT  SVC
FMT01        72   61    0    0   14    6   70    0    0   94   -/-   0    0   D
FMT02        59    0    0    0   18    0   70    0    0   89   -/-   0    0   N
FMT03        80   31    0    0    9    0   24    0    0   95   -/-   0    0   D
ONLINE      LINE  DSR            SYSTEM RDY
```

*Individual Agent
Performance Display*

time until the queue settles back to "normal." Gate call limiting permits this to happen, and the gate reject count informs the supervisor on how many calls were subsequently rejected by the system.

Here's a good example of how this limiting ability might help a telemarketing center: Assume that a major snowstorm hits your city. Only 50 of your 250-agent-force are able to reach your office building. You know you'll never be able to handle your "normal" call level with just 50 agents, so you set the limit count so callers in queue beyond that limit receive a busy signal and are not held for long periods of time in queue. Once the backlog of calls is eliminated or your agent force is increased, management ends the Gate Reject Count. This type of sophistication is what separates the ACD from other telecommunications systems and why so many telemarketers are looking seriously at changing to the ACD.

DNIS Reports. If a telemarketing center uses dialed number identification service, these reports can provide statistical information on the number of calls received by each DNIS number. Armed with this data, the managers of the center can evaluate market data, sales data and so forth. They'll know exactly how many calls came into the center for each product or service they handle. They'll know the exact day, hour and precise frame of time that the heaviest number of calls for a product were received in their center. Data like this can make a telemarketing service center valuable to its radio and TV clients, because it can show them *precisely* when the *top response* to their advertising is achieved.

With this detailed information in hand, advertisers can make more intelligent purchases of media time. As an example they might see that it is better to advertise in a less expensive TV market than in a more costly market because responses from the latter generated fewer calls than did the former.

Transaction Codes. These reports can provide transaction information on up to 200 individual codes. Each time an agent handles a call, he keystrokes coded information on all kinds of data gathered during the course of the call. For a sale of a yellow widget, the agent causes a code for "yellow" to be entered. Assume that at the end of the workday 145 yellow widgets were sold. In contrast, only 34 red widgets were sold, while Widget Kits generated sales of 1,550. The software tallies *all* the agents' transactions codes for the period, giving the telemarketing center a strong picture of the widget response. This data is valuable to the advertiser, who might decide to emphasize red widgets in advertising (or perhaps kill production of red widgets?), while beefing up their Widget-Kit promotion (where it appears they have a winner).

PABX Reports. Assuming a telemarketing center includes PABX with the ACD, these reports provide a basis for evaluating the traffic load on individual PABX terminations. Reports are sorted by department number and extension numbers.

JOINING AUTOMATED TELEMARKETING SYSTEMS WITH THE AUTO-MATIC CALL DISTRIBUTOR

Both hardware vendors and software producers have addressed the specialized needs of service centers and other businesses in which telemarketing becomes essential. A number of vendors now market software packages that enable telemarketers to run sophisticated programs for both inbound and outbound calling. One of these has been developed by Rockwell and called the Galaxy CONTACT System for Marketing™. It links the Galaxy ACD with the Tandem NonStop™ computer and provides a complete telemarketing solution that can increase the scope and profitability of such an operation.

The user of such a system can implement and manage diverse telemarketing and sales campaigns *simultaneously*. It improves the effectiveness and efficiency of agents as they qualify prospective customers, make sales calls, develop scripts and fulfill orders. Managers can evaluate overall marketing success using the many sophisticated reports this software can generate. Agents can have access to many different scripts, each of which can be customized with a variety of subscripts.

Scripts can be assigned according to campaigns, DNIS data records, or by trunk. Inbound calls can be matched automatically to scripts, and scripts can be added, modified or deleted on-line. In telemarketing campaigns, thousands of campaigns can be defined and each can be individually designed. Form letters and brochures can be sent to designated customers and prospects automatically. The system customizes each form letter. Mass mailings can be handled and three different letters or mailings can be assigned to each mass mailing. Labels and all files are queued for printing, automatically.

The CONTACT system handles accurate call scheduling for agents, so they'll make the most efficient use of their work time. Agents can review their call lists, add, delete or postpone calling. All scheduled calls are then dialed automatically. Reports generated by this calling help management track sales volume, media impact, survey results, aggregate calls and other data.

CRT menus help agents and managers control their work and maximize productivity. Many other types of databases, such as media analysis records, agents' files or ACD configurations can be easily accessed and managed. Two types of autodialing are possible with the Galaxy system:

System Controlled Autodialing. Helps improve the productivity of agents by routing, dialing and then connecting calls to the ACD. If a voice is detected at the other end of the line, the call is queued and connected immediately to the next available sales agent. If a voice is not detected, the call is released and another is dialed.

Agent Controlled Autodialing. Automates outdialing for *prescreened* prospects. Some software systems will validate each phone number and then devise and execute the least expensive call-route to reach the prospect. Performance reports list the calls completed by each sales agent, the length of each call, the cost of each call and a great deal more.

There must be a software interface between the mainframe and the telecommunications system in order to permit this type of automation to function. Interfaces sufficient to link most computer systems are X.25 or SNA/SDLC. The important thing to remember is that automated telemarketing systems joined with ACD's provide tremendous operational efficiencies and cost savings.

NEEDS ANALYSIS--HOW TO DETERMINE YOUR NEED FOR AN ACD AND IDEAS FOR VENDOR SELECTION

I'm occasionally asked by telemarketers what it takes to determine whether an ACD is right for their business. One of the first things I tell them is that ACD's are a *strategic* business asset. This concept is especially true *if they have an urgent need to answer or make calls and process a high volume of calls, inbound or outbound.*

Telecommunications equipment is typically less than 5% of the total operational costs, so those contemplating the purchase of ACD equipment should carefully consider the benefits of management efficiencies outlined earlier in this chapter. It is wise to exercise caution in making a decision on price alone, when there are so many other factors to be considered.

That is not to say, however, that price is not a major consideration. Telemarketers should keep in mind that the ACD's price is usually greater than a PBX's price. But, and this is very important, ACD's are designed to be *more cost-effective* in a different arena. Modularity is another big factor in selecting an ACD system: Consider future growth patterns. If the telemarketer expects to grow significantly, the system purchased should have the ability to match that growth. Some ACD's will reach a certain size and that's that. Nothing will get them over the hump to where they'll stay cost-effective. Discover if true modularity is possible before deciding to purchase an ACD.

There are important questions you must ask in your selection process. For example, can the manufacturer supply you with an uninterruptible power supply if you cannot afford being one second off the air? Are there software programs that are available and ready to serve you through the ACD? Does the manufacturer's ACD have a proven *uptime* record?

Does the ACD vendor have a nationwide team of skilled people to guide in the selection, installation and maintenance of the ACD? Are knowledgeable sales engineers on hand around the clock to help if there's an emergency, and to give on-going solid advice?

Can the ACD in question provide the telemarketing company with "dedicated workstations" for its agents? In other words, can the ACD be made to interconnect with a computer data base so the sales reps can have direct access to a variety of scripts and data? How is the connection accomplished?

Can the ACD handle DNIS calling? Can it handle least-cost routing? Can it be connected with audio response units? Does it provide clear on-screen data to supervisors and can it print out detailed periodic and merged reports for long-range analysis? How many printers will it serve? How many agents can be connected to the ACD? How many trunks? How long a lead-time period is required from the signing of the contract to the cutover of the system into actual use?

Most of all, remember that *price* alone may not give the best value; it may not always be the best solution to a telemarketer's long-range goals.

Consider all the factors in making a decision. **Figure 18-12** presents a typical needs analysis checklist. These needs vary, of course, from company to company and from consultant to consultant.

REQUEST FOR PROPOSAL (RFP)

Requests for proposals for ACD systems are similar to RFP's that are generated for most capital equipment. They generally range between 90 to 120 pages and ask the manufacturer for detailed information about equipment, both hardware and software, prices, shipping, installation, testing, cutover to service and maintenance agreements.

Figure 18-12
A Typical Needs Analysis

1) Call Volume.

Busy hour	Under 1,000	( )	1,000-5,000	( )	Over 5,000	( )
Average hourly	Under 500	( )	500-2,000	( )	Over 2,000	( )
Monthly	Under 20,000	( )	20,000-100,000	( )	Over 100,000	( )
Annual	Under 250,000	( )	250,000-1M	( )	Over 1M	( )

2) Percentage of Calls   Inbound (%)   Outbound   (%)

3) Number of telemarketing sales representatives (TSR's) and supervisors employed:

Current:

TSR's	Under 25	( )	25-49	( )	50-100	( )	Over 100	( )
Supervisors	Under 3	( )	4-6	( )	7-9	( )	Over 9	( )

Next 12-18 months:

TSR's	Under 25	( )	25-49	( )	50-100	( )	Over 100	( )
Supervisors	Under 3	( )	4-6	( )	7-9	( )	Over 9	( )

4) Number of hours of training provided to new TSR's:

Under 40   ( )   40-120 ( )   Over 120   ( )

5) Number of call centers: ( )   **Number of locations receiving telephone calls:** ( )

6) Number of hours/week call center(s) is (are) open:_____ hours/day   _____ days/week

7) Number of trunks: Under 50   ( )   50-200 ( )   Over 200   ( )

8) Overflow from one geographical region to another?   Yes   ( )   No   ( )

9) Types of telephone system(s) now used for volume calls:

( )   PABX
( )   Key systems
( )   ACD
( )   Single lines
( )   UCD
( )   Other _____

10) Which of the following are used with your primary telephone systems?

( )   ACD
( )   T1 Multiplexers
( )   Channel service units
( )   Management reports
( )   PABX
( )   Staffing analysis software
( )   Audio response units
( )   Automated telemarketing devices
( )   Other _____

11) How are management reports currently used?

( )   Traffic analysis
( )   Productivity
( )   System utilization
( )   Other _____

12) Provider of primary trunk service:

( )   AT&T
( )   U.S. Sprint
( )   MCI
( )   Other _____

13) Annual telecommunications expenditures:

Equipment	Under $500 K	( )	$500K-$3M	( )	Over $3M	( )
Services	Under $1M	( )	$1-$5M	( )	Over $5M	( )
Personnel	Under $2M	( )	$2-$8M	( )	Over $8M	( )

14) Goals of your current call-handling capability:

( )   Reduce cost
( )   Increase revenue
( )   Improve service
( )   Other _____

15) Additional features/capabilities you would like to have in your system:

_____

_____

Generally, a manufacturer will take from 30 to 45 days to analyze the RFP and answer the questions and proposals contained it it. The RFP should be as detailed as possible, to assure that the manufacturer describes each and every element of the equipment, and the purchaser needs to check the manufacturers' RFP in detail to assure that the ACD will perform exactly as wished. Quite often, the RFP will be tied to a contract, so it is very important that all the vendor's technical answers be clear and able to be implemented as stated.

Usually, the manufacturers' response to a request for proposal will be many times the size of the purchaser's RFP, because much more space is required to describe all the elements of the ACD system than to ask for the information.

MAJOR MANUFACTURERS OF ACD SYSTEMS

Integrated systems.

*   *AT&T*, 295 North Maple Ave., Basking Ridge, NJ 07920. Telephone (201) 221-2000.

*   *AT&T*, in Canada, 1500 Don Mills Road, Suite 500, Don Mills, Ontario M3B 3K4. Telephone (416) 449-4300.

*   *Digital Transmission, Inc.*, 315 Eisenhower Lane South, Lombard, IL 60148. Telephone (312) 620-1170.

*   *Fujitsu Business Communications*, 3190 Mira Loma Ave., Anaheim, CA 92806. Telephone (714) 630-7721.

*   *InteCom, Inc.*, 601 InteCom Drive, Allen, TX 75002. Telephone (214) 727-9141.

*   *InteCom, Inc.*, in Canada, TTS, 460 Isabey Street, St. Laurent, Quebec, H4T IV3. Telephone (514) 342-6051.

*   *Inter-Tel, Inc.*, 6505 West Chandler Blvd., Chandler, AZ 85226. Telephone (602) 961-9000 or (800) 523-8180.

*   *ISOETEC Communications, Inc.*, 7 Thorndal Circle, Darien, CT 06820. Telephone (203) 655-6500.

*   *ISOETEC Communications, Inc.*, in Canada, NEDCO, 505 Locke Street, St. Lawrence, Quebec H4T IX7. Telephone (514) 341-3700.

*   *Mitel, Inc.*, 5400 Broken Sound Blvd. NW, Boca Raton, FL 33431. Telephone (305) 994-8500.

* *Mitel, Inc.*, in Canada, Mitel Corporation, 350 Legget Drive, P. O. Box 13089, Kanata, Ontario K2K IX3. Telephone (613) 592-2122.

* *NEC America, Inc.*, 8 Old Sod Farm Road, Lelville, NY 11747. Telephone (516) 753-7000.

* *NEC America, Inc.*, in Canada, NEC Toronto, Suite 801, Commerce Courte, P.O. Box 123, Commerce Courte Postal Station, Toronto, Ontario M5L IE2. Telephone (416) 363-2431.

* *Northern Telecom, Inc.*, 2150 Lakeside Blvd., Richardson, TX 75081. Telephone (214) 437-8000.

* *Northern Telecom, Inc.*, in Canada, Northern Telecom Canada, Inc., 304 The East Mall, Islington, Ontario M9B 6E4. Telephone (416) 232-2000.

* *Plant Equipment, Inc.*, 28075 Diaz Road, Temecula, CA 92390. Telephone (714) 676-4802.

* *Rolm Corporation*, 4900 Old Ironsides Drive, Santa Clara, CA 95050. Telephone (408) 986-1000.

* *Rolm Corporation*, in Canada, Rolm Canada, 4 Lansing Square, Willowdale, Ontario M2J 1T1. Telephone (416) 498-7656.

* *Siemens Information Systems, Inc.*, 5500 Broken Sound Blvd., Boca Raton, FL 33431. Telephone (305) 994-7524.

* *Siemens Information Systems, Inc.*, in Canada, Siemens Electric Limited, 1180 Courtney Park Drive, Mississuga, Ontario L5T 1P2. Telephone (416) 673-1995.

* *Solid State Systems, Inc.*, 1300 Shiloh Road NW, Kennesaw, GA 30144. Telephone (404) 423-2200.

* *Tadiran Electronic Industries, Inc.*, 10801 Endeavor Way, Suite A, Largo, FL 33543. Telephone (813) 541-5724.

* *Telephonic Equipment Corporation*, 17401 Armstrong Ave., Irvine, CA 92714. Telephone (714) 250-9400.

Stand-Alone ACD Systems.

* *ACD Technologies, Inc.*, 2360 East Devon Ave., Des Plaines, Il 60018. Telephone (312) 827-7700.

TELECOMMUNICATIONS (ACD)

* *Aspect Telecommunications*, 1733 Fox Drive, San Jose, CA 95131. Telephone (408) 279-5511.

* *Automation Electronics Corporation*, 11501 Dublin Blvd., Dublin, CA 94568. Telephone (415) 828-2880.

* *Candela Electronics*, 926 West Maude Ave., Sunnyvale, CA 94088. Telephone (408) 738-3800.

* *Conversational Voice Technologies Corporation*, CVCT Center, 4205 Grove Ave., Gurnee, Il 60031. Telephone (312) 249-5560.

* *Dacor Electronics, Inc.*, 8 Industrial Ave., Upper Saddle River, NJ 07458. Telephone (201) 825-4640.

* *Data Plus*, 7205E Lockport Place, Lorton, VA 22079. Telephone (703) 550-7914.

* *ISOETEC Communications, Inc.*, 6 Thorndal Circle, Darien, CT 06820. Telephone (203) 655-6500.

* *Metro Tel Corporation*, P.O. Box 698, 15 Burke Lane, Syosset, NY 11791. Telephone (516) 364-3377.

* *Qualitel Services, Inc.*, 2871 Metropolitan Place, Pomona, CA 91767. Telephone (714) 596-1675.

* *Ring Group of North America*, 230 Community Drive, Great Neck, NY 11021. Telephone (516) 487-0250.

* *Rockwell International Corporation*, Switching Systems Division, 1431 Opus Place, Downers Grove, IL 60515. Telephone (312) 960-8000.

* *Startel Corporation*, 17661 Cowan Ave., Irvine, CA 92714. Telephone (714) 863-8700.

* *Teknekron Infoswitch*, P.O. Box 612487, DFW Airport, TX 75261. Telephone (817) 354-0661.

* *Telcom Technologies*, 761 Corporate Center Drive, Pomona, CA 91768. Telephone (714) 620-7711.

* *Telephone Support Systems, Inc.*, Triad 1, 2001 Marcus Ave., Lake Success, NY 11040. Telephone (516) 352-6800.

* *Telephonic Equipment Corporation*, 17401 Armstrong Ave., Irvine, CA 92714. Telephone (714) 250-9400.

* *U.S. Takachito Corporation*, 10722 Los Vaqueroa Circle, Los Alamitos, CA 90720. Telephone (714) 761-3844.

COST VARIANCES

As indicated earlier, there are substantial cost variances between ACD systems. It must be kept in mind that integrated ACD/PBX systems offer a great deal less in the way of functionality than do the stand-alone ACD's.

It also should be indicated that multiple features may be added to many of these ACD systems. It is much the same as purchasing a new car. You've selected the basic model of the car. But then, do you want tinted glass? Power steering? Cruise control? Stereo tape deck? Tilt wheel? Etc.

Each end-user has different requirements: different numbers of agents, different trunking requirements, different numbers of supervisors, etc. The comparison of the price of one system versus another can have costs varying considerably.

To make the most cost-effective decision, it is important that you understand your operations and business applications. Do you want to improve efficiency and productivity, or increase growth? Are you concerned about payback or flexibility or competitiveness? Whatever the success factors, once determined, you should look for the best equipment to support your business situation.

Talking with the vendors' sales engineers and asking intelligent questions will help you narrow down to systems that appear to be correct for your business. In some cases, perhaps only one or two of the many companies will be in a position to actually handle the job.

A final point to remember about pricing: Manufacturing techniques are rapidly changing the size, power and pricing of telecommunications equipment. New micro-sized components, more information capacity per circuit board and higher quality in both the design and manufacturing process can radically affect the cost.

INSTALLATION, CUTOVER AND MAINTENANCE

One of the most important factors in the ACD decision-making process is the quality of the vendor's technical service. This can run all over the map, from total commitment to service to practically no service whatsoever.

However, the mere fact that a vendor doesn't provide service should not frighten away a potential purchaser. There are a number of telecom service companies that can be hired to handle the details of installation, general maintenance and emergency service.

Some manufacturers provide total service, from assisting in site selection, to pre-installation, shipping and installation, testing, cutover to service and , finally, ongoing maintenance and emergency

356

assistance. In other words, they offer *a complete turnkey service*.

Much of the decision-making process in considering service can hinge on costs. One telemarketer could have a technical service contract that provides once-a-week basic maintenance. Another might have a contract guaranteeing that a technician will be on site within two hours of an emergency call. I've visited a number of sites and have seen highly skilled technicians who are full-time employees of the firm itself. These companies have such skilled personnel they can do nearly everything to maintain the equipment, even to the point of installing and cutting over a new system.

There are ACD manufacturers who have their own maintenance personnel permanently located on users' sites and, of course, charge them for this service.

But it should be noted that ACD's run on sophisticated software programs. When there are problems with these programs, the telemarketer may need to have the manufacturer do an analysis. If a user decides to purchase a software upgrade, the skills of the manufacturer quickly come into play--to assure that the new program runs correctly. It is important that the purchaser understand the vendor's capacity to create, install, test and maintain its software programs.

Some vendors provide on-line remote software analysis for their users. Here, a telephone link is established between the vendor's test-bed and the customer's hardware and software. Engineers (perhaps thousands of miles distant) can then "see" first-hand what the problem is. They can often correct the problem on the spot, or arrange a temporary solution while software is adjusted at the factory.

These matters are generally included in the purchaser's request for proposal. Even before this, the telemarketer should have determined the vendor's capacity to handle service and maintenance and may have eliminated from consideration those firms that didn't meet their particular requirements.

CONCLUSION

There are so many considerations surrounding an intelligent approach to the ACD as a tool for the telemarketing community that one is hard pressed to look at the core of it, to see what really matters.

The key term in all of this, I believe, is "SURVIVAL."

To contribute to a telemarketing company's survival, the initial consideration for the communications system is that it must contribute to the long-term objectives of the telemarketer's business. *It must make the business more competitive.* It must offer significant benefits without creating excessive costs. Put simply, *it must REDUCE the cost-per-transaction of doing business.*

Second, *the system offered must be FLEXIBLE.* It must readily adapt to the rapidly-changing business conditions found in the business of telemarketing. It must not be so specialized that even minor changes in the business environment will strand the purchaser's investment in the product.

Third, the system *must have the capacity to GROW with the business,* and to grow with the increasing demands coming from within the business.

Fourth, *the system should be COMPATIBLE with the existing communications equipment already in place at the business.* No matter how capable or exciting the ACD seems to be, if its adoption requires major changes in existing systems, it is unlikely to be cost-effective.

Finally, the system should be *compatible with the telemarketer's strategic OBJECTIVES.* The ACD cannot be "the tail wagging the dog." It must underpin the goals and growth of the business.

With these precepts firmly in mind, telemarketing managers can begin to examine and evaluate the variety of business communications systems in the marketplace.

----

¹Galaxy is a registered trademark of Rockwell International Corporation.

CHAPTER 19

Telecommunications (General)

Charles E. Yates
Vice President-Market Planning, Business Markets Group
American Telephone & Telegraph Company (AT&T)
Basking Ridge, New Jersey

Without a doubt, a carefully managed telemarketing program is a must for any business to succeed today in moving its products and satisfying its customers. Applications from order taking and customer service to sales support and account management can be handled by telephone as a key part of an overall market strategy.

By definition, *telemarketing is the careful integration of applied information technology and management systems to enhance the full range of traditional marketing activities*. Telemarketing encompasses a broad range of applications--promotion management, order processing, customer service, sales support and account management.

Promotion Management. This application is essentially the combination of communications technology and traditional promotion techniques, such as coupons, discounts, sweepstakes and contests. *Promotion management* applications may enable callers to vote, hear a pre-recorded informational message, or interact with selected company personnel.

Order Processing. Basically, *order processing* is the taking and processing of orders by telephone. This application can be--and often is--expanded to include cross-selling, add-on sales and catalog selling. With the number of two-income families on the rise, catalog sales are enjoying a healthy business boom that is expected to continue.

Customer Service. The next application--*customer service*--is generally considered the information a company provides customers before or after a sale is made. This can include product information, the most convenient dealer location, account status, emergency "help" hotlines, repair scheduling and dispatch, successful complaint handling and proper product use and care.

Sales Support An increasingly important function--*sales support*--uses a telemarketing staff as an adjunct or aid to direct field sales people. The trained sales support specialists help the sales force or branch office by generating and qualifying successful leads and profitably handling marginal or "costly to visit" remote accounts. Sales support programs are generally used to couple inside resources with outside sales to handle specific products or projects.

359

Account Management. The most complex telemarketing area is *account management.* Here, the full client relationship is established and maintained by a single telemarketing salesperson or account executive. That person is responsible for all selling and servicing activities just as any "outside" salesperson would be.

To get a perspective on the market impact of telemarketing, consider the fact that in 1987 telemarketing generated nearly $120 billion in sales revenues, according to National Telemarketing, Inc. *By 1990, that figure is expected to exceed $400 billion.* Today, 300,000 companies make telemarketing part of their sales strategy--from small start-up businesses to giant sales and service centers. And together, these operations employ more than two million people.

ADVANCED TECHNOLOGY ASSISTS TELEMARKETING

Telemarketing gives companies the ability to establish innovative programs that can give them a strong competitive edge. Recent advances in technology are making telemarketing an even more effective business tool to help increase a company's efficiency, productivity and profitability. Technology, coupled with intelligence in software systems, enhances the telemarketing effort by taking routine activities and automating them, allowing companies to respond quickly, more personably, and more professionally than ever before.

This is especially important today because companies are finding that the time they have to respond to customers' demands is shrinking, while the amount of information they must process is dramatically increasing.

Even though technology plays a major role in strengthening telemarketing operations, business managers are continually asking what, how and where they should automate to gain improved performance. The best course of action is to focus not on the technology itself, but on solutions for improved results.

Today, a framework exists to "unbundle" the value of applied technology into more understandable, identifiable functions.

As part of this framework, a telemarketing center's operations are described in terms of five major functions (see **Figure 19-1**):

* *Marketplace access.*

* *Customer interaction.*

* *Fulfillment.*

* *Human resource management.*

* *Business impact and planning.*

The first three functions can be thought of as making up the direct business transaction; the last two as center and business support for the telemarketing operation itself. All five functions work together--

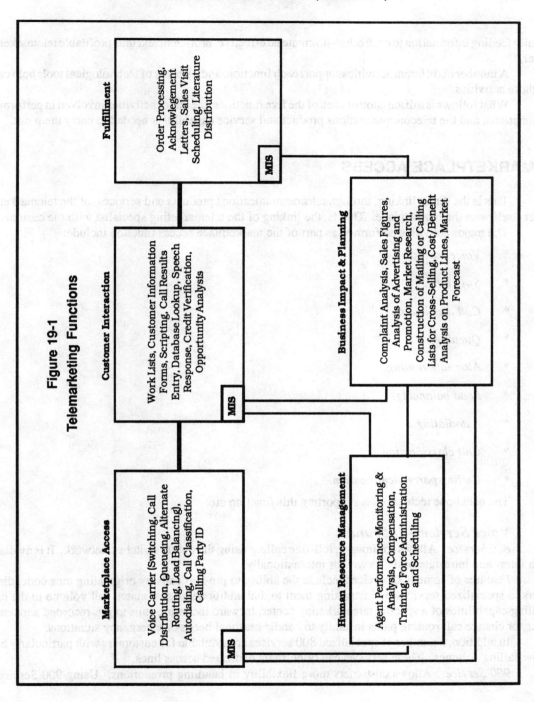

Figure 19-1
Telemarketing Functions

Fulfillment

Order Processing, Acknowlegement Letters, Sales Visit Scheduling, Literature Distribution

MIS

Customer Interaction

Work Lists, Customer Information Forms, Scripting, Call Results Entry, Database Lookup, Speech Response, Credit Verification, Opportunity Analysis

MIS

Business Impact & Planning

Complaint Analysis, Sales Figures, Analysis of Advertising and Promotion, Market Research, Construction of Mailing or Calling Lists for Cross-Selling, Cost/Benefit Analysis on Product Lines, Market Forecast

Marketplace Access

Voice Carrier (Switching, Call Distribution, Queueing, Alternate Routing, Load Balancing), Autodialing, Call Classification, Calling Party ID

MIS

Human Resource Management

Agent Performance Monitoring & Analysis, Compensation, Training, Force Administration and Scheduling actually feeding information to each other--to create an effective, proficient and thus profitable telemarketing center.

A number of different activities support each function, and a variety of technological tools help carry out these activities.

What follows is a discussion of each of the five functions, the major activities involved in performing the functions, and the telecommunications product and service capabilities needed to carry them out.

1. MARKETPLACE ACCESS

This is the direct linking, through telecommunications products and services, of the telemarketing center itself with the marketplace. That is, the linking of the telemarketing specialist with the customer.

The major activities performed as part of the marketplace access function include:

* *Voice carrier.*

* *Switching.*

* *Call distribution.*

* *Queuing.*

* *Alternate routing.*

* *Load balancing.*

* *Autodialing.*

* *Call classification.*

* *Calling party identification.*

The backbone technologies supporting this function are:

Voice Services--Inbound

800 Service. Allows for inward, toll-free calling using the public switched network. It is available on an inter- and intrastate basis, as well as internationally.

Features of some 800 services include the ability to pre-sort calls by originating area code, direct callers to specialized services by instructing them to dial additional digits, match call volume to the call-handling capabilities of a specific telemarketing center, forward incoming calls to pre-recorded announcements, or change call routing paths instantly to handle seasonal needs or emergency situations.

In addition, a number of specialized 800 services are available for customers with particularly high or low calling volumes. These services can often share dedicated access lines.

900 Service. Allows customers more flexibility in handling promotions. Using 900 Service, a company can offer customers pre-recorded product or service information, can ask customers to register an opinion on a specific topic or can connect the customer with a company representative for further information.

The 900 Service is a one-way national mass calling service that permits simultaneous connection by thousands of people to a sponsored information announcement or call-count program. It is available on an interstate and international basis. The service includes a number of features, such as the ability to offer variable length messages--from 15 seconds to several hours--and a call forwarding capability that allows sponsors to conduct in-depth interviews with a selected number of callers.

Voice Services--Outbound

WATS. Provides volume discounts on outbound calls only. WATS has time-of-day and day-of-week prices, and a volume-usage tapered price schedule. It is available for both interstate and intrastate calls, as well as internationally.

Long Distance Optional Calling Plans. Offers businesses a discount on long-distance service in addition to any regular time-of-day, day-of-week discounts already applicable. For a monthly fee, a business receives a percentage discount on direct-dialed long-distance messages. The plans are offered on an interstate and intrastate basis.

Data Network Communication Services

In addition to voice services, several offerings that allow information to be sent electronically among locations are also available. These services include dedicated private lines as well as data over switched networks and provide telemarketing centers with the ability to send data back and forth whenever necessary.

Private Line Digital Services. Provide businesses with virtually error-free data transmission at speeds of 2.4, 4.8, 9.6 and 56 kilobits. The services are available in more than 100 major metropolitan areas in the U.S. and can be connected to Canada's digital network.

Packet Switching Services. Allow customers to communicate with multiple independent data systems using a standard protocol.

Redi-Access. This is a public data network jointly provided by AT&T and Control Data Corporation. It allows businesses to efficiently integrate a wide range of applications running on multiple independent data systems into a unified corporate data network. The service, which offers low delay/high throughput data transmission, is available in more than 150 cities, 24 hours a day, seven days a week.

Software Defined Network Service (SDN). This is a private network offering designed strictly by AT&T for businesses with very high traffic. SDN carries voice and data traffic between customer locations, as well as to off-network points. SDN is customer controllable and its pricing is based on communications usage, time of day, distance, access and optional features. SDN provides flexible centralized management with extensive reporting capabilities.

Premises-Based Call Handling Systems

Private Branch Exchange (PBX)/Automatic Call Distributors (ACD's). The call handling capabilities of PBX's and PBX-based or stand-alone ACD's allow for the distributions, queuing, announcement handling and alternate routing of calls so a telemarketing center can effectively manage incoming calls. ACD's, either stand-alone or PBX integrated, are offered by a variety of telecommunications companies.

There are a variety of call management products on the market today to enable a telemarketing center to effectively take or make calls for as few as 20 or as many as 1,000 telemarketing representatives.

Typically, PBX/ACD's can be classified as inbound or outbound systems or a combination of both.

Synthesized/Computerized Speech. Another type of inbound call handling system is a relatively new technology available in a variety of configurations. It uses synthesized or computerized speech to enable a business to employ a computer to handle repetitive or relatively simple customer information exchanges. This system can be stand-alone or used in conjunction with a live system to free telemarketing representatives to handle more complex customer calls. The premises-based system works like this:

Telecommunications specialists create a customized speech vocabulary made up of the various responses to customer inquiries. This vocabulary is then stored on a computer using a pre-recorded, digitized human voice. During the customer inquiry process, the required responses are selected from the vocabulary based on information given to the system by a caller using a touch-tone telephone. Built-in features and prompts aid customers along the way.

For example, customers can enter order information directly into the database by pressing the proper touch-tone buttons for their account number, item numbers and quantities. Since telemarketing reps are not involved in these calls, these systems can operate 24 hours a day if necessary, resulting in improved customer service, reduced operating costs and increased sales opportunities.

Automated outbound call handling systems are of two types--*predictive* and *preview.* With predictive systems, the system dials a call ahead of a rep in anticipation of when the rep will be free. The system transfers only "live" calls to agents. When the system reaches a busy signal, it continually re-dials. All unanswered calls are placed on the bottom of a list to be tried again.

This type of configuration is particularly effective in telemarketing operations where there are a large number of people to be called and the probability of reaching each person is uncertain.

With preview systems, telemarketing representatives can actually preview information about a particular customer before or at the time a call is placed. The rep simply presses a button when ready, and the system dials the call. This type of configuration is useful for reps maintaining ongoing relationships with customers because it allows the rep access to personalized information about the customer.

Auto Dialers. The actual devices that assist telemarketing representataives in call setup as well as in the sales process. The capabilities of these dialers range from simple rep-initiated dialing to paced, predictive dialing by a computer. These devices can be purchased independently or integrated into the PBX/ACD operation. Automatic dialers can also integrate prerecorded sales messages into the call session. However, these messages must be introduced to customers by a live representatative.

Integrated Services Digital Network (ISDN). Today, ISDN is adding even greater dimension to telemarketing.

With ISDN, customers can send voice, data and video over the same lines and access a host of advanced service features. For example, in inbound call handling situations, ISDN will be able to provide a telemarketing representative with the phone number of the calling party. The rep can then *instantly call up the customer's database* and thus add a much more personal touch to the call.

At the same time, ISDN could provide an intercept message telling customers to hang up if all representatives are busy and their call will be returned in a specified amount of time. This would be a boon to customers who don't have time or patience to wait on "hold."

Many of the applications possible through ISDN are a few years away, although trials using Automatic Number Identification (ANI) are underway.

2. CUSTOMER INTERACTION

This is the second of the five telemarketing functions, and it is the actual execution of a business transaction between a telemarketing representative and the customer. The rep needs to have customer information, product information and often additional facts on hand to deal effectively with each customer.

The activities performed as part of this function include the full range of selling and servicing activities, as well as the design, preparation, and maintenance of the system needed to support these transactions. Activities could also include generating work lists, completing customer information forms, entering call results, database search, speech response, credit verification and opportunity analysis.

The technology required to support the rep consists primarily of computers, data terminals and applications software.

Computer Systems. Studies have shown that businesses are looking for a number of important characteristics in processors used for telemarketing:

* *Multi-user, multi-task operating systems that allow users to share computer resources and to perform more than one job at a time, or switch from one application to another in real time.*

* *Fast response time so reps can quickly and efficiently serve customers. This means frequently that telemarketing centers should have a processor dedicated to the telemarketing operation and not share a processor or use the corporate mainframe.*

* *Ability of a business to customize and add applications as needed.*

* *Ability to expand a system according to changing needs.*

* *Minimum down time to ensure customers continuous access to the system.*

* *Mainframe connectivity for transfer of business and customer information.*

* *Multi-function communication capability to allow the center to move and interact with information stored both within the company and outside locations.*

Software. A full range of application software is available today to support telemarketing transactions. The software is tuned to support specific telemarketing transactions, such as billing, inventory control, etc., and can run on various operating systems, including MS-DOS and UNIX. Companies can choose to use or develop their own software or to purchase programs from a wide variety of outside vendors.

Telemarketing Representative Workstations. Typically, representative workstations are defined as the telephone and data terminal needed to transact business. This can include simply the devices

365

themselves or a rep's entire work space or environment.

The newer, lightweight telephone headsets provide an ideal solution to improving telemarketing rep productivity. They free up the reps' hands to provide greater comfort and improve communication clarity.

Special features include *receiver amplifiers* and *noise cancelling* via noise-cancelling microphones and voice switching (the microphone transmits only when the volume reaches a pre-determined level and, thus, background noise is cancelled out). This equipment is ideal for large, busy centers.

A full range of workstations are on the market today, from basic asynchronous terminals, through synchronous displays that encompass multiple windows, touch screens, and integrated voice and data. Specially designed rep voice terminals provide special call handling features and displays that enhance the representative's performance.

With today's workstations, telemarketing representatives can have simultaneous on-line and batch access to as many as three different synchronous and one asynchronous host computer to allow them to work with appropriate company databases. Ancillary equipment, such as printers, modems, and controllers provide the necessary administrative aids and network links.

These terminals can be anything from an independent PC, which a representative involved in brokerage or real estate transactions might use, to a video-graphics terminal connected to a large mainframe.

Even in an almost totally manual telemarketing environment, the move today is toward more computerized and automated workstations. This saves time and increases the productivity and effectiveness of representatives during calls. At the same time, technology is moving toward having voice and data in the same device for even greater efficiency of operation.

3. FULFILLMENT PROCESSING

The third telemarketing function can be looked at two ways: one, as the actual material response or information sent to a customer after a transaction; and two, as all of the parts of the business system needed to complete a customer transaction, including shipping, billing, accounts receivable, and inventory updates.

The following types of technology can be applied to support the fulfillment function:

Local Area Networks (LAN's). These can be thought of as large "pipes" used to move information among the various components in one location, such as a building or a campus.

The networks link computers, terminals and printers to allow reps to exchange information, transfer files, access databases and share system resources. The distribution medium can be standard low-cost telephone wiring or coaxial cable. These networks also facilitate the transfer of information from the telemarketing center to other departments for transaction completion and fulfillment.

Facsimile/Electronic Mail. Transfer of information from one place to another can be accommodated quickly via facsimile or electronic mail.

Facsimile is the electronic transmission of an original paper document from one point to another, using regular telephone lines. Using this technology, a telemarketing rep could send information, such as specs of product diagrams, to a customer during or immediately following a transaction.

366

The basic components are a fax machine--available from a variety of vendors--and a telephone. Today, some companies offer fax machines with telephone touch-tone pads built in.

In contrast, electronic mail is the electronic transmission of information. In this case, the user creates the message in electronic form using a keyboard. Both senders and receivers must subscribe to the same electronic mail system, although many systems can "gateway" to users on competitive systems.

Both services can be very time and cost effective.

4. HUMAN RESOURCE MANAGEMENT

The fourth telemarketing function provides effective and efficient ways to use personnel to achieve the business goals of a telemarketing center. Various software systems aid in this effort as well as maintain an efficient balance of staff, network services and terminal equipment.

Historically, this function was part of the Call Management System (CMS) agent reporting capability with ACD's. The movement today is toward more distinct use of system and operations information to manage, develop and train staff.

The type of reporting available includes individual representative performance reviews, as well as group reports that show the number of calls handled, length of each call, percentage of reps available to receive calls, etc. These reports are an aid to understanding the overall quality of representative/customer relationships.

In a nutshell, this information *allows a business to react to changing call volumes in a center, analyze trends and ascertain rep performance.*

Force Management Software Programs. These programs can generate reports that can provide key business benefits in the form of labor savings, improved call service and reduced administrative work.

These reports produce information that can be used to ascertain the number of representatives a center will require, and how those reps should be scheduled for lunch, breaks, and vacations. In addition, the reports provide historical data to help forecast future manpower needs for a center.

Service Monitors. Monitoring of service allows telemarketing managers to sample representatives' performance and maintain standards of quality, and is often part of a center's PBX. A supervisor can tell the switch which stations to access at various times.

Monitoring can be accomplished using a tone--so agents will know when they are being supervised--or without a tone. While service monitoring can be an effective aid in training and development, it must be carried out with concern for the employee and in accordance with local legal requirements.

5. BUSINESS IMPACT AND PLANNING

The fifth function takes all of the information gathered from the entire telemarketing operation and

367

enables managers to make decisions affecting the overall direction, success, and profitability of a business.

Processors and computer networks can capture information from the telemarketing center for use in planning business strategies. This information can aid in manufacturing scheduling, purchasing, advertising and sales promotion analysis, market research, market forecasting, complaint analysis, etc.

The underlying technologies include computers, call management systems and specific software, all of which are used to take source data and generate management reports. All of the results generated from the other functions feed into the business impact and planning function to allow for the dynamic allocation and re-allocation of resources.

This allows a corporation to make effective, strategic use of the broad base of information collected within any telemarketing operation.

ADJUNCT TELEMARKETING TECHNOLOGIES

Teleconferencing. Teleconferencing services are becoming an increasingly important resource to telemarketing center managers. These services can allow the staff of remotely located telemarketing centers to be part of important company conferences, such as sales organization meetings, new product introductions, product change announcements and marketing program presentations.

Teleconferencing can also facilitate the training of representatives by allowing instructors to reach more people in more locations in less time. Students and their instructor in a central classroom can be connected to students in one or more remote sites, sharing the same written and visual materials.

And teleconferencing can enable groups of employees to create or revise telemarketing support materials without having to travel to meetings.

There are three basic forms of teleconferencing:

* *Audio, which is a basic conference call of two or more people that may be enhanced by visual support tools, such as interactive writing devices, viewgraphs, slides, freeze-frame video and facsimile.* While a basic confer- ence call can be conducted from any office, audiographic calls usually take place in a facility set up expressly for this purpose.

* *PC Networking involves the exchange of graphics between personal comput- ers to allow users to produce and interactively edit data, text, and graphics.*

* *Business video can be interactive or broadcast. It offers real-time exchange of visual signals, voice, data, and graphics.* This type of video offers one- way broadcasts to people in multiple locations.

Crisis and Disaster Management Systems. In recent years, it has become imperative for telemarketing managers to institute plans to cover possible business crises and disaster situations that could face a telemarketing center. In a business crisis situation, a company would need to get information out to the public quickly; in a disaster situation, a fire or storm may shut down a telemarketing center, and back- up facilities would be needed immediately.

TELECOMMUNICATIONS (GENERAL)

Today, applications exist to handle the needs of centers facing service interruptions, calling overloads or business crisis situations, such as the Tylenol tampering of a few years ago.

For example, in telemarketing center recovery, a storm might disable a center's operations or a special promotion may have caused a temporary calling overload. Using 800 services, telemarketing managers can create back-up systems to ensure that customers can get through. Calls can be re-routed to other centers, if one telemarketing group is out of service; or calls can be redirected to an interim facility to lessen calling volumes.

In computer disaster recovery, the overriding objective is to guard against the loss of critical data. If a company cannot provide its own backup processing location, other companies are available to offer this kind of service on an emergency basis.

In business crisis intervention where a company needs to let people know important information quickly or may need to recall a product because of a problem, 800 and 900 services can be quickly set up to handle the special calls. Teleconferencing capabilities can also be used to reach people--especially employees--with up-to-the-minute information.

As telemarketing continues to play a vital role in overall business strategy, crisis management programs are becoming an integral part of the business impact and planning function.

TELEMARKETING AT WORK (A CASE EXAMPLE)

It's clear to see that there are a wide variety of technological tools to help put a telemarketing center together in an effective and efficient manner.

Here's a look at how these technologies can work together to optimize one telemarketing application--debt collection.

A large national company found that its collection representatives spent almost half their time unproductively--by reaching busy signals, no answers, or network intercepts when attempting to reach customers.

To solve the problem, the company elected to install an advanced outbound call management system in one of its regional offices. The results were outstanding--*representatives in the center increased their productivity by 60 percent or more.*

The outbound call management system uses the latest technology to support each collection agent. It works like this:

* *System recognizes central office answer supervision and human voice responses, then passes only "live" calls to the telemarketing reps.*

* *A speech response system that provides automatic dialing, call classification, switching and human voice response to touch-tone or voice input.*

* *Computer processors driven by custom-designed software. These perform administrative functions for the entire system, such as start up and shutdown, control of all system resources, dynamic pacing of calls based on rep*

availability, and report generating to help effectively manage the system. The processors also distribute data to representatives.

* *Multi-function workstations with multi-tasking windows to allow agents to access multiple databases simultaneously.*

* *Outbound WATS provides economical long-distance service for the entire system.*

All of these technologies work in concert to ensure the efficiency of each agent and the telemarketing center as a whole.

PUTTING IT ALL TOGETHER--AN INTEGRATED SYSTEM

Just as the careful integration of telemarketing into an overall marketing strategy is becoming crucial to the success of most businesses today, so the careful integration of all parts of a telemarketing system are crucial to the success of the telemarketing center itself.

All of the resource technologies of a center--from network services, switches, processors, software, and rep workstations--must work together smoothly so that critical information can be moved into a center, among its various components and from the center to other parts of the business in a timely, accurate, easily understood, and useful manner.

Information is an asset. It must be managed as one.

It is imperative that business managers just beginning to set up a telemarketing center, as well as those who want to add applications or increase a center's automation, first develop a blueprint of their goals and then work with telemarketing experts to decide on the information systems that will help them reach those goals.

Once this is done, a telemarketing operation will take off quickly to increase profitability and help a business better serve its customers.

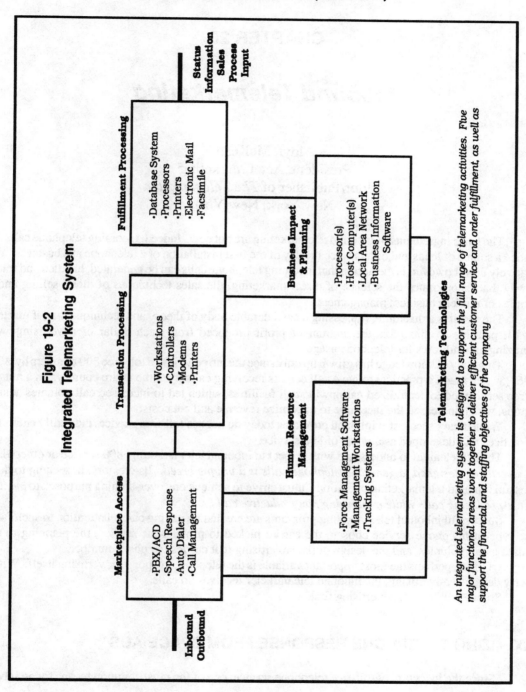

Figure 19-2
Integrated Telemarketing System

An integrated telemarketing system is designed to support the full range of telemarketing activities. Five major functional areas work together to deliver efficient customer service and order fulfillment, as well as support the financial and staffing objectives of the company

CHAPTER 20

Inbound Telemarketing

Aldyn McKean
President, Actel Marketing
Editor/Publisher of *The Telemarketer*
New York, New York

The basic ingredients of inbound telemarketing are not new. Indeed, incoming telephone calls have provided a source of leads and orders since the day of the first installation of a telephone at a business. What *is* relatively new, however, is the notion that incoming telephone calls can be generated, handled and tracked in a way that incorporates the science of direct marketing, the sales techniques of direct selling and the principles of modern business management.

The result is a discipline possessing a considerable body of theory and technique that, if mastered, makes it possible to maximize the amount of profit produced from each dollar of advertising, while minimizing expenditures for telephone usage.

This body of knowledge has grown up only since the introduction of toll-free 800 numbers by AT&T in 1967, which made it practical to have call centers receiving calls from the entire country. In a nutshell, toll-free service led to centralized nationwide call facilities, which led to increased call volumes at single locations, which increased the incentive to maximize revenue and cut costs.

While many successful inbound programs today do not use toll-free service, they still benefit from the practices that developed as a result of 800 service.

The key element to understand with respect to inbound telemarketing, 800 service or otherwise, is that *advertising designed to generate telephone calls is a unique breed.* Its creators, in seeking to design successful inbound telemarketing operations, must strive to achieve one over-arching purpose: to *maximize revenue-producing calls while minimizing nonproductive calls.*

Successful inbound telemarketing programs are created by paying careful attention to such factors as the type of telephone service chosen, the carrier picked to provide the service, the planning to meet fluctuating call volumes, and the design of the advertising that carries the phone number.

Of these, perhaps the most important variable is the telephone-response advertising itself. Without properly designed advertising, the inbound telemarketer receives no calls.

So, we will look at advertising first.

MAXIMIZING TELEPHONE RESPONSE FROM SPACE ADS

Since the inception of toll-free telephone service, one of the most common means for an inbound telephone marketer to reach new customers has been space ads (or ads in newspapers and magazines) that carry telephone numbers. In the beginning, telephone ordering was looked on by most marketers simply as an adjunct to mail ordering. The space ads (or print ads) from this period--and indeed many even today-- reflect this bias.

Designing Successful Telephone Response Space Ads.

Successful telephone response space ads have a few things in common with all successful ads. First of all, the headline and artwork must attract the reader's attention. The best ad copy for the world's greatest product will never be read if the headline and art in the ad do not attract attention. If the product being advertised is not well known, then solid product information should be provided. The chief benefit(s) to the user of the product should be stressed-- either implied by the artwork or stated explicitly in the copy.

In addition to the above tenets, which all print ad designers should observe, there are other factors that must be taken into account by the creators of telephone response advertising.

To be successful, a telephone response print ad must convince readers to take prompt action, put down the periodical and pick up the phone. Remember, a prospective customer who does not call before throwing away the magazine containing the ad is a lost customer.

Quick action can be encouraged by offering a premium to the first x-number of callers. Or the ad can read "limited time offer, while supplies last," or some other phrase that will indicate that the reader might lose out if a call is not made soon. If you feel these approaches are too hard-sell, you can simply encourage the reader to "call now" or "call today."

It will also increase the response to your ad if you mention a specific *benefit* that the reader will realize by dialing the 800 number--the most obvious of which is promptness of delivery. For example, the Buckingham Corporation's ad for Wines-by-Wire tells prospective customers that their "gift of Mouton-Cadet can be delivered overnight."

Companies that offer toll-free customer service can increase their response by emphasizing this fact in their order-generation or lead-generation ads. Whirlpool, General Electric, Geico Insurance, and General Motors have been effective in doing this.

Applications of 800 Number Space Ads.

As marketers gradually realized that 800 numbers in print ads could increase response by 20% or more, and could produce up-scale credit card buyers, the ads became more sophisticated, as well as more numerous.

A study by Advertising Information Services of recent issues of 21 major daily newspapers revealed that over 5% of the national ads they carried displayed 800 numbers.[1] Approximately 15% of the ads in *Time* and *Newsweek* carry 800 numbers, while the figure is over 20% for *Fortune* and *Business Week*. Not only are 800 number print ads becoming more numerous and sophisticated, but the applications for the 800 numbers being advertised are becoming more varied.

Orders. The original and still most common use of print ads bearing 800 numbers is in generating orders. Retailers, catalog houses, specialty item sales companies, publishers of subscription periodicals and others are advertising their wares in periodicals and enabling buyers to purchase by phone.

A recent variation on this idea is the advertising of the ability to deliver gifts ordered by phone. This application of the space ad with a phone number is particularly prevalent during the holiday season and is utilized by subscription publications, liquor distributors, florists, and others.

Wine and liquor distributors who offer the gift-by-telephone capability include General Wine & Spirits Company, which encourages readers of up-scale publications to call "Whiskey-Gram" and have a bottle of Chivas sent to a friend; Foreign Vintages, Inc., which offers its Amaretto liqueur; the Joseph Farneau Company, from whom a gift selection of Bolla wines is available; and the Buckingham Corporation, which advertises, "a gift of Mouton-Cadet can be delivered overnight."

Leads. A fast growing use of the print ad/800 number combination--particularly in business-to-business sales--is the generation of names, addresses and phone numbers of prospective customers. Xerox and IBM are using print ads to generate telephone inquiries for office equipment and computers. A majority of the financial ads in the business sections of major daily newspapers now carry toll-free numbers. Over 75% of the financial ads in the Sunday *New York Times* Business Section include such numbers.[2]

Merrill Lynch, for example, uses the financial pages of major dailies to help generate leads, which are then screened and qualified. The company advertises that booklets containing economic forecasts or information on particular securities can be obtained by calling an 800 number. Telephone reps at Merrill Lynch's telephone center are trained to capture the caller's name, address, and telephone number and to ask questions that will determine if the caller is planning to purchase securities or would like to talk to a Merrill Lynch account executive.

Callers are sent information about Merrill Lynch, and an account executive from a nearby office is notified of their interest. Those callers who are planning to buy securities are classified as "hot leads" and are usually contacted within a day by an account executive.

Dealer Locator. Magazine and newspaper readers are frequently encouraged to call an 800 number to find out the location of the nearest dealer who carries a particular product. Among the companies that advertise 800 numbers in print in order to provide dealer locations are Panasonic, Sony, Pitney Bowes, Fedders, Smith Corona, GE, Fiat, Jaguar, Armstrong Cork, and Piper Aircraft.

Pre-Buy Information. Other companies offer to answer the questions of prospective buyers over the phone or to send callers pamphlets containing information on certain products. Approximately 5% of the calls received at Whirlpool's Cool-Line are from people wanting more information on a product prior to purchase.[3] Whirlpool's ability to provide that information by phone results in sales that otherwise might not occur. Xerox, in a four-page ad in *Fortune*, offered to send prospective customers copies that had been produced by Xerox's XL-10 Imaging Process.

Catalog Requests. Numerous catalog houses advertise their 800 numbers in periodicals to enable readers to call and request a copy of the catalog. Among the companies that gather a significant portion of their new customers in this way are Spiegel and Sears Roebuck.

Emphasizing the Phone Number.

When 800 numbers first began to appear in space ads, they were generally squeezed into the ad as an afterthought to a mail-back coupon. Often the phone number was printed in typeface smaller than that of the copy in the body of the ad. The typical ad did not mention any particular benefit of using the toll-free number. The standard procedure was simply to tell the prospective customer to "order your widget today by filling in the coupon below, or call 800-____-____."

A fact that far too many advertisers overlook is that the 800 number itself may be the most important element of an ad. If if is printed in small type at the bottom, it is not going to be used by as many people as it would if it were emphasized more. There are several ways to emphasize the 800 number that may result in increased response to an ad.

Position. Instead of placing the 800 number at the bottom of an ad, why not place it in the body copy-- or even in the headline? One of the best reasons that the previously mentioned ad for Xerox in *Fortune* was effective, is that the 800 number was encountered by the reader in the middle of the ad.

Graphics. There are several ways to use graphics to add emphasis to your 800 number. Whirlpool, for example, employs pictures of satisfied users of the Cool-Line number. Other alternatives are to show a finger dialing a phone and include the 800 number in the picture some way. Even extremely simple graphics can be effective. Macy's uses a small graphic representation of a telephone next to the telephone ordering information in some of their ads. If there is not space for anything else, simply drawing a box around the 800 number will add emphasis.

Typeface. Advertisers who have gone to the trouble and expense of installing 800 service to better serve their customers ought to make it easy for potential customers to find and read the telephone number. However, all too many print ads carry 800 numbers that are printed in such small type that, at best, they are discovered only after the reader has donned a pair of bifocals and, at worst, go completely unnoticed. Always print an 800 number in large enough type so that it cannot be overlooked by a potential customer.

Combinations of the Above. Each of the above means of emphasizing the 800 number in print ads has been used by advertisers to increase response. However, more could be done in the way of combining them. One could, for example, position the 800 number in body copy *and* print it in a large typeface *and* use a graphic depiction of a telephone or telephone-using customer.

Avoiding Over-Emphasis. While advertisers tend for the most part to err on the side of under-emphasizing the 800 number, it is also possible to commit the opposite error. If you splash your 800 number across the page in two-inch high letters and devote little space to explaining the features and benefits of your product or service, the result will be that you will receive a lot of nuisance calls, lots of calls from people with questions, an enormous number of calls from unqualified prospects, and not too many orders. It is best to do some testing in local publications or regional issues of national publications in order to determine the proper emphasis on the 800 number.

It is always a good idea to permit both mail and telephone response to a print ad because there are people who will only use one response medium or the other. When both a coupon and telephone number are used, the percentage of orders coming via the two response media will provide a gauge of how much emphasis should be put on the phone number versus the coupon. If one medium accounts for 75% or more of the response, you should try putting more emphasis on the other.

DIRECT MAIL PLUS PHONE NUMBERS

Direct mail pieces bearing phone numbers have been used to market products ranging from magazine subscriptions to luxury automobiles. Telephone response to direct mail can bring in orders and leads for businesses as well as memberships and pledges for nonprofit groups. The direct mail/telephone response combination is ideally suited to conducting tests of new products or new marketing ideas because of the speed with which results can be read.

Early Mailers Made Poor Use of Phones. As was the case with early space ads, when phone numbers were first used in direct mail they were generally regarded as being of secondary importance to the return-mail order cards. As a result, early telephone response direct mail pieces did not take full advantage of the potential offered by telephone response. Often the telephone number was squeezed into the return-mail card as an after-thought.

Planners frequently did not know how to decide whether to offer telephone response to direct mail. What's more, they frequently did not know how to design a direct mail piece in order to make optimum use of telephone response. Many of their early mistakes are repeated today by marketers who are unfamiliar with the particular requirements of direct mail intended to generate telephone response.

When to Use--or Not Use--Telephone Response. The results achieved by inserting 800-numbers in direct mail pieces will vary depending on several conditions. Some direct mail marketers routinely experience increases in total response of 20% or more when adding telephone numbers--particularly toll-free numbers--to their mail pieces. However, others have been disappointed by the results they achieved.

One problem with the unsuccessful campaigns can be increased bad debt. When open credit is extended to consumers in a trial offer, whereby the product is received before it is paid for, 800 numbers can increase bad debt--particularly if the free trial part of the offer is emphasized.

In two tests conducted by Rapp & Collins, Inc., in which open credit was extended to customers who ordered the products of Wilshire Marketing, the bad debt rate doubled when 800 numbers were added to a direct mail promotion that previously contained no phone numbers.[4] These results are by no means surprising.

The reason that toll-free numbers increase response is that they are *easier to use* than return-mail coupons. This means they will produce response from people with a weaker interest in the product being sold. Obviously such people are less likely to pay. The moral is that whenever a customer receives a product before paying for it, the free-trial offer must be deemphasized when telephone response is accepted--unless an increase in bad debt can be tolerated. On the other hand, there are a variety of circumstances under which 800 numbers can improve the results achieved with direct mail:

Tested Lists. If you are mailing to a list that has previously tested well for responsiveness and back-end payment, you can offer telephone response with less risk.

Continuity Programs, Subscriptions, Memberships. If products are to be received in a series of shipments, risk is reduced because shipment can be stopped if payment is not received.

Credit Card Payment. If, instead of extending free trials, you are requesting payment by credit card prior to shipment, then the telephone offers an excellent source of paid orders. The only potential problem here is fraud, which ordinarily accounts for smaller losses than nonpayment.

Lead Generation. When you are attempting to generate and qualify leads with direct mail, there is no better response mechanism than the telephone. Telephone reps can be trained to qualify leads and provide your field sales force with the best leads in the shortest time.

MAXIMIZING RESPONSE TO DIRECT MAIL

As with print ads, it is important in direct mail pieces to construct an offer that is designed for telephone response; to mention personal service, convenience, and speed of delivery; and to use artwork and the position of the phone number to emphasize telephone ordering.

For each direct mail campaign there is an optimum amount of emphasis that should be placed on telephone ordering to maximize telephone response without significantly cutting mail response. If mail orders are desired in addition to telephone orders and if, as is often the case, they cost less to handle, telephone ordering should not be overly stressed in the mail piece. However, failure to push the telephone option significantly can result in losing orders that might otherwise have been received. The only way to determine the optimum emphasis on the telphone ordering option in your mail campaign is to test.

In some cases. the telephone orders represent up to 90% additional business, business that has not been "cannibalized" from mail response. This was the case, for example, for *TV Guide*, according to its subscription manager Ken Armstrong, when that magazine first added 800 numbers to its direct mail promotions.

"Our volume of mail orders remained constant," Armstrong noted, *"while we added 25% to 30% more orders on the telephone."* [5]

In situations such as this, the phone number should be strongly stressed.

INCREASING CATALOG SALES WITH 800 NUMBERS

A few years ago it was possible to order by phone from only a small percentage of direct order merchandise catalog companies. Today a majority of such companies use 800 numbers. As more and more catalog houses have tested toll-free ordering, it has become clear that catalogs will pull more and greater sales if they carry an 800 number. What's more, an inbound telephone operation can in most cases be cost-effective for catalogs that generate orders averaging as little as $15.00 each.

ADVANTAGES OF TELEPHONE ORDERING

Printing a phone number in your catalog will provide benefits to your operation and to your customers. The advantages to customers are quicker service, more accurate service, more personal service, greater convenience and (in the case of operations with on-line computers) the ability to know if the desired item or color is out of stock. All these factors contribute to one of the chief advantages of telephone ordering for the catalog company: customer loyalty.

Increased Customer Loyalty. Because of the previously mentioned service benefits, a telephone customer is more likely to be a loyal customer. When asked about customer loyalty, Mark Dahlquist, president of Maid of Scandinavia, had this to say:

"We get five to 10 letters a day thanking us for prompt service, which we could not provide without 800 number ordering. Our customers develop a rapport with our operators. One even sends our operators a batch of cookies every Christmas. Another came to town and took an operator out to dinner." [6]

Now that's customer loyalty! Did you ever achieve that with mail order?

Increased Number of Orders. A 1982 survey showed that 800 numbers in catalogs nearly always increase the number of orders received. The survey was conducted by Esther Lazaros for an MBA thesis for the New York University Graduate School of Business Administration.[7] Results were computed from questionnaires returned by 182 consumer catalog companies that use 800 numbers. *Nearly 97% of the respondents who reported adding 800 numbers to a catalog that did not previously have them noted that the number of orders received increased in the first six months of using 800 numbers.* Of those who reported such an increase, 90% felt that the 800 number was at least partially responsible and 68% felt it was the sole cause.

The increase in orders experienced by the respondents was correlated to a variety of other factors. The most significant variable here was found to be the 800 number's location in the catalog. *A huge 83.3% of the respondents who printed the number on every page experienced a significant increase in the number of orders as compared to only 53.8% for those who showed the 800 number on the order blank only.*

Catalogs with higher-priced products were more likely to show significant increases in orders after adding 800 numbers. The survey revealed that 69.4% of the catalogs whose products averaged between $51 and $100 showed significant increases, while only 37.8% of those with products averaging under $25 showed such increases. Catalogs appealing to men were more likely to show significant increases in the number of orders than catalogs appealing to women. Nearly two-thirds (64.8%) of the male-oriented catalogs showed significant increases while only 41.0% of the female-oriented ones did.

Increased Size of Orders. Telephone buyers, because they are generally credit card buyers, tend to order more merchandise and higher-ticket items. The Lazaros survey showed that nearly 74% of the catalogers who added 800 numbers reported an increase in the average order size within the first six months.

Those who showed an increase in average order size were asked to what they attributed it. Some 45% did not know or did not respond to this question. Of those who did respond, 61% attributed the increase in order size solely to the 800 number while an additional 22% attributed it to the 800 number in combination with some other marketing activity.

In addition, a majority (53%) of respondents reported that the average size of telephone orders exceeded that of mail orders. About a third (35%) reported no difference in average order size between mail and phone, while 11% indicated that mail orders were of greater average value. Those surveyed were asked by what percentage telephone orders were greater or less than mail orders. The mean response to this question indicated that *a phone order could be expected to be 23.7% greater in value than a mail order.*

Expansion into New Markets. The telephone will enable you to obtain orders from groups who are traditionally not catalog buyers. A wife employed outside the home, for example, is far more likely to buy by phone than is a full-time homemaker.

Increased Holiday Orders. The telephone enables your customers to order from your catalog in the last days of the Christmas rush, which they could not do otherwise. Pat Houlahan of Shepler's Western Wear remembers a near-Christmas caller who said, *"Hi, this is Johnny Cash. I'd like a coat sent to the Rev. Billy Graham, but I don't have charge cards."* The order was shipped, a check arrived a few days later and Mr. Cash has been a good customer of Shepler's ever since.[8]

378

Up-Sells. A customer on the telephone can be sold an additional item or a more expensive item.

Competitive Advantage. A catalog with an 800 number can pull customers away from one that does not because of the convenience and faster service.

Quicker Reaction Time. The telephone enables a catalog marketer to achieve a much quicker reading in tests of merchandise, layouts, prices, premiums, etc.

Earlier Action on Overages and Shortages. The quicker reaction time means earlier action on overages and shortages. Furthermore, any overages can be moved out through up-selling.

A BATTLE PLAN FOR GOING 800

Let us assume that you are now convinced of the advantages of placing an 800 number in your catalog. How do you proceed?

Plan and Test. You will want to allow at least three months from the time of your decision to go with an 800 number until you mail out your first test catalog in order to plan your campaign. Devise an initial test that will give you enough response to read the results, but not so big as to be unmanageable.

Take Advantage of Other's Expertise. Setting up a database, installing telephone equipment and hiring and training staff are not simple operations. If you do not have experience with telemarketing or do not have an in-house database, you should consider placing your program--at least at the beginning--with an outside telephone response center. But be careful! Only about 10 of the major tele-response centers are set up to handle catalogs effectively. If you decide to bring the operation in-house, hire a reputable consultant to help you.

Test Out of House. Even if you wish to bring the operation in-house, you may wish to test first with an outside center. The experience of Alden's Catalog provides an instructive timetable for such a procedure.

Alden's first tested toll-free numbers in one state only in December 1977. (You should avoid the holiday season for your test.) The calls were handled by one of the major teleresponse centers. In April 1979-- after 15 months of testing, analysis, and working out the bugs--the program was expanded to all states except Alaska and Hawaii. Again, the calls were taken by an out-of-house center. In February, 1980, after another 11 months of a roll-out campaign and careful planning and analysis, the operation was brought in-house at Alden's. (If Alden's planning and analysis had been as extensive in other areas, the company might still be in business.)

Allow for Your Catalog's "Personality." Every catalog has a unique image or "personal-

379

ity.'' The telephone can either enhance or obscure it. If you place your telephone response business out-of-house, make sure the center you choose can design a program to suit you and does not try to mold you to their set-up. Also, make sure the telephone reps are trained in such a way that they are aware of the nature of your catalog. Of course, the same goes for an in-house operation.

Provide Accurate Information. Your operation will be only as good and as efficient as the information provided to your telephone reps. You will probably want a computerized database. Whatever your decision on computers, make sure that the information you give your telephone reps is accurate and up-to-date. You should assign a particular person to be responsible for this task. Also make sure all telephone reps have copies of all catalogs in use.

Anticipate Peaks and Valleys. You already know from your direct mail experience that you will be jammed with orders during certain seasons (such as pre-Christmas) and less busy during others. The telephone will magnify this situation. If you get 20% more orders by adding 800 numbers during your off-peak test, expect 30% more during peak season. Make sure that your center, whether in-house or not, has the lines and staff to handle your peaks. There is no easier way to lose an order than to have a customer experience constant busy signals.

Expect Non-Order Calls. When your customers see an 800 number, they will want to use it for complaints and customer service questions. You can cut down on this somewhat by printing a notice near the 800 number that tells customers that it is only for orders and that other problems should be directed to another number. Even if you do this, however, you will still get customer service calls. Make sure your telephone reps or your tele-response service are prepared for them.

Be Ready for Credit Card Problems. Telephone orders are credit card orders, so you'll face the problems of stolen cards and invalid or expired numbers. Be sure to have procedures in place to deal with these situations.

Print the 800 Number Repeatedly. Do not just print the toll-free number on your order blanks. Order blanks can get ripped out and lost, and customers who have gotten to the order blank are probably about to buy already. Print your 800 number prominently every three to four pages in your catalog. That way you will pick up sales from impulse buyers.

Offer a Benefit. When you print your 800 number, tell your customers how they can benefit from using it. Don't say, *''For faster order processing...''* That's not a benefit. You might say, *''So that you can enjoy your choice of fine widgets within two weeks, call toll-free.''*

WHAT'S AHEAD FOR CATALOGERS?

Where once a catalog house might have turned to toll-free ordering to provide a competitive edge over other catalogs, in the future 800 numbers may be vital for a catalog's survival.

As more and more catalogs adopt 800 numbers, more customers will expect to be able to shop by phone from any catalog. The future will also see an expansion of customer service applications for 800 numbers. Many catalog companies already handle service calls via toll-free lines. For example, Shillcraft (the hook-it-yourself rug catalog) has an extensive toll-free customer service center with telephone representatives to help customers choose colors for their rugs or design their own custom rugs.

THE EFFECTIVE USE OF TELEVISION TO GENERATE INBOUND CALLS

For the inbound telemarketer, television always exercises a powerful attraction. It is a medium that sets marketers to dreaming of massive call volumes, massive numbers of orders, and massive profits. Unfortunately such dreamers usually wind up with massive headaches.

To reap the profits and minimize the headaches in television direct response requires careful attention to all the following elements:

1) *The product (or service or cause).*

2) *The television commercial.*

3) *Media-buying.*

4) *Testing.*

5) *Call handling.*

6) *Source tracking.*

7) *Fulfillment.*

APPLICATION OF DIRECT RESPONSE TV

Applications of the direct response TV commercial have become increasingly diverse. Current users of the TV and telephone media mix are engaged in the following:

Order Generation. The oldest type of direct response commercial is still the most common. In the 1950's advertisers began soliciting orders for records and kitchen utensils on television. Today orders are being generated for magazine and newspaper subscriptions, exercise equipment, power tools, video cassettes and an array of other products.

Reservations Solicitation. Sheraton Hotels pioneered the use of the television commercial to encourage calls to an 800 reservations number. Today airlines, car rental firms, and other hotels do the same.

Lead Generation. Direct response TV is being used by both consumer and business-to-business marketers as a means of generating leads, which are then followed up by mail, outbound telephone, or sales visits. Insurance, investments, office equipment, and high-ticket consumer products have been successfully marketed in this fashion.

Dealer Locator. A number of advertisers urge viewers to call for the name and location of their nearest dealer who carries the advertised product. Dealer locator calls can also serve as lead generation calls if the callers' names are captured for later follow-up.

Pledge Solicitation. Nonprofit organizations, such as Save the Children Foundation, have made extensive use of TV commercials to generate pledges.

Continuation of Advertising Message. Recent use of the phone call in response to a TV ad has been to continue the advertising message. Carrier Corporation, for example, urges viewers who are suffering from the heat to call an 800 number. Callers reach a tape recorded message that gives detailed information about the effectiveness and efficiency of the Carrier Heat Pump air conditioning system.

PRODUCT SUITABILITY

If you are contemplating the use of TV direct response as a means of generating orders in a one-step campaign, your first task should be to gauge the suitability of your product or service for direct response advertising. To be successful at TV order generation, you should be certain that your product meets the following criteria:

Uniqueness. The most important criterion for TV direct response is uniqueness; your product must be unique or must be offered at a price that is unique. If you are selling ordinary socks or paper clips that are no different from those available at the corner store, stay away from direct response TV. In a few instances products that are widely available in stores have been successfully marketed through direct response TV when they could be offered at a price substantially below the regular store price.

Price. Until the mid-1980s, most direct response professionals argued that no product with a price of over $20 could be successfully sold on TV. Many higher-priced products had been tried and failed.

However, as cable stations have begun to deliver upscale audiences, orders have been generated for products with much higher prices. The Jack Nicklaus *Golf My Way* video cassette was successfully marketed by requesting a single credit card payment of over $70. The Dahon Folding Bicycle sold well at $219.99-- collected in three credit-card payments of $73.33 each.

These high-ticket success stories still represent the exception and not the rule, however. All of the record collections, periodical subscriptions and household gadgets that make up the bulk of the products marketed in one-step order generation campaigns sell for $29.95 or less--the majority sell for $19.95 or less.

Mark-Up. Marketing costs per unit sold will usually be significantly higher in TV direct response than with other direct marketing media. Thus the mark-up must be greater to pay for these costs and still show a profit. If a product is to be sold for $19.95, the unit cost of the product should be no more than about $6. Mark-ups of 300% and even 400% are common in TV direct response.

Mass Appeal. You don't reach specialized markets economically by television. Your product should appeal to a broad cross section of the public if you expect to use TV successfully. There have been a few exceptions to this rule lately. Obviously, if you can sell a product for $70 its market does not need to be as broad as a product that sells for $20. Products targeted narrowly to sports enthusiasts, Spanish speakers, blacks, or doctrinal Christians have proven successful on, respectively, ESPN, SIN, BET, and CBN. Nevertheless, broad mass appeal is still essential for success on most other networks or stations.

STEP ONE: CHOOSING AN AGENCY

Occasionally advertisers will attempt to produce their own direct response commercials without the help of a direct response advertising agency. They usually come to regret this decision. An experienced direct response agency will not only be able to create an effective commercial, but will be able to purchase air time at a considerable saving--perhaps as much as 50%. Since the cost of air time will be the major expense in a TV response campaign, such a saving can be decisive in determining the campaign's success.

There is a great deal of difference between an ad that is designed to produce sales in retail outlets and one that is meant to generate direct orders. A direct response ad is unique in that it must motivate the viewer to take immediate action. As a result, direct response ads present a different set of creative problems from other types of advertising.

In addition, media buying practices for direct response commercials are totally different from those for traditional image ads. For all these reasons, you should be certain that you select an agency that has specific experience in direct response television.

Bear in mind that it is common for an agency with little or no direct response experience to claim to have such experience. You should ask to see tapes of successful *direct response* commercials that the agency has produced. Then contact their clients to make certain that the campaigns were indeed successful.

THE DIRECT RESPONSE COMMERCIAL: HOW EXPENSIVE?

In recent years, direct response television commercials have become increasingly sophisticated. It was once possible to shoot a direct response commercial on video tape in one or two takes and wind up with an ad that could deliver a sufficient number of orders to make the campaign profitable. Such a commercial could once be shot for as little as $3,000.

Today's TV viewers, however, have become accustomed to more creative and elaborate commercials. In order to achieve credibility with these viewers, it is necessary to spend considerably more money. Even so, the average direct response commercial still costs less than the average image commercial.

A direct response commercial can cost anywhere from $10,000 to $100,000 to produce. The amount you pay will depend on your own specific needs. The more up-scale your target audience and the more competition your product faces in the marketplace, the more you will require high-quality production and special effects. The result will be higher costs.

If your product is a household gadget or record targeted to the mid-scale audience, you should be able to produce a serviceable commercial for about $12,000 to $20,000. A commercial with an appealing, quality look can be produced for $30,000 to $50,000.

Time and *Newsweek,* who continually battle each other for subscribers, have opted for elaborate commercials with special visual effects and musical scores. The production costs involved in such efforts can range from $60,000 to $100,000. Bear in mind that production costs have tended to rise at the rate of about 10% per year.

If you decide to hold the line on costs, then you must make this clear to your producer *before* production begins. You should ask for and receive an itemized budget for the production of your commercial. Go over this budget item by item. Once you have approved the initial budget, it quickly becomes more difficult to cut costs.

You may want to request a Studio Cost Summary Form from the Association of Independent Commercial Producers (100 East 42nd Street, New York, NY, 10017, 212/867-5720). This form itemizes all the elements that make up the total cost of producing a commercial.

FILM VERSUS TAPE

A commercial can be shot either on film or video tape. It used to be the case that tape was cheaper and film resulted in better quality. In recent years, however, the differences between tape and film--in terms of both price and quality--have been virtually eliminated.

Today the choice between film and tape is based primarily on more subjective criteria: what sort of "look" is desired and what effects will be used. A commercial that is shot on film can be given a softer, more mellow look and will have a greater sense of depth and perspective. Shooting directly on state-of-the-art C-format, 1-inch video tape will result in more vibrant colors as well as greater definition and clarity. In addition, certain special effects are more easily accomplished with film, while others lend themselves more readily to tape. Creative requirements will determine the choice.

End tags, in which the phone number and ordering information are shown, are ordinarily shot on tape in order to yield the greatest possible sharpness and clarity. Regardless of how the commercial was shot, editing is usually done on tape since computer tape editing will permit greater speed and precision.

HOW LONG SHOULD THE COMMERCIAL BE?

Direct response commercials are usually longer than image commercials because they have

384

different requirements. A direct response ad must drive viewers to their phones immediately; must describe an attractive offer (including price, delivery terms, and possible free trials or premiums); and must give a phone number.

Most direct response commercials that are designed to produce orders or pledges in a one-step campaign are 120 seconds long. But with 120-second spots becoming increasingly difficult to buy, more and more advertisers are experimenting with shorter spots; several have made them work. *Newsweek* and Hanover House, for example, have successfully generated orders with 60-second spots.

A number of advertisers have found success by using a media schedule involving both 120-second and 60-second spots. The longer spot is used to provide a detailed sales pitch while the shorter spot serves as a reminder and reenforcement.

For lead generation programs in which it is not necessary to state prices and offers, 30-second spots can be effective. For example, a 30-second spot created by Chicago's Eicoff agency for Spectrum Cable TV has been successful in generating calls from potential cable subscribers.

ELEMENTS OF AN EFFECTIVE COMMERCIAL

Because a direct response commercial must stimulate an immediate action, its components are different from those of the traditional image advertisement used by mass marketers. To be successful, a direct response commercial should include all the following elements:

Attention Getter. The first task of a direct response commercial is to get the viewer's full attention. This may be accomplished through dramatic effects, as in the case of the *Time* commercial that shows a rapid succession of pictures of world events accompanied by introducing a celebrity who is known and recognized by the target audience.

Demonstration of Product or Need. The best products for TV direct response are those that can be demonstrated. It was an effective demonstration of the product that made the Ginsu Knife commercial the success that it was. When the product is a record, the demonstration usually involves showing the recording artist in performance.

If the product itself cannot be demonstrated, then dramatize a situation in which the product will be needed. Allstate Insurance, for example, combines the attention getter with the demonstration of the need for its homeowners insurance by showing a family watching helplessly as their home burns down. The Vertronix Corporation, in its ad for a home burglar alarm, shows a thief approaching the darkened window of a house.

If you depict a problem or need, you must then show how your product solves it. For example, Allstate showed a home being rebuilt, and Vertronix depicted the would-be thief scurrying away after activating the alarm.

Price. It goes without saying that viewers should be told how much the product costs. The price should both appear on the screen and be heard in the voice-over. Ideally, the price should remain on the screen for four seconds or more and should be repeated. Otherwise, you will pay for a good many phone calls from people who call merely to ask the price.

Product Reminder. Just prior to giving the ordering instructions, the commercial should tell viewers once again what they will get if they order. In the case of the Ginsu Knives, the entire collection is shown as a group and each type of knife is mentioned for at least the second time in the voice-over.

Ordering Instructions. The final element in the direct response commercial is ordering instructions. The 800 number should appear on the screen for at least 20 seconds in a two-minute spot and for 15 seconds in a 60-second spot. Each digit of the phone number should be read and repeated in the voice-over. In addition, viewers must be told that they can use major credit cards or order C.O.D. Credit card orders can be encouraged by showing pictures of the credit cards along with the 800 number.

THE CHOICE OF SPOKESPERSON

Many direct response advertisers find that the offer is most effectively delivered by an on-camera spokesperson. Others find the best results by using an off-camera voice-over. Still others use a combination of both. Time, Inc., has had success in encouraging phone calls by having a telephone representative wearing a headset stress the premium offer before and after the main commercial.

When it is vital to establish credibility--such as when selling high-ticket products or insurance policies--a celebrity is often used to good effect. It is often possible to avoid large up-front fees for celebrities by agreeing on a commission to be paid based on the sales generated by the commercial.

A spokesperson, particularly one who is a celebrity, should be chosen carefully. A good celebrity spokesperson meets all the following criteria:

Respected by Target Audience. The spokesperson should be someone who is recognized and admired by the specific target group you have chosen. Thus older, respected entertainers such as Arthur Godfrey, Art Linkletter and Lorne Green have all been effective spokesmen for insurance products targeted to senior citizens. Roger Staubach and George Kennedy, both service veterans, have been effective in generating calls for life insurance that is designed for veterans.

Credible for Specific Product. A spokesperson must be appropriate to the product. Each of the above-named insurance spokesmen has a carefully cultivated image as basically conservative, trustworthy and respectable. They thus lend credibility to the insurance offers. The insurance companies have wisely avoided using glamorous actresses as spokeswomen. However, these same actresses might make excellent spokeswomen for a product such as *People Magazine*.

Effective Presenter. The fact that a person is a celebrity does not necessarily mean that she or he can effectively demonstrate your product. Indeed, a celebrity will often attempt to displace your product as the center of attention. Choose someone who can speak clearly and persuasively and who can show enthusiasm for your product without overshadowing it.

386

Response Vehicles. Should you accept C.O.D. orders? C.O.D. rejections can run as high as 30%, yet many campaigns are more profitable because they permit C.O.D. ordering. The rejection rate is typically higher with higher-priced products. Thus it is usual for marketers of low-ticket products to accept C.O.D.'s, while C.O.D. ordering will often not be permitted for products costing over $30.

Even if you accept C.O.D. orders, you can encourage the use of credit cards. The TV commercial may advise viewers to *"avoid C.O.D. charges by using a major credit card."* The telephone representative who takes the call can ask for a credit card and remind callers that they can avoid C.O.D. charges by using their cards.

You should also include a mailing address in your ad, particularly if you target an older audience. You can often get 20% to 30% of your orders prepaid by mail.

MEDIA BUYING FOR DIRECT RESPONSE TV

Direct response advertisers do not usually find it economically feasible to buy commercial time at the same rates or even in the same way as typical mass marketers. When mass marketers buy commercial time, they select a specific position in a specific program airing at a specific time on a specific day; and they pay a set price. For direct response buyers the situation is quite different. Direct response media buys are usually done in one of two ways.

Spot Buying. Direct marketers often engage in a practice called "spot buying." This means that the TV station will air the commercial at no particular time. Spot buying is done either within certain "dayparts" or on a "run of station" (ROS) basis.

The weekly broadcast schedule is usually divided into six dayparts: daytime, early evening, prime time, late evening, Saturday and Sunday. A direct marketer might request that a commercial be aired a total of 10 times during the week in the late-evening time period. The broadcaster will sell time on this basis at a considerable discount.

An even greater discount may be obtained when time is bought on an ROS basis. This means that the TV station will air the commercial at any time, whenever it wants.

The advantage of spot buying is its low cost. There are also disadvantages. First of all, a direct response commercial can be preempted if another advertiser is willing to pay full price for the same time. Thus you may request 10 airings during the week, but you may actually get only six or seven. Secondly, the broadcaster may run your commercial during a program that does not attract your target audience.

Per Inquiry. Many TV stations and cable networks will air commercials on a per inquiry, or "PI," basis. This means that the advertiser pays the broadcaster (or cablecaster) an agreed-upon fee for each response received. The broadcaster may insist that the advertiser use one particular telemarketing service bureau, so that response will be accurately measured.

This approach offers real advantages to both the advertiser and the broadcaster. Since the broadcaster is being paid based on response, only those commercials that are really pulling will be run. If a commercial bombs, the advertiser does not have to pay for a whole commercial schedule. What's more, the broadcaster will tend to run commercials during those programs that attract the appropriate audience.

Unfortunately, the availability of PI spots is drying up. Image advertisers are devoting more of their media budgets to cable networks than ever before and are paying full price for the best positions. This has meant that fewer positions are left for PI ads. In 1981, one major cable network filled 90% of its commercial positions with PI ads. Today only about a third of the advertising on the major cable networks is direct response advertising and only 10% of that (3% - 4% of the total) is PI.

FIRST AND THIRD QUARTERS WORK BEST

In broadcast advertising the year is divided into quarters, with rates varying substantially from one to the next. Rates are lowest during first quarter (January, February, and March); they are also very low during third quarter (July, August and September).

First quarter is a particularly attractive time for direct marketers to purchase commercial time because, not only are rates low, but those people who are most likely to buy tend to be at home watching TV.

Third quarter is often a time of testing for direct marketers. Those commercials that work during third quarter will be "rolled out" during the following first quarter.

MEDIA BUYING IS A JOB FOR PROS

Direct response media buying, like direct response commercial production, is best done by people who have specific direct response experience. Good media buying for direct response commercials requires a keen understanding of the audience of each station during the various dayparts. The media buyer must know which daypart is right for his commercial.

For direct response media buyers, there are no cut-and-dried rates or schedules as there are for other advertisers. A good direct response media buyer spends considerable time on the telephone coaxing and haggling with broadcasters and cablecasters.

The larger direct response ad agencies have their own media departments. For smaller agencies and entrepreneurs, there are independent media buyers. Whether you use a large agency media department or an independent, make certain that your media buyer has experience in direct response media buying.

The major agencies and independents, because they buy so much time, are able to buy it more cheaply. In addition, they will carry the clout necessary to ensure that as few of your commercial airings as possible are preempted.

Finally, the experienced agencies and independents will offer better analysis and control. Their personnel will know as quickly as possible whether or not it will be profitable to air a commercial in a particular daypart on a particular station.

Testing. Like all good direct marketers, the direct response TV advertiser must test in order to determine the most effective offer and creative approach. Usually, a test is run by conducting what might be called an "AB flip-flop." This means that commercial A is run for one week on station 1 while commercial B is run on station 2. The following week commercial A runs on station 2, and commercial B runs on 1. The results are then compared to see which commercial is most effective.

As with all other aspects of direct response TV, comparing the results of this type of testing requires considerable experience. Remember that since time is bought on a spot basis, there is no guarantee that the same number of commercials will air or that they will air at precisely comparable times on the two stations.

Sourcing. Whether you are testing creative approaches or just checking the effectiveness of your media buys, *it is imperative that each and every telephone call be accurately attributed to the TV station and commercial that generated it.*

In the early days of TV direct response, advertisers attempted to do their sourcing by asking callers what station they were watching when they saw the ad. The problem with this method is that it is not accurate. Callers often do not know or do not remember what station they were watching. A cable station may be on channel 4 in one neighborhood and on channel 5 in another section of the same city.

When the media schedule consists of stations that do not broadcast to overlapping areas, a longitude-latitude look-up system can be used. This is usually based on the caller's ZIP code or telephone area code and exchange. However, with more and more direct response advertising being done on nationwide cable networks, this approach has become less useful.

The most accurate sourcing method involves using different telephone numbers on different stations. The telephone rep who takes the call asks the caller what number was dialed and then knows on what station the ad was seen.

With Dialed Number Identification Service (DNIS), this method becomes even simpler. DNIS makes it possible for the 800 number that was dialed by the caller to be known automatically. A pulse sent with the incoming 800 number telephone call from the local phone company central office lights an LED display or is recorded directly onto the call record.

CALL HANDLING

Unless you are generating millions of calls annually, you will find that the most economical means of handling calls generated by TV ads will be to use a service bureau. The most important thing for TV advertisers is to select a service bureau that has experience in handling TV response and has sufficient lines and staff to do an adequate job. An experienced ad agency or independent consultant will know which service bureaus can handle TV response.

If you are selecting a service bureau on your own, you may wish to begin by consulting *The Directory of Telephone Marketing Service Agencies,* available for $80 from Actel Marketing, in New York City (212/ 674-2540). You should be prepared to pay a personal visit to the service bureaus you select in order to be certain that they really have the line and staff configurations that they claim.

A successful TV direct response campaign must be carefully monitored at all times. Each element of the program must be designed with care by experienced pros. Enormous rewards await those who are skilled at tapping the potential of direct response TV.

MAKING TELEPHONE-RESPONSE ADS WORK ON RADIO

Radio has proven to be a difficult medium for generating telephone response. Many direct marketing professionals advise against using telephone response ads on radio at all, while most others warn that this should be done only under certain specific circumstances. Nevertheless, there are numerous cases of telephone-response radio commercials producing excellent results.

Disadvantages of Radio. Several qualities inherent in the medium pose problems for direct marketers. These qualities must be borne in mind when planning and executing radio campaigns.

* *Lack of Intrusiveness.* Radio is often a background medium for the listener who is actively engaged in conversation, housework, shopping, or other activities. It is much more easily "tuned out" than television. Thus, radio does not generally have the intrusiveness necessary to motivate the listener to make an immediate response. Radio tends to work best for informational or image advertising in which the effect of spots is cumulative. In other words, awareness builds in proportion to the frequency of message delivery. In direct response, the advertiser generally is looking for an immediate reaction.

* *No Visual Cues.* Sound without sight is a disadvantage to telephone marketers for two reasons. First, consumers are less likely to buy a product that they cannot see. Secondly, they are less likely to remember or record correctly a telephone number that they have only heard.

* *Listeners Not Able to Record Number.* Many radio listeners are in environments--such as cars, stores, and work places--in which they cannot conveniently write down a telephone number.

* *Shortness of Spots.* Few radio stations are willing to run spots longer than 60 seconds. Direct response television spots are often 120 seconds long. It is nearly impossible to convey in 60 seconds of sound what is conveyed in 120 seconds of picture and sound.

* *Difficulty in Sourcing.* Because there are many more radio stations than television stations, each radio station has a much smaller market share than an average television station. Thus, many radio stations must be used to obtain satisfactory levels of audience "reach." Add to this the fact that people often do not know what radio station they're listening to, and it can be seen that sourcing problems are enormous. If sourcing is to be done automatically, many 800 numbers will be required. If sourcing is to be done by asking where callers got the phone number, many of them will not know to what station they were listening.

* *Changeability of Formats.* Radio stations can and do change their formats
with little or no advance notice. An advertiser may buy time on an all-news
station for a product oriented to older consumers only to have the station
change its format to teen rock.

Advantages of radio. While the disadvantages of radio are significant, there are several
advantages that make radio a useful medium for direct marketers under certain circumstances.

* *Listener Loyalty.* Unlike TV viewers, radio listeners tend to be more loyal to
one particular station. The result is that as an ad is repeated on a particular
station, many listeners who did not respond after hearing it the first time will
have additional opportunities to listen to the terms of the offer, record the
800 number, and call.

* *Specialized Formats.* Because radio stations and even some radio networks
tend to specialize in certain formats--such as all news, talk shows, jazz, rock,
etc.--it is possible to pinpoint those stations to which your target audience
would most likely listen.

* *Lower Cost per Spot.* Because radio spots cost much less than television
commercials, it is possible to begin a campaign on radio with a relatively
modest investment.

* *Ability to Change Ads.* While a television commercial cannot be inexpensively changed, a radio spot can. This ease of change offers direct marketers
greater flexibility for testing various approaches.

SUCCESSFUL USE OF TELEPHONE-RESPONSE RADIO ADS

Given the disadvantages that radio presents, can the medium be used to generate telephone
response? Yes, under certain circumstances and when great care is taken in devising the radio campaign.

Several periodicals--including *Time, Newsweek, The Wall Street Journal, Book Digest, Smithsonian
Magazine* and *Cricket*--have successfully used 800 numbers on radio to attract subscribers. Merrill Lynch
and other brokerage firms have employed radio spots to generate calls from potential investors. In addition
a number of products that are related to the formats of particular stations, including jazz record series and
books about composers of classical music, have been marketed via telephone response radio spots.

What are the ingredients of a successful telephone response spot?

Product. The first question to ask before buying radio time is, *"Is my product or service suited
to direct response radio spots?"* You may answer "yes" to this question if your product or service offers
an immediately identifiable personal benefit *and* can be understood easily without being seen. Products
related to health or self-improvement often do well on radio because they offer immediate benefits.

391

Among the products that can be easily understood without being pictured are books, magazines and records. Products such as *Prevention*, the health magazine, or *The Wall Street Journal* and *Barron's*, financial publications, which both offer immediate benefits and are easily understood without pictures do *extremely* well on radio.

Target Audience. Products oriented to individuals over 30 and at least slightly up-scale will do better than other types of products on radio. In general, it is wise to stay away from the under-24-year-olds on radio. Ordinarily, it is the slightly up-scale person who responds to radio spots.

Attention Getter. Given that radio is a nonintrusive medium and offers no visual cues, it is essential to get the attention of your target audience in the first five seconds of the spot. Thus the right "headline" is vital.

The following was used by Ellentuck and Springer Advertising for *Prevention Magazine* with excellent results: *Can you recognize your body's danger signals?"* No one interested in health could ignore the message that followed. Another attention getting headline is this one by Wunderman Ricotta and Kline for Merrill Lynch: *"You can prosper during recession."* Both these headlines make the listener ask questions: *"What are my body's danger signals?"* and *"How can I prosper in a recession?"* Thus, they hold interest.

It may not be important that everyone listen to your spot, but your target audience should. This Ellentuck and Springer headline for *Cricket* is a good example: *"If you're the parent or loving relative of a 7 to 10 year old. . .."* This headline speaks directly to the target audience; others can "tune it out."

Time of Day. Direct response commercials should *not* be aired during drive time, roughly 7:00 to 9:00 a.m. and 4:30 to 6:30 p.m. The most effective time to air direct response radio spots has proven to be 8:00 p.m. to 11:00 p.m. However, different times of day may be right for different products. The magazine *Working Woman*, for example, is going to miss most of its target audience if it airs on a weekday between 9 and 5. A magazine such as *Ladies Home Journal*, on the other hand, might do well with a daytime spot.

Time Allowance for Offer and Phone Number. Radio spot copy writers often forget that an 800 number, though it looks like one word in a script, is actually nine words when read on the air and 18 words when repeated. Time must also be allowed for giving the terms of the offer. Copy writers and production people must allow 20 seconds at the end of a radio spot to explain the terms of the offer, read the telephone number, and repeat it.

Format. Careful attention must be paid to the format of a station on which a spot is to air. Generally, a station with more listener involvement will be best for direct response. Following is an approximate ranking of radio formats starting with those that generate the most listener involvement to those that generate the least:

1) *Listener talk shows.*

2) *News.*

392

3) *Public affairs and features.*

4) *Classical.*

5) *Jazz.*

6) *Rock, country-and-western.*

7) *Middle-of-the-road.*

8) *Easy listening.*

SPECIALIZED USES OF THE RADIO

Radio's unique characteristics can be used to perform at least a couple of specialized functions. Radio spots can be used to test direct response concepts prior to incurring the expense of television commercials. They can demonstrate which offer or which creative approach will capture the most people.

Thus, the risk involved in subsequent television advertising is reduced. It is analogous to a direct mail test prior to a roll-out. Radio spots have also been used in a supporting role to alert consumers to direct response print ads appearing in magazines or newspapers.

PROJECTING TELEPHONE RESPONSE TO ADS

One of the questions most frequently asked by marketers starting a telephone response ad campaign is: *"If I purchase a certain amount of air time or print space, how much response will I get?"* The neophyte telemarketer is often surprised to learn that there is no reliable answer to such a question. There are so many factors that affect the rate of response to an ad, and those factors vary so much from one case to the next, that it is impossible to predict accurately what the response to a given ad will be until it has been tested.

Range of Potential Response Is Enormous. It might be supposed that a rule of thumb could be divised for predicting the response to an ad based on the number of people who will see it. However, past experience shows that the number of people who see an ad is not a reliable guide to results.

Two recent newspaper ad campaigns for consumer goods illustrate the point. In both cases the advertisers had done extensive market research to determine where their potential markets were. Both advertisers purchased large ads in Sunday newspapers that would reach those markets. In one case ads placed in newspapers with a combined circulation of 3 million pulled only 56 responses. The other ad pulled 30,000 responses from newspapers with a 2 million combined circulation. That's a response rate of 1 in 54,000 in the first case as compared with a 1-1/2% response in the second.[9]

393

FACTORS AFFECTING RESPONSE RATE

The difficulty inherent in projecting response to an untried ad is apparent when one begins to examine all the factors that can bear upon it. However, if one keeps all these factors in mind, the wide variance in response rates begins to make some sense and trends emerge.

Type of Campaign. One of the most decisive factors in determining the response rate to an ad is the type of campaign being waged. A campaign that involves giving away free samples will, all other things being equal, produce more calls than one designed to generate leads. A lead generation campaign is likely to produce a higher response rate than a similar campaign that requests orders. A campaign designed to produce C.O.D. or credit card orders will generate more calls than would another campaign for the same product that permitted only credit card orders.

Type of Product. Certain kinds of products pull better than others. Offers for records and subscriptions to periodicals have been made to work well in just about every medium. On the other hand, a whole variety of highway safety products, from seat belts to emergency flashers, have been advertised with 800 numbers and have not sold.

Creative/Copy. The creative work that goes into an ad is one of the most powerful--and at the same time one of the most indefinable--determinants of the eventual response. Simply put, the creative effort can make or break a campaign.

Corporate Image. Some manufacturers are better known or perceived as being more reliable than others. Thus, they can generate greater response to their ads. Xerox, for example, can often pull a greater response than its competitors in similar ads for copiers.

Market Segment. Some market segments are more inclined to order by telephone than others. The 25-to-35-year-old group, for example, is more inclined to place phone orders than the over-60 group.

Portion of Audience in Target Group. The percentage of viewers or readers of your ad that are part of your targeted market segment will obviously affect your response rate. The higher the percentage, the higher your response rate.

Medium. Some media work better than others in generating 800 number calls. Television, in general, out-pulls radio. Print is more effective than outdoor advertising.

Media Context. The same commercial will pull better in one program than in another even if both programs have the same or similar viewership. Likewise, a print ad may do better in one magazine than another.

Position. One page of a periodical may be better than another page in the same publication. In a magazine the best positions are usually the back cover, the inside front cover and the first six right-hand pages. A late commercial position in a TV program may be better than an earlier one.

Emphasis on the Phone Number. The more emphasis placed on the phone number in an ad, the more likely it is that a person who decides to buy will choose the telephone as the means of doing so. With print ads in which a mail ordering option is offered in addition to the phone number, the percentage of response taken by phone will increase dramatically as the phone number is given greater emphasis in the ad. An ad in which the maximum emphasis is placed on the mail-back coupon while the minimum emphasis is given to the phone number will typically pull 75% mail response to 25% phone. These figures can be exactly reversed by reversing the emphasis in the ad.

Number of Previous Exposures of Ad. The response to an ad will usually increase with each successive time that the target audience is exposed to it up to four or five times. After approximately the fifth time, the response will level off. Eventually a saturation point is reached. Response to subsequent airings of the ad will taper off gradually then soon decline sharply. This tendency holds true in both print and broadcast advertising, however, in broadcast the saturation point will usually be reached more quickly and the decline in response will be more sudden.

This point is illustrated by a series of ads that aired on network TV during successive NFL Sunday Game of the Week programs. The commercials offered coins commemorating the 1976 Montreal Olympic Games. About 1,000 calls were handled when the first ad was aired. On the second Sunday the number doubled. It doubled again on the third Sunday and again on the fourth. On the fifth airing the call volume leveled off and subsequently declined.[10]

Time, Day and Season. Finally, the time of day, the day of the week, and the season of the year can all affect response.

HOW TO PROCEED

The foregoing is not meant to cause readers to despair of ever being able to anticipate call volumes. Rather it is intended to encourage cautious planning and testing. Once an ad has run, future response can be projected. When it has run four or five times, the projections can be made more accurately. If the response to the first use of an ad is marginal, it may pay to run the ad again since the response rate may increase.

A good rule to follow in initiating a telephone-response ad campaign is to cost-justify on the basis of your worst-case projection and to plan your telephone lines and staffing around your most optimistic projections. In calculating a worst-case projection, start with a figure of .1% response in space and broadcast, and .5% in mail. Adjust these figures up or down depending on the influence of the factors discussed in the preceding paragraphs.

If, for example, you have placed maximum influence on the phone number and your ad will appear on the first right-hand page of a targeted magazine, you might adjust your worst-case projections up to .5%.

The optimistic projections should ordinarily fall close to one-half percent for general television, 1%

- 3% for space and 4% or more for mailing. Again, these figures should be adjusted up or down based on the specific situation.

SOURCING INCOMING CALLS

It is essential in managing any inbound telephone marketing program to know exactly how many calls have been generated by each advertisement or promotion. If calls are being generated by different media--such as TV, space and mail--it is essential to know the quantity and quality of response generated by each medium. If different TV stations or different magazines are used, it is important to determine the number of responses generated by each station and each publication per dollar spent for advertising. When this is done, future advertising dollars can be spent more wisely.

In order to do any effective testing--whether it be of the creative approach, the offer, or some other element of the ad--it is necessary to know which ad generated which calls. Without this knowledge it is impossible to compare the results from one ad with those of another.

"Sourcing" is the term by which telemarketers refer to any of the various processes that are used to determine which ad in which medium generated a call. It is of crucial importance in inbound telemarketing to know what methods of sourcing calls are available and to know which methods are right for which applications. A sourcing technique that works well in one case may not be appropriate in another application.

ASKING THE CALLER IS ASKING FOR TROUBLE

In the early days of telephone response marketing, the most common method of sourcing a call was to ask the caller, *"Where did you see our number?"* The problem with this approach is that it simply does not yield the most accurate results.

An example of the problems that this method of sourcing can lead to is provided by a 1979 marketing campaign for the GE Spacemaker microwave oven. Young & Rubicam designed print ads for the microwave unit in which readers were encouraged to call an 800 number to find the location of their nearest dealers.

To provide sourcing information, the designers of the campaign instructed telephone reps to ask callers where they had seen the ad. Approximately 10% of all callers said they had seen the ad in magazines or other media in which the ad had not appeared. Many callers reported that they had seen the ad on television when, in fact, ads had appeared only in print.[11]

An additional 3% of the callers had been told about the ad by another party and did not know where it had appeared. Thus a total of at least 13% of all calls were not attributed to their true sources, and this does not include cases in which callers saw the ad in one publication but identified it as having appeared in another publication in which the ad also ran.

If calls are taken in response to television advertising, the problem is even worse because many people simply will not know what station they were watching. If ads appear on more than one station at a time, it becomes impossible to do accurate sourcing by asking callers where they saw the ad.

The problem is exacerbated because cable operators often put a station on a different channel number than the one on which it broadcasts. A caller whose cable channel is 21 may actually be watching broadcast channel 9. When relying on callers to identify where a TV ad was seen, it is common to have as many as 20% of the calls either not sourced or incorrectly sourced.[12]

ZIP CODE MATCH

If it is unreliable to ask callers where they saw an ad, how then is the source of the call to be determined? A method that can be used when handling calls in response to broadcast advertising is the *ZIP code match* routine. This method can only be used in an automated environment in which orders are entered directly into a computer. It requires the purchase of some software or extensive programming.

The usual procedure is to enter into a computer the longitude and latitiude of every ZIP code in the country. The longitude and latitude of each broadcast station that is to carry advertising is also entered. The computer is then programmed to use the caller's ZIP code to determine the nearest station carrying the ad. This station is then assumed to be the one that the caller was watching. The chief advantage of this method of sourcing is that no time is wasted on the phone in gathering extra information that is used only for sourcing purposes.

Unfortunately, there are disadvantages as well. This method of sourcing cannot be used if advertising is being done on two stations in the same market or on a cable network that is carried in a market where broadcast advertising is also being aired. In addition, while this method may be more accurate than asking callers where they saw the ad, it is not 100% accurate. Callers who saw the ad while traveling out of town are likely to be incorrectly assigned. What's more, this method is of no use in most space or direct mail campaigns.

USING DIFFERENT NUMBERS

The sourcing method that has come to be the most often used in major broadcast telephone response campaigns is that of using different telephone numbers in different ads and different media. This method comes close to being 100% accurate. As soon as it is known what number a caller dialed, the source of the call is known.

Most organizations that handle response to television advertising maintain a large number of phone lines that all terminate in the same service group. This means that, no matter which of the numbers was dialed by the caller, the call can be routed to whichever station is free at the time. This makes for an efficient operation but complicates sourcing. It may mean that, in order to determine what number was dialed, the telephone rep must ask the caller. This can add to the length (and therefore the cost) of the phone call. It can also create confusion for the caller who will not understand why the telephone rep would not already know the number of the phone being answered.

The option of using different numbers as a sourcing mechanism is only available to those telephone marketers who maintain a large number of incoming 800 trunks. Basically, you can get only as many 800 numbers assigned as you have 800 trunks. If you have only one or two trunks, you get only one or two numbers. This usually means that broadcast advertisers, who must maintain large numbers of incoming trunks to provide adequate coverage, can use different numbers for sourcing while print and mail advertisers cannot.

It is sometimes possible to combine ZIP code matching and the different number system. Some calls--given their originating points--could only have been generated by one specific TV station. In this case, the computer terminal screen will tell the telephone rep that no further information is needed to determine the source of the call. For calls that might have been generated by two or more TV stations, the telephone rep will be cued to ask what number was dialed.

DIALED NUMBER IDENTIFICATION SERVICE (DNIS)

Since January 1983, AT&T has offered a service that eliminates the need to ask 800 number callers what number they dialed. This offering, now available from all major 800 service providers and called Dialed Number Identification Service (DNIS), makes it possible for a 4-digit LED display to light up and reveal the specific 800 number that was dialed for each incoming call received.

The catch here is that in order to be able to use DNIS, it is necessary to purchase or lease equipment that is prohibitively expensive for all but the very largest operations. However, most of the major inbound telemarketing service bureaus that handle TV response now offer sourcing by DNIS.

EXTENSION NUMBERS

In smaller operations (usually not handling broadcast response) where there may be as few as one or two incoming lines, it is not possible to obtain enough different phone numbers to source properly. An excellent solution to this dilemma is the use of extension numbers. The phone number would be advertised as, for example, "800/222-5000 Extension 16." The caller will then ask for extension 16. The telephone rep can then record the number 16 as the source code and then reply, *"This is extension 16; did you wish to order the widget?"* If the caller fails to ask for an extension, the telephone rep simply asks, *"What extension did you want?"*

This is a simple means of handling sourcing in a space or mail campaign. It is impractical for broadcast, however, because it greatly increases the amount of information that the listener must remember or record.

NAMES

An alternative to using the rather impersonal extension numbers is to use names. For example, your ad might read, *"Call 800/222-5000. Ask for Lee Porter."* A different name can be used for different ads. If names--such as Lee, Chris, Pat, Charlie, Jody, and Aldyn--that could apply to either sex are used, anyone can take the call.

The primary drawback to this procedure is that if your customers are to have repeated contacts with your company, they will probably figure out the ruse and may feel that they have been deceived. Where repeated contacts with the same customer are desired, it may be wise to stick with extension numbers as opposed to names.

CHOOSING THE RIGHT METHOD

One of the methods described here will be right for your program. It is important to take some time to choose the right one. If you are advertising exclusively on TV and are on no more than one station per market, ZIP code matching may be the most cost efficient approach. If you are on stations that serve overlapping areas, you will want to use different numbers on different stations. If you are going to use a service bureau, you may want to use one that offers sourcing by DNIS.

If you have a small operation and advertise only in space or mail, you will need to choose between using extension numbers or names. If repeated contacts with customers are desired, extension numbers are preferable.

INBOUND TELEPHONE SERVICE OPTIONS IN A DEREGULATED ENVIRONMENT

The range of service options available to today's inbound telemarketers would astound the industry's pioneers of just three decades ago. For them there was one giant provider of long distance service: AT&T. Some telemarketers even got local service, telephones and switches from AT&T as well. What's more there was only one type of telephone service in widespread usage.

Since the introduction of toll-free 800 service in 1967 and the breakup of AT&T in 1984, the inbound telemarketer inhabits an entirely new world. Today a telemarketer can choose service from several long distance common carriers--including the three majors: AT&T, MCI, and U.S. Sprint--as well as regional telephone operating companies and a variety of resellers. Not only is there more than one long distance service provider, there are many types of service available from each carrier.

TYPES OF SERVICE

The three major carriers all offer a variety of types of service that can be used by inbound telemarketers. With the exception of 900 Service--which is at present offered only by AT&T--every type of service is offered by all three companies. In some cases, the three companies' offerings even have the same or very similar names. The terms ''long distance,'' ''800 service,'' and ''FX,'' for example, are used in the names of products offered by all three of the major carriers. While the names are similar, the features and pricing can vary significantly from one carrier to the next.

399

POTS. The basic type of telephone service with which we are all familiar and which continues to serve almost all homes and businesses has for years been referred to by telecommunications professionals as "POTS," an acronym for "plain old telephone service." It could be argued that in the post-divestiture world there really is no such thing as "plain old service," since intra-LATA service is provided by the local exchange carrier and long distance service by a long distance common carrier or reseller.

Ordinary long distance service is also called "MTS" or "Message Toll Service," a name given to it by AT&T but changed to AT&T Long Distance after divestiture. Most telemarketers who receive calls only from within their own local areas still serve their customers with POTS. Many nationwide marketers who have toll-free numbers request that local customers or intrastate customers call an ordinary local number. There are a few nationwide marketers, such as L.L. Bean, that ask all their customers to call their POTS number at their own expense.

800 Service. Toll-free 800 service is now offered by all major long distance carriers. Volume discounts as well as time-and-day discounts are available from all providers. Each carrier also allows its 800 subscribers the ability to accept calls from only specified areas.

800 Readyline. Traditional 800 service requires dedicated lines that can only be used for handling the incoming toll-free calls. With 800 Readyline, introduced by AT&T in 1987, it is possible to accept 800 number calls over existing business telephone lines. In 1988, Sprint introduced its own version of the service called FonLine 800. The service is used primarily by small businesses that want to offer toll-free calling but expect calls on only an occasional basis. The service is inexpensive compared to traditional 800 service and can be initiated without the addition of more telephone lines.

Megacom 800. In 1985, AT&T--in response to competitive pressure from Sprint and MCI-- introduced a service to keep its highest-volume 800 service users from changing carriers. Sprint with its Ultra 800 and MCI introduced similar services in 1988. Megacom 800 Service is designed for businesses that log at least 800 hours of interstate 800 service usage per month per location. The service makes it possible for these companies to reduce the cost of their toll-free calls. It also makes it possible to be more flexible in determining the areas that will be served.

Subscribers to normal AT&T 800 Service must elect to receive calls from any of six geographic service areas. Each successive service area (or band) permits calling to additional states. Rates vary according to the size of the area over which service is offered; the distance that calls actually travel is irrelevant to their cost. Toll-free calls can only be limited by designating a small service area from among those available. With Megacom 800 Service, subscribers can receive calls from any specified location or group of locations in the U.S., Puerto Rico and the Virgin Islands. Billing is based on the duration of all calls and the distance from the caller's area code to that of the Megacom 800 Service subscriber. (Sprint and MCI do not use the service area system. Thus with even the basic 800 service options of these carriers, calls are billed based on time and distance.)

With Megacom 800 Service, subscribers can elect to receive calls *only* from one or more of the six geographic service areas--such as areas 1, 3, and 5. It would also be possible to create a unique toll-free calling area by selecting any combination of service areas and area codes from around the U.S. (This is possible for subscribers to the basic 800 offerings from Sprint and MCI, also.)

INBOUND TELEMARKETING

For example, a New York subscriber who wishes to take calls only from adjacent states plus California could designate Service Area One and the California area codes. These would then be the only areas from which calls could be received; the subscriber would not have to handle or pay for calls from other areas.

Several alternatives are available for making connections from the premises of the subscriber to the AT&T, Sprint, or MCI network. Subscribers can purchase access to the network from a local exchange company, from their chosen long distance carrier, or from another vendor; or they can provide their own access. This is accomplished through dedicated T-1 terminations.

Remote Call Forwarding. Remote Call Forwarding (RCF) is a service that makes it possible to maintain a local number in a distant city without having an actual telephone in that city. The service is inward only. Customers can call in, but the subscriber cannot call out over an RCF line. If RCF is desired to connect cities in different LATA's, the service can be obtained from any of the three major common carriers. Intra-LATA RCF service is arranged by the local exchange carrier. Subscribers to RCF pay a relatively high monthly fee as well as the cost of forwarding calls via the designated long distance carrier. RCF is appropriate whenever there is desire to establish a local presence and the expected volume of calls from other cities is not great enough to justify using 800 service.

FX Service. Foreign Exchange (FX) Service provides a direct link from one city to another. It is designed for users who have a constant flow of calls between a business and a specific distant city. FX differs from RCF in that it is a two-way service. Calls can be placed to or from the distant city. Like RCF, it is available from all three major carriers but must be obtained from the local exchange carrier when the points to be linked are within the same LATA. It involves a substantially higher monthly fee than does RCF. Because of the high monthly fees, the service is only cost effective where there is a very high volume of calls between a business and a distant city. In typical marketing applications, 800 Service combined with out-WATS will ordinarily be more cost effective.

900 Service. Dial-It 900 Service was developed by AT&T to facilitate handling massive call volumes for programs that involve polling or the playing of recorded messages. The service has been engineered to facilitate the handling of massive bursts of telephone calls. Indeed, 900 numbers have been broadcast on nationwide prime time network television and 100% of the calls generated have been handled. This would be impossible with any other type of telephone service.

At the time this encyclopedia went to press, 900 service was available only from AT&T. However, both Sprint and MCI have plans to offer the service in the future.

Ordinarily callers to a 900 number reach a recorded message. (In the case of the 900 number offered by the National Aeronautics and Space Administration [NASA], callers can listen in on live conversations between NASA Ground Control and orbiting astronauts.) For purposes of polling or voting, it is possible to advertise two or more different 900 numbers and maintain a count of the calls going to each number.

With 900 service, unlike 800 service, the caller pays a small amount--typically 50 cents for the first minute and 35 cents for each additional minute--for each call. For a while it was AT&T's practice that when call volumes reached a prescribed level, AT&T would share revenue with the sponsor of the 900 number. However, this practice was discontinued in 1988. It is possible to arrange what AT&T calls premium billing.

With premium billing, the subscriber is permitted to charge callers an amount up to two dollars per call over the basic charge. This premium amount is then collected by AT&T and forwarded to the subscriber.

It is not possible to have all 900 number calls put through to live representatives, thus the service cannot be used for order taking and lead generation. Nor can all calls be put through to voice recorders that would gather information from callers. However, it is possible to connect a specified number of callers--who would be selected randomly--to a live representative or voice recorder. This makes it possible for 900 numbers to be used for sweepstakes and contests where winners reach live representatives (or voice recorders) and losers hear a pre-recorded message.

976 Service. Local telephone operating companies offer 976 service to enable local information providers to transmit recorded messages by phone to callers. The most familiar 976 applications are the local time and weather information services available in most cities.

700 Service. In 1987, 700 numbers began to be used for conference calls and gab lines. Callers pay a fee that is established by arrangement between the sponsor (or subscriber) and the carrier and which appears on the user's phone bill. Callers to 700-number gab lines generally hear a recorded message telling them the subject for the gab line they have called and charges involved. By 1988, gab lines for singles who wished to chat or arrange dates were popular in several major cities.

At the time this encyclopedia went to press, it was anticipated that AT&T would soon announce a new service that might use 700 numbers (or might not). The service, which had for years been rumored to be in development and which had always been referred to as "700 service," would combine features of the 976, 800 and 900 services. Like 976, it would enable subscribers to provide recorded information and to charge fees to callers that would appear on their phone bills. The sponsors of the service would have wide latitude in setting the fees they would charge. Some of the routing features of 800 and 900 service were also expected to be available with the new service.

800 SERVICE FEATURES

In 1982, AT&T began to introduce a number of call routing features that allow subscribers to be more flexible and responsive in managing calls to their 800 numbers. The first seven features described below make up what AT&T calls its Advanced 800 Features. All of these features were--at the time of publication of this encyclopedia--expected to be available from Sprint in early 1989 and from MCI soon thereafter.

800 Time/Day Manager. The first two Advanced 800 features, 800 Time Manager and 800 Day Manager--which together replaced a service that was originally called Variable Call Routing--allow 800 service subscribers to have calls rerouted to different locations based on the time of day and day of the week. Time Manager and Day Manager will allow greater flexibility by making it possible to specify that call routes be shifted based solely on the hour of the day, soley on the day of the week, or both.

For example, suppose a catalog operation in New York takes its own 800 number calls Monday through Friday from 8:00 a.m. to 5:00 p.m. At other times calls are routed to an outside service agency in

Utah. The cataloger would use Day Manager to specify that all calls on Saturday and Sunday be re-routed to Utah and would use Time Manager to direct weekday calls to Utah between 5:00 p.m. and 8:00 a.m.

800 Area Code Routing. Area Code Routing, originally called Custom Call Routing, allows 800-Service subscribers to route their 800 number calls to various destinations, based on the area codes where the calls originate. For example, if an airline has reservations facilities in Philadelphia, Atlanta, and Denver, it is possible to route calls from the East and Midwest to Philadelphia, calls from the South to Atlanta, and calls from the Plains States and West to Denver.

800 Single Number Service. Single Number Service permits the use of a single 800 number where two or more would otherwise be necessary. The most common use of this service is to make it possible for intrastate and interstate callers to dial the same 800 number in order to reach a company. The service is now free to AT&T, Sprint and MCI 800 subscribers.

Prior to 1982, when Single Number Service was introduced, telemarketers had to advertise two different 800 numbers if they wanted to take both intrastate and interstate calls. This was because the two types of calls required two separate groups of lines. With Single Number Service, telemarketers need only advertise one number, even though the calls may be handled by different groups of incoming trunks. Single Number Service can also be used when a company has different groups of lines that serve different AT&T service areas or bands.

800 Courtesy Response. Another Advanced 800 offering, 800 Courtesy Response, permits callers to hear recorded messages under certain conditions specified in advance. Courtesy Response can, for example, be used in conjunction with Time Manager and Day Manager. Callers can be routed to a recorded message if their calls are received during hours when the call center is closed. These hours would be specified by the 800 service subscriber.

800 Call Allocator. Call Allocator makes it possible to apportion calls to two or more call-answering locations by setting the percentage of calls each location should recieve. For example, if you want 30% of your calls to go to your Chicago branch, 30% to your Seattle branch and 40% to your Atlanta branch you could ensure that calls are apportioned as closely to those exact percentages as possible. The percentages specified must be expressed in whole numbers. Thus, if you wished to break your calls into approximately even thirds, you would specify 33%, 33% and 34%.

800 Command Routing. Command Routing allows telemarketers to respond to spontaneous needs--such as shut-downs, emergencies, power failures, or unanticipated peaks in call volume--by pre-determining alternate ways for 800 number calls to be routed. On command from the telemarketer, calls could be switched to a planned alternate route. If, for example, a call-answering facility in one city were shut down by a snowstorm, calls could be quickly re-routed to another branch operation or to a service bureau. However, the alternate route must be determined in advance.

800 Call Prompter. 800 Call Prompter will allow callers to hear a recorded message that instructs them to dial an additional digit or digits in order for their calls to be properly routed. For example, customers might dial an 800 number and then hear a recorded message that tells them to press the number "1" on their telephone keyboard if they wish to enter an order, "2" if they require service, or "3" if they have a billing problem. When customers press the appropriate keys, their calls are routed to the appropriate departments--even if those departments are on opposite sides of the country.

The codes used to determine the routing of calls can have up to 15 digits. Thus, ZIP codes, account numbers, I.D. numbers, or social security numbers could all be used. For example, callers could be asked to enter their ZIP codes and then be routed to the geographically closest location.

The chief drawback of this service is that it can only be used with Touch-Tone phones. The network is not yet engineered to recognize codes that are dialed on rotary telephones. It is necessary to provide some mechanism for handling calls that "default." (A default occurs whenever a caller enters a code on a non-Touch-Tone phone, enters an incorrect code, or enters no code.) These calls may be routed to any answering location to be handled by a live representative or by an answering and recording device. Another option is to employ Courtesy Response in order to allow people who place defaulted calls to hear a recorded message.

800 Routing Control Service. Routing Control Service allows subscribers to have direct access to the AT&T network so they can prescribe changes in call-routing patterns. Subscribers can perform such re-setting by entering commands directly into terminals located on their own premises and thus avoid the time and expense of formal service orders. The service was originally introduced in January, 1984, to allow 800 Service subscribers who use Variable Call Routing to reset the time of day and day of the week that the destination of their calls are shifted.

Subsequently it became possible to use Routing Control Service to change any of the commonly-varied call-routing parameters for any Advanced 800 Service feature. Subscribers to Area Code Routing, for example, can use Routing Control Service to change the way calls from a particular area are routed. This is done by simply entering instructions in a computer terminal. This service is available 22 hours a day, seven days a week. (Two hours per day are set aside for network maintenance and billing functions.)

Advanced 800 Combinations. By combining different Advanced 800 Service features, it is possible to custom-design highly flexible systems for handling 800 number calls. It is possible to combine any service feature with any and all others.

For example, imagine a large catalog company with a dozen incoming call centers. The company could use Area Code Routing to divide the country into two or more regions each with its own destination or set of destinations for calls. Within each region Call Allocator could be used to control the percentage of calls handled at each incoming call center. It could be stipulated, for example, that 30% of the calls from the West go to Seattle, 30% to Los Angeles and 40% to Denver.

Time Manager and Day Manager could be used to shift early morning calls to Eastern centers that would open before the Western ones. Late at night when all centers are closed, Courtesy Response could be used to allow callers to hear a recorded message. If a center in one city were shut down because of a snow storm, calls could be rerouted to centers in other cities with Command Routing. Callers could be referred within each center by using Call Prompting. It would even be possible, by combining Area Code Routing, Call Prompter and Call Allocator, to specify that the call center in Los Angeles should handle 30% of all billing inquiries from the Southwest and 20% of all service calls from California. Routing Control Service could then be used to automatically change any routing instruction relating to any feature.

The cost of all Advanced 800 Features is based on the number of different possible call paths or "branches" established. For example, if Call Allocator is used to apportion calls among three call centers, the number of branches would be three. Thus, the more call centers you have to route calls to and the more features you employ, the more you pay.

Dialed Number Identification Service (DNIS). In order to facilitate more personalized service and the sourcing of incoming calls, AT&T introduced Dialed Number Identification Service (DNIS) in 1983. DNIS, as was previously noted, makes it possible for 800 service subscribers who have several different 800 numbers in a single service group answered at the same location to be able to identify which 800 number was dialed as each call arrives.

In order to subscribe to DNIS, you must have a compatible terminal device--most likely an automatic call distributor (ACD) or Private Business Exchange (PBX). Many ACD's and PBX's are not DNIS-compatible. In addition to the terminal equipment, video display terminals or telephone instruments with LED displays are also required. When a call for one of your 800 numbers arrives at your local telco switching office, the 800 number dialed by the caller is automatically determined and a four-digit signal is out-pulsed with the call to your terminal equipment to be displayed on the VDT or LED.

DNIS is used primarily to accomplish two objectives: improved sourcing and more personalized service. The primary users are telemarketing service agencies that take calls for several different advertisers and companies with several different units sharing the same telephone answering facility. If different 800 numbers are assigned to different advertisers or to different corporate divisions, the telephone representative will be able to answer the call with the name of the advertiser or division.

800 Band Advance. As previously mentioned, AT&T's 800 and WATS services are based on service areas or bands. An 800 service subscriber can choose service from any of six different service areas. A company that takes calls only from within its own state would need only to have intrastate service (which is sometimes referred to as "Band 0"). Band 1 service usually permits a company to take calls only from adjacent states. Band 2 adds more states in the region. Each band is successively larger and includes all areas in lower-numbered bands, except that intrastate calls are only possible with Band 0. Band 5 includes the entire country. Calls on a Band 1 line are cheaper than calls on Band 2, Band 2 calls are cheaper than Band 3, etc.

Companies with very large call volumes, in order to save money, sometimes have different groups of lines serving different bands. Thus, a company in Nebraska might take calls from Iowa on lines dedicated to Band 1 service and calls from Maine or California on Band 5.

Band Advance makes it possible for such companies to have a call "advance" to lines serving another band when the lines that would otherwise serve that call are busy. The call will automatically hunt lines serving successively higher-numbered bands until a free line is found. In our Nebraska example, if an Iowan places a call and all of the Nebraska firm's Band 1 circuits are busy, the call could be rerouted via the firm's Band 2, 3, 4, or 5 lines. The usage charges for calls bumped to a higher band are billed at the higher rate. This service is provided not by AT&T but by the local exchange carrier. It is available only where the local exchange carrier has tariffed it and where central office switching equipment can handle it.

405

SELECTING THE INBOUND LONG DISTANCE CARRIER

With so many common carriers and resellers offering so many different kinds of long distance telephone service (and with local exchange carriers offering intra-LATA service) the task of choosing your long distance service provider or providers can be confusing. Following are the most important criteria to consider when making the choice, as well as some advice on comparison shopping.

Price. Obviously the cost of service will be an important consideration. For most types of service there will be initial set-up fees, monthly fees, and usage charges. For telemarketers, who ordinarily pack their phone lines with the maximum possible amount of call traffic, the set-up and monthly fees will be negligible compared to the usage fees--except for services, such as FX and Megacom, that are designed for high-volume users.

In addition to determining the basic usage charges, it is important to know if volume or time-of-day discounts are offered. If so, how great are the discounts and at what levels of volume or what times of day do they become effective? A telecommunications consultant will be essential to helping you project your call traffic patterns and determining--given those patterns--which carrier or combination of carriers will offer the best bargain.

Transmission Quality. The quality of the sound that will be heard by your customers on your phone lines is of vital importance. Simply put, if your customers cannot understand or hear clearly what your reps are saying, they will not buy your products. Never, never sacrifice transmission quality to save a few dollars in usage fees.

The first question to ask about a long distance service is, *"How will calls be transmitted?"* U.S. Sprint emphasizes its fiber optic network in its advertising, and for good reason. Fiber optics offers the most consistently high-quality transmission of voice available. Satellite circuits tend to be the least reliable. Don't be sold by a sales pitch from a carrier. If you are told that your calls will be handled via a fiber optic network, find out exactly what percentage of the network is fiber optic.

The telecommunications trade publications occasionally run surveys of the users of various long distance services or conduct their own tests. These can be helpful in determining which carriers offer the highest quality service.

Whenever possible, it is best to test a service before having a lot of lines hooked up. Try to find another user of the service who will allow you to monitor calls or conduct test calls over their lines. If you are unsure about sound quality, it is a good idea to have a single test line installed before ordering an entire group of lines. The transmission quality of a service offering--particularly when obtained from a reseller--can vary widely from one geographic location to another. Therefore, it is important to do your testing at a location in the same area (and preferably served by the same telco central office) as your planned telephone center. Also, have friends or associates in various parts of the country call you on the test lines. You will want to listen for volume, distortion, background noise and echo. If you find a problem in any of these areas, do not order the service for a marketing application, period.

Reach. You must know--particularly if you expect to take international calls--what regions within the U.S. can be served by the service you are contemplating. Just because you are not taking calls from Alaska, Canada, the Caribbean, or Europe today does not mean that you won't want to tomorrow.

Network Capacity. Another factor that you will want to check in tests or surveys is network capacity. How often is it impossible to get through because the carrier's network is at full capacity? Even if you are only considering inbound service, you can test network capacity by placing outbound calls. Network capacity is particularly important if you plan to serve customers in other countries. Even among the three major carriers, there are wide variations in the extent to which international networks are blocked.

Routing and Control Features. It is anticipated that the years 1989 to 1995 will see an explosion of routing and control offerings from the long distance carriers. The Advanced 800 features described in the preceding pages are only the beginning. While all the currently available Advanced 800 features will probably be available from all three carriers by 1990, each carrier is working on offerings that it hopes will not soon be duplicated by the others.

Terminations. Will your chosen carrier permit either switched or dedicated terminations? "Termination" refers to the manner in which the incoming trunks are connected to your phone system. A switched termination implies that calls are routed through the local telco central switching office like other ordinary calls. A dedicated termination, such as a T-1 circuit, makes it possible to bypass the local exchange. This may provide cost and call-handling advantages. Dedicated T-1 terminations are available with MCI's basic 800 service, while AT&T's and Sprint's basic 800 services can only be offered through a switched termination. The only way to get dedicated T-1 terminations for toll-free service from AT&T is to upgrade to Megacom 800 (or Ultra 800 in the case of Sprint), which, as previously stated, is only cost effective at the level of 800 hours of usage per month per location.

Billing. The method of billing may be of crucial importance. How long must a call be connected before a call is billed? Is usage rounded up to the nearest minute or nearest tenth of an hour? Do you receive a detail of all calls with your monthly bill? With Sprint 800 service call details are provided with each bill.

Will you be billed according to bands or service areas or will your bills reflect the actual distance that calls travel? With AT&T's basic 800 service, if you order Band 5 service, you pay the Band 5 rate even if a call comes from a neighboring state. Only with Megacom 800 does AT&T bill for the actual distance a call travels. With MCI or Sprint 800 service, however, you are always billed for the actual distance a call travels based on a series of ranges.

Reporting. The reports offered with telephone service vary widely from one carrier to another and from one service to another. Among the reports that are important to telemarketers are call details, busy reports, and forecasts.

The most significant advantage of Sprint or MCI's 800 services over AT&T's basic 800 offering is that they provide a summary of calls received. MCI's call detailing will provide for each call: the calling number (if the call originated in an equal access exchange, otherwise the area code and sometimes the exchange will be provided), the date, time, duration of call and fee for the call. The report can be organized in numerical order by area code and number or by time of day and day of the week. The report can be issued monthly, quarterly, or on request. None of this is offered to basic AT&T 800 Service subscribers.

Your carrier should be able to provide you with busy reports, i.e., summaries that show by the quarter hour how many of your incoming trunks were busy and how frequently all your incoming trunks were occupied. The reports should also tell, when your center was busied out and how many calls were presented but reached busy signals. This information is used for planning phone lines for future campaigns.

Your carrier should also be able to provide forecasts of future call volume and should be able to vary the assumptions on which the forecasts are made. Given those forecasts, the carrier should be able to help you plan your future need for trunks. AT&T even has software available that can be used to schedule your telephone reps into shifts according to seniority and personal preference based on the forecasts you or they produce.

PLANNING FOR THE FUTURE IN INBOUND TELEMARKETING

Clearly the world of inbound telemarketing is changing rapidly. New advertising media and methods are being developed, new carriers enter the industry as others die, new long distance services are continually being developed while new features are added to existing ones. All of this will mean greater opportunities for future inbound telemarketers. But some things will remain as true in the future as they are today. The telemarketers who succeed will be the ones who learn the scientific discipline of telemarketing, who stay informed of the changes that affect their businesses, who offer value and service to their customers and who carefully plan and test each new idea or campaign.

----

[1]The results of the study, commissioned for *The Telemarketer* newsletter (published by Actel Marketing, New York) were reported in *The Telemarketer*, Vol. 7, No. 4, July 25, 1986, p. 4.

[2]*Ibid.,* p. 5

[3]*Ibid.*, Vol. 7, No. 20, March 25, 1987, p. 4.

[4]*Ibid.*, Vol. 7, No. 5, August 11, 1986, p. 3.

[5]*bid.*, Vol. 1, No. 19, March 10, 1981, p. 1.

[6]*Ibid.*, Vol. 7, No. 21, April 10, 1987, p. 4.

[7]Lazaros, Esther, *The Effectiveness of 800 Numbers in Direct Mail Catalogs*, published by the Direct Marketing Association, New York, 1983.

[8]*The Telemarketer*, Vol. 7, No. 21, April 10, 1987, p. 5.

[9]*Ibid.*, Vol. 7, No. 7, September 10, 1986, p. 2.

[10]*Ibid.*, Vol. 7, No. 7, September 10, 1986, p. 3.

[11]*Ibid.*, Vol. 3, No. 6, August 25, 1982, p. 7.

[12]*Ibid.*, Vol. 6, No. 18, February 25, 1986, p. 3.

CHAPTER 21

Service Bureaus

Paul Mohr, President
Direct Marketing Systems, Inc.
Wynnewood, Pennsylvania

Seldon Young, President
NICE Corporation
Ogden, Utah

Traditionally, telemarketing service bureaus have either accepted inbound client telephone calls or placed outbound client telephone calls.

Inbound calls may include (but are not limited to) catalog orders, media advertisement orders, and dealer-locator or product information inquiries. Outbound calls may include (but are not limited to) market survey questions, calls to qualify prospects or telephone sales calls.

However, telecommunications and computer technology advances have allowed contemporary telemarketing service bureaus to evolve into more comprehensive information processors. This enhanced role has increased both available bureau services and overall value-added bureau functions (for client projects).

Contemporary service bureaus no longer just take or place telephone calls.

As internal bureau data processing systems have grown in scope and complexity, bureaus have begun to offer clients both new services, and services generally purchased from other industries (vertical integration). These vertically integrated bureaus offer clients "one-stop shopping," through services such as:

* *New project planning.*

* *Project analysis (offer, target market, fulfillment).*

* *Call analysis (script, media).*

* *Operator-assisted call processing (usually supported by on-line computer data base).*

* *Automated call processing (computer totally processes call, much like bank-by-phone systems).*

* *Lead/inquiry management.*

* *Product fulfillment.*

* *Marketing database information.*

* *Creative consulting.*

Consequently, clients must re-evaluate how they purchase their direct-response project services to ensure that they assemble the optimum mix of service bureau and internally controlled functions.

FUTURE ENVIRONMENT

Two major trends will dominate (and accelerate the growth of) the future service bureau environment:

1. *Both consumers and businesses will increasingly accept telemarketing as a sales/distribution mechanism.*

2. *Businesses must accommodate an evolving global marketplace which will continue to erode regional and national market boundaries.*

Telemarketing service bureaus, which can manufacture information faster and more economically than most in-house telemarketing operations, will continue to expand their value-added services and play a greater role in client business strategies.

Highly automated bureaus will function as major nodes in a global information network and will have multiple sites (made possible by telecommunications and data processing technology) to accommodate national or regional characteristics. These future telemarketing service bureaus, positioned as information processors, will produce value-added products (information) which will flow globally, directed by market-place needs.

WHEN TO USE A SERVICE BUREAU

Clients use telemarketing service bureaus for several reasons, to either perform complete projects, or to augment internal telemarketing departments. Specific situations include:

* *Balance call load.*

* *Support successful pilot projects.*

* *Short-term projects.*

* *Employee constraints.*

410

> * *Don't understand the business.*
>
> * *Distribute costs.*
>
> * *Financial control.*
>
> * *Cross-project expertise.*

A professional, comprehensive telemarketing service bureau helps clients to plan, implement, and service projects far more successfully than inflexible, dedicated resources.

Balance Call Load. A service bureau can process call overflow (peaking) not appropriate for in-house telemarketing operations. Often, clients with internal telemarketing groups will use service bureaus to process call volumes, which exceed internal capabilities, through two techniques:

1. *For specific projects, clients use bureau telephone numbers to shift call-load.*

2. *AT&T's enhanced WATS (Custom Call Routing, or Call Allocator).*

Custom Call Routing routes inbound calls to either client or bureau centers, based upon the caller's area code. The Custom Call Allocator feature allows clients to define call-distribution percentages (based upon inbound call count), to direct inbound calls between centers.

Each approach allows service bureau clients to distribute inbound calls between centers, to ensure that call-loads are optimal, and call-response does not degrade.

Support Successful Pilot Projects. Service bureau clients may use internal telemarketing operations to "tune" pilot projects, until project sales and revenues are acceptable, then employ a service bureau to process far larger call volumes during the project roll-out. Bureau clients who decide to expand their internal operations to support project roll-out often discover that they cannot cost-effectively manage a full-service center with the same skills or resources used for small, internal groups.

For example, based upon successful internal pilot projects, a major financial services corporation, which decided to process all calls, spent three years to develop their center, which processed projects at twice the bureau cost and half the bureau productivity.

Short-Term Projects. Clients may use a service bureau to accomplish short-term projects, with no additional, in-house staff. A service bureau can provide project flexibility, and avoid unnecessary, on-going costs for under-utilized telemarketing facilities.

Employee Constraints. Telemarketing techniques are staff-intensive. In addition to the management difficulties in this environment, many firms wish to reduce fixed-employee expenses and remain flexible to react quickly to dynamic market conditions. Consequently, service bureaus, which must be extremely successful at staff-management, allow clients to utilize this labor-intensive communication technique, yet remain flexible.

411

Don't Understand the Business. Many service bureau clients don't have, or may not wish to acquire, the skills required to run a successful telemarketing center. In addition, to obtain the proper labor pool, telemarketing centers must often be located far from a client's normal business site.

Consequently, many clients cannot justify a sub-optimal telemarketing center at their corporate location, or the additional administrative overhead of a decentralized site in a good labor pool. To these clients, telemarketing is a communication technique, not their primary business.

Distribute Costs. A service bureau distributes center costs across many clients, to minimize individual client capital requirements. These requirements include:

* *Facility.*

* *Telecommunication equipment.*

* *Computer equipment.*

* *Management.*

Very few clients could cost-justify the resources required to provide the services of a comprehensive telemarketing service bureau.

Financial Control. Internal client telemarketing operations often incur hidden costs, or costs distributed across multiple departments, which require sophisticated cost-allocation systems to accurately identify product or project sales/service expenses. However, clients can easily calculate service bureau effectiveness and profitability, since the bureau's bill uniquely identifies all sales and service costs related to specific products, or projects.

Cross-Pollination. Service bureaus have experience from many clients, across several industries, who use multiple advertising and fulfillment techniques.

Consequently, bureau customer service representatives (CSR's) can provide valuable insight when clients plan, implement, and adjust telemarketing programs to maximize either product profitability or service effectiveness.

HOW TO USE A SERVICE BUREAU EFFECTIVELY

Often, service bureau clients seem to "work in a vacuum" as they plan their product sales/service projects. In early project design phases, bureau customer service representatives (CSR's) can provide invaluable media or script advice which will allow clients to maximize project potential faster, with lower costs.

Later, as the project "rolls-out," and service bureau telephone sales representatives (TSR's) talk to customers, the bureau can identify:

* *What script and product benefits work best.*

* *What customers want from the product or service.*

* *Additional products or services that customers are apt to purchase.*

Consequently, bureau CSR's can provide valuable input to tune product scripts or offers, to maximize project back-end profit or service benefits.

Not a Commodity. However, some clients inaccurately perceive telemarketing services as commodity items which they purchase at the lowest possible price. If these clients treat their service bureau as a "commodity vendor," valuable bureau resources are often inefficiently used or ignored for several reasons:

* *Clients provide inadequate project information, as they try to maintain business confidentiality.*

* *Project coordination is sub-optimal, since client-bureau communication is difficult, and often inaccurate.*

* *Clients do not use bureau CSR input to adjust project scripts and offers.*

Consequently, the client does not benefit from valuable bureau insights, based upon past projects, and direct customer contact.

In addition, if the client does not carefully involve the service bureau in project implementation, project coordination becomes cumbersome, as several client departments try to adjust their overall offer, based upon market reactions. A direct-response project's major strategic advantage is the ability to modify the product/service offer, based upon market results.

Consequently, fast, accurate project change to market response is critical to maximize profit or service benefits. Therefore, poor, overall project coordination and communication, which occurs when a service bureau is treated as a distant, commodity item will minimize potential project success.

Marketing Department Extension. Clients should use professional, comprehensive tele-marketing service bureaus as an extension of their marketing, advertising and fulfillment departments. With a broad range of experience and resources, a bureau can perform several key tasks to increase overall project profits or service benefits:

* *Offer analysis.*

* *Media analysis.*

* *Customer service.*

* *Fulfillment analysis.*

Based upon this information, and past-project experience, a customer service-oriented service bureau can consult with clients to determine if potential projects will be profitable. Service bureau clients should consider these invaluable bureau assets when they select and use their telemarketing resources.

For example, a service bureau client offered a self-help book, which generated a high order rate during pilot project tests. Based upon pilot project analyses, the bureau projected a 35%-40% COD rejection rate (a potential several hundred-thousand dollar project loss) and advised the client to:

* *Carefully analyze back-end cancellations.*

* *Expand the project slowly, based upon past experience with this type product.*

However, the client decided to expand the project quickly anyway. Two months later, this client had lost over $300,000 on this project, caused by a COD rejection rate which eventually reached 45%.

HOW TO SELECT A TELEMARKETING SERVICE BUREAU

Potential clients should evaluate three major telemarketing service bureau characteristics to identify the optimal bureau for their projects:

1. *Functional capabilities.* Service level the bureau can provide.

2. *References.* How successfully the bureau has previously performed these services.

3. *Price Structure.* Total client cost to obtain this service level.

Although each potential client may have unique call processing requirements, these three bureau features allow clients to compare centers to determine their optimal price/performance choice.

Functional Capabilities. Service bureau call-throughput (successfully processed call volume), either inbound or outbound, is directly related to:

* *Total number of center telephone lines.*

* *Total number of telephone service representatives (TSR's) available to use these lines.*

* *TSR quality and capability.*

* *Telecommunications and data processing support systems to enhance TSR efficiency and effectiveness.*

Clients must determine the proper mix of these bureau capabilities required to optimize both call-processing performance and service bureau fees. Low call-processing fees may imply inadequate center facilities to provide acceptable client services, while elaborate, but under-used facilities will generate unnecessarily high service costs. In addition, client requirements may range from simple, large call volumes (usually inbound) to sophisticated, low call volumes (usually outbound).

References. Service bureaus will usually give their best customers (current customers content with bureau service levels and price) as references. These customers will verify that the service bureau can perform specific services for stated prices. However, potential clients should attempt to evaluate how quickly and accurately bureau customer service representatives (CSR's):

* *Correct either bureau or client project errors.*

* *Modify ongoing projects, based upon client requests.*

* *Recommend project modifications, based upon call response, to increase project profitability or service level.*

Clients should augment satisfied customer references with information from references not on the service bureau's customer list to determine how the bureau handles project problems (ask the bureau for customers not on their reference list). Probe both good customers, and customers not on the published reference list to determine:

* *How does the service bureau resolve project problems?*

* *Did the service bureau correct the problems quickly?*

* *How did the service bureau correct the problems?*

If the bureau won't provide unlisted customers, ask published reference list customers if they know any of the bureau's other customers.

Price Structure. Generally, service bureau prices depend upon the service-level which clients require, and call-volumes, since most bureaus offer discounts for large call-volumes. Bureau clients must carefully balance their requested service-levels to optimize call-throughput and cost-per-order.

As clients analyze several bureaus for similar services, low call-rates for any specific center may imply lower service levels (higher busy rates), which:

* *Decrease center call-throughput.*

* *Increase average cost-per-order.*

Or, lower costs for comparable services may imply that this center may be "buying the business," and intends to increase call-rates later.

Clients who shift business between centers to obtain the lowest call-rates lose valuable customer service benefits, and incur costly project learning-curves. Although this strategy may minimize total project call cost, it usually does not maximize overall project profitability. Consequently, clients should base any decision to select (or change) bureaus upon both call-cost and overall service quality.

415

VARIOUS CALL-RATE STRUCTURES

Potential clients must evaluate a telemarketing service bureau's total call-rate structure, which includes several different project rate components:

* *Inbound call charges.*

* *Outbound call charges.*

* *Inquiries and complaints.*

* *Front-end charges.*

* *Back-end charges.*

References will identify if a bureau can provide appropriate service-levels. The bureau's total call-rate structure defines the complete cost for this service.

Inbound Call Charges. Inbound call-rates are usually based upon two price structures:

1. *Rate/call (dynamic rate).*

2. *Rate/minute/call.*

Since call length is directly related to script complexity, average scripts (average complexity) are usually priced dynamically, while difficult scripts (which imply longer calls) are priced at a per-minute rate.

Dynamic call-rates, or rate per call, include a base cost for specific call-information items. Each additional question or inquiry response is charged separately. For example, the base call's cost may include specific information-capture per call:

* *Caller's name.*

* *Address.*

* *City, state, ZIP code.*

Additional call segments are dynamically priced:

* *Phone number--specific rate.*

* *Credit card number--specific rate.*

* *Sales order--specific rate.*

* *Additional questions--specific rate.*

Usually, calls which last longer than three minutes are priced at a rate per minute, per call. Often, difficult calls are priced at per-minute rates. Based upon possible call segments, the bureau

416

charges a specific rate per minute for each call. Per-minute rates usually result in higher total call costs than dynamic rates.

> ***Outbound Call Charges.*** Outbound call-rates are usually based upon three call structures:
>
> 1. *Hourly.*
>
> 2. *Hourly + profit incentive (PI).*
>
> 3. *Profit incentive + back-end cancellation rebates (fee rebates, based upon sales cancellations).*

HOURLY CALL RATE

Hourly rates tend to minimize telephone sales representative (TSR) pressure to perform, and subsequent ''cheating,'' which occurs when TSR's:

> * *Modify the sales offer to increase sales volume (which usually creates unsatisfied customers and increased back-end sales cancellations).*
>
> * *Create fictitious sales (a short-sighted tactic, which often occurs under incentive-based fee structures).*

Also, hourly call-rates imply job stability. Consequently, TSR's are more inclined to perform thoroughly. However, straight hourly call-rates may not maximize project profitability or service levels.

HOURLY PLUS PROFIT-INCENTIVE CALL RATE

Hourly plus profit-incentive (PI) outbound call rates are specific call rates per hour, with an additional fee for each sale, negotiated for each project. However, since hourly plus PI call rates are usually structured to include service bureau costs/call, plus a marginal profit/call, the bureau can substantially increase their total project profits with increased sales volume.

Consequently, bureau TSR's are under greater pressure to perform, which increases project sales volume, but may encourage TSR ''cheating'' (described in previous paragraph).

For hourly plus PI call rates to function properly, the service bureau must have adequate supervisory or quality control staff to ensure that TSR's:

> * *Sell the correct product offer.*
>
> * *Really make each sale that they report.*
>
> * *Conduct pleasant, persistent and consistent sales presentations.*

Usually, the hourly plus profit incentive is the most successful call-rate structure for both the bureau and client.

PROFIT INCENTIVE PLUS BACK-END CANCELLATION REIMBURSEMENTS

Profit incentive (PI) plus back-end cancellation reimbursements (BCR's) are specific fees/sale, with a BCR for each customer that later cancels, negotiated for each project. This call rate is advantageous to the bureau client, since the client only pays for product sales (no sales, no costs). Service bureaus usually test PI plus BCR jobs for 100-200 hours at an hourly rate, then negotiate the PI rate, based upon test results.

The back-end cancellation reimbursement provides an incentive for high service bureau quality. However, this call-rate structure pressures TSR's to make the project successful quickly, which encourages cheating (TSR may change the product offer to increase sales volume). Although the back-end cancellation reimbursement eventually protects the bureau client from false sales, valuable outbound list names have been wasted to create unsatisfied customers.

(Note: Sales cancellations imply either service bureau or fulfillment failures, and must be carefully analyzed to determine appropriate corrective action.)

Since the service bureau is paid "up-front" for declared sales, back-end cancellation reimbursements can create a dangerous business situation. Bureaus with cash flow difficulties have an incentive to report "marginal" or false sales as true orders, and hope that they can later generate cash to pay cancellation reimbursements. Or, client fulfillment failures can cause an honest, effective bureau serious financial damage.

For example, a credit card client engaged a bureau to perform a project with a profit incentive back-end cancellation reimbursement fee structure. However, client order fulfillment was delayed by 30 days, an unusually long period. Consequently, many customers either forgot they ordered the product, or were angered by the delay, and the order rejection rate increased drastically. The service bureau paid over $500,000 in back-end cancellation credits.

Inquiries and Complaints. Service bureaus usually have different rate structures for inquiries and complaints than for sales (inbound or outbound) calls. Although inquiries often take longer than sales calls, bureaus often price inquiries lower than sales calls. Complaints, which are also longer than sales calls, are often priced higher than sales calls.

Front-End Charges. Each service bureau may have unique policies and prices for front-end efforts to prepare projects for the call process. Potential bureau clients should evaluate front-end project fees for services such as:

* *Computer programming.*

* *Computer data input.*

* *Script set-up.*

*   *Administrative (clerical, secretarial).*

*   *Other charges not included in the call-rate structure (inbound or outbound).*

In addition to these possible front-end charges, clients should evaluate possible back-end project charges, to develop a total cost/call analysis.

For example, a communications firm accepted a service bureau contract with open-ended charges for project computer programming and administrative set-up efforts. First-year set-up charges for this project were $15,000, on a $50,000 project (front-end costs not justified by project scope).

Back-End Charges. Several possible back-end project charges, in addition to call-rates, are:

*   *Call disposition (back-end data) data transmission charges (FAX, TWX, Telex, additional file copies).*

*   *Magnetic tape charges for call disposition records sent via computer tape media.*

*   *Administrative functions (clerical, secretarial).*

Since all service bureaus vary their total call-cost structures, potential clients must include all charges related to a specific project to develop an accurate cost/order analysis.

For example, after a major project began, an insurance company discovered that order transmission, TWX, FAX, and secretarial charges increased projected project call-costs by 25% (a significant increase).

CALL QUALITY CRITICAL

Although call-rates are an important part of this analysis, call quality, verified through references and call monitoring, is equally important, since low call-rates may produce poor sales volume or quality.

(Note: Determine how the service bureau you select defines bureau bills to the call process, and verify your bills monthly, at a minimum.)

SERVICE BUREAU CUSTOMER SERVICE FEATURES

Direct response projects must quickly adjust to market conditions to maximize profit or service benefits. Clients who include telemarketing techniques in their projects must react immediately to market response, or:

*   *High inbound call volumes can overload an under-staffed center.*

*   *Outbound calls can waste valuable list names with ineffective scripts.*

Consequently, telemarketing project "tuning" requires fast, accurate project coordination, which bureau customer service representatives (CSR's) can provide when they help clients to:

* *Modify projects.*

* *Develop and modify scripts.*

* *Analyze offers.*

* *Analyze complaints.*

Modify Projects. Service bureau CSR's should provide daily project updates to clients:

* *Market script response.*

* *Sales statistics.*

* *Media analysis.*

Only the service bureau can provide this information, which defines the market response (feedback) required to enhance project success.

Once bureau clients make project "tuning" decisions, based upon market feedback, CSR's must quickly and accurately implement:

* *Script changes.*

* *TSR retraining.*

* *Temporary project interrupts (allow time for corrective action, yet restart with minimal disruption).*

These modifications, which allow the overall project to adjust to market response, are critical to maximize project profit or service benefits.

Develop and Modify Scripts. Script size directly affects the variables that control client sales volume:

* *Calls/hour.*

* *Contacts/hour.*

* *Sales/hour.*

Consequently, optimum script length and content, are needed to maximize project success.

Inbound scripts are generally brief, to maximize call-throughput/hour, since these calls usually peak immediately after advertisements occur (script length is the primary variable). Outbound scripts, which are pleasant, persuasive, and concise, must initiate customer action (script content is the primary variable).

Since clients often ask service bureaus to help develop project scripts, bureau CSR's should understand how to:

* *Write initial scripts for pilot projects.*

* *Test and modify the initial script to improve performance.*

* *Design scripts to process any customer variation of the original offer.*

CSR's must explain bureau script set-up variables to clients (how scripts function in the bureau computer system) to ensure that clients do not develop technically infeasible scripts. In addition, based upon customer contract, CSR's should recommend script adjustments to increase call success.

For example, a related newscast may negatively affect market response to a product offer, and skew sales statistics. CSR's should immediately inform the client of this issue's impact, and recommend script changes to minimize the newscast's effect.

Clients should share previous script efforts (and results) from either internal or other bureau centers with a new service bureau to minimize script "learning-curve." Since telemarketing is a highly dynamic sales technique, any information which assists a bureau to develop the optimal project script can significantly increase overall project success.

Analyze Offers. Since telemarketing service bureaus perform client calls which create customer contact, bureau CSR's can help clients to understand what's happening in their sales environment and should suggest offer modifications to:

* *Increase call up-sells.*

* *Increase credit card orders (decrease bill-to and COD orders).*

* *Decrease cost/order.*

* *Increase overall revenue/call.*

Analyze Complaints. Service bureau clients will probably experience customer complaints or sales cancellations caused by:

* *Product offers which confuse (or deceive) customers.*

* *Inadequate product information (at the bureau).*

* *Product fulfillment failure.*

* *Ambiguous scripts.*

* *Over-ambitious TSR's.*

These can generate negative public relations, or higher costs/satisfied sale. In addition, unsatisfied customers represent lost future sales potential for more, or different, client products. Therefore, clients can use CSR insights to quickly "tune" (correct errors) projects to minimize both customer complaints and cancelled orders.

421

Professional service bureaus with comprehensive quality control procedures generally receive most customer complaints from product fulfillment failures. Although the customer has paid (credit card or check) for the client's product, the item has not been received. Usually, fulfillment failures cause complaint calls to peak suddenly. When this happens, bureau CSR's can assist clients to quickly identify and correct customer complaint sources, to minimize total project cost/sale, and maximize future sales to current customers.

INBOUND PROJECT MANAGEMENT

Inbound service bureau clients should understand five major project management concepts, to either assess, or manage, both inbound bureaus and projects:

* *Inbound customer service.*

* *Call busy ratios.*

* *Industry response norms.*

* *Project reports.*

* *Center review.*

These concepts will help bureau clients to obtain the resources required to implement highly dynamic projects, which will quickly and accurately adjust to market response (feedback).

Inbound Customer Service Functions. It is difficult to predict new project offer results, script effectiveness and call-volumes accurately.

Consequently, bureau customer service representatives (CSR's) must react quickly to:

* *"Tune" projects.*

* *Ensure adequate media separation and analysis (identify which advertisement initiated each inbound call).*

* *Coordinate project data transmission.*

Often, clients who use television advertisements heavily must purchase available TV spots on short notice. Bureau CSR's must have access to available telephone numbers, and ensure that new numbers are quickly assigned to correctly separate media response. Otherwise, the bureau will assign inbound calls to incorrect media sources, which will hinder project "tuning" and decrease potential project success.

MEDIA ANALYSIS

Often, inbound clients may not notify a bureau of all the television or radio stations involved in a project. The bureau may subsequently apply sales statistics to the wrong station, which creates false media analysis data.

Consequently, clients may cancel advertisements on a station that generates acceptable sales volume. Bureau CSR's must continually monitor client media analysis to detect such errors, and initiate corrective action.

Both the bureau and client should carefully document media sources (as applied to specific telephone numbers) during each project life-cycle, to minimize lost sales and project cost incurred through incorrect media analyses.

DATA TRANSMISSION

Bureau CSR's must ensure that clients receive project results in formats acceptable to client processing systems (manual or automated). Project results may include orders in several formats (magnetic tape, printouts, mail labels), and media analyses, sent several ways (FAX, TWX, Telex, courier).

Call-Busy Ratios. Inbound telemarketing service bureaus measure their center's call throughput with call-busy ratios (percent inbound calls that receive a busy condition). Busy ratios are critical to inbound center call-throughput, and directly affect client sales volume and average cost/sale.

The term "busy ratio" has several definitions:

* *All call-attempts received at the service bureau switch.*

* *All call-attempts received at the central office (CO) that serves the service bureau.*

* *All call-attempts intercepted before the service bureau CO (This information must be requested from AT&T).*

Inbound bureau clients should verify how their center defines and uses busy ratios to maximize center call-throughput.

Inbound center busy ratios strongly affect project success. Even the best offer won't meet client sales projections when processed through an inbound center which has a high busy ratio during the project's "window-of-opportunity" (immediately after project media spots).

Additionally, a high center busy ratio may cause clients to change a successful offer, or cancel a project that could perform well.

Although an inbound bureau may quote a 5% busy-ratio, this ratio may be based upon average daily call-traffic. Inbound clients should also review center busy ratios hourly, for 24 hours (all centers can provide this information) to avoid high call traffic periods (call-load spikes), which would artificially decrease overall project performance.

Clients can integrate busy-ratio tests into their pilot projects, and subsequent roll-outs. Run a pilot project (a test call batch) to estimate average project cost/call, and use this estimate to manage your project. If the project rolls out, and average cost/call increases:

* *Drastically for a specific hour(s).* Did your service bureau have a busy hour/ day, which caused traffic blockage (unacceptably high center busy-ratio)?

* *Drastically, for long periods.* Did a storm, building construction, or some physical disruption cause route blockage?

* *Did your media spot run full-time (or is this media source saturated)?*

A client who suspects unacceptable busy ratios for a specific period should test call into their bureau center during that time to determine the effective busy-ratio for their project. The client should immediately notify the bureau if call-throughput is unacceptable, and request that customer service recommend solutions.

Clients should carefully track inbound busy ratios, which are major project success/failure factors.

Industry Response Norms. Direct response projects, which focus on immediate prospect reaction, are particularly susceptible to product fulfillment delays, which may cause customers to cancel product orders (or pledges).

Figure 21-1
Sample Order Cancellation Rates

Days Delay	3	4	5	6	7	8	9	10	11	12
Sample Base Cancellation Rate	2%	2%	2%	2%	2%	2%	2%	2%	2%	2%
Additional Cancellation Rate	0%	2%	2%	4%	4%	8%	8%	16%	16%	32%
Total Cancellation Rate	2%	4%	4%	6%	6%	10%	10%	18%	18%	34%

Consequently, clients should review both internal and bureau communication functions, to ensure that product fulfillments:

* *Minimize product shipment delays.*

* *Maximize fulfillment accuracy.*

Inbound client order cancellations escalate exponentially (after the third day), for each day's fulfillment delay. Therefore, if normal project fulfillment delay is 3-4 days, bureau order response-time (to transmit orders to client) can significantly affect project profitability.

Quickly fulfilled inbound projects generally experience a 15%-40% cancellation rate. However, for every day's delay beyond three, inbound clients may expect to experience an additional order cancellation rate, which increases exponentially, and doubles every two days (See **Figure 21-1**).

Project cancellation rates can range from 0%-60% (based upon the offer and target market), however, assume that our sample project has a hypothetical 2% cancellation rate, if products are fulfilled within three days.

Since each cancelled order loses not only the sale (profit), but postage and handling expenses, average project cost/sale will increase significantly with a high cancellation rate. Both the service bureau and client must react very quickly to problems which might delay order fulfillment in order to ensure maximum project effectiveness. Therefore, the ability to correct project errors quickly and accurately is a key factor that clients should assess when they review bureau references.

PROJECT REPORTS

Each inbound client may have specific reports that they use to manage projects; however, three reports are most commonly used:

1. *Media Analysis.*

2. *Up-Sell Analysis.*

3. *Inquiry/Order Ratios.*

These reports track key projects results, to provide market response feedback necessary to "tune" and manage both front-end and back-end efforts.

Media Analysis. The *Media Analysis* identifies which advertising media (usually radio or television stations) generate the highest sales, based upon several formats:

*   *Hour by hour (sales per hour per station).*

*   *Station by station.*

*   *Print media by print media.*

*   *Credit card vs. COD.*

*   *Bill-to vs. credit card.*

*   *Total calls per station.*

*   *Total credit card orders per station, bill-to, etc.*

Clients should review the *Media Analysis* daily, to determine how to adjust their media campaigns to maximize project success.

Up-Sell Analysis. Since up-sells add additional time to each call, whenever service bureaus must increase call-throughput (volume), bureau TSR's tend to ignore up-sell opportunities, and accept only the basic sale. However, the bureau will probably still charge clients for the up-sell questions.

Consequently, if client up-sell analyses indicate mixed strong and weak up-sell periods, clients should request that bureau customer service representatives recommend corrective action.

Inquiry Order Ratios. The *Inquiry/Order Ratio* report identifies the total number of inquiries (or complaints) to orders, and may be used to identify project problems. High inquiry/order ratios imply either fulfillment failures, or unclear advertisements (advertisement may have offered Master Card and Visa payment options, but no COD). If the advertisements have successfully run previously, fulfillment failure is indicated.

Inbound Center Review. To assess an inbound center for potential projects, clients should look at several center characteristics:

* *TSR work environment.*

* *General center atmosphere.*

* *Adequate staff for total call volumes (based upon center call analysis system).*

* *Station loading (taking calls, waiting for calls).*

Additionally, clients should make their own test calls into a potential center, to evaluate the overall call process.

OUTBOUND PROJECT MANAGEMENT

Outbound service bureau clients should understand five major project management concepts, to either assess, or manage, both outbound bureaus and projects:

* *Outbound customer service.*

* *Service bureau management.*

* *Quality control techniques.*

* *Project reports.*

* *Center review.*

These concepts will help bureau clients to obtain the resources required to implement high-quality, flexible outbound projects, which will yield maximum sales results and conserve prospect lists (a critical project resource).

Outbound Customer Service Functions. Continual and daily client and bureau customer service representatives (CSR's) project contact is critical to create a responsive feedback mechanism between market response and project management (to "tune" the project). Fast, accurate outbound project feedback and adjustment are probably more critical than inbound project response, since outbound efforts are more:

* *Expensive (per hour).*

* *Complex (difficult to "tune").*

* *Dependent upon prospect lists--a sub-optimal project will waste valuable
  names and not create sales, or even worse, create unsatisfied customers.*

Outbound clients should remember that once a prospect is unsuccessfully called (poor script, or offer), that name (a valuable resource) is probably lost forever, and cannot be restored.

Consequently, both optimized feedback response and call quality control are critical project customer service functions.

Project feedback, based upon market response, is a major outbound customer service function. Based upon project feedback (prospect/customer script response) CSR's must:

* *Recommend offer and script changes.*

* *Retrain TSR's immediately to correct errors, or enhance successful scripts
  and/or offers.*

* *Help clients understand what other products or services they could offer to
  their customers.*

If this project "tuning" doesn't happen immediately, TSR's may lose sales, or sell an incorrect offer, which creates unsatisfied customers. The service bureau CSR's must have some effective way to manage prospect lists, to ensure that TSR call-queues remain full, otherwise:

* *Outbound call-flow will decrease, when TSR's run out of names.*

* *TSR's moved to other projects will experience a learning curve when they
  return to the original project, which will decrease their overall effectiveness.*

* *Client order-flow will be irregular, which may negatively affect project
  analysis.*

Generally, prospect lists are the limiting factor in successful outbound projects, thus list management is a key customer service function.

Service Bureau Management. Outbound clients should require bureau upper management to become directly involved with projects, and not function merely as center administrators. Service bureau management commitment is critical to outbound project success, since bureau management controls center resources, and direct response projects (with constant "tuning") have dynamic project requirements. Also, bureau upper management has the overall perspective, based upon many projects, to help clients develop and implement successful outbound projects more rapidly.

Outbound Project Reports. Several reports are generally used to track outbound project results:

* *Revenue/hour.*

* *Dials/hour.*

* *Total incorrect numbers/day.*

* *Total outbound hours/projects.*

* *Contacts/hour.*

* *Sales/hour.*

* *Sales conversion ratios.*

* *Sales/contact.*

These reports allow CSR's to "tune" projects for maximum success, otherwise, clients may use up prospect lists and miss project sales goals.

For example, a major service bureau implemented an evening outbound project to call Millionaire Club members, based upon a client list. Prospect contact was dramatically low, approximately one contact/25 calls (normal contact rate should be one contact/12 calls). Service bureau management reviewed both *Dials/Hour*, and *Contacts/Hour Reports*, and concluded that project dials were excessively high because TSR's were not able to reach prospects with client list telephone numbers. A review quickly revealed that the client's list contained prospect business (not residence) telephone numbers, and was useless for an evening project.

QUALITY CONTROL TECHNIQUES

Telemarketing service bureaus use four quality control techniques to ensure that their TSR's perform high-quality, outbound calls:

* *Monitor calls.*

* *Tape calls.*

> * *Verify sales on-line.*
>
> * *Recall sales.*

The appropriate mix of all four techniques, (implemented by either TSR supervisors, or quality control staff) maximizes the number of TSR's who correctly sell the proper offer to real customers.

> ***Monitor Calls.*** Bureaus monitor TSR calls for several reasons:
>
> * *To ensure that the TSR presents the correct offer.*
>
> * *To review overall TSR performance and suggest how TSR's may improve their sales technique.*
>
> * *To ensure that the overall sales presentation is pleasant, persuasive and consistent.*

Calls may be monitored by either TSR supervisors, or center quality control staff.

> ***Tape Calls.*** Bureaus may tape all TSR sales or conversions to verify that the sales actually occurred. Usually, the sale is taped only after the customer agrees to purchase the offer. The bureau should review all taped sales calls and recall all potentially false orders (based upon management experience).

> ***Verify Sales On-Line.*** TSR supervisors may come on each TSR's line, as they make a sale, to speak to the customer and verify that each sale did occur, and that the offer was correct.

> ***Recall Sales.*** Service bureaus may recall (sales only, not on survey calls) a percentage of customers who purchased a client offer the next day to verify the sale. Next day sales recalls will identify most project sales rejections (usually, outbound projects have a 6%-13% cancellation rate on total project sales). Sales call-backs also help bureau supervisors to identify which TSR's have a higher than average cancellation rate and take corrective action.

Initially, bureaus will usually recall 40%-60% of project sales, to verify that call, offer and script quality are acceptable. However, as the project evolves, recalls may be decreased to 20% of sales, to minimize cancelled orders that would otherwise remain sales ("buyer's remorse affect"). All four quality control techniques are necessary to create high-quality sales and satisfied customers.

OUTBOUND CENTER REVIEW

To review outbound centers for potential projects, clients should assess several center characteristics:

> * *Line load.*

* *Supervisory load.*

* *Overall center performance.*

Line Load. The characteristic of *line load* measures available outbound telephone lines/TSR, and directly affects overall project call-throughput. Low line/TSR ratios will reduce both prospect contacts/hour and project sales/hour, and since outbound project rates are hourly, overall project profitability will decrease. For most outbound projects, a 1:1 line/TSR line load ratio is optimal.

Supervisory Load. Our second characteristic, *supervisory load* measures available TSR supervisors/TSR, and directly affects overall project performance and call-quality, since supervisors perform quality control functions previously defined. Usually, a 1:15 supervisor/TSR ratio (or better) is acceptable for outbound projects.

However, difficult (complex) projects may require a 1:8 (or better) supervisor/TSR ratio to ensure acceptable performance and quality levels.

Overall Center Performance. Potential outbound service bureau clients should verify that the:

* *Center follows the procedures it has defined for performance and quality.*

* *Physical facilities are neat and clean.*

* *TSR's have scripts and rebuttals readily available for help in an easy-to-use format.*

* *TSR's project a good self-image (dress affects performance, even in telephone sales).*

* *TSR's have training procedures for their own sales skills and product knowledge.*

* *Bureau applies appropriate project incentive plans.*

These characteristics will help potential clients to identify centers to process successful, high-quality outbound projects.

INDUSTRY CONCERNS/PROBLEMS

According to *Telemarketing Intelligence '87*, a report from Schlenker Research Services, the service bureau industry is not without its problems.[1]

When executives at 64 of the leading service bureaus were asked to select the "most significant problem you are currently facing," various concerns were raised.

Consumer receptivity is a continual issue, affected by more frequent, as well as pre-recorded sales calls. Another concern is perceived industry image, which may largely explain the generally favorable reaction toward formal accreditation. And, of course, they were concerned about government legislation that would inhibit or restrict telephone sales calls.

However, the most critical problem, in the minds of telemarketing service bureau executives, concerns high turnover rates and, in turn, recruiting and hiring good people. Motivating TSR's, keeping up their spirits and enthusiasm, and ensuring their reliability also causes some concern.

FUTURE

Looking to the future, however, there is great optimism within the service bureau industry.[2] *Telemarketing Intelligence '87* reports that key executives at the leading service bureaus project:

* *Significant organizational growth.* Most respondents (83%) expect to add work stations within the year.

* *New locations.* Most respondents (66%) expect to start activities at new locations within the next three years.

* *Billings.* Typical increases in annual billings are 33%.

* *Purchase intentions.* Plans to purchase of computer terminals, hardware and software are very encouraging--especially strong intentions to purchase computer terminals within the next 12 months (36% say they definitely expect to purchase).

* *Industry growth.* The service bureau industry is in a dynamic and growing phase--1988 was excellent and a high rate of growth is expected again this year.

----

[1]Barry Schlenker, *Telemarketing Intelligence '87*, Service Bureau Study, Schlenker Research Services, 1987, pp. 7, 9, 10.
[2]*Ibid.,* pp. 6, 8, 10.

CHAPTER 22

Catalog Telemarketing

Richard L. Bencin

For some unknown reason, most catalog marketers, and writers on the subject, give very little attention to telemarketing. Some effort or space is devoted to *telecommunications*, such as automatic call distributors (ACD's), WATS lines, monitoring and quality control systems, that sort of thing. But virtually nothing is done with the true telephone marketing and sales side of catalog merchandising.

It seems that most of the catalogers are far more interested in improving response, fulfillment and back-end collections than anything else. They spend something like 95% of their effort in these and related areas. Little of their thought or effort goes to telemarketing.

As further evidence of the general disdain for telemarketing among catalog marketers, few of them have attempted to use outside professional telemarketing consulting services. Apparently, most catalog houses feel that telemarketing is merely an order-taking function not requiring any real expertise.

Because of this attitude, many catalog marketers relegate the development of their telemarketing function to inexperienced personnel (little wonder they call their telephone sales reps "operators"). They simply forget about that segment of their business. After hours, some don't even bother with human "operators," relegating their evening and night incoming orders to telephone computers. Are these computers able to answer simple questions? Substitute out-of-stock items? Cross sell? Up sell?

Of course *not*. Respected catalog houses, especially the major ones, should know better. By degrading the telemarketing sales position to a minimum wage order taker, many of the supposedly *avant garde* catalog merchandisers make the same mistakes as the "storekeepers" with their low-paid, poorly trained, nonmotivated sales clerks.

Shouldn't the personnel handling the incoming telephone catalog operation be true telephone sales representatives? And for business-to-business catalog marketers, especially with expensive and sophisticated merchandise, professional outbound telemarketing is a must.

BUSINESS-TO-BUSINESS CATALOG TELEMARKETING

A weak case might be made that consumer catalog sales operations can do without sophisticated telemarketing. When it comes to business-to-business catalog marketing, there's no case. Consider some of the major differences. Business-to-business marketing:

* *Sells more sophisticated and expensive products, services, or systems.*

* *Requires better quality control of telephone selling.*

432

* *Demands more qualified sales personnel, often with considerable technical education.*

* *Requires more training.*

* *Often requires coordination of inbound and outbound marketing efforts.*

* *Needs more sophisticated selling.*

* *Representatives usually get higher pay, incentives, and status.*

These differences apply even more directly to business-to-business telemarketing. A fine example of this was the Xerox Corporation's success with selling office copiers from a mini-direct response catalog in 1981. In 1982, *Xerox World* was able to announce proudly that 8,000 office copiers were sold through mail order/telemarketing within the first year of the program. Here's how the telephone was used:

> *"The task is then to convert as many of these [mini-catalog] respondees to customers as possible. A certain proportion are converted by follow-up telephone contact. That represents thousands of machines sold--some 8,000 last year--to people who've never even looked you in the eye."*

These fine telemarketing sales reps were so professionally dedicated and motivated to their jobs that they would take a day from their own weekend to attend telemarketing training--without pay.

The Xerox telephone sales reps were an enthusiastic group. With the author, they reviewed and discussed getting through customer screens (secretaries), handling sales objections and even how to turn prospect objections into positive sales appeals to help close the orders.

And close they did.

It is easier, less time-consuming and less expensive to increase the telephone sales closure and size of order rates by 25%-50% than it is to increase the initial direct response by that much. Not that the other catalog elements are less important. It's just that telemarketing is *just as important as any other element.*

MISAPPREHENSIONS ABOUT TELEMARKETING

The telemarketing effort (or lack of it) is often one of the weaker links in the chain of catalog marketing.

Telephone response, unfortunately, has been deemed an order-taking function by many catalogers. Tremendous selling opportunities to increase conversion rates, cross-sells (sell related items), up-sells (sell more profitable items), or provide out-of-stock replacements are often overlooked. Also, potential profit-building outbound telemarketing efforts are totally disregarded by many catalog operations.

The key to unlocking this problem is turning the emphasis of senior catalog management more toward the goal of increasing the size of the catalog order instead of thinking solely in terms of response rates. Nowhere is the prejudice toward "response" more evident than in the selection and training of catalog telemarketing managers.

Catalog telemarketing managers are often recruited from customer service or administrative backgrounds. Often, these managers have no prior sales or marketing experience whatsoever.

Of particular concern are the huge corporations entering into significant catalog marketing operations. They often use internal personnel from completely unrelated areas. It seems that many companies still believe "a good manager is a good manager, no matter where you place that person."

Well, that's an old axiom--proven in many areas. But it fails when applying to a sophisticated direct marketing area such as catalog marketing, especially if training or assistance is not provided.

Consultants and specialists often receive frantic calls from newly assigned catalog telemarketing managers asking for help. The basic requests are for information to read or seminars to attend about catalog telemarketing.

Clearly, many senior catalog managers have not even considered training their catalog telemarketing managers. No wonder we often see the catalog telemarketing centers as merely order-taking entities. The expertise to develop a high-powered selling unit is totally lacking.

If we take the new (or at least *additional*) perspective of increasing order size, the following implications apply to the telemarketing operation:

* *Consider the telemarketing operation as a selling entity rather than just an order-taking facility.*

* *Hire the best possible catalog telemarketing manager to manage the telemarketing center. If one is not available, get outside consulting assistance to develop the telemarketing program and to train the telemarketing catalog operations management.*

* *Periodically review the development of the catalog telemarketing center (look for computer-assisted programs, sales training development, quality control, etc.)*

* *Evaluate rates of inquiry conversions to sales, growth of size of orders, cross-sells, and up-sells.*

In other words, spend the appropriate time and effort to increase individual order profitability. Response rate, plus the size of the order, *combine* to spell success.

INSTANT CATALOG TELEMARKETING ANALYSIS

Catalog executives can take an "instant catalog telemarketing analysis" by making a quick physical review of their facilities and by asking a few pertinent questions of the telemarketing management.

The first step is the "eyeball review." This involves simply walking through the telemarketing operations area looking for the following:

* *Minimum size of the telemarketing cubicles at 5' X 5' (no divided counter tops or minuscule stalls).*

CATALOG TELEMARKETING

* *Minimum of 6' between back-to-back telemarketers.*

* *Acoustical material on the floor (carpets), cubicle dividers, walls (carpets or acoustical tiles) and ceiling (noise reduction material).*

* *Temperature stabilized at 68 to 70 degrees Fahrenheit, with no drafts, hot or cold spots, or other discomforts and adequate humidity.*

* *Conference and training facility available.*

* *Telemarketing supervisor's and manager's offices equipped with complete station monitoring equipment, both through the telephones and listen-only external speakers. All telemarketing stations should be on the same system.*

Some readers may be wondering how important these "nit-picking" considerations really are, and it's not impertinent, given all the larger problems of sales and direct marketing. But the fact is, they're *critical.* If the telemarketing facilities are too crowded, hot and noisy, both telemarketers and customers will perceive the telephone operation as a "boiler room." Also, without complete station monitoring equipment, supervisors and managers will not be able to control, direct, and properly supervise the quality of the operation.

Once the "eyeball review" is completed and changes or improvements are in progress, it's time to ask the manager and supervisors the following questions:

* *How often are individual telemarketer reviews given regarding the calls heard through the monitoring equipment? (Weekly should be minimum.)*

* *How often are telephone sales training sessions conducted, e.g., product benefits, cross-selling, up-selling, out-of-stock replacements, etc.? (Again, weekly training is minimum.)*

* *Are outbound telephone calls made to regular customers? How often?*

* *What outbound telephone effort is being made to follow-up on initial inquiries where no immediate sale is made?*

* *Are scripts being used? How often are alternate scripts being tested to compare against the control script(s)?*

* *What analysis has been made to review potential CRT-driven scripts? Cross-selling? Up-selling? Out-of-stock replacements? Objection handling? Questions/responses?*

* *Has "rifle cataloging" been tested against mass catalog mailings? (Outbound phone calls to qualify; catalogs sent only to receptive prospects; outbound calls to close.)*

435

* *What back-end analysis of the telemarketing effort has been made? (Closure rates by SIC/size, size of orders by SIC/size, script comparisons, rifle vs. mass catalog marketing, part-time vs. full-time telemarketers, commissioned vs. hourly, etc.)*

Unfortunately, the replies to these questions by most telemarketing managers and supervisors in catalog operations will often be "never," "seldom," "haven't considered it," or a blank stare.

Professional catalog telemarketing can go a long way to precluding the problem of catalog glut. Catalog sales management must understand a telemarketing operation can make or break their business.

ORDER-TAKING VS. ORDER "MANAGEMENT"

We've already discussed the fact that many catalog marketers do not attempt to cross-sell or up-sell their catalog merchandise. This doesn't mean, however, that the "order-taking" mentality must inevitably continue.

In fact, catalog CEO's or appropriate division heads should consult with their directors of telemarketing to determine the current progress in developing the "incremental catalog sale."

Cross-Selling. First, a definition of cross-selling is necessary. Simply, the term refers to the attempt by a catalog telephone sales rep to sell additional related items along with items requested by a catalog customer. The cross-selling could be as a result of either an inbound or outbound telephone call.

Examples of this would be indices for notebooks, supplies for copiers, a stand for a typewriter, etc. Calling up the associative, companion items on a computer's CRT screen obviously is quite helpful, especially if the product line is broad.

Also, the proper selling presentation can be programmed into the computer. This eliminates omissions and nonrelated product selling attempts, and assures correct selling dialog.

Up-Selling. This means the attempt to sell a more appropriate, a more feature or benefit-laden, or more expensive product than the one originally requested by the customer. Also, up-selling can be simply increasing the *quantity* of the order

Care must be given to recommending the best product for the requirement of the purchaser. Up-selling can be implemented best if questions are raised to better understand the needs of the customer. Appropriate features and benefits are then reviewed to acquaint the customer with the additional value of the upgraded product.

Suggestion of a more sophisticated electronic typewriter with greater memory, to handle more extensive revisions, would be one example of an up-sell. Again, better satisfying the customer's needs helps to make the up-sell the practical extension of improved customer service and profitability.

The computerized CRT, obviously, helps with prompting the appropriate questions during the up-sell attempt. Product complexities and depth of the total product line are major determining factors regarding the need to computerize this particular selling opportunity.

436

Out-of-Stock Replacement Items. One of the greatest advantages of taking a live telephone catalog order is the capability to conduct a two-way communication exchange. For example, orders taken through the mails sometimes can't be fulfilled because of out-of-stock conditions. And, by the time a follow-up letter or telephone call is placed, it may be too late to substitute for the item.

Unfortunately, most catalog marketers simply mail an "out-of-stock" notification form, losing orders and revenues as a result.

Certainly, if out-of-stock situations are apparent while a catalog telephone sales rep and a customer are talking over the phone, closely related replacement items should be suggested and sold by the telephone sales rep. Again, an on-line computer relating immediate stock availability is of great help in determining the deliverability of the merchandise ordered.

Also, CRT prompts to help guide the telephone sales reps to the appropriate replacement item(s) are very helpful.

Managing the Order. Telephone response, unfortunately, has been deemed an *order-taking function* by many catalogers. Tremendous *selling opportunities* to increase conversion rates, cross-sells, or provide out-of-stock replacements are often overlooked.

Cross-selling, up-selling and selling replacement items in out-of-stock situations help significantly to increase the size of the catalog order. Astute catalog telephone selling techniques can help to enhance order size up to 50%. Not a bad return for simply converting "order-taking operations" to "selling catalog merchandise centers."

But it all takes the right investment and commitment--in people and facilities. Response rates *plus* the size of the orders, all managed by the right people, are the "names of the game."

ARE 800 NUMBERS REALLY NECESSARY?

There are some catalog "experts" who claim, despite their experience in consumer catalog operations, that it's not necessary to provide a toll-free number for response when marketing directly to businesses. Their logic is based on the assumption that business people really don't care if they have to make a business toll call. The cost, presumably, is considered inconsequential.

Okay. That's one way to look at the issue. There remain a few questions, however:

* *Aren't small and medium-sized businesses concerned about telephone costs? (And, remember, more than 90% of all businesses fall into this category.)*

* *How unconcerned about costs are the nearly one million new businesses that come on-line every year--many of them very small, often with staffs of one or two people?*

* *And what about the millions of professionals--doctors, lawyers, sales reps, etc., who have second offices in their homes where they can't use the "company" lines?*

The business executive's lack of interest in telephone costs is a myth. The overwhelming majority of both consumer and business-to-business catalog marketers, knowing this, use 800 numbers. In fact, there is significant evidence that supports the following statements about 800 service:

* *It increases the number of orders (generally a 15%-25% increase).*

* *It increases the size of orders (generally a 25%-40% increase).*

* *It provides a greater opportunity for both cross-selling and up-selling.*

* *It establishes a competitive advantage by pulling from catalogers who don't provide 800 number service.*

* *It provides a quicker reaction time to gauge the response to various tests, layouts, prices, premiums, etc. Also, it provides a more responsive reaction to overages and shortages.*

* *It links the 800 number's ability to increase orders with the frequency with which it is printed within catalogs.*

And these are just the advantages of *inbound* 800 service. Given that the more sophisticated, higher-priced business merchandise doesn't always sell upon the initial inbound telephone call, consider the advantages of *outbound* WATS!

BUSINESS-TO-BUSINESS CATALOG MARKETING--RIFLE METHOD

Most business-to-business catalogers use conventional methods of catalog distribution. For example, 100,000 catalogs are mailed to a list and the hope is that 2%-3% will respond.

That's 2,000 to 3,000 responses, and a lot of wasted paper.

As the responses come in, order-takers cover the phones and go through the mechanics of accepting the order. They don't do much selling for the most part. Under these conditions, the telephone is merely the conduit for the response. The catalog mailing was the trigger, and a very expensive one at that.

Some savvy business-to-business catalog marketers are exchanging their shotguns for high-powered rifles, however. And they're succeeding.

Instead of mass mailing their catalogs, marketers are using telemarketing to identify the precise decision-maker, qualify, presell the catalog mailed and subsequently, to close the catalog sale by virtue of a follow-up outbound telephone call. Instead of, perhaps, a 2% response rate on millions of catalogs, these esoteric catalog marketers are experiencing close ratios of 20%-30% of a much smaller mailed base.

Procedurally, here is how it works:

1) *Telephone calls are made to each prospect listing to determine the exact name and title of each company's decision-maker.*

2) *An introductory one-to-two page letter is then sent to each of the identified buyers--within a #10 envelope, typed directly (without labels) and with first-class postage stamps. These mailers, especially if stamped confidential and without outside advertising on the envelope, will get through to the buyer.*

3) *A telephone call by a trained telephone sales rep (not an order-taker) is then made to the prospect to discuss the benefits of doing business with the vendor company (via catalog and telephone).*

4) *If the prospect agrees to review the catalog and receive a second telephone call to discuss both the catalog and telephone only specials, the catalog is mailed.*

5) *After the catalog mailing, a telephone call is made to the expectant potential buyer and a sale is attempted and often consummated.*

6) *Through SIC/size and ZIP code analysis, the most responsive list segments are constantly re-evaluated so that true "electronic top-down selling" can take place--catalog marketing directed by telemarketing and computers can be very scientifically target oriented.*

Many business-to-business marketers using this rifle approach now totally reject the shotgun approach, considering it too expensive and too inefficient. That might be too strong a position, however. The astute business-to-business cataloger should be testing both methods. Perhaps both can work in different market niches, or, it may be that a complete reversal of catalog market strategy is in order.

However, effective testing with sophisticated telemarketing and back-end, test cell computer analysis are mandatory for a qualified review of the rifle type of catalog marketing. It must be given a fair opportunity to work.

It may be that once properly evaluated, the rifle approach to catalog merchandising will end up being an extremely effective method of getting around or through the "catalog glut."

COMPUTERIZING CATALOG TELEMARKETING

There are still quite a few manual telemarketing operations around. In a recent survey of telemarketing centers, 53.6% were discovered to be completely manual. Partially automated centers comprise another 42%, while completely automated centers (i.e., paperless) are a minority of 4.4%.

These statistics represent an unfortunate state of affairs. Manual catalog telemarketing centers are at a decided disadvantage compared to their fully computerized counterparts. Consider just a few of the general problems manual operations face:

* *Manual searches and posting.*

* *No easy access to account history and inventory.*

439

* *Lower productivity.*

* *Difficult management.*

* *Lower revenue per call.*

* *Less accuracy.*

* *Slower fulfillment.*

* *Greater customer dissatisfaction.*

Even if you have already implemented computerized telemarketing centers, the level of sophistication is probably nowhere near as high as it could be. Software design and implementation within automated catalog telemarketing centers can become quite sophisticated. Program enhancements should, therefore, constantly be evaluated.

If computer hardware is available, the following should be placed in memory and programmed to be available:

* *All catalog items (including descriptions, variations, benefits, etc.).*

* *Customer histories (including special ordering instructions and credit history).*

* *Order format sequence (with checks and balances).*

* *Telemarketing responses fully prompted (with appropriate branching with respect to the customer's replies).*

* *Edit programs (ZIP codes to be checked automatically against city/state, check digits for charge cards, item number/description cross check, etc.).*

* *Objections and questions with appropriate responses.*

* *Substitution, cross-sell, up-sell and promotional items, all cross-referenced from items requested by the customer.*

* *Fulfillment procedures.*

It's probably readily obvious that we are considering here automation beyond the simple loading of the catalog, forms fill-in, and fulfillment paperwork. This leverage of the computer's power for improved catalog telemarketing provides many benefits, which are worth examining in detail.

Error Reduction. Computerized catalog telemarketing helps the telephone sales representative to focus on selling. Many of the burdensome, redundant procedures and manual searching/processing can be computer programmed so that the customer can receive the greatest attention. If they're not automated, they distract from the selling effort.

Catalog items and customer histories can be accessed quickly with less error and time involvement. Computer edit programs can automatically assist with ZIP and city/state cross checks, check digit routines for charge cards, item number and description cross checks and others.

All mathematical calculations can be done automatically. This includes multiplication of unit prices, subtotals, sales taxes and totals.

Increased Productivity. Because of error reduction programs, less search time through manual records and catalogs, sequenced order handling, branched scripting, automated prompts and less paperwork between calls, call productivity as well as quality should improve.

For the outbound follow-ups on original catalog inquiries, follow-up dates and times, reasons for the call back, etc., can be further programmed for even greater productivity performance improvement. Even the dialing of the calls can be completely automated.

Increases in completed calls per hour of 60% to 300%, after switching from a manual environment to a fully automated one, are not uncommon.

Again, an existing automated telemarketing catalog center can also be improved for both a better quality and quantity performance. An ongoing systems design with telemarketing savvy can become a great catalog center asset.

Increased Sales. Branched scripting, or prompting, can assist greatly in providing the telephone sales rep with the most complete and convincing sales order presentation. Even the anticipated questions or objections can be met head on with positive responses that can help to increase the size of the order and to close the sale itself.

For each series of catalog items inquired about, there are natural cross-sells, up-sells and out-of-stock replacements. All of these can be used via computer prompting to help the catalog telephone sales rep.

It should be clear by now that we are *selling* by phone, and not merely taking orders from inquirers. Sophisticated systems design and computer programming is certainly one way to help the cataloger to become a much better marketer.

Faster Fulfillment. In a manual catalog telemarketing operation, paperwork must process through order entry *before* order fulfillment. And this situation is made even worse if the order-taking center is at a significant mailing distance from order entry--perhaps at least a three-day delay before merchandise is packed and shipped.

With a computerized catalog operation, however, once the order is captured, it is transmitted directly to the computer database. Order transmittal is, therefore, electronic, and computer print-outs can help to move merchandise out the same or the next day.

Documentation should include mailing labels, stock picking instructions, packing lists and, of course, the actual customer invoices. In addition, sales letters, proposals or contracts for larger, more expensive merchandise can be created virtually on-line and the sales cycle shortened. The result is better customer service, along with more responsive selling and quicker cash flow.

ENCYCLOPEDIA OF TELEMARKETING

Easier Management. An automated catalog telemarketing center is much easier to manage than a manual one. It provides for better analysis, direction, and control.

The number of completed calls per hour, average talk time, revenue per sale and other data can be tracked as closely as hourly and daily. Supervisors can become quite responsive with this kind of quick feedback.

In effect, automation provides instant analysis and correction.

Also, compensation programs, sales contests and "instant motivators" can be implemented easier, faster and better. Easier-to-manage computerized telemarketing programs definitely help to improve the telephone sales rep's quality and quantity of sales orders.

In summary, because of the enormous potential of computerized telemarketing within a catalog environment, it behooves all catalogers to review its total merits. It appears that electronic catalog selling helps to receive orders in the most efficient, complete, and saleable way.

Response is not the only game to play. There is also the matter of how one handles the response once it's in--a lesson many still need to learn.

This Chapter has been reprinted with permission, from *Strategic Telemarketing*, by Richard L. Bencin, ISBN 0-915601-02-8, c 1987, available direct from Cresheim Publications, P.O. Box 27785, Philadelphia, PA 19118, 1/800-792-6732.

442

CHAPTER 23

Customer Service Telemarketing

Warren Blanding
Chairman of the Board
Marketing Publications, Inc.
Silver Spring, Maryland

Whether they sell by phone or in person, whether in corporate purchasing offices, homes, or across a retail counter, professional salespeople know instinctively that *telemarketing equals customer service.*

Professional selling is making it easy for potential customers to reach the buying decision, justify it and be comfortable with it. The essence of customer service is to meet the customer's expectations in the actual delivery of the service or product, and make it a positive experience to the extent that customers will continue to buy from that particular source.

MANAGEMENT'S STAKE IN GOOD CUSTOMER SERVICE

"You can't do business from an empty wagon," the saying goes. And no selling effort is better than the customer service plan that supports it. If customers can't get the goods or services they've contracted to buy, or if they are poorly treated in the process, they won't remain customers. Thus an effective customer service system has to provide a good logistical support, but it also has to have good people and policies that customers perceive as fair.

This is simple common sense. But it's only the tip of the iceberg. For telemarketing management in particular, the damage done by poor customer service goes far beyond lost sales and little repeat business. Good salespeople won't continue to work in an environment where their efforts are not supported by customer service of equal quality.

THE BIG PICTURE

Sales and customer service are subsystems of the firm's overall marketing system. Each affects the other, and both affect the whole. The notion that customer service is a reactive rather than interactive or proactive function has long since been discarded in marketing-oriented companies.

In recent years, it's been demonstrated that customer service quality directly affects the "intent to re-buy" and, thus, corporate growth, profits, and market share.

443

Customer service has four main impacts on an organization's marketing results:

1.   *Cost of servicing the order which, in turn, affects profit margins.*

2.   *The customer's willingness to accept the product or service based on availability, order cycle, time, etc.*

3.   *Future purchases by these same customers based on their degree of satisfaction with the way the transaction was handled and their perception of the vendor as somebody they care to do business with. There are two separate elements to be measured here:*

     a.   *Account retention.*
     b.   *Account growth.*

4.   *Reduction in future selling costs, here again with two dimensions:*

     a.   *Easier cross-selling /order enhancement with established customers.*
     b.   *Direct order placement, bypassing salespersons as established customers order directly from customer service.*

In an ideal world, a customer makes the buying decision and then receives the product or service in the most convenient way, when and where wanted, finds that it meets expectations and is satisfied with the associated sales administration, i.e., billing, instructions, warranty service, handling of returns, exchanges and refunds, etc.

In the real world, these results occur only to the extent that sales and customer service are truly integrated as a marketing system. This requires coordination of the actual telemarketing project with the development of strategic customer service procedures, standards, and measurements.

PROVIDING VALUABLE FEEDBACK

Another important contribution by customer service to telemarketing is immediate feedback on problems in product availability, customer dissatisfaction, delivery, etc., that may suggest rescripting, promotion of different products, or other changes in the telemarketing campaign.

Since telemarketing presentations can be changed quite readily, and since uniformity is easily assured--unlike field sales, where control and uniformity of presentations are difficult to maintain--this feedback from customer service operations can help minimize potential losses as well as maximize profitability of the telemarketing operation.

THE TELEMARKETING/CUSTOMER SERVICE PLAN

The immediate goal of telemarketing is to generate the highest volume of sales at the lowest selling cost. Performance can be readily tracked.

Customer service has as its goals fulfilling orders and handling inquiries, complaints, paperwork, returns, and exchanges, etc., at levels that are cost-effective for the company and satisfactory to its customers to the point where they will remain customers and, over time, increase their purchases either in actual volume or by moving up to the top of the line.

Unfortunately, many companies concentrate on sales goals, but pay little or no attention to the business of setting strategic, cost-effective customer service standards to support those sales and build repeat business.

THE "RIGHT" STANDARDS

When they have customer service standards, most companies will acknowledge privately that their standards reflect what they *can* do rather than what they *should* do. This is another way of saying that few companies actually research customer needs and preferences on customer service features, but assume that if they don't hear too many squawks from customers their present levels must be satisfactory.

This is of course a false reading. Customers who find service adequate, but not exceptional, are easily wooed away by competitors offering something better. Customers who are dissatisfied with levels of service will seldom voice their dissatisfaction, but will simply seek another source. Actual complaints initiated by customers tend to relate to a specific incident or problem rather than overall service levels.

This lack of research into customer service preferences is all the more damaging because it's tantamount to ignoring the value of the right level of customer service as a marketing strategy for retaining and cultivating customers.

STANDARDS ARE A MANAGEMENT RESPONSIBILITY

Although customer service standards are often set by customer service or sales managers based on their best judgment of what is affordable and what is needed competitively, standards are in fact a top management responsibility. The amount of money that is spent on customer service is an investment not at all different from the firm's investment in advertising, merchandising and other marketing efforts. There are cases, for example, where beefing up customer service has proven more cost-effective in increasing market share than spending a comparable amount for advertising.

Given this, management has to be the ultimate decider of what customer service standards should be and, therefore, how much money the firm will spend to achieve them. What's more, since customer service standards have to be supported by various departments within the company, it's usually necessary to have a top management mandate to that effect.

THE THREE STEPS IN SETTING STANDARDS

The most common standards for customer service concern product availability and order cycle time.

445

And they're interconnected: a "ship-same-day" standard, for example, cannot be met if products are not in stock. So there must also be a standard for product availability: 90%, 95% or whatever, according to the degree to which management wishes to meet the ship-same-day standard.

There are many other standards, of course: standards for how quickly the telephone is answered, how long customers have to wait in queue to be serviced, the percentage of inquiries to be handled on-line, how quickly complaints, refunds and exchanges are to be handled. As well as standards for line item fill, there will be standards for complete order fill, dollar fill, substitutions achieved, orders accepted as filled, etc.

It should be noted that these are mainly quality or strategic standards, not standards of output like the number of orders, keystrokes or transactions per hour, calls per day, etc., which are engineered standards developed by industrial engineering methods.

Step 1: Setting Strategic or Quality Standards.

Thus, the first step in setting standards, in our example, would be a management decision that a ship-same-day policy would have actual strategic value for the firm. This would be done via an assessment--research plus such management sciences as simulation-- of the benefits of such a policy in terms of increased sales volume and market share.

Step 2: Feasibility and Engineering Standards.

Feasibility such as a ship-same-day standard would need to be determined. Can the company meet it under present conditions? For example, does it have the systems, procedures and manpower to turn orders around and actually ship them within a single day? Equally important, does the company maintain sufficiently high levels of inventory to actually fill such orders?

If the answer to these questions is "no" (as it often is), then the next question is: *"What will it cost us to upgrade the system and the inventory to the point where we can realistically meet our strategic ship-same-day standard?"* Here, again, careful cost analysis and management science come into play to cost out an operating plan supported by the necessary levels of inventory.

Of course it follows that management has to approve the commitment of resources envisioned in this second step of setting standards. And, as might be expected, it sometimes finds the price steeper than it's willing to pay.

As an example, consider a company which currently ships 90% of its orders complete and on time might wish to increase this to 100%. It's quite easy to project costs for this improvement. In most cases, it would actually require doubling the inventory--a staggering 100% increase in cost for a 10% improvement in service.

So, management may decide to settle for a somewhat lesser level of service using calculations reflected in **Figure 23-1**. In short, management may decide to practice the art of the possible. It's extremely important that these exercises be performed, because a substantial financial commitment may be required-- and management must support it.

Step 2 is completed by developing the engineered standards, whereby the required levels of performance can be maintained within the cost constraints that have been decided on. For example, it may be determined that to ship 955 of orders on the same day, a standard of 80 orders per day, per customer service rep may be required, with corresponding standards for picks per hour in the warehouse, packs per hour in the shipping department, etc.

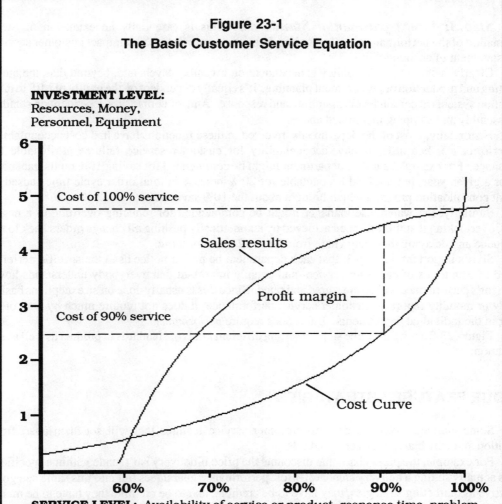

Figure 23-1
The Basic Customer Service Equation

INVESTMENT LEVEL:
Resources, Money,
Personnel, Equipment

Cost of 100% service

Sales results

Profit margin

Cost of 90% service

Cost Curve

60%   70%   80%   90%   100%

SERVICE LEVEL: Availability of service or product, response time, problem resolution, technical or application advice, upselling, cross-selling, etc.

Traditional cost curve relates required investment level to desired service level. Note that the cost curve rises sharply after 90% service level has been reached, and that a 10% increase in service will often double the cost of rendering that service, and equal or exceed the revenue that the improved service brings. There are, of course, procedural changes that can improve service without adding cost; many of these involve reducing the number of signoffs required on adjustments, eliminating acknowledgements and similar paperwork. In general, however, the cost of rendering "100% service" is justified only when the market is willing to pay the extra cost, as in the case of life-saving pharmaceuticals, critical parts for heavy machinery and similar items. Federal Express and similar premium transportation services are also an excellent example of situations where customers are willing to pay premium prices for high levels of service.

Step 3: Interdepartmental Standards. This is essentially an extension of Step 2--a determination of the performance levels required from all departments which impact customer service, and a clear statement of accountability.

Clearly, a ship-same-day policy is dependent on inventory levels and, beyond that, the quality of forecasting and production or procurement planning. It's equally dependent on the ability of MIS to maintain information systems at certain levels of uptime and response. And, of course, it's dependent on standards of order assembly and shipping mentioned above.

Historically, most of the departments involved in these functions have had cost accountability for their performance, but little, if any, accountability for customer service failures attributable to that performance. For example, a traffic department might be commended for saving 10% on its transportation costs for a given year, but not held accountable for 20% increase in total order cycle time caused by the shipment consolidation program which brought about the 10% savings.

Similarly, the warehouse manager might be commended for reducing overtime to a negligible amount, overlooking that this had been achieved by automatically pushing all change orders back to the end of the queue and delaying them anywhere from 24 to 72 hours or more.

So it's important, in Step 3, that each department be put on notice as to the specific performance expected of it in terms of customer service--and equally important that everybody understands how each department's performance will be measured and rated. Since this is usually done on an exceptions basis, with a weekly or monthly report on customer service performance, it does not require much by way of record keeping in the individual departments. But it does require *performance*!

Figure 23-2 shows the three steps in setting different kinds of standards in product as well as service organization.

"UNIQUE FEATURE" STRATEGIES

Some marketers elect to develop customer service features that will set them apart from the competition and which are, in effect, standards.

For example, the pizza chain that discounts the price if delivery isn't made within a specified time frame is actually setting a delivery standard. Most performance guarantees fall into this same category. To be effective as marketing strategies, they have to be credible, and to be credible they have to be monitored as carefully as conventional standards.

WHEN THE BEST CUSTOMER SERVICE ISN'T NECESSARILY THE BEST

A number of books and recent articles about customer service have created the impression that the answer to most of today's problems is simply to develop "excellent" customer service. Nothing can be further from the truth.

Developing a customer service strategy means defining the procedures and policies that will achieve the firm's goals at the least cost. For example, many industrial and commercial firms classify customer by

Figure 23-2
Strategic (Customer Service) Standards

QUALITY STANDARDS	FEASIBILITY STANDARDS	INTERDEPARTMENTAL STANDARDS
Inquiries: ___ handled on-line within ___ minutes.	Database scope and ease of access by personnel for update, retrieval.	Timely database update: ___% of "live" inquiries answered on-line.
Complaints: ___% resolved on-line; ___% within ___ days.	Set automatic adjustment levels, cut signoff requirements.	Sign-off to be completed within ___ (hours/days).
Order turnaround: within ___ working hours/days.	Order entry systems, inventory, personnel, shipping capacity.	Inventory reorders met, timely release by other departments (Sales, Credit).
___% line fill, complete order fill, dollar fill, etc.	Inventory levels and balance.	Responsibility of Finance and Manufacturing to maintain inventory.
Errors: maximum allowable error rate.	Systems and procedures, design of work, training of personnel.	Accountability of departments involved.
Field Service: response within ___ hours, MTBF, etc.	Staffing, dispatch system, training, productivity measures.	Parts, technical support, design and engineering.
Consumers/general service levels: length of queue not to exceed ___ persons; length of wait ___ minutes.	Staffing requirements, systems and procedures, size, layout and number of service positions, provision for monitoring	Timely response from other departments as required.
Courtesy levels: specific routines or scripts, standards of helpfulness.	Time requirements, staffing training, provision for observation.	Limitation on emergencies and other departures from regular procedure.
Priorities by class of customer, type of situation, etc.	System capacity, decision rules, staffing.	Accountability of all departments involved.

449

sales volume and/or channel or type of business and develop different customer service configurations for each. "A" and "B" customers tend to get better service than "C" and "D" customers; hospital and public utilities get better service than wholesalers and jobbers, and so forth.

In price-sensitive industries selling generic or commodity-type products, providing high levels of customer service may be an excellent way for one company to differentiate itself from its competitors. The only problem is that high levels of service may require price increases to cover the added costs of the "excellent" customer service--and this may price the company out of the market.

In another situation, a company may decide to "de-market" certain less profitable classes of business in order to concentrate on its primary markets. A standard strategy for doing so is simply to reduce service levels to the accounts in question. (In a business-to-business situation, this would not normally be considered a violation of FTC regulations as long as it applied to a class of customers.)

In short, while it's generally true that "good" customer service will generally increase sales and market share, marketing strategy dictates that it be the "right" customer service for a given situation. . .and not necessarily the "best."

Similarly, marketers should be extremely cautious in using the term "customer satisfaction" as a goal for the firm's customer service strategy. The real goal is to motivate customers to continue purchasing from the company, to increase their purchases, to recommend it to others, etc. And it's simply more practical to zero in directly on the motives that will cause them to do so rather than rely on a highly subjective term like "satisfaction," which could mean a thousand different things to as many different customers.

SPECIFICS OF CUSTOMER SERVICE MANAGEMENT

Although there are some fundamental differences between customer service operations in a consumer environment and those in industrial or commercial settings, these relate mainly to the size and frequency of purchases. And, they're not nearly as pronounced in telemarketing in any event. The customer service management elements described here are essentially generic, and would naturally be modified to suit individual situations.

Order Entry. Telemarketing differs from much of current industrial/commercial selling practice in that order entry is frequently performed by the telemarketers as part of the sales function. In inbound telemarketing, e.g., catalog sales, some firms use personnel who simply take orders and enter them into the system, usually in a highly standardized computer-assisted mode. Other companies may elect to train personnel in order enhancement, substitution, inquiry conversion, closing, and other selling techniques.

The type of product or service being sold is, of course, a major determinant of the way orders are entered. Custom or special-order goods or services require considerably more detail than stock items ordered by number, and, of course, accuracy in order entry is at a much higher premium. Customer or high-ticket orders may require several levels of verification and sign-off, whereas stock orders may be entered at one location and remotely printed out at another--the most suitable regional warehouse, for example, or the location where a particular item is stocked.

It's still the practice in some companies for the order-entry person--telemarketer or otherwise--to write the order out on a standard form and turn it over to off-line data entry personnel for actual keypunch entry. In some types of situations, this is more cost-effective and produces a higher level of accuracy. In others, it's just unwillingness to break with the past.

The manner in which orders are entered may also be influenced by other practices in the firm. For example, direct marketing firms which consolidate small orders and ship them to a break-bulk point may assign order-entry personnel by territory: all calls originating within certain area codes will be automatically routed to these people. The same results can be obtained in outbound telemarketing, of course, simply by confining calls to specified areas.

In a corporate telemarketing center handling products for several divisions of a company, it may be desirable to batch order entry by product line rather than randomly. One firm does this by means of time sequence:

* *8 to 9 a.m.--veterinary medicine.*

* *9 to 10 a.m.--ethical pharmaceuticals.*

* *10 to 11 a.m.--over-the-counter drugs.*

* *11 a.m. to 12 noon--instruments and equipment.*

The pattern repeats in the afternoon, and the batches are relayed intact to the warehouse to facilitate order assembly and shipping.

Another firm batches its orders by size as well as by time. It handles all small orders in the morning using a specific order-picking configuration, and then changes the picking faces and assembles large orders in the afternoon. For reasons of motivation as well as productivity, morning orders are zone-picked by workers working alone within their zones. In the afternoon, the zones are expanded and workers work in teams of two.

Order Entry by Customers. Direct order entry by customers using either touchtone telephones or computer terminals is already quite common and will become more so. With the development of translators and third-party systems, compatibility of computer software and language is less and less of a problem. Although the most pure computer-to-computer ordering systems are in industrial markets, there's no reason to believe that the practice won't spread rather quickly to consumer markets as well.

On the other hand, some companies are finding it more practical to move back to hard-copy orders received by mail or, increasingly, by facsimile and then entered into the system off-line. In some cases, this is being done using optical scanning equipment, and this application is expected to increase significantly within the next five years.

Clearly, economics have a lot to do with a firm's order-entry methods. High-volume situations with a requirement for immediate confirmation--e.g., car rental firms, airline and hotel reservations, critical supply situations--require an on-line, real-time system. Many direct-marketing organizations are moving in that direction also; customers don't like to place an order by phone and then learn by mail six or seven days later that the item they ordered won't be available for another month.

In such situations, a real-time system enables the order-entry person or telemarketer to confirm

451

availability and/or offer substitutes for items not available. A substitution program may involve offering the customer a higher-priced version of the same product at the lower price as an investment in customer retention, or it may simply be a matter of offering a different color or materials, e.g., wood vs. plastic, etc.

Yet there may not be sufficient economies of scale to warrant an on-line, real-time system, and consideration may have to be given to an off-line batch system.

Immediacy is implicit in telemarketing, and whatever order-entry procedure is adopted must reflect that immediacy. This is equally true of the actual logistics of fulfillment, order assembly, packing, shipping, etc. Although credit is not normally a customer service function from the telemarketer's point of view, customers don't make the distinction. Calling customers who have not been pre-cleared, or delaying firm orders unduly while credit is checked is equally inconsistent with that immediacy.

There is an increasing trend towards the use of third party organizations for both order entry and fulfillment, particularly where computer-to-computer transactions are involved and it's not economical for smaller firms to maintain compatibility with customers with different computer systems.

Order Cycle Time. Historically, many firms have measured their customer service effectiveness by means of an "order cycle" that begins when the order is received and ends when it is placed for shipment. The problem with this approach is that it doesn't measure the total elapsed time from placement of the order until the time he or she actually receives it.

Today, customer service departments recognize this difference, and, of course, a principal reason for the use of the telephone for order placement is to reduce the "inbound" segment of the cycle. The other two segments are the internal processing/order assembly segment and the actual delivery segment. These should be continually monitored to assure that they meet the customer needs and expectations that have been identified as critical to account growth and repeat business.

It's fundamental to sound customer service management to regularly measure customer service quality in terms of order fill, order cycle time, accuracy, courtesy and efficiency of personnel, and similar measures. Most of these are internal measures which should be applied continuously.

Total order cycle time is often measured by using prepaid reply postcards enclosed with customer shipments. The card carries the order number and asks the customer to answer two or three questions about date of receipt, condition of the packaging and, in the case of consumer goods, satisfaction with the product.

As the response cards are received, the data is added to existing data or order receipt, time of processing, and so forth, to give a total profile of the order cycle. This, in turn, enables pinpointing the bottlenecks or trouble spots in the order cycle. If orders are received by mail, allowance must be made for the inbound segment. In industrial marketing, allowance may have to be made for the time lag between requirements by the actual customer and issuance of a formal purchase order by his or her purchasing department.

Accuracy: Allowable Error Rate. Nobody likes to admit that there is such a thing as an "allowable error rate" in customer service. Yet it's unrealistic to plan for a 100% error-free operations, when the costs of error prevention may be greater than the value of the merchandise being sold. Clearly, customers don't like errors, but, in actuality, quick and no-hassle correction of errors often creates a more lasting and positive impression on customers than filling orders directly in the first place.

With this in mind, companies are increasingly assessing the tradeoffs between error avoidance before the fact and error correction after the fact. This requires a high level of response when errors do occur. Very often, the company gives the customer a credit or certificate against future purchases. This usually mollifies the customer and assures that he or she will continue buying the service or product.

Product Damage. While in-transit product damage to purchased goods is technically the responsibility of the customer in terms of filing claims against the carriers involved, in actual practice many customers are not in a position to do so and resent being told it's their responsibility. To counter this, some firms sell on a "delivered" basis (also known as FOB customer's dock), which means that the title remains with the seller--and thus responsibility for in-transit damage--until the goods are actually signed for by the customer. Another way of dealing with this practice by some sellers is to offer customers insurance against damage in transit for a small added fee. In industrial marketing, larger firms often provide assistance to their smaller customers in filing claims against carriers.

Customer Service Failures and Customer Complaints. Closely related to the subject of errors and accuracy is the issue of customer service failures in general, and the complaints they generate. A customer-service failure is sometimes simply a failure to meet standards of line fill or order cycle time, and, thus, known to the seller before it's known to customers. But other failures, such as errors in order assembly, shipping or billing, as well as actual product defects, may remain unknown to the seller until the customer actually complains about the problem.

Unfortunately, the response of many companies to such complaints is highly defensive and centers on requiring customers to prove that they are entitled to an adjustment or refund rather than assuming the customer has made the complaint in good faith and, thus, making a quick settlement and getting back to business as usual.

A few companies are acknowledging that, when they ultimately pay the claims or complaints that are proven to be valid, it has cost them more to weed out the few unjustified claims (which are seldom more than 10% of the orders) than if they had automatically resolved all complaints below a certain dollar amount-- *often as high as $400 or even more.*

Figure 23-3 shows one way of computing the amount a company can automatically refund a customer without investigation and still come out ahead in terms of costs and customer good will. What some companies do is determine the point below which 80% of all claims fall, and set policies to pay these automatically, without investigation. The premise is that these 80% typically represent only 20% of the total dollars, whereas the remaining 20% of complaints usually represent 80% of the dollars and should be scrutinized much more carefully.

As noted above, complainers whose complaints have been well-handled represent a higher proportion of a firm's repeat and "buying up" customers than do non-complainers. Making it easier for customers to complain pays for itself in increased customer loyalty and in increased sales. A strategy for fast and fair complaint handling is particularly appropriate for telemarketing, where the customer often depends entirely on the representations of the telemarketing rep in reaching a buying decision--and, without prompt and responsive attention to his or her complaints, will probably never do so again.

But it's not enough to just recognize the importance of responsive complaint handling. Most personnel tend to resist complaints no matter how frequently they're told that complaints are opportunities. To overcome this resistance, customer service management must write specific decision rules for the major

453

Figure 23-3
Automatic Complaint Settlement
Breakeven Points

Cost of Investigating a Complaint	Amount That Can Be Paid Out Automatically by Claim Validity or "Customer Honesty Level"					
	90%	80%	70%	60%	50%	40%
$10	$100	$50	$33	$25	$20	$10
$20	$200	$100	$67	$50	$40	$20
$30	$300	$150	$100	$75	$60	$30
$40	$400	$200	$133	$100	$80	$40
$50	$500	$250	$167	$125	$100	$50
$60	$600	$300	$200	$150	$120	$60
$70	$700	$350	$233	$175	$140	$70
$80	$800	$400	$267	$200	$160	$80
$90	$900	$450	$300	$225	$180	$90
$100	$1,000	$500	$333	$250	$200	$100

This table shows the breakeven on complaint handling, i.e., the amount that can be paid out automatically, based on the cost of handling the complaint and the percentage of valid claims. In most business-to-business transactions, the cost of investigating a complaint is $40 or more, and the validity ratio is usually at the 90% level -- that is, 90% of the complaints are usually paid out after investigation in any event. Thus, by reading over from the $40 investigation cost and down from the 90% validity point, we see that the breakeven point is $400. This means that the company can automatically pay out on any claims of $400 or less and still come out ahead. Of course, the numbers will vary from company to company, but they will seldom be under $100. Additionally, prompt settlement of complaints has been proven to be a strong incentive to repeat and increased purchases for complaining customers.

categories of complaint. This minimizes the issue of personal judgment, which can sometimes result in "reprisals" against particularly demanding customers and, in fact, eliminates repetitive and inconsistent decision-making altogether.

THE CUSTOMER SERVICE DEPARTMENT AS A TELEMARKETING UNIT

Every customer contact affects the company's ability to sell, for better or for worse, whether it's with a discourteous (or courteous) driver of company-identified highway equipment, a hurried (or helpful) switchboard operator, or a member of the sales force calling in person. It's often overlooked that an extremely high percentage of customer phone calls are from people who have:

* *Already made a purchasing decision and simply want to place an order.*

* *Actually entered the order and/or bought the product and are calling in reference to it.*

* *Been motivated to buy and are calling for information that will help them make the best decision.*

Most of these calls come to the customer service department, and virtually all have an important characteristic in common that distinguishes them from conventional telemarketing or even personal sales calls: *There is virtually no sales resistance on the part of the customer!* The customer is calling primarily for help in buying, and in some instances will actually say, "*Can you help me? I'm looking for a _____ that will _____...*" or "*Which do you think would be best?*" In this context, the customer service representative (CSR) is perceived as an advisor rather than as a salesperson trying to make a sale. It's a unique opportunity to practice "passive" telemarketing, which is really not passive at all, but is called that to distinguish it from conventional outbound telemarketing which, quite often, must deal with prospects who have not made a buying decision and, therefore, present considerable sales resistance to overcome.

Passive telemarketing takes a number of forms, including:

1. Inquiry Conversion. A customer calls to inquire about a product or service and the CSR persuades the customer to place an order. This can be done via scripting, computer screen prompts, and, sometimes, extemporaneous performance by a skilled CSR.

2. Setting Up Appointments for a Formal Sales Presentation. This is an intermediate step in situations where the sale must be closed in person.

3. Qualifying Leads. This is a variation on Number 2, in which the CSR handling the inquiry uses probing techniques to determine whether this is a worthwhile lead that should be followed up by a salesperson, or whether it is best handled simply by mailing literature.

4. Steering. In this instance, the CSR must direct the customer to a dealer or distributor and must rely on the customer to initiate the contact. This requires careful scripting in order to motivate the customer to do so.

5. Order Upgrading or Enhancement. This can take several forms:

* *Upgrading to weight-break or price break.*

* *Upgrading to a higher-priced version (but only after probing to determine the customer's real need).*

* *Add-ons of related or "companion" products.*

* *Introduction of new products or services on the basis of their newness rather than their relatedness.*

6. Substitutions. This is generally, but not always, a planned strategy to capture a sale that would otherwise be lost because of lack of stock. Many real-time programs will show the CSR that a stock-out condition exists, but that certain other items can be substituted, either because they are the same product, but employ different materials, or because they are the brand-name version of a private label product (or vice versa), meet the same military specifications, and so forth. In some instances, the company may offer the higher-priced version at the same price as the item which was ordered but is not available.

Substitution strategies can be quite sophisticated. At one tire company, for example, CSR's call dealers by appointment and are guided through the ordering process by computer. The screen carries a forecast of what the dealer is likely to order in terms of tire sizes, grades and quantities. In adjacent columns, the screen shows stock on hand and, if it is not sufficient to cover the dealer's order, suggested substitutions which can be offered at the same price. The objective is to sell the dealer a full truckload lot, because, if this isn't possible, the dealer may not order at all.

7. Pricing and Estimating. This is an important competitive tool, quite often computer-supported, but also requiring considerable skill on the part of the CSR. What it sometimes means is that the firm that can come up with a firm price that's in the ball park may get the business simply because customers don't always want to wait for others to grind out their estimates.

Passive telemarketing can be quite profitable because there is so little actual selling cost involved. A few companies are *recovering the entire cost of running their customer service departments* through one or more of the strategies described above. But the majority of companies aren't even making an organized approach to this rich and lucrative source of revenue.

OUTBOUND OR PROACTIVE TELEMARKETING

Outbound or proactive telemarketing in the customer service department is operationally similar to regular telemarketing, but frequently with these distinctions:

CUSTOMER SERVICE TELEMARKETING

Marginal Customers. "Prospects" are often regular customers whom the firm can no longer afford to contact via field sales personnel. To compensate for what might be perceived by the customer as "down-grading," these marginal customers are handled via a strong sales-service relationship in the customer service department (and usually with excellent results).

Opportunity Situations. Outbound telemarketing by customer service personnel is frequently handled on an opportunistic basis, i.e., when there's a lull in regular customer service work. This enables the department to carry more people than it might otherwise be allowed, and enables better handling of seasonal surges as well as added sales from the telemarketing itself. One warning, however: *These stints of telemarketing must be formally assigned by the manager, based on his or her familiarity with the work flow.* If they are left to the discretion of CSR's, some CSR's may not telemarket at all, while others may neglect their regular work because they prefer telemarketing.

Buying Influences. Telemarketing calls may be made to "influencers" rather than actual buyers. For example, in one firm which manufactures laboratory equipment, each CSR is required to make one call per day to a hospital lab technician who is actually using the firm's equipment. The purpose is to determine if the technician is satisfied with the equipment, has any misunderstandings or problems that need clarification or solution, etc. The premise is that, although the technician does not actually make buying decisions. . .

* *If he or she isn't getting good results or high utilization, it may be perceived as a failure of the equipment rather than a lack of knowledge on the part of the technician.*

* *Problems of adjustment or calibration may come to light which the technician might be constrained from reporting for fear of being blamed for causing the problem. Fixing these will increase productivity and accuracy.*

* *Satisfaction on the part of the employee with the equipment is a morale factor which enhances his or her self-esteem, as well as the manager's self-esteem for having made a good choice of equipment as well as personnel.*

* *Good equipment performance and productivity build a good reputation for the equipment. In the hospital environment, which is given to large-scale group buying, this is a key factor in future purchases from the manufacturer. Although hotline or troubleshooting calls are inbound, i.e., originated by customers, they have basically the same goal of maintaining satisfaction with equipment products and should be considered a legitimate form of tele-marketing.*

Early Warning and Product Recall Telephone Calls. While not selling as such, these calls are often critical to future sales relationships. They include notifying customers of impending problems like strikes or shortages, or assisting them in the implementation of product recalls for quality or other

457

reasons--a typically sensitive situation which requires skilled handling in order to maintain confidence in the firm's products and their integrity.

CUSTOMER SERVICE *IS* TELEMARKETING

The process of selling never ends. Although it's often described as "customer acquisition"--which is a primary role of field sales, advertising and sales promotion and, of course telemarketing itself--in actual fact selling is the process of creating satisfaction with the sale and, with it, paving the way for future sales to the same customers.

This is a major mission of customer service--to establish confidence in products and vendors alike, to nurture accounts so they will buy in greater volume as well as variety. Because customer service is the primary and most frequent contact for the majority of customers, it is a prime medium for telemarketing strategies which may be outside the scope of conventional telemarketing departments.

Today, customer service is recognized as a major marketing strategy and an integral part of the total selling process, as is telemarketing. Which is why customer service *is* telemarketing, from beginning to end.

CHAPTER 24

Distribution Channel Telemarketing

Peg Fisher
President
Peg Fisher & Associates, Inc. (PF&A)
Racine, Wisconsin

Uncontrollable market forces affect the entire distribution channel from the manufacturer to the wholesaler-distributor, to the dealer and finally to the user.

As changes are made in one channel in response to market forces, impact is felt throughout the distribution pipeline. Market forces are the basis for nurturing and growth of new forms of distribution which in turn force change upon or replacement of old ways of doing business. Survival depends upon management's ability to evaluate important trends and restructure as necessary to be able to meet changing market demands.

This chapter is designed to position the need for telephone sales within the larger context of market forces. It begins with an overview of trends impacting manufacturing, followed by an overview of important trends in the merchant wholesale-distribution industry.

These overviews will help the reader understand how market forces are bringing on a period requiring aggressive restructuring along all routes within the distribution channel. I hope to demonstrate reasons why firms are moving away from traditional methods for bringing products and services to the marketplace.

At a time when management must know how and why costs are incurred, and how and why results are achieved, the benefits of telephone sales hold definite appeal. Telemarketing's flexibility, manageability, inherent productivity, and cost-effectiveness all help in implementing the changes being made to meet today's marketing challenges.

AN OVERVIEW OF FORCES AFFECTING MANUFACTURERS

There is a general excess of manufacturing capability in our economy, and excess capacity means a buyer's market. Competitors are all fighting for their share of a shrinking marketplace, and price concessions are often made in an attempt to retain or gain market share. Price concessions result in eroding margins for the manufacturer.

Manufacturers are reevaluating their distribution channels, as well as studying how those channels affect market share and profitability. They are examining costs and seeking better ways to control them in order to remain competitive while passing savings along to users.

Other important trends affecting manufacturing are:

* *The decline of heavy industry.*

* *The success of mid-sized manufacturers.*

* *The simultaneous rise of service and high technology firms.*

The more important results of these trends have been:

* *A shrinking traditional market.*

* *The increasing need to find and create new outlets.*

* *The erosion of profits, the requirement to cut costs.*

* *Increasing pressure for new product innovations.*

* *The requirement to develop marketing strategies to identify new and changing markets and meet new demands.*

Though many manufacturers have historically depended on the health and growth of their selected distributors to find markets for their products, they are faced today with the need to reach decisions and make choices having repercussions throughout the distribution channel--sometimes to the detriment of their present distribution network.

Further, some manufacturers are being challenged by the restructuring decisions being made within their distribution network. In the wake of uncontrollable market forces, some distributors are moving into manufacturing. They are now direct competitors of their former suppliers. Although they may keep a supplier's line, they sell their own brand name of cutting tool or cleaning compound or paper product of "equal" quality at less cost. Distributor restructuring may also result in inventory consolidation strategies and dropping a supplier's line. Either way, the manufacturer experiences the erosion of market share.

Market pressures on manufacturers require restructuring and cost cutting to be able to deliver savings to users. For some, choices made will determine viability in the future. For others, choices will determine the manufacturer's ability to compete in a global economy.

THE CHANGE MASTER

The restructuring decisions made by large businesses in particular are viewed as the harbingers of what is to come for others. Large firms are seen as the change masters in our economy. Others watch them closely and may follow in their footsteps.

Change masters are "*Those people and organizations adept at the art of anticipating the need for, and of leading, productive change,*" according to Rosabeth Moss Kanter, author of *The Change Masters*.

The restructuring plans and implementation steps of leading industrials like GE and DuPont are

460

having major repercussions in the distribution pipeline. Their response to market forces will determine how or if general line distributors will be able to do business with them in the future. Their decisions and the forthcoming results may further impact the ability of the general line distributor to do business with other leading businesses.

A closer look at these examples helps explain their restructuring choices and the impact on other routes in the distribution channel.

General Electric. GE through its GEMIMS (General Electric Maintenance Inventory Management Service) plans to replace some 3,200 MRO (maintenance, repair, operations supplies) suppliers to their plastics group by substituting direct buying from manufacturers by GEMIMS. Plans are eventually to have GEMIMS buy for all GE plants and then enter the open market and sell to other large industrial MRO users.[1]

GE's choices stem from cost-cutting objectives. They need to reduce the high cost of acquisition and possession of products used to maintain and operate their plants. Integrated product purchasing through GEMIMS is intended to achieve better management control of inventory for all manufacturing locations.

The resulting quantity buying power for multiple versus single locations will achieve cost justified discounts from vendors. Additional cost savings are expected to be realized through the use of sophisticated computerized systems which will reduce labor and paperwork processing costs.

GE's choices impact both distributors and manufacturers. Direct buying from vendors means significant business loss to distributors that have served the separate plants in the past, aside from some specialized distributor services. The choice for the manufacturer is to sell direct to GEMIMS or lose the business. For the manufacturer that wants to protect its distribution network, it is difficult to stand back and not sell direct while allowing a competitor to take over the business.

Some manufacturers attempt to hold back from direct selling. One of PF & A's clients had a policy of selling through independent distributors despite the growth of large discount retailers and homecenter type businesses that buy direct through their respective headquarters. This manufacturer realized loss of market share among the highly price-conscious and DIY (do-it-yourself) users market as a result of the policy.

Finally, in response to growing market pressures and market share loss, they now actively pursue these business relationships to the detriment of traditional distribution channels.

DuPont. Another example of manufacturer restructuring is the DuPont Company's response to growing market pressures. They decided to drop all but three large multi-locational distributors. Their objective is to save on acquisition and possession costs by eliminating in-plant inventories and using state-of-the-art computerized inventory management and order entry systems to reduce paperwork.[2]

To achieve increased productivity and reduced costs goals, the three selected distributors are responsible for supplying 35 major manufacturing plants and numerous construction locations with all industrial and electrical MRO requirements traditionally supplied by hundreds of local and regional distributors.

Dana Corporation. Manufacturer restructuring does not always eliminate sales through traditional distribution channels, but it can effect the loss of major business for some and an increase for others. In 1986, the Dana Corporation announced its restructuring as part of their plan for competing in a changed global market. They are closing 40 of 60 major production plants to be replaced with 65 smaller scattered locations across the country that will also serve as assembly and distribution centers. To the independent distributors that serviced the big plants, the result is lost sales that can only be replaced with sales to new types of customers.[3]

Summary. Change masters among manufacturers are responding to market forces by changing from old and traditional methods in favor of new methods for achieving their goals. They realize their ability to remain competitive requires making difficult and complex choices to achieve better production and operations methods and cost controls. As plans are implemented, these in turn force choices on other routes within the distribution channel.

HOW TELEPHONE SALES ADDRESSES IMPORTANT TRENDS IN MANU-FACTURING

Shrinking market share. . .increased competition. . .global markets. . .direct buying. . .distributor restructuring. . .eroding margins. . ..

These forces cause manufacturers to get more involved with the sales and marketing of their products. Versus leaving sales responsibility in the hands of the distribution network, manufacturers are taking over part and sometimes all of the selling function and doing a better job today than ever before to insure their advertising dollars are well spent.

The following situations demonstrate how telephone selling helps manufacturers address important trends faced in today's market.

Situation #1. Manufacturers use various forms of advertising to generate leads and product inquiries. Their objective is to create product awareness and help build market share. Historically, responses from potential buyers were directed to distributors for follow-up and qualification of buyer need.

This traditional method for handling inquiries has come under scrutiny for good reasons. Manufacturer evaluation of this method finds distributors often ignore leads, or follow-up is not timely because the distributor's field sales force concentrates its time calling on existing customers versus prospective users. Further, the lack of distributor feedback on lead quality means manufacturers cannot evaluate the use of their advertising dollars or the quality of their lead sources.

Traditional methods for handling advertising responses are being replaced by manufacturers who understand the problems inherent in dependence upon the distribution network. Telephone prospecting and telephone sales organizations are being set up to change all this. Their implementation puts control over advertising back in the manufacturers' hands, provides better support to the distribution network, and in some cases is designed to build and maintain direct sales with the manufacturer.

Solution #1. In response to advertising and trade inquiries, an immediate mail follow-up from the manufacturer insures timely response. The mailing may include names and addresses of distributors in the prospect's area. Following the mailing, telephone calls from the manufacturer qualify need and interest in the product. Depending upon the prospect's needs, lead disposition can take any number of directions.

DISTRIBUTION CHANNEL TELEMARKETING

For example, telephone sales may be directed to select out any accounts having sufficient quantity requirements to buy direct, or accounts located outside of a distributor's active selling area. These accounts then become the account base for active telephone sales solicitation to build a sales relationship and assume full sales responsibility. Remaining qualified leads may be directed to the distribution network.

Another option is to have TSR's establish an ongoing sales relationship with any qualified account having sales potential. TSR's would take orders from these accounts and coordinate the order processing and paperwork through their selected distributor located nearest to the customer. Coordination by the manufacturer insures the distributor has their product available to sell versus substituting a competitive line or the distributor's own house brand.

Situation #2. Some areas of the country may not be adequately covered by distributors because sales potential is small or accounts are far away from the distributor's primary selling territory. However, taken together, there may be geographically distant accounts and small accounts that warrant sales coverage if coverage can be cost-effectively provided.

Similar to this situation is a territory that once had distributor coverage, but due to merger or acquisition or because the distributor dropped the manufacturer's line, that area of the country no longer has active distributor sales coverage. Replacing the distributor is not a simple process since another in that area may be entrenched with a competitive product.

Solution #2. As a counter-strategy to losing market share to a competitive line and not responding to user needs, manufacturers are setting up their own telephone sales functions to assume full sales responsibility for accounts and prospects in areas such as this. Telephone sales functions are supported with new types of mailings and customer education materials such as catalogs, product literature, video presentations and samples.

Situation #3. Cost cutting moves by manufacturers have resulted in the restructuring of some of their field sales forces. For example, eroding sales and margins in a sales region that used to support six field staff can only support the cost of less than three today. The regional sales manager's responsibility is now divided between this restructured region and another similar region having reduced sales potential due to shrinking markets and a reduced sales force compliment as a result.

Field sales staff who call on distributors in these regions face a larger geographical area to cover and a significant increase in travel time. *One supplier was able to document an average annual time spent driving at 221 days a year as a result of restructuring!* The cost efficiencies gained through reduced staff deployment were offset with productivity losses and reduced face-to-face time with distributors in these regions.

Solution #3. Manufacturers set up telephone sales functions to supplement field sales efforts. TSR's perform sales tasks formerly done by field sales. These include setting up individual account profiles having names and titles of all distributor personnel who need product and applications knowledge during their customer dealings. Telephone staff handle individual mailings on products and specification sheets, point of sale (POS) and co-op advertising materials, samples, manufacturer developed training materials and videos, catalogs, price sheets, and so forth.

Regularly scheduled calls are made to distributor personnel. These are designed, for example, to provide technical and product applications assistance, to promote the use of co-op advertising, to explain and sell distributors on participation in manufacturer-sponsored promotions, to insure smooth working relationships and understanding of manufacturer policies and procedures, to take orders during outbound calls and educate customers on who to call to place orders, to handle special orders, to expedite and solve related problems.

As manufacturers continue to be pressured by market forces beyond their control, the use of various forms of telephone sales is expected to increase.

AN OVERVIEW OF THE MARKET FORCES THAT ARE AFFECTING WHOLESALER-DISTRIBUTORS

The wholesaler-distributor faces one thing that is constant: change. Find a market force not affecting this industry today and for certain it will be there applying pressure tomorrow! In many ways, the market forces expected to shape the role of this industry parallel the forces impacting manufacturers.

Loss of distributor market share is aptly demonstrated in the examples cited earlier of the restructuring motivated by cost-cutting in the distribution pipeline by GE with GEMIMS, DuPont, and Dana Corporation. Changes made in their response to market forces affect literally thousands of wholesaler-distributor's share of market. Also cutting into market share are other alternate and non-wholesale channels which are expected to grow faster than traditional channels. What was once the purview of the wholesaler-distributor is now the business of the direct seller, discount retailers, national account line hards, co-ops and others.[4,5,46]

The erosion of the U.S. customer base and shrinking traditional supplies markets mean increased competitive pressures and the resultant margin erosion, with competitors cutting costs to gain or retain customers. Simultaneous with the shrinking traditional heavy industry base is the growth of new markets with different needs and ways of buying.

The wholesaler-distributor is squeezed in the middle between users and suppliers, both looking to reduce their own costs and improve their own efficiencies in the distribution pipeline.

The Pressure From Suppliers. The distributor's function as the nation's inventory manager provides suppliers the local or regional warehousing of product needed to meet demand. Suppliers look to distributors to find markets for their products as well as create markets through value-added offerings and services. Distributors are pressured by suppliers to help them reduce their costs and improve their efficiencies in order to remain competitive. For the distributor, however, it is not what is in stock that counts nor is it the number of customers that buy a given product. It is what the distributor can sell at a profit that matters--to the distributor.

The Pressure From Customers. Customers look to distributors for more than just delivery that is faster. Their primary need is for help to improve their cost structure to keep them competitive. The 1987 National Association of Wholesaler-Distributors (NAW) describes the reasons for seeking distributor value-added services as follows:

* *Help reduce their costs.*

* *Increase their productivity.*

* *Make their job easier.*

* *Increase their sales.*

* *Improve their knowledge and skills.*

* *Improve the flow of information to their management.*

Selling at a profit for the distributor covers a variety of costs and services that have traditionally been middle-channel distribution functions. If the distributor did not incur the costs and provide the services, they would have to be assumed by some other route in the distribution channel because they cannot be eliminated.

Customers pressure distributors to provide these services or lose their business to a competitor or to an alternate distribution channel. For example, a former owner of an independent building supplies dealership used to rely heavily upon local distributors when he was an independent dealer. But competitive forces and price competition made him decide to join a large co-op having hundreds of store locations and headquarters purchasing to achieve buying leverage with vendors. Today, this dealer's purchasing from distributors is only on an exception basis. As he explained, "*Our retail prices are sometimes less than what the distributor pays his vendor. I don't need the distributor in this business.*"

Historically, distributor response to customer pressure has been to provide equally good service to all customers. Although the services provided have resulted in overall sales gains, these are accompanied by declines in return on net worth and return on assets because of an underlying failure to keep costs in line with sales and margins.

As one industry leader and president of a wholesaler-distributor firm explained:

> "*I have an upgraded computer, a trained field sales force, better depth of inventory than our competition, the best inside sales people in the area, a new telephone system, good vendor relations. You name it, I've got it. In return, sales are flat, margins are eroding, and my employees are burned out from the pressure and threatening to quit. The servicing demands are keeping everyone busy with people working from crisis-to-crisis. We have constant pressure for more support staff, while we're losing ground. We are working harder and longer but making less in the end.*"

Summary. Market forces are causing owner/managers of distributor firms to have to re-evaluate their role. Supplier pressures, customer pressures, and the changing marketplace require aggressive restructuring away from the old and into new ways of doing business if they are to remain viable.

The challenge for the distributor is more than just relying on the health of external forces such as American manufacturing for their prosperity. They need to determine which services they should be offering to what markets where they can make a profit.

And they need to achieve efficiencies in their internal business practices.

THE CHANGE MASTERS

Shrinking margins. . .a changing industrial base. . .new growth industries. . .alternate distribution channel growth. . .eroding margins. . .changing market demands. . . .

A myriad of changes face the distributor today. What is he doing to respond to these uncontrollable forces in the marketplace?

There are two types of responses needed:

1. *Distributors need to decide upon new offerings to take to the market to penetrate existing accounts and develop market share in new areas.* Two key factors predicted to influence wholesaler-distributor growth:

   a) New value-added services, and

   b) Diversification into new product lines.

2. *Distributors need to make internal organizational changes to effect efficiencies and cost saving.* For example, they need to gather and use marketing intelligence, increase their use of technological support, achieve productivity increases, and reduce operating costs.

VALUE-ADDED SERVICES AND DIVERSIFICATION

The change masters among wholesaler-distributors will offer new value-added services because of their appeal to both suppliers and customers.

Value-added services are ways for distributors to expand market share as well as take over functions that manufacturers now perform for themselves, but would prefer to outsource. Often, distributors are in a better position to carry out regional activities (e.g., re-manufacturing, repair, assembly and product applications sales support) effectively and economically.

Value-added services also interest customers who outsource their own in-house production and quality assurance work to distributors having the capability at lower operating costs. Other value-addeds of interest to customers include:

* *Cutting-to-length.*

* *Special packaging and labeling.*

* *Special stocking programs.*

* *Preventive maintenance programs.*

* *Hazardous materials control and disposition.*

* *Various computer applications such as electronic order entry, electronic mail, management reporting, etc.*

The change masters will evaluate diversification into new product lines. This includes considering greater breadth within the existing product offerings, consolidation of vendors to increase buying leverage with those remaining, as well as offering totally new lines.

For example, in response to GE's restructuring, an industrial distributor has taken on new lines in the paper and packaging equipment distribution industry. This diversification presents new market share opportunities to the distributor through expanded market share within the existing industrial user by sales of new products and related services. It also opens up opportunities for building market share with a whole new type of user base.

The business forms distribution industry is another example of why distributors are taking on new lines. Traditional business comes from sales of custom and stock business forms. Sales erosion of this traditional business has resulted from the expanded use of desktop publishing and computers in general among the customer base. In response to this new market force, business forms distributors now sell computer supplies, software and software compatible forms, forms handling equipment, printers and document storage devices, for example.

Like the industrial distributor cited, this type of diversification provides opportunity to build upon prior customer relationships to penetrate and increase market share among traditional users. And, it opens the door for developing new markets.

Offering new value-added services or diversifying into new product lines is only part of the challenge for the distributor. Keeping costs in line with sales and margins is what really counts. If the distributor cannot make sufficient margins, offering new services and lines may simply compound an existing problem. The distributor needs to evaluate the services offered today. He needs to evaluate to whom they are offered and how they are provided. Working harder and longer but making less in the end is not the objective.

INTERNAL ORGANIZATIONAL CHANGES

Distributors will make internal organizational changes in a number of areas as needed to effect efficiencies and cost savings. Some of the key areas of change are addressed here. These are followed by a discussion of how telephone sales can help the distributor implement and use anticipated changes.

Having the right information can be an important competitive advantage to the distributor who should play an ever-increasing role as a marketplace information gatherer. Distributors will place increased emphasis on *market intelligence* gathering *and* use of marketing intelligence.

The objectives to be achieved include:

1. *Learning what segments in a distributor's marketing territory are growing and which are not.* Market intelligence will help the distributor decide upon appropriate restructuring. It can be used to support strategic responses to market forces, i.e., be the information base that determines which value-

467

added services and which product lines present sales and profit opportunities to the firm.

2. *Understanding each individual customer's changing needs in light of their business opportunities, restructuring and their use of competition.* As customer's needs change, continuing to sell in the traditional way only forces the account to seek out a supplier who is organized to meet his needs. Information gathering about individual accounts is key to maintenance of repeat business and adjusting service offerings to the account accordingly.

3. *Segmenting the existing customer base to insure profit contributors are not subsidizing sales to low or non-profitable accounts.* Most distributors pride themselves on offering equally good service to all customers. This strategy often is ineffective, since it actually costs distributors to sell to certain accounts. The only way small accounts (or large accounts that only purchase certain low margin commodities) can be made profitable is either by providing fewer services to these customers (thus reducing the distributor's cost to sell them) or to *significantly reduce the cost of sale.*

Having marketing intelligence available keeps the distributor in tune with the realities of the marketplace and its changing needs. But he needs a way to manage this information. This is just one reason why distributors are expected to increase their use of *technological support.*

Technology might be described as the engine that drives the change in productivity for the wholesaler-distributor. Historically, technology expenditures concentrated on handling company financials. Today:

> *". . .EDP costs should increase significantly in sales and marketing so wholesaler-distributors can get better information about their markets and the needs of their customers. . . (EDP) will also improve sales productivity by providing the inside and outside sales forces with better support. . .."* [7]

Predicted increases in automated systems purchasing between vendors and customers alone is expected to free inside sales from time-consuming multi-line order taking and related tasks.

Distributors will emphasize *productivity increases.* Having increased technology support will provide the tools to assist with measuring individual performance.

Putting technology into the hands of field sales will not only provide them support data and information about their customers, but will serve management as a measurement tool and accurate sales reporting system which is severely lacking among wholesaler-distributors in general. Many have no sales reporting systems in place today. Those that do often have limited reporting because *"My people don't like to spend their time on paperwork."*

The upshot of a management attitude that fails to reinforce the importance of productivity reporting is marketing intelligence stuck uselessly in the heads of field sales people. When a field sales person retires or leaves the company for a competitor, the company is left with an unknown territory and the difficult challenge of starting over.

The development of technology and productivity measures to help redirect staff activities will help distributors achieve the goal of *reduced operations costs*. Sales and marketing costs as a percentage of sales are expected to have a noticeable reduction.

In order to maintain profit levels in spite of shrinking margins, distributors are evaluating their traditional methods for taking products and services to the market and considering less costly options that afford management better control over the selling function.

Summary. Aggressive restructuring away from the old and into new ways of doing business is needed by the change masters among wholesaler-distributors if they are to achieve acceptable profits and be able to grow. They must become users of market intelligence, increase their technological support, achieve productivity increases and reduce operations costs. They must evaluate their product and value-added service offerings in light of changing market demands.

HOW TELEPHONE SALES ADDRESSES IMPORTANT TRENDS IN WHOLE-SALE-DISTRIBUTION

Overall trends in the wholesale-distribution industry indicate increasing emphasis on redirecting field sales and inside sales roles. The primary reason given for expanding the inside sales function to include sales tasks is the reduced cost of sales advantage to the distributor.

Although reduced cost is a definite wholesaler-distributor need, moving sales tasks away from field sales to telephone sales provides much broader benefits.

The following discussion explains how telephone sales helps to address and implement key organizational changes, to reach decisions about new offerings designed to meet changing market demands, and to implement those decisions.

How can telephone sales help with needed productivity increases? It can significantly increase the account coverage and sales and prospecting call potential compared with field sales. On the average, although distributors would like to believe otherwise, field sales contacts range from three to five calls a day. The range for full-time telephone sales staff, depending upon product and support systems provided to the staff, is from 25 to 35 daily sales presentations, sometimes more.

Historically, distributors have assigned field sales a "territory." They pay field sales for volume or margins in that territory. But, compensation is no measure of which accounts in that territory received sales contact. *In fact, many, if not most, receive little or no contact because the field sales reps concentrate on large or key accounts only who eat up their time while prospecting is ignored.*

On the other hand, telephone sales has the capability of actively soliciting literally hundreds of accounts on a regular basis. Comparing field to telephone sales productivity is like comparing a Ford Escort to a Lamborghini Countach. Call frequency projections can help put the true potential of telephone sales into perspective (see **Figure 24-1**).[8]

Daily call potential and annual potential is one measure of productivity. Consider another: using field sales to announce and explain new value-added services and new products is a very time-consuming

469

endeavor. By the time they physically get around to their assigned accounts, competitors have an opportunity to make inroads.

Lack of field sales reporting systems means management never really does know which accounts "get the message." Since smaller and geographically isolated accounts typically get limited if any sales contact, and prospecting is a back-burner function for field sales that concentrate calling on present users, the potential for achieving market share gains and existing account penetration through new offerings is held back.

Figure 24-1
Call Frequency Projections

Daily # Outbound Contacts	Annual # Sales Days	Annual Call Potential	# of Accounts and Average Annual Contact Potential				
			100	150	200	250	300
15	221	3,315	33.1	22.1	16.5	13.3	11.0
20	221	4,420	44.3	39.4	22.1	17.7	14.7
25	221	5,525	55.3	36.8	27.6	22.1	18.4
30	221	6,630	66.3	44.2	33.2	26.5	22.1
35	221	7,735	77.4	51.6	38.7	30.9	25.8

Telephone sales productivity can overcome this inherent problem with a field sales force. Depending on the size of the total account base and prospective users, it can take a few days to a few weeks to announce and explain new offerings, answer questions, qualify need and interest, handle follow-up mailings and samples and begin taking orders.

Another important measure of sales productivity is the time required for a new-hire sales person to begin contributing to company profits, when his sales and margins are greater than his cost to the company. Managers frequently explain it takes from six to 12 months before a field person makes his presence known on the bottom line.

The contribution to profits by telephone sales staff can begin to show by the end of the first month, most likely within the first three. From the time of initial start-up, staff experiences concentrated customer contact and a resulting "fast" learning curve.

How can telephone sales help reduce operations costs? The cost of a field sales call depends on the market covered. Client statistics indicate a range from about $75.00 a call to well beyond $250.00 a sales call. Comparisons with telephone sales reveal a minimum cost reduction of 70% up to 90% and more. Though telephone sales staff base salaries and commission structure often parallel field sales, lower operating costs automatically result since automobiles and related insurance, travel and entertainment are virtually eliminated while sales productivity is significantly increased.

Frequently, telephone sales gross margins overall are higher by as much as 15% over field sales. This stems from better management direction of sales personnel to concentrate their activities on selling higher margin products. Also, many telephone sales functions at least initially begin selling to smaller users where discounting practices do not apply.

Staff proximity to management has inherent management time and related costs savings. Coordination and communications takes less management time overall. Because the job tools and account records used by staff are readily available for management review and results analysis, it takes less management effort and time to redirect staff, to identify and correct training needs, to coach and counsel on "joint" sales calls. Versus having to plan a day out of the office making joint calls with a field salesman, management can schedule an hour's time and accomplish the same objective with TSR's.

How can telephone sales help gather and use market intelligence? Of all the positions in the company, telephone sales is in the primary position to both gather and use market intelligence. Earlier, three reasons were given for needing market intelligence:

1. *To learn what segments in a distributor's territory are growing and which are not.*

2. *To understand individual customer's changing needs.*

3. *To segment the customer base to insure profit contributors are not subsidizing sales to low or non-profitable accounts.*

Once management determines which market segment to go after, telephone sales activity can be directed to prospecting in that new area. They can concentrate their calls to qualify need and interest, gather information about the potential users, and to sell. The information gathered will provide the kind of detail needed by management to either support planned redirection or change it.

One of the key job tools used by telephone sales staff is the account profile record. It contains considerably more than just basic mail list information (the *Addendum* to this chapter provides some examples). During initial and follow-up calls, TSR's build and maintain these records, which are used to define sales strategies by account, and to identify specific sales call objectives with customers. The distributor's need to understand individual customer's changing needs is an objective that is possible with telephone sales through these records and related sales call notes.

The benefits to management of these staff job tools should not be underestimated. When the TSR's have information about the customer's type of business, names of buyers and buying influences, type of equipment on which product is used, use of competition, interest in JIT (just in time) or use of it, problems the customer experiences with his customers and so on, this is specific market intelligence of importance.

Because TSR's maintain contact frequency with hundreds of accounts within brief time frames, account information is timely. Further, it can be used to "target" existing accounts having potential for new value-added services and products.

The gathering and use of market intelligence by the telephone sales staff is one of the major benefits of telephone selling to the wholesaler-distributor. Another spin-off benefit is the timely update of the company's mailing lists--a task often neglected by field staff who do not like doing paperwork.

The use of market intelligence to segment the customer base is important to TSR's for two reasons. Telephone staff use this information to manage their sales time by concentrating call frequency where the greatest potential exists. It is also a measure of productivity since sales results achieved by telephone staff can be measured against prior profit contributions by their accounts.

How can telephone sales use increased technological support to the benefit of the company? The active calling and management of hundreds of accounts by one telephone sales person needs computerized systems support to enhance productivity. Manual systems can be used. But TSR's find themselves spending hours daily just updating records, handling customer profiles and follow-up call note sheets, communicating address changes to others in the company, tracking results, pulling together individual mailings.

Management typically has data needs that can only be answered through time-consuming efforts, e.g., how many mailings were sent, how many orders were taken during calls, how much time was spent on calls versus call planning and follow-up. Without computer support, support staff spend an inordinate amount of time just providing management with data to the detriment of staff productivity.

Although significant amounts of market intelligence are gathered on customer profiles, summarizing that information manually is almost impossible. Manual operations typically forgo the analysis of data and information gathered until they can be set-up on a computerized sales management system.

TSR's need:

* *A fully integrated computerized support system that ties their sales management system together with other company systems.*

* *They need sales history by account, telephone territory sales and profit information with comparative data from prior years.*

* *Inventory information for use during customer calls.*

* *Order-entry capability for use when orders are placed during calls.*

* *Word processing integration for creating customized mailings and writing quotes and proposals, as well as for updating the 's master direct mail file.*

A fully integrated support system increases telephone sales productivity, provides management with the flexibility for creating of sales and productivity measures, and helps to maintain customer master files.

WHY DISTRIBUTORS IMPLEMENT TELEPHONE SALES

The change masters in wholesale-distribution implement telephone sales for a variety of reasons. And the reasons are expanding as management learns the how-to's of staffing and supporting and measuring and managing this new method of selling.

DISTRIBUTION CHANNEL TELEMARKETING

The following examples demonstrate why two different distributors implemented telephone sales.

Situation #1. A building materials distributor with 11 branch locations analyzed its margins by product type and concluded their profits on commodities did not warrant field sales call costs. Since customers shop strictly for price on commodities, customer requests for pricing from field sales could not be effectively handled. They in turn had to call the branches or headquarters from the customer's location, but often lost orders since branch prices were not competitive and no one at headquarters was available to immediately coordinate with vendors on pricing. Since individual branches did their own commodities buying, they could not achieve vendor price concessions for quantity purchasing through centralized buying.

Solution #1. The only way low-profit contributing products could be turned into profit contributors was to provide less costly services to these product buyers. This firm decided to eliminate field sales selling of commodities and assign these products to a telephone sales function responsible for sales to all accounts. Consolidated buying for all branches and a central warehouse put this distributor into a more competitive price category due to quantity purchasing. Customer requests for pricing now come direct to telephone sales personnel, who check inventory and coordinate immediately with vendors. Quick handling and competitive pricing have made commodity sales a profitable product category. Not only does the customer receive better, more timely service and better prices, the distributor has reduced his sales expenses significantly to be able to continue providing commodity lines to the customer base at an acceptable profit.

Situation #2. An industrial supplies distributor with a full-line of MRO determined they had literally thousands of house accounts and inactive accounts for whom no one had sales and profit responsibility. The prospect of hiring and managing more field sales personnel was considered too time-consuming and expensive a service. They needed a way to quickly qualify sales potential in these accounts. They wanted to reduce their sales expense ratio sufficiently to make calling on smaller accounts profitable.

Solution #2. This distributor initially set-up a two-person telephone sales function to qualify accounts. The qualification process eliminated some accounts from the distributor's master file, determined that small volume potential customers were only to be set-up for direct mailings from the company, and established two new telephone account territories having sales potential sufficient to warrant telephone sales contacts. *Within the first 12 months of operation, the TSR's were averaging over $35,000.00 a month each in sales at 36% gross margin average.* Average sales per telephone sales person increased during the second year of implementation, and the function has subsequently been expanded to call on accounts pulled from field sales. *This firm's long-range objective is to eliminate field sales and build their business through catalog and telephone selling.*

Situation/Solution #2 is the most common start-up telephone sales application in the wholesale-distribution industry

TORN BETWEEN THE OLD AND NEW

In my work with corporations throughout the distribution channel, I find many frustrated owner/

managers torn between the old and new, attempting to deal with a perceived dichotomy. On the one hand, they see their existing "known" field sales organization. On the other, telephone sales is the "unknown" concept shrouded by misperceptions, lack of understanding of the how-to's of implementing and fear of its impact on the existing field sales group and the customer. All too often, the tactical decision is to leave things as they are and hope for the best.

But time continues to pass, and the marketplace and buyers' needs continue to change. New computer and telecommunications technologies are readily available and affordable even to the smallest supplier, and the market intelligence potential that this represents must be able to be used. Once-successful responses to the marketplace are no longer in tune with its needs. The old tried-and-true strategies that fit a former time can only lead to decline and eventual failure.

CONFUSION ABOUT TELEPHONE SALES IMPLEMENTATION

A new marketing strategy, like telephone sales, isn't something that can be implemented in a day. It is here that confusion abounds among owner/managers and among many trade associations that represent the wholesale-distribution industry. Failure or disappointing results often stem from this confusion.

There are two primary steps to implementing telephone sales:

* *Step one is management planning.*

* *Step two is staff selection and staff training.*

Planning is a management function, since telephone sales must be integrated into the existing organization. It requires

* *A marketing strategy.*

* *An account base.*

* *Job definition.*

* *A compensation plan.*

* *Direct mail support.*

* *Results measures.*

* *Training tools.*

* *Job tools and support systems.*

* *Someone responsible for and capable of managing day-to-day operations.*

Though it is the key to successful implementation, management planning is often ignored.

474

DISTRIBUTION CHANNEL TELEMARKETING

Telemarketing is viewed instead as just another inside sales skill versus a new way to take products and services to the marketplace.

Two important job definitions are in order. One is for the "inside sales" function as it is traditionally used in the distribution channel--a customer service and sales support position. The other is for "telephone sales" which is a selling position capable of handling some or all of the steps in the selling process typically handled by field sales today.

These functions are not the same. *To expect customer service staff to be capable of assuming a selling role automatically is just plain folly.* Yet, all too many managers proceed as if this should work.

Most inside sales operations are usually very busy, often understaffed, and responsible for performing a myriad of customer service tasks that are critical to customer satisfaction and maintenance of repeat business. However, it is typically not a function that is measured by management. As a result, owner/managers often do not know all the many important tasks performed by inside sales.

That being the case, it appears to be a simple thing to management to tell inside sales people that they have added job responsibilities beyond those they already handle, i.e., to call customers and prospects and to assume selling responsibility.

Because of the heavy workload, most inside sales reps don't have the time to pick up the telephone and call a customer. They are too busy answering incoming telephone calls and responding to customer requests. To expect to implement telephone sales on an as-time-is-available-basis in the first place simply confirms management's lack of commitment to the importance of the function.

If existing inside sales reps are to be assigned additional responsibilities, then their job must be redefined to afford them the time to be able to do these new job tasks with the consistency required to achieve results. In other words, they will need support staff to handle tasks they presently perform. This presumes that the inside sales staff in question possess the personal characteristics of a salesperson and want a sales versus a service job. A good customer service person does not necessarily have what it takes to be successful at sales.

There are many fine trade associations that represent the distribution channel. Since the early 1970s, trade associations have been sponsoring annual convention presentations for owner/managers on the how-to's of telephone sales implementation. However, some perpetuate the confusion between inside sales and telephone sales.

Association-sponsored workshops for inside sales staff provide telephone sales skills training but ignore the management planning issues. Though attending staff gain knowledge and skill, they do not have the authority, responsibility, and often lack the marketing knowledge and company marketing strategy information required to be able to set up a telephone sales function.

Telephone sales implementation data reflects owner/manager confusion. For example, 1986 data on industrial merchant wholesaler-distributors from a survey conducted by the Southern Industrial Distributors Association reveals that for firms smaller than $5 million in revenue, the average number of field sales people is 4, the average number of telephone sales people is .5. For firms larger than $5 million, those numbers are 13 and 1, respectively.[9]

Primary sales tasks remain with field sales in industrial distribution. The same is true among distributors in the PHCP (plumbing-heating-cooling-piping) industry. An in-depth research study of this industry finds 33% of 1,850 respondents have telephone sales responsibility in an assigned account base. However, only three of that group had full-time selling tasks and one of the three qualified his response by explaining he also had purchasing and counter sales responsibility.[10]

The state of the art among manufacturers, according to an early 1987 survey among 322 members of the American Supply & Machinery Manufacturers Association, indicates a majority have increased their ratio of inside sales to outside sales. The objectives they hope to achieve through this response to rising field sales costs is reduction of the sales expense ratio and increased sales volume.[11]

Summary. Owner/manager perceptions of a dichotomy between the old and the new must be put into a broader perspective through analysis of buyer's needs, and analysis of the uncontrollable forces shaping the specific distribution channel in question. The objective is to restructure the sales and marketing group.

But, restructuring doesn't just happen. Owner/manager understanding and knowledge is needed to effect the implementation process. And that understanding must include the definition of the marketing strategy to be implemented via telephone sales.

Appropriate distribution channel response to uncontrollable market forces depends on the primary market changes affecting the individual firm or the industry and upon the types of products and services being sold. The following examples demonstrate and explain the reasons for different types of responses.

A MACHINE TOOLS DISTRIBUTOR EXAMPLE:

Industry Trend in the US:
In the past, this distributor's customers were primarily large manufacturers having ongoing capital purchasing plans. Buyers were sophisticated and understood the benefits of new technologies in machine tools designed to increase production capabilities, reduce per unit production costs, and maintain or increase high quality production standards.

Machine tool prices ranged between $50,000 to $250,000 and more. The distributor's field sales engineers built a relationship selling strategy with buyers and called on these same accounts year after year.

Today, the distributor faces the erosion of the traditional heavy industry customer base and the growth of highly innovative but smaller potential users. The growth of small users is due in part to large manufacturers outsourcing to small job shops.

This means the distributor must sell more individual transactions to smaller users who do not buy every year. Since buyers are not sophisticated and knowledgeable about new machine tool technologies, they require more in-depth education and hand-holding. Further, buyers are difficult to find. A two-man operation today can turn into a 40-man production plant in a matter of weeks and have machine tool needs as a result. Or, a mid-sized manufacturer might get approval on a bid that requires immediate purchase of new machines in order to expand production and quality control capability.

Simultaneous with changing market trends is the response of the machine tool builders who are bringing out new high-technology machine tools at less cost. Prices start at about $15,000. Although these tools have applications for larger users, a key market in which to build market share is the small end user.

Distributor's Solution:
A telephone prospecting and small machine tools sales function was developed with the following objectives:

DISTRIBUTION CHANNEL TELEMARKETING

1. *Mail literature to potential users to help develop awareness of the distributor's products and value-added capabilities.*

2. *Conduct follow-up telephone calls to qualify need for various types of products including the small-end machine tools, and to determine buying plans and funding arrangements. Qualified accounts were classified into immediate need, within three months, six months, one year, and so on for appropriate scheduled follow-up.*

3. *Immediate and short-range leads for larger machine tools are sent to field sales engineers for in-person follow-up.*

4. *Immediate and short-range needs for small machine tools are assigned to telephone sales to promote attendance at product demonstrations to show how new technologies fit a user's manufacturing and quality control requirements. Closing on these sales is the responsibility of the telephone sales person at the time of the demonstration or through follow-up telephone sales calls.*

5. *Through ongoing direct mailings and telephone contacts, this distributor is building a database on all potential users in his marketing area as well as educating them about products and applications. The end result will be a detailed market intelligence data base on all potential buyers and their capabilities.*

The Result:

1. *Very specific marketing intelligence is being developed which will keep this distributor in touch with changes in the marketplace.*

2. *Sales of small machine tools are accomplished through TSR'S without the need for field sales engineer involvement.*

3. *The distributor can now target specific direct mail pieces and product specifications to real potential users versus mass mailings. This has been a significant side benefit of telephone prospecting implementation to this distributor and his supplying machine tool builders.*

A BUILDING MATERIALS DISTRIBUTOR EXAMPLE:

Industry Trend in the US:

Historically, this industry sold through two-step distribution. Suppliers sold distributors who in turn sold dealers or retailers who sold to the contractor. With the growth of the DIY (do-it-yourself) industry and other price-conscious buyers, two-step distribution channels found themselves with new forms of competition. Aside from the broad line chains like K-Mart, there are increasing numbers of discount retailers, home centers, co-ops, and programmed wholesalers that cater to the consumer and the contractor. Multi-billion-dollar sales growth in this segment is eroding distributor market share and taking large amounts of business that was once sold by the independent distributor.

Since these newcomers represent hundreds of locations, direct buying from manufacturers by their respective headquarters in large quantities achieves highly competitive pricing--*often below the independent distributor's costs.*

Trade Association Solution:

The National Building Material Distributors Association represents the independent distributor. NBMDA commissioned the design of a customized management planning workshop which reflected important industry trends and taught owner/managers the how-to's of implementing telephone sales functions designed to decrease selling costs, provide increased and better account coverage, and help penetrate new markets to replace the eroding customer base. A total of thirteen regional workshops were sponsored by NBMDA and attended by 250+ owner/managers of distributor firms. In response to manager request, NBMDA then commissioned the development of a self-instructional staff level skills training program on the how-to's of telephone selling.

The Results:

1. *29% of those attending implemented new telephone sales functions.*

2. *26% of those attending made significant changes to their existing telephone sales functions to increase profitability and expand applications.*

3. *Outside sales functions were redirected to activities where they would yield greater return on investment.*

4. *Distributor customers experience better service, more frequent contact and timely response to their needs.*

5. *Members have definitive customized management and staff training tools needed to manage and expand their operations.*

6. *Follow-up surveys indicate that sales increases were achieved of up to 100%![12]*

Summary. These examples demonstrate how understanding market forces can be used to restructure traditional sales and marketing organizations. Perhaps more important, they demonstrate businesses that took the time to understand the answer to a very important question:

"What does a buyer need from me in order to be able to buy from me?"

In other words, does the buyer need someone's physical presence to place an order, to understand what a supplier sells, to know the credit terms and policies of the supplier? In fact, these examples and others in this chapter prove field sales contact is not a primary reason for selecting a supplier.

WHAT DO BUYERS NEED FROM SUPPLIERS?

The change from an industrial to an information-based economy has affected more than just suppliers. It has affected buyers who place value on timely, accurate information required to make intelligent buying decisions. They seek suppliers who are organized to meet their need for information. Time is not only money to a supplier, it means money to a buyer.

PF & A's research over the past ten years among thousands of buyers of technical products proves it is the *buyer's needs* that should determine how a supplier's sales and marketing team is organized. We ask buyers a series of questions about telephone sales implementation as follows:

"Mr./Ms. Buyer, what would you think if our client (the buyer's supplier) *had a telephone sales person assigned to you who:*

* *Was educated on products and product applications?*

* *Had information about your buying practices and product needs--in fact, who kept an up-to-date profile on your company as well as its buying history?*

* *Could give advice on the best way to buy to get the best price based on your quantity requirements?*

* *Called you with appropriate product and application recommendations-- including new product explanations, specials, promotions, and discounts?*

* *Had cross-referenced specifications on competitive products?*

* *Could take and develop quotes and provide accurate information immediately on delivery, inventory availability, back-order status, special products ordering and lead times?*

* *Was available for you to talk with about application questions and problems?*

* *Had back-up support staff to handle your inbound calls to place orders, handle returns, credits, and defective materials inspection arrangements?*

Buyer response to these questions is decidedly positive! What could be more time-efficient than having someone like this available? A sales organization structured like this definitely has a competitive edge. The role of telephone sales has taken on increased importance where it counts: *among buyers.*

PF & A's research does not stand alone. Research specific to merchant wholesaler-distributors proves the role and importance of outside sales contacts has decreased significantly as a factor that influences a buyer's selection of a supplier. The National Association of Wholesalers-Distributors (NAW) 1982 *Future Trends* study cited contact with outside sales as the #1 buyer selection factor in 1970, but predicted it would be #8 in importance by 1990.[13] However, NAW's 1987 study goes beyond those predictions for the future stating *"Panelists believe that over the next five years this trend (away from outside sales) will accelerate even more than was predicted in the 1982 study."*[14]

The 1987 study, *Facing the Forces of Change*, emphasizes significant change between outside sales and inside sales roles. Although the study lumps together the telephone sales and inside sales functions--presuming because both use the telephone as the primary communication tool with customers--predictions are indeed important. *"...the sales personnel will perform different tasks, since they will be relieved of many routine ones, such as order taking, field sales and pricing. The computer will allow the sales force to serve existing customers better and to generate new customers through telemarketing, cold calls, new account development and adding value for current customers."*[15]

Summary. The state-of-the-art of telemarketing implementation in the distribution channel proves telemarketing can and does work for owner/managers who function as change masters. They work to restructure their sales and marketing organization in line with changing market needs and corporate goals.

Yet, the old objections to implementing keep surfacing. These objections indicate the need for objective analysis to replace existing attitudes about telephone sales, to eliminate preconceived ideas, and to stop the short-range tactical decision making that prevents the "aggressive restructuring" needed to improve productivity in the distribution channel.

OWNER/MANAGER OBJECTIONS TO TELEPHONE SALES IMPLEMENTATION

Owner/Manager: *"If we implement telephone sales, we'll threaten the field sales group. They'll quit and go to a competitor."*

Like the owner/manager, field sales fear change from the way things used to be. But the marketplace is the change master, not one or more field sales people. And owner/managers must be the analyzers of the marketplace, the gatherers of input from all possible sources including field sales, the decision-makers about what strategies will be implemented for the good of the entire organizations' viability.

Owner/Manager: *"Our product is much too technical to sell by telephone."* Or, *"You can sell commodities, but not proprietary products by telephone."*

These types of comments typically come from owner/managers who have never analyzed the buying process, i.e., what the buyer needs in order to be able to buy. Even successful case studies fall on deaf ears with these managers because they are not what these people want to hear. We are dealing with attitudes and misperceptions and lack of objective management analysis when comments like these are expressed. No more, no less.

Within the industrial distribution channel, carbide cutting tools used in the metal working industry are generally perceived as technical products--even by people outside the industry. That being the case, the following example may prove a point to the nonbelievers.

A regional sales office-based telephone sales function was implemented in early 1987 by this supplier. Sales overall were up 40% with December, 1987, sales up 75% from December 1986 sales. Without a doubt, according to this firm's president, the increase is attributed to telephone sales. What is most exciting about this example is that telephone sales is still considered a start-up operation. The results achieved in less than one year of implementation are excellent thus far, since considerable time was spent during this period setting up the function and recruiting personnel. Major bottom-line contributions should be forthcoming in 1988 and beyond.

Within the building materials industry, proprietary products are those considered unique in some way, and owner/managers insist they require field sales demonstration, e.g., a new type of roofing or paneling. Yet, PF & A's experiences in these industries prove just the opposite. We set up telephone sales functions designed to sell both commodity lines and proprietary products, and it works.

One supplier has a national accounts group. A small cadre of national account executives are responsible for developing programs, pricing, advertising strategies, and for selling the product promotion package to various national account headquarters. Although headquarters were buying the packages, there was no sales organization to call on the hundreds of individual store locations throughout the country that are represented by national accounts. Their solution: sell both commodity and proprietary products to the respective national account store locations by telephone with a primary sales objective to promote proprietary lines. The result: market share data prove overall penetration on both proprietary and commodity lines sales to national accounts. These results are particularly significant in those markets showing loss of share on sales through the traditional distribution network serviced by field sales people.

Owner/Manager: *"We can't afford the cost of implementing telephone sales."*

There are costs involved to design a telephone sales marketing strategy, to develop support materials and systems, to recruit and train and put the physical set-up in place. And, management time and related costs are an obvious and needed commitment. But, a professionally designed operation can virtually pay for itself within a few months of implementation and continue to contribute to profits into the future. Cost is not the real issue. Attitude is. Many businesses that balk over implementation costs simultaneously hire a new field salesperson expecting a break-even on that investment, hopefully after a year, and never give it a second thought.

Owner/Manager: *"Someone else tried telephone sales in our industry. It didn't work. We know it won't work in our industry."*

What another company does or does not do is not the issue. What an owner/manager does with his company counts. Typically those making a comment like this do not know anything about the telephone sales function in question, aside from the fact that it didn't work. Without direct involvement or analysis of the implementation strategy, there is no way to know why another's operation failed. PF & A's evaluation of unsuccessful operations typically finds the demise *was due to lack of management planning in the first place.* In fact, some operations are designed to fail to prove a point within the company or the industry. The most common reasons for failure we find are:

1. *There was no business plan or marketing strategy defined for the function.*

2. *The accounts assigned had no sales potential for the products or services*

being offered, or, the potential was too low to warrant sales calls of any sort.

3. *The wrong staff were hired for the job, and the job was never defined.*

4. *No results measures were put into place.*

5. *There was no compensation plan to reward for performance; in fact, success meant increased commissions to field sales staff versus those doing the job.*

6. *TSR's were never trained for the job.*

7. *No one was responsible for managing and directing the function.*

8. *The telephone sales group was not integrated into overall existing company operations.*

There are two common ways for owner/managers to implement telephone sales functions in the distribution channel. Neither work. The first way is to approach some unsuspecting inside salesperson, tell him to "sell," and explain he should continue doing his present job and fit the selling time in whenever possible.

The second most common approach to implementation is to schedule a staff level workshop on one day and expect staff to begin telephone selling the following day. Support systems, forms design, job descriptions, compensation plans, direct mail support, account base assignment, coordination with other internal operations, telephone equipment, computer equipment--you name it--are simply ignored.

When someone says *"We tried it. It didn't work."* typically, that means company management just didn't do its job.

Owner/Manager: *"If we cut back on field sales calls, our customers will think we don't care about them and my competition will eat our lunch!"*

The use and expense of field sales is seen as a value-added service by owner/managers. This perception reinforces costly field sales calls on anyone and everyone, even low sales potential accounts that cost the supplier money to make even one sales call. Erroneous perceptions frequently prevent objective analysis.

The real question any business needs to ask and answer is:

> *"What does the customer/prospect need from me in order to be able to buy my products and service?"*

The answer to that question should determine how the sales group should be organized. Seller perceptions just plain don't count. Consider the GE representative who stated the following in defense of GEMIMS buying direct versus through distributors:

> *"In most cases there isn't any value-added; the distributor is just selling commodities."*

Whether the distributor is selling commodities or what he perceives as proprietary or technical product, if a buyer places no value on a supposed value-added service, then there is no value no matter what the seller thinks.

The above owner/manager reason for not implementing telephone sales further ignores a known reality about field sales in the distribution channel. Reliance on field sales has an inherent lack of account coverage potential built into this sales strategy. Field sales may have an assigned territory for which they receive commission on all sales, but that has nothing to do with the accounts on which they call and concentrate their time. *Most accounts in larger territories are simply ignored.* They receive no contact. Others may get an annual, bi-annual or quarterly contact. But, no one is working with these accounts. And, they constitute the majority in the territory because it is physically impossible to cover them all.

Concern over a competitor's field sales contacts presumes quality calls. PF & A experience traveling with field sales often finds them implementing a milk-route sales mentality, i.e., if it's Tuesday, then they call on accounts X, Y, and Z. Having a sales strategy and specific sales call objectives have little or nothing to do with making these unannounced calls, which often end up having the field salesperson calling his inside sales people to answer a customer's question.

Summary. Owner/manager objections to telephone sales implementation are not always what they appear to be initially. Avoidance of telephone sales, especially among merchant wholesaler-distributors, stems from overextended sales managers who spend the majority of their time calling on accounts--not managing sales staff. The lack of market intelligence gathering, of field sales reporting, of data analysis and the use of that data directly reflects the need for someone who has the time to manage.

When sales managers realize the implementation of telephone sales requires a time commitment, the most immediate response is to try to offload the task and related decisions to someone without the required experience and authority, or to short-shrift the planning process. From inception, the operation is doomed to limited success or failure as a result.

At this time, the state-of-the-art of telephone sales implementation in the distribution channel is basic and has not been fully tested. But the trend overall is toward greater utilization. Uncontrollable market forces are in turn forcing management to make choices and reach decisions about changing the sales and marketing organization. There is a definite and proven need for better, more cost-effective, more efficient and productive sales strategies. Telephone sales can be such a strategy when properly designed and supported. Its continued and expanded use by the change masters in the distribution channel is expected to influence others having the same goals: profitability and growth.

RECRUITING AND TRAINING FOR TELEPHONE SALES

Telephone sales in the distribution channel has been successfully implemented with technical and commodity products. Yet many owner/managers will cite anything and everything for not implementing or not being successful, e.g., *"Our product is too technical."* Or, *"We tried it; it doesn't work in our industry."*

To help ensure the successful implementation of telephone sales in technical products application, we recommend developing recruiting specifications for purposes of defining the knowledge, skill, experience, and education needed for someone to be able to do the job. Once developed, it is common for a client

483

to eliminate people formerly under consideration for the position because they do not meet these requirements.

Simply put, the more complex the telephone sales job, the more complex the recruiting criteria and vice versa. For example, recruiting specifications for a full-line technical products salesperson include:

1. *Company-specific knowledge:* for example, pricing, procedures, use of sales reports, CRT, order entry and use of various forms, information flow, who to call for what reasons, bid preparation, vendor contacts.

2. *Product knowledge:* for example, types of products, product application, product reference sources including use of specification sheets and other literature, samples and their use, vendors, competitive products, product features and benefits.

3. *Customer knowledge:* for example, types of customers and their differences, how customers buy, when, what, and why they buy, use of JIT, blanket orders, upcoming projects, names and titles of buyers and buying influences.

4. *Sales and telephone sales how-to's:* for example, how to define sales strategies by account type, how to set specific sales call objectives, how to sell company features and benefits, how to sell product features and benefits, how and when to schedule calls, to qualify sales potential.

Presuming you cannot recruit someone having the required experience, the next best approach is to hire the most appropriate candidate and provide the training needed to be able to do the job. For many firms, this means hiring staff initially for the inside sales/customer service function for six to 12 months or more prior to promotion to telephone sales. The benefits of having the right people in the job are demonstrated by these actual client examples:

Correct Recruiting Example. An electronic components and assembly house supplier started its telephone sales function in early 1986 to sell relays, capacitors, R.C. networks, cable assemblies, the full line of electronic supplies and assembly. One telephone sales person was selected from the customer service/inside sales function having 2 1/2 years experience with the company working with products, literature, customers and vendors. Within the first six months, sales averaged $20,000 a week. *The first 12-months' sales exceeded $600,000 which surpassed all prior experiences working with new outside sales staff.* The second 12-months' sales are expected to easily exceed $1,000,000. A second telephone sales person was just recently brought in from the customer service/inside sales area to begin building another new account base for the firm.

Poor Recruiting Example. A full-line industrial supply house staffed its new telephone sales function with two former "telemarketing trained" people from their local telephone company. Neither had product or industry knowledge prior to hiring. They were provided catalogs, product literature and a list of accounts to call. No product training was given nor was it seen as needed by management. After 12 months,

DISTRIBUTION CHANNEL TELEMARKETING

I was called in to see why they only achieved $225,000 in sales. The first question the telephone sales staff asked during our interview was: *"What is all this stuff we're supposed to be selling?"*

Was This Investment Worth It? One manufacturer client in the building materials industry has no internal source from which to recruit telephone sales staff for its new operation located at a regional distribution center. The solution was to hire two people having experience using building materials in former jobs, who had customer service/order entry and sales backgrounds in related industries, and who understood distribution. Immediately after hiring, they were provided a full 10 weeks of intensive training planned to address their knowledge and skills development needs. They were sent to work in a customer service operation in another part of the country, travelled with outside sales reps to call on representative types of accounts similar to those they would be selling by telephone, visited manufacturing operations for product training, received hands-on CRT and company orientation training and, finally, telephone sales training--all prior to ever picking up a telephone to call an account.

Was this investment worth it? Within the first four months, this two-man operation broke even on all costs incurred to set up including training and office equipment. *At the end of the first year of implementation, these people are considered among the top salesmen in the country for this company in comparison with all field salesmen.*

Summary. Recruiting qualified personnel is a common problem cited among firms in the distribution channel. Recruiting is considered a time-consuming task for management. Yet, once someone is recruited, training needs are virtually ignored and productivity suffers accordingly. The excuse is there is no time available to train. The results of this attitude are the only real thing that counts. The results include the following costly situations in time and dollar terms:

* *Staff will quit because they realize they do not know how to do the job and will not be offered the training. In fact, when they ask for help, people get angry with them. This puts management back into a time-consuming and costly recruiting mode.*

* *Results that could have been achieved in a few months are not forthcoming until years of trial-and-error implementation.*

* *The corporate image suffers from often thousands of unprofessional calls made by unprofessional staff.*

In response to recent significant turnover, one owner/manager recently complained *"My customers just won't take the time to help me train my people anymore!"* What he was really saying is he expects someone outside his company to train his people to make money for him. That is probably why his margins have eroded so badly these past few years and will probably continue to do so.

The knowledge and skills needed to be able to do the job must be clearly defined before hiring. If you cannot find the right person, select the next best and invest into training to develop the knowledge and skills needed. Technical product selling has been successfully achieved over the telephone in the industrial, welding, electrical, electronics, building supplies, machine tool industries and many, many more.

ADDENDUM: CUSTOMER PROFILE EXAMPLES[16]

Following are examples of customer profile records used by telephone sales staff in various distribution channel firms. The account information gathered by staff is used to define by-account sales strategies and specific sales call objectives.

----

[1]*Modern Distribution Management*, P.O. Box 370, Claverack, NY 12513. May 18, 1987.

[2]*Ibid.*, June 7, 1985, June 24, 1985, April 30, 1986 and September 21, 1987.

[3]*Ibid.*, November 14, 1986.

[4]"Programmed Wholesalers, Wholesaler Groups," *Building Supply Home Centers*, August 1987, pp. 102-128.

[5]"1987 Wholesaler Giants," *Building Supply Home Centers*, September 1987, pp. 46-74.

[6]*Facing the Forces of Change*, pp. 12 and 27.

[7]*Ibid*, page 67.

[8]*Planning Your Telephone Sales Operation*, Peg Fisher & Associates, Inc., New Edition, Sixth Printing, September, 1987. Available from PF & A, 1201 S. Wisconsin, Racine, WI, 53403, page 1.10.

[9]Data presented at the June, 1987, Triple Industrial Supply Convention by the Southern Industrial Distributors Association, 11 Corporation Square, #200, Atlanta, GA 30329.

[10]*Supply House Times*, October 1983, pp. 178-196, 7574 Lincoln Avenue, Skokie, IL 60077.

[11]*Industrial Distributor*, May 1987, page 14, 249 W. 17th Street, New York, NY 10011.

[12]"Proven Sales Increases Up to 100%: An Industry Case Example," available from Peg Fisher & Associates, Inc., 1201 S. Wisconsin, Racine, WI 53403.

[13]*Future Trends in Wholesale Distribution: A Time of Opportunity, 1982*, available from Distribution Research and Education Foundation, 1725 K Street, #710, Washington, DC 20006.

[14]*Facing the Forces of Change*, page 87.

[15]*Ibid*, page 87.

[16]*Planning Your Telephone Sales Operation*, pp. 3.6,3.9--3.15.

Figure 24-2
Customer Information Record (Example 1)

Set-up date: _____ Credit info. sent date: _____
Telephone #: (   ) _____ Credit approval date: _____
Fax #: (   ) _____ Line of credit: $ _____
                                     Acct. rep.: _____

Company name: _____ Cust. #: _____
Mailing address for quotations/samples: _____
City: _____ State: _____ ZIP: _____ # Yrs in business: ____

Headquarters: ___ Yes ___ No   (If "Yes")   Centralized buying? ___ Yes ___ No
                                  (If "No")   Number of company locations: _____

NAME   TITLE   PRODUCTS PURCHASED   EXT. #
1. _____/_____/_____/_____
2. _____/_____/_____/_____

Type of business: _____
            Brochure requested/received: _____ Yes _____ No
Type of customers you sell: _____
Average annual volume in our products: $ _____
Brands used: _____
Competitive suppliers: _____
Do you use JIT inventory management system? _____ Yes _____ No
    If "Yes," for what products? _____
            Annual usage: _____
Are you interested in blanket orders or timed releases from stock?   _____ Yes _____ No
    If "Yes," for what products?_____
            Annual usage: _____
Do you have special requiements for getting product approval? _____ Yes _____ No
    If "Yes," explain: _____
How do you buy electronic components? _____ Monthly _____ As needed _____ By the job _____ Other
Do you have any upcoming projects design and engineering plans?   _____ Yes _____ No
    Engineer names: _____ Ext. #: _____
                    _____ Ext. #: _____
Any special delivery/labeling/packaging instructions? _____ Yes _____ No
    Explain: _____
    _____

Do you accept partials? _____ Yes _____ No
Do you have assembly done outside your firm?   _____ Yes _____ No
    If "Yes," for what?   _____ Cable   _____ Printed circuit boards
                          _____ Electro-mechanical   _____ Panels
                          _____ Other (please explain): _____
                          _____

Figure 24-3
Account Information Record

Credit status: _____
Annual volume: _____
O.S. contact initials: _____

Account #: _____
Set-up date: _____

Delivery route: 1 2 3 4 5 6
Accept B.O.'s: ____ Yes ____ No
Call day: M T W Th F   am / pm
Locations: _____

Company name: _____ Cust. #: _____

Mailing address : _____
City: _____ State: _____ ZIP: _____ # Yrs. in business: ____

Shipping address : _____
City: _____ State: _____ ZIP: _____ # Yrs. in business: ____

CONTACT NAME   TITLE   PRODUCTS   EXT. #
1. _____ / _____ / _____ / _____
2. _____ / _____ / _____ / _____
3. _____ / _____ / _____ / _____

Account type (check):

☐ Lumber yard   ☐ Home center   ☐ Hardware store   ☐ Decorating center   ☐ Carpet store   ☐ Paint store

Other (specify): _____

Total # employees: ____   # O.S. ____   # Counter ____   # Yard ____

Holds open houses/
DIY clinics: ____ When: _____   Products involved: _____

Customers served: ____% Contractor   ____% DIY   ____% Municipal
Other (specify): _____

Services offered: (List services account offers its customers and person responsible, e.g., general contracting, home/commercial building design, kitchen planning, installation, etc.)

_____   _____
_____   _____
_____   _____
_____   _____

In-store displays: (Specify the type/product/supplier of product)

_____   _____   _____
_____   _____   _____
_____   _____   _____

Figure 24-4a
Customer Information Record (Example 2)

Credit type: _____

Customer #: _____

TS #: _____
OS #: _____
Driver: _____

Customer name: _____ Telephone : ( ) _____
        Call Time: M T W Th F (Circle One)   am pm Other: _____

Mailing address : _____
        City: _____ State: _____ ZIP: _____

Shipping address : _____
        City: _____ State: _____ ZIP: _____

Special shipping requirements: Partials: Y N   Backorders?   Y   N   Other:

CONTACT NAME   TITLE   PRODUCTS   EXT. #
1._____/_____/_____/_____
2._____/_____/_____/_____
3._____/_____/_____/_____

Type of business: _____
Type of metal welded: _____
_____

Equipment used: Brand name:
_____   _____
_____   _____
_____   _____
_____   _____

In-store displays: (Specify the type/product/supplier of product)

_____   _____   _____
_____   _____   _____
_____   _____   _____

Processes used: (MIG, TIG, PLASMA, other) _____
_____

Type of welding systems in place: _____
_____

489

Figure 24-4b
Customer Information Record (Example 2, Continued)

Types of safety equipment used: _____

Equipment rental needs: _____

Repair service needs (Who does repair/how satisfied): _____

_____

Welding lab testing needs: _____

Staff training needs: _____

PURCHASING HISTORY:

Industrial gases:			*Weld/cut. supplies:*			*Filler metals:*		
1	Oxygen	____	10	Brush/abras	____	19	Mild stl. electrds.	____
2	Fuel/acetylene	____	11	Wheels/belts	____	20	Mild stl. autowire	____
3	Nitrogen	____	12	Fluxes/chem.	____	21	Non-ferris	____
4	Inert	____	13	Silver solder	____		Electrodes/wire	____
5	Specialty	____	14	Tools	____	22	Flux cord wire	____
Other prod./serv:			15	Tips	____	23	Subarc flux	____
6	Equip. rental	____	*Medical gas/supplies:*			24	Other	_____
7	Repair serv.	____	16	Gases	____			_____
8	Lab testing	____	17	Inhalation				_____
9	Other	_____		Mach., etc.	____			_____
		_____	18	Anesthesia				_____
		_____		Mach., etc.	____	25	Safety equipment	____

SALES POTENTIAL:

Potential equipment needs: _____

_____

Potential supply needs: _____
                (Use coding from above "Purchasing History")

Potential service needs: _____
                (Use coding from above "Purchasing History")

COMPETITIVE INFORMATION: What products/equipment/services are currently purchased
      from a competitor?

ITEMS   SUPPLIER   REASON

_____

_____

_____

Figure 24-5a
Customer Information Record (Example 3)

INTERNAL OFFICE INFORMATION

Account volume size: $ _____

Customer #: _____

Branch: _____

Credit limit: $_____

Salesperson name: _____

Credit class: (Circle one) A B C D

Call frequency schedule: _____

ADDRESS/SHIPPING INFORMATION

Customer name: _____ Telephone : ( ) _____

Mailing address : _____

City: _____ State: _____ ZIP: _____

Shipping address : _____

City: _____ State: _____ ZIP: _____

Special shipping instructions, e.g., limitations on trailor height, unloading flat-bed trucks, customer's lift truck capability: _____

_____

_____

Preferred carrier (if appropriate): _____

Delivery days & hours: Mon: ____   Tues: ____   Wed: ____   Thurs: ____

                     Fri: ____   Sat: ____   Sun: ____

TELEPHONE NUMBERS/WHO BUYS WHAT INFORMATION   Call zone (Circle one) +1 1 -1

Buyers names/titles	Products purchased	Telephone #/ext. #
_____ /	_____ /	( ) _____
_____ /	_____ /	( ) _____
_____ /	_____ /	( ) _____

COMMENTS   (E.g., individual buyer preferences, attitudes, problems, names of others you talk with and their titles, etc.)

_____

_____

_____

_____

_____

_____

Figure 24-5b
Customer Information Record (Example 3, Continued)

SALES HISTORY/PLANNING INFORMATION

PRODUCT	SUPPLIER	BUYING FREQUENCY	TL	1/2TL	1/4TL	OTHER

Primary product

_____ _____/_____ /___/___/___/_____
_____ _____/_____ /___/___/___/_____
_____ _____/_____ /___/___/___/_____
_____ _____/_____ /___/___/___/_____

Secondary product

_____ _____/_____ /___/___/___/_____
_____ _____/_____ /___/___/___/_____
_____ _____/_____ /___/___/___/_____
_____ _____/_____ /___/___/___/_____

Other

_____ _____/_____ /___/___/___/_____
_____ _____/_____ /___/___/___/_____
_____ _____/_____ /___/___/___/_____
_____ _____/_____ /___/___/___/_____

If _____ is used, any brand preference? _____

Any use of co-op advertising on _____? _____

Figure 24-6
Customer Information Record (Example 4)

INTERNAL INFORMATION

Customer #: _____
Credit code:_____
TS name: _____
OS name: _____

Bank/trade reference: _____
SIC code: _____ # Employees _____
Delivery route: _____
Delivery days: _____
Volume code: _____
Call frequency schedule: _____

ADDRESS INFORMATION AND ORGANIZATION:

Customer name: _____ Telephone : ( ) _____

Mailing address : _____
    City: _____ State: _____ ZIP: _____

Shipping address : _____
    City: _____ State: _____ ZIP: _____

    Special shipping instructions: _____
_____
_____

Type of company: OEM _____ User _____ Reseller _____ Other _____
Description of nature of customer's business: _____
_____

% of customers by type: _____ % (type) _____ % (type) _____ % (type) _____ % (type)

Buyer names/influencers   Title   Products Purchased   Ext. #

_____/_____/_____/_____
_____/_____/_____/_____
_____/_____/_____/_____

Other names/titles: _____
SALES INFORMATION: _____ % of total purchases/our product; Accept back orders: Y N

Sales potential: (U = uses; P = purchases from us; T = target sales potential)

Product category:	#1 ____	#5 ____	#9 ____	#13 ____	Etc.
	#2 ____	#6 ____	#10 ____	#14 ____	
	#3 ____	#7 ____	#11 ____	#15 ____	
	#4 ____	#8 ____	#12 ____	#16 ____	

Sales strategy (sales/profit quota by year; tie-in with customer's JIT systems; blanket order objectives on "X" products and target product and product "mix" objectives, etc.): _____
_____

493

CHAPTER 25

Fund-Raising Telemarketing

Richard L. Bencin
Donald J. Jonovic, Ph.D.

It's an amazing fact that many non-profit organizations overlook outbound telemarketing's power to increase the success of fund-raising efforts. Most organizations seem content with using direct mail for the bulk of their solicitations, with only *limited* telemarketing and face-to-face visits to the top 100 or so of the most generous past givers.

Some larger institutions use inbound "phonathons" associated with network, local, or cable TV. A few others use print or direct mail along with an 800 number for response. *Outbound* telemarketing efforts, however, are seldom made in conjunction with the overall fund-raising campaign.

Consider the evidence: There were 17 non-profit winners (four gold, four silver, and nine bronze) of the 1987 58th annual International Echo Awards, sponsored by the Direct Marketing Association. Only *one* of these used outbound telemarketing in their programs!

This low telemarketing usage is particularly remarkable since telemarketing is, by far, the largest component of the direct marketing spectrum. Compare 1988 telemarketing expenditures of $45.4 billion with the following:[1]

* *Broadcast $30.9 billion/annum.*

* *Newspapers $29.5 billion/annum.*

* *Direct mail $19.0 billion/annum.*

* *Magazines $8.2 billion/annum.*

SOME IMPORTANT CAVEATS

Still, for those organizations with the inclination to try a "do-it-yourself" program, it's quite possible to implement very successful outbound telemarketing (there are excellent telemarketing service agencies that provide specialized fund-raising services, and telemarketing often deserves at least some experimentation on the service-agency level).

Organizations have done so, and some of them have more than tripled donations over the results of their prior direct-mail programs. Cautions abound, however.

The fund-raising organization *must* be able to make the following commitments in order to be successful:

* *Provide senior-level management support to both the form and substance of the program.*

* *Enlist the services of a qualified telemarketing consultant.*

* *Secure the services of an excellent staff supervisor who can function as an outstanding motivator and sales trainer/coach of the telephone team captains and volunteers.*

* *Provide a large base of qualified volunteers (outgoing, verbal, persistent, resistant to rejection, etc.) ready and willing to make the necessary solicitation calls.*

* *Obtain the appropriate central facilities and telephones that would be conveniently located, well-equipped and fully suited to telephone calling with regard to space, acoustics, supervision, etc.*

Assuming that these commitments will be made, let's take a closer look at how to set up an in-house program using volunteers.

TRAINING MANUAL

The first step is to develop a functional, effective *Training Manual*. The following are the minimum features required in a working manual:

Simplicity. Because most volunteer assignment periods are very short (often one month) and the personnel are relatively inexperienced, the training must be simple, easy to learn, and virtually word-for-word. Hence, the need for a simple training manual.

The procedures, script and objection/question responses would, therefore, be designed for maximum performance with the least amount of risk and nominal performance assumed. However, individuals can and should be encouraged to "personalize" their presentations and maximize their performance.

Contents. The manual should cover, at least, the following topics:

* *Notes to volunteers.*

* *Contribution letter.*

* *Getting by the "screen" (calls to businesses only).*

* *Contribution script(s).*

* *Objections/questions and replies.*

* *Queries.*

* *Weekly Summary Report.*

* *Prospect sheets.*

* *Special payment options/procedures.*

Notes to Volunteers. In this section, basic procedures, along with the requirement for reading the manual, should be described. Team captains can use this section for preliminary review with the volunteers.

Here is an example of a "notes" section:

Notes to Volunteers (Example)

1. *Your responsive attendance at our first training meeting and subsequent calling sessions would be greatly appreciated. Please read all training material prior to the initial sessions.*

2. *Please make the commitment to call all designated prospects given to you. The calls should be made in a timely manner with your best possible effort.*

3. *At the conclusion of each calling session, please provide your team captain with the Weekly Summary Sheet and the completed prospect sheets you were provided before the session. Please note that completed calls, revenue pledged, and calls yet to be completed should be summarized by category for the _____ (organization name).*

4. *Should you be asked any question, or be given a complaint about the organization that cannot be answered immediately, please complete a Query and forward it to your team captain. Someone on the administrative staff will call the inquirer within two business days.*

5. *If, for any reason, you cannot make a particular calling session, please try to arrange an alternate plan with your team captain so that you can make your assigned calls.*

6. *Please accept our most sincere thanks for helping with our telephone fund raising. We couldn't make it without your help.*

Contribution Letter. A letter requesting a contribution should precede the outbound telemarketing call, and should be sent under the signature of the chief executive officer of the non-profit organization. Long copy generally sells better than short copy, so you can usually safely tell the complete story.

The major reasons for contributing should be highlighted and all appropriate supporting material/ brochures should be included with the envelope. Remember, postscripts tend to be among the most read parts of any letter, and this could be a good place to comment about a forthcoming phone call.

Getting by the "Screen." This section is applicable only to those volunteers who are calling on businesses. Many company executives will have "screens" or "gatekeepers" charged with eliminating unwanted phone calls. The volunteer will have to get by these screens in order to make their appeal to the designated person.

This is why the "heavy-hitter" volunteers should be put on this aspect of the project. Confidence and experience are important for getting by the screen. So, too, are prepared suggestions of approaches to typical screen comments, such as the few examples below:

Getting by the Screen (Examples)

* *Screen: "May I ask who is calling. . ."*

  Response: "Certainly. Who am I speaking with please?

  Mr./Ms. _____, this is _____. The spelling is _____. I've got some rather important information to discuss with Mr./Ms. _____, would you please put me through to him/her? (The slowdown of the receptionist/ secretary by the name spelling may cause him or her to put the call through without further challenge.)

* *Screen: "What is this call in reference to. . ."*

  Response: "I'm calling with an urgent request from General Hospital, and need to speak with Mr./Ms. _____ directly."

* *Screen: "Can I help you. . ."*

  Response: "Yes. I'd like to speak to Mr./Ms. _____."

* *Screen: "He's/she's out of town" (or "in a meeting" or "can't be disturbed," etc.)*

  Response: "I understand. . .can you tell me when would be a more appropriate time to call Mr./Ms. _____ back?"

* *Screen: "Why do you want to speak to him/her?"*

  Response: "Our President, Mr. _____, has sent Mr./Ms. _____ a letter

497

about an urgent need at the hospital. He asked me to call on his behalf.''

Contribution Script. Dual scripts may be required, one for businesses and one for individuals called. However, for the sake of simplicity, and since some volunteers will be calling on both, an attempt should be made to design a universal script.

The script should be easy to read, with brief, hard-hitting sentences. The script should tell the story without being overly long. It should also reinforce the direct-mail letter, which has served as an excellent ''ice breaker'' for the telephone caller. Note the reference to the prior letter in the following script example:

Contribution Script (Example)

*   *Hello, Mr./Ms. _____, this is _____ calling from General Hospital. (Pause)*

*   *Our President, Mr. Tom Jones, sent you a letter recently. Did you receive it and have a chance to read it?*

*   *As Mr. Jones said in his letter, because we have outgrown our surgery facilities here at General Hospital, we have an urgent need to build a new Surgery Center.*

   By doing so, we'll be able to handle the increasing number of operations and more complex procedures such as hip replacements and cardiac bypasses.

   Also, I might add, we should be able to reduce our hospital costs over the long run by handling more operations on an outpatient basis. We'll also be able to reduce our bed capacity requirement at the hospital.

*   *So we can better serve the community by improving our surgical care and reducing long-term hospital costs, won't you help us with your contribution?*

If ''yes'':

Thank you. How generous can you be in giving us your helping hand?

Thank you very much, Mr./Ms. _____. We'll be sending you a pledge envelope for your contribution. Please fill it out, write the check and return it as soon as possible, okay?

Thanks again, and good bye.

If ''no'':

I understand. Could I verify your address?

Thank you for your time.

FUND-RAISING TELEMARKETING

Objection/Questions and Responses. By consolidating questions and thinking through what 90% of the anticipated objections might be, the objection/question list should be boiled down to about 10. The replies must be short, to-the-point, and logical.

Replies, when possible, should be phrased to lead to an appropriate request for a contribution. Committing these replies to memory will help the telemarketers, since each reply could turn a potentially terminating comment into a *positive reason* for support.

Objection/Response (Examples)

"I CAN'T AFFORD IT/TIMES ARE TOUGH/I'VE BEEN LAID OFF…"

*   *Mr./Ms. _____, I can sympathize with your position.*

*   *That's why General Hospital would be appreciative of even a small contribution, say $20 or $30.*

*   *Could you help us out with just that much?*

If still "no":

*   *If this is a difficult time, could you pledge a contribution for our Surgery Center in three months? (Or six months?) We'd be happy to remind you at that time.*

"DOESN'T GENERAL HOSPITAL HAVE THEIR OWN MONEY TO BUILD THE SURGERY CENTER?"

*   *It's true that we are a high productivity hospital that's been well managed. That's why $7 million in financial reserves have been set aside for the project.*

*   *But it's an unfortunate fact of life that reimbursements from the Federal Government and others are based on historical costs and not true replacement costs.*

*   *So we still need an additional $4 million to complete the new Surgery Center. That's why we're calling on you. Won't you help us?*

"I'VE ALREADY GIVEN TO THE UNITED WAY."

*   *Mr./Ms. _____, it's wonderful that you've given to the United Way, but the funding for the Surgery Center at General Hospital is a special, one-time only program. It will not be funded by the United Way.*

"WILL THIS CONTRIBUTION BE USED BY GENERAL HOSPITAL FOR ANY OTHER PURPOSE THAN THE SURGERY CENTER?"

* *Mr./Ms. _____, unless you specifically ask us to accept your contribution for another purpose, your gift will only be used to help build our new Surgery Center.*

"WHAT RECOGNITION WILL BE GIVEN TO CONTRIBUTORS?"

* *We will prominently list all donors on huge wall plaques right within the waiting area of the new Surgery Center.*

* *Those individuals and businesses giving special contributions will be appropriately recognized.*

* *General Hospital wants the community to know who has supported this much-needed facility. We expect the new Surgery Center to serve our area for quite some time to come.*

ANY QUESTIONS/COMPLAINTS THAT CANNOT BE ANSWERED IMMEDIATELY

(Question)

* *Mr./Ms. _____, I really don't have a specific answer to your question. I'll be happy to have someone on our administrative staff call you back within two business days. Would that be all right?*

(Complaint)

* *Mr./Ms. _____, I'm sorry to hear that you've had that problem at General Hospital. If you'd like, I'll be happy to have someone on our administrative staff call you back within two business days. Would that be all right?*

(Prepare the General Hospital Query and submit it to your team captain.)

Queries. The query form should be used when the volunteer on the phone cannot answer a question or handle a complaint. Both the appropriate remarks from the "Objection/Response Examples," as well as an easy-to-use form, should provide the facility to handle these situations adequately.

Administrative personnel designated to respond to the queries/complaints should get back to the appropriate potential donor within two business days. This prompt response should promote good public relations as well as help the telephone volunteers if they still are attempting to close for a contribution.

Results of the queries should, therefore, flow back to the original volunteer for this reason.

Weekly Summary Report. This report will help to consolidate and organize data for all concerned. Each week's activity should be summarized by volunteer, team captain, and the overall program.

Various source categories, such as previous donors, businesses, and former patients/members/graduates should be summarized by the following:

* *Total completed calls.*

* *Total number of pledges.*

* *Total dollar value of pledges.*

* *Calls yet to be completed.*

Analysis of the summary data will show everyone the quality of the job being done. Perhaps more importantly, analysis will make clear the job *remaining* to be done.

Also, this back-end analysis of the prospect sources will help management estimate just *when* the goal will be reached--and *how many* callers and team captains will be needed.

ORGANIZATION

A number of important management and organizational issues should be addressed before the project begins to ensure the most effective and efficient program possible:

Computer/Manual Clean Up of Prospect Lists. Before providing prospect lists to team captains and telephone volunteers, it's important to "clean" them. Specifically, all individuals and businesses that have already given to the campaign should be removed from the lists. Also, previous donors, businesses and former patient/member/graduate lists should be checked for duplication.

Prospect Sheets. Each potential donor should have a sheet which includes complete name identification, title (if business), address, phone number, amount previously given (if donor) and source (previous donor and type, business or former patient/member/graduate). Also, if special payment instructions apply, a special "remarks" section should be made available.

Ideally, these forms should take the form of 8 1/2" X 11" computer printouts. Three-hole punched, these forms allow easy organization and follow up, since binders for team captains could be maintained with appropriate indices separating work still pending by volunteers. If such printouts aren't available, 3"X5" cards, indices and "recipe boxes" can also work well.

Special Payment Options/Procedures. These options should be worked out prior to the start of telemarketing. Give consideration to options such as the following:

* *Monthly payment plans (duration, monitoring procedure).*

501

* *Post-payment pledges (follow-up reminders, calls).*

* *Credit cards (if applicable).*

* *Employee deductions.*

The telephone callers should be briefed well enough to understand all payment options available, and be able to explain each of these plans to donors.

Manpower Requirements. In most cases, the initial telephone solicitation should be scheduled to last for one month, and team captains/telephone volunteers should be asked to spend four hours per week for four weeks. Schedules should be drawn based on the time assumptions made, available telephone volunteers and the prospect calls to be made.

Prospects. The first month's calling efforts should be organized to provide for contacting all prior donors and a significant sample of incremental prospects (should new prospect lists be considered). This sample should be evaluated as to close ratios and average contribution size to help determine if a second month's effort is required, and to which kind of prospect. This data can also help to determine the potential productivity of future campaigns.

Location. An office location within the organization's headquarters is often ideal. Look for a single, general area with cubicles (or open offices) that can provide a sense of togetherness while allowing some telephone privacy. Other important considerations are proper acoustics and proximity to food, vending and other break facilities.

Some organizations that lack sufficient facilities of their own have been able to find organizations willing to donate such space for use during the program.

Follow-Up Correspondence. Responses to contributors should be developed so that pledges are both verified and processed. Provisions should also be made for reviewing special payment arrangements. Needless to say, requests for payment should be made as appropriate.

PROGRAM IMPLEMENTATION

Generally, fund-raising programs are implemented in the following order:

Selection of Team Captains. The project supervisor should select his or her team captains on the basis of competence and supervisory capability. The team captains will be responsible for selecting, training and supervising their quota of volunteers, and they will be charged with maintaining and monitoring all administrative activity relative to each team's performance.

These are key assignments, so selection of the captains should be done with great care. The professional telemarketing consultant should be used to provide an initial "train the trainers" program to both the project supervisor and the team captains.

Training of Telephone Volunteers by Team Captains. Team captains should train volunteers in the following tasks:

* *Request all telephone volunteers to pre-read all training material, contribution letters, brochures, etc.*

* *Conduct an initial meeting to discuss and review the Training Manual.*

* *Explain all administrative requirements (i.e., prospect sheets, Queries, Weekly Summary Sheet).*

* *Conduct role plays of the script and objections/responses from the Training Manual.*

Weekly Procedure. Each week, individual telephone volunteers should receive the appropriate number of prospects to call. Volunteers should be asked to make their best effort at completing as many *quality* calls as possible.

Because not all calls will result in contacts, more prospect sheets should be distributed than the number of expected completions. Prospect sheets, *Queries,* and *Weekly Summary Sheets* should also be distributed and/or monitored and assembled for accurate summarization and return to the organization's office or headquarters.

Follow-Up Correspondence Procedure. All pledges should be followed up by the organization's administrative staff so that the applicable correspondence can be mailed to contributors who made pledges. Correspondence should be tracked so that returns and non-returns can be determined on an ongoing basis.

Query forms, too, should be directed to the personnel who can best respond to the questions/ complaints of the prospects called. Annotated forms should be returned to the calling center so that appropriate telephone volunteers can be informed of the results and, thus, be in a position to make follow-up calls if contributions are still possible.

Motivation. Motivational programs should include lunches or dinners, refreshments, and prizes for top telephone personnel. A significant prize should be offered to the most successful volunteer telemarketers in the following categories:

* *Top revenue producer calling on new prospects.*

* *Top revenue producer calling on previous donors.*

Additional prizes could be offered to *other* telephone personnel with the highest number of actual contributions within the same categories. These prizes can offset situations where a revenue category is won due to a contribution "windfall."

Properly organized and executed, telemarketing can be a powerful tool for fund raisers. While no approach is ideal for every situation, telemarketing offers the advantage of relatively uncomplicated setup

503

and detailed measurability.
It can and should be tried in just about every fund-raising effort.

Direct Marketing, May, 1988, p. 35.

504

CHAPTER 26

International Telemarketing

Eugene B. Kordahl
Vice President-Marketing
International 800 Telecom Corporation
Randolph, New Jersey

It doesn't take a great deal of knowledge of U.S. foreign trade balances to realize that many countries in Western Europe are selling much more to our country than we are to theirs. Among those enjoying the greatest positive imbalances are Denmark, France, Netherlands, the United Kingdom, Norway, Switzerland, and Sweden.

Even developing countries within the Western Hemisphere, such as Mexico and the countries of South America and the Caribbean Basin, seem to have mastered the unilateral knack of selling goods and services to the United States. If you have any lingering doubts about this imbalance, you need only look at the nationality of brands we use regularly.

Competitors from abroad are looking at us, realizing how parochial we are in our business dealings with the rest of the world, and saying to themselves, *"We can sell our automobiles, radios and televisions to the U.S. almost without fear of competition."* In many ways they are right. We didn't even begin thinking globally until the last decade or so.

But our competitors have. Some countries are already using *telemarketing* to enter our markets, a technology many of our marketers have only begun to recognize. Most U.S. business people, for example, are not even aware that toll-free international 800 service exists. No wonder companies in other countries seem to be in a better position than we are when it comes to selling internationally by telephone.

IMPETUS FOR INTERNATIONAL TELEMARKETING

To add confusion to this volatile international economic picture, the discussion early in 1987 of a 200% U.S. tariff came as a rude shock to many European countries. Exporters of food and drink products (e.g., French brandy, Danish ham, Dutch cheese, and Belgian endive), were put on notice that Americans could react officially in a tough way. The shock involved may have been part of the impetus for some of the increased telemarketing activity between Europe and the United States.

Harrod's Foray. The first indication that the balance of trade was having an effect on the prospects of telemarketing came in late December of 1985. Harrod's, the famous London department store, ran a full-page ad in the Sunday, December 29th, *New York Times*, offering three order-by-toll-free-phone cashmere sale items. As a result of that ad, which featured an international 800 number as the response device, 2,500 U.S. orders were received, amounting to more than $300,000 in sales. Over the eight-day period of the sale, Harrod's averaged 312 orders per day (17 orders per hour), and the value of the average order was $120.

This "experiment" opened the door to a second offer in July of 1986, in which Harrod's advertised English crystal and flatware. Another full-page ad in the *New York Times* with an international 800 number encouraged callers to ask for an eight-page color brochure offering additional merchandise. To add to the telemarketing effectiveness, a brochure was mailed on July 1st, five days before the publication of the *New York Times* ad, and was targeted to lists of customers who had previously shopped in the London store, had used Harrod's regular charge card, and those who had applied for value-added tax (VAT) rebates.

The majority of the calls to the 800 number had been made to request the brochure, but Harrod's also received many orders in the $2,000 to $3,000 range. The average order was $240.

In their comments about the overall test, Harrod's stated that total sales from the second test far exceeded their expectations, and in combination with the mail drop, considerably increased the total overall response to their international telemarketing campaign. The phone bill for Harrod's ran about $1 per minute, with the average call running about 2.5 minutes.

French Invasion. Hot on the heels of Harrod's international retail efforts, Galleries Lafayette, the famous Parisian retailer, featured their first direct-response promotion in the United States in the November, 1987, issue of *Elle*.

Galleries Lafayette targeted the fashion-conscious *Elle* woman, who *"Knows that Paris is the capitol of fashion."* Toll-free international calling was encouraged and the caller to France would reach an English-speaking TSR and order from a selection of fur coats, hats, and muffs. Each product offered was exclusively designed for Galleries Lafayette.

This test run was a joint venture of France Telecom and American Express.

Others, Too. A group of European retailers, as part of a multi-vendor, international direct-sales campaign, reportedly paid American Express approximately $6,000 for a one-third page ad in an eight-page section taken by American Express in *The New Yorker* Travel Supplement. The supplement was called "Destination Europe."

Each retailer advertised a specific list of products. The cost to each retailer included the costs of creating the ads, setup of the telephone lines, provision of the computer software package to receive and ship the orders, and the telephone charges for the first 500 orders that the retailers received.

"This is a low-risk opportunity for British retailers to promote themselves in the U.S. markets," said Peter Hessey, Director of National Accounts at American Express (U.S.). Hessey had also assisted the Harrod's test the year before.

The retailers involved with this most recent test were Mappin & Webb, Silversmiths, Hanley's Toy Store, Gieves & Hawkes, Selfridge's Department Store, and Swaine, Adeney, Brigg.

Clearly the international telemarketing breakthrough has been made. Europeans (soon to be followed by others?) have invaded the American marketplace with enthusiasm.

Fortunately, they still have a lot to learn

Yet, so do the Americans.

THE WEAK DOLLAR AND TELEMARKETING

The dollar's decline and its actual impact on the telemarketing industry has not been fully understood by many. In 1985, Treasury Secretary Baker, concerned about growing protective measures being applied by other countries, engineered a program designed to speed the decline of U.S. currency. Since then, we have seen the dollar decline at remarkable speed.

Unfortunately, the decline has only recently had any significant effect on the trade deficit, and the potential for further narrowing seems doubtful without aggressive marketing.

Many experts have criticized the failure of American businesses to take advantage of the changing exchange rate. The Reagan Administration criticized U.S. industry for failing to exploit the weak dollar by selling to world markets, and former Federal Reserve Chairman, Paul Volker, echoed the criticism:

"The great question is whether management can and will seek out and exploit the new competitive opportunities abroad made possible by better aligned exchange rates."

While the jury is still out on American management, nations like Taiwan, who produce American brand name products such as Wilson, Schwinn and South Korea's Hyundai, Samsung, and Gold Star, are rushing to compete for the U.S. dollar in this free-wheeling global economy.

Further, the Japanese are not responding to the changing economic marketplace the way we Americans expected. The expectation was that the Japanese manufacturers would pass along their cost increases via price increases to American consumers, yet they have decided instead to absorb the difference in slimmer profit margins, lay-offs, and salary reductions. Toyota Motors, for example, is facing a massive reduction in profit in 1988, while Nissan had already slipped into the red.

Figure 26-1
Comparison of Typical U.S. and Japanese Prices

Product	U.S. Price	Japan Price
Revere Ware small sauce pan	$18.00	$65.47
Black & Decker steam iron	36.00	99.77
Chips Ahoy (chocolate chip, 12 oz. package)	2.19	4.60
Johnson & Johnson Baby Powder (9 oz. container)	2.15	3.51
Ritz Crackers (12 oz. box)	2.09	3.42
Levi Jeans	32.00	62.35
IBM Personal Computer (PS/2 Model 30-021)	2,295.00	3,452.88

According to *The New York Times* of March 2, 1988, the weakened U.S. dollar had failed to bring an increase in sales of U.S. products in Japan. A price comparison of U.S. products domestically and in Japan is instructive (see **Figure 26-1**).

In Japan, many prices for American goods have, in fact declined, but few have fallen in proportion to the fall in the dollar. Because of the American reluctance to cut prices, many American products still remain much costlier in Japan than in the United States.

Part of the cause is the fact that many U.S. branch offices in Japan are not allowed to set their own prices. As a result, they have been slow to bring prices into line with the realities of the international currency exchange. Also, some American companies actually manufacture their products in Japan and, therefore, have not benefited from the weaker dollar at all.

There is one part of the phenomenon, however, that telemarketing *can* directly address. American companies selling consumer products often cannot control the final prices in the Japanese stores. The setting of the final retail price is up to the Japanese distributors, who often do not pass along price cuts, but instead keep the extra margins for themselves. However, a direct marketing/telemarketing campaign, held on an international scale, seems to be a practical approach to achieving more competitive pricing.

Japanese customers browsing in American catalogues featured in Japanese stores are beginning to get the notion that they can save a great deal of money by dealing *directly* with the United States. The problem, however, is that the international 800 numbers direct to the U.S. are not quite in place. This situation should soon be rectified.

HIGH COST OF U.S. PRESENCE IN JAPAN

Smaller high-tech companies have had trouble coping with the weaker dollar's purchasing power in Japan. The already high cost of operating in Japan has climbed even higher with the weakening of the dollar.

Previously, the cost of running a modest office in Japan with one American and one clerical person was approximately $500,000 a year. Today, in 1988, the cost is approximately $1 million per year.

John P. Stern, a U.S. electronic industry representative in Japan, has stated that he knows of several companies that have closed their Tokyo offices as the stronger yen complicated their already severe problems. Slack demand and difficulty in breaking into the Japanese market could not justify the cost of opening or maintaining an office.

An Alternative. In lieu of having an office in Japan, smaller high-tech manufacturers, as well as other service and manufacturing companies, have an excellent opportunity to provide a presence in Japan by investing in the comparatively modest cost of an international 800 line to Japan from their corporate headquarters in the United States. And for the American firms already established in Japan, toll-free numbers in other parts of the Orient have proven worthwhile.

INTERNATIONAL GROWTH OPPORTUNITIES.

The real opportunity for export seems to be in the field of manufacturing. In fact, certain economists are saying that without more growth in manufacturing, the huge U.S. trade deficit will not be reduced dramatically, at least not without a recession.

Lester C. Thurow, professor of economics at MIT has said that the export of services alone won't significantly affect the deficit. He noted that the U.S. ran a tourist deficit of $12 billion, and that seven of the 10 largest banks in the world are now Japanese. Agriculture, once a strong earner of export dollars, cannot do the trick either, in his opinion. The only remaining alternative, according to Thurow, is *manufacturing*.

508

INTERNATIONAL TELEMARKETING

The big question, of course, is what sort of manufacturing will be the most compelling for the export market. Will it be capital-intensive, employing skilled workers with the latest technology?

Paul A. Volker, former chairman of the Federal Reserve Board, described the challenge of balancing trade accounts as a manufacturing problem. The growth in production needed to effect this trade balance, Volker said, is in advanced products where we can have an edge. As things now stand, we are not investing in industry at a high enough rate to support that growth.

This once again highlights the American's non-global economic attitude. There are great opportunities for those manufacturers who are willing to make an effort in international marketing by establishing a presence in foreign markets.

In a report released in 1987 by the Commerce Department, the top 10 exporting industries were listed as follows:

* *Semiconductor devices.*

* *Optical devices/lenses.*

* *X-ray apparatus.*

* *Biological products.*

* *Medicinals, botanicals.*

* *Lithographic services.*

* *Electronic connectors.*

* *Radio/TV equipment.*

* *Wood pallets, skids.*

* *Surgical appliances.*

For the aggressive telemarketer, *with knowledge of foreign needs for these products*, there is much opportunity for a proactive international telemarketing program.

The dollar has fallen significantly against such key currencies as the yen and the German mark. This, in turn, has made American products such as tractors, machine tools, and other industrial products cheaper overseas.

As a result, U.S. products are being bought by foreign buyers. Jack Pierson, owner of Preco Industries in Lenexa, Kansas, has said, *"For the guy in Japan who's just starting to consider buying our products, the lower price he pays out in yen now is a real eye opener."*

Export is beginning to attract all types of U.S. industrial companies. A chemical division based in St. Louis, a valve manufacturer in Cleveland and a manufacturer of industrial flow meters in Racine, Wisconsin are all increasing their export activities based on the experiences they've had in testing the export market.

509

An owner of a furniture company in the United States was traveling through Europe last year and came to a startling conclusion:

> *"I discovered that my products were a lot better and a helluva lot cheaper than what my European competitors could offer."*

That executive caught "export fever." He went on to say that his products were not high-tech, that a lot of people around the world were making furniture, but:

> *"What we have is priced properly and will beat them on quality."*

Small U.S. exporters are discovering that they are suddenly competitive in everything from carpets and saw blades to computer stations and microwave systems. Many of these fledgling exporters are now considering telemarketing as a viable channel of international marketing.

Leading companies here in the U.S. are already using the innovative international 800 to benefit their worldwide marketing, sales, and services. Hundreds of companies are now using toll-free services to allow their foreign customers and prospects to contact them with the ease and convenience of a local phone call.

Digital Equipment Corporation, for example, uses the international toll-free network to enhance European customer service operations as well as their computer diagnostics. Through the use of the world-renowned Service 800 facilities from Europe, DEC can now maintain the lowest down time among computer manufacturers in Europe. Their international 800 network is quite extensive and allows DEC to have a presence in every major marketplace for a fraction of the cost it would require to maintain a local office.

Another world leader using international 800 service is International Paper Company's Plywood Division. It has experienced a 20% share of market in Europe *without a physical presence in Europe*. The Plywood Division takes orders from European customers via Service 800 lines in Amsterdam and London directly into the United States.

The obstacles to exporting are much lower than many people might think. Harrell Freemen, of Freeman Engineering in New Orleans, said that the paperwork involved wasn't nearly as formidable as he expected it to be. His telecommunications equipment firm, which produces mobile telephones and other products, was impressed when exporting began in 1987. Overseas sales grew so fast that they totalled 20-25% of the company's $2 million in sales in 1987.

Still, it is interesting to note that only 39,000 American manufacturers, about one in 10, are exporting. The top 250 U.S. multinational firms account for 85% of U.S. exports, a statistic that prompted Charles F. Valentine, a partner responsible for international trade advice at Arthur Young, to observe the greatest impact on the deficit will come from small and medium-sized companies. New players will develop products quickly and sell them in niches that larger companies typically (or even necessarily) overlook.

Telemarketing, clearly, will be one of the marketing channels used.

The secret, according to one industry pundit, is to offer something nobody else can.

He should have added that the rest of the secret is to let the world know about what you're offering.

MARKETING REQUIRED

The U.S. trade deficit will not disappear until Americans purchase fewer foreign goods or U.S.

companies improve upon their overseas marketing. The decrease in the value of the U.S. dollar has not created the expected outstanding export response for the many reasons I've suggested, ranging all the way from the fact that some trading nations have tied their currencies to the U.S. dollar, to the import duties and trade restrictions that exist overseas.

It's interesting to note that the Japanese and the Koreans have discovered ways to overcome these obstacles using good management, patience and professional salesmanship. Industries world-wide who buy their raw materials in U.S. dollars are actually finding their raw materials costs *declining*.

The German chemical industry, to give but one instance, pays for more than half of its oil-based feed stock in dollars. Consequently, many of its raw materials costs are declining along with the dollar. German chemical sales in the U.S. rose 18% through August of 1987.

There are some who argue that foreigners don't want our products. If you believe that myth, then you haven't seen the customs area of any foreign nation as residents return from the United States. Their suitcases are crammed with American goods ranging from fabrics to metal products.

Foreigners have developed *for* foreigners such products as American Ice Cream, California Chicken, American Hamburgers, Texas Hot Sauce and the New York Deli. Responding to the complaints of international travellers about the inability of buying a decent hot dog, a box of popcorn or a jar of peanut butter in many countries, many producers have rushed to fill the void--*both* U.S. and overseas competitors.

Statistics reveal that U.S. exports of frankfurters and variety meats, such as lunch meat, represent areas of strength for the U.S. It is obvious that foreign consumers like the taste and quality, as well as the presentation of American hotdogs and lunch meat.

However, just because American meat producers have a significant portion of that market at the moment, there's no guarantee that they're going to keep it. Remember the state of the automobile industry 25 years ago? We simply scoffed at the Japanese auto productive capacity at the time, and look where we are today. The same volatile situation exists with many other American industries that already export.

International telemarketing can help American businesses to protect their markets with two-way verbal communication. Selling and servicing customers can be made much easier. And language is not a barrier. The tongue of international commerce is English and every day, business transactions occur between buyers and sellers who do not claim English as their native language.

The development and protection of marketing channels demand creativity, planning, patience, and sales savvy. The basics of marketing remain the same for international marketing as they are domestically. Objectives must be established and appropriate strategies selected. In fact, marketing expertise gained in Newark or St. Paul can be valid and useful abroad.

Since the entry into international marketing must be viewed as a long-term and ongoing project, there are costs and risks of this market entry, but not much different from those found in America. The benefits can be immense.

"Today," according to Dr. James C. Makens, a member of the faculty at the Babcock Graduate School of Management at Wake Forest University, *"each product or service sold abroad represents a step toward a correction of the trade deficit, and a return to a long-term national, economic health. The task is not purely nationalistic. Foreign markets represent opportunities for sales and profits. After all, that's where most of the world's population can be found."*

511

WHERE ARE THE INTERNATIONAL TELEMARKETING OPPORTUNITIES?

In reviewing the U.S. total exports to individual countries between the years 1980 and 1986, a number of major markets emerge as telemarketing opportunities awaiting exploitation. The developed countries of Europe, South and Central America, Africa, the Far East, South Pacific, and the Caribbean Basin have been increasing their mutual exports. This is certainly the time for medium and large-size American companies to start developing opportunities through the planned use of international telemarketing.

Europe's Common Market. Total U.S. exports to the Common Market represent an interesting picture for the marketer interested in developing international trade. Of the 12 Common Market countries, 11 have *decreased* the number of American products coming into their countries, while only one (Ireland) has increased its imports of American products.

This leaves a very large potential marketplace with a very strong need for American know-how, products and services that is not being filled at this time. The entrepreneur or marketing professional who doesn't see this as a grand opportunity is still thinking in a typically parochial American way.

Non-Common Market Countries. Interestingly enough, non-common Market countries such as Austria, Norway, Sweden, and Turkey have all increased their imports of U.S. goods and services over the past seven years. Of the 28 developed countries listed in the Department of Commerce's International Trade Administration Reports, 10 of those nations are importing more U.S. goods, while 18 are not. It would seem that there is a growing need for the use of marketing and specifically, telemarketing, to these various countries by American producers of goods and services.

Western Hemisphere. The developing countries of South America, the Caribbean Basin, as well as Bermuda and some of the other islands in the French West Indies, Greenland, etc., reflect a growing need for U.S. products. Of the 37 nations in the Western Hemisphere, 17 have increased their imports of U.S. products and services, while 20 have reduced theirs.

Part of the problem with the implementation of telemarketing is that telephone service from AT&T does not include inter-country service (e.g., Venezuela to Argentina) that marketers want. Fortunately, Service 800 of Nyon, Switzerland, *does* provide this service.

Asia, Middle East and Africa. Africa and Asia represent a golden opportunity for those who are looking for marketplaces that seem virtually untapped by the American exporter. In East Asia, we find that four governments are increasing their imports from the United States. They are Hong Kong, South Korea, Singapore and Taiwan. Overall, East Asia has increased its imports of U.S. goods. Five of the 14 other Asian countries have increased their imports from American while the other nine have decreased their imports.

The Middle East, representing 15 countries, reflects an increase in U.S. imports in four of the countries within the past six years, while 11 of the countries have decreased their imports.

Africa, represented by its 56 various governments, reflects that in the past six years, 15 of the nations have increased their imports from America, while the balance have either remained stable or decreased them.

512

The Pacific. Of the remaining developing countries, which are the six island nations in the Pacific, four have increased their imports from the U.S., while two have decreased over the past years. This region, too, represents opportunities for the aggressive marketer.

Socialist Economies. Between 1980 and 1986, both China and the U.S.S.R. decreased their imports of American goods, yet China recently began reversing that trend. Seven Eastern European nations are decreasing their imports from the U.S. with the exception of Hungary. Interestingly, international toll-free service was recently inaugurated between Budapest and the U.S., and 94 other countries.

Of the world's remaining centrally planned economies, only Cuba and Vietnam have increased their imports of American goods.

An Instructive Example. International consumers are increasingly enamored of American products and services. An excellent example of this is a company called Catalog International, Inc., (CII) of Beverly Hills. This firm has set up consoles in one of the major Japanese department stores where shoppers can browse through American catalogs and place orders through the CII network. Once the order is received from the consumer, CII places the order with the U.S. cataloger and Nippon Express, the Japanese freight airline, ships the merchandise directly to the customer.

The Japanese consumer is willing to pay a 20% surcharge, as well as the import duty, rather than purchasing items at the Japanese retail prices which are 30 to 40% higher than U.S. catalog prices.

While the CII test is relatively unique, it does portend the future for those of us interested in international telemarketing. CII expects to have a total of 20 consoles working by the summer of 1988, with the expectation of an additional 8,000 consoles a year or so thereafter.

Potential. As of January 1, 1984, there were a total of 59.7 million business lines in the world. Of that total, 20.2 million (34%) were in the U.S. alone. Impressive as that proportion might seem, it also means that there is a healthy 66% of all business lines *overseas*, waiting for international contact from the U.S.

The markets are there. The infrastructure is there. Why aren't we?

CURRENT WORLD POSITIONING OF TELEMARKETING

Let's look at the current position of telemarketing, the trends internationally, and the future expectations of telemarketing in Europe and Asia.

Figure 26-2 is a partial listing of countries showing their number of service bureaus and in-house operations that were identified in December of 1986. Although the numbers have surely increased since this count, the trend is indicative of the various attitudes toward telemarketing and its international implications.

While this does not give us a total picture of the current European telemarketing operations, there were a total of 65 service bureaus in Europe and 709 in-house centers identified as telephone sales centers in 1986. When Canada, Japan, Australia, and Hong Kong were added to the picture, we had a world total of 102 service bureaus and 1,689 in-house telephone sales centers, compared to 82 telemarketing service bureaus and 140,000 telephone sales centers in the U.S.

513

ENCYCLOPEDIA OF TELEMARKETING

A further indicator of what is going to be happening in the near future is that computer use, while in its infancy abroad, has been growing exponentially because foreigners have studied U.S. hardware and software experiences and have learned from us. The have used our experience to get a jump ahead of us in technology. In recent travels abroad, I noted a great emphasis on sophisticated software, some of which goes beyond what the U.S. telemarketer is used to.

Europe is leading the entire non-U.S. world in developing telemarketing. They are competitive today, and soon will bring direct competition to the U.S. from both telephone service bureaus and in-house operations in Europe. This competition should start to reach an impressive size as quickly as 1990.

In a recent closed-circuit television conference about telemarketing in London and New York, participants noted that the international 800 number is the fastest growing tool in telemarketing on both sides of the Atlantic. There was a great deal of reference to Harrod's and others' uses of the international 800 service to penetrate American markets successfully.

Figure 26-2
Relevant European Telemarketing Statistics

	Credit Card Penetration	Telemarketing Service Bureaus (TSB)	In-House Telephone Sale Centers
Austria	23%	4	20
Belgium	23%	3	40
Denmark	13%	3	20
France	66%	3	50
Netherlands	18%	4	70
Norway	57%	3	20
Sweden	57%	5	25
United Kingdom	59%	15	100
West Germany	31%	15	200

Some of the benefits of using international 800 were discussed by the panelists. Included were the advantages of personal contact, the immediacy of being able to place an order, the specific city selectivity, the "time clock" feature of 800 service which allows call forwarding to different locations depending upon the time of day, and the prestige value connected with being an "international" consumer. (The specific city selectivity feature allows a marketer to advertise a local phone number in a foreign city with automatic call routing via Service 800 to the marketer's headquarters in another country.)

American marketers will have to learn to provide foreign markets with the opportunity to buy directly from U.S. merchants and manufacturers. The logical way is person-to-person contact on an international basis.

There is a growing interest among telemarketers from all over the world in the newly organized World Telemarketing Association. This will be an association of practicing professionals that will allow the methods and techniques of professional telemarketing to be shared among all who are interested.

In by-passing the "pioneer days" of the U.S. experience, our international brothers are already using information gained in seminars and trade shows to gather strength that escapes too many American telemarketers. Sophisticated techniques are becoming more visible, and the desire for database management is very strong overseas.

In some of the Eastern European, Warsaw Pact nations, a 1970s attitude toward telemarketing still prevails. However, this thinking is changing rapidly, due primarily to the evidence that international 800 service can draw more and more tourists to these various countries.

INTERNATIONAL TRENDS

New exporters can find sales much faster by focusing on markets and starting small. Dedication is needed to be a successful exporter. More important than having substantial resources is top management's time and a commitment to getting the process started.

Encouragingly, small U.S. exporters are discovering that they are suddenly competitive because of the weak dollar, which provides them with an opportunity to sell goods and services at a lower price than foreign competitors. It has been noted by the Small Business Administration in Washington that the prices of U.S.-made goods, which have been falling so fast, have created a condition where many foreigners are now knocking on the doors of U.S. manufacturers, particularly small manufacturers, *asking them* to bid overseas business for the first time.

Will the U.S. lose even more economic strength? It's an important question, and the answer is yes-- if we don't take the bull by the horns to counteract the foreign international telemarketing invasion that has already started. It will surely continue to grow over the coming years. The dynamic growth in Europe in the next five years, coupled with the growth and higher technology that the Orient will be bringing to the marketplace, will increase sales pressures from every point of the compass.

We will see innovation in the use of satellites and other high-tech equipment. Certain European countries will become telemarketing leaders with innovative and dynamic marketing thrusts toward lucrative markets, specifically the United States.

Global telemarketing is the leading edge of tomorrow. The internationalists have experience with buyers in one country and sellers in another. All they have to do now is add the telephone, as many are already doing with enthusiasm.

International WATS-type services are being introduced by major carriers such as AT&T, MCI and Sprint in the United States. Quietly, though, Service 800, the well-known European provider of international 800 services, has made itself available to the rest of the world for the past 13 years, and has added substantially to the demand for more international telemarketing.

Interestingly, we can start our international telemarketing using the wealth of experience from our domestic use of 800 service. Now, however, we have the added dimension of being able to be extremely accurate in our use of the 800 number, down to the point where we can be city-specific.

It's great to have a service that covers an entire nation, but when only two or three cities out of the entire nation account for the majority of the nation's business, city-specific is certainly the attractive method of using international Service 800.

ENCYCLOPEDIA OF TELEMARKETING

As this overview of international telemarketing implies, we can feel confident that the rest of the world is alive and healthy, and is watching the U.S. for ideas and trends. We will continue to hear from our competitors abroad.

Our world *wants* and *needs* U.S. products and services. All we have to do is market intelligently.

Will the U.S. lose even more economic strength?

The answer, again, is a resounding yes--if we don't climb aboard the international telemarketing bandwagon *now*.

CHAPTER 27

Anatomy of a Boiler Room

Richard L. Bencin
Donald J. Jonovic, Ph.D.

Some people say telemarketing was born in a "boiler room"--and it's hard to dispute them. Fact is, there's a little bit of the boiler room in many telemarketing operations.

This atavism is understandable. After all, telemarketing is a relatively new marketing discipline, still close to its rather dubious, humble beginnings. But understanding needn't imply acceptance. The stigma of the boiler room's unprofessional character remains a part, albeit small, of telemarketing's reputation. Its full potential won't be released until that stigma is erased.

It's important, therefore, to understand the elements that make up a typical boiler room. Armed with this understanding, telemarketing managers will be better able to eliminate these negative features if and when they occur in new or ongoing operations.

Let's look at a real-life example.

ADVENTURE IN A BOILER ROOM

You are about to enter the front door of a major service club's telemarketing center. You've already noticed the neighborhood --not a place you'd care to be caught after sunset. Unconsciously, you feel for your wallet as you approach the door.

Once inside the building, you're struck by the hallway stretching off in front of you. The tile on the floor looks as though it was part of the first run of linoleum. The few tiles you can see under the grime, that is. On the right wall are old, metal-framed windows. The slats are veneered with dust on the inside; the glass is opaqued by mottled industrial grime on the outside. The left wall is made up of movable partitions that have obviously been moved far more times than design specs called for. Some are pinned with curled and yellowed cartoons depicting different variations of workplace misery. The humor seems strained.

Rounding one of the partitions to the left, one is assaulted by chatter and squeaking erupting on all sides from numerous rows of 2' by 4' desks, abutted to each other, manned (or womanned) by slouching, dishevelled telemarketing "reps." It is summer. It is hot. Fans of all sorts and sizes whir and clatter on many desks. The only water cooler is almost empty, and the cup dispenser is missing.

Somehow, the bright mood with which you began the day has vanished, too.

Welcome to a boiler room.

You haven't seen the worst of it, however. The run-down, sub-human, inadequate facilities are only

517

one common feature of such operations, and you're here to get the full details. Grimly, you open your briefcase and pull out an inspection checklist. The next few hours run something like this:

PERSONNEL

* *Telephone sales supervisors tell you they don't have job descriptions in writing, only vague verbal understandings.*

* *Their jobs, they say, do not include monitoring, personnel reviews, setting sales targets, interviewing, or many other essential responsibilities.*

* *The telephone sales reps [TSR's] are not reviewed formally.*

* *TSR's start and quit as if through a revolving door--and when they stay on the payroll, they're often not on the job.*

* *TSR's who show talent are almost immediately moved to the outside sales force. If they don't want to do that, they're locked into the minimum-wage boiler room.*

* *TSR's commissions are lower than those of the outside sales force.*

* *TSR'S receive no production incentive overrides, as do the outside sales reps.*

* *Supervisory pay is far below national averages for outbound, consumer telemarketing operations.*

You put down your clipboard for a moment and search out a telephone sales supervisor. Over a cup of coffee in the dingy break room, you ask her for her impressions of the operation.

"We've got lots of problems," she says, *staring into her coffee cup. "The TSR's really feel like second-class citizens, and they're probably right. It's no wonder we can't get the attitude up. The people we have aren't up to any reasonable standards and we can't hire good ones. Quality applicants are looking for salary and commission. We offer minimum wage for full and part-time people.*

"This is Friday. We're in the middle of a heat wave. I can predict with almost complete certainty that only a couple of reps are going to show up tonight."

"How can you know that?" you ask.

"Because it's what happened last Friday night, and the Friday night before."

You go over and talk to some of the reps on break.

"I'm really surprised someone like you is here," one young woman says. *"I*

518

didn't think anybody cared enough to bring in a consultant. They sure don't care about us. Don't ask what we think. We don't have any say. We never even have meetings anymore."

"I wish you luck," another says when you explain you are a consultant. *"You're gonna need it."*

TRAINING

* *Product training is minimal and often outdated.*

* *No monitoring equipment or program exist for training.*

* *Trainees are forced to listen to one-sided sales conversations (equipment's not available to allow them to hear prospect replies).*

* *Supervisors are unable to coach via call analysis.*

* *Scripts are used in training, but not required for live telephone sales.*

* *Supervisors and TSR's receive no telemarketing publications.*

You pull one of the senior managers off in a corner to discuss the training program.

"Well," he tells you, *"It's a little overblown to call it a training program. Actually, the whole thing is done in bits and pieces because we don't have the people to put together any full-scale program. Sometimes I wonder if it isn't best to learn by doing the actual calls. . ."*

PRODUCTIVITY

* *No call accounting equipment exists (e.g., Station Message Detail Recorder, add-on equipment that measures telephone activities by station).*

* *No monitoring equipment is used.*

* *No reports are maintained regarding calls attempted or calls completed (record-keeping is limited to orders and hours worked).*

* *Productivity, per activity reports, is abysmal.*

You notice in your travels around the shop that TSR's indulge in a great deal of aimless chatter during sales calls. You select one at random and ask what the call or sales quotas are.

"Quotas? Gee, we used to have those, back maybe two years ago. But not now."

"Well," you ask, *"do you at least have scripts to help guide the calls?"*

519

"Nope. We just try to get 'em to listen by acting like we're running a survey. Look, I just call down this list here cut out of the phone book, then ask about five or six questions to see if they're already members. If they aren't, I promise to send them some stuff. All this takes a lot of time."

You stare at the rep for a moment, bemused and nonplussed, then ask him to go on with his calling. He phones name after name on the list. Some, you can tell by the address, would have no use for membership. Fully a third of the people he calls are already members, but they still get treated to the same, time-consuming phony survey.

By now, the heat is getting to you and you feel vaguely depressed. Still, you're here to work. *Maybe something can be done*, you think as you walk toward the manager's office. *With a lot of management attention, this mess can probably be turned around.*

The manager, however, is gone for the afternoon.

A MATTER OF ATTITUDE

There's a common thread running through the fabrics of most boiler rooms--a negative attitude toward customers, prospects, and telemarketing personnel. This attitude usually resides at bone depth and is very difficult to change, because, generally, it represents the basic perceptions of senior management.

The senior managers of boiler room operations usually try to implement telemarketing in the quickest and cheapest way. Some (fortunately few, but even few are too many) will resort to illegal, or at best unethical, activities. It seems almost everyone has a favorite story about telephone calls selling phoney land deals, imitation gold and silver, even counterfeit copier toner. Achieving professionalism in these situation is not only unlikely. It is probably impossible.

The senior management of boiler room operations tend to have very distinctive management styles. They "manage" mostly by memo and very seldom are seen on the floor or out with their people. The little contact they have with their people is usually characterized by fear and intimidation. These managers don't delegate. They *abdicate*.

In many senses, operators of telemarketing boiler rooms are like ineffective managers everywhere. They don't manage people. They *use* them, usually poorly. They tend to fixate on immediate results at the expense of long-term growth and profitability. Prospects are means to quotas. Customers are forgotten as soon as the order is taken. The telemarketing operation, itself, is only a means to these quotas, so it's squeezed as dry as possible. Sometimes, an intelligent and aggressive line manager of telemarketing can push through some of his or her staff or equipment needs. But "too much" push can often be taken as disrespect or outright mutiny.

For senior management of the boiler room, the telemarketing operation is not a tool. It's a bludgeon used to beat both the prospect and the employee into submission.

At least the prospect can hang up. The TSR is stuck in close, cramped, improperly heated or cooled quarters. Room overtones often shroud the callers with a din of white noise. You can almost see, feel and hear the steam pipes and clicking water meters--a true "boys in the basement" environment. No wonder they're called "boiler rooms."

The typical operation uses divided 30"-wide countertops, small cubicles, and atrocious acoustics. Some might condescend to use 4' deep dividers (5' should be standard, with 5'-wide cubicles, 25 square feet of space per TSR), but they leave the TSR's sticking out half-way into the aisles, which serve as sluices for sound. These "upgraded" operations may not look like boiler rooms, but they certainly sound a lot like the bowels of some old tramp steamer. Add to this cacophony the anarchy caused by a lack of professional scripting, call monitoring, and performance review, and the boiler room devolves quickly into a zoo.

One often wonders why these hapless people stay as long as they do. Boiler rooms often pay little more than minimum wage. Little wonder they're characterized by high turnover, robot-like script presentations and a lack of overall concern and interest on the part of the TSR's. Training is a one-time, half-hearted effort, leaving the disoriented TSR up to his or her own wits to survive the job.

Survival is a real problem. Hire, demand performance, and fire if it's not forthcoming. So what if the boiler room doesn't provide the facilities, or the environment, or the training, or the scripting to make the expected performance possible? These people are a "dime a dozen." It's cheaper just to get somebody else. Presumably, management of these operations is looking for "naturals," people who are internally motivated to make up coherent and effective scripts, and sell lots of product under subhuman conditions. Surely, lots of such people exist out there.

THE 10 SYMPTOMS OF "BOILERROOM-ITIS"

Boiler rooms come in all sizes, at many levels of complexity. Some might do better in the physical plant area, but even worse in training and supervision. Others might truly be little more than run-down hovels, but slightly better at training. Still, boilerroom-itis is a terminal disease with a very definite set of symptoms. Here are the 10 most common.

1) Not Providing Proper Expertise. The number one reason why many telemarketing programs fail is the mistaken belief that telemarketing is easier to manage than field sales. Telemarketing managers require expertise in database development, script design, telephone facilities management, computerization, "scientific marketing" (test call analyses and program enhancements), quality control, human resource planning/control and synergistic direct marketing.

2) Token Commitment and Resources. Telemarketing will work, but only if the proper commitment is made in time, effort, expertise, and funding. Program tokenism leads only to mediocrity at best, and failure at worst.

3) Ignorance of Database Management. As most direct mailers already know, database management is vitally important to a direct marketing program's success. Telemarketing is no different. Management must understand database management with all of its ramifications of list segmentation, customer/prospect analysis and back-end (post sale) list evaluation.

4) Defective Human Resource Planning. There are many potential areas for failure in the area of human resources: "burnout" of outbound telemarketing sales reps (lower productivity after four

521

hours on the phone), improper selection and training, lack of appropriate compensation, and the absence of viable career paths. Also, major distinctions should be made between in-bound and out-bound telephone sales personnel. The later requires significantly more salesmanship and an insensitivity to rejection.

5) Lack of Professional Scripts/Call Guides. Operating a telemarketing operation without professional scripts or call guides (script outlines) invites lower productivity and sales because of the inability of management to control and measure performance. Well-written scripts delivered naturally by trained telephone sales reps can be one of the most powerful tools of telemarketing.

6) Improper Facilities Management. Lack of acoustical partitions, cramped space and uncontrolled extremes of humidity and temperature usually lead to disgruntled employees, low performance and high turnover.

7) Failure To Capture Pertinent Marketing Data. Most telemarketers record only the most basic of operational data from their telephone program: completed calls, sales recorded, sales dollars and perhaps, a few other mundane statistics. However, the real beauty of telemarketing is its potential to record infinite marketing information about survey data recorded and the analyses of ongoing control tests. "Scientific marketing," for example, can determine which list, script, or offer provide the greatest response. Further, types and sizes of businesses can be determined that provide the best qualification rates, sales ratios and largest orders.

8) Insufficient Quality Control. Telemarketing has the potential to direct, control, and measure the telephone presentations. Without proper monitoring equipment and regular weekly reviews with supervisors, quality control quickly dissipates.

9) Failure To Provide Computer Expertise. Computer knowledge is required in developing and maintaining a database for prospects and customers. Marketing data analysis should always be processed via computers as well as sophisticated branched scripting.

10) Failure To Understand Telemarketing's Synergy with Direct Marketing. Telemarketing must support or be supported by other direct marketing disciplines such as direct mail, print and broadcast direct response, catalog, and others. To attempt a telemarketing program without relating to other direct marketing channels will often isolate the effort and thereby lessen its total effectiveness.

There may, indeed, be a little of the boiler room in many telemarketing operations, but that's not the fault of telemarketing.

It's the fault of management. . .and only management can correct the fault.

CHAPTER 28

Taking the Reins of a Troubled Telemarketing Center

Richard L. Bencin
Donald J. Jonovic, Ph.D.

Whether it's done by a telemarketing manager or an outside consultant--or both--turning a troubled telemarketing center around is no easy task. Usually, much has to be done, often in a very short period of time before the roof *really* caves in.

For the purposes of this chapter, we'll assume that a newly appointed telemarketing manager has been asked to manage a telemarketing center that's in real trouble. What follows are some insights into the process he or she might follow in an effort to shore up the walls and rebuild.

First things being first, the new manager will have to grasp quickly the overall requirements of the position, ideally through a series of meetings with senior and peer-level managers. The objective IS to clarify:

*   *The requirements of the position.* Duties, policies and a listing of the
    products and/or services being marketed are good starting points.

*   *Responsibility and authority.* A definitive statement of each must be clearly
    made, preferably in writing, so that the new manager can know when he or
    she must review potential changes with senior management. Knowledge of
    these limits also helps to describe the scope of the position and its impact on
    the rest of the organization.

*   *The goals to be met and problems to solve.* Here, it's important not only to
    list the goals and problems, but to set priorities. When trouble sets in, it's
    critical to know what must be done first so that productive rebuilding can
    occur. Foundation first, then the walls, the roof, and so on.

These basics taken care of, the manager can begin the turnaround process, which has three stages: situation analysis, recommendations, and implementation. But before we get into the process itself, we should back off and look at the key to a turnaround's success: the telemarketing manager.

HIRING THE TURNAROUND MANAGER

Managing a telemarketing turnaround requires analytical ability, creativity, problem-solving

523

ability, and a facility at juggling many balls at one time. Getting the job done requires a lot of energy, a great deal of experience, and powerful skills at selling the project internally. Needless to say, there's no surplus of such people anywhere.

Because telemarketing is a relatively young industry, prospective telemarketing managers with 10 years' experience, or even five, are difficult to find. Often, the best that can be done is to recruit an individual with at least three years' experience in a *variety* of related successful experiences: supervision, training, program development, and computers/telecommunications.

It's important to understand, however, that telemarketing "savvy" should almost always outweigh specific product experience in judging the qualifications of a telemarketing manager. Clearly, the manager will have to learn product capabilities and the nature of the market, but the skill in short supply is *validated telemarketing expertise*.

Typical Salaries. According to the *1987 National Telemarketing Salary Guide*, prepared by Telemarketing Recruiters, Inc., of New York, salary ranges for outbound, in-house telemarketing managers/ directors are as shown in **Figure 28-1**. Inbound centers pay slightly less.

Figure 28-1
Typical Salary Ranges
Telemarketing Managers and Directors

	LOW	AVERAGE	HIGH
Business-to-Consumer			
Manager	$25,000	$37,000	$45,000
Director	$37,000	$58,000	$75,000
Business-to-Business			
Manager	$28,000	$42,000	$53,000
Director	$41,000	$62,000	$82,000

Since telemarketing management salaries are increasing faster than management salaries in general, expect to pay increases of 10%-15% annually, especially at senior levels.

Too often, salary offers to outside people are too low to support successful, experienced management personnel. There is tremendous leverage potential inherent in a superior telemarketing manager, something senior management too often fails to factor into their pay considerations.

In many industries, a competent manager with 20 full-time telephone sales reps could potentially produce as much as a 200-person national field sales force--with significantly lower sales costs. On the other hand, an under-qualified manager, or an inappropriate in-house transplant, could spoil the entire operation. In situations like these, millions in sales could be foregone in order to save a few thousand dollars in salary.

TAKING THE REINS OF A TROUBLED TELEMARKETING CENTER

Commission or Salary? While every situation and circumstance is unique, it is generally preferable to pay the bulk of a telemarketing manager's compensation in salary. This is a very competitive level in the telemarketing industry, and individuals qualified for these positions tend to focus on *guaranteed* compensation, particularly if they will be asked to relocate. Financial institutions, after all, are interested more in guaranteed income when considering mortgage loan applications.

Business-to-Business vs. Business-to-Consumer. Although business-to-business telemarketing generally requires greater sophistication in products, markets, presentations and so forth, and although business-to-business often involves a higher average sale value, business-to-consumer telemarketing can have equivalent challenges. Consider these: higher call volumes, a greater number of orders, larger centers, and more sophisticated computer and telecommunications systems.

The tendency is often to pay business-to-consumer telemarketing managers less, but we believe this is misguided. Upgrading management talent for consumer telemarketing could go a long way toward increasing productivity and overall performance.

More importantly for the industry, an improved management cadre at the consumer level could contribute to a more sophisticated marketing approach. It could also help relieve some of the anti-consumer telemarketing pressures.

What To Look for in a Resume. Certain experience and skills are essential to success as a telemarketing manager. When that manager is expected to reverse the decline of a troubled center, those qualities become critical.

Here are some of the more important considerations:

Direct Marketing Experience. Since most telemarketing operations don't operate in a marketing vacuum, experience with other direct marketing disciplines is vital. Look for knowledge and/or experience in direct mail, catalog, print, and broadcast.

Find the individual who:

* *Understands the complex interrelationships among the various alternate channels and telemarketing.*

* *Relates to the concept of "target marketing" as it concerns strategy, methods, database applications and tactical sales management.*

Data Processing/Telecommunications Skills. A telemarketing manager without data processing and telecommunications skills can be a severe corporate liability. Operations productivity and quality could both suffer as a result, swamped by a sea of paper, busy signals, and chaos.

Unearth the candidate who:

* *Can develop batch or CRT computer-assisted telemarketing environments.*

* *Is able to manage databases, analysis systems, and marketing strategies to the point of becoming a "scientific marketer."*

* *Has a deep appreciation of sophisticated telephone systems such as ACD's, SMDR's, least cost routing, monitoring, etc.*

* *Has a systems and/or communications background related to telemarketing.*

Supervisory/Managerial Ability. A telemarketing center manager will have to possess skills in leadership, organization, and motivation. He or she must be able to develop supervisors and TSR's into self-reliant, high-quality telemarketers.

Locate the person who:

* *Will motivate subordinates to meet and exceed center sales targets.*

* *Shows an ability to recruit effectively, manage a variety of simultaneous telemarketing programs, and is adept at managing the "bottom line."*

* *Can develop sales and supervisory personnel, and ready them for more challenging telemarketing positions.*

Training Development/Implementation. The development of training programs on getting past the "screen," using scripts, handling objections and closing the sale are essential to a successful telemarketing operation.

Search for a person who:

* *Can develop and execute telemarketing training programs.*

* *Has the ability to create instructors' guides for supervisors/sales trainers.*

* *Understands both group development and one-on-one coaching techniques.*

Fundamentally, the resume should describe a creative individual who can quickly grasp marketing problems and opportunities, not only as they relate directly to telemarketing, but also to the growth and profit goals of *your* organization.

Should the Manager Also Be a Program Developer? It's a natural mistake to ask a telemarketing turnaround manager both to create programs and to manage the telemarketing center. This is something like asking a math professor to write the textbook he's expected to use in teaching. While some have the dual capabilities, this can often be an unnecessary condition of employment that severely limits the pool of potential candidates.

Often, a much better alternative is to hire a consultant to analyze the current program and its problems, then to ask that consultant to help in the search for a capable turnaround manager. The consultant could also help with new program development, as necessary, as well as conducting periodic operations reviews to help with ongoing management of the center.

Conducting the Search. Few human resource managers, marketing executives, or CEO's fully understand the often esoteric needs of a telemarketing center. Even fewer know where to look for the right candidate to manage the turnaround.

The typical in-house approach is to use the local metro newspapers, the *Wall Street Journal*, and/or direct marketing/telemarketing trade publications to advertise for candidates. Then that onerous task requires one to wade through piles of resumes from "boiler room" supervisors, telco reps-turned-telemarketers and all sorts of pretenders.

It can work, but it's often a lot like choosing to cross the country by mule train.

Consultants and executive search firms offer a better choice *if* discretion is used in selection. Regarding search firms, we'd strongly recommend using either a direct marketing executive placement firm or a general agency that has a specialty in telemarketing.

The expense will usually be higher, but the result, both in time saved and candidate quality, are generally well worth the price.

SITUATION ANALYSIS

Assuming a competent, experienced telemarketing manager is in place, his or her first step in managing the turnaround is to analyze the situation. This analysis includes seven basic areas of review:

1) *Strategic direction.*

2) *Location/facilities.*

3) *Database/lists.*

4) *Personnel.*

5) *Training.*

6) *Productivity and quality control (performance management).*

7) *Miscellaneous.*

Strategic Direction. Through ongoing discussions with senior and peer management, the telemarketing manager must work to refine the definition of the center's strategic direction. This is particularly important given telemarketing's synergy with other functions within the organization, particularly marketing.

Marketing management, in particular, should have a creative interest in telemarketing's potential as a complement to direct mail, catalog, print, broadcast, field sales, and customer service. With a center clearly in trouble, much of this synergy has probably been lost or at least greatly disrupted, and marketing's interest may have waned.

This is why one of the manager's first jobs will be to position (or reposition) telemarketing into its appropriate role in the overall marketing strategy. Lead generation, for example, may become a complete selling process, aided by direct mail and video brochures, and the entire field sales operation could change as a result of thoughtful application of "telefocus marketing." The telemarketing manager can only achieve these goals with the full cooperation of others in the organization.

Potential applications should be discussed and analyzed by key management as a team. The entire purpose and thrust of the telemarketing center may change as a result of this team analysis, but achieving this focus should be the telemarketing manager's primary task.

Location/Facilities. Center location is a vital consideration, particularly in a turnaround situation. Should the center be centralized or decentralized? Are employees properly sourced? What are current and proposed facility requirements?

For example, the new manager might find that a consolidation of telemarketing facilities from regional centers to a single, centralized environment may offer some cost savings, improved productivity, and better control. Or, perhaps, *de-centralization* may be the answer.

The current center(s) should be analyzed from the viewpoints of functionality, support systems, telecommunications, computerization, and amenities. Here are the kinds of questions the telemarketing manager should be asking:

* *Do we have enough space to accommodate current and proposed plans?*

* *Are current support systems (management control systems, monitoring, records/reporting systems, etc.) adequate?*

* *Does computerization of the center offer major advantages, or, if already in place, is the center's MIS capability being properly used?*

* *What about the center's layout, acoustics, cosmetics--are they adding to or detracting from the productive effort? Do they enhance the effort to attract quality personnel?*

Database/Lists. Telemarketers too often overlook the vital importance of databases and lists. Yet these are two of the most important ingredients in telemarketing success.

The newly assigned manager should examine the troubled center's level of sophistication, asking questions such as:

* *Is the database manual or automated?*

* *Can appropriate customer/prospect profiles be designated?*

* *Are current prospect lists and sources satisfactory?*

* *Have the prospect lists been purged against the customer list?*

* *Does the center understand the tiers of descending prospects by SIC and size (backed by empirical data)?*

TAKING THE REINS OF A TROUBLED TELEMARKETING CENTER

* *What are the future needs and requirements of the telemarketing center's database?*

Database capability, future requirements, MIS support, marketing analysis needs and other relevant database issues must, therefore, be reviewed by the telemarketing manager. Center turnaround often depends on this investigative analysis.

Personnel. Telemarketing is essentially a people business. The right telemarketing management team, as well as TSR's, are absolutely essential in order to turn around a center's poor performance. Sales growth is dependent on this living heart and soul of the business.

Thus, an important piece of analysis for the turnaround manager is a personnel file review of the management team and the TSR's. Turnover and absenteeism should be studied. Background, including both education and practical experience, as well as prior performance reviews should be examined carefully.

Still, nothing beats one-on-one personal interviews, and the careful observance of how the line management staff interacts with the TSR's. Attitude, energy levels, knowledge, communication abilities, and management dynamics can all be observed within the context of the normal work day.

Individual meetings with members of the management team should include discussion of their perceptions of the problems, opportunities and causes of the center's poor performance. Since the center is, by definition, troubled, these conversations will require a great deal of sensitivity and leadership on the part of the new manager. The managers are being evaluated and they know it. But, with proper direction, the telemarketing manager should be able to elicit meaningful insights while he or she is examining knowledge, communications ability, attitude, and commitment to helping improve the performance of the center.

A complete review of labor policies, hours, compensation and benefits is clearly in order, since it can uncover obvious trouble spots or opportunities for improvement. For example, inadequate compensation is often a major problem. If the center is paying "boiler room" wages, it's probably getting what it pays for.

Also of particular interest to the turnaround manager is the *span of supervisory control*. Are the supervisors handling too many TSR's to be efficient and productive (eight to 12 TSR's per supervisor is ideal)? Are lead communicators (TSR's with part-time management duties) being used to help with the supervision as well as being groomed for management? Is there enough time for supervisors to monitor TSR's and provide ongoing coaching and training?

Other key questions about the management staff:

* *Do they understand their duties and responsibilities?*

* *Is their background and training adequate?*

* *Are they providing thoughtful performance reviews for their TSR's? Targets? Incentives?*

* *Can they grow with the job?*

Training. Training is often a powerful tool in accomplishing a telemarketing center turnaround. And we're not simply talking telephone sales techniques.

Often, the lack of product knowledge or a misunderstanding of administrative procedures is at the

529

core of poor TSR sales performance. If the TSR's don't fully understand what or why they are selling, they won't have the necessary belief in their products or the appropriate understanding of how their prospects and customers can benefit.

The telemarketing manager, therefore, should review both the initial and ongoing product, administrative and sales training programs. Often, tele-sales operations provide an initial training program, but then completely overlook the value of ongoing coaching and training.

Some, unfortunately, don't even provide a formal training program up front. They just seem to depend on the infamous OJT (on-the-job training). Usually, this is an exercise in learning the worst of habits from the rest of the marginal TSR performers.

Training methods should also be reviewed. Be sure to look for the necessary role plays, monitoring with feedback analysis, script rehearsals, objection handling exchanges, etc.

Finally, it's worth asking about the trainers, themselves. Do *they* need training?

Productivity/Quality Control (Performance Management). Although every issue discussed to this point impacts the center's performance, one must delve into those issues that directly affect the measurements of the jobs at hand.

Here are some specific areas that must be examined in detail by the telemarketing manager:

* *Scripts.* Are scripts being used? Are they in need of review or complete re-write? Do supervisors base their reviews on script presentation skills?

* *Monitoring.* If monitoring is available, is it being used effectively? Can all supervisors and managers, as well as the center manager, "silent monitor" all TSR telephone calls? Are listen-only speakers and/or ongoing coaching available for the benefit of new trainees? How often are TSR's being reviewed (once weekly should be the minimum)?

* *SMDR (Call Accounting).* Can TSR telephone connect time be determined per telephone hour, per day, etc.? How long, on the average, are TSR's spending on the telephone each hour? (Twenty five to 35 minutes connect time per hour should be expected of an efficient manual center; more, if the center is automated). Is it productive time?

* *Productivity Reports.* Are the appropriate productivity reports available? Can call attempts, presentations, completed calls and sales per hour be determined?

* *Marketing Analysis Reports.* Does the center have the capability of deter-mining the *best selling matrix* of events for maximum productivity? For example, can the impact of such factors as list, script, mailer, level of contact, offer, part-time vs. full-time TSR productivity and market area be determined?

* *Quotas*. Are quotas being used, and are they reasonable? Do the telemarketing management and the TSR's understand the relative importance of the quotas to the success of the operation?

We have frequently run into situations where *scripts are not required, monitoring capability does not exist (or is unused), management doesn't know what the TSR call-connect time is (or doesn't choose to use the SMDR reports even if they're available), quotas are unknown and reports consist only of sales and hours recorded!*

Many centers, for example, average *less* than 15 minutes connect time per TSR-hour. However, without monitoring or call management systems, management is simply unaware of the situation.

The turnaround manager, as well as his or her senior management, must understand that telemarketing has the *potential* to be completely measurable, targeted and controlled. It's up to the center management to dig out all the constraints in the way of reaching ultimate potential.

Miscellaneous. There are, of course, many other issues deserving of the new manager's attention. Some apply to all troubled centers. Some are unique.

For example, it's worth asking whether the organization is represented in the appropriate national and local telemarketing and/or direct marketing associations. Which periodicals are being used regularly?

The entire range of administrative and fulfillment procedures deserves careful attention. Also, customer service, even if it's separate from the telemarketing operation, should be reviewed, since its performance can impact significantly on the ongoing productive efforts of the telemarketers.

RECOMMENDATIONS/IMPLEMENTATION

After all the questions, discussions and analyses are completed, the next step is to recommend actions to be taken. In this report, problems and opportunities should be carefully delineated, along with the appropriate action.

These recommendations can be implemented singularly or in group serial fashion, depending on the individual situation. The telemarketing center manager, especially if the actions recommended are beyond his or her authority, should present and discuss the recommendations with the appropriate managers. Even if all recommendations could be carried out within the complete scope of the center manager, communication with the balance of the marketing team always makes sense.

At bedrock, implementing is done by, with, and through *people*. The new telemarketing manager's success will hinge on his or her ability to communicate changes to the staff, to encourage supervisors and TSR's to involve themselves in the changing environment, and to make the hard decisions that must be made.

Turning around a troubled telemarketing center takes skill, empathy, courage and commitment.

And, once begun, performance improvements should never end.

531

CHAPTER 29

Step-by-Step for Startups: A Review

Thomas A. DePrizio
President & CEO
U.S. Telemarketing, Inc.
Atlanta, Georgia

The startup of a telemarketing program, no matter how modest or elaborate, represents a marketing milestone in the life of any organization. It's an undertaking that clearly signals management's intent to step boldly into the future.

If you've been charged with the job of introducing this dynamic sales tool into your organization, congratulations. You now occupy one of the most challenging, exhilarating--and terrifying positions of your career.

Establishing a telemarketing program is not extremely difficult, nor is it a piece of cake. It requires hard work, persistence, and determination, but, more than anything, it requires good planning. A well-reasoned telemarketing plan *will* result in a highly successful program and improved sales.

Conversely, a well-intentioned, but impulsive leap into the telemarketing unknown will almost surely guarantee disaster.

The purpose of this chapter is to remove much of the mystery and trepidations surrounding the establishment of a telemarketing program by walking you through a startup. . .step by step.

SQUARE ONE: TELEMARKETER, KNOW THYSELF

The first step in establishing a telemarketing program is to make sure that you fully understand what telemarketing is and what it can and cannot do for your organization.

Probably the best working definition of telemarketing is this: "the *planned* use of the telephone to assist in the sales of a product or service which is an *integral* part of the company's overall marketing activities." "Planned" and "integral" are the operative words here.

Telemarketing is an intricate marketing process that does not operate in a vacuum. It's vital that management recognize telemarketing as an integral, ongoing part of your organization's marketing efforts, not as a quick-fix panacea for a period of temporarily flagging sales.

It's also important, right up front, to differentiate between telephone sales and telemarketing. Although telephone sales is one element of the telemarketing process, it is just that--*one* element. The sole purpose of telephone sales is to sell over the telephone, period. A telemarketing program, however, is a

532

comprehensive telephone marketing system which can be distinguished by three key characteristics:

* *It is planned.*

* *It is continuous.*

* *It is integral to the organization's overall marketing scheme.*

Indeed, it's not uncommon to find a telemarketing program that is being used not as an independent selling medium, but as an auxiliary marketing component that "synergizes" the entire marketing effort.

Taking pains to ensure that all concerned in a potential telemarketing venture understand the nature of the telemarketing beast and how it differs from its sub-set cousin, telephone sales, is critical, since for the program to be successful, two conditions must be met:

* *All levels of management support the program.*

* *The program must be respected as an important component of the overall organizational marketing plan.*

The human relations groundwork should be laid early to guarantee that your colleagues are buying into telemarketing from an informed position. This effort will more than pay for itself in the final results.

DIVING IN: DEVELOPING A TELEMARKETING CALL PROGRAM

Now that you've paved the way for the ultimate success of your telemarketing program, it's time to get down to work. In conceptualizing your telemarketing plan, you will have to consider four crucial elements:

1) *Market* (to whom you want to sell).

2) *Offer* (what you want to sell).

3) *Medium* (how you will sell).

4) *Message* (what you will say).

Market. The first, and probably most essential step in the development of any budding telemarketing program is to identify and understand your market. When targeting markets for telemarketing, balance the difficulty of the market to be penetrated with the telephone contact cost.

According to the classic product/market matrix, which forms the basis of all sales (**Figure 29-1**), there are four product/market combinations. The toughest to sell is new product/new market. The next toughest is current product/new market. New product/current market is an easier sell, while current product/ current market is the easiest.

It helps to keep this scale of sales difficulty in view when weighing the potential cost effectiveness of your telemarketing program. Depending on where your operation falls in the matrix, your costs will be

533

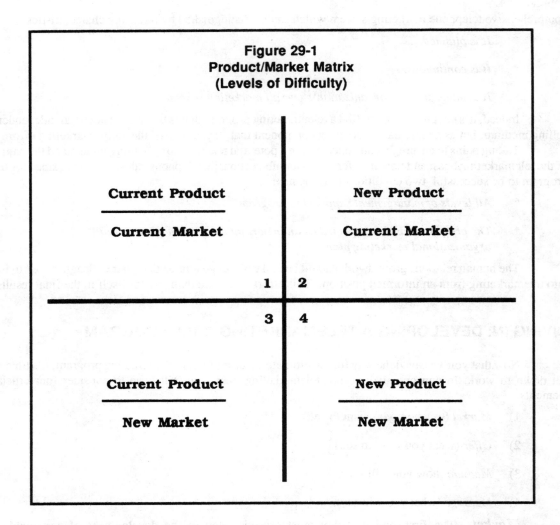

Figure 29-1
Product/Market Matrix
(Levels of Difficulty)

Current Product	New Product
Current Market	Current Market
1	2
3	4
Current Product	New Product
New Market	New Market

relatively higher or lower than average. Remember, however, when determining whether telemarketing makes economic sense, to compare potential cost levels to other marketing channels (e.g., field sales).

Be selective. Focus your market.

Next, recognize that the telephone has more than one use as a sales tool. The six best applications for telemarketing are:

* *To gather information.*

* *To provide information.*

* *To qualify or generate leads.*

* *To sell a product or service.*

* *To manage cash flow.*

* *Customer service.*

As you've probably noticed, five of the six uses constitute sales support functions. Keep this in mind as you identify markets and determine how telemarketing will be used by your organization.

Your next step is to find a way to reach the markets you selected. This is the stage at which client telephone lists must be obtained or compiled. There are two types of telemarketing lists: *response* and *compiled.*

A *response* list is an active list of people who have already responded to direct media such as direct mail, television, commercials, etc., which have primed them for the product or service you are selling. Response lists can be generated from in-house promotional programs or rented/bought from compatible organizations. Since the client has already indicated interest in what you have to offer, this should be an active, fertile telemarketing list.

Don't overlook the obvious. Current and past customers are generally considered your best prospects for additional sales.

The *compiled* list is a list of companies or individuals who meet a set of common criteria. This kind of list is more broadly based than a response list, and is usually a "passive" list, since the qualifying factors often are factors other than response.

The decision on the kind of list to use should be based primarily on your knowledge of the market. Cost of the list, in general, should not be an important factor, since the quality of the lists used will *directly* affect the success of your telemarketing program.

AN OFFER THEY CAN'T REFUSE

Even if your company has just developed the most miraculous product in the universe, for which customers will beat down the door once they hear about it, you will need to develop an *offer*.

A complete offer is comprised of three elements:

1) *The product or service.*

2) *The price.*

3) *A delivery system.*

The delivery system--the means by which the customer receives the product or service and the vendor receives payment--is the most important and most often overlooked aspect of the complete offer. While this statement might surprise most people experienced in direct marketing, keep in mind that the telephone, by nature a non-visual, intangible medium, is still viewed with distrust by many people. Therefore,

535

the seller must reduce the buyer's risk as much as possible by offering attractive terms of sale.

Assuming the product/service is attractive and offered at a reasonable price, the sale will be made or undone on the basis of speed of delivery, credit options, iron-clad guarantees, ease of return, etc.

TELEMARKETING + EXISTING SALES PROCESSES = SYNERGY

With markets and offer(s) defined, you've reached the point in the telemarketing planning process where you will need to widen your scope, examine your organization's existing sales processes and determine which will best support the telemarketing function.

Telemarketing should not be a stand-alone medium. For all its sales effectiveness, the telephone is a one-dimensional communication medium, solely dependent on a voice message.

The client/customer/contributor/member on the other end of the line lacks the benefits of cues provided by other media--body language in person-to-person contacts, illustrations in direct mail or broadcast, the verification (referability) inherent in print. Many potential customers have little confidence in a disembodied voice making "trust me" promises over a telephone wire.

The onus is on the telemarketer to prove sincerity and credibility, and the most effective way to do this is to enlist the aid of other media. But there are many other media. How do you select which to use?

The traditional sales process, as it is practiced in the United States, has four elements:

* *Conversation.*

* *Demonstration.*

* *Illustration.*

* *Credibility.*

Think about how most products or services are sold, whatever the medium. First, there is some form of discussion about the product or service (conversation). Second, the customer is shown how the product is used or will provide a benefit (demonstration), usually through example (illustration). Finally, the customer is given some guarantee of delivery and performance (credibility).

The telephone is capable of presenting only one of these with any efficiency: conversation. Thus, the other three must be supplemented by an auxiliary medium, selected on the basis of the complexity of the product or service being offered.

Four basic types of auxiliary media support exist:

* *Broadcast (television and/or radio).*

* *Print advertising (newspaper, magazine, billboard, etc.).*

* *Direct mail.*

* *Field sales.*

536

I have listed these media in a specific order--their ability or efficiency to present complex messages. Broadcast has the least ability. Field sales, the greatest ability. Clearly, the more complex the product or service being sold, the further up this hierarchy we must go in selecting auxiliary media.

The complexity of the product/service will similarly determine the sequence in which the chosen support media are used. Some sequencing rules of thumb exist, which you should find useful.

Generally, when broadcast support is used, the broadcast message is aired first, followed by the telephone sales call. The broadcast spot builds credibility and paves the way for the telemarketer by giving the consumer a wealth of information about the product in advance. Not only does the viewer see, hear and learn about the product but he unconsciously gives the sales idea more credence because of the inherent credibility of the television medium.

Print accomplishes a similar result when introduced *before* the sales call.

When dealing with field sales support, telemarketing is almost always used first in the sales sequence, most often to generate leads and set up sales appointments.

The decision about when to introduce direct mail into the sales sequence is entirely dependent on the specific product or service being offered. Specialty products further require a double shot of media support such as a telephone call to introduce the idea, followed by a direct mail piece to provide complicated explanatory material, followed by a phone call to sell the product.

Regardless of the media mix employed to support the telemarketing program, an essential point to remember is that the initial presentation must be augmented by a telephone sales call within a maximum of seven to 10 days.

Sales Force as Partners. Another vital aspect of integrating the telemarketing program into the existing sales process is sensitivity to the feelings and needs of the sales force. Fear, anger, resentment, and a number of other ''unpleasant'' emotions often start building, eventually turning into a tidal wave of resistance to the telemarketing process when the sales force is not informed and involved in the program. Nothing will kill a telemarketing program more quickly or efficiently than a threatened field sales force.

Remember, your sales associates, more often than not, view the telemarketing plan as direct competition until you disabuse them of this false notion by involving them in the program and letting them see how it can *complement* their efforts.

CUE PLEASE! WHAT'S MY LINE?

Okay, now you've zeroed in on your market, obtained call lists and determined the most effective media mix for your program. What next?

Script writing.

After all your strategic planning and analyzing, you can't just dial the phone and chew the fat. As previously discussed, the message in a medium like the telephone is all-important, and its quality is paramount to success.

The best guarantee of consistent quality in a telemarketing message is the existence and use of a quality script. . .

537

Alarm bells!

I know from experience that the idea of scripting causes many newcomers to telemarketing programs to break into cold sweats. The image they form is of a TSR on the phone, routinely reading a script and giving a forced and wooden presentation.

Not so. Far from limiting the telemarketer, scripting frees telemarketing representatives to plan and control their calls. This avoids verbal scrambling and bungling, and confers a greater sense of assurance and authority.

The purpose of scripting is to give TSR's a well-planned, carefully thought out call pattern, while at the same time allowing enough flexibility for differences in personal style and response. The script must convey your message quickly, clearly, and sensitively. It is important, always, to keep both the sales objective *and* the needs of the customer in mind when preparing scripts.

Telemarketing is an interactive medium, and must allow not only for the transmission of your message, but the customer's responses and, sometimes, objections.

While Chapter 11 of this Encyclopedia will provide you with a detailed guide to script preparation and use, a brief discussion of the various script types and call guides will be useful here.

There are three basic kinds of telemarketing scripts:

* *Verbatim.*

* *Guided.*

* *Outline.*

Verbatim Script. A verbatim script is one that is followed word for word. This type of script is generally aimed at the business-to-consumer audience. The message is usually brief, approximately 350 to 500 words--and the call itself lasts about three to four minutes. Verbatim scripts require little response from the prospect and include few closed-ended, probing questions.

Guided Script. The next level in scripting is less restrictive, and allows the TSR the flexibility to adjust the direction of the conversation according to the flow of a particular conversation. The guided script works best in business-to-business call programs, but may be used for business-to-consumer calling when the product or service offered requires some probing. The presentation of a guided script runs approximately 500 to 750 words, and requires five to six minutes to deliver. This script includes two to three open- and closed-ended probing questions. It is usually delivered by a representative with an experience level of at least two months.

Outline Script. This is probably the most difficult level of scripting. TSR's are given total flexibility. This isn't to suggest that they simply pick up the telephone and improvise. The outline script, which is used almost exclusively in business-to-business calling, is comprised of words and ideas written in outline form. A probing sequence is essential to this type of presentation. An outline script requires at least seven minutes, but should never run longer than 10, unless you are confident that the caller and the prospect already have a strong relationship. The outline-script call should be handled either by a very skilled representative, or by one who has developed a working relationship with the customer.

538

STEP-BY-STEP FOR STARTUPS: A REVIEW

The central point to consider when writing and using telemarketing scripts is that telemarketing is a people business, and regardless of the type of script used, there can be no substitute for a thinking, caring, intelligent TSR.

Call Guides: A Roadmap to Better Business. Another major grouping of scripts, "call guides" are complete business-to-business sales packages comprised of six key elements:

* *Program overview*--in which the philosophy of the sales campaign is stated.

* *Script prompts*--cues, transitions and probing questions that chart the flow of the call, and enable the TSR to rebound quickly when presented with client objections.

* *Feature/benefit menu*--a listing of the product/service's most important features with a corresponding listing of its benefits.

* *Key selling point(s)*--a technique to focus in on particularly attractive features of the product and the company.

* *Objection menu*--lists the most common objections and likely responses.

* *Technical question sheet*--a listing of the most frequently asked technical questions, with answers.

RECRUITING

The day you begin your recruiting program is the day your telemarketing program moves from the shadowy world of dream into the searching (and often harsh) light of reality. To this point, your telemarketing program has been an attractive theory (which, in the eyes of sceptics, at least, may or may not prove sound).

Since telemarketing is a people business, those who represent it have to be pre-eminently suited to this highly interpersonal field. Telemarketing representatives are a particular breed with readily identifiable character traits. They must be screened, hired, and trained with the utmost care and attention.

The single most important quality a TSR must possess is a good telephone voice--defined as well-modulated, enthusiastic, confident, and mature. A "good telephone voice" doesn't have to be of broadcast quality, but it should meet a high standard of speech refinement. If you are not instantly impressed favorably by a candidate's voice quality, don't consider him or her for a position on your telemarketing team.

Other desirable personality traits are: pleasant demeanor, good telephone presence, enthusiasm, confidence, and authority. Candidates should demonstrate a real desire to do the job, and give evidence of a propensity for influencing others somewhere in their background. Previous sales experience is, of course, extremely helpful.

Making It All Worthwhile: Compensation. The TSR's role is demanding, stressful, and often lonely. It's a job not just anyone can, should or wants to do.

For those who want to do the job, compensation is a prime motivator. These are people who are goal-oriented and ambitious, and who expect to see quick returns on expended effort. Your first objective, when trying to determine proper compensation that will satisfy budget constraints, senior management, and the needs of the reps themselves, is to find the best ratio of incentives to base salary.

Because telemarketing is a results-oriented and not task-oriented business, incentives act as self-motivators for the TSR's. They also serve as productivity boosters for the unit as a whole. Incentives are an extremely important coefficient in the compensation formula, in ways that go beyond purely money.

The most widely used distribution in the industry is 65% salary, 35% incentive. This ratio is comfortable enough to give the TSR a sense of security, and challenging enough to make him/her competitive. When designing your incentives program (see, also, the more detailed discussion of compensation in Chapter 9 of this Encyclopedia), remember to pump a healthy sense of fun into them--the more interesting your incentives, the better motivators they will be.

And don't forget to offer similar incentives for the telemarketing unit management. Never underestimate the importance of motivating the motivators.

Here are three questions to ask yourself in designing your compensation program:

* *What constitutes good job performance (quantitatively)?* How many calls, closes, etc., do you expect a TSR to make?

* *How much am I willing to pay for good performance?* Much may depend on what you can afford to pay, but try to assess the true value of the TSR's position in the company's overall sales activity.

* *How much of the money that I am willing to pay am I willing to put at risk?* This is staking-the-odds time. In other words, how much are you willing to pay in base salary?

We Know You're Out There: Writing the Classified Ad. Once you've determined the type of person you seek and how much you are willing to pay, it's time to cast the classified ad "net."

A display or block ad with a border, though more expensive than a per-word or per-line ad, is most likely to give you the results you want. It attracts the attention of the calibre of applicant you're seeking and projects a professional image for the company (see **Figure 29-2**). Spend the money!

Now that that's settled, let's discuss the five points that should be covered in the ad:

1) *Who you are.* This is your chance to let your corporate star shine. Go ahead. Brag a little (or a lot). Show your company at its most appealing. Just as you want to know why you should hire an applicant, they want to know why they should come to work for you.

2) *What you want people to do.* Don't lead the applicant on a merry dance, or be coy or otherwise evasive. Don't pull any punches, either. Tell the applicant exactly what it is he or she will be doing. Most important of all, don't use any euphemisms for "telemarketing."

Figure 29-2
Classfied Ad Example

"Tired of Being Part of the Telephone Room Masses?"

Our $70 million, growth-oriented, public corporation is opening a new division at a new facility in the heart of the Loop. Become involved in a multi-media, direct-marketing approach assisting our field sales reps.

If you have:
·Minimum 1 year telemarketing experience.
·College education or 4 years' business experience.
·High energy level and are a self-starter.
·Excellent communications skills...

Then take this opportunity to **Break Away** from mundane hourly tele-marketing jobs and come to a new professional environment.

We offer:
·Attractive base salary.
·Incentive compensation.
·Excellent benefit package.
·Training.
·Career progression.

So if you're dead-ended at a telemarketing center and feel you're under-paid, then send your resume for a $20,000 first-year package to:

**Productive Work Space
12345 Main Street
Anywhere, USA 12345
Attention: Mr. Robert Jones**

Equal Opportunity Employer

3) *What you'll pay them to do the job.* Here's the carrot. Compensation should be described, along with all that the term implies--base salary, incentives, bonuses, vacation and other benefits.

4) *What qualifications you require.* Here, list requirements for voice quality, level of education, previous sales experience, industry expertise, etc.

5) *What action you want them to take.* Ask for response by resume. Try not to accept telephone calls (a twist of irony). Initial contact with the applicant should be made by telephone, true, but with *you* initiating the call so that *you* retain complete control. This will help you judge all the important qualities of voice quality and presence under the closest to normal conditions possible.

The Telephone Interview: A Very Revealing Call.

The telephone interview will confirm with greater certainty and effectiveness than any other single step in the hiring process, whether a candidate that looked good on paper has what it takes to cut it in the telemarketing "jungle." What is occurring here is actually an on-the-job test before a candidate has been given the job. The phone is the ultimate pre-screening tool and should be used for all it's worth.

Before you reach for the phone to dial the candidate's number, however, pause a moment to remember your objective--to judge telephone presence and quality. Don't view the interview as an opportunity to go on a heady, no-risk power trip in which you "test the candidate's mettle" by seeing how well he or she will react under pressure.

That approach will succeed only in making the applicant nervous, suspicious and, perhaps, even resentful. Tension affects voice quality, so play the conversation in a low-key way. Make the prospect comfortable. What you'll receive in return is the best gauge available of future job performance.

Try to call the candidate within five days of receiving his or her resume. This should ensure that the enthusiasm and interest are still alive. It will also project a more professional image for your organization. During the interview, rate the candidate for voice quality, mannerisms, clarity, continuity, and enthusiasm.

Set up a one-hour interview if, and only if, you are totally satisfied with the candidate's telephone presence. *There are no other redeeming factors in this field.* If you haven't enjoyed talking with this person for the last five minutes, neither will your clients. You may also choose to further qualify candidates at this point by briefly reviewing their education, employment history, outside interests, etc.

Some basic questions that should be asked during the interview include:

* *A description of the previous five years of employment.*

* *An explanation of any unemployment during that period.*

* *Professional and personal objectives.*

* *Outside interests, particularly how the candidate relaxes. (No, this information is not "none of your business." Telemarketing sales is a high-stress occupation, and you need to now whether this person knows how to "let down.")*

542

*   *A topic of choice for open discussion.*

These questions have been chosen because they all focus on the candidate, giving him an opportunity to expound on a subject he knows best--himself. This puts all candidates on an equal footing and allows the interviewer to concentrate on the medium, not the message.

TELEMARKETING MANAGEMENT: THE BUCK STOPS HERE

Any department within an organization, regardless of the nature of its responsibility, is only as good as its management. This truth is exceptionally self-evident in a telemarketing unit.

Telemarketing is management-intensive because it is a high-stress, results-oriented function that relies heavily on the sales ability of its personnel. People selling to people require deft and sensitive handling.

Managers who loathe getting involved in the nitty gritty of the everyday operation don't belong in telemarketing. A telemarketing manager doesn't have to be "one of the troops," but he or she had better know what it feels like to be a staff member, usually by learning the staff's jobs as well as they do.

The three central characteristics of a good telemarketing manager are:

*   *Good sales sense.*

*   *Good sense of people.*

*   *Good sense of numbers.*

At minimum, the telemarketing manager's responsibilities will include setting objectives for the unit, developing call guides, training, monitoring, coaching/counseling, and gaining familiarity with the organization's resources.

The telemarketing manager should, in all events, be a consummate "people person," who knows how to spur his staff on to unprecedented heights of self-realization. He should also possess the requisite finesse to act as a corporate diplomat for the telemarketing program, quelling interdepartmental fears and territorial disputes, and promoting the professional image of his unit. The legitimacy and degree of acceptance the telemarketing program achieves within the organization will be directly proportional to his or her accomplishments in these areas.

TRAINING: DOING IT RIGHT THE FIRST TIME

At last, you've reached the point where you can stop talking about telemarketing and start doing something about it. You have a group of warm bodies, lists, an offer, etc. What do you do? Point them in the direction of the phones?

Not quite. Unfortunately, TSR's are trained, not born, and your training sessions will have to be, like every other step in the startup process, very well-planned.

The basic telephone sales techniques that should be taught at these sessions are voice, rate of speaking, tone, volume, and listening. The telephone selling skills that should be taught are those that are included in the classic tripartite "anatomy of a call"--opening, dialog and close. Because of their ultimate importance to the success of the telemarketing program as a whole, these techniques and skills will be explored at length and in detail in this section.

Training Game Plan. Let's begin at the beginning. Before you assemble your first training class populated with eager faces, stop and think about what it is you want to impart to these fresh (for your purposes) minds. First, recognize that there are two distinct and equally critical segments in telemarketing training:

1) *Telephone sales training.*

2) *Product/company informational training.*

Never, ever attempt to introduce both types of training at once. You will simply confuse, discourage, and frustrate the trainees.

I won't go into elaborate detail about product/company informational training here, except to say that all the fancy telephone sales techniques won't be worth the cost of the phone call unless the telemarketing representative has a thorough working knowledge of what he or she is selling and for whom.

This issue of product/company training is a wonderful juncture at which to strengthen the diplomatic bonds between the telemarketing unit and the organization's existing sales force. Invite the star sales associates to guest lecture on products/services. Since it is genuinely important that TSR's understand the company's business philosophy, you can also involve other marketing managers or even a member of senior management to brief them on these issues. Such cooperative training involvement will do double duty as an interdepartmental "harmonizer."

Hands-On Teaching. Reaching the hearts and minds of raw telemarketing rep recruits requires the same techniques as reaching clients--you have to engage their minds. *All* training should be hands on, since telemarketing is a field in which you really do only learn by doing. Five teaching methods specifically designed and tailored to the field of telephone sales can be employed:

* *Lecture.* This is the straightforward verbal impartation of information.

* *Workshop.* This is a combination of lecture, class discussion, and exercises.

* *Role play.* This is perhaps the most important and least appreciated part of the training process. It is so vital that it should consume about 50% of the total training time. It's a terrific confidence booster and can be great fun. However, since it is a serious and important teaching tool, role play should be scripted, covering each part of a telephone sales call. Each trainee should role play each situation at least once, and role plays should always be critiqued first by the players themselves, next by fellow class members, and lastly by the instructor.

* *Call guide development.* This is similar to a workshop, except that the

544

purpose is to develop working, effective scripts/call guides.

* *Live calls.* The baptism of fire, carefully monitored and exhaustively critiqued. Never unleash your fledgling TSR's on an unsuspecting public without first having put them through a segment of live-call training. On the last day of class, take the group into the telephone sales area. Require each student to make a live call to a customer/prospect/suspect, in which a full presentation that satisfies a call objective is accomplished. The trainee may have to make several calls to realize his or her goal, but then what could more closely reflect real life? Don't be too shocked if a sale is actually made during the training session.

In general, provide plenty of good, constructive criticism, pointing out specific areas in which the trainee evidenced weaknesses. Make concrete suggestions for improvement. And, finally, liberally praise areas of strength.

Imparting Wisdom: Teaching Telemarketing Sales Techniques. Now that we've discussed how to teach, it's time to consider what should be taught.

The initial 120 seconds of a sales call will make or break the sale. The first 30 seconds are the most critical. Of course, the most essential telemarketing challenge--and basic problem--is one of engaging the prospect's interest in the caller and his message. But let's put first things first. The TSR's message isn't even going to get a chance to hit the airwaves if the client is put off by the TSR. Although there is no accounting for personal taste, there are several telemarketing sales techniques that may be acquired to help the TSR firmly gain the prospect's ear.

Voice. The first, and probably most important technique that could be taught is voice. Most people have voices, to be sure, but most could be better if they were developed. The voice is of paramount importance in telemarketing sales because it's the element that gives the customer his or her first impression of the telemarketer--and we all know the importance of first impressions.

It is *not* advisable to change or disguise the voice in phone presentations, but it is vital to convey enthusiasm and sincerity. It may be trite, but nevertheless accurate, to say that smiling while talking (as mega-telemarketer AT&T recommends) transmits a positive vocal impression. Also, the TSR will have to learn to avoid letting the deadly sound of argumentativeness creep into his or her voice. Few mistakes can kill a call faster.

Speech Rate. Although the rapidity or slowness of speech generally goes unnoticed in face-to-face conversation because voice is supported by visual cues, pace becomes obvious and often obtrusive in telephone conversations.

If the TSR speaks too swiftly, the customer, lacking the aid of visual contact, may not pick up on the message being relayed. Alternatively, if speech drags, the customer may get ahead of the TSR and could eventually lose interest in the conversation.

Studies have shown that the ideal rate of speech for telephone conversation is approximately 180 words per minute. A trainee can easily learn to adjust his rate of speed by practicing with a prepared 180-word statement.

545

ENCYCLOPEDIA OF TELEMARKETING

Tone. The tone of voice a TSR presents on the phone sets (and please excuse the pun) the tone of the call. Voice tone is the telephone personality. It accurately indicates and conveys the telemarketer's mood and personal faith in the product, service, and/or organization being represented.

However, tone is the most difficult voice quality to self-evaluate. When we speak, we are usually so involved with what we are saying that we are totally oblivious to how the message is coming across.

Tone can be judged in two ways:

1) *Ask a co-worker to listen while you are making a sales call, then have him or her critique your performance.*

2) *Tape record your calls, and judge for yourself.*

Remember, tone registers before words.

Listen Up. Equally important to the success of a telemarketing call is the TSR's ability to listen. Remember, communication is a *two-way* process. If it's not an interactive conversation, it's a private speech to a captive and probably lost audience of one.

The best way to improve listening ability is to exercise a healthy respect for the customer and his thoughts. The TSR should frequently run down this listening "checklist":

* *Limit your own talking.*

* *Think like the customer.*

* *Ask questions.*

* *Don't interrupt.*

* *Concentrate on what the customer is expressing.*

* *Listen for ideas, not words.*

* *Interject occasionally, to indicate understanding of what the customer is saying.*

* *Turn off personal worries.*

* *Be prepared.*

* *React to ideas, not the person.*

* *Don't argue mentally.*

* *Don't jump to conclusions.*

* *Listen for overtones.*

546

Anatomy of a Call. A telephone sales call is comprised of three main components:

1) *The opening.*

2) *Needs establishment.*

3) *Needs satisfaction.*

The opening, actually the first 30 seconds of the opening of a sales call, is the single most important phase of the entire call. In the opening, the tone of the conversation is set and interest is (we would hope) piqued. If the client isn't engaged in the first 30 seconds by what the TSR is saying, and how it's being said, the customer's lost for good.

The second part of the body of the call, needs establishment, is also known as the dialog phase. The primary purpose of this part of the call is to ask questions that determine the client's needs.

The concluding segment of the call is the close, in which the client's needs, which were discovered in the dialog phase, are satisfied or the telemarketer illustrates how they could be satisfied.

Fine-Tuning Telephone Sales Skills. There are eight basic sales skills that can be developed and refined to improve the telemarketer's rate of success. Each will be examined here in some detail because each is important.

1) *Introduction of self and company.* A self-introduction is more than a nicety of telephone manners. It is your calling card, the element that creates the customer's first impression of the telemarketer and the organization he or she represents. The telemarketer must speak clearly, audibly, and with some degree of enthusiasm. A good introduction is comprised of three elements:

* *The prospect's name.*

* *The telemarketer's name.*

* *The name of the TSR's organization.*

2) *Securing the prospect's attention.* To get the prospect's attention, an engaging lead-in statement must be made. Keep in mind that in making a bid for attention, the goal is to focus on the telemarketer, not the product or service (which will come later).

3) *Creating interest.* Here, the focus shifts from the telemarketer to the product or service. Interest-getting statements will closely tie in to benefits, directly answering the client's unspoken question: *"What's in it for me?"*

4) *Probing.* This is one of the most important skills a TSR can acquire, since asking directed questions is the most direct route to establishing need. It's only through establishing need that the TSR can sell.

The heart of probing is questioning or interviewing. What the TSR wants to gain here is relevant information about the prospect's business. Two basic types of questions are asked to accomplish this task: open and closed-ended.

Open-ended questions are generally not answerable by one or two words. Instead, they're designed to get the prospect to "open up" and to involve him more in the conversation. Most of a customer's real needs can be elicited in responses to open-ended questions. They also tend to be the most effective opening.

Closed-ended questions, on the other hand, are generally answerable in one or two words. They can be just as useful as open-ended questions, but in a different way. The TSR can use them to zero in on a specific point, to obtain a very specific piece of information, and/or to bring the customer back on track if he goes off on a tangent. In any event, probing is best accomplished by incorporating a deft mixture of both open-ended and closed-ended questions.

5) *Paraphrasing.* This device allows the TSR to clarify statements made by the client by rephrasing a statement of need. In this way, he can ensure that the client's needs, which were elicited through probing, have been understood by the TSR. The need can then usually be tied into a benefit provided by the product or service being sold.

6) *Presentation of features with corresponding benefits.* Let's first get clear on our definition of "benefits" and "features." A *benefit* is the good the prospect will derive from a product or service. A *feature* is a characteristic of the product or service being sold. Features are inherent in the product. This includes such attributes as color, size, shape, quality of workmanship, weight, height, width, etc. It is imperative that the TSR understand that benefits sell, not features. Benefits meet the customer's need, features make the product or service more attractive and believable. It's important not to confuse the two when trying to make a sale.

7) *Meeting objections.* The thought of responding to objections can be paralyzing to a novice TSR at first, but objections are not difficult to handle if they are clear (see Chapter 12 of this Encyclopedia for a detailed discussion). The problem often lies in determining exactly what the prospect is objecting to, and what is at the root of the objection.

The best way to clarify the subject is to paraphrase or probe the objections the prospect has stated. Price objections often must be paraphrased or probed to determine whether the prospect objects to dollars or doubts value. Stalling tactics that are not objections should almost always be probed.

Once the objection is clear, it should be met with information or proof. To determine whether or not the prospect accepts your answer, simply ask.

Finally, know when the horse has breathed its last, and put the stick down.

8) *Summarizing and closing.* This is the moment of truth. The close of a sale to a TSR is like the final paragraph of a novel to a writer. It's both a relief and a letdown. The close is, at once, a culmination of all the effort, and the essence of what selling is all about.

There are three types of close: *direct, assumptive,* and *contained choice.* Sensitivity and intuition are required to choose exactly the right type of close to use.

In the *direct close*, the TSR asks for the order in plain and simple language: *"May I place your order, Mr. McGillicuddy?"* Short. Sweet. To the point. This type of close is used when the customer responds positively to a benefit and features presentation.

The *assumptive* close is slightly more oblique. The TSR zeroes in with this type of close after the customer has sent out a buying signal or a statement that indicates he has made the decision to buy, but is tying up loose ends. For example, if a client says, *"Does the shelving come in gun-metal gray?"* he's sending out a strong buying signal. Go for it? The answer is: *"Yes it does. May I have the shipping address?"*

The *contained choice* is a little more intricate than either the direct or assumptive close, but involves the prospect more. This is the type of close to use when a client is still fence-straddling. Interestingly, the contained choice close is the most preferred by many TSR's, probably because it requires less prospect manipulation and mental arm wrestling.

A final point on closes: *never* close in the face of an objection.

REPORTING IN: CONTROL SYSTEMS AND MEASUREMENTS

Every business operation needs a control system. This gives it accountability, viability, and the most important "-bility," the possibility of a future.

The central purposes of a control and measurement system are to manage, monitor and measure a program. A telemarketing program is not static. It doesn't open for business on Day One, and then continue to operate on the same basis for the next 20 years--or even 20 days, for that matter. So, the telemarketing program manager will have to maintain a detailed, accurate reporting system that charts what the program is doing and a record of precisely how it's doing it--good or bad. This is the only way to pinpoint and adjust to needed change.

The goal in this aspect of telemarketing management should be to produce reports that lead to decisions (see Chapter 15 in this Encyclopedia for more detailed information on reporting systems). There are two inviolable axioms to live by when maintaining a control and measurement system:

* *Collect only actionable data.* This means collect only the information you need to know, not information that's nice to know. One good test of whether you're building a solid database or just making another sacrifice to the paper gods (sometimes referred to as "senior management") is to ask yourself the question, *"Is this actionable?"*

* *If it's irretrievable, it's unusable.* Obvious as this one may seem, it's not. Knowing how to collect and store information so that it is instantly retrievable is essential.

Transforming the reporting system into a well-oiled machine will require the design and development of two essential forms: a *customer call record* and a *daily activity report*. A customer call record should be kept by each TSR. This report should include statistics such as demographic information and a running history of the account. The two benefits of keeping a log such as this is that it will act as a good briefing device to keep the telemarketing representative familiar with the account, and, should the TSR responsible for the account leave (expect a 30% to 50% annual turnover in this field), the customer call record will give his or her replacement a useful history of the account.

The second mandatory report, compiled by the unit manager, is a *daily activity report*. This report, based on statistics provided by each telemarketing representative, details activity such as number of dialings, presentations and presentation results. This acts as a good overview of the program's activity.

While it's wise to eventually record and store such information on an automated database, it's probably advisable to generate reports manually in the beginning.

Draw Me a Picture: The Flow Chart. A flow chart detailing the entire telemarketing program process and the external operations with which it interfaces in the organization is another essential document. This document literally gives both the telemarketing staff and outside managers a clear picture of the program, what it is and how it functions.

Big Brother Is Listening. The key to maintaining a fresh, dynamic telemarketing program is *monitoring*. Only by monitoring the individual and collective progress of the program can the telemarketing manager know where needed adjustments are to be made.

Monitoring should consist of a systematic, point-by-point analysis of existing operations. The individual progress of TSR's should be documented by monitoring a sampling of five live sales calls with their prior *written consent*. Monitoring should be done without the TSR's knowledge at the time, so that the

550

manager can get an accurate picture of the quality of performance. Ideally, monitoring should be done on a weekly basis.

Monitoring results should be recorded according to the same format every time, and management should look for progress in areas where the TSR was weak, or slippage in areas of previous strength. Monitoring results should be reviewed with the TSR as soon as possible after the monitoring is completed. This session should be viewed as a combination consulting/teaching opportunity for the manager.

If monitoring indicates that a TSR is not performing acceptably by the end of his third month of employment, termination is called for. A three-month trial is adequate time to determine whether someone can cut it in this field or not. One final point: remember that a monitoring program must be systematic and continuous to be of any value. A pattern must emerge in order for areas of needed adjustment to be identified.

Paperwork: Whose Job Is It, Anyway? TSR's may be required to submit data for customer call records and other reports, but they should *never* be involved in the clerical or administrative support functions of the program. TSR's are hired to *sell*. So, let them sell. Any time taken away from sales activity can be directly converted into lost sales. Don't sell yourself short--include an administrative support position in your staffing proposal.

The Crystal Ball Complex: Projecting Revenue vs. Expenses. A time-honored formula exists for computing revenue/expense expectations:

$$(TSR) * (P) * (V) * (R) * (D) = Revenue$$

Five considerations must be entered into the formula to solve the equation. They are:

* *Number of TSR's on the project (TSR).*

* *Number of presentations per TSR per day (P).*

* *Average value of sale per presentation (V).*

* *Expected close/presentation ratio (R).*

* *Number of work days in the month (D).*

This is the "bottom-to-top" approach. You set a goal to be attained, and the formula works out what it will take to attain that goal. For example, you've hired three TSR's. You figure they can each realistically make 25 presentations a day, averaging $500 per order, with a close ratio of one to five. There are 20 working days in this particular month. When the figures are inserted in the formula, you realize you can expect 1,500 presentations per month. If 300 sales are made at an average of $500 per order, you can expect $150,000 per month in business.

With a new operation, realistically plan on making 25% of projected results after the first month. By the second month, look for 50%, the third month 75%, and, by the fourth month in operation, expect your program to live up to your original projections.

But don't make the mistake of getting locked into your first projected formula. The introduction of a telemarketing program into a company may be hindered or aided by a number of unknown variables.

Rework your formula as soon as you begin to see inconsistencies in the results.

CUBICLE, SWEET CUBICLE: THE IMPORTANCE OF ENVIRONMENT

Anyone who works in an office spends at least half of his waking hours in the workspace allotted by the organization. It's a sobering thought, indeed, to realize that the space we return to day after day is as much home as our homes. Yet, until very recently, management gave little attention to the impact the often sterile environments had upon employee performance.

The importance of a work environment (see Chapter 14 in this Encyclopedia for a more detailed discussion of habitat) is nowhere more crucial than in the high-stress atmosphere of a telemarketing operation. The massive efforts that have gone into the planning of the program can be quickly forfeited by not providing a climate conducive to this unique field.

The four critical environmental factors management must contend with when designing the layout of a telemarketing unit are:

* *Lighting.*

* *Ventilation.*

* *Distractions.*

* *Acoustics.*

Each of these factors will be dealt with, but the ideal telemarketing environment will, in a nutshell, be clean, bright, well-lighted and ventilated, and will have minimal noise distraction. It will not be overly isolated, and it will provide sufficient rest rooms, break areas, refreshment facilities and personal lockers.

Lighting. The telemarketing area should be well-lighted to create a more cheerful atmosphere, as well as to provide adequate illumination for the close work that is involved in data gathering and script reading. The inclusion of some natural light, if possible, will be a morale booster.

Ventilation. This is probably one of the most important environmental factors to be considered. Poor ventilation is the telemarketer's hidden enemy. Unseen, unheard, and unfelt until it's too late, poor ventilation will sap the strength of your TSR's, leaving them too warm, uncomfortable, lethargic, and unmotivated. Therefore, make sure the telemarketing area can be independently climate controlled, and that the ventilation system is regularly inspected and maintained.

Distractions. Noise and visual distractions will eat into call effectiveness if they are excessive. Distractions can be reduced by providing adequate, partitioned space per telemarketing representative. There should be no major traffic in the area, and acoustical side panels should be provided to muffle the sound produced by nearby telemarketing co-workers. Above all, be sure your layout is designed so that the TSR can preserve a sense of privacy. The work he or she is performing is tough enough without having the added

552

handicap of self-consciousness to combat.

Acoustics. Anyone who has tried to carry on a telephone conversation in a public place understands the importance of acoustics to telemarketing. Deadening sound is very important to the TSR's concentration and stress level. He or she needs to be able to shut out, mentally, all distractions in order to concentrate and preserve a professional conversational tone. This can be aided by installing a dropped, sound-absorbing ceiling, carpeting the floors, and surrounding each work area with sound-absorbing cubicles.

Furniture. After the environmental factors have been attended to, it's time to go shopping for furniture. Telemarketing's furniture requirements are relatively minimal, but they're vital to the comfort and satisfaction of the staff. Each telemarketing representative will require a 60" X 30" work surface and an adjustable chair with very good back support. The importance of selecting a high-quality chair with good support cannot be overemphasized, given the sedentary nature of the work conducted in it. The chair should have arm rests and casters to enable free movement. Don't cut corners in this department. Plan to budget from $1,000 to $1,200 per TSR for furniture.

COMING ON-LINE: CHOOSING TELEPHONE EQUIPMENT

The question to ask when considering what telephone equipment to lease or purchase is not which brand is best, but what type of equipment does your operation need to meet your needs adequately?

Before you run out to the phone store to compare Brand X with Brand Z, take a good, hard look at your company's existing telephone system to determine if it has sufficient trunk lines to handle your unit's demands (see Chapters 18 and 19 and Appendix D of this Encyclopedia for a detailed discussion of telephone and telecommunications equipment). If it does, don't go to the needless high cost of installing a new service.

One important caution, however; don't use your organization's existing systems if that would entail sharing lines.

Not only is the telephone system the heart of your operation, it *is* your operation, and if you scrimp here, you'll bitterly regret it later. The amount of equipment and service needed for the new telemarketing operation is actually minimal and inexpensive when integrated into the company's existing system. Each TSR will need a touchtone telephone, a comfortable headset, and a WATS line. This initial setup will cost about $500. The cost of all new equipment and a new system independent of the company's existing system will be a minimum of $10,000. It is also advisable to budget an additional $2,000 for a call accounting system (a device that attaches to the telephone switch to provide printed out reports of telephone activity on each line in the unit), regardless of the type of system you choose.

EPILOGUE: THE TELEMARKETING STARTUP IN REVIEW

Now that you've walked through a telemarketing program startup step by step, you're probably experiencing one of two emotions: elation or dejection. Or maybe you're just plain worn out. Well, welcome. Starting a telemarketing program is hard work, and lots of it.

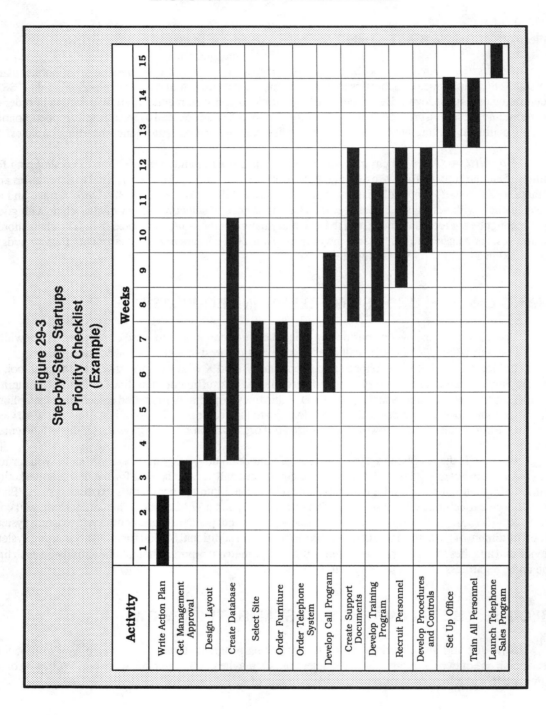

Figure 29-3
Step-by-Step Startups
Priority Checklist
(Example)

STEP-BY-STEP FOR STARTUPS: A REVIEW

Success, often undreamed of success, is practically guaranteed if you have the enthusiasm, commitment, and energy it takes to plan, promote, and gain management support for an undertaking of this nature.

When all is said and done, there is only one differential that will determine the ultimate success of your proposal to expand the sales frontier of your company, and that is *good planning*. A telemarketing program must be systematic and an integral part of the company's overall marketing efforts.

Above all, know your market. Your medium and your message will fall on stone-deaf ears if the need for your service hasn't been clearly established.

Finally, be confident, and give yourself *a lot* of credit. After all, you're the one who had the vision to recognize telemarketing as the sales tool of the future.

You weren't wrong.

CHAPTER 30

Telemarketing: Yesterday, Today, and Tomorrow

Steven A. Idelman
Chairman & Chief Executive Officer
Idelman Telemarketing, Inc.
Omaha, Nebraska

YESTERDAY

The telemarketing industry is undergoing a period of dramatic change and growth. In the last quarter-century, telemarketing has grown from an unrespected stepchild kept hidden in the back rooms of business into a promising adolescent, who has emerged to capture the attention of the entire nation.

Despite the common misconception that telemarketing is a new field, telemarketing has its roots in the first three decades of this century. The groundbreakers for today's telemarketing were the steel and the financial industries. While those pioneering efforts were sometimes little more than bare-boned and primitive attempts to fit established face-to-face selling methods to the phone lines, they revealed the potential of Dr. Bell's remarkable invention.

Telemarketing's roots are in what now seems like the dark and dreary past. The industry's unusually colorful history is checkered with "boiler room" pioneers who managed with minimal business expertise; their specialty was fast-paced hyperbole. Some went well past hyperbole to pure telephone con artistry. To many, "phoner" became synonymous with "phony."

The old school telemarketer was frequently short on concern for his employees. Sometimes, the conditions the early telephone salespeople had to endure were beyond the imagination of today's newer generation of telemarketers.

One old school entrepreneur was especially noted for his ability to find unbearable (and extremely cheap) locations for his phone rooms. On one occasion he rented a windowless basement room of a building that should have been designated as an endangered historical landmark. It was dark, dingy, cold and far beyond simply "damp." What little lighting existed was provided by bare bulbs. The walls were not peeling, but only because they had never been painted. That phone room epitomized the old "boiler-room" mentality.

In those days, there were very few requirements beyond the ability to close a sale, in almost any manner possible. The only restriction on personal conduct was "sell or leave." It wasn't unusual to see six packs of beer or bottles of cheap bourbon adorning the desks of the salesmen. On-the-job drinking frequently went hand in hand with on-the-job training.

One day the old school owner left the operation for several hours. Upon his return, he saw that the basement was flooded with water up to the bottom of the sales reps' chairs. Perched on top of those chairs were his salespeople, phoning away...at least most of them were. In the absence of any management, one of the people had increased his normal pace of drinking on the job. In fact, he was drunk as a skunk.

Just as the owner reached the water level, the inebriated salesman passed out and fell face down, floating in the water. When he didn't move, a couple of the salesmen started to get up and rescue the unfortunate guy. But they were immediately frozen by the owner's cry--"*Keep calling and leave the drunk where he is. The first man who touches him is fired!*"

It may be hard to believe, but I know that is a true story, because *I'm* one of the guys who had the audacity to try and help out the drunk. In fact, that experience was a part of my early incentive to play a role in helping telemarketing move into the legitimate business theater. Fortunately for the industry, I was not alone in that desire. Many legitimate and concerned telemarketers survived and prospered.

Still, we were not terribly sophisticated and our management teams were extremely limited. The old school approach meant that an entrepreneur, who was well versed in phone sales, would set up what was essentially a one-man shop. The founder was the source of all expertise and had hands-on control of virtually every aspect of the company. If the founder was out because of illness, marketing trips, or vacation--well, good luck! Often the entire operation took a vacation when he did, or worse yet, they came to work anyway.

I *know* the problems of yester-year because I've been there. In April of 1981, after serving my seven years of apprenticeship, I opened my own 45-phone shop. I ran the operation like a madman. My wife worked with me and we did it all, everything from recruiting and hiring to training to program development to supervising. We were flying!

I forgot only one minor thing. Since I was totally occupied with the daily operation, I had no time for marketing our services. After 90 days I had to lay off almost everyone. I went back to marketing, and after a reasonably short time we were again off and running.

I wish I could say that that was the last time I had problems of short-sightedness or lack of preparation. But I can't. Like most of the old school telemarketers, I made my share of mistakes learning the business. Those who paid their dues, and survived, learned a lot. We *had* to.

One of the early pioneers who helped the industry change and mature was the late Murray Roman. In 1962, under the direction of a young and innovative Ford executive named Lee Iacocca, Mr. Roman carried out a 20-million-call project. At the time, the sheer size of the project and the unprecedented sophistication of the systems were staggering. But he made it work. And the successful results helped establish telemarketing as an acceptable part of the marketing strategy in the American business community.

Telemarketing's past is marked by colorful characters and is checkered with mistakes. Yet the lessons learned in that sometimes painful process continually moved us forward. The yesterdays of telemarketing were built upon entrepreneurial adventures in experimentation and innovation. They were rich with the development of new concepts and expanded applications for a new industry.

In a sense, telemarketing's past was a struggle toward maturity and a search for a stronger identity.

TODAY

In today's emerging present, we find ourselves still in the process of redefining our identity. Telemarketing and the image of telemarketing *have* changed, and are actively changing--some for the better (growth and corporate acceptance) and some for the worse (more angry consumers).

Telemarketing is rapidly being accepted as a viable and profitable force in the business community. Over 90% of the Fortune 500 companies employ telemarketing as a part of their overall marketing strategies. Household names such as JC Penney, Sears, Allstate, Spiegel, Montgomery Ward, and Citibank--just to name a few--have joined the telemarketing fold. And as telemarketing moves into the boardrooms of America's largest corporations, the era of the old "seat of the pants, wing-and-a-prayer" manager is rapidly moving into the past.

If any single issue can characterize the status of today's telemarketing, it is the issue of growth. Recent research indicates that dealing with telemarketing's remarkable growth is the number one concern of its managers.

The following statistics were compiled from various industry sources, including Rudy Oetting, Aldyn McKean, the DMA, the ATA, and the *1986 Annual Guide to Telemarketing* by Fishman & Kordahl.

In 1980 there were 15 telemarketing service bureaus which had been in operation for at least two years; in 1986 that number had increased to 78--with over 1,600 more that started up and died a quick death in 1986 alone! In the corporate world of 1985, 82,000 firms were involved with telemarketing; by 1986 that number had grown to over 140,000 firms, representing industry growth of over 20%. The average business-to-business telemarketing sale increased from $250 in 1980 to $1,500 in 1986, with projections of a $1,700-2,000 average by 1990. In 1986 total telemarketing revenues (inbound and outbound) in the United States were $118 billion: projections for 1987 were $142 billion, with expectations of 15%-20% growth per year through 1990.

Telemarketing applications and industries using them have grown dramatically. Today anything from fine art to soap, from diapers to computers, from credit card protection to legal services protection is sold by phone.

That growth presents us with unparalleled opportunities and unprecedented challenges. On the positive side, we are faced with learning how to better manage our operations both financially and operationally. On the downside, telemarketing--like any "hot new industry"--has attracted more than its fair share of the "Florida swampland" and "naked options" type of get-rich-quick scam artists. Warnings to the public about the abuse of credit cards and misleading pitches for vacation travel have become increasingly common.

Control of Growth. As a group, we are searching for the essential factors and the most effective techniques to capitalize on that explosive growth while somehow keeping it under control. We are searching for the ways to establish and prove new methods, procedures, and structures. We are struggling with the best means of integrating modern technologies into our work. We are searching for answers to critical personnel development and retention issues. And we are working to establish a permanent and clearly defined role in the corporate marketing repertoire.

The vast majority of managers responsible for creating the new image and capabilities of the industry are recognizing that they require guidance and assistance in the endeavor. The demand for substantive information is extremely high. Presentations at industry conventions have received rave reviews and urgent requests for additional information and guidance. The industry's publications have rushed to print summaries of those presentations.

Telemarketing is undergoing a dynamic transition. It is experiencing the internal and external pressures of increased acceptance and greater demand. That brings today's telemarketers their own special challenges.

Yet we have to assume that if rapid growth can be handled in traditional business environments such as manufacturing, retail, and more traditional service businesses, then rapid growth can also be managed in the telemarketing environment. Once you get past the telemarketing specific issues, business growth is business growth, and you must consider the production, service, and execution needs of your company.

So the biggest hurdle is in recognizing the problems with growth which are unique or at least unusual about the telemarketing environment. The following are among the most important:

* *The concerns about the use of call guides or scripts.*

* *The sensitivity of call transmission quality versus the importance of lower cost, list selection, and database management.*

* *The question to automate or not to automate.*

* *The design and placement of facilities.*

* *The problems of inconsistent call loads.*

* *The coordination (and often friction) with field sales and marketing staffs.*

* *The requirements of fulfillment and customer service.*

* *The impact and demands of existing and pending telemarketing legislation.*

And, of course, there are the problems created by being only as good as your last call. Any telemarketing unit--whether in-house or service bureau--can easily plummet from favor even more rapidly than it can climb to the heights of acceptance.

The full list is extensive.

Labor Issues. But the biggest telemarketing difference is in the area of labor issues, especially in the area of consumer telemarketing. In a traditional business environment the labor force is generally comprised of full-time employees who are working to support themselves on a full-time basis. In telemarketing this isn't generally true, especially not in consumer telemarketing. And while the business-to-business environment more closely approximates the traditional business environment, it still has to deal with the unique problems presented by telemarketing:

* *The impact of frequent rejection.*

* *The intensity/burnout factor.*

* *The youth of the industry and its people.*

* *The lack of perception of telemarketing as a "high profile" career path.*

* *The lack of formal telemarketing preparation and training in the country's educational institutions.*

* *The frequent perception of chaos in a fast-paced and change-driven industry.*

Transition means change, but changes created by the process of growth rarely come easily...especially on people issues. And telemarketing--more than most industries--is people intensive. As the industry changes, effective management and development of the people are becoming increasingly critical.

As of 1988, the demand for quality telemarketing services was growing faster than the industry's ability to grow the necessary amount of qualified managers. The industry needs dramatic improvement in its ability to deal with the retention of qualified people. That's a hard, cold fact, regardless of the hype you hear about how great everyone's people are.

All too often, the concern about turnover comes after the fact. Work on retention shouldn't start at the point problems actually begin to appear. It doesn't even start in the training or in the interview. All those are important, but you have to start with the image you put out in the marketplace with your ads.

The recruitment ad should be simple, classy and easy to follow. No "make your dreams come true," no gimmicky disguising of what the job is, no misleading hyperbole or impossible promises. That just disappoints a lot of job applicants and sets the company up to be disappointed with an extremely high turnover rate. Say what it is, say it in a persuasive way. . .and that's it.

This whole industry generally accepts high turnover as a part of the business. Some companies expect to solve the problem with lavish ergonomics, extraordinary benefits, and basic phone rep salaries in the $35,000 range. That approach *alone* all too frequently results in an environment that isn't very productive--although there are exceptions to every rule. But usually The Rule rules: *It requires a lot more than money and comfortable chairs to keep TSR's both happy and productive.*

Research into motivation has repeatedly shown that money is pretty far down the list of what satisfies people in a job and keeps them around. Money *is* an important factor and always on the list--especially in the decision of whether to take the job initially. But there are other factors that consistently score higher than money. Most of them have to do with the people's feelings about their places in the company and the company's feeling about them. Money draws people initially, but it doesn't keep them. Management must fulfill other needs to sustain satisfaction and to reduce turnover.

It is primarily a matter of giving individual attention to each and every employee. For this reason, broad scale decentralization with branch offices all across the country is frequently not ideal. The more you decentralize, the harder it is to maintain control and to maintain the kind of values and understanding and energy that promote individual attention.

One telemarketing CEO with four branch operations in the same city, in the name of motivating his people, held a monthly "open house" with different employees invited to attend each meeting as representatives of the employee work force. What the CEO failed to understand was that an open house in *his* office was more intimidating than it was motivational! The poor guy missed the point of individual attention. The attention is best given on the employee's turf or, at least, at a neutral location.

We need to understand thoroughly that people are our only real asset in telemarketing. They are certainly the single most important asset that can help us sustain effective growth over the long run.

A growing telemarketing organization needs a lot of people, and the number of talented and knowledgeable people out there today is definitely limited. The moment those people start to feel like numbers in a faceless organization, they loose the feelings of caring from and involvement with the company. People begin to lose their initial loyalty. Their natural incentive to grow with the organization dies.

There is a lot that can be done, and a lot that needs to be done. But much of it is basic. Things like following up on people. Call the ones who didn't show up yesterday. Not to beat them up, but to say *"We really missed you yesterday. We really need you, and it's not the same without you."* Those are the keys; *we missed you, we need you.*

One of the telemarketing industry's leading professionals was interviewed for a management position several years ago. He was asked "What is your philosophy of management?" His answer had been formulated during many years of managing salespeople and running his own companies.

He said *"If you want your people to perform for you and for your company, you must get them to think that you care about each one of them as a person. But if that caring is only pretended, they'll soon sense it and cut your legs out from under you. So you either honestly care about the people, who they are, what they want, what they need, and how you can help them achieve what's important to them, or you stay out of management. Really care about them as human beings and show that you care, or don't make the mistake of calling yourself a manager."*

The industry is growing quickly, and choices aren't always easy when you embark on managing growth. The answers to some problems come with trial and error. But you will experience change--and remember one of the *first* rules--people are inherently resistant to change! You have to make sure that they perceive that change as a natural evolutionary process, not one of chaos and upheaval.

The key is constant, accurate, and comprehensive communication of your objectives, your strategies for attacking those objectives and the rewards of achieving them. Without that there will be confusion, hesitation and unfocused energy.

The way to approach change with your people is extremely important. There are three primary choices:

* *Mandate.* Sometimes mandating change is the only choice, but it is best to save it for the major and urgent issues.

* *Internal marketing and involvement.* Selling people on new ideas and approaches is often the best way to go, even if it leads to debate. It certainly is better than mandate if mandate would create lasting resentment.

* *Test it in small areas.* This approach can work very well in many situations, with the added bonus of many good and workable suggestions from the people involved. . .before the new systems are fully implemented.

While caution and compromise on people issues sometimes seems the hard way to go, its long range effects on attitude, receptivity to change, and maintaining an atmosphere of discussion and innovation are extremely valuable.

Keeping your existing work force happy and productive is a challenge. But it's an even better trick to have large infusions of new labor and still to give the newest people that same close feeling of involvement that your veterans have. The key to that is the ability of the floor managers and supervisors to empathize with the people and familiarize them with the organization.

This is frequently a problem area because most phone room supervision is home-grown and promoted from within the phone rep ranks. Often the incentive for a good rep to take the promotion is "*to simply get off the phone.*" Telemarketing's work force is generally young, and the supervisors frequently lack enough life experience to handle the new level of authority. If abused, that supervisor's authority can turn into a destructive power trip. And only an excellent supervisory training program--complete with follow through and reinforcement after the course is completed--can effectively manage the development of the highly energetic, but sometimes immature, telemarketing supervisor.

Commitment to Excellence. Today's telemarketing environment needs more enlightened management and more constantly reinforced commitment to excellence.

"Commitment" and "excellence" should be more than mere buzzwords. Unless we make that commitment and base all of our actions upon it, we pose dramatic risks of creating mediocre communications and slipshod operations that are a threat to the industry. Today we *need* that commitment, but the even more sophisticated and demanding telemarketing environment of the future will *demand* that we do it. That means that management must pledge itself to providing every possible means of support and development that has proven productive and important in the more traditional and better-established areas of the business world.

Policy and procedure manuals which can be updated easily should be created for every department of your company. While this can be a major expenditure of time and money, it is one of the best investments you can make. The learning curve time of your people will be improved and the frequency of costly mistakes will be reduced when you have good sales, supervisory, and operations manuals in place. It's *not a substitute* for classroom or on-the-job training, but when the rubber hits the road, it's good to know there's a steering wheel guiding where your people go. If telemarketing is to be fully accepted as an equal member of the marketing community, it is a step that we must take.

We bit that bullet a few years back. We were growing even faster than we would have liked, and we recognized we could no longer put it off. We knew the key was the ability of our floor supervisors and management. Our supervisors had to be even better than they were in the handling of people issues. They had to have greater ability to understand, relate to, empathize with, teach, coach and motivate their people.

This situation is a critical area, and the problems that arise in it are frequently ducked with the explanation of "*Well, that's just telemarketing.*" That's just plain stupid!

What really is the problem is that as you're growing rapidly, and your key people are getting busier and busier. While lip service is given to the need to solve the problems, nobody has the time to do it.

We decided to hire a consultant to help us improve and standardize our management training and to create additional manuals. And we selected someone who specialized in people issues, whose credentials were excellent, who had a strong telemarketing background, and who could be trusted to handle it properly while we were tied up constantly with the growth process. Using a consultant was expensive, but the results were well worth the cost, because the consultant concentrated on solving the problem areas--which allowed the company's management personnel to continue growing the organization.

If you really care, doing the kinds of things that will bring the desired results and loyalty and retention will increasingly become second nature to you. Finding things to praise about people and their work will be easy. The feelings behind your words are felt. Innovation flourishes. Pride in work quality abounds. The commitment to excellence is mutually reinforced throughout the company.

Developing a happy, stable and productive telemarketing workforce can be done. If you take the steps required, you can have talented and effective supervisors and managers. You can have 90%-98% TSR attendance, with people who put out that extra effort whenever you need it. And they'll be happy to stay with you. Then you can afford to turn over whom you *want* to turn over, instead of wondering why a talented new group of people wound up with an 80% attrition rate in a matter of a few weeks.

Do loyalty and satisfaction happen automatically and without effort? Of course not. Not any more than they happen in a good marriage or in a close-knit family. They require constant sensitivity and communication and dedication to making it work. But the rewards in terms of productivity and satisfaction are enormous.

Service Bureaus. For service bureaus, the issues of productivity and satisfaction take us to the *clients*. Happy clients are still *the* bottom line. And to have happy clients, the industry needs to do a better job of both managing and educating those clients.

The proper management of the client starts with your company's marketing effort. All too often, our marketing efforts are little more than pure hyperbole. We *all* tend to do it. Our TSR's are the best. Our program development is the best. Our "everything" is the best. Our telemarketing ads and brochures say the same thing--*"We're the best."*

That's dangerous. You'd be wise not to hype your communications, because ultimately you will be held accountable for the promises you make. In other words, there is nothing worse than promising someone the moon if all you are capable of delivering is the mountain top; if you had only promised to carry them halfway up the mountain, you would have looked like a champion when you took them all the way to the peak.

Instead of making unreasonable promises, the industry would be much better off if the clients were told--in each and every case--exactly what is reasonable to expect.

Today we're in a marketing game where the victors are the ones who do the best job of convincing the client that their approach--either automated or manual--is the way to go. That's unfortunate because, frankly, the buying marketplace--the client marketplace--isn't yet fully prepared to make that decision.

The only answer is for the automated shops to admit that automation alone is not the final answer, *and* for the manual shops to acknowledge that there is more to doing the complete job than can be done manually. The fact is that some programs work best for the client with automation while others are still most effectively run manually. Ultimately, service bureaus may need to be partly manual and partly automated if they are to serve a wide variety of markets.

You can do very well--developmentally, strategically and productively--for one client and still not maintain the account if you are not able to overcome the client's confusion or preconceived ideas about the marketplace and about modern techniques of telemarketing. We need to get them to understand the importance of maintaining continuity of their internal management teams who do the analysis and interface with the vendor, whether the vendor is "in-house" or an outside service; to understand the importance of giving consistent and accurate back-end data; to accept our expertise in our field; to listen to our input about techniques and how to target lists and techniques, and to accept the validity of that input.

We need to do a more accurate and more comprehensive job of educating the client markets about our business and how we work. We have to let them know exactly *what* we need from them and *when* we need it. Explain *why* we do it that way and *what* it accomplishes for the client. Explain how we work differently than others. The marketing approach in telemarketing cries out for the educational, consultative approach. The planning for growth requires a solid and consultative marketing plan. When the client truly understands how you work, why you work that way, and what it does for them, they can truly work with you to help make their programs successful. They'll understand what is *going* to happen, what *is* happening, and what the *realistic expectations* should be.

      Growth. If we make sense to our clients and make their programs work, they'll respond and grow with us, whether we're in-house shops or service bureaus. But they won't respond in the way we want if we are satisfied just being big job shops and executing calls. We have to help improve their programs, make them work, and keep them healthy and growing. We have to analyze the programs and proactively recommend real and positive changes for improvement. If we do that...if we help our *clients* grow...our clients will help *us* grow.

      Since handling the problems and challenges that are either caused by or magnified by growth is the single factor which most characterizes today's telemarketing, it is important for a telemarketing unit to be clear about its objectives, priorities and approaches to managing growth. There are three basic approaches: Growth for Growth's Sake, Growth for Immediate Profitability and Survival, and Controlled Growth. There are many sound reasons for choosing and establishing the Controlled Growth philosophy.

      Growth for Growth's Sake assumes that bigger is better, and ultimately that biggest is best. But biggest isn't always best. If the growth comes without regard to the continuance of standards of excellence, or to the development of the people resources, or to the long range profit performance of the company--if the growth costs too much in terms of the essence of the company--then bigger isn't better and the growth can be an uncontrolled cancer. Growth for Growth's Sake just can't be justified--not at *any* point, or for *any* reason.

      Growth for Immediate Profitability and Survival may be acceptable in the short term if there is serious need for quick profits or quick volume. When it's needed as a quick fix to manage a shoestring budget in order to stay in business, it's hard to argue with it. If you have a lot of talent that needs to be promoted quickly, that kind of growth may be required. There's a saying that all telemarketers can relate to: *"Why is it that, when an opportunity is lost, it is usually found by our competitors?"*

      Yet, whatever the reasons, that type of growth brings the danger of compromising excellence. Continuing growth of that type almost assures mediocrity. When we realize that we have to grow in the wrong ways and for the wrong reasons, it's time to open our eyes to the need for the Controlled Management of Growth.

      Controlled Growth is growth that is planned for and anticipated, for which the company has the financial and people resources at any given time such that the growth that is being undertaken does not cause harm to the existing clients or projects, nor does it decrease margins so much as to make the business financially unhealthy. This requires planned, focused, budgeted efforts and execution. It requires knowing *when* to say no to a client or project (be that in-house or with a service bureau), when that business is not right for telemarketing or for your specific operation.

      Controlled Management of Growth requires a philosophy that precedes any desire for growth, which is defined by the quality of service which you wish to provide. If you define that quality as excellence, then the real question for controlled growth is *"How do we grow because big looks good and profitable for today, without regard to the effects on the foundations which made it possible?"*

Controlled growth starts with a plan and with a strong foundation. From the smallest building to the largest skyscraper, the true strength and longevity of that structure will primarily be determined by the plan for its structure and the foundation upon which it is built. If you put up a cheap "quick fix" structure on a poorly laid foundation, you wind up with a building with massive structural weaknesses. Sooner or later, the foundation starts to crack and the mortar starts to separate. What cost a pretty penny to put up in the first place stops looking pretty, starts to crumble and fall, and costs far more to repair than the additional amount that would have been required to build it right in the first place.

Starting out with the expectation of growth doesn't mean having to start big. You *can* effectively start small, if you start with the right foundation which allows for future growth. Then you can plan for gradual addition in modules, reinforcing the structure as you build it larger. You can then build the skyscraper one floor at a time. The addition of fixed personnel expense in a growing telemarketing firm is like the addition of each new floor. But the plans have to allow for those additional building blocks of the structure, or you only build a shaky tower that's like a house of cards. When the wind blows strongly in the wrong way, it begins to quiver and fall.

Controlled growth calls for the planning for future growth and the recognition of what it was that put you in the position to be able to grow. When you have *defined* your market and *defined* your approach, you can begin to plan for the modules of supervision, management, training, program development, fulfillment, and client services which must grow as the company grows, to remain strong.

Controlled growth sometimes means sacrificing short-term profits in the interest of long-term excellence. Perhaps you've heard *"Never get too far from the well"* or *"Always dance with the lady what brung you."* Those sayings carry a lot of truth.

As an example, let's say that you know that what made you successful to date was a monomaniacal commitment to excellence and hands-on management by knowledgeable and talented people who shared that commitment, and that one of the keys to your success is 70 hours of training for new TSR's. Then the ABC company says *"Here's four million calls,"* or your Executive V.P. of Marketing says *"We need to add on these 11 new sales programs immediately."* In either case, you know that in order to do it you can only have 10 hours of training for new TSR's, and you don't have the time to find the kind of fixed expense managers that you need. If what you try to do is throw the extra weight on the shoulders of your already maxed-out people, and hope they hold up, what you're *going* to do is take a big part of the project in, bill out a lot of money, make a lot of profit, *and* burn out a lot of well trained management people and a lot of TSR's who *didn't* have proper training.

If your actions conflict with the keys that have built your success, you've gotten too far from the well...and you're not going to be able to continue playing the game that way very successfully. You can't deviate too far from the game plan. You have to stick with it even when it may appear that it isn't going that well.

You may have to convince the Executive V.P. of Marketing that his immediate plans are too ambitious. You may have to turn down business that you would love to have and know would be good for your company under the right conditions. Given the courage of your convictions in the plan, you have to be able to stay with it. You also need to have the courage to change the game plan when you realize the plan was wrong. And in today's telemarketing, the opposite approach is too often used...properly managing growth is one of the many great challenges issued to the telemarketing of tomorrow.

TOMORROW

The issue of handling today's growth situation in telemarketing, leads us to the "tomorrow" part of "Telemarketing: Yesterday, Today, and Tomorrow." In the same way that individual telemarketing companies and telemarketing units have to face the issue, the industry needs to look to its future and its growth.

With certain qualifications, the future looks extremely bright. Telemarketing is in the process of moving into a new maturity which will determine its capacity to effect profound changes in the marketing strategies of every astute Marketing Director, President, and Chairman of corporate America. And an exciting and thriving future can be achieved. . .if we are sensitive and responsive to the critical issues which will determine the shape of that future.

The concept of "*the future is what we make it*" is certainly true in our industry. And it raises four important challenges for telemarketing's future. Each deals with the issue of quality.

Methods of Presentation. The first concerns the quality of the contact and the presentations that we offer to the prospects. The industry believes that the live operator call is the best way to approach telemarketing. Perhaps that's because the marketplace just isn't ready for the electronic approach, or because much of the marketing community isn't knowledgeable enough about technology to create an acceptable method. In either case, the marketplace has told us that today's state of the art electronic methods are not all acceptable, and some of the automated calling technology--including ADRMP--is being outlawed.

But if we fail to give our communicators the proper training, people may just get tired of poor quality, live presentations and collectively slam the phone in the face of telemarketing. If that happens, we will be just as vulnerable to having our *live presentations* outlawed, as well.

If that should happen, a tremendous source of employment and economic stimulation would be lost to us and to this nation. If we are to avoid crippling the industry, we must make sure that we have quality training for quality communicators who give quality presentations.

Marketing of Telemarketing. The second area of concern for quality is in the *marketing* portion of *telemarketing*. Over the past several decades of growth, we have developed much more sophistication in our telephone techniques and we have gone quite far in enhancing our ability to move beyond simple telephone sales. But truly to earn the right to use the term *telemarketing* we must go further.

If we can overcome the problems and keep the industry moving forward, we can anticipate that the size and complexity of telemarketing programs will continue to grow. The level of marketing expertise of our clients--whether internal or external--will certainly continue to increase. The number and the subtlety of suitable telemarketing applications can be expected to explode to remarkable new levels. The range of quality and complexity of products and services offered by phone can be expected to rise dramatically. As was shown in the research statistics, both the total dollar volume and the average size of a telemarketing order will continue to grow. And the sheer volume of calls will be staggering.

If the industry is not only to keep pace, but also to stay a step ahead of the complexity of challenges and opportunities that the future will bring, there is a very significant need for improvement in the quality and sophistication of the industry's marketing capabilities and techniques.

* *We must continue and accelerate our development of "telemarketing specific" direct marketing rules, guidelines, strategies, and methodologies.*

* *We need to look beyond our existing hardware and software capabilities to imagine the possibilities for new magnitudes of sophistication in list selection, target marketing, segmentation, demographics, psychographics, and customer needs identification and profiles.*

* *We must further expand database management to include individual TSR profiles, consisting of more than sales, hours and conversion ratios.*

* *We need to be able to know, realistically, what each TSR's back-end cancellation rate is. Today, in most cases, the only quantitative measure of TSR performance is front-end sales productivity numbers. The real measure of any TSR's value is not fully defined without the back-end numbers. This will require a distinct awareness of the need by telemarketing professionals, as well as by the clients they serve--and frankly, will be tough to do in a purely manual environment.*

We must improve our ability to coordinate with and use state-of-the-art marketing research, direct mail, print advertising, and the electronic media. And we must create the systems, software, and hardware required to use effectively the innovative new methodologies we have developed.

With the improvement in the quality and sophistication of those areas must come the development of more effective methods of results projection and program analysis. We need to increase our sales and research capability while improving our back-end results and order fulfillment techniques.

Management Workforce. Accomplishing these things will require dedication, persistence, innovation and increased education. That raises the third quality issue for our future: The quality of our management workforce.

With any business, part of the problem in developing your management team is answering the question "*Whom do we want?*" You either want the brightest mind you can find, perhaps just out of college with a little work experience, or you want someone with a proven track record who's pretty happy and not even looking for a change.

But there are some problems here. First, the supply of telemarketing personnel with a strong management track record is very limited. Next, the business and public image of telemarketing--while rapidly improving--often leads both new graduates and talented prospects, who are experienced in other business areas, to reject telemarketing as a serious career choice. And the self-images of people with a traditional business background make it hard for them to take the jobs that start at 2:00 in the afternoon and ends around 10:00 at night. That's especially true when it means only one--maybe two--days off a week, and that not necessarily on the weekend.

Further, no matter how talented a person is, he/she can never become a successful *telemarketing* supervisor or floor manager until first spending time as a TSR. Until someone has experienced the work and its demands--including the frustration, the rejection, and the patience required to do the job well--it's virtually

567

impossible for them to bring true empathy to the job. And without that empathy they just can't supervise properly. The superstar might be able to learn it in a week or a month, but it usually takes longer. Yet that is an expensive development time, and the talented and aggressive superstar may be unwilling to spend the time required to develop the proper base of experience.

Any company starts with an entrepreneur, a founder, a leader who knows the industry and gathers around him a group of specifically trained and educated people who can share his values and carry his insights and vision into execution. From medicine to high tech to agriculture, there's a farm system called the nation's educational network. IBM goes to campus and recruits the brightest young minds and talents who have been trained in electrical engineering or computer science. The graduate of Harvard Law School is interviewed by the firms in need of those talents. People are developed through the traditional educational process and are integrated into the company with a good existing base of knowledge of that particular type business.

However, unlike most traditional industries, there is no "farm system" or educational system for the education, training and development of those key management people for telemarketing. There is no formal conduit through which hands-on telemarketing knowledge and experience is passed. There *are* some night courses available in a few schools. And we are hearing about plans for the first telemarketing courses to be offered by universities. But there are no degree programs in telemarketing anywhere in the nation.

Seminars, trade show conferences, and courses offered by national and local industry associations and organizations such as the DMA and the ATA currently provide the best available formal education. But such sessions can rarely go beyond the scope of an effective, general introduction to subject matter that would take a full-course outline and many weeks to teach in real depth. The telemarketing *degrees* come from the school of hard knocks and on-the-job training.

That is a reality that does not bode well for the future of the industry. We have to rely too much upon on-the-job training and, as a result, the people who move into management all too often don't have the kind of background and education to properly prepare them to *run* the organization. Even if a CEO has the educational background and years in the business, the most difficult part of the industry's growth is that we have to home grow our own talent from within. Does that mean we train and promote our TSR's up to management? Yes, that can be done. It is what we have been doing.

If you're a service bureau or if you're like many in-house operations--a non-Fortune 1000 company where TSR's may be paid in the $17,000 to $35,000 range--you're probably paying an hourly wage. And the hourly wage you can offer will largely determine the kind of labor you can get. If you underestimate the importance of getting bright, articulate, communicative, quick learning people you might try to get by with $3.50 or $4.25 an hour wage--and it will look good on the financial statement *for a while*. But the second you decide to grow that way and decide to build your company that way, you've limited yourself internally with the quality of people you have available to promote.

It's a problem you might have when you first start, particularly if you begin with very little money and a small budget. You might be tempted to pay minimum wage for your TSR's. Well, that might work over the short term for consumer oriented, tightly scripted telemarketing. However, not only will the TSR's not be the people you need for business-to-business work, but when you try to promote from within, you may have to go through 1,000 people to find the 20 that you need.

In order to grow the business you need to have a better pool of people to draw your supervisors from, and you have to increase the base wage of your TSR's to attract them. As you up their wages--from minimum wage to $5 to $8 an hour plus bonuses and incentives--you can get all the good supervisory talent you need.

TELEMARKETING: YESTERDAY, TODAY, AND TOMORROW

As you continue to grow and promote from within, the quality of that original pool of talent becomes even *more* important as the supervisor is promoted to manager, department head, and director. What originally appeared to be a question of simply filling the phones takes on an entirely new meaning and dimension. And you have a new--but similar--set of challenges as you develop people for program development, fulfillment, training, and personnel.

But if we are to develop the kind of long-term quality people that the projections for our future indicate we will need, this situation has to change. We need to encourage the development of formalized telemarketing training programs. We need to provide more information to the public to improve the image of telemarketing as a viable career choice. We need to encourage the development of more night courses, more college offered classes, and a widespread national base of university offered degree programs.

Image and Acceptance. To accomplish those objectives, we will have to deal with the fourth "quality" challenge of the future: the overall image and acceptance of telemarketing.

We have to make sure that our internal quality control is assured. It is clear that what *you* could do by yourself as a 30-50 phone shop, you can't do alone as you grow into a much larger shop. But that means more than the quality assurance within the individual firms that we are responsible for. In the same way, as our industry undergoes the tremendous growth that is anticipated for the future, we cannot--*as individual firms*--maintain the quality assurance that we need as an industry.

Managing the growth of individual telemarketing firms was addressed earlier. Now it's time to re-address some of those ideas, while thinking in terms of the *industry's* growth.

The telemarketing industry can choose to grow for growth's sake, or we can choose to have controlled growth. If the industry's growth comes without regard to the continuance of standards of excellence, or to the development of people resources, without concern for the long-range profit performance of the industry, or if the growth costs too much in terms of the essence of the industry, then bigger isn't better and the growth can become an uncontrolled cancer.

We have to open our eyes to the need for the Controlled Management of Growth on an industry-wide basis. We need to assure that the industry's growth is planned for and anticipated, that the industry has the financial and people resources to assure that the growth does not cause harm to the clients or to the public, nor does it reduce margins to the point of destroying the industry's financial health. This means that--as an industry--we maintain planned, focused, budgeted efforts and execution. It requires that we develop the ability to say "no" to a situation that is bad for the public or for the industry.

Like the individual telemarketing companies, the telemarketing industry needs to determine a philosophy that precedes any desire for growth. The most important questions to be asked in determining that philosophy are "*What is the* quality *of service which we, as an industry, wish to provide?*" and "*How do we grow the telemarketing industry* while *maintaining and improving our standards of excellence?*"

Maturation is an essential part of healthy growth. We are in an industry that has a serious need to mature in its efforts to police itself. If *self* regulation is done properly, we can largely forestall regulation by *mandated* legislation. If we fail to mature in our response to this need, there's going to be unnecessary and overly restrictive legislation passed that will take the regulation of the business out of our hands.

Maybe not tomorrow, and maybe not next month, but somewhere down the line someone will get hit for improper telemarketing procedures, in a way that will stimulate overly restrictive legislative action on a much broader and much larger scale than we have seen to date. But if we can demonstrate that we are making a proactive commitment to meaningful action of self-regulation, we can reduce the negative impact of that kind of legislation.

Outbound phone shops make calls representing major names in corporate America. In effect they are selling a commodity. And as much as we don't want to admit it, they do cause a good deal of stress to buyers and prospective buyers. It can be reduced dramatically through ethical and knowledgeable telemarketing procedures, but that stress does occur. There's the interruption factor, the pressure to make a decision, and the back-end stress.

In the case of less than ethical telemarketers, they just cause outright harm to the prospects and buyers, as well as endanger the image and future of the industry. That's the case even if the cost of the product or service is only $49.95. Who says that $50 isn't just as important to that buyer as $5,000 is to someone who buys sugar options from a phone room operation? If we are not sensitive to that reality, it will come back to haunt us.

Those TSR's who sell options, commodities, bonds, and other types of products are required to pass a test and become licensed. The assumption behind those laws is that uniform standards of training, testing, licensing, and the potential for punishment of offenses will reduce the probability of the buying public being exposed to misrepresentation or fraudulent tactics. History has shown that the larger an industry gets, the greater the possibility for abuse *and* for reactive legislation.

We have to be very cautious in this area, but we have to get more actively involved. While it might be easier to wait to see what happens, we don't want to get caught up in a situation that winds up throwing a monkey wrench into the ability of the industry to operate.

This is an extremely serious subject, but maybe this little story can put it into perspective in a little lighter vein. You probably have heard of "the three great lies"...but you might not have heard the business version of the three great lies. The first is still *"The check is in the mail."* The second is *"Whatever your needs are, we can serve them."* The third great business lie is the one told when someone arrives at your company's door and says *"Hi! I'm from the GOVERNMENT and I'm here to HELP!"*

We need to make sure we don't face a legal process that requires 12 months of study for an individual to become a licensed TSR. That would be devastating. We're in an industry that is constantly under attack by certain segments of the press as being arm twisting, high pressure, misleading, etc. There *is* that element in telemarketing. And every true case brought to the public's attention affects the entire industry through guilt by association.

Perhaps a firm doing outbound telemarketing should be required to go through an approval process to become a licensed or certified telemarketer. To be clear, this is in regard to licensing the *firm*, not the individual rep. The company, in order to be licensed, would have to be willing to answer questions about where they operate, how long they have been in business, the kinds of solicitation they do, the controls on quality, the security of proprietary list data, etc. Those are basics.

Perhaps telemarketing companies also should be required to submit a minimum of three typical scripts they have created, letting them substitute *"the ABC company"* for the client's name. The scripts would be judged not for sales effectiveness or creativity, but for adherence to prescribed standards of ethics. In addition, the firm should present an outline or synopsis of their hiring and training process. This could be submitted in a general proposal form that gives away no proprietary procedures. The firm would also have to agree to "on location" spot reviews by the board which reviews the firms for the initial and renewal licensing or certification.

TELEMARKETING: YESTERDAY, TODAY, AND TOMORROW

The industry has made some headway in this direction. For example, the Direct Marketing Association has created TPS, the Telephone Preference Service, to help consumers request that they not receive solicitation calls. The consumer can request that their names be removed from calling lists, and TPS compiles those "*do not solicit*" into lists that companies may subscribe to and use to purge their own lists.

TPS, as valuable as it can be, is effective only for those companies who choose to use the service; there is no requirement that companies purge the names of those people who have requested that they not be called from their lists. TPS is a step in the right direction, but we need to do more. We need to *require* adherence to certain standards of regulation, just as the SEC does. (If you question whether this approach will work, just ask Ivan Boesky!)

If we're glad we're in the business, why should we ignore those consumers who have taken the time and made the effort to let us know that they really don't want to be called? And why should we be ashamed to say "*Let us know if you don't want to receive a phone call.*"?

There are many possible approaches. Maybe we're afraid that if we advertise, people who would never otherwise put their name on the list will do it. Maybe we're afraid that if we talk about it too much, we'll come under too much scrutiny by the public and by governmental bodies.

But we certainly seem to be afraid. Suggestions have been made that the industry's leading firms pool some financial resources to create an extensive campaign to educate the public about telemarketing, about what's positive about it, about how to recognize *good* telemarketing and how to recognize and deal with *bad* telemarketing. What has been the common response? "*For God's sake, what are you suggesting? We don't want to make the consumer more aware!*"

That response is the remnant of the old school of thought--but it's a leftover that doesn't really cut it today, and certainly won't tomorrow.

Under any circumstance, as provisions are made to allow more of the public to add their names to "*do not call*" lists and as some states pass more restrictive legislation, there will probably be some list shrinkage. That's going to happen with or without self regulation. There are other similar situations. Some of what is going to happen with the bells and whistles of automation will assist in cutting the less ethical and less skilled firms out of the marketplace. But the public doesn't hear the bells and whistles. Their perception of telemarketing is shaped by the approach and actions--good, bad, or indifferent--of the grass roots TSR when the phone conversation begins, whether that TSR works for an automated or a manual firm.

Some of these suggested actions might seem agreeable. But we should give serious consideration to establishing self-regulating bodies and procedures that can--at the very least--bring some measurable control and *enforceable* standards to the industry. While we might not *all* like the structures and standards that would result from our combined efforts, waiting for legislation to be enacted will result in rules and guidelines that *none* of us like--some of which are already being enacted in some states.

The most successfully regulated industries have been ones who structured the regulatory systems themselves. The old AT&T/Bell System did it by creating the most advanced research facilities in the world (Bell Labs), obsoleting their own products and services with new and better ones, and creating their own competition. Finally, they were the ones who suggested the outlines for government regulation of the industry, including regulation of how much they could charge and how high a profit margin they could make. Would it have happened anyway? Almost assuredly. Would those regulations have been as acceptable to the industry if they had simply fought all internal and external regulation? Not at all likely.

There are other good examples. The Chicago Board of Trade. The New York Stock Exchange. They

571

are self-regulated industries. They report to an even higher authority called the Securities and Exchange Commission, which they helped create.

It will *not work* if it is a traditional government or legal panel making the rules. It *can* work if the panel or board overseeing the certification is one composed of real experts in the industry. (Of course, then we can argue for hours about who the experts are!)

We don't want to inhibit the growth and the future of outbound telemarketing, but something has to be done if we are to protect the buying public and our own industry. Decisions will have to be made about what standards are to be followed, what panel guidelines should be, how to encourage participation, and how to enforce the standards. So long as there is no formal body in charge of the regulations and standards, the results of the efforts will be mediocre at best.

Anyone in the industry knows there is concern about what will happen, from a regulatory standpoint. We've seen the passage of asterisk bills and the outlawing of ADRMP's. We hear about attacks on monitoring and tape recording. We have seen the passage of special telemarketing taxes and the attempts to pass licensing regulations.

A lot of people discuss it and just keep going on with business as usual. Others have actually gotten out of telemarketing rather than be caught in what they perceive to be an approaching death of the industry through governmental regulations that may effectively *outlaw* outbound telemarketing. The DMA, the ATA and other industry organizations and associations have established legislative committees and hot lines to help track troublesome situations and to forestall pending legislation. Yet many of the companies in the industry aren't particularly concerned because they feel they barely would be affected, no matter what regulations might come down. Perhaps they are right. What if they are not?

It is essential that we begin *now* to study the examples and the methods of those industries which have managed the development of the successful regulation of their industries. Then we need to take action based on those successful precedents.

This is not nearly as critical for inbound telemarketers as it is for the outbound side of the business. Nor is it of as immediate a concern for the business-to-business telemarketer as it is for the business-to-consumer sector. Yet a failure to improve will affect both the innocent *and* the guilty. It won't matter to the public perception where the problem breaks; the inbound, the outbound, business-to-business and business-to-customer will all suffer through guilt by association, whether or not it is justified. All sides need to join together on this issue.

Telemarketing has come a long way, and with our concerted efforts and continued nurturing it can go much further. If growth has been managed in the more established traditional industries, it can be managed in telemarketing. If turnover can be managed in traditional industries, it can be managed in telemarketing. If self-regulation can be instituted in traditional industries, it can be instituted in telemarketing. These things can be done, *if* we are sensitive to the key issues. That's really the only difference: To what issues do we sensitize ourselves, and then what positive actions do we have the foresight and the courage to take?

If we dedicate ourselves to making the telemarketing industry as good as it can be--providing the best possible service to the public and to our clients--we will grow into an even stronger and more influential industry. We will fulfill the predictions being made about our future, because word-of-mouth support-- whether among the clients or among the public--is what this and any service industry is about.

Reflections of Yesterday/Today and the Challenge of the Future. Our yesterdays were

TELEMARKETING: YESTERDAY, TODAY, AND TOMORROW

a time of development and a time of establishing the early guidelines. They were days of rough and tumble seat-of-the-pants management of bare-bones telephone sales.

Today's telemarketing is in the process of evolving into a more refined and more mature business marketing medium. It has become a broadly accepted marketing method, having gained recognition as a valuable, cost efficient and highly productive tool. It is gaining increased sophistication and complexity as we combine the lessons of the telephone sales past with the experience and the established principles of other marketing and database management disciplines. And we are struggling with the problems inherent to any industry that grows faster than the educational and personnel bases that are required to support it. Yet--for the most part--we have met the challenges and laid the foundation for a strong, healthy, and vibrant new maturity.

Our tomorrows will be shaped by the strategies we develop and the actions we take to achieve full acceptance as a unique and required tool in the methodologies of any competent marketing organization. We will find ourselves facing (and dealing with) the problems inherent in any high-impact, high-profile, business practice that personally touches the lives of the majority of people in both their business and personal lives.

Telemarketing is a growth industry, and the future holds many challenges. The bigger the industry and the bigger the work force, the *more* we need leadership, and the bigger and stronger the leadership needs to be. Telemarketing is, and will remain, a unique field with its own set of rules and requirements.

The yesterdays are gone. The tomorrows will be what we make them. The industry will be carried into full recognition and power by a new breed of specially educated and trained telemarketing managers who will have the expertise to balance traditional business techniques and values with the special requirements of the fast-paced, high-production, high-quality, innovative growth environment that *is* today's telemarketing.

The stage is set for us--the actively participating members of this and the next generation of professional telemarketers. Our role today is to expand upon the foundation built by the early pioneers of our yesterdays, by stepping out boldly and making the aggressive plans today, that will lead us to that bigger and better tomorrow.

That *is* the challenge.

EPILOGUE

Dr. Gary S. Goodman
President, Goodman Communications Company
Editor/Publisher, *Telephone Effectiveness Newsletter*
Glendale, California

As is appropriate in an "epilogue," especially considering the unique nature of this Encyclopedia, the time has come to take a more philosophical view of our transition into the future of telemarketing. After all, this is *not* the end, only the beginning.

I'd like to close this hands-on and strategic volume with a little philosophy on telemarketing's core asset: its people.[1]

ZEN AND THE ART OF TELEPHONE SELLING

In 1974, a best-selling book with a most unusual title appeared in stores across the United States: *Zen and the Art of Motorcycle Maintenance*. People naturally wondered what Eastern philosophy had to do with fixing bikes. Robert M. Pirsig took more than 400 pages to make a very convincing argument that the two activities are linked in a special way.

Pirsig demonstrated through the device of a personal travelog that the same frame of mind needed to mend a motorcycle was required for reaching inner peace. He wasn't seeking converts to a religion, but he was interested in finding out just what combination of elements resulted in producing things of quality.

Quality is a very elusive thing, as Pirsig was to discover. Just when you think you understand it, it seems to slip away from you. Pirsig believed that quality wasn't something one could put into a product like two tablespoons of sugar. It was a frame of mind with which the process of creation was pursued. If you have a quality frame of mind as you undertake a project, your chances of creating a quality outcome are high, assuming you possess the technical knowledge needed to do what you want to do. If you simply try to finish the task without caring about it, or you "technique it," as some have labeled overly expedient work, you will tend to come out with a substandard product.

Telephone selling is an activity that requires a quality frame of mind to produce success. A manager with whom I spoke recently seems to embody the non-qualitative frame of mind that produces failure. He said, "*I really pity those people who have to sell by phone. They must have the worst job in this company.*" This fellow was responsible for developing new telephone sales representatives! Imagine the success he was having with that attitude. There is no question that his dim view of the job was communicated to recruits who probably picked up his attitude, and who subsequently failed.

The manager suffered from a problem that Pirsig identified in his book. The fellow was seeing only the surface value of the job, and the deeper structure of selling by phone never entered his consciousness. He

574

never saw the possibilities for quality in that assignment. There is nothing inherently bad about the job. It was the frame of mind of the manager that took the quality away from it.

Perhaps the real problem that some people have with telephone selling is that they simply don't understand success. Success can be boring. That's right, boring. Success works somewhat like the assembly line. Once you fashion the system for efficiently producing positive results, the process simply requires maintenance, and seldom are major repairs needed. Very often repetition is at the basis of success. And repetition is likely to be boring. One of the major hurdles people have to surpass is handling boredom in the telephone selling situation. Because tele-reps should be required to follow scripts as they sell, this process can be rather grueling.

Boredom can be dangerous. Research on the impact of boredom on individuals is fascinating. One study that was conducted in the 1960s arranged for subjects to be confined to sensorially non-stimulating rooms, consisting only of a bed, bathroom facilities and white walls and floor. Subjects were paid for their efforts based on the length of time spent in the room. The longer the stay, the higher the pay. At first, subjects were very pleased that they were making money for literally doing nothing. After a few hours, however, most seemed to become visibly agitated. They couldn't fall asleep, and several reported that their thinking processes were severely impaired. Others claimed that they were beset by uncontrollable hallucinations.

The experimenters concluded that our well-being is closely related to the kind of sensory stimulation to which we are exposed. Most people aren't equipped to entertain themselves and keep themselves cognitively aroused without outside intervention. As in the study, where putting up with boredom was an index of success, most subjects opted for the failure that brought with it relief in the form of normal stimulation.

Telephone salespeople do something similar. They stray from a proven, successful presentation because they crave novelty. Rather than build their personal frustration tolerance, which is something veteran tele-reps must do, the strays cause excitement through performative failure. If we could ask their unconscious selves why they do this, they would say, ''*Because at least failure is interesting*.''

What does all of this have to do with Zen, anyway? Zen masters can stare at a brick wall for hours on end, and see quality in what they are doing. They actually see inside of themselves as they gaze outward. They use the wall and the staring technique as a method through which they can perfect their self-discipline. Seeing how long they can stare and enjoy it is interesting to these practitioners. .

Telephone selling really isn't boring. It holds forth the prospect of tremendous stimulation and personal gratification. Think about it. During the typical hour of selling, the average tele-rep may meet as many as 20 new people to whom he or she must adjust. This art of code switching or modifying oneself to adapt to another is very involved and really a lot of fun. Moreover, we never know what opportunities for profit and novelty await us from one call to the next.

A number of manufacturers decided to do their own experiment. Noting that the traditional worker was rebelling against the assembly-line method of production as being dehumanizing, managers began to recruit from the ranks of the handicapped and retarded. They found that their new workers had lower absenteeism, higher job satisfaction and produced at a better level than their predecessors. Some attribute this success to the idea that the new workers knew no better than to enjoy what others saw as inherently distasteful work. Another view is that the new workers saw the potential for quality in what they were doing, and brought this winning attitude with them as they performed. No one taught them to be bored with what they were doing.

Management has an obligation to show tele-reps how to enjoy their jobs by seeing quality in them. This often requires training tele-reps so they aren't simply told to follow a script, but they also are shown *how and why the script is constructed* for the purpose of producing certain effects. Managers need to keep their level of enthusiasm high and make sure to communicate the benefits of being involved in a telephone selling effort.

Discipline is the key factor in producing a smoothly operating telephone sales cycle. Master boredom and understand the essential nature of success. You'll then be geared to succeeding in telemarketing.

Even if you aren't a Zen master.

THEORY T: A REALISTIC MANAGEMENT STYLE FOR TELEMARKETING

How can we get telemarketers to do the best job possible? Should we offer them huge salaries, juicy commissions and appetizing bonuses? What about cruises on luxury liners, or weekends off at resort hotels? I know of one company that insists on offering sales representatives trips to other cities to attend seminars because the top producer has a terrible home life, and the only prize worth hustling for, in his estimation, is a vacation away from his family!

Some companies believe that placing someone's name on a trophy as the representative of the month, quarter or year, is the finest sort of recognition available. No matter what perks are involved, managers and bosses are basing their reward system on a philosophy that may or may not consciously be understood or articulated. This can lead to problems when the best representatives leave the job for greener pastures, and you may have no idea as to what turned them on and turned them off. Lots of dollars and energy are wasted in training people who aren't going to fit into the lifestyle that telemarketing often requires. And it becomes a nightmare trying to appeal to each individual on your sales staff to customize an incentive plan that will be meaningful and effective.

There are companies that make it for all kinds of reasons. Some utilize a very strict method of supervision and behavioral control, whereas others are advocates of an easy going style that allows sales representatives to modulate their pace of work and determine the overall office atmosphere in which they sell. No matter what management style you use, it pays off to be aware of what you're doing, for the purpose of consistency, predictability and efficiency.

Theories X, Y, and Z. Douglas MacGregor wrote a landmark article in 1957 entitled, "The Human Side of Enterprise," in which he detailed the differences in two management philosophies he designated as "X" and "Y." *Theory X* managers, according to MacGregor, operate from several assumptions about human behavior that the author felt were suspect. For instance, *Theory X* managers are said to believe that people are by nature indolent, or lazy, and the only way to motivate them to work is through the carrot and stick. It is the possibility of being rewarded and/or punished that will make an otherwise listless employee get off the dime and get something done, according to this school of thought.

If employees can respond only to the carrot and stick, it stands to reason that supervisors must be present at all times to administer these rewards. Without rapid reinforcements, productivity will drop off completely, leaving the enterprise to decay almost immediately. *Theory X* managers put the locus of control outside of the employee. Left to his own resources, it is suggested, the worker would not be able to summon the self-discipline and self-sacrifice that are required in the workplace.

Theory Y assumptions are quite different. The employee is assumed to be inner-directed by certain higher-order needs and drives. While satisfying physical, social, and safety needs is important, it is not paramount for the *Y* worker as it is thought to be for the *X* worker. The *Y* employee wants self-respect and self-actualization, according to MacGregor. Consequently, this individual is seeking meaning and satisfaction from the job, and these kinds of individualistic motivations cannot be fulfilled in an *X* type of atmosphere. Their satisfaction comes from within, and it is the task of the company to facilitate the worker's quest for these values.

Theory Z is the latest management philosophy to surface, and it owes its articulation to the success of Japanese companies that have achieved significant productivity through its implementation. *Theory Z* emphasizes the compact between worker and company. This is a bond that is much stronger than most American patterns. The worker in a large Japanese company can look forward to stable employment, even in recessions, in trade for his commitment to be maximally productive and to shape his conduct to company aims. What have come to be termed *quality circles*, or tightly knit workgroups, are utilized extensively to define and resolve problems. *Theory Z* managers stress complete involvement of the worker

What Style Is Right for Telemarketing? Many business people examine management philosophies such as those just mentioned and then resolve to adopt one school of thought or other because they like it, or because they feel it is trendy or because they think that they would like to be managed that way. As you might guess, these are inadequate rationales. We need to ask ourselves what style works best, and proceed to implement it, irrespective of how comfortable it appears at first impression.

Theories X, Y, and *Z* all possess certain strengths as well as drawbacks. *X* is a highly authoritarian model that requires close supervision and active management. There are many *X*-oriented businesses that are quite successful despite what some business school faculties might predict. Many family companies operate on a paternalistic basis, where one person's voice predominates, and others are left to implement his or her policies without deviation. Some individuals respond favorably to an *X* style of leadership, and they are happy to comply with the orders of those who seem to know what they're doing. Others find little or no room for self-expression in an *X* atmosphere, and they rebel and ultimately leave.

The *Y* type of company can be summed up as permissive. *Y* managers don't care how you go about your job, as long as you get the job done. In theory, this sounds logical and practical. Why should someone care how I do something, as long as I reach my production targets by the end of the week or month? Permissiveness, in actual operation, has its shortcomings as a philosophy. B.F. Skinner, the most eloquent proponent of behaviorism in the twentieth century, framed the problem as follows:

> *Permissiveness is not. . .a policy; it is the abandonment of policy; and its apparent advantages are illusory. To refuse to control is to leave control not to the person himself, but to other parts of the social and nonsocial environments.*[2]

Y managers may be deluding themselves by thinking that good results will come by letting employees find their own way. If Skinner is right, it is more likely that workers will adopt methods that seem to be working for others, or they'll experiment on their own. In telemarketing situations, I've found that both approaches are inefficient. Imitating another salesperson rarely is going to capture the essence of that

577

salesperson's strength. Groping in the dark on your own assumes you are not only a born telemarketing genius, but that you'll be able to replicate your successful sales presentation after you have happened upon it. This is highly unlikely.

A typical *Y* philosophy, with its do-your-own-thing methodology, is the weakest format for telemarketing operations. If there is a successful organization that employs the *Y* method, it is very likely that management is beholden to the people who are presently employed, for they alone might know what it is they are saying that is responsible for success. Consequently, management is unlikely to be able to fashion a winning formula that it can give to new trainees to make them successful. As a result, managers are tied to the people they have on board now, and these people can set their own terms for commission plans and the like. In the short term, a *Y* style may seem to work, but in the long run, it fizzles.

A *Z* style seems better suited to manufacturing than to telephone selling. The former is, by nature, a team enterprise, where selling on the phone is inherently individualistic. Moreover, the womb-to-tomb employment compact between worker and manager is completely unrealistic in a telemarketing situation, where the rigors of the job are such that turnover is relatively significant.

Toward Theory T. If we are able to keep an employee one year in a telemarketing unit, we're ahead of the game. It is the unusual telemarketing operation that enjoys a longer term relationship than this.

Given high employee turnover, how many of us can afford to wait for a period of weeks or months for a new person to become productive? Only the largest corporations can afford the financial drain that comes from assigning the wrong people to various jobs, and then setting forth to make them successful in them. The rest of us have to be more prudent. We have to make quick decisions, while leaving as little to chance as possible. Unlike Hamlet, we can't argue with ourselves over the question, "*To Manage or Not to Manage.*" Manage, we must, and the sooner the better. *Theory T* operates from this as well as other assumptions, which we'll examine next.

People are lazy as well as energetic. I avoid making generalizations about the inherent nature of human beings, because I've seen that people are capable of acting in both predictable as well as bizarre ways, depending on a lot of factors. Unlike MacGregor, whose ideas we examined, it doesn't matter to me how we classify people when it comes to their energy while they are not on the phones. I don't care if they sleep in their cars during lunch breaks, as long as others don't see them and they return in time for the afternoon shift.

People will do what we ask out of compliance, identification, or internalization, and it is not terribly important why they are behaving as we wish, as long as they do so. Compliance, identification, and internalization tend to be correlated with *Theories X, Y,* and *Z,* respectively. *X* employees perform their duties out of compliance with the direct orders of managers, who are always present to assure that their orders are executed. Compliance, as a motivated response mechanism, is costly because it requires continuous energy on the part of worker as well as supervisor, who must be present to praise and correct the work product.

Identification requires that the employee feel that he is working because there is a reward in it for him, whether it is the paycheck at the end of the week, or whatever the paycheck will purchase. The worker, who is responding out of a sense of identification, is easier to manage because he tends to keep his own nose to the grindstone in a quasi-voluntary way. When he lapses into nonproductiveness, he need only be reminded that he is losing commissions or their equivalent in buying power.

The internalized worker applies himself to the job because he wants to and because he finds higher-order meaning in the work he does. In a sense, the internalized employee comes to find himself in his work, and he only works for the paycheck as a secondary motivational factor. Teachers, artists and others who are classically referred to as the underpaid are said to derive psychic income from their jobs that compensates them for their economic shortfall.

The internalized worker is, by far, the easiest to manage, for he really manages himself. The teacher doesn't come to class 15 minutes early because she fears her principal will punish her if she's late. She arrives early because it corresponds with her sense of professionalism. In fact, this person would resent a chastising principal because it would impeach her sense of total commitment. By contrast, the worker who operates out of mere compliance would dislike the reprimand because she got caught.

Compliers, identifiers and internalizers have differing views of the extent to which their relationships with their employer are adversarial. The complier is most likely to foster the most animosity and resentment toward management, followed by the identifier. The internalizer is least likely to resent his or her employer.

This discussion might imply that it is better to hire and work with internalizers as they might seem to be model employees. This is true to a point. Internalizers can be easy to get along with, as long as their perception of the job and yours coincide. If you try to introduce rapid changes, and especially those that require close compliance, internalizers can see the change as a threat to their expectations related to the job, and they can rebel. In any mature workplace, there tend to be a few internalizers present, who are often viewed by newer employees as credible sources. If these people rebel, there must be something fundamentally wrong, it would seem to others. The reaction can then become generalized throughout the work force. *Then you have a real problem!*

It's unrealistic to believe that all or most telemarketers can or will become internalized while they work for you. The inherent nature of the task militates against this outcome. Selling by phone isn't as glamorous or intrinsically rewarding as teaching or fine art, and people can't be expected to get the thrill out of the business that you or I might get. Generally, the most we can hope for is identification, but the least we can insist on is compliance.

And, insist, we must. I have found that people who comply with my instructions are likely to become successful very quickly. When they do, they like the job and they tend to like themselves. They also make plans that include their job as the centerpiece of their productive activity. This leads to identification, and occasionally, internalization. If we don't insist that they comply initially, they'll probably fail, and it won't be long before they are fired or they quit. If they won't comply when they first come to work, you won't get them to comply later on.

In the final analysis, it doesn't matter to me why they are producing, whether it is out of a sense of compliance, identification or internalization, as long as I get the results I need. By being able to classify their motivational state, I am able to give them the kind of supervision they require.

Telemarketing managers should appreciate that their function will require a different management style than that which might be used in other corporate departments.

Whenever a telemarketing function is installed into an existing organization, several predictable things occur. The entrenched sales bureaucracy becomes threatened. Field salespeople, as well as their managers, worry that their jobs may be replaced by lower-paid, more highly efficient phone clones. Customer service grows concerned as workers there clamor to have a shot at joining the new and glittering department, with its new furniture and generous commission structure. The credit department might grow uptight because it is suddenly deluged with applications to process, and its historic inefficiency is for the first time being

579

noticed and challenged by this upstart function. In short, the new department puts a strain on everyone, and it isn't long before tour buses of employees, vendors and customers are being shuttled through the new phone room, which serves to lower telephone performance and make the telemarketing function resemble the existing departments.

The outside influences exert pressure on the telemarketing operation and its management to become homogenized as is the rest of the organization. Instead of being truly productive, a higher corporate value prevails: *looking productive*. This means that neatness and sterility are placed above efficiency. Have you ever known a printer who could work all day and not get his hands dirty?

Telemarketing managers need to have the backbone to stand up to the personnel department, which may try to populate the staff with the same sort of do-nothings that are found in every nook and cranny of the organizational behemoth. Don't let this happen.

Some of the Old with Some of the New. *Theory T* is perhaps most akin to *Theory X* in the final analysis. Without embracing some of the limiting assumptions that *X* managers make about human nature, we can see that a closely supervised operation is desirable. People require explicit direction, and we have a responsibility to ourselves, our companies, and our employees to show people a tried-and-true path to productivity.

At the same time, we should do what we can to create a climate that is hospitable to those who already may be productive, and who are most likely to be motivated out of a sense of identification or internalization. If the two goals are incompatible, however, in any particular situation, we should opt for control, predictability, and stability. And these outcomes are most likely to be generated by a *Theory T* management philosophy.

THE IMPORTANCE OF BEING DIFFERENT

Upon completing a recent nationwide telemarketing project for a firm in a glamorous industry, I was struck by a problem that may be more widespread than I initially considered. I noticed that people in positions of influence, such as supervision and marketing management, were unconsciously cloning themselves by hiring folks with the same traits. Looking around, I saw nothing but look-alikes.

How could I tell this hiring practice was going on? For the most part, those who were being hired were what one savvy manager called, "pretty people," or folks who made a pleasant appearance but didn't have the mental power to perform effectively. This sort of inbreeding, known for its deleterious effects, was contributing to the slow death of the organization in other units, and it promised a speedier demise in the telemarketing division.

Bertrand Russell, the great philosopher, once pointed out that people elect to have children for two reasons: the desire to survive death, and the narcissistic wish to see "little thems" running about. In some sense, managers who spawn mirror images of themselves also show a form of self-love that can stifle innovation, inhibit change, and lower the chances of collective survival. The rigors of changing market conditions require differentiation and adaptation. Ironically, by hiring folks just like ourselves, we may be actualizing a corporate death wish.

EPILOGUE

The telephone is an inherently democratic medium. Much of its strength as a marketing tool resides in the fact that it is blind. We can be young or old, black, brown, white or yellow, tall or small, and still do an effective job, if we have been well trained. There is some sociological evidence to support the contention that the non-mainstreamers have the best chance of doing well in telephone work.

People who are sociologically different from ourselves are referred to by some social scientists as being *marginal*. Marginality brings with it some obvious detriments in the form of alienation and discrimination, but it also confers benefits. Sociologists point out that marginal people often develop very refined communication skills because they must deal effectively with mainstreamers who possess most of society's rewards. Only by adapting to the changing communication requirements of various situations can the marginals survive and prosper.

As a requirement of their craft, actors must be professionally marginal in order to develop insights into characters and to learn to respond to different types of people naturally. It may be this window into the world that contributes to the great success that actors often encounter in telephone work.

Several organizations have benefited from the telephone skills of sightless persons. These employers have found that such staffers bring to telephone work a degree of empathy and sensitivity that is rarely found in visually endowed people.

In denying us a visual channel of communication in most situations, the telephone liberates us from some of the biases inherent in face-to-face communication. It is highly unlikely that someone will ask us our age on the phone, but a youthful or mature appearance could stand in the way of closing a sale in person.

Unless we hire people who are different from ourselves, and from our narrow conceptions of the right kind of employee, we will be denying our organizations short-term success, and perhaps, long-term survival.

----

[1]Parts of this Epilogue were adapted from a book by Gary S. Goodman, *Gary Goodman's Breakthroughs in Telemarketing*, New York: Prentice Hall Press, 1987.
[2]Skinner, B.F., *Beyond Freedom and Dignity,* New York: Bantam, 1971.

APPENDIX A

The American Telemarketing Association

Ron Weber
President, American Telemarketing Association
President, Ron Weber and Associates, Inc.
Orange, Connecticut

The American Telemarketing Association (ATA) is a non-profit trade organization representing telemarketers (companies using telemarketing in the broadest sense) who have joined together to promote their business interests and to solve mutual problems. The Association is the only organization which deals exclusively with telemarketing interests.

The Association offers educational programs to increase the professionalism of the industry, its members and their staffs, recognizing that it has a responsibility to be the creative and innovative force in developing and presenting its programs.

Legislative issues are of key concern to the ATA. It has developed a network of members to deal with legislative issues at the Federal, state and local levels. The Association recognizes its need to concentrate a great deal of its resources on legislation and regulatory issues in the telemarketing industry.

Twice a year, the national Association conducts meetings which gives those in the telemarketing industry an opportunity to meet and network on common issues, visit exhibits of services and products available to the industry, and participate in educational programs to increase the professionalism of the industry members. In addition to the national Association meetings, each chapter conducts regional meetings during the year.

ATA BACKGROUND

The ATA was founded in August 1983 by 20 corporate members, who each contributed $500 to provide a total $10,000 capitalization.

Growing rapidly from the original core group, the Association planned and held three successful National ATA meetings within 18 months:

1. *Philadelphia, PA, February 1984.*

One-day conference, speakers only.

2. *Kansas City, KS, June 1984.*

One and one-half day conference, speakers, and AT&T center tour.

3. *Houston, TX, November 1984.*

Two and one-half day conference, speakers and exhibitors.

By the third conference, increased management responsibilities and increased financial stability allowed the ATA to consider a professional management firm with the resources to manage its rapid growth potential.

The ATA engaged its first professional association management firm on February 1, 1985.

When the Association's management firm began operations, the ATA had industry recognition as the first and only national association dedicated to telemarketing. Consequently, the Association's goals were to build a solid, comprehensive organizational structure to service the rapidly expanding telemarketing industry.

At the end of 1987, there were close to 900 members served by the national organization and through nine regional/state chapters and one international chapter.

The regions and states that have chapters include: New England, Middle Atlantic, Potomac, Southeastern, Southern Region, Midwestern, Minnesota, Northern California, and Southern California. There is a newly formed chapter in the United Kingdom.

The ATA headquarters is located at:

The American Telemarketing Association
5000 Van Nuys Blvd.
Suite 400
Sherman Oaks, California (91403)
(1-800-441-3335)

MISSION STATEMENT

The ATA's mission is to serve those industries and professions that utilize telemarketing in their businesses.

Specific elements of the ATA mission are as follows:

* *Monitor and report on proposed state and Federal regulations that affect the
telemarketing industry.*

* *Educate the public and legislators at Federal, state, and local levels about
professional telemarketing techniques and benefits, to ensure that implemented regulations are fair to both the public and the telemarketing industry.*

* *Provide educational seminars that encourage the growth and increase the
professionalism of the telemarketing industry.*

583

* *Provide telemarketers with a forum for communicative networking in all aspects of the profession.*

* *Generate and distribute functional statistics and case studies to help telemarketers improve their current operations.*

* *Support telemarketers' interests at both regional and national levels.*

GOALS

1. *To serve the collective needs of the telemarketing industry by monitoring, reporting and providing feedback opportunities on Federal, state and local legislation and regulations affecting the telemarketing industry.*

2. *To provide targeted educational programs for the following groups:*

   a. *Industries using telemarketing.*

   b. *Special market segments.*

   c. *ATA members and their staffs.*

   Such programs will be prepared by the members of the Association to promote their professionalism, management, and technical skills.

3. *To educate the public, legislators, regulators, and the business and professional communities about the nature and proper utilization of telemarketing.*

4. *To provide a forum for communications and networking.*

5. *To supply the industry with valid market research, statistics and case studies.*

Goal #1. To serve the collective needs of the telemarketing industry by monitoring, reporting, and providing feedback opportunities on Federal, state, and local legislation and regulations affecting the telemarketing industry.

Strategies:

1. *Assemble information on pending and existing legislation and regulations at Federal and state levels.*

2. *Interpret trends in legislative/regulatory fields.*

3. *Disseminate information to members.*

584

4. *Collect feedback to change legislation and regulations, and take appropriate action.*

5. *Meet with responsible legislators and regulators at Federal and state levels.*

6. *Develop and publicize ATA's business ethics guidelines.*

7. *Promote positive public image for telemarketing.*

8. *Provide special legal advice for special legislative problems on an* ad hoc *basis.*

9. *Provide membership with tools to obtain legislative information independently.*

10. *Establish telemarketing industry legislative policy guidelines.*

11. *Exhibit at key legislative conferences and seminars, (e.g., National Association of Attorneys General, National Conference of State Legislators).*

12. *Meet with Federal Communications Commission officials.*

13. *Develop state-by-state alert-notice network.*

14. *Propose industry-wide self-regulation policies.*

Goal #2. To provide targeted educational programs for the following groups:

A. *Industries using telemarketing.*

B. *Special market segments.*

C. *ATA members and their staffs, including middle management.*

Such programs will be prepared by the members of the Association to promote their professionalism, management, and technical skills.

Strategies:

1. *Identify special market segments.*

   a. *Financial, banking, brokerage.*

   b. *Retail.*

   c. *Manufacturers.*

   d. *Wholesale distributors.*

    e.   *Direct sales.*

    f.   *Fund-raising organizations.*

    g.   *Insurance.*

    h.   *Customer service.*

2. *Determine matrix of programs.*

3. *Investigate ATA membership to verify market segments.*

4. *Establish mechanism to determine needs of special interest groups by survey, committee, or task force.*

5. *Determine programs, including, but not limited to, the following:*

    a.   *Statistics.*

    b.   *Operating ratios.*

    c.   *Training.*

    d.   *Communications.*

    e.   *"Hot" line.*

    f.   *Case histories.*

    g.   *Speakers bureau.*

6. *Publish education report.*

7. *Develop certification program.*

8. *Provide continuing education through seminars and workshops.*

9. *Provide chapter-education programs.*

10. *Provide speakers bureau.*

11. *Develop reference library.*

12. *Publish home-study courses.*

13. *Develop and publish case histories.*

14. *Provide forum for industry members.*

15. *Review existing industry education programs and publish strengths and weaknesses.*

Goal #3. To educate the public, legislators, regulators and the business and professional communities about the nature and proper utilization of telemarketing.
Strategies:

1. *Prepare editorials and press releases for trade press, business, and professional press and newspapers.*

2. *Establish on-line "bulletin board."*

3. *Place institutional advertising.*

4. *Exhibit at selected industries' shows.*

5. *Coordinate with consumer organizations.*

6. *Establish liaison with other interest groups.*

7. *Retain professional public relations organization to represent ATA.*

8. *Select industry image.*

Goal #4. To provide a forum for communications and networking among industry members.
Strategies:

1. *Publish monthly newsletter.*

2. *Publish semi-annual member services referral directory.*

3. *Conduct annual meeting.*

4. *Conduct regional conferences in cooperation with ATA chapters.*

5. *Offer annual national exposition of vendors' products and services.*

Goal #5. To supply the telemarketing industry with valid, empirical market research, statistics, and case studies.
Strategies:

1. *Establish committees to:*

   a. *Provide market research on statistics, demographics, trends and technological achievements, lists of telemarketing and segmentation users.*

b.   *Case studies.*

c.   *Public opinion research.*

ATA TELEMARKETING STANDARDS AND ETHICS GUIDELINES

Guideline Purpose. Guideline principles apply to both in-house telemarketing service vendors, whether calls are directed at businesses or consumers. The ATA believes these guidelines should define this industry's high professional standards and preserve the industry's future as a viable business technique.

The ATA cannot, and does not, dictate telemarketing practice. It is our intent, with this document, to recommend professional telemarketing standards and ethical behavior.

Document Uses. Education of businesses, consumers and legislative groups on the telemarketing industry and definition of voluntary standards for ethical telemarketing practices so that guidelines may be established by which the telemarketing industry can measure its performance.

Telemarketing Definition. Telemarketing is planned, professional telephone use to advertise, market or provide service functions. Telemarketing may be the only method to advertise, market or provide a service or may be used simultaneously with other techniques. Telemarketing programs can be outbound ("seller" initiates calls), or inbound ("buyer" initiates calls). Professional telemarketing programs have clear goals and are closely supervised.

The telemarketing industry is dedicated to providing a valuable service through telemarketing that affords the public (both consumer and business) economical, convenient access to products and services.

Telemarketing Applications. Businesses use telemarketing to perform a broad spectrum of advertising, marketing, and service functions:

*   *Sales support (in conjunction with field sales).*

*   *Market research.*

*   *Consumer surveys.*

*   *Lead generation.*

*   *Lead qualification.*

*   *Information hot lines.*

*   *Reservations service.*

*   *Technical support.*

APPENDIX A: THE AMERICAN TELEMARKETING ASSOCIATION

* *Customer service.*

* *Direct mail/advertising follow-up.*

* *Customer satisfaction surveys.*

* *Account management.*

* *Order taking.*

* *Catalog sales.*

* *Fund raising.*

* *Subscription sales.*

* *Renewals.*

* *Product announcements.*

* *Special promotions.*

Telemarketing Business Benefits. Telemarketing provides organizations (both profit and non-profit) a cost-effective method to communicate quickly with a large segment of their targeted prospect population. Since telemarketing communication is interactive, both "buyer" and "seller" can obtain important data, register opinions, offer information, and finalize agreements.

Telemarketing supplements other advertising and marketing channels, and allows businesses to maximize their total marketing investment through more timely and effective results.

Telemarketing Consumer Benefits. In many U.S. households, all adult members are employed. Consequently, telemarketing's convenience has become an important merchandising technique. Telemarketing is a personalized, interactive method for consumers to learn about products, services, or opportunities. When the consumer has limited time, or is immobile, telemarketing delivers products and services and makes buying opportunities possible with local and distant vendors.

Many consumers would be greatly inconvenienced without telephone business techniques such as:

* *Travel reservations.*

* *Catalog purchases.*

* *Subscription renewals.*

* *Charity donations.*

* *Banking services.*

* *Insurance purchases.*

* *Food and medicine purchases.*

* *Personal services.*

With a broader market available to vendors, more choices available to consumers, and sales costs frequently reduced through telemarketing, consumers may benefit from lower, long-term product and service prices.

Telemarketing Economy Benefits. The telemarketing industry's rapid growth has benefitted the general U.S. economy. *U.S. News and World Report*, May 8, 1983, predicted over 8,000,000 new telemarketing job opportunities by the year 2000. People who learn new telemarketing skills are generally more marketable.

Individual businesses have greater growth potential when they use telemarketing to obtain:

* *Better marketing information.*

* *Broader market bases.*

* *Lower business costs .*

AMERICAN TELEMARKETING ASSOCIATION TELEMARKETING GUIDE-LINES

The ATA endorses these guidelines for professional telemarketing practice:

1. *Telemarketing call recipients can expect that there is a reason for the call and the call purpose will be accomplished efficiently, courteously, and professionally.*

2. *Both company name and the communicator who makes or receives calls should be clearly identified when every call begins.*

3. *The communicator should approach each call courteously and never use abusive language or rude manner.*

4. *The communicator will accommodate the business person's or consumer's time constraints and, if necessary, schedule a future recall.*

5. *All telemarketing offers to the business or consumer public should be legal, legitimate, and have recognized value. All offers should be fulfilled according to the offer terms.*

6. *Repeated calls, with the same offer, should not be made to the same prospect/ customer.*

7. *Except for public safety, by previous agreement, or calls to current customers, the business or consumer public can expect a live communicator to introduce the call. (The public's time has as much value as ours--the professionals in this industry.)*

8. *All telemarketing equipment should be carefully monitored to ensure proper operation. Equipment use should be supervised to ensure professional application to telemarketing programs.*

9. *Telemarketing organizations should follow all Federal and state telemarketing regulations.*

AMERICAN TELEMARKETING ASSOCIATION TELEMARKETING OPERATIONAL GUIDELINES

The ATA endorses these guidelines as operational telemarketing standards:

Hours/Days of Operation
Outbound Calls:

*   *Business calls should occur during normal business hours.*

*   *Consumer calls should occur between 9:00 a.m. and 9:00 p.m., local time. Exceptions require prior consumer agreement.*

*   *Consumer calls should not occur on major national holidays: Christmas, New Year's Day, Thanksgiving. If calls occur on other national or state holidays or recognized religious days, sensitivity should be shown for consumer inconvenience.*

Inbound Calls:

*   *Hours and days of operation should be clearly advertised when inbound calls (toll free or consumer paid) are invited through advertising, catalogs, direct mail, media presentations, or other methods to avoid caller inconvenience.*

Telephone Service Levels
Outbound Calls:

*   *Sufficient telephone service should be provided to avoid communicator contention for available lines. This allows communicators opportunity to*

591

meet their performance goals and maximize productivity.

* *With automatic dialing equipment, sufficient communicators should be scheduled to ensure that every telemarketing call recipient will speak to a live person immediately. Exceptions are public emergency, or when the call recipient has been previously notified about pre-recorded messages and has agreed to accept such calls.*

Inbound Calls:

* *The "seller" must provide sufficient incoming lines to accommodate antici-pated call volumes. This affords the "buyer" the advertised opportunity and protects the telephone network from blockages, which could affect regional or national telephone service limits.*

Target Audience. These guidelines recommend that all calls initiated by a telemarketing group be directed at a targeted prospect or customer audience. We do not condone random or sequential number calls with no concern for the offer applicability to the call recipient.

The ATA recognizes that market research applications must use random sampling techniques to ensure study validity. The telemarketing group should, however, show sensitivity to the call recipient's willingness or resistance to participate in the research survey.

Personnel. Telemarketing managers should follow these standards, as a minimum, when they select and train all telemarketing personnel. These standards apply to personnel on full or part-time, short or long-term assignments.

1. *The communicator should know the targeted audience's language.*

2. *The communicator should speak clearly and be easily understood.*

3. *The communicator should understand the call subject matter and be able to respond to most probable questions.*

Training. Communicators should receive, as a minimum, training in the following areas:

1. *Product, service, or offer.*

2. *Message presentation.*

3. *Performance measurements.*

4. *Record-keeping procedures.*

5. *Appropriate business etiquette and behavior.*

Management. Professional telemarketing should always be performed with a telemarketing manager's on-site direction and control. This stipulation protects communicators, as well as the prospect or customer.

The telemarketing manager should train, guide, motivate, and control communicators to ensure:

1. *That the communicators follow their planned presentation.*

2. *A connection with the organization that offers the product, service, or opportunity.*

The telemarketing manager provides quality control to ensure that the offer is made truthfully, professionally and that the prospect or customer call is processed efficiently.

Quality Control. Managers in a telemarketing center should regularly monitor communicators' performance by listening to business calls being made or received while they are in progress. Monitoring of communicators' business calls provides a means for employers to observe and evaluate employee performance and give objective feedback. Monitoring also helps employees by identifying performance deficiencies so additional training can be received to give them added skills and improve performance.

This guideline also provides a means to protect consumers/customers and the employer against possible unethical practices by individual communicators. Monitoring protects the employer's right to supervise and regulate the quality of work being performed in his/her behalf or in behalf of his/her clients.

Presentations. In all telemarketing situations, both the company which makes or receives the call, and the communicator should be clearly identified when the call begins. Telemarketing call recipients can expect a reason for the call, and that the purpose will be accomplished efficiently, courteously, and professionally.

Environment. Telemarketing activities should be conducted on a business or institutional premises, and controlled by a responsible telemarketing manager.

Communicators should have sufficient work area and privacy to fulfill their task requirements. Work areas should have space for reference documents and product, service or opportunity information.

The telemarketing work environment should be professional, without distractions which could affect call efficiency.

The telemarketing organization should have a pleasant work place, conducive to meeting performance objectives. It should contribute to the sense of pride telemarketers have about their work.

FUTURE FORCES

Telemarketing is playing a larger role in the growth of broad-based industries and professions. ATA is an organization of those industries which are concerned with the effective utilization of telemarketing. Since telemarketing is a technique used by many industries, ATA also serves specialized market segments.

Because telemarketing is growing at a rapid rate, many entering the field are not properly trained or experienced. ATA will continue to diversify its educational programs for members at various experience levels.

Legislative thrust is key to the future of the telemarketing industry and to the ATA. With the potential increase in restrictive legislation in areas such as: asterisk bills, taxes, automatic dialing and recorded message players, unsolicited calls to consumers and businesses, monitoring of business calls, restrictive use of credit cards over the phone, the hours of operation, technology and restraint of competition, ATA must continue to take the leadership role to prevent unwarranted and dangerous regulation of the industry.

Employment and career issues as well as the availability of telemarketing service representatives will be key issues in the next five years. ATA will continue to develop professional and career path opportunities for TSR's. Additionally, supervisory and management level personnel must be developed in far greater numbers.

Technological breakthroughs in telemarketing already exist, but the *implementation* of these technological advancements will increase. ATA must address technology issues as they apply to the industry.

ATA also must enhance its marketing role in educating industries, professions, and services in the value of effective use of telemarketing within their own groups.

APPENDIX B

The Direct Marketing Association/Telephone Marketing Council

Jonah Gitlitz
President and Chief Executive Officer
Direct Marketing Association
New York, NY

AN OVERVIEW OF THE DIRECT MARKETING ASSOCIATION

In 1987, the Direct Marketing Association celebrated 70 years of service to the leaders of the direct marketing field, both here and abroad. Clearly, the growth and development of direct marketing is reflected in the growth and diversity of DMA--the primary association in the field.

From its early beginnings in 1917 as the Direct Mail Advertising Association to 1973, when our name was changed to the Direct Mail/Marketing Association and then, in 1983, when we became DMA, the Association has responded, as the name changes indicate, to the growing and changing needs of its membership. Today, we number more than 2,600 domestic companies and 6,000 members.

As the complexities of the field have multiplied, so have the responses of the Association. Both direct marketing and the Association are now in the mainstream of American business activity.

Today, just as direct marketing includes many media, the Association has adapted a multi-faceted approach in the service of its membership. We now have 14 special groups, and respond to the specific problems of a diversified membership. Business-to-Business, Card Pack, Catalog, Credit Card, Financial Services, Non-Profit, Research, and Telephone Marketing are only a few of those Councils.

Through these and other groups such as the Industry Leader Groups, we are able to provide unparalleled networking and educational opportunities. Working together, peer groups develop programs that answer needs and solve problems unique to each group.

The Association is particularly strong in the area of government affairs. DMA maintains a full-time professional lobbying staff in Washington that is supplemented by legal and economic counsel, both in Washington and at the state level.

We are now heavily involved in litigating the Postal Rate Case that is pending before the Postal Rate Commission. DMA's legal and economic counsels have prepared intensive testimony calling for a reduction in proposed rates.

In 1987, the Association, in cooperation with Doubleday, was responsible for administering a national non-delivery test on properly addressed third-class mail. The study revealed that non-delivery rates

595

were unimproved over those recorded in a 1983 test. DMA representatives met with the Postmaster General, Preston R. Tisch, to attempt a resolution of this most serious problem for direct marketers.

Lobbying goes on at both the state and Federal levels over many other issues. This year, DMA led a coalition of non-profit organizations in mounting a successful campaign to prevent the elimination of special postal rates for non-profit mailers.

At both the Federal and state levels, we have been deeply involved in opposing the imposition of sales/use taxes which would require out-of-state direct marketers to collect and remit sales taxes to the individual states. A recent example of DMA activity on the state level is our appearance as *amicus curiae* in the case of D.H. Holmes Company, Ltd., versus the Louisiana Department of Revenue and Taxation.

DMA has long been active on telemarketing issues, and 1987 was no exception. In Rhode Island, the Association helped pass an amendment to a new law that exempted most of DMA's telemarketing members from burdensome registration requirements. In Indiana, similar efforts saved mail and telephone marketers from having to send customers a written contract for purchases over $25. In a later section of this appendix, I will further detail DMA activity in the telemarketing area.

We work very hard to keep our membership apprised of the wide variety of legislation that would affect them. This past year, for example, Government Affairs, in cooperation with the Conference Department presented two seminars designed to clarify details of the use tax issue. *Washington Report*, a monthly publication, covers details of legislative matters pertinent to direct marketers and is supplemented, as the need dictates, by *Washington Alerts*.

Our Conference Department develops and executes nearly a dozen conferences throughout the year. Those popular meetings (almost 8,000 attended this year's Annual Conference) provide specific segment information as well as broad industry overviews. All of these resources are designed to meet members' educational, informational, as well as networking needs.

For the past 57 years, DMA has rewarded excellence in the direct marketing field through its international ECHO Awards competition. The highly coveted award this year attracted a record-breaking 1,429 entries.

Through the Information Central Facility, we serve our members' informational needs. In the past year that department responded to over 14,000 inquiries. A database system provides nearly instantaneous segment information on 1,200 topics. The reference collection, which is also available to members without charge, includes 500 reference books, 2,500 ECHO portfolios and 250 video cassettes. That department produces the direct marketing industry's source book, the *DMA "Fact Book"* with its statistical supplement which is revised annually, as well as the *Direct Marketing Manual*, a practical resource covering every industry segment, that is supplied to every member, when their company joins the Association.

The Consumer Acceptance Task Force is a major initiative that is bearing fruit already for direct marketers. The first steps have been taken toward meeting its four-year (1987-1990) goal of expanding the universe of people who shop at home, by mail or telephone.

The initiative has two goals. It seeks to improve the industry's customer relations process as well as enlighten the consumer about the benefits of shopping direct.

To meet the first of those goals, the Customer Relations Committee of the Task Force has produced and circulated to our membership "Recommended Practices for Customer Satisfaction." That Committee is now preparing suggested performance benchmarks for the various business segments. These detailed guidelines are intended to raise the level of performance in the customer service/fulfillment areas.

APPENDIX B: DIRECT MARKETING ASSOCIATION/TELEPHONE MARKETING COUNCIL

The second goal, to increase consumer use of shopping at home, is being met through, first, a new booklet entitled "Shopping at Home: A Consumer Information Guide." The Guide informs the consumer of the most useful techniques for shopping by telephone or mail.

Secondly, a "Shop-at-Home Center" has been established whose director and staff work intensively with consumer media (as well as our own member companies) to develop wide-ranging articles and programs about the virtues of the shop-at-home process.

The Ethics Department is charged with administering our very important self-regulatory programs, Mail Preference Service and Telephone Preference Service, by which consumers can arrange to have their names removed from mail and phone lists of national marketers.

Recently developed, too, in consultation with key representatives of consumer agencies and several non-profit organizations, is the Non-Profit Mail Preference Service which performs a similar function for that segment.

In a project involving the Food and Drug Administration and the Council of Better Business Bureaus, DMA this year sent health fraud information to mailer segments of our membership. The mailing encouraged members to use strict acceptance standards for health, diet, and fitness advertising.

The Dialogue Series, begun in 1985 as a means of bringing together DMA members and consumer agency representatives for candid discussions, continued in 1987 to be an important program. Held in major cities around the country, the twice-yearly meetings have proved a good indicator of how concerns of consumers and perceptions of direct marketing vary by geographic region.

This year, Dialogue IV in Los Angeles and Dialogue V in Dallas gave the DMA a new sense of the need for consumer education materials in Spanish. Heightened respect for DMA's self-regulatory functions, fostered by the Dialogues and other consumer programs, resulted in an invitation to participate in the National Association of Attorneys General Conference and in a cooperative effort with the Postal Inspection Service.

In a move to increase the visibility of direct marketers with high ethical standards, DMA provided an information kit and Membership Directory to 190 local members of the Councils of Better Business Bureaus. Our work in the ethics area is ongoing.

DMA, through its active Public Relations/Communications Department, has become the authoritative resource for the direct marketing trade press, general advertising media and business publications. In 1987, that department responded to more than 1,300 media inquiries and attracted positive media attention to the convenience of shopping at home and to the industry's commitment to ethical business practices.

Projects conducted by the Research Department aided the DMA Task Force on Consumer Acceptance as well as individual member segments. The Department this year conducted a series of focus groups with light buyers to study consumer attitudes about shopping at home.

Noting a trend of increasing demand for comparative salary figures, the department has completed three compensation and job description surveys for the list business, direct response advertising agencies and the telemarketing business. Underway is a survey for the catalog industry, which focuses on consumer buying habits.

Ever-increasing demand for education led to record enrollments in the Education Department's 15 seminars. Indeed, "Managing the Telephone Marketing and Sales Operation" was one of the best-attended seminars this past year.

To make these learning opportunities broadly available to the direct marketing community, the courses were offered, last year, in nine different cities across the country.

DMA also conducted a total of 96 in-house educational programs at such companies as IBM, American Transtech, Omaha Steaks, L'Eggs Brands, WNET/13 and AT&T.

Separately chartered, but very much a part of DMA, both in spirit and fact, is the Direct Marketing Educational Foundation. For 22 years, the foundation has emphasized programs for students and professors as the prime strategy for expanding and improving the teaching of direct marketing at the college and university level.

And the numbers demonstrate that the strategy has been successful. DMEF records show that more than 100 colleges now include at least one full course in direct marketing, and several have multiple courses. This represents quite a remarkable achievement: in 1965 there were no direct marketing courses on any college campus in America.

The Association continues to grow and change, as does the direct marketing field. We will continue to seek the means and methods that will help to keep our membership among the most forward-looking in an ever-changing society.

Membership inquiries are welcome, and should be directed to the Membership Services Department at the New York City office *(6 East 43rd Street, New York, New York 10017; 212/689-4977)*.

THE TELEPHONE MARKETING COUNCIL OF DMA

The importance of the DMA Councils, 14 of them, within the Association framework cannot be underestimated. They are the means by which the needs of each segment is served, and they evolved through our understanding of the needs of our business and its explosive growth. The Councils reflect the diverse and evolutionary nature of direct marketing and DMA's commitment to providing individualized services.

All of the Councils function with the support of professional DMA staff who are permanently assigned to each group and each elects an operating committee, develops projects and programs and many provide a quarterly newsletter to keep members abreast of current activities, events and opportunities for interaction. All of the Councils provide the framework for meeting specific informational and networking needs.

The Telephone Marketing Council of the Direct Marketing Association was formed in 1973 and has made significant contributions to the industry. Its programs have been in the hands of a dedicated leadership since its founding by such pioneers as Murray Roman.

The Council has been instrumental in the creation of two milestones. First, "Ethical Guidelines for Telemarketers" and, secondly, the highly important legislative weapon, Telephone Preference Service. "Ethical Guidelines" serve to inform DMA members of specific issues of conduct which are of paramount importance to a maturing industry. TPS not only aids consumers who do not wish to receive telephone sales calls, but stands as persuasive proof to legislators that the industry is not only interested in, but capable of, self-policing.

Another very significant contribution was made by the Telephone Marketing Council to the development of the consumer booklet, "Guidelines for Telephone Shopping," that was prepared in association with the United States Office of Consumer Affairs.

The Councils have a primary commitment as educational forums, and the telephone group is no exception. In 1982, the Council presented the first "Telephone Marketing: Issues and Answers" program

598

in Los Angeles. In subsequent years, the program was repeated in New York City and in Atlanta, and gave rise to the first Telephone Marketing Day in 1984. The now-yearly event is the product of very sophisticated advance planning and includes an award honoring those individuals who have established telephone marketing as a significant part of the direct marketing process.

From the original award, presented to pioneers in the industry, has grown the annual Telephone Marketing Excellence Award that is offered to an individual or company that has made a significant contribution to the industry over the course of the year.

Provided to the Council membership, as well, is an ongoing monthly program of highly targeted educational topics, and members frequently volunteer their services as teachers at DMA seminars.

STATE LEGISLATION AND TELEMARKETING

Each year states propose legislation which would restrict or even ban certain telephone solicitation calls, and each year DMA vigorously opposes these measures. 1987 produced more than 105 bills in 40 states.

Telephone solicitation bills can be roughly divided into five areas:

Asterisk Bills. An asterisk or "do not call list" bill would require the telephone company or some public agency to keep lists of all consumers who do not wish to receive telephone solicitation calls. Telemarketers would have to obtain the list from each telephone company or agency in the state and delete "no call" names from their calling lists. This would place a burden on everyone involved--the telephone company to compile the list, the consumer to pay for the service, the state to enforce the law, and the telemarketer to comply. Such measures are introduced each year, but only one (in Florida) has passed to date.

Hours. Restrictions have been proposed in some states which would severely limit calling hours for telemarketers. DMA has actively and successfully opposed such measures.

Registration of Telephone Solicitors. We see a growing number of states proposing bills to require telemarketers to register with the state before doing business. These bills respond to growing consumer complaints about "scams" and closely resemble a California law enacted in 1985. DMA worked closely with the sponsor of that bill and with the attorney general's office, and was able to effect important exemptions.

DMA carefully monitors all registration bills and cooperates with legislators, staffers, and regulatory officials to exempt businesses otherwise registered in the state, or to clarify definitions.

This past year, we have been involved in five states where bills similar to the California legislation have been introduced. The thrust of our efforts is always to support requirements that aid the states in prosecuting unlawful activities, while preserving the rights of lawful businesses.

Monitoring. The ability of employers to monitor or listen in on their employees' solicitation calls is very important to telemarketers. The process becomes a valuable training tool to help ensure accurate, high-quality contacts between employees and customers. When done properly, it helps the employee to improve his skills and provides a measure of service quality control which benefits the customer as well.

These are the points that we consistently make with legislators across the country and with which we have been effective. The battle, however, is ongoing.

ADRMP'S. States have taken several different approaches to dealing with consumer complaints about "computer calls" or auto-dialed recorded message players (ADRMP's). These efforts range from outright prohibition to requirements that recorded messages disconnect when the called party hangs up.

It might be useful to review the guidelines established by the Telephone Marketing Council with regard to telemarketing and ADRMP's. These guidelines are used by DMA in determining our position on various ADRMP proposals:

* *The equipment must immediately release the telephone line when the called party hangs up.*

* *Permission should be obtained from an individual by a "live" operator before the recorded message is played.*

* *Telemarketers should avoid calling telephone subscribers who have unlisted or unpublished telephone numbers unless a prior relationship exists.*

* *Random or sequential dialing techniques should not be used for solicitation.*

THE FEDERAL REGULATORY AND LEGISLATIVE ARENAS

With the divestiture of AT&T came a new agenda of concerns for DMA at the federal level: in Congress, in the courts and at several of the regulatory agencies.

The anti-trust consent decree, resulting in the break-up of the AT&T system, opened doors for the regional and local telephone companies to enter new unregulated lines of business including telemarketing, direct mail marketing and associated support services, including list development, fulfillment, supervision and maintenance.

As a safeguard, in the interest of DMA members, DMA has participated in several Federal District Court proceedings and filed formal comments with both Congress and the Department of Justice. In each of these arenas, DMA has emphasized its position that it does not oppose the entry of individual Bell companies into direct marketing but must have assurances that conditions of fair competition are maintained and that any direct marketing activities will not be subsidized by revenues derived by the holding companies from their telecommunications service activities.

DMA is also an active participant in several FCC rate proceedings, including measures to offset the negative impact of the new interstate directory assistance charge and to assure the accurate and fair assessment of rates for WATS, 800-WATS Megacom and the new 800 Ready, as well as other telephone services used by direct marketers.

In congress, DMA is currently working to oppose legislation that would require an audible intermittent "beep" tone to accompany all monitored telephone calls.

600

CONCLUSION

What is abundantly clear to us at DMA is that like-minded business people have entirely too much at stake *not* to be aggressively self-governing. This the message we deliver, along with the substantive proof, to legislators across the country.

APPENDIX C

Telemarketing Books/Magazines In Print

Richard L. Bencin
Donald J. Jonovic, Ph.D.

It seemed logical to include a bibliography in the *Encyclopedia of Telemarketing,* since, to our knowledge, no comprehensive listing of telemarketing "books in print" exists for the industry.

We discovered very early in our search that book references were universally incomplete. Even the best, in fact, listed *less than half* of the books available. It's simply not possible to go to even a major metropolitan library and conveniently find all of the telemarketing books in print.

Some reference sources have yet to accept the classification of "telemarketing." Some books are listed under "telephone selling," a few are buried within various sundry categories such as "marketing" and many simply cannot be found. As a certain sign of the industry's relative youth, some publishers of telemarketing books have never gotten around to listing their volumes in Bowker's "Books in Print" or even the Library of Congress cataloging system.

Therefore, in order to go beyond the immediate,, and clearly inadequate sources, we found ourselves becoming detectives. Compiling this bibliography/book review required interviews with owners of private book collections, reviews of bibliographies of known books, sorting through a variety of independent book catalogs and writing to hundreds of book publishers throughout the U.S., Canada, and Great Britain.

It took us six months, several hundred telephone calls and many letters of request for review copies to finally secure this listing. We believe it to be complete--in fact, as far as we know, it's the first comprehensive listing of telemarketing books in print. Inevitably, however, even the most "complete" list is found to be incomplete. If we have missed any books on this field, it has not been through carelessness or lack of effort, and we request that any author, publisher, or reader who is aware of an omission please bring it to our attention.

A TREASURE CHEST

The books listed here, at varying levels of completeness, competence and quality, represent a valuable resource for the telemarketer. They probably represent more than a thousand collective man/woman-years, covering the entire gamut of telemarketing startups, case studies, examples, vignettes, anecdotes and real-life stories. If an idea has been tried, or a mistake made, it's likely to appear in one of these volumes.

Some of the books reviewed here have enjoyed extensive marketing and competent promotion and, as a result, are probably known to most serious students of telemarketing. However, many have suffered virtual isolation, with limited and in one case we know of, *terminated* distribution (in one case, we received the *last* known copy of the book).

We hope that our listings will help resuscitate some of the excellent volumes now nearing extinction.

Ultimately, the reader will have to be the judge of the value of these volumes. Still, this collection does contain entire volumes on some relatively esoteric telemarketing subjects-- retail telemarketing, fund raising, building circulation, computers, managing telemarketing growth, telemarketing "breakthroughs," customer service, telephone techniques, financial telephone sales and wholesale/distribution channel telemarketing.

Consider this not-so-random sampling of chapter titles:

* *Zen and the Art of Telephone Selling.*

* *Electronic Shopping.*

* *International Telemarketing Trends.*

* *The Eleven Commandments.*

* *Telefocus Marketing.*

* *The Bottom Line.*

* *From Rolls Royces to Pink Elephants (Sold over the Phone!).*

* *The Challenge of the Future.*

* *Checklist for Setting Up an Inside Selling/Telemarketing Function.*

* *Telemarketing by Computer Can Double Productivity.*

* *Bank Marketing--A New Frontier.*

* *Techniques for Stores with Multiple Locations.*

* *ABC's of Complaint Handling.*

* *The Mathematics of Telemarketing.*

* *Consumer Attitude Survey.*

* *19 Ways to Get All of the In-Person Interviews You'll Ever Need.*

* *Newsletter Marketing by Phone.*

* *Theory T: A Realistic Management Style for Telemarketing.*

603

* *The Importance of Being Different.*

* *Phonegotiating: Reach Win/Win Agreements By Phone.*

* *Comparing Prices of Service Bureaus.*

* *When To Automate.*

* *The 27-Point Hiring System.*

* *Telemarketing Scripts You Can Adopt.*

* *How to Handle Any Objection Ever Made.*

* *Pick the Cherries Not the Pits.*

* *Tracking Your Program for Success.*

* *The Sixty Telemarketing Canons.*

* *Fighting Back: The Consumer's Guide to the Telephone.*

* *Inquiries: Closing the Advertising Loop Electronically.*

A CHRONICLE OF TELEMARKETING'S GROWTH

A final note. A study of copyright dates on these books provides a remarkable "core sample" of telemarketing's history--and its growth.

From the 1960s, only *one* book survives in print--the "granddaddy" of them all: *How To Increase Sales and Put Yourself Across by Telephone*, by Mona Ling. Copyright date, 1963. This book was recently (1987) re-published by Prentice Hall. For a telemarketing book to remain in print for *25 years*, it must have something going for it.

The 1970s added only *three* telemarketing books still in print today. Most notable of these is Murray Roman's classic *Telephone Marketing: How To Build Your Business by Telephone*. Roman's book was a first-of-its-kind volume in that it positioned telemarketing as an organized, proactive, and productive marketing channel, right alongside direct mail, catalog, etc.

In the 1980s, however, we witness a relative explosion of new titles. In this decade *(as of December 1988)*, 66 books have been published that are still in print. An impressive 94% of *all* telemarketing books in print have been generated within the last eight years!

Interestingly, very few of the telemarketing authors are repeat performers. Most seem to "do their thing," and then go on to other pursuits. The industry's most prolific author seems to be Dr. Gary S. Goodman who has *six* recent book credits. His *Breakthroughs in Telemarketing* is his most notable--good reading, competent writing. The other multiple book authors in telemarketing are Eugene Kordahl, Murray Roman, Warren Blanding (customer service telemarketing), Mary D. Pekas and Richard L. Bencin.

HOW TO USE THIS BIBLIOGRAPHY

We've organized the books in print by general subject (listed below). Each book review includes publisher and copyright date information, a listing of chapter titles, and a brief description.

Use the Subject Listing to gain broad access to book titles, and the Index of this Encyclopedia for more detailed subject reference.

Subject Listing:

Telemarketing Books in Print

Breakthroughs.

Building Circulation.

Campaigns/Applications that Work.

Computers.

Customer Service.

Do's and Don't's.

800 Numbers.

Encyclopedia.

Fund Raising.

Hiring.

Incoming Call Management.

Insurance.

Insurance, Investments and Real Estate.

Lists, Databases and Direct Mail.

Managing Growth.

ENCYCLOPEDIA OF TELEMARKETING

Objection Handling.

Reference Texts.

Retail.

Scripts.

Startups and Managing a Center.

Startups and Managing a Center: Business-to-Business.

Startups and Managing a Center: Small Businesses.

Strategies.

Telephone Allocation.

Telephone Sales for Outside Sales Reps.

Telephone Sales Skills.

Telephone Sales Skills: Corporate Environment.

Telephone Techniques.

Wholesalers/Distributors.

Magazines, Newspapers and Newsletters

Magazines/Newspapers: Direct Marketing.

Magazines/Newspapers: Fund Raising.

Magazines/Newspapers: Technologies & Techniques (Inbound/Outbound Phone Calls).

Magazines/Newspapers: Telemarketing.

Newsletters: Customer Sales Rep Telephone Skills & Techniques.

Newsletters: Customer Service.

Newsletters: Direct Marketing.

Newsletters: Fund Raising.

Newsletters: Incoming Call Management.

Newsletters: Telephone Sales Rep Skills & Techniques.

Newsletters: Telemarketing.

Telemarketing Books in Print

BREAKTHROUGHS

Gary Goodman's Breakthroughs in Telemarketing, Dr. Gary S. Goodman. Englewood Cliffs, NJ: Prentice Hall, Division of Simon & Schuster, Inc., 1987.

The Random House College Dictionary defines *breakthrough* as "a significant development...that removes a barrier to success." This book should remove barriers in one's pursuit of effectiveness in telemarketing and management. There are 30 chapters dedicated to solving 30 obstacles. Each chapter is preceded by a summary encapsulating some of the major ideas, and each chapter moves quickly from point to point.

Some telemarketers might tell you that telemarketing and management are for everyone. After all, to be effective, you only have to "smile and dial." As competition increases, and as people become more resistant to sales calls by telephone, we're finding that it requires much greater sophistication and commitment in order to be successful in this rapidly changing field.

This book covers in depth such difficult problems as employee recruitment and turnover, and new ideas are offered for handling them. A new management philosophy, "Theory T," is geared specifically to telemarketing.

Salespeople will find some chapters motivating and others instructive.

Chapter titles:

* *The Need for Breakthroughs in Telemarketing and Management.*

* *How to Defrost the Cold-Call.*

* *How to Get Through Screening.*

* *The John Wayne Effect.*

* *Change Beliefs and You'll Change Your Paycheck.*

* *Selling Can Be Beautiful.*

607

ENCYCLOPEDIA OF TELEMARKETING

* *High-Pressure Selling.*

* *Zen and the Art of Telephone Selling.*

* *Multistage Versus One-Shot Telemarketing.*

* *What Ever Happened to Telephone Selling?*

* *Winning Through Negativity.*

* *Vital Differences in Face-to-Face and Telephone Selling.*

* *Improving Your Listening Skills.*

* *A Close That Almost Always Works.*

* *Is Your Voice a Turn-on or Turn-off?*

* *Pitfalls To Avoid in Telemarketing.*

* *How To Boost Profits Through Upselling.*

* *Theory T: A Realistic Management Style for Telemarketing.*

* *To Script or Not To Script.*

* *How To Pay Telemarketers.*

* *Eleven Key Ideas in Telemarketing Management.*

* *How To Screen Telemarketing Applicants by Phone and Reduce Employee Turnover.*

* *You Can Get Good Help if You Know Where To Look.*

* *How To Make Your Answering Machine a Money Machine.*

* *Humanizing the Telemarketing Process.*

* *A New View of Telemarketing Management.*

* *Critical Stages in Telemarketing Training.*

* *The Importance of Being Different.*

* *Ten Ways To Increase Office Productivity by Phone.*

*   *How To Choose a Telemarketing Consultant.*

Format: paperback. 148 pages.

BUILDING CIRCULATION

Building Circulation Through Creative Telephone Marketing, Jim Atkins and Dave Gotthelf. New Canaan, CT: Folio Magazine Publishing Corporation, 1981.

An important book for anyone contemplating building circulation for magazines, newsletters, books seminars and other related products or services.

The book contains people and company resources, scripts, case examples, objection/responses, how to's, and the mathematics of building both initial and renewal subscriptions. Actual results of many programs--some well-known and some relatively obscure--are revealed with detailed data.

Although some of the numbers used in the math may be somewhat outdated (1981 publishing date), the described process for insuring profitability is on target.

Chapter titles:

*   *How To Use This Monograph.*

*   *Should You Use an Outside Service or an In-House Operation?*

*   *Selecting and Using Outside Services.*

*   *Operating Your In-House System.*

*   *Getting the Most from Your 800 Number.*

*   *Testing with the Telephone.*

*   *Telephone Marketing for the Consumer Magazine.*

*   *Special Problems of Trade Magazines.*

*   *Converting Agency Subscription Orders.*

*   *Converting Free Circulation to Paid.*

*   *Newsletter Marketing by Telephone.*

*   *Marketing Books, Seminars, Other Products or Services.*

*   *Equipment and Operations.*

*   *Customer Service and Follow-up.*

609

*   *Hiring a Consultant.*

*   *Glossary of "Telephonese."*

*   *Supplier's Directory.*

*   *How Publishers Use an 800 Number in Their Promotions.*

Format: paperback. 265 pages.

CAMPAIGNS/APPLICATIONS THAT WORK

Successful Telemarketing: Opportunities and Techniques for Increasing Sales and Profits, Bob Stone and John Wyman. Lincolnwood, IL: NTC Business Books, an imprint of National Textbook Company, 1986.

This book shows many successful applications of telemarketing by many corporate giants such as General Electric, AT&T, Merrill Lynch, American Express, Beech-Nut Nutrition Corporation, Whirlpool, IBM--as well as small and medium sized firms.

Provides step-by-step guidelines for launching a successful telemarketing program. Major applications are reviewed within order processing, customer service, sales support, sales promotion and account management. Lead generation and qualification are given special attention.

Rudy Oetting, chapter contributor to "The Mathematics of Telemarketing," provides some interesting data regarding industry cost norms. Inbound/outbound costs, development of worksheets and sales cost comparisons (field vs. TSR's) are intriguing.

Chapter titles:

*   *The Scope of Telemarketing.*

*   *The GE Answer Center.*

*   *The AT&T National Sales Center.*

*   *Telemarketing in the Advertising Process.*

*   *Telemarketing in the Sales Promotion Process.*

*   *Telemarketing in the Selling Process.*

*   *Telemarketing in the Fundraising Process.*

*   *Developing and Maintaining a Database.*

*   *How To Do Market Research via Telephone.*

APPENDIX C: TELEMARKETING BOOKS/MAGAZINES IN PRINT

* *The Mathematics of Telemarketing.*

* *Telemarketing in the Training Process.*

* *Making the In-House/Service Organization Decision.*

Format: paperback. 236 pages.

Telemarketing Campaigns That Work!, Murray Roman. New York, NY: McGraw-Hill Book Company, 1983.

Describes in A-to-Z detail 18 classic telemarketing campaigns that worked. It shows the strategies behind each campaign--the method used in day-to-day implementation--and the results. In fields ranging from banking to consumer retailing, service companies, industrial products and executive seminars, it describes just what goes into a successful telemarketing campaign.

Included are discussions of how to prepare a telemarketing campaign on behalf of new products, how to determine, using only limited capital, whether a sufficient market exists, how to develop specific lists for telephone marketing, how to screen prospects by telephone, how to increase sales lead follow-up efficiency, how to discover and measure responsiveness, how to record prospect information quickly and simply, how to balance direct mail and telemarketing efforts, how to penetrate markets outside one's own geographical area, how to pretest a script to make it smooth and effective, how to schedule optimum calling times, how to build and update a list for repeated calls, how to use a computer and CRT's, how to improve the rate of payment on "yes" responses, how to turn marginal accounts into profitable accounts and how to use the telephone as a fund-raising tool.

The book presents several entire telemarketing scripts for useful comparison--and examples of materials employed and actual results achieved in telemarketing campaigns which provide important hard data for analysis. In addition, supporting charts, consumer surveys, FCC decisions, agency versus in-house program criteria and ethical guidelines are all included to reinforce key points.

Chapters and appendices:

* *Publishing.*

* *Bank Marketing--A New Frontier.*

* *"800" Success Stories: 3 Companies--25 Million Incoming Calls.*

* *Marketing Communications Services.*

* *Nonstore Marketing.*

* *Incremental Sales to Business.*

* *Maximizing Sales Force Productivity.*

* *Building Nonprofit Associations and Fund-Raising Campaigns.*

611

ENCYCLOPEDIA OF TELEMARKETING

* *Expanding Your Contributor Base with Phone.*

* *Establishing and Refining In-House Telemarketing Facilities.*

* *Intracompany Applications.*

* *The Range of Telemarketing Applications.*

* *FCC Memorandum Opinion and Order in the Matter of Unsolicited Telephone Calls.*

* *Roster of States' Legislation.*

* *The Direct Marketing Association Guidelines for Ethical Business Practices.*

* *What Your Customers Think About Telemarketing.*

* *The Inappropriateness of Longer, Literate Taped Messages.*

* *Louisiana National Bank Survey of Customer Response.*

* *Montgomery Ward's Survey of Customer Response.*

* *Sample Results of Telemarketing.*

* *Criteria for Selecting an In-House or Agency Workshop.*

Format: hard cover. 282 pages.

Telephone Magic: How To Tap the Phone's Marketing Potential in Your Business, H. Skip Weitzen. New York, NY: McGraw-Hill Book Company, 1987.

Offers fresh ideas and an original approach for using the phone to best advantage in the marketing mix. Written in non-technical style, it provides 300 practical ways to use the phone to improve service, increase sales and cut costs.

Using numerous case histories, the author demonstrates the best ways for businesses, entrepreneurs, and service and nonprofit organizations to use the phone to create new pathways to profits. To help achieve the right marketing mix for the Information Age now dawning, the book analyzes the best technique for using the phone.

When used at the right time and in the right way, the telephone is the most effective marketing tool now available. This book shows how to integrate the new telephone techniques and technologies into a marketing mix that is responsive, flexible, cost-effective, and highly profitable.

Chapter titles:

* *Promotion.*

* *Advertising.*

* *Prospecting.*

* *Selling.*

* *Research.*

* *Services.*

* *Products.*

* *Distribution.*

* *Pricing.*

* *Packaging.*

* *Creating a New World.*

Format: hard cover. 192 pages.

COMPUTERS

All About Marketing Information Systems, Datapro Research Corporation. Delran, NJ: Datapro Research Corporation, a Subsidiary of McGraw Hill, 1988 (updated quarterly).

A regularly updated information service that provides management strategies, planning guidelines, and evaluations of systems and services for direct marketing.

A major section of the information service--Telemarketing Systems--includes both management strategies for implementing telemarketing systems and in-depth evaluations of available hardware and software.

Approximately 150 pages are devoted to Telemarketing Systems. Other major sections include: Marketing Research Systems, Customer/Market Database Systems, Order Fulfillment Systems, Sales Analysis/Productivity Systems and General Purpose Hardware and Software.

Telemarketing topics include:

* *Telemarketing Facilities Planning.*

* *Inbound Telemarketing Systems: Technical Planning.*

* *Multiuser Telemarketing Systems.*

* *PC Telemarketing Software.*

* *Telephone Services for Telemarketing.*

* *Telephone Usage Management Systems.*

Format: Three-ring binder. 800 pages.

Step Up to Automation, Judy F. Lanier and Gary D. Banko. San Jose, CA: SofTel Publications, 1987.

Provides an in-depth understanding of how to implement a productivity system and shows the pitfalls and traps to avoid. Takes readers through a step-by-step proven process for successful automation. Selecting a system can be either exciting or painful. This book helps make the process both a pleasant and rewarding experience.

Co-authored by Judy Lanier, a leading industry expert, and Gary D. Banko, a systems engineer, this concise guide provides information in the way sales and marketing professionals prefer: straightforward reading, lots of how-to details. . .no fluff and no technical talk.

The book explores necessary issues such as: developing a needs analysis and a request for proposal (RFP), selecting the right software and hardware, choosing a vendor and installation and training.

Chapters and appendices:

* *Realistic Expectations.*

* *Two Stories on Automation.*

* *When To Automate.*

* *Developing a Master Plan.*

* *Justifying a System.*

* *LAN Tutorial.*

* *DOS Tutorial.*

* *Hardware Tutorial.*

* *Glossary of Terms.*

Format: paperback. 90 pages.

CUSTOMER SERVICE

Guide to Customer Service Excellence, Editors of *Customer Service Newsletter*. Silver Spring, MD: Marketing Publications, Inc., 1985.

Twenty-four proven ways are described to improve customer service operations and increase productivity, profitability and market share.

APPENDIX C: TELEMARKETING BOOKS/MAGAZINES IN PRINT

Telemarketing chapters include discussions on design and layout of a customer service department, a checklist of professional telephone techniques, evaluation of telephone performance (outstanding), a checklist for setting up a telemarketing function, and how to turn customer complaints into sales leads.

An excellent overall guide for customer service management truly interested in upgrading their facility.

Chapter topics:

* *Developing a Statement of Mission for the Customer Service Department.*

* *A 15-Point Checklist for Organizing and Activating a Customer Service Department.*

* *Checklist for Design and Layout of the Customer Service Department.*

* *Guidelines for Planning and Writing a Customer Service Manual.*

* *A Short-Form Policy/Procedure Manual for the Customer Service Department.*

* *A Sample Manual for Credit and Collection Policies.*

* *Guidelines for Maintaining Good Distributor Relations.*

* *A Customer Service Checklist for Manufacturers and Distributors.*

* *How To Set Relevant, Practical Customer Service Standards.*

* *Productivity Improvement in Customer Service: How To Do It Without Consultants and Engineers.*

* *Formulas for Allocating the True Cost of Productive Labor in Customer Service.*

* *Sampling Service Quality with Business Reply Cards.*

* *Single-Page Customer Questionnaires that Pull High Responses.*

* *Checklist of Professional Telephone Techniques.*

* *How To Evaluate Telephone Performance of Individual Reps.*

* *Checklist for Setting Up an Inside Selling/Telemarketing Function.*

* *The Rep Evaluation Grid for Inside Selling Activity.*

* *Form for Analyzing Potential Bottlenecks in the Order Cycle.*

* *How Carboline Reduced Error Rates by 75%.*

* *Cancelled Order/Lost Business Reports: "Early Warning System."*

* *Potential Sales Leads from Customer Complaints.*

* *Model for an Incentive Contest for Customer Service Personnel.*

* *Contingency Planning--Answering the "What If" Questions.*

* *Forecasting and Allocation Checklist: When Product Shortages Occur.*

Format: paperback. 62 pages.

Inside Selling/Telemarketing for Customer Service Representatives, Warren Blanding. Silver Spring, MD: Customer Service Institute, Marketing Publications, Inc., 1986.

A phone-side guide written for customer service representatives, this self-study workbook covers the full range of telemarketing. Most importantly, it talks the reps' language--and answers their questions and concerns about telemarketing. This down-to-earth workbook covers telemarketing on inbound calls, including order upgrading and converting inquiries into sales; the seven basic steps of outbound telemarketing; overcoming phonophobia; using scripts, scenarios and software; listening and speaking skills.

The actual call is covered in depth, including: planning the call, qualifying the customer, opening the call, making the presentation, overcoming objections, closing the sale, and making post-sale follow-up.

Chapter titles:

* *Inside Selling/Telemarketing: What Is It?*

* *Inside Selling/Telemarketing Is Much Less Complicated and Difficult than Most People Think!*

* *Beware of Phonophobia!*

* *Your Telemarketing "Tool Kit."*

* *Outbound Telemarketing--Getting Ready To Go.*

* *Converting Inquiries into Sales.*

* *Converting Complaints into Sales.*

* *ABC's of Complaint Handling.*

Format: spiral bound. 129 pages.

DO'S AND DON'T'S

Telemarketing's 100 Do's & Don't's, Staff of *Telemarketing* magazine. Norwalk, CT: Technology Marketing Corporation, 1986.

Designed to help telemarketers prevent pitfalls and costly mistakes.

This professional guide provides profitable pointers in virtually all areas of the telemarketing process. Chapter sub-topics include critical issues such as in-house or outside agency, integrating the marketing mix, recruiting, training, automating the telemarketing operation, scripting, list selection, integrating telemarketing with field sales, converting customer service into sales and many others.

The unique do's and don't's summarizations help to reinforce much of the narrative. A speed reader's delight.

Chapters/appendices:

* *Management Commitment.*

* *Planning.*

* *Marketing Strategy.*

* *People.*

* *Ergonomics.*

* *Telecommunications in Action.*

* *Telemarketing Techniques.*

* *Additional Telemarketing Applications.*

* *The Last Word: Ethics.*

* *Checklist for Selecting a Telemarketing Service Vendor.*

* *The 27-Point Hiring System.*

* *A Telemarketing Work Station That Fits.*

* *Analyzing Your Long Distance.*

* *Telemarketing Scripts You Can Adopt.*

* *Direct Marketing Association Guides for Telephone Marketing.*

Format: hard cover. 141 pages.

800 NUMBERS

The Effectiveness of 800 Numbers in Direct Mail Catalogs, Ester Lazaros. New York, NY: Publishing Division, Direct Marketing Association, Inc., 1983.

The objective of this study was to determine if offering toll-free, 800 service for merchandise ordering, as opposed to mail ordering only, would profitably increase the sales of the catalog company. The hypothesis tested was that an 800 number for ordering consumer merchandise from direct mail catalogs increases sales 22%. The research seeks to differentiate companies using the 800 number with limited success. Research objectives include establishing the association between the significant factors for a company's business such as product line, market, price of product, and the success of the toll-free ordering system. The research also examines the differentiating factors among those companies having greater success from those with limited success.

Chapter titles:

* *The Study.*

* *Benefits of Toll-Free Ordering.*

* *Guidelines for Offering Toll-Free Service.*

* *Drawbacks to Toll-Free Ordering.*

* *The Future.*

* *Conclusions and Recommendations.*

* *Findings.*

* *Appendices.*

Format: paperback. 94 pages.

ENCYCLOPEDIA

Encyclopedia of Telemarketing, Richard L. Bencin and Donald J. Jonovic, Ph.D. Englewood Cliffs, NJ: Prentice Hall, Division of Simon & Schuster, Inc., 1989.

Combines many of the best minds and authorities in the business in a collaborative effort to bring the full impact of telemarketing's evolution to professionals and novices alike. It's a handbook within which covers every important facet of telemarketing and its key related disciplines. Each topic area is an "expert system" in print--a data processing specialist deals with computers and telemarketing, a specialist in database marketing writes the chapter on list management, etc.

Although the contributors share a level of expertise, they vary greatly in background, experience and interest. Represented are publishers, authors, leading consultants, and executives of telemarketing specialty

618

services. Also participating in the book are founders, presidents and chairmen of the American Telemarketing Association, the International Customer Service Association, the Direct Marketing Association and the Telephone Marketing Council of the DMA. They are not only telemarketing leaders, but also telemarketing pioneers who represent hundreds of years of experience, and have been present at the creation of thousands of telemarketing operations.

Chapters with contributing authors:

* *Why Telemarketing (Richard L. Bencin/Donald J. Jonovic, Ph.D.).*

* *Integrating Telemarketing with Other Direct Marketing Disciplines/Field Sales (Richard L. Bencin/Donald J. Jonovic, Ph.D.).*

* *Telefocus Marketing (Richard L. Bencin/Donald J. Jonovic, Ph.D.).*

* *Consumer Programs (Richard Herzog).*

* *Business-to-Business Programs (Gene Sollo/Peg Kuman).*

* *Organization and Staffing (Connie Caroli/Hal Crandall).*

* *Profiles of Telephone Sales Reps (Michael J. Marx, Ph.D.).*

* *Training (Jeffrey C. Wooden).*

* *Compensation/Motivation (Lee Van Vechten).*

* *The Sales Call and the Selling Skills Required (Art Sobczak).*

* *Scripts and the Offer (Richard L. Bencin/Donald J. Jonovic, Ph.D.).*

* *Handling Objections (Richard L. Bencin).*

* *Databases and Data Banks [Lists] (Ed Burnett).*

* *Habitat (Gere Picasso).*

* *Systems (William Fawns).*

* *The Bottom Line (Dwaine L. Canova).*

* *Computers (Richard Brock/Judy Lanier).*

* *Telecommunications [ACD] (John A. Pollpeter).*

* *Telecommunications [General] (Charles Yates).*

619

ENCYCLOPEDIA OF TELEMARKETING

* *Inbound Telemarketing (Aldyn McKean).*

* *Service Agencies (Seldon Young/Paul Mohr).*

* *Catalog Telemarketing (Richard L. Bencin).*

* *Customer Service Telemarketing (Warren Blanding).*

* *Distribution Channel Telemarketing (Peg Fisher).*

* *Fund Raising Telemarketing (Richard L. Bencin/Donald J. Jonovic, Ph.D.).*

* *International Telemarketing (Eugene B. Kordahl).*

* *Anatomy of a "Boiler Room" (Richard L. Bencin/Donald J. Jonovic, Ph.D.).*

* *Taking the Reins of a Troubled Telemarketing Center (Richard L. Bencin/ Donald J. Jonovic, Ph.D.).*

* *Step-by-Step for Startups [A Review] (Tom A. DePrizio).*

* *Telemarketing: Yesterday, Today and Tomorrow (Steven A. Idelman).*

* *Epilogue (Dr. Gary S. Goodman).*

* *The American Telemarketing Association (Ron Weber).*

* *DMA/Telephone Marketing Council (Jonah Gitlitz).*

* *Telemarketing Books/Magazines In Print (Richard L. Bencin/Donald J. Jonovic, Ph.D.).*

* *Telecommunications [Peripheral Equipment] (Neal H. Shact).*

* *Glossary of Telemarketing Terms (Richard L. Bencin/Donald J. Jonovic, Ph.D./Eugene Kordahl/Lee Van Vechten/Judy Lanier).*

* *General Research (Barry Schlenker).*

Format: hard cover. 800 pages.

FUND RAISING

More Dialing, More Dollars: 12 Steps to Successful Telemarketing, Michael E. Blimes and

620

APPENDIX C: TELEMARKETING BOOKS/MAGAZINES IN PRINT

Ron Sproat. New York, NY: American Council for the Arts, 1985.

The authors demonstrate in practical, step-by-step fashion how the telephone can be used to increase the rate of success 30% to 50% or more when soliciting contributions, members, or subscribers.

The book discusses how to make a telemarketing program work by giving 12 essential steps to setting up and conducting a successful telemarketing campaign.

The methods described have been used successfully by a variety of organizations, both large and small. An important book for anyone who wants to increase fundraising income, membership, and subscription sales.

Chapters (steps):

* *Why the Telephone?*

* *Is Telemarketing for You?*

* *Assess the Prospective Audience Potential.*

* *Establish the Goals and Set Objectives.*

* *Plan the Campaign.*

* *Prepare the Campaign.*

* *Determine Evaluation Control Criteria.*

* *Develop Script(s) and Probable Responses.*

* *Train Staff and Callers.*

* *Test the Program.*

* *Revise Scripts and Responses.*

* *Conduct the Program.*

* *Report the Results.*

* *Evaluate the Program.*

Format: paperback. 93 pages.

Telephone Fund Raising, Jonathan A. Segal and Janet B. Allen. New York, NY: Plenum Press, A Division of Plenum Publishing Corporation, 1987.

This book provides the information needed to develop and maintain a lucrative telephone fund-raising program. It describes a model program, taking one through every step of the process.

The authors teach how to prepare a list of contributors, how to write scripts, how to negotiate large

621

pledges, how to develop a coterie of top-notch callers (how to find them and train them, for example), how to contact potential contributors (whom to call, when to call and so on) and how to structure and administer the program.

Also included are sample dialogues, 20 keys to negotiating, pledge validation, paid callers or volunteers, gaining support of the board of directors, record keeping and many other key issues.

The principles discussed can be applied to any nonprofit or political cause, regardless of its financial needs. The approach is practical, ethical and conforms to the highest standards of the fund-raising profession.

Chapter titles:

* *Negotiating Large Pledges.*

* *Developing a Coterie of Top-Notch Callers.*

* *Contacting Potential Contributors: The Mechanics.*

* *Structuring and Administering Your Telephone Fund-Raising Program.*

Format: hard cover. 213 pages.

Telepledge, The Complete Guide to Mail-Phone Fund Raising, Louis Arthur Schultz. Washington, DC: The Taft Group, 1986.

This manual will help fund raisers to conduct the processes of designing, installing, and managing a telepledge mail/telephone solicitation program. The author states that this solicitation program has had wide application among nonprofit organizations in the United States, and has proven successful in the effective and efficient solicitations of large numbers of prospects who cannot or should not be solicited face to face.

Use of this solicitation system is intended to raise general giving levels, increase the size of the average gift, create new donors, improve the public relations of the organization, identify potential major donor prospects, and collect valuable information on the donor population as a group or as individuals.

Part I of this manual--Sowing the Seeds--lays out the steps necessary to design and install a telepledge program. Part II--Reaping the Harvest--tells how to conduct an ongoing solicitation program.

Part/Chapter titles:

Part I (Sowing the Seeds).

* *Telepledge Concepts.*

* *Typical Telepledge Results.*

* *Telepledge System Flow.*

* *Telepledge Mailings.*

* *Prospects.*

* *Determining Program Size and Duration.*

* *Staffing.*

* *Estimating Telepledge Pledges.*

* *Equipment and Physical Facilities.*

* *Estimating the Telephone Budget.*

* *Telepledge Installation Event Sequence.*

Part II (Reaping the Harvest).

* *Telephone Fund-Raising Ethics.*

* *Callers.*

* *Caller Training--Annual Fund.*

* *Caller Training--Capital Campaign.*

* *Telepledge Management.*

* *In Conclusion.*

* *Appendix: Sample Letters.*

* *Glossary.*

Format: three-ring binder and cassette tape. 201 pages.

HIRING

The Telemarketing Manager's Hiring Bible, Eric J. Adams. San Francisco, CA: Herman Advantage Publishing, 1987.

This book is the most comprehensive hiring guide available. It leads the reader step by step through the complete process of recruiting, screening, evaluating, interviewing, and selecting TSR's who are right for the organization.

It helps to calculate hiring costs and turnover rates. The book even shows how to stage a full-day workshop for managers and colleagues.

The "Bible" is based on years of experience developing hiring programs for some of America's major corporations.

Assisting the author/publisher with content were Micahel J. Marx, Ph.D., Steve Friedland, M.S., Alex Englemen, M.S., and Rhonda Rockwell, Ph.D.

Chapter titles:

* *Getting Started.*

* *The High Cost of TSR Selection.*

* *Recruiting.*

* *The Tele-screen.*

* *Evaluating.*

* *Interviewing.*

* *The Final Decision.*

* *A Hiring Workshop You Can Sponsor.*

Format: three-ring binder with one cassette tape. 78 pages.

INCOMING CALL MANAGEMENT

What Senior Managers Need To Know About Incoming Call Centers, Gordon F. MacPherson, Jr. Bowie, MD: SLN, Inc., 1988.

This unique, illustrated book helps telemarketing executives, managers, and supervisors to manage an incoming call center. The author is President of the Incoming Calls Management Institute in Annapolis, Maryland.

Includes all of the basics of maintaining appropriate incoming call service levels for different kinds of industries. The graphics, examples and clear-cut text help one to get up to speed *quickly* on this vital topic.

Chapters titles:

* *Calls Bunch Up.*

* *There Is No Such Thing as an Industry Standard Service Level.*

* *The Vital Element in Planning: Service Level Linkage.*

* *Productivity Declines as Service Level Improves.*

* *What First-Level Supervisors Do To Maintain Service Level.*

* *ACD Reports Can Be Misleading.*

* *Why a Single Correct Ratio of Trunks to TSR's Doesn't Exist.*

* *Your Slowest TSR Could Be Your Best.*

* *Environmental Comforts Are Critically Important.*

* *Telecommunications Support for Incoming Call Centers.*

* *How To Buy the "Least Expensive" Telephone System.*

* *An Incoming Call Center Is a Socially Significant Place.*

Format: paperback. 72 pages.

INSURANCE

Everyone's Guide to Opening Doors by Telephone, Sam Aronson. (See Telephone Sales for Outside Sales Reps.)

INSURANCE, INVESTMENTS AND REAL ESTATE

Successful Farming--By Phone, Steve Kennedy. Yorba Linda, CA: Calculated Industries, Inc., 1987.
   In today's competitive real estate sales market, a key to getting ahead and staying ahead is targeting your professional services--the primary function of real estate "farming" *(selecting prospects claimed as yours to cultivate).*
   This book explains in detail how to apply the concepts of telemarketing to the realtor's real estate "farm." Step by step, it covers everyting one needs to know about "farming" successfully.
   A unique book for the real estate professional attempting to build his or her business.
   Chapter titles:

* *Introduction to Farming by Phone.*

* *Staking Out Your Farm.*

* *Telemarketing: Wave of the Future.*

* *Successful Home Strategies.*

* *Your Farm Phone Directory.*

* *Selling Yourself over the Phone.*

* *Tips on Telephoning.*

* *The Farm Call Script.*

* *The Opening.*

* *Questions Keep the Conversation Going.*

* *How To Handle Objections.*

* *The Critical Close.*

* *Wrapping It Up.*

* *When Your Phone Rings.*

* *Keeping in Touch by Phone.*

* *You Can Do It!*

Format: paperback. 287 pages.

Successful Telephone Selling in the 80s, Martin D. Shafiroff and Robert L. Shook. (See Telephone Sales Skills.)

LISTS, DATABASES, AND DIRECT MAIL

Handbook of Direct Mail Lists and How To Profit from Their Use, Ed Burnett. Englewood Cliffs, NJ: Prentice Hall, Division of Simon & Schuster, Inc., 1988.
    This 768-page volume is truly an encyclopedia of data on lists connected with valuable "How To" tips to follow in order to save and make money in direct mail. An ideal text for students and a good refresher for experienced practitioners with complete coverage of the mathematics of direct mail.
    Of special interest to telemarketers is the chapter on "How to Use Telecommunications in Direct Mail Operations" as well as the overall in-depth analysis of database and lists.
    Chapter titles:

* *Some Easy Lessons on How To Fail in Direct Marketing.*

* *Everything You Need To Know About List Markets.*

* *How List Bearers and List Managers Operate.*

* *How To Deal with the Other Direct Mail Professionals.*

* *How To Rent a List from the Viewpoints of the Owner and User.*

* *Criteria.*

* *Specialized Types of Lists and How They Work.*

* *Compiled Lists for Consumer and Business Marketing.*

* *How To Test Mailing Lists.*

* *The Mathematics of Direct Response.*

* *Special Mathematical and Computer Based Direct Response Techniques.*

* *How To Use Merge/Purge.*

* *Database vs. Databank: A Look at What They Can Do for the List User.*

* *The How To's of Marketing for Catalog Operations.*

* *How To Use Telecommunications in Direct Mail Operations.*

* *Response Is the Name of the Game (Direct Mail Is Just One of the Players).*

* *Neither Rain Nor Snow...A Look at Modern U.S. Mailing Practices.*

* *How To Cope with List Problems and Abuses.*

* *Rental Practices and Problems.*

* *A Look into the Future.*

Format: hard cover. 768 pages.

MANAGING GROWTH

Managing Growth in Outbound Telemarketing, Steven A. Idelman and Grady L. Dobbs. Englewood Cliffs, NJ: Prentice Hall, Division of Simon & Schuster, Inc., 1988.

Addresses the problems that managers of growth must face, with the premise that growth can be brought under control with active management of change and a persistent commitment to quality and value. It gives step-by-step instructions and real life "hands on" examples. It concentrates on application and action, on the practical and purposeful steps required to produce high quality, cost-effective results through proper planning and execution, financial monitoring and management, staffing and structuring, training and compensation, operational and marketing strategies, management development and management of people.

ENCYCLOPEDIA OF TELEMARKETING

This book is a telemarketing management resource, containing unique insights, effective techniques and valuable answers to the hard questions about how to manage telemarketing's dynamic growth successfully.

Chapter titles:

* *The Philosophy Underlying Growth.*

* *Planning for Growth.*

* *Structuring for Growth.*

* *Money Matters (You Bet It Does!).*

* *The People Issues.*

* *Creating a Growth Atmosphere.*

* *The Marketing Effort.*

* *Managing the Client.*

* *The Downstairs of Growth.*

* *Putting It All Together.*

* *The Challenge of the Future.*

Format: hard cover. About 300 pages.

OBJECTION HANDLING

The Sales Script Book, Gerhard Gschwantdner and Dr. Donald J. Moine. Fredericksburg, VA: *Personal Selling Power,* 1986.

A unique text listing the most common recurring sales objections and many suggestions for replying to them. Designed for field sales or telephone personnel, this book helps to provide suggestions for building prepared, creative replies to repetitive objections.

Many of the book's responses are memory joggers or creative prompts that enable more lengthy retorts to objections. Consultants or telephone service agencies could use the book as an ongoing reference document for objection handling techniques.

Chapter titles:

* *How To Use This Book.*

* *Attention-Getting Scripts.*

APPENDIX C: TELEMARKETING BOOKS/MAGAZINES IN PRINT

* *Getting Through the Secretary.*

* *Your Price Is Too High.*

* *I Am Too Busy to Talk with You.*

* *I'm Too Busy; Talk to Our Purchasing Manager First.*

* *It's Too Complicated.*

* *I Don't Want To Take Big Risks.*

* *I Want To Work with a More Established Company.*

* *I Plan To Wait Until Fall.*

* *I Only Buy American Products.*

* *We Tried Something Like It, But It Didn't Work.*

* *Your Competitor's Product Is Better.*

* *We Expect Hard Times Ahead.*

* *Your Product Is Too New.*

* *Business Is Slow Right Now.*

* *I'm Not Interested.*

* *We Won't Buy from You.*

* *The Machine We Have Is Still Good.*

* *We Are Satisfied with What We Have Now.*

* *I Have To Think This Over.*

* *I Need To Talk to My Boss About It.*

* *I Can't Afford It.*

* *I'll Buy a Used One.*

* *I Want To Get a Couple Prices First.*

629

* *I Have To Get 2 More Estimates.*

* *I Don't Have Any Money for This.*

* *I Can Get the Same Product for Less.*

* *Give Me a 10% Discount, and I'll Buy Today.*

* *You've Got To Do Better Than That.*

* *Your Sales Script Book.*

Format: three-ring binder. 101 pages.

REFERENCE TEXTS

Directory of Telemarketing Centers (1988), Aldyn McKean. New York, NY: Actel Marketing, 1988 (updated annually).

     A directory of the major telemarketing service agencies in the U.S. Includes discussions about telemarketing agencies vs. in-house operations, selection procedures for choosing a telemarketing service agency and general pricing criteria.

     Each service agency is described regarding: parent corporation, telephone center locations, business telephone numbers, key officers of the company, description of services, average number of reps on duty (inbound/outbound), years in business (inbound/outbound), toll-free numbers, type of business by percentage (inbound/outbound), media breakdown by percentage (inbound/outbound), volumes of completed calls (inbound/outbound), data capture method, script cueing method, recorded message capability, call distribution system, automated dialing system, busy reports available, types of transmission available, credit card checking procedures, in-house fulfillment availability, client information (companies, products and type of service) and additional services available.

     This is an important book for any company contemplating using a telemarketing service agency. Chapter titles:

* *Outside Vendors vs. In-House Operations.*

* *How To Choose an Out-of-House Telemarketing Service.*

* *Comparing Prices of Telemarketing Service Bureaus.*

* *Telemarketing Service Bureaus (and Parent Companies).*

Format: paperback. 261 pages.

DMA Fact Book and *1987 Supplement to the Fact Book*, Direct Marketing Assn. New York, NY: Direct Marketing Assn, Inc., 1986 (*DMA Fact Book*), 1987 (*1987 Supplement to the Fact Book*).

APPENDIX C: TELEMARKETING BOOKS/MAGAZINES IN PRINT

A reference work that many direct marketers are turning to for information guidance and bottom-line statistical facts. More than 320 tables and charts highlight the latest critical research findings, show important industry growth and usage trends, provide valuable expenditure, production and operating cost figures and quantify marketers' outlooks and expectations concerning key issues.

The *1987 Supplement* contains contributions from 55 outside direct marketing firms and professional associations and seven major DMA research studies--representing a 104% increase in the total number of charts and tables over the 1986 Supplement.

This 1987 volume is an excellent complement to the *Fact Book's* ninth edition, which provides an encyclopedic overview of direct marketing and direct response advertising. Written by acknowledged experts, the *Fact Book* offers 17 chapters regarding essential information on lists, direct mail, catalogs, telemarketing, research, production, and more--with emphasis on the specific market techniques used in business-to-business, consumer, financial services, and circulation promotion--just to name a few.

This reference work can be obtained as a set or individually.

Chapters of the *DMA Fact Book*:

* *Direct Marketing--An Introduction.*

* *Mailing Lists.*

* *Direct Mail Directions.*

* *The Catalog Industry.*

* *Telemarketing.*

* *The New Electronic Media.*

* *Print Media.*

* *Business-to-Business Cataloging.*

* *Business-to-Business Mail.*

* *Subscription Marketing.*

* *Continuity Planning.*

* *Financial Services.*

* *The Non-Profit Sector.*

* *International Direct Marketing.*

* *Research.*

631

* *Consumer Attitudes.*

* *USPS.*

* *Legislation.*

* *Ethics.*

* *Printing and Production.*

* *Education.*

* *A History of Direct Marketing.*

* *Glossary.*

Format: paperback. *DMA Fact Book* is 158 pages. *1987 Supplement to the Fact Book* is 191 pages.

First Annual Guide to Telemarketing: 1986, Eugene B. Kordahl and Arnold L. Fishman. Lincolnshire, IL: Marketing Logistics, Inc., 1987.

This authoritative, 210-page study tracks the telemarketing industry since 1980. The new publication represents a joint effort between Eugene B. Kordahl, President, National Telemarketing, Inc., and Arnold L. Fishman, President, Marketing Logistics, Inc. Predictions of a 15-20 percent growth per annum for the rest of the decade for the telemarketing industry are extrapolated from the data collected.

The guide provides a valuable information resource for serious telemarketing practitioners. It's divided into three parts: the Telemarketing Economy, the Telemarketing Firm, and a Glossary/Directory of Suppliers.

Sections:

Part One. The Telemarketing Economy.

* *Telemarketing Economy.*

* *Telemarketing Growth.*

* *Telemarketing User Segmentation.*

* *Telemarketing User Sales Leaders.*

* *Telemarketing User Company Profiles.*

* *Telemarketing Supplier Segmentation.*

* *International Telemarketing Trends.*

* *Trends.*

Part Two. The Telemarketing Firm/Company Dynamics.

* *Sales.*

* *Automation.*

* *Sales Force Integration.*

* *Operation Location.*

* *Sales Center Planning.*

* *Financial Planning.*

* *Promotional Planning.*

Part Three.

* *Glossary.*

* *Directory of Suppliers.*

Format: hard cover. 210 pages.

Telemarketing Intelligence 1987, Barry Schlenker. Morganville, NJ: Schlenker Research Services, 1987.

A comprehensive study on the current use and anticipated growth of telemarketing in American business.

More than 700 completed in-depth interviews with proprietary (in-house) telemarketing organizations conducted under standard market research procedures. These 707 telephone interviews, averaging over 30 minutes each, developed more than ''70,000 bits of information'' compiled and presented in approximately 100 tables. The information is current and comprehensive.

More than 60 completed in-depth interviews with the nation's largest service bureau organizations, conducted under standard market research procedures. These 64 telephone interviews, averaging over 30 minutes each, gathered valuable information and insights on current experience and anticipated developments.

A total of 600 telephone interviews with a representative sample of adults in the continental United States to assess consumer attitudes toward telemarketing sales calls. The interviews covered topics such as receptivity to receiving calls, degree of annoyance and the perceived need for laws or regulations.

This study provides the help to evaluate current strategic and tactical positions and potential opportunities in telemarketing--one of the most dynamic business developments in the country today.

Two separate reports are available: ''Report 1: In-House Telemarketing Operations,'' and ''Report 2: Telemarketing Service Bureaus and Consumer Attitudes Toward Telemarketing.''

Summaries, conclusions and table categories include:

* *Conclusions and Observations.*

* *Summary of Findings.*

* *Tabulated Survey Findings.*

* *Current Telemarketing Operations and Expected Growth.*

* *Personnel Hiring, Training, Performance.*

* *Automation: Computer Terminals/Hardware/Software.*

* *Telecommunications Related Equipment and Services.*

* *Attitudes and General Information.*

* *Consumer Attitude Survey.*

Format: spiral bound. Report 1: 210 pages and Report 2: 200 pages.

RETAIL

How To Increase Sales via the Telephone, Alan H. Jordan. New York, NY: Sales Promotion Division, National Retail Merchants Association.

A book for retailers interested in building their business through telemarketing. Taking advantage of the sales that can be generated over the telephone may deliver those extra dollars so necessary if retailers are to survive these difficult times of economic uncertainty. Yet all too often many stores fail to realize the importance of using the phone. Increasing customer loyalty, suggesting merchandise and developing customer prospect lists, are just a few of the many ways small to large size retail stores can generate a great deal of incremental revenue.

Chapter titles:

* *Selling Over the Phone.*

* *Getting More Customers in Your Door.*

* *Who Are Your Current Customers?*

* *The Automatic Tape Answering Machine.*

* *Creative Marketing--Building a Nationwide Customer Base.*

* *Using the Phone To Obtain Free Publicity.*

* *A General Discussion of the Techniques.*

* *Coordinating a Mail Campaign with Telephone Solicitation.*

* *Need Circumstances.*

* *Techniques for Stores with Multiple Locations.*

Format: paperback. 67 pages.

SCRIPTS

Words for Telemarketing, Steven R. Isaac. Brentwood, NY: Asher-Gallant Press, Division of Caddylak Systems, Inc., 1988.

This book presents a wide range of ideas on structuring communications, and is useful for fund raising, customer service, market research, and inbound and outbound telemarketing applications.

Telephone script writing is broken down into easy-to-learn pieces to show quickly how to write scripts that get results. Valuable tips include phrasing that helps get a caller past secretaries, the 13 most persuasive words in the English language and how to use them, an easy way to start a script, 10 techniques for handling objections and four proven techniques to get a "yes" decision.

Also included are more than 15 prewritten scripts that can be used as they are, or adapted to fit "customized" situations.

Chapter titles:

* *Why Scripting for the Telephone?*

* *The Unique Characteristics of the Telephone as a Communication Medium.*

* *The Seven Basic Rules of Telephone Script Writing.*

* *The Step-by-Step Process of Development.*

* *Getting Through to the Right Person.*

* *The Introduction.*

* *Present/Probe.*

* *Closing.*

* *Reassurance.*

* *Script Formats.*

635

* *Scripting Objection Responses.*

* *The Magic of Words.*

* *Where We Use Telephone Scripts.*

* *Scripts and Objection Responses from Actual Telephone Programs.*

Format: paperback. 166 pages.

STARTUPS AND MANAGING A CENTER

The Complete Guide to Telemarketing, Peter M. Moloney and Joel Davis. Salem, NH: Ideabank
Publishing, Inc., 1986.

A comprehensive, step-by-step analysis of setting up an in-house telemarketing center. The book
is well-written and functionally organized as *each* chapter contains Objectives, Prerequisites, an Overview,
and a Summary. Color coded dividers help one to locate pertinent sections.

Some of the more interesting topics within the chapters are: 45 Reasons To Use Telemarketing, Ten
Steps to Starting a Telemarketing Program, The Situation Assessment Checklist, Estimating Cost Effective-
ness, Guidelines for Success, List Criteria, Developing the Sales Information Manual (SIM), Evaluating
Phone Service Vendors, Nine Guidelines for a Positive Environment, How To Lure Qualified Applicants and
Day-to-Day Motivation.

Chapter titles:

* *Telemarketing Fact and Potential.*

* *Ingredients for Success.*

* *Assessing Your Present Situation.*

* *Selecting Your Telemarketing Opportunity.*

* *Defining Meaningful Objectives.*

* *On Your Mark, Get Set...*

* *Compiling and Preparing Prospect Lists.*

* *Packaging Your Message.*

* *Designing Jobs and Call Report Forms.*

* *Selecting Phone Services.*

* *Selecting Equipment.*

* *Setting Up the Calling Environment.*

* *Developing a Compensation Plan.*

* *Hiring Telephone Personnel.*

* *Improving Telephone Sales Techniques.*

* *Managing the Telemarketing Function.*

Format: three-ring binder. 364 pages.

How To Plan and Manage a Telemarketing Operation, E. Patricia Birsner and Jacqueline L. Larkin. Boston, MA: American Management Association Extension Institute, 1985.

This book is designed specifically for the practicing telemarketing manager and the future telemarketing manager. It provides private, self-paced individualized study; learning and self-evaluation through instructional programming; and communication between the student and the staff of AMA instructors through assignments and a final examination based on the case study as pioneered by Harvard University. Paralleling a business school course of study, the curriculum makes available a stable, inclusive, and continuing transmittal of practices and perspectives to those working managers who, on their own time and at their own pace, want to continue their education.

Each chapter includes Learning Objectives, Summary and Instructional Programming. Answering the questions following each chapter offers a chance to check comprehension of the concepts and reinforce understanding.

Chapter titles:

* *The Telephone as a Marketing Tool.*

* *The Applications of Telemarketing.*

* *The Telemarketing Process.*

* *Communications Theory and Telemarketing.*

* *Writing the Telephone Sales Package.*

* *Selecting Telephone Sales Personnel.*

* *Training the Telemarketing Sales Staff.*

* *Evaluating the Telemarketing Operation.*

* *Glossary.*

*   *The First Examination.*

*   *The Practice Case.*

*   *The Examination Case.*

Format: three-ring binder. 212 pages.

In-House Telemarketing: A Master Plan for Starting and Managing a Profitable Telemarketing Program, Thomas McCafferty. Chicago, IL: Probus Publishing Company, 1987.

Describes those aspects of telemarketing that can either support a company's traditional marketing approaches or provide significant advantages over them. It also identifies the kinds of marketing challenges that are "naturals" for telemarketing.

Establishing and supervising a telemarketing program may appear at first to be a relatively easy task. But like so many "relatively easy tasks" in business, the creation of a successful telemarketing program often proves elusive. It generally requires years of experience to master the trade and acquire the pivotal insights that can make the difference between a successful telemarketing center and a failed one. The knowledge and experience of telemarketing presented in this book will provide a short-cut to telemarketing success.

Concentrating on how to create, plan, and manage an in-house program, this guide covers equipment and facilities, sales strategies, script writing and testing, sales training and more. Includes evaluation techniques and other often overlooked aspects vital to success. Examples include the TM Software Checklist, Role Playing Critique Form, and the Telemarketing Center Budget Checklist.

Chapter titles:

*   *What Is Telemarketing?*

*   *The Unique Characteristics of Telemarketing.*

*   *Selecting and Preparing the Customer Prospect List for Telemarketing.*

*   *Key Issues on Staffing the Telemarketing Center.*

*   *Planning for Higher Telemarketing Productivity: Tracking and Measuring Telemarketing Results.*

*   *Planning the Telemarketing Facilities: Space and Equipment.*

*   *Budgeting the Telemarketing Center.*

*   *Integrating Telemarketing into Your Existing Marketing Program.*

*   *Telemarketing Follow-Up Systems: The Importance of the Call Report.*

*   *The Telemarketing Reference Guide.*

* *Training, Coaching, and Motivating TSR's.*

* *Inbound Telemarketing.*

* *A Sample Inbound Sales Call Report and Order Form.*

* *Dealing with Credit Fraud.*

* *Insights into Teleresearch.*

* *Sources for More Information.*

* *The Tele-Reference from Telecross.*

* *Checklist of Things To Be Done To Set Up a Telemarketing Center.*

Format: paperback. 337 pages.

Startup Telemarketing: How To Launch a Profitable Sales Operation, Stanley Leo Fidel. New York, NY: John Wiley & Sons, 1987.

Should help owners and managers of small-to-midsize businesses--and marketing managers in larger companies--get a telemarketing operation up and running fast, while avoiding the hassles and headaches that often plague the business. Helps marketers determine where telemarketing can generate the greatest return, including some innovative telemarketing applications in use today.

Provides an exhaustive startup checklist to ensure efficiency right off the bat. Plenty of logistical support--how to lay out the operation, recruit, train and compensate sales staff, and implement advanced selling techniques. Record keeping forms and scripts included.

Chapter titles:

* *The Telemarketing Revolution.*

* *Telemarketing Applications.*

* *In-House Telemarketing Versus Telephone Service Bureaus.*

* *Telemarketing and Other Marketing Methods.*

* *The Entry-Level Approach.*

* *Target Marketing by Telephone.*

* *Creating a Telemarketing Environment.*

* *How to Recruit and Hire Telemarketers.*

* *How To Train and Coach Telemarketers.*

* *Designing Your Compensation Program.*

* *Advanced Telephone Techniques.*

* *The Psychology of Selling.*

* *Computerizing Your Operation.*

* *Resources for Telemarketing.*

* *Sample Telemarketing Manual.*

Format: hard cover. 287 pages.

Strategic Telemarketing, Richard L. Bencin. (See Strategies.)

Successful Telemarketing, Peg Fisher. Chicago, IL: Dartnell Corporation, 1985.

If you're responsible for developing your organization's sales and marketing plan, this manual should help considerably. A compilation of guidelines, how to's, models and examples illustrate effective telephone use in conjunction with other marketing methods.

The manual reflects experience setting up both in-house telemarketing operations as well as consulting others on the process in two primary commercial and industrial groups: manufacturers and wholesaler-retailers. Examples from service industries are also included.

Decision-making points appear throughout the manual. To help reinforce understanding of the importance of reaching sound marketing decisions, case examples abound. Consequences of what can happen if the proper decisions are not made are detailed.

Chapter titles:

* *What Is Telemarketing?*

* *Identifying Profitable Accounts.*

* *Selecting Your Marketing Strategies.*

* *Getting the Most from Direct Mail Support.*

* *Designing Your Internal Support System.*

* *Setting Up the Work Areas.*

* *Selecting the Best Manager.*

* *Selecting Your Telemarketing Staff.*

* *Custom Designing Your Job Tools.*

* *Gathering Sales Information.*

* *Measuring Results.*

* *Developing Job Standards.*

* *Training Your Staff.*

* *How To Pay Your Staff.*

* *Gaining Staff Cooperation.*

* *Putting It All Together.*

Format: three-ring binder. 346 pages.

Telemarketing Management System, Maynard A. Howe, Ph.D., and Roger J. Howe, Ph.D. Del Mar, CA: Mc-Graw Hill, Inc., (Mc-Graw Hill Training Systems), 1988.

Aimed at easing the setting up and running of a telemarketing department. The book contains five volumes of detailed procedures and forms for everything from acquiring hardware to making the sale and managing the staff.

Each manual is full of concrete information that takes one step-by-step to greater profitability by reducing the cost of sales and increasing productivity. Comprehensive and practical self-study, how-to guides, forms, checklists, worksheets, and samples are included.

Volumes:

Volume 1: The Business and Marketing Plan.

* *Telemarketing Business Plan Tutorial.*

* *Telemarketing Applications, Sales, and Marketing Programs and Mission.*

* *Personnel, Facilities, and Financial Plan.*

* *Sample Telemarketing Business Plan.*

* *Writing the Telemarketing Business Plan.*

* *Resources.*

Volume 2: Personnel Selection, Compensation, and Evaluation.

* *Defining the Telemarketer's Position.*

* *Compensation.*

ENCYCLOPEDIA OF TELEMARKETING

* *Recruiting Candidates.*

* *Evaluating and Selecting Candidates.*

* *Hiring Candidates.*

* *Orientation.*

* *Performance Review Process.*

* *Employee Exit Interview.*

* *Retaining Telemarketers.*

* *Resources.*

Volume 3: Facilities and Equipment.

* *Telemarketing and the Physical Environment.*

* *Creating the Telemarketing Center.*

* *Automating the Telemarketing Operation.*

* *Telecommunications Systems and Equipment.*

* *Telemarketing Facilities Survey and Needs Statements.*

* *Recources.*

Volume 4: Call Management.

* *Sales Inquiry and Lead Tracking.*

* *Business Development.*

* *Customer Referral.*

* *Customer Service.*

* *Customer Survey.*

* *Correspondence.*

* *Automation.*

642

* *Resources.*

Volume 5: The Sales Call Guide--Planning, Scripting, and Selling Skills.

* *Communication Skills.*

* *Precall Planning.*

* *Establishing Rapport with the Customer.*

* *Determining Customer Objections.*

* *Recommending a Customer Action.*

* *Obtaining Customer Commitment.*

* *Dealing with Obstacles.*

* *Wrapping Up the Sale.*

* *Forms.*

* *Resources.*

Format: three-ring binders (5). 908 pages.

Telemarketing: Setting Up for Success, Michael R. Burns. Norwalk, CT: Technology Marketing Corporation, 1987.

A handbook for the new supervisor or manager entering the challenging telemarketing field. It is also intended for newcomers to the telemarketing industry, communicators, TSR's (telephone sales representatives) and telemarketing sales and support staff.

The objective of this book is to provide an outline of basic, but important aspects of the telemarketing function. Critical topics addressed: personnel selection, facilities arrangement, guidelines for telephone service and equipment selection, list selection and segmentation, precall/postcall planning with sample scripts, the development of effective scripts, sales strategies, training and comparison of manually operated telemarketing systems versus automated telemarketing systems.

This book is a training resource for neophytes in the telemarketing field. It is written in a comprehensive manner and assumes virtually no prior knowledge of telemarketing.

Chapter titles:

* *What Is Telemarketing?*

* *Steps for Establishing a Telemarketing Operation.*

* *Personnel.*

* *Facilities--More Than a Desk and a Phone.*

* *List Sources--Whom Do You Call?*

* *Telemarketing Methodologies.*

* *Scripting Basics--Techniques and Examples.*

* *Sales Strategies.*

* *Training for Successful Telemarketing.*

* *Operations.*

* *Glossary of Terms.*

Format: hard cover. 173 pages.

Telephone Marketing: How To Build Your Business by Telephone, Murray Roman. New York, NY: McGraw-Hill Book Company, 1976.

In this trail-breaking volume, one of telemarketing's pioneers reveals proven result-getting concepts, strategies, and techniques of telephone marketing.

It's filled with facts, figures, examples, case studies, do's and don't's, checklists, charts and rules of thumb. It tells how fast a caller should speak. It includes a detailed step-by-step blueprint for planning, conducting and perfecting telephone marketing campaigns.

Because success in telephone marketing depends on careful analysis and planning, the book shows how to develop an accountable telephone marketing plan, structure systems for specific sales programs, design call and program support materials such as taped messages, scripts and communicator response modules, establish controls, record-keeping and cost-accountability procedures for a "production line" system, devise recruiting and training programs for supervisory personnel and telephone communicators, analyze and evaluate programs, project cost and response factors, pretest before program implementation to develop scripts, operator norms, response feedback, and cost per order.

Quite clearly, this book was written for the marketing professional of its day, but even though much of the cost and reference data is now outdated (1976 publication date), many of the original ideas are still sound. One of the classic books on telemarketing and still selling well after 12 years.

Chapter titles:

* *The Multimedia Sales Challenge.*

* *A Modern Approach to Today's Market.*

* *The Range of Applications.*

* *Identifying Your Market--Whom Do You Call?*

* *Your Promotional Message--What Do You Say?*

* *Get Ready, Get Set--Who Will Say It For You?*

* *The Interdependency Factor.*

* *Telephone Economics.*

* *The ''800'' Route to Sales.*

* *Some Guidelines for the Independent Salesperson.*

* *The Eleven Commandments.*

* *The Future State of the Art.*

Format: hard cover. 218 pages.

Total Telemarketing, Robert J. McHatton. New York, NY: John Wiley & Sons, Inc., 1988.
  The objective of this book is to deliver in-depth guidance on all of the practical aspects of telemarketing sales operations. It helps determine if telemarketing is the right choice, discusses how it can integrate into marketing and promotion plans and shows how to analyze costs and benefits.
  It contains advice on equipment and service options, how to do research while selling, figuring the ''break even'' rate, timing and seasonality, kinds of products to telemarket and which to avoid, how to obtain ''hot'' lists, handling credit collections and customer service, telemarketing and the law.
  The book can also serve the seasoned telesales manager as a ready-reference tool, training manual and idea book for an expanding operation. The chapter, ''Understanding the Maze,'' is a guided tour through the complex environment created by the divestiture of AT&T.
  Chapter titles:

* *Dialing for Success.*

* *Managing the Phone Operation.*

* *Economics of Telemarketing.*

* *Understanding the Maze.*

* *An Introduction to Success.*

* *The Telephone Script.*

* *Opening New Accounts.*

* *Hiring and Training the Telecommunicator.*

645

* *Telephone Language and Etiquette.*

* *Prospecting.*

* *A Unique Approach to Closing.*

* *Selling Existing Accounts.*

* *Surveys.*

* *The Art of Inbound Telemarketing.*

* *How To Handle Complaints.*

* *The Telephone and the Law.*

* *The Ethics of Telemarketing.*

* *Success Stories.*

* *Telemarketing Organizations.*

* *Periodicals on Telemarketing.*

* *Glossary of Telemarketing Terms.*

Format: paperback. 246 pages.

STARTUPS AND MANAGING A CENTER: BUSINESS-TO-BUSINESS

Business-to-Business Telemarketing, Jeffrey Pope. New York, NY: AMACOM (American Management Association), 1983.

This book, which focuses on outbound business-to-business telemarketing, assumes the reader is serious enough about telemarketing to be considering a telemarketing center. The author believes if an organization wants to use telemarketing in a planned, systematic way, it will want to move toward such a center. The center doesn't have to be elaborate, he believes, but requires at least three or four phones to begin to get the *control* that is the key to effective telemarketing.

The author assumes that a company will be utilizing telemarketing to *supplement*, not replace the personal sales force, and tells what to do with telephone marketing, how to do it--and also explains why. It's written as a step-by-step guide to telephone marketing.

Chapter titles:

* *The Time Is Right for Telemarketing.*

APPENDIX C: TELEMARKETING BOOKS/MAGAZINES IN PRINT

* *Why Business-to-Business Telephone Marketing Can Succeed Where Consumer Telephone Selling Fails.*

* *Telemarketing Success Factors.*

* *The Business-to-Business Sales Triangle.*

* *Segment Your Sales Effort.*

* *Prospecting.*

* *Profiling.*

* *Qualifying.*

* *Selling.*

* *Servicing.*

* *Where Can Telephone Marketing Work for You?*

* *Ad, Mail, Phone, or Personal?*

* *Inbound, Outbound, or Both?*

* *In-House or Outside Supplier?*

* *The Telephone Marketing Pyramid.*

* *Planning the Program.*

* *Script Writing.*

* *Training Telephone Representatives.*

* *Technical Briefings.*

* *Establishing a Control System.*

* *Lists.*

* *Mailing Literature.*

* *Cost Factors.*

* *Setting Up a Telephone Marketing Center.*

647

* *Analyzing and Reporting Results.*

* *Ten Steps to a Successful Program.*

Format: Three-ring binder. 185 pages.

Telemarketing for Business, Eugene B. Kordahl. Englewood Cliffs, NJ: Prentice Hall, Division of Simon & Schuster, Inc., 1984.

This comprehensive looseleaf guide provides up-to-date information and proven guidance to making the most of telemarketing. It shows how to set up, implement, operate and maintain a successful telemarketing program. It gives a step-by-step master plan that has been worked out in detail and proven in the business world.

Its major thrust is aimed at businesses that wish to sell products and services to other businesses in the commercial/industrial market. Interested marketers, ranging from owners and managers of up-scale small businesses (eight million dollars or more in gross sales) to corporate giants should find this book useful.

The book shows how to increase sales at lower cost, improve customer service, speed development of new products and achieve dramatically higher market penetration.

An invaluable guide for both new or established business-to-business telemarketing centers.

Chapter titles:

* *Consumer vs. Business Telemarketing.*

* *Developing Your Own Basic Telemarketing Plan.*

* *Work Habitat.*

* *Telephone Equipment.*

* *Market Identification and Lists.*

* *Personnel Requirements (Human Resources Planning).*

* *The Telephone Sales Manger's Preparation for Training the Communicator.*

* *Training the Communicator.*

* *Introducing the Program to Your Company.*

* *Managing Communicators: Motivation & Evaluation.*

* *Telemarketing and Data Base Management.*

* *Fulfillment.*

* *Maintaining Your Program.*

* *What Some Other Companies Have Done with Telemarketing and Telesales--10 Case Histories.*

* *Glossary of ''Telephonese'' and Telephone Marketing Terms.*

* *Glossary of Telemarketing Telephone Equipment.*

* *Glossary of ACD Manufacturers.*

* *Glossary of Common Carriers.*

Format: three-ring binder. 324 pages.

STARTUPS AND MANAGING A CENTER: SMALL BUSINESSES

Building Sales Through Telemarketing, Jan Watrous-McCabe. Hinsdale, IL: CES, Inc., 1988.

Positioned for the small business market, this book covers the basics while not being intimidating to the reader. Especially appealing to the small business person should be the relative ease, albeit professional approach to the intricacies of going into telemarketing for the first time.

The author guides the individual through telemarketing basics: sales skills, listening and verbal skills and how to develop a quality telemarketing script. The book provides a self-paced individualized study. Learning and self-evaluation are provided by the practice case at the end of the text.

Chapter titles:

* *Telemarketing Basics.*

* *Listening Skills.*

* *Verbal Skills.*

* *Sales Skills.*

* *Steps of the Call.*

* *Types of Telemarketing Scripts.*

* *Developing a Script.*

* *Practice Case.*

* *Examination Case.*

Format: three-ring binder. 71 pages.

STRATEGIES

Integrated Direct Marketing, Ernan Roman. New York, NY: McGraw-Hill Book Company, 1988.

Integrated direct marketing (IDM) is the art of creating coordinated multimedia direct-response campaigns. Instead of asking individual experts to build response rates to direct mail, telemarketing, broadcast and print media, etc., in isolation, today's marketing managers must learn to deploy their forces in mutually supportive, carefully organized and thoroughly integrated campaigns to cut through the clutter and win the hearts and minds of the target market.

This book shows how it's done, beginning with an explanation of the theory behind direct-response media integration, then exploring the practical issues that must be tackled to achieve success. While IDM is a new concept for most businesses today, some of the top direct-response marketers in the country have already proven that the technique can dramatically increase the return on marketing dollars invested. This book reveals their secrets of success through in-depth case histories from AT&T, IBM, Citicorp and others, along with authoritative insights and how-to guidelines from America's leading direct marketing consultants.

From all of these materials taken together, the reader should gain a firm grasp of the fundamental concepts of IDM, practical tips and techniques to be put into action immediately, and a vision of the phenomenal growth potential available to those with the insight to embrace IDM today.

Chapter titles:

* *A New Marketing Philosophy.*

* *Creating Synergy Through Media Selection and Deployment.*

* *Strategic Planning for IDM Success.*

* *Issues for Implementing IDM at Your Company.*

* *The Creative Challenge of IDM.*

* *New Tactics for Database Marketing.*

* *Toward an IDM Future.*

* *Making It Work--A Management Checklist.*

Format: hard cover. 288 pages.

The Marketing Revolution, Richard L. Bencin. Philadelphia, PA: Cresheim Publications, an imprint of Swansea Press, Inc., 1984.

This book puts the concept of telemarketing into the perspective of the new strategies under which modern companies and organizations operate. The author helps the reader step outside of the typically narrow focus of telemarketing books to take a useful and valuable wider view. His contention is that an understanding of the many trends affecting marketing in general is necessary to capture the full power and potential of the medium.

The book is thoroughly researched and filled with interesting ideas and information drawn from virtually every key marketing, direct marketing and telemarketing publication, as well as the well-known and respected specialists in these fields. The author presents a wide-ranging review of the ideas of every major writer and thinker in marketing today, developing for the reader a clear picture of the opportunities and risks facing marketers.

The Marketing Revolution is important reading for marketers, in general, but can be particularly useful for telemarketers. The chapter devoted to telemarketing outlines telemarketing's growth, its benefits, uses and primary applications. The emphasis is on defining the rationale for telemarketing as a coordinated part of the organization's overall sales and marketing strategies.

A carefully documented overview of the most pervasive marketing trends today, each of which impact on and are affected by telemarketing.

Chapters (Marketing Megatrends):

* *Mass Magazines to Specialty Magazines.*

* *In-Person Shopping to Convenience Shopping.*

* *Field Sales to Alternate Marketing Channels.*

* *Storekeeping to Retailing.*

* *Indirect Sales to Direct Marketing.*

* *Telephone Selling to Telemarketing.*

* *Image Advertising to Direct Response Advertising.*

* *Network Television to Cable Television.*

* *In-Store Shopping/Print Catalogs to Electronic Catalogs.*

* *Imprecise Marketing to Scientific Marketing.*

Format: hard cover. 219 pages.

Strategic Telemarketing: How to Fit This New Medium into Your Marketing Plans,
Richard L. Bencin. Philadelphia, PA: Cresheim Publications, an imprint of Swansea Press, Inc., 1987.

This book takes marketing and telemarketing managers beyond the usual tactical approach. It goes beyond scripts, space design and equipment to take the first strategic look at the new medium, and defines how it can fit an organization's overall marketing strategy.

It covers the nuts and bolts, describing in detail many of the specific mechanical aspects of a telemarketing operation. In this sense, the book could be considered a primer for the neophyte telemarketing manager. But the bulk of the book goes beyond discussion of tactics into the applications telemarketing can have as a functioning part of an overall marketing effort.

This "synergy" discussion is, perhaps, the book's most significant contribution.

According to the author, telemarketing can only work when it's part of an overall, sophisticated marketing program. It must be carefully planned, with substantial commitments of personnel and financial support from management. Telemarketing is a process, and this book shows how to understand, organize, and manage that process, especially how to integrate it with field sales efforts.

Chapter titles:

* *Telemarketing in Today's World.*

* *Strategic Implications of the "New" Medium.*

* *Planning and Controlling the Telemarketing Program.*

* *The Basics of Telemarketing.*

* *Handling Objections.*

* *Computers and Telemarketing.*

* *Auditing the Results.*

* *How To Get Help.*

* *Catalog Telemarketing.*

* *Inquiries: Closing the Advertising Loop Electronically.*

* *The 10 Biggest Mistakes Telemarketers Make.*

* *Integrating Field Sales with Telemarketing.*

* *A Telemarketing Glossary.*

Format: hard cover. 182 pages.

TELEPHONE ALLOCATION

How Many Phones Do You Really Need?, Paul S. Bender and Warren Blanding. Silver Spring, MD: Customer Service Institute, a Division of Marketing Publications, Inc., 1986.

Today, customer service managers are under a great deal of pressure to cut costs and increase productivity in handling the inbound telephone calls that increasingly occupy the time of their personnel. This book is written to help them.

Its step-by-step method for telephone planning was developed primarily for managers of small to medium departments which do not enjoy the economies of scale--and the engineering support--available to their counterparts in credit card companies, hotel and airline reservation centers, insurance companies and other large organizations. Ideally each system should be fully engineered to the individual company, however, that is not always practical.

It's axiomatic that before you can go someplace you have to know where you're starting from. The first chapters of this book will help one to make an assessment in terms of call content and practices--and what one might do to reduce some calls, eliminate others, and handle still others by alternative means.

The chapter on setting objectives on call content and quality is worth special attention, because this is the final determinant of how many phones are needed and the caliber of the people who will be manning them.

Chapter 5 deals with the actual calculations and is basically a do-it-yourself technique for testing the relative cost of different options: shorter calls and longer holds, longer calls and shorter holds, more people and better service, fewer people and lower costs, etc.

Chapter titles:

* *Profile Current Call Patterns.*

* *Identify Avoidable and Reducible Calls.*

* *Improve Call Balance.*

* *Set Objectives for Call Content and Quality.*

* *Making Your Calculations.*

* *Queuing Tables.*

Format: paperback. 43 pages.

TELEPHONE SALES FOR OUTSIDE SALES REPS

Cold Call Techniques (That Really Work!), Stephan Schiffman. Boston, MA: Bob Adams, Inc., 1987.

Salespersons are faced with the constant, bewildering problems of "getting those appointments," and turning a list of names and phone numbers into a calendar filled with solid prospects waiting to meet with them.

This book is a clear, step-by-step, guaranteed (by the author) guide to success in this often-neglected, vitally important area.

The author asserts that the plan has worked for thousands of salespeople at top companies across the country and will help sales reps to: discover the one simple phrase that can turn around the vast majority of objections, learn how to be one's own sales manager, find out how to monitor calls and set goals based upon personal statistics, determine exactly how much time per week should be allocated to cold calling, and see how business is like a war. . .and learning what one's role is on the battlefield.

Chapter titles:

* *The One Successful Way To Call.*

* *Getting an Appointment.*

* *Handling Objections.*

* *Soft Selling: Persistence and Enthusiasm.*

* *"How'm I Doing?"*

* *The Perils of Reinventing the Wheel.*

* *Business as War.*

* *Conclusion: The Lemonade Stand.*

* *Sample Scripts.*

Format: paperback. 118 pages.

Everyone's Guide to Opening Doors by Telephone, Sam Aronson. San Mateo, CA: Talmud Press, 1981.

This book/tape presentation is considered by some to be the definitive guide for telephone-appointment setting and persuasion projects.

A system shows how one can get a face-to-face interview for every two phone calls to people who can say "yes" to a proposition. Twenty-seven tested scripts are provided along with Persuasion Guidesheets with real examples actually detailed and recorded.

The telephone-appointment setting procedures were proven under a year-long test under the sponsorship of a multi-billion-dollar sales organization, The Equitable Life Assurance Society of the United States, and they can be used for selling, job finding, fund raising and persuasion projects (calling a meeting and getting a big turnout, getting a raise, etc.).

Chapter titles:

* *How To Use This Book.*

* *How Important Is Getting In?*

* *Getting Started with Two Easy Telephone Scripts.*

* *Closing the Sale or Other Transaction.*

* *A Name, A Name, My Kingdom for a Name!*

* *Good Work Habits and the Magic of Working Jointly.*

* *Selling Insurance--How I Sold 14 Out of 10 Mortgage Cancellation Cases!*

*	*Selling Real Estate.*

*	*Raising Funds for Charity.*

*	*Calling a Meeting--And Getting a Big Turnout!*

*	*Getting a Better Job.*

*	*Scoring in Public Relations.*

*	*Making Up with an Angry Friend.*

*	*If You Specialize in Wholesale.*

*	*Getting a Raise--Making Up Your Own Script.*

*	*19 Ways To Get All the In-Person Interviews You'll Need.*

*	*Additional Closing Techniques--Sophisticated but Learnable.*

*	*Becoming Permanently Motivated--Something Brand New.*

*	*Converting Telephone Approaches into In-Person Ones.*

*	*Final Tips for Success.*

Format: paperback and a two-sided cassette tape. 349 pages.

How To Increase Sales and Put Yourself Across by Telephone, Mona Ling. Englewood Cliffs, NJ: Prentice Hall, Division of Simon & Schuster, Inc., 1963.

This is the oldest telemarketing book in print. Originally copyrighted in 1963, it was recently re-published in 1987.

It's a complete primer for field sales reps in helping them to make qualified appointments by telephone. Practical ways for sales reps to increase their face-to-face selling time with the most likely prospects are included.

Special chapters feature making appointments by telephone in real estate and insurance.
Chapter titles:

*	*The Creation of a Verbal Universe.*

*	*Why Telephone Skills Will Increase Sales.*

*	*How To Prepare and Organize for Telephoning.*

*	*Important Factors in Developing a Presentation.*

ENCYCLOPEDIA OF TELEMARKETING

* *How To Write a Presentation.*

* *How To Get Appointments by Telephone.*

* *How To Get Insurance Appointments by Telephone.*

* *How To Get Real Estate Appointments by Telephone.*

* *How To Overcome Objections.*

* *The Many Kinds of Buyers.*

* *The Expert Buyer.*

* *The Open-Minded Buyer.*

* *The Individualistic Buyer.*

* *The Indecisive Buyer.*

* *The Timid Buyer.*

* *The Logical Buyer.*

* *The Complainer Buyer.*

* *The Price Buyer.*

* *The Bully Buyer.*

* *The Emotional Buyer.*

* *The Stubborn Buyer.*

* *The Flirt Buyer.*

* *Modern Telephone Shopping.*

* *How the Secretary Should Handle Telephone Calls.*

* *Development of Listening Skills.*

* *How To Improve Your Speech.*

* *Effective Management Communications.*

Format: paperback. 262 pages.

How To Win More Business by Phone, Bernard Katz. London, England: Business Books, Ltd., an imprint of The Hutchinson Publishing Group, 1983. (Available in the U.S. through Brookfield Publishing Company, Brookfield, VT.).

This book contains advice on how to plan and execute telephone selling calls and provides a comprehensive guide to all practical aspects of selling by phone. Topics include selecting who to phone, the preparation needed for each call, how to overcome objections, how to be in control of the call, how to close the sale and how to combine telephone selling with other methods of marketing.

The book is for sales people, sales managers and for any reader who wants to win more business. Chapter titles:

* *How To Prospect for Business by Phone.*

* *How To Get Appointments.*

* *How To Match Benefits to Needs.*

* *How To Overcome Objections and Win.*

* *How To Communicate on the Phone.*

* *How To Plan the Sales Call.*

* *How To Plan the Sales Presentation.*

* *How To Close That Sale.*

* *How To Plan for the Repeat Sale.*

* *How To Answer the Telephone.*

* *How To Write the Follow-up Letter.*

* *Self-Help Test.*

Format: paperback. 200 pages.

Phoneworks Sales Lead Prospecting Manual, Walter T. Hupalo and Charles D. Wiemers. Washington, D.C.: Inmark Corporation, 1988.

This is a guide to creating a more productive sales-lead generation system by quickly identifying qualified potential customers and their needs and setting up face-to-face meetings with sales reps.

Provides proven "how to" techniques and concepts to make the phone a more creative, productive sales prospecting medium for quickly identifying potential buyers, zeroing in on their needs and setting appointments. It provides concise, fast reading for sales people, regardless of level of experience.

Helps to create the tactics field sales reps need to fight the battles in the field, dominate the territory,

657

and beat competition to the sale.

Sections:

* *A Comparison: Phone vs. Face-to-Face Presentations.*

* *The Marketing Mix: Where Your Sales Leads Come From.*

* *Self Management: Sales Prospecting in a Planned and Systematic Manner.*

* *A Good Ear: Listening as a Strategy and Tactic.*

* *Do's and Don't's: Basic Rules to Better Sales Lead Prospecting by Phone.*

* *The Art of Using Questions.*

* *Projecting a Desirable Image: Your Voice Is an Asset.*

* *The Path to the Decision-Maker: Getting Through to the Right Person.*

* *Getting Past the Gatekeeper: How to Beat the Screener.*

* *Overview.*

* *Making Your Introduction.*

* *The Body of the Presentation.*

* *Going for the Close.*

* *Handling Questions and Objections.*

* *Accurate Note Taking.*

* *Forms Addendum.*

Format: spiral bound. 104 pages.

"Salesman Calling," H. Gordon Bethards. Skokie, IL: Century Communications, Inc., 1984.

In 1975 a script was written for a sound tape under the title, "Pay Phone Pay." The intended audience were sales representatives who normally sold face-to-face.

The script has been edited and shortened and reproduced in print. However, the dialogue style has been retained. The narrator is Bill and the author is Gordon. They are the principal speakers, but there are also 16 skits employing 23 different actors.

This book is not about telephone selling per se. It's about using the telephone to complement face-to-face selling. It's about how a seller can increase coverage, save time and gain sales through simple, easy-to-learn-and-practice telephone techniques.

It also deals with the subject of telephoning for appointments. The emphasis is not on how to get appointments, but rather on why one should ask for appointments. Included are six reasons why telephoning in advance of a personal visit will help sales grow.

Chapter titles:

I. Complement Face-to-Face Selling.

*   *Ask for the Order.*

*   *Solving Problems.*

*   *Planning Is the Key.*

*   *A Planned Call.*

*   *A One-Time Proposition.*

*   *Qualify the Prospect.*

*   *Again, Ask for the Order.*

*   *To Call or Not To Call.*

*   *Summary I.*

II. Telephoning for Appointments.

*   *When To Telephone.*

*   *Courtesy.*

*   *Importance.*

*   *Preparation.*

*   *Confirmed Appointments.*

*   *Time Savings.*

*   *Productivity.*

*   *Summary II.*

Format: paperback. 75 pages.

Using the Telephone in Selling, Patrick Forsyth. Brookfield, VT: Gower Publishing Company, 1985.

The author first reviews the basics of telephone techniques, and explains where the telephone fits into the buying process. He then takes the reader step by step through the process of planning a call, making it and following it up. There are chapters on arranging appointments and on the sometimes difficult business of handling incoming calls (including complaints).

The text itself is laid out in workbook style, with charts, forms and checklists where appropriate, and contains exercises designed both to reinforce the points made in the text and to help relate them more directly to the reader's own circumstances.

The package includes an audio tape with a variety of examples linked to the text.

Chapter titles:

* *Why Use the Telephone?*

* *Telephone Technique.*

* *The Buying Process.*

* *Before the Call.*

* *Getting Through to the Right Person.*

* *Making the Call.*

* *Making Appointments.*

* *Incoming Calls-Inquiries/Complaints.*

* *After the Call.*

* *Analyzing Performance.*

* *Summary and Review: Using the Audio Tape.*

Format: paperback and audio cassette tape. 73 pages.

TELEPHONE SALES SKILLS

Advanced Telemarketing: Blueprint for Telemarketing Sales Success, Mary D. Pekas. Sioux Falls, SD: Telemarketing Institute, Inc., 1985.

This book is the core material for the *Conversational Soft Sell*™ approach to telemarketing. In it are the building blocks of an effective sales approach done in a non-threatening, soft-sell manner.

Readers will learn to write their own telephone sales scripts for products, services and appointments in their own language following a scientifically designed approach to identifying personality types.

Sections:

APPENDIX C: TELEMARKETING BOOKS/MAGAZINES IN PRINT

* *Introduction.*

* *Opening.*

* *Fact-Finding.*

* *Persuading.*

* *Closing.*

* *Mind Programming of Permanent Forms by Spaced Repetition.*

* *Sales Analysis Overview/Opening Practice.*

* *Opening Analysis/Fact-Finding Practice.*

* *Fact-Finding Analysis/Persuading Practice.*

* *Persuading Analysis/Closing Practice.*

* *Closing Analysis/Objection Answer Development.*

* *Objection Answer Individualization.*

* *Objection Analysis/Mind-Writing of Sales Conversations.*

* *Mind Programming of Objections.*

* *Completed Sales Conversations.*

* *Ideas on Ongoing Workshops That Can Be Conducted.*

* *Appointment-Securing System.*

Format: three-ring binder. 236 pages.

Basic Telemarketing, Mary D. Pekas. Sioux Falls, SD: Telemarketing Institute, Inc., 1985.

This book is a course designed to develop a professional telephone style. It focuses on telephone fluency and delivery through the four elements of conversation: word, voice, listening and attitude.

Once learned and practiced, the exercises contained within the text should provide the TSR's with the framework for lifelong telemarketing skill building and renewal.

The basic TSR text is accompanied with an Instructor's Manual and an action tape series. Sections:

* *Introduction.*

* *Mind Power.*

* *Word Power.*

* *Voice Power.*

* *Listening Power.*

* *Telephone Lab/Record Management.*

* *Suggested Reference Books.*

* *Telephone Lab Sample Scripts.*

Format: paperback and six, two-sided tapes. Book is 348 pages. Instructor's Manual is 158 pages.

Gary Goodman's 60-Second Salesperson, Dr. Gary S. Goodman. Englewood Cliffs, NJ: Prentice Hall, Division of Simon & Schuster, Inc., 1985.

The objective of this book is to teach the reader to master the telephone sales process and make every second count.

Specifically, and *within 10-second increments*, the book teaches how to psych up before getting on the phone, build rapport with strangers, establish credibility, create desire, construct appealing offers, engineer commitment and seal the deal.

All within a 60-second call. A most unique book.

Chapter titles:

* *Your 60-Second Psych-Up.*

* *The First 10 Seconds, Building Rapport.*

* *The Second 10 Seconds, Positioning and Credibility.*

* *The Third 10 Seconds, Describing Your Products and Services.*

* *The Fourth 10 Seconds, Fashioning the Offer.*

* *The Fifth 10 Seconds, Creating Commitment.*

* *The Final 10 Seconds, Sealing the Deal.*

Format: hard cover. 100 pages.

How To Be a Successful Telephone Sales Representative, Gail Cohen. New York, NY: American Management Association Extension Institute, 1984.

A complete telephone sales skills course including six two-sided cassettes and a workbook. Summaries are provided in the workbook to assist in studying and reviewing course material. Cassettes refer

662

to various exhibits contained in the workbook.

A case study is provided. By considering the situation presented in the case and answering questions based upon the information learned in the body of the course, one can sharpen his or her knowledge of the subject of telephone sales.

A Pre-Test and Post-Test have also been included. Grading is done by the Course Service. Chapters and tape sides:

* *History, Use and Benefits of Telephone Sales.*

* *Preparing for Successful Telephone Sales.*

* *Establishing Contact and Creating Interest.*

* *Probing for Relevant Facts.*

* *Preparing and Delivering the Sales Message.*

* *Asking for the Sale.*

* *Understanding and Preparing for Objections.*

* *Handling Objections.*

* *Setting Objectives and Organizing for Results.*

* *A Case Study: Phil A. Buster Realtors, Inc.*

Format: paperback and six two-sided cassette tapes. 138 pages.

Phone Power: How To Make the Telephone Your Most Profitable Business Tool, George R. Walther. New York, NY: G.P. Putnam's Sons, 1986.

This book is written for profit-motivated executives, results-oriented telemarketers, time-pressured secretaries, problem-pummeled customer service agents and anyone else who relies heavily on the telephone in business.

It provides techniques and strategies to save time handling disorganized, overly talkative callers; negotiate more favorable agreements without leaving your office; end "phone-tag" frustrations and reach whomever you call much faster; create favorable first impressions and start off on a positive footing; defuse irate complainers and build bridges of rapport; and increase one's success ratio, whether selling products or collecting past-due accounts. It shows how to cut literally hours each week from the time spent on the phone. It gives secrets to connecting with people--and to making sure people you *don't* want to talk to never connect with you.

This book offers examples from major companies such as American Express, General Electric, and Clairol, all of which have used the telephone to increase their profitability, as well as simple tips that secretaries and receptionists can use to make office life easier.

Chapter titles:

* *Phone Tag: Avoid Being "It."*

* *Opening Doors: Ease Through Any Labyrinth.*

* *Phone Time: Accomplish More in Less Time.*

* *Power Talking: Project More Authority with Your Voice and Words.*

* *Phone Relations: Elevate Your Organization's Public Image.*

* *Wired Emotions: Deal Positively with Irate, Disturbed and Demented Callers.*

* *Phonegotiating: Reach Win/Win Agreements by Phone.*

* *Dialing for Dollars: Collect Past-Due Accounts and Cut Back on A/R Problems.*

* *Profitable Telemarketing: Meeting Your Customers' Needs.*

Format: hard cover. 192 pages.

Prospecting Your Way to Sales Success: How to Find New Business by Phone, Bill Good. New York, NY: Charles Scribner's Sons, 1986.

Anyone who does any prospecting or selling by phone--from securities, insurance and real estate brokers to fund-raisers, suppliers and bankers--knows the frustrations and rejections of "cold calling." Here the author shares his techniques for creating a successful telephone prospecting campaign.

"Old School" methods, with their don't-believe-a-customer-who-says-no philosophy, can be time-wasting and demoralizing. The author suggests stopping the attempt to grind a "yes" out of a prospect who says "no" (and means it). Instead, he suggests getting results by finding more and better qualified prospects. This book is written to help in finding customers who are ready to buy now ("cherries") while screening out unqualified, uninterested customers ("pits").

This book helps in the design of a complete, customized telephone prospecting campaign, from the first call to the final close. Topics include how to qualify prospective customers; how to study a product or service and design an appropriate sales message; how to create, order, evaluate and maintain a "bathtub" of lists; how to develop and test scripts, including sample scripts for a variety of products and services; how to make more calls and how to close and when to close.

Also included are special tips on motivation, time management, and record keeping, charts to help keep track of progress and a special section on troubleshooting common problems that will fine-tune a prospecting campaign to peak performance. A final chapter addresses the particular problems of sales managers.

Chapter titles:

* *Prospecting: The Old School Versus the New School.*

* *Applying the Principles of the New School.*

* *What You Say: To Script or Not.*

* *Script Writing Part I: Finding Your Cherries with the First of Two Calls.*

* *Script Writing Part II: Appointment Scripts.*

* *List Development--Part I: Filling the Bathtub.*

* *List Development--Part II: How to Keep the Bathtub Full.*

* *Managing Your Prospects.*

* *How You Sound.*

* *How to Make More Calls.*

* *Breakout: Putting it All Together.*

* *For Managers Only (Or How To Work Some Magic with Your Sales Force).*

Format: hard cover. 242 pages.

Reach Out and Sell Someone: Phone Your Way to Profit and Success Through the Goodman System of Telemarketing, Dr. Gary S. Goodman. Englewood Cliffs, NJ: Prentice Hall, Division of Simon & Schuster, Inc., 1983.

This book shows step-by-step how the telemarketing alternative to personal sales visits can increase sales by increasing selling time. According to the author, these techniques, tested in every major industry in America over the past 14 years, have helped thousands of salespeople increase their profits. From opening calls smoothly, to handling objections, to closing the sale, this book explains the requirements for selling any product or service better.

It includes such information as answers to the 30 most-asked questions about telemarketing, 60 golden rules of telemarketing (what you should know, have at hand, think, do and not do when you sell by telephone), how to overcome the fear of rejection (and how to develop the go-for-it attitude on each and every call) and how to manage and motivate telemarketers.

Chapter titles:

* *The Thirty Most-Asked Questions About Telemarketing and Management.*

* *The Psychology of Telemarketing.*

* *The Sixty Telemarketing Canons.*

665

* *The Anatomy of a Telemarketing Call.*

* *How To Handle Resistance and Objections.*

* *Managing Telemarketers.*

Format: paperback. 141 pages.

Selling on the Phone, James D. Porterfield. New York, NY: Wiley Press, a Division of John Wiley & Sons, Inc., 1985.

This book is designed to teach sales personnel (not their bosses) how to develop a successful selling system before they make their first call (and their first mistake).

Step by step, this activities-oriented handbook shows how to determine what's important about a product and how to use this product knowledge to sell, how to qualify the potential customer, how to handle more informed buyers, how to manage customer objections and how to close a sale.

This five-step selling system is intended to help basic selling skills become second nature. Numerous self-assessment exercises pinpoint areas that need improvement immediately, and frequent applications activities help decide what techniques best complement personal style.

Chapters/appendices:

* *An Introduction to Telemarketing.*

* *What Goes into a Sale.*

* *How To Use Product Knowledge to Your Advantage.*

* *A Basic Sales-Call Strategy.*

* *Prospecting.*

* *The Attention-Grabber.*

* *Analyzing Needs.*

* *An Action-Getting Presentation.*

* *Answering Objections.*

* *Asking for the Order.*

* *Building Obstacle-Free Communication Channels.*

* *Your Positive Mental Attitude.*

* *Using Words That Sell.*

* *A Teleselling Voice.*

* *Effective Listening.*

* *Performance Evaluation Test.*

* *Call Flow Pattern.*

* *A Sample Multi-Call Work Plan.*

* *Developing a Script.*

Format: paperback. 146 pages.

Selling Skills for the Non-Salesperson: For People Who Hate To Sell But Love To Succeed, Dr. Gary S. Goodman. Englewood Cliffs, NJ: Prentice Hall, Division of Simon & Schuster, Inc., 1984.

This book is geared for the person who has to persuade others in everyday life but doesn't have the title "salesperson."

Written in a lively way, this book shows how to be attractive to other people and have them like you, build credibility and an aura of expertise, create winning sales presentations, handle difficult people and master objections, overcome the psychological hurdles of selling, develop telephone skills, determine which prospects are worthwhile and which ones to avoid, before investing precious time and much more to help become a successful persuader.

Chapter titles:

* *The Selling Game.*

* *How To Put Your Best Self Forward.*

* *Profile of the Successful Salesperson.*

* *Anatomy of a Sale.*

* *Mastering Objections and Difficult Customers.*

* *Professional Telemarketing Techniques.*

Format: paperback. 138 pages.

Selling Successfully by Telephone, Harrold Hayden. New York, NY: Sales Builders, Division of *Sales & Marketing Management*, 1977.

This basic telephone selling training program is divided into two segments. Part I (which includes Cassette #1 and the Administrator's Guide) is designed for the manager and/or trainer and utilizes an interview format to give a feel for the variety of ways the telephone can be used to sell more effectively and the benefits of doing so. The booklet itself is designed to enable the effective administration of the telephone selling program.

Part II (which includes Cassettes #2, 3 and 4 and the Workbook) is the training program itself, and is designed to be used in training a sales staff to perform effectively with the telephone in hand.

This program is designed to enable one, with a minimum of manager involvement, to train staff to utilize the phone with great effectiveness.

Chapters and tapes:

* *How To Plan a Telephone Sales Campaign.*

* *How To Plan a Telephone Sales Call.*

* *How To Get Selling Points Across.*

* *How To Close the Sale.*

Format: a spiral binder workbook; paperback administrator's guide; and four cassette tapes. 81 total pages.

Successful Telephone Selling in the 80s, Martin D. Shafiroff and Robert L. Shook. New York, NY: Harper & Row, Publishers, Inc., 1982. Paperback: Barnes & Noble Books, a Division of Harper & Row, Publishers, Inc., New York, NY, 1983.

Successful selling over the telephone, as with personal sales visits, depends on learning the right techniques and practicing them. This book is aimed at teaching those techniques, which the authors believe can work for everyone.

Moreover, a central premise of the book is the assertion that almost anything can be sold by telephone. In certain industries the telephone has been the conventional marketing tool for years; the selling of securities is a prime example. But products rarely associated with telephone selling can also be sold by phone, according to the authors, including high-ticket items like life insurance, real estate and even fine art.

This book is intended to help a reader discover the methods that work for the top telephone salespersons in the country, methods that can help guarantee success. The authors ask the reader to forget any preconceived notions about the limitation of telephone selling.

Many actual selling experiences of the authors as well as other top salespersons across the U.S. are detailed. The Acknowledgments list a veritable Who's Who of successful salespeople.

Chapter titles:

* *The Telephone: A Cost, Time and Energy Saver.*

* *Using Your Time Profitably on the Telephone.*

* *Getting Through to the Right Person.*

* *The Initial Approach.*

* *The Telephone Presentation.*

668

* *How To Handle Every Objection Ever Made.*

* *Closing the Sale.*

* *Follow-Up.*

* *Servicing the Customer.*

* *Attitude and Self-Image.*

* *How To Sell Yourself on the Telephone.*

* *Speaking Effectively.*

* *Listening.*

* *Women in Telephone Selling.*

Format: both hard cover and paperback . 171 pages.

Telemarketing: High Profit Telephone Selling Techniques, Gerald J. Ortland. New York, NY: John Wiley & Sons, Inc., 1982.

This book offers a self-paced professional short course covering every aspect of telemarketing, from basics to advanced selling methods, in an easy, step-by-step format. The material covers techniques developed by the author over a dozen plus years of successful telephone selling including developing prospects, overcoming telephone anxiety and closing the sale over the phone.

This book allows the reader to pace learning and to monitor the program on an ongoing basis through exercise and review materials. Each chapter opens with a list of the key concepts that one encounters as each chapter is read. Most chapters contain at least one brief quiz (Quick Quiz) that should be used to reinforce the points made in the prior reading material. At the end of the chapter there is a brief chapter summary followed by a Checkpoint Test, which gives one an opportunity to measure the mastery of the chapter material.

Chapter titles:

* *Conquering the Fear of Selling.*

* *Developing and Maintaining Self-Confidence.*

* *Speaking and Listening Effectively.*

* *Turning Negative Replies into Advantages.*

* *Never Apologize for Calling.*

* *Preparing and Using Winning Sales Presentations.*

* *How To Get and Stay Motivated.*

* *Your Telephone Headquarters: An Overview.*

* *Planning, Developing and Operating Your Headquarters.*

* *Communicating with and Through Your Secretary.*

* *Forms for Controlling Your Telephone Business.*

* *Telephone Marketing Advantages.*

* *Expanding Your Business.*

* *The Telephone in Marketing and Advertising Promotional Efforts.*

* *Overcoming Competition by Servicing Clientele.*

* *Closing Telephone Sales Professionally.*

* *You Alone Create Your Own Destiny.*

Format: three-ring binder. 171 pages.

Telephone Sales Training System, Eugene Kordahl, Randolph, NJ: National Telemarketing, Inc., 1983.

A complete *telephone sales training system*, this manual uses programmed learning under a closely managed environment. Readers are asked to answer questions, fill in a blank, make a choice or, in short, *do* things while they learn.

The book positions programmed learning as being very desirable to ensure uniform understanding of the material. However, the manager of the telephone sales operation is very actively involved as a facilitator of the sales training material.

Role playing, preparing the training facilities, preparing the personnel and training equipment are all part of the author's system of telephone sales training.

Sections:

* *Introduction.*

* *Manager's Workshop Manual.*

* *Basic Telephone Techniques.*

* *Sales Instruction Manual.*

* *Product Application.*

Format: three-ring binder. 119 pages.

APPENDIX C: TELEMARKETING BOOKS/MAGAZINES IN PRINT

Telephone Selling Report (Volumes I - IV), Art Sobczak. Omaha, NE: TeleMarketing Design, Inc., 1988.

These manuals contain the complete set of articles from Volume I through Volume IV of *Telephone Selling Report*, covering June 1984 to May 1988. Because this information is timeless, these ideas and tips are just as valuable today (and will continue to be so in the future) as the day they were first published.

Each article has been categorized by topic for easy access. These topics are clearly identified in the Table of Contents, on the divider tabs, and at the top of each page. Furthermore, the spine and tabs of each Volume are color-coded for quick identification.

Selling by phone is a skill. As with any skill, its mastery requires continual exposure to new ideas, review of previously covered material, and practice to transform the ideas into habits. The articles in these Volumes provide information useful in increasing sales and profits.

The author is extremely widely read. That knowledge, combined with his long experience, means that these Volumes represent one of the most comprehensive sources of telephone sales skill information anywhere.

There are many ways to use the manuals. Managers can adapt various articles to fit their own situations, and incorporate the ideas into their own training programs, or use complete topics/articles for sales meeting discussions. More importantly, individual telephone reps can use these Volumes to work independently on selected areas needing improvement.

Sections:

*   *Self Improvement.*

*   *Communication: Speaking.*

*   *Communication: Listening.*

*   *Screeners.*

*   *Opening Statements.*

*   *Probing.*

*   *Sales Message.*

*   *Closing.*

*   *Objections.*

*   *Call Management.*

*   *Customers.*

*   *Resources.*

*   *Telemarketing.*

* *TeleTips.*

Format: spiral bound. Volume I through Volume IV. 526 pages.

Winning by Telephone: Telephone Effectiveness for Business Professionals and Consumers, Dr. Gary S. Goodman. Englewood Cliffs, NJ: Prentice Hall, Division of Simon & Schuster, Inc., 1982.

This book, according to the publisher, is for people who are tired of being victimized by "blabbers" and "ramblers" who never get to the point; frustrated by being put on hold and transferred from department to department when seeking information; or exasperated with having to make *another* callback because of forgetting "just one little thing."

It offers tips for solving these and other common telephone problems and making one's calls more productive and profitable. It presents techniques for making the most out of every call, including how to manage time effectively on the phone by controlling conversations and smart call planning, how to develop a "telephone ear" to quickly react to the other person's "hidden agendas" for the call, and what to do when there's a problem listener on the line.

There are also discussions of how to manage conflict calls and difficult people without getting angry and defensive yourself, how to develop a "power voice" to sound credible, trustworthy and authoritative on-the-spot, while organizing ideas in seconds, how to use the telephone to build the professional image of the caller's organization, and how to "fight back" as a consumer.

Chapter titles:

* *Tele-Time Management.*

* *Developing the Telephone Ear: Listening Problems, Opportunities and Tips.*

* *Developing Your Power Voice: Building Credibility and Persuasiveness.*

* *Customer Relations: Handling Telephone Conflict.*

* *The Telephone in the Professional Office.*

* *Fighting Back: The Consumer's Guide to the Telephone.*

Format: paperback. 144 pages.

You Can Sell Anything by Telephone!, Dr. Gary S. Goodman. Englewood Cliffs, NJ: Prentice Hall, Division of Simon & Schuster, Inc., 1984.

What would happen if you put a half-million-dollar computer, a $200,000 Rolls-Royce, and a $10,000 Salvador Dali work of art together? You'd be looking at three very pricey items that the author claims can all be sold by telephone using the techniques he has developed.

This book takes the reader through several case studies on how to sell anything, no matter how great or small; which words to use and which to avoid in building a winning sales talk; how to think and sound like a savvy telemarketer; and how to overcome secretarial screening agreeably, master phone-fear and call reluctance and control conversations with finesse and ease.

Chapter titles:

* *From Rolls-Royce to Pink Elephants.*

* *How To Sell Yourself Over the Phone.*

* *The Anatomy of Success: Developing Patterned Sales Presentations.*

* *How To Sell Any Product or Service by Phone.*

* *Special Challenges in Telemarketing.*

* *There Is an Answer for Every Objection!*

Format: paperback. 119 pages.

TELEPHONE SALES SKILLS: CORPORATE ENVIRONMENT

Telemarketing: The Corporate-Caller Skills Program, Barry Z. Masser and William M. Leeds. New York, NY: MacMillan Publishing Company, 1984.

This training and reference tool devoted to the professional business-to-business telemarketer, field sales reps and their supervisors is presented in three sections:

Part I is devoted to program-building. While, in normal circumstances a company's management will plan and do most of the implementation work on a telemarketing program, the authors believe an adept caller should fully comprehend the process and be able to accomplish the initial steps if need be.

Part II concentrates on caller skills. This, according to the authors, is the substance that separates just another caller from a top income producer. Every topic in Part II is built from caller experience in companies deeply involved and dependent on telemarketing.

Part III is on strategies and controls, the substance that holds a program together and gives it direction and purpose. It is the area of frequent difficulty in otherwise good telemarketing programs and is, therefore, a beneficial knowledge area for today's caller and tomorrow's marketing tactician.

Chapter titles:

* *What It Takes To Reach the Top as a Caller.*

* *A Survey of the Distribution Systems You'll Be Dealing with.*

* *Sources of Potential Customers.*

* *The Structured Approach and Its Applications.*

* *The Components of a Powerful Telemarketing Program.*

* *Getting the Information You Need To Build a Strong Presentation.*

* *Setting Up Your Calling Environment and Starting the Program.*

* *Dealing with Screens.*

* *How To Qualify Prospects Tightly and Accurately.*

* *Incremental Closing.*

* *Overcoming Objections.*

* *Sharpening Your Sensitivity Through Better Listening Skills.*

* *Building Your Effectiveness Through Hard-Hitting Language.*

* *Using Your Voice to Maximum Advantage.*

* *Telephone Courtesy.*

* *Using Literature Packages to Your Advantage.*

* *Effective Follow-Up Tactics for More Closes.*

* *Telemarketing by Computer Can Double Productivity.*

* *Feedback Systems for Telemarketing.*

* *Intelligence Gathering Through Telemarketing.*

* *Extra Performance Through Self Motivation and Stress-Avoidance Techniques.*

* *The Caller's Quick-Reference Troubleshooting Guide.*

Format: three-ring binder and two cassette tapes (six modules). 210 pages.

TELEPHONE TECHNIQUES

Telephone Dynamics, Universal Training System Company staff. Wilmette, IL: Universal Training Systems Company, 1970.

This book presents an advanced program in productive telephone usage developed specially for personnel who make and receive important business calls.

The techniques used in this program were perfected over a period of years, in connection with custom training programs created by Universal Training Systems Company for many leading companies. These audio-visual programs were commissioned by firms such as GE, American Hospital Supply, Montgomery Ward and Inland Steel for a variety of specialized business objectives: telephone selling, credit and collection, supervisory and management training, computer systems training, etc.

It was found that the Audiograph, a special audio-visual method, was the most effective way to train people in productive oral communication. This unique combination of pre-recorded dialogue, sound effects, and other stimuli, reinforced by printed materials, involves looking, listening and actual participation. The result is a stimulating, enjoyable learning process whose effectiveness has been proven in a variety of business applications.

Materials are presented in dramatic, fast-moving form with interesting use of music, sound effects and dialogue, interspersed with recordings of actual telephone calls. In Audiographic instruction the learner listens and critiques actual examples of proper and improper usage. To reinforce his learning, he records his own voice. The learning process is further reinforced through use of an illustrated workbook in which, while listening, he enters answers to simple quizzes. This forms the basis of a permanent reference source which helps maintain his new level of proficiency.

Topics:

* *Background of Telephone Use.*

* *Explanation of Program.*

* *The Differences Between Face-to-Face Communication and Telephone Communication.*

* *The Telephone Communication Pathway.*

* *The Dynamics of Telephone Personality.*

* *Telephone Courtesy.*

* *Island of Communication.*

* *Greeting the Caller.*

* *Probing.*

* *Critique of Calls.*

* *Closing Calls.*

* *Pronunciation Guide to Words Most Frequently Mispronounced.*

* *Handling Incoming Calls.*

* *Screening Calls.*

* *Effective Message Taking.*

* *Probing for Additional Information.*

* *Focusing the Conversation.*

* *Transferring Calls.*

* *Cooling Off the Irritated or Angry Caller.*

* *Proper Call Placement.*

* *Long Distance Calling.*

* *How To Learn Contact Names.*

* *Penetrating the Call Screen.*

* *Setting Up Appointments.*

* *Sales Calls.*

* *Service Calls.*

* *Collection Calls.*

* *Closing the Call.*

Format: paperback and two, two-sided cassette tapes. 40 pages.

WHOLESALERS/DISTRIBUTORS

Successful Telemarketing, Peg Fisher. (See Startups and Managing a Center.)

WIN-WIN Telemarketing for Wholesalers--Distributors, S. Michael Zibrum. Washington, D.C.: The National Association of Wholesaler-Distributors, 1986.

    This package is designed to meet the needs of all key players in a successful wholesale distribution telemarketing program: The Chief Executive Officer (CEO), the telemarketing administrator and the telemarketer. The package contains three modules, plus an audio training cassette and accompanying workbook.

    Module One--The Chief Executive Officer (CEO) Guide teaches the CEO how to create the type of program that meets a company's needs and goals using situation analysis. In addition, it helps the CEO select the right administrator for his or her telemarketing program.

Module Two--The Telemarketing Administrator Guide helps the administrator design and implement a successful telemarketing program for a company. The program explains how to find the best people to carry out a program by recognizing key personality traits.

Module Three--The Telemarketer Guide is a hands-on training guide accompanied by a workbook and an audio cassette. The telemarketer learns to recognize basic buyer and seller conversational styles, how to handle questions and objections, and how to keep meaningful records for day-to-day telephone interaction.

Key conversational elements as the presentation, the trial close and the fallback are brought together on audio cassette by a fictional telemarketer.

The program provides wholesaler-distributors with a practical, hands-on approach to establishing a successful telemarketing operation. Its three modules, audio training cassette and workbooks are packaged in an easy-to-store three ring binder. Each module is full of forms which help one plan, organize and execute the program.

Modules/chapters:

Module One (CEO Guide).

* *The Role of the CEO in the Telemarketing Program.*

* *Re-Introduction to Telemarketing.*

* *The Situation Analysis: Tailoring Your Program.*

* *Long-Term Considerations of the Telemarketing Program.*

Module Two (Telemarketing Administrator Guide).

* *The Telemarketing Administrator and Program Success.*

* *Where To Find the Business Base.*

* *Goal Setting for Your Program.*

* *Selecting the Right Telemarketer.*

* *Establishing the Work Area.*

* *Procedure for Starting Your Program.*

* *Tracking Your Program for Success.*

Module Three (The Telemarketer Guide).

* *The Role of the Telemarketer.*

* *Preparing for Your Calls.*

677

* *Developing Your Telephone Technique.*

* *Sales Aides To Improve Performance.*

Format: three-ring binder, three module books, three workbooks and one two-sided cassette tape. 191 pages.

Magazines, Newspapers and Newsletters

MAGAZINES/NEWSPAPERS: DIRECT MARKETING

Catalog Age, Stamford, CT: Hanson Publishing Group, Inc.

Catalog Business, New York, NY: Mill Hollow Corporation.

Direct Marketing, Garden City, NY: Hoke Communications, Inc.

Direct - The Magazine of Direct Marketing Management, Stamford, CT: Hanson Publishing Group, Inc.

DM News, New York, NY: Mill Hollow Corporation.

Sales & Marketing Management (Canada), Downsview, ON, Canada: Sanford Evans Communications, Ltd.

Target Marketing, Philadelphia, PA: North American Publishing Company.

MAGAZINES/NEWSPAPERS: FUND RAISING

Fund Raising Management, Garden City, NY: Hoke Communications, Inc.

MAGAZINES/NEWSPAPERS: TECHNOLOGIES & TECHNIQUES (INBOUND/OUTBOUND PHONE CALLS)

Inbound/Outbound, New York, NY: Telecom Library.

MAGAZINES/NEWSPAPERS: TELEMARKETING

Telemarketing, Norwalk, CT: Technology Marketing Corporation.

TeleProfessional, Waterloo, IA: TeleCross Corporation.

NEWSLETTERS: CUSTOMER SALES REP TELEPHONE SKILLS & TECHNIQUES

CSR Hotline, Freehold, NJ: FGI and Affiliated Publishing Companies.

NEWSLETTERS: CUSTOMER SERVICE

Customer Service Newsletter, Silver Spring, MD: Customer Service Institute.

NEWSLETTERS: DIRECT MARKETING

Business-to-Business Direct Marketer, Colorado Springs, CO: Maxwell Sroge Publishing Company.

The Catalog Marketer, Colorado Springs, CO: Maxwell Sroge Publishing Company.

Friday Report, Garden City, NY: Hoke Communications, Inc.

Non-Store Marketing Report, Colorado Springs, CO: Maxwell Sroge Publishing Company.

NEWSLETTERS: FUND RAISING

FRM Weekly, Garden City, NY: Hoke Communications, Inc.

NEWSLETTERS: INCOMING CALL MANAGEMENT

Service Level Newsletter, Bowie, MD: SLN, Inc.

NEWSLETTERS: TELEPHONE SALES REP SKILLS & TECHNIQUES

Telephone Effectiveness Newsletter, Glendale, CA: Goodman Communications Corporation.

Telephone Selling Report, Omaha, Nebraska, TeleMarketing Design, Inc.

TSR Hotline, Freehold, NJ: (SPI) Self-Paced Instructions International, Inc.

NEWSLETTERS: TELEMARKETING

The Telemarketer, New York, NY: Actel Marketing.

The Van Vechten Report, Freehold, NJ: FGI and Affiliated Publishing Companies.

APPENDIX D

Telecommunications (Peripheral Equipment)

Neal H. Shact
President
CommuniTech, Inc.
Elmhurst, Illinois

Telephone peripheral equipment is rarely discussed because it is overshadowed by the greater glamor and expense of sophisticated telephone systems. Yet, peripheral equipment is the crucial interface between the human being and the technology. Peripheral equipment, quite simply, makes these large systems--and the people who use them--work better.

Even so, information and help on this equipment, along with the equipment itself, is often difficult to find. The peripheral industry's most competent experts, for example, are usually found in small, highly specialized firms. When large organizations offer peripherals they usually do so as a convenience and accommodation for their end-users. Major PBX and ACD vendors are structured to provide service, support and expertise on their main product lines that they manufacture. Thus, the level of support they can provide on a peripheral add-on basis is often limited.

It seemed suitable, then, to devote a section in this Encyclopedia to this critically important stepchild of telephone technology. I will focus, here, on a few of the most valuable peripheral products, and discuss how they can benefit your organization. Telephone headsets are given the most emphasis because they are the most commonly found peripheral in the telemarketing industry, and because they represent significant productivity enhancements at a minimum investment.

WHY USE TELEPHONE HEADSETS?

Virtually every telemarketing consultant recommends the use of telephone headsets. Why?

The reasoning is basic. Headsets are one of the most cost-effective ways to increase productivity and decrease expenses. One frequently cited study has showed the *headsets yield up to a 43% increase in productivity.*

By using a headset, the number of physical body movements necessary to answer each call is decreased. There are fewer reaching motions. The effort to position the headset between the shoulder and the ear is eliminated. Most obvious of all, both hands are left totally free to type or write information.

Multiply needless body movement by hundreds of calls per day, remove that wasted motion with headsets, and you have an employee who is less stressed and less fatigued. Elimination of this unnecessary stress produces a more effective work force.

There is another subtle, yet major benefit to using headsets. Employees using headsets can read information from a terminal more quickly, because an employee not using a headset probably has his neck slightly bent and his head tilted while cradling the phone. The headset user holds his head upright, allowing the eye to scan and read information much more quickly along a horizontal plane.

You can demonstrate this phenomenon with a simple test. Read the next paragraph of this article holding this book at a slight angle, then reread the paragraph holding it as you normally would. It is easy to see that your reading speed rapidly increases.

Another important reason for using telephone headsets is that they allow telephone sales reps to talk more comfortably. When TSR's are not comfortable with ears inflamed, exhausted from straining to hear, and have necks painfully crooked, is it any wonder that they become fatigued? With headsets they will be productive longer, and maintain a higher level of enthusiasm.

KINDS OF HEADSETS AVAILABLE

When most people think of headsets they think of a switchboard operator wearing a traditional in-the-ear model. While that is still a popular model, there are three other basic styles available: over-the-head monaural (similar to a Sony Walkman where you would hear out of one ear), over-the-head binaural (the same as monaural except that you hear out of both ears) and under-the-chin. With the exception of the Danavox under-the-chin model, all manufacturers make their own versions of the other styles.

In-the-Ear Models. As mentioned earlier, the most commonly thought of headset is the in-the-ear model pioneered by *Plantronics* (345 Encincal Road, Santa Cruz, CA 95060) and commonly known as the StarSet. It has been in production for 27 years. The design has not remained static and many improvements have been added over the years. While its popularity has declined (mainly because there are now so many other choices), it remains the most popular headset model in use.

ACS Communications (250 Technology Circle, Scotts Valley, CA 95066) offers two versions of the in-the-ear set, one version is called the Contourmount, which is virtually a copy of the StarSet except that it offers the option of noise cancelling (which will be discussed in the next section). The second version, the MicroSet, is similar in design but varies in two ways: Its weight is 1/3 of the StarSet's and it offers foam tiplets that do not have to be inserted fully into the ear canal.

Unex (Five Liberty Way, Westford, MA 01886) offers two versions of in-the-ear headsets, the Ventel I and II. Both headsets offer optional noise cancelling. The difference between the two models is that the Ventel I uses an ear tip that is inserted into the ear canal and the Ventel II uses a foam covered earbud that sits in the ear but external to the ear canal.

GN Netcom/Danavox (6400 Flying Cloud Drive, Minneapolis, MN) has just introduced a new model which is worn on the ear but does not need an eartip or headband. The design allows the set to be hung over the ear and suspends a small speaker outside of the ear itself.

Over-the-Head Headsets. Lightweight, over-the-head headsets were introduced by ACS Communications in 1978. The design proved to be very popular, especially with the influx into the industry of men who wanted a more masculine headset than the traditional Plantronics StarSet model.

682

APPENDIX D: TELECOMMUNICATIONS (PERIPHERAL EQUIPMENT)

ACS's success was followed by the introduction of Plantronics Supra, Ventel's Unex and the Danavox 900 Series. All of the manufacturers offer single and dual ear headset models. The dual ear headsets, also called binaural headsets, *are probably the best suited models to the telemarketing industry.* By delivering sound to both ears, binaurals allow the best concentration, and the most effective competition with outside noise. The experience is similar to wearing a stereo headset--the user feels like he or she is "right there" and really involved with the caller.

Under-the-Chin Headsets. Danavox is the only manufacturer that offers an under-the-chin model. This brand has unique appeal to wearers who do not want something in their ears and do not want to "mess up" their hair.

FEATURES AVAILABLE

Noise Cancelling. Headset manufacturers are responsive to the demands of the market and have introduced many features, both optional and standard, which make the headsets more practical, comfortable and easy to use. Here we will look at some of the most valuable features for telemarketers.

Of all of the features available with headsets used in a telemarketing environment, *the most important is the ability to handle background noise.*

In a large center, room noise rises throughout the day. As it becomes harder to hear, reps speak louder, increasing noise levels, etc. For telemarketers, noise is more than just an inconvenience. It has a direct relationship to productivity. When conversations must be repeated, call duration increases, which usually leads to a requirement for more staff and equipment (which, of course, can increase noise. . .).

Headset manufacturers have long sought to reduce the background noise transmitted via headsets. One approach is the use of true *noise-cancelling* microphones. These microphones only transmit sound originating within about one inch of the microphone. No other sound is transmitted.

But this approach has a drawback within a telemarketing environment: it demands perfect microphone positioning. Without it, the *headset user's voice* will also be cancelled. This technology worked well with highly trained people such as pilots, astronauts, and military personnel but was difficult to implement in the office marketplace where less skilled personnel had problems in properly positioning sensitive microphones. GN Netcom/Danavox and Unex's Ventel headsets eliminated this problem by using noise cancelling microphones with more limited capabilities that were easier to use.

The second approach to noise reduction was pioneered by Plantronics and uses *voice switching technology.* This technique only allows the microphone to transmit when volume reaches a predetermined level. When the headset user is not talking, or is pausing during the conversation, no sound is transmitted. When the headset user speaks at a normal level the microphone is "live" and all background and room noise is transmitted.

ACS's noise cancelling TelecTret headset line is the only product that marries these two technologies. They use a noise-cancelling microphone that provides between eight and 12db noise reductions (about 24db is perfect) and achieves near-perfect voice switching. This technology is an option on most of their existing line of headset products.

683

Mute Switch. A mute switch allows the wearer to turn off the microphone while listening to the other party. This feature is a real benefit for telemarketers who may need to check with a supervisor for assistance without breaking the conversation flow.

Volume Control. All telephone headsets come with volume control unless they are going on telephones that have volume control built in. This feature allows the user to increase volume, which is often necessary with the variety of telephone line connections found today. Telemarketers also find it useful toward the end of a shift when they become tired and are straining to hear calls.

HOW TO SELECT A TELEPHONE HEADSET

The process of selecting which headsets to use can be fairly complex. Not only is there a bewildering number of models and features, users regard them as a highly personal choice. After all, it is the only piece of work equipment that TSR's will be physically attaching to their bodies. Any selection process should include the input of the users. The result of failure to do so can be seen in many organizations, perhaps your own, in the piles of headsets users refuse to wear.

Telephone System/Sets Determination. The first step in selecting a headset is to determine what type of telephone system and telephone sets you will be using. With the tremendous variety of phone equipment on the market and lack of standardization, *it is essential to choose headsets that are compatible with your phone system.*

All of the leading manufacturers make headsets that are compatible with virtually all phone systems, but in order to do so, they have made a variety of models. If you are in the process of choosing a phone system or expect to be changing shortly, delay your headset purchase until the phone system choice is finalized.

Needs/Features Analysis. The second step is to analyze your needs and determine what features are needed. You can call each of the four major headset manufacturers directly or work with a distributor who specializes in telephone headsets and discuss your specific needs with them. This latter route is preferable because you only have to deal with one person who can help you eliminate manufacturers whose products do not offer the features you need.

An added benefit of working with a distributor is that as long as you're making a large-quantity purchase, they will often allow you to try several models or brands so that your people can hear how they sound on your phone system and feel how comfortable they are over an extended period of time.

Trial. The third step is to arrange the trial. Arranging an evaluation serves several purposes beyond simply choosing the "best" headset. It is really the beginning of the implementation process. By getting employees' input, you are allowing them to "buy into" using the headsets chosen. After all, it is harder to complain about having to use headsets that you yourself have selected. If this is the first time headsets are being used in your organization, this step is even more important.

684

APPENDIX D: TELECOMMUNICATIONS (PERIPHERAL EQUIPMENT)

For the employees who may still complain about having to wear a headset and do not want to, remember, *this is a productivity tool that can increase efficiency by up to 43%* This is now a management issue: you can let employees help choose *which* headset they will use, but cannot let them decide *if* they will be used.

When setting up a trial remember to let employees try each headset for several days. After only a few hours, all of the headsets feel pretty much the same. Since they will be wearing these headsets all day, every day, you'll want to make sure they are as comfortable as possible over an extended period of time. Failure to implement this step may result in employees avoiding wearing the headsets, complaints about headset "problems," or unnecessary returns for repair that end up as "no trouble found" bills.

The feedback obtained from telemarketers at this stage centers on comfort and how well they can hear. There are differences because each telephone headset has a slightly different sound, just as do stereo speakers in a store.

What is frequently overlooked during the trial is *how the headset wearer sounds to the people he or she is talking to*. It doesn't make any sense to have a comfortable employee who can hear well talk to customers who think your employee sounds terrible! Yet, most evaluations are conducted without ever taking this variable into account. Always place a test call to those employees who are testing the headsets.

Headset Evaluation Worksheet. To aid you in conducting an effective evaluation, there is a *Headset Evaluation Worksheet* (**Figure D-1**) at the end of this appendix. There is room to rate several models according to the criteria that our customers have told us are the most important.

HOW HEADSETS ARE SOLD

All headsets are sold through a network of distributors and dealers. None of the manufacturers sell directly but all of them will refer you to a distributor in your area and will provide assistance regarding compatibility and model selection.

The distributors range from highly specialized experts in headsets to large supply houses who stock thousands of products.

THE REAL COST OF A HEADSET

There are many aspects of the cost of a telephone headset. There is the initial purchase price, annual price (which factors in the costs of consumable parts and repairs), lifecycle cost (which includes the costs of consumable parts and repairs), and finally, the cost of aggravation--what's involved when the headsets need repairs. The total costs can add up to be significantly greater than the initial purchase price.

Depending on the features and style of the headset, all of the manufacturers' products have a suggested price that ranges from $120 to $190 per unit. In quantity, it is common to find headsets selling at a discount. Do not confuse them with headsets that carry a lower list price, as they are probably what the industry refers to as "consumer-grade" and will not last in a rugged telemarketing environment.

On an annual basis, your headset budget will include the cost of consumable spare parts such as ear tips and cushions, voice tubes and replacement clothing clips. This can easily add $10 per headset.

Beware of the company that offers headsets but does not carry spare parts! The same people who were so friendly and so competitively priced for the initial buy, may tell you to go elsewhere when you critically need an inexpensive part. This same warning applies to additional headsets that are purchased after your initial order. A reputable headset distributor will allow you to purchase additional units after your initial purchase at the same rate as long as there has not been a manufacturing price increase.

Annual repair costs can become significant. All of the manufacturers have repair charges of $40 to $60 for headsets that are currently being manufactured. There are also separate repair facilities such as ours at CommuniTech where we repair out-of-warranty headsets for $35, and typically repair them more quickly than the manufacturers could.

How often the headsets need repairs is largely a function of how well they are being cared for. Annual failure rates can range up to 20%. Most employees have no idea what a headset costs and tend to treat them in a cavalier fashion.

We strongly recommend having employees sign a liability form. When employees know they will be held accountable, they take better care of the headsets which will reduce your cost.

Of course, it is impossible to quantify the cost of aggravation, but if you could, you would want to purchase headsets from a company that would be willing to handle as many of the labor-associated problems as possible.

Let's examine a worst case scenario and hope it never happens to you. It would take place in an environment where the company decided to let the employees use whatever headset they personally preferred, which means they have bought headsets from *all* four major manufacturers.

Employees frequently ask for a different headset, which results in numerous small purchases. This problem becomes compounded when a headset fails. Each different manufacturer must be contacted to get a return authorization and time must be spent determining whether the headset failed during the warranty, or afterward, which would affect whether the repair was billable. If a working headset is sent to a manufacturer as an in-warranty failure it will be billed for testing and refurbishing. Last, but not least, someone must spend time following up to make sure the headsets are returned from repair.

As you can see, there are many logistical considerations associated using headsets that are not apparent when a prospective buyer begins the search. There can be many hidden costs. Expert headset vendors can minimize or eliminate these costs because they specialize in not only selling, but servicing telephone headsets. When making your headset purchase look for *the lowest overall cost* for features required, not just the lowest initial purchase price.

HANDSETS

Headsets, with their built-in volume control capabilities, are the best way to beat surrounding noise. But there are still some operations which, for various reasons, have not opted to put in headsets.

For those of you who fall into that group, there may be a good, inexpensive way to beat the noise problem. *Walker Equipment*, the leading manufacturer of telephone handsets, has a broad array of specialized handsets.

APPENDIX D: TELECOMMUNICATIONS (PERIPHERAL EQUIPMENT)

Walker Equipment (a subsidiary of Plantronics, the headset manufacturer) makes volume control and transmission control handsets that directly address the problem of surrounding noise.

Their Walker W-6 handset line overcomes noise with a built-in amplifier that allows you to set your listening level loud enough so you can hear the person at the other end of the line. The amplifier is capable of *increasing volume up to 10 times*. With the W-6 you can choose between two volume control options, both built into the handset. One is a rotary wheel which, when set, retains the volume at the level you've chosen. The other is an electronic touchbar which automatically resets the volume to its "normal" setting when you hang up. "Basic" W-6 models are priced around $40.

Another "noise-defeating" handset is the Walker PT series. These handsets contain a built-in "muting" touch bar that lets you stop your phone's transmission whenever you want. By using this option while you're listening, you will reduce the annoying "sidetone" (surrounding noise that gets picked up by the phone's microphone) that makes it difficult to understand the person on the other end of the line. Like a mute button, it also allows you to hold private aside conversation without being heard over the phone. The PT series "basic" price is around $20.

And, for people who want *both* volume control *and* the mute capability of transmission control, Walker has married the two into the Walker W-8's starting at $47.

All these Walker handsets are also available with an optional noise-reducing microphone at a slight additional charge. For further details call an authorized Plantronics distributor or dial 1-800-HANDSET and be connected with Plantronics in Santa Cruz, California.

CONFIDENCERS

A confidencer is a noise-cancelling microphone that replaces the microphone element in a telephone handset. They are inexpensive, easy to install and can make a dramatic difference in the amount of background noise transmitted. The largest manufacturer of this equipment is Walker. There is also a much smaller company, *Roanwell Corporation*, located in New York (180 Varick St., New York, NY 10014).

POWER PROTECTION EQUIPMENT

What happens to your telemarketing organization when you lose electric power? Will your phone and computerized telemarketing systems crash? Will all operations grind to a halt? If you have not planned for back-up power, its probably just a matter of time before you wished you had the capability.

Last year we experienced a three-hour blackout. Fortunately we had our computers and phone systems supported with back-up power systems and disruptions were minimal. While my employees continued to be productive, my next door neighbors, an insurance agency, complained about how much money they lost.

How much would you lose?

DataShield Uninterruptible Power Supplies (UPS's) from *PTI Industries* (269 Mt. Hermon Road, Scotts Valley, CA 95066) are reasonably priced equipment that can help avert disasters. DataShield has recently introduced UPS's that range in size from 400 Watts to 10 KVA. This means that you can provide back-up power on anything from a small PC to a computer room and a large PBS or ACD.

Traditionally, organizations that have used UPS's had large centralized UPS systems, a situation analogous to the role of mainframe computers in the computer industry. Just as PC's changed the role of computers in a company, so has this new generation of smaller inexpensive UPS's. Organizations have the alternative of using smaller UPS's in addition to, or instead of centralized units. The benefit of using several smaller UPS's is that they do not need specialized personnel to wire, install or transport.

The first consideration when buying a UPS is to choose the proper size. First determine what equipment will be supported. Next check the power consumption which is usually found on the back of the equipment. The rating is usually listed in amperes (amps) but may also be listed in watts. With this information you can call DataShield and their marketing people can help you select the appropriate unit.

The second consideration is to determine how long you would like to keep your equipment running. Do you want to keep running throughout a several hour disruption, or do you just want to be able to safely shut down your computers? How long is a typical outage in your area? Lightening prone areas or businesses in areas with a lot of new construction are usually the most affected. How quickly is power restored?

PTI Industries may be new to the UPS business, but they are no stranger to the power protection business. They have been making surge protectors and stand-by power supplies for five years and have an outstanding reputation. In fact, *PC Magazine* rated DataShield surge protectors #1 in their May, 1986, evaluation of surge protectors.

Their line of stand-by power supplies ranges from 200 to 1,500 watts. They are able to support phone and computer systems from 20 minutes to eight hours. These systems are very economical and some models offer transfer times of as little as one millisecond.

For customers seeking the additional assurance of on-line, back-up power and the protection of voltage regulation, DataShield introduced their line of Uninterruptible Power Supplies.

DataShield UPS's boast some unique technological breakthroughs. Perhaps the most unusual is the solid-state design of their SS400 and SS700 (440 and 700 VA) systems. This design eliminates the need for large costly transformers. By being smaller and lighter (32 and 39 pounds) than competitive systems, they are also up to 30% less expensive and more easily transported.

These models have 200 joules of surge protection built in which is comparable with the protection provided by the best surge protectors on the market. The UPS's use industrial grade sealed lead acid batteries and will provide power for five to 20 minutes. This is enough time to safely shut down a computer system to prevent disc drive damage.

The SS400 and SS700 sell for $995 and $1,195. DataShield's large UPS systems range in size from 2KVA to 10KVA. They use a ferroresonant technology and static bypass. This combination allows the UPS to handle up to 500% overload conditions. This technology allows excellent price-performance and the ability to handle the startup requirements of the most demanding new computers (starting up demands the most power). Prices on the 2KVA unit are $5,100 and range up to $12,500 for the 10KVA model.

CALL ACCOUNTING

Any business that uses the telephone can benefit from a call accounting system. Especially when

APPENDIX D: TELECOMMUNICATIONS (PERIPHERAL EQUIPMENT)

the employees' job function requires them to be continually on the phone as they are in the telemarketing industry. A telemarketing firm with under 200 telephones can generate well over 100,000 calls in a month.

Businesses often use call accounting for a simple reason. It reduces phone costs, and any dollar savings from the telephone directly increases a company's profits. A call accounting system saves money in two ways: by decreasing telephone abuse and increasing trunk efficiency. Detailed station reports allow you to spot check for telephone abuse and misuse. These reports can reduce a monthly phone bill *by up to twenty percent.*

Call accounting also saves money by providing traffic analysis reports. These reports help you determine what type of telephone services you should use and what they cost per minute on a trunk-by-trunk basis.

Two things happen when a company grows:

* *First, someone is given the task of managing telecommunications, regardless of their experience or expertise in this area.*

* *Next, he or she begins adding telephone lines until complaints about phone service stop.*

As a result, the organization is typically overtrunked, and the trunks are not configured for optimum efficiency. *It is not uncommon to find firms paying for WATS lines that have not been working for months!* A good traffic analysis package will help optimize a company's trunks, thereby trimming another probable ten percent off the telephone bill.

Thus, by catching telephone abuse and misuse and by streamlining trunks, a call accounting system can often pay for itself within six to nine months. At the same time, the system provides for smooth and accurate allocation of phone costs to the company's accounting center.

After the telephone bill has been reduced by a potential 30%, a network-optimum package can tie all of this information together to build some "What if" scenarios. These help to determine exactly what the most economical facilities are for specific needs. The end result of working with a good network optimization package is the least possible network cost--and peace of mind.

With call accounting, telemarketing organizations can also provide meaningful and motivational reports directly to the salespeople and their management. These reports may be set up in a variety of configurations. One such report gives an analysis of all incoming and outgoing calls handled by each salesperson.

This type of report is an excellent tool for tracking the productivity of each salesperson. Call accounting gives the ability to input client/project codes. Using these codes, one can report on each account worked on for either incoming or outgoing calls and identify the person doing the work.

Thus you are able to simplify both commission tracking and customer billing.

In the near future, telephone companies will provide the capability to automatically identify *incoming callers.* This will save time and increase accuracy in reporting by eliminating the need to input client/project numbers.

One other major productivity analysis made possible by call accounting systems is the ability to determine *talk time* by telephone sales reps. Hourly, daily or weekly productivity reviews can help determine the true "phone time per hour" by individual TSR's, teams or the entire operation.

689

NETWORK MONITORING

In addition to providing call accounting systems, *TelWatch* (400 E. Diehl Rd., Naperville, IL 60560) manufactures a product called NetWatch that produces a broad spectrum of information about usage patterns (traffic), line availability, signalling problems and general transmission quality for any type of telephone trunking facility. It produces reports in understandable English that can be retrieved remotely via a "dumb terminal" data device and a modem.

Because NetWatch works by actual observation of signals on the lines, it can locate intermittent problems or problems that occur only in high traffic. It can find a line with crosstalk, for example, because the noise on that line will appear to be higher than the noise on other similar lines.

Another application of NetWatch is general quality surveillance. Rather than use the information to find a problem line via a noise or level or traffic pattern that is different from the others, you can use the box to see how *all* the lines are doing. *If two vendors are providing WATS lines with identical geographical calling patterns, the lines with the highest quality level delivered and the lowest noise will be readily apparent.* NetWatch can also characterize the working "return loss" which is a measure of the echo margin on the facilities.

For larger telemarketing organizations served via digital facilities, NetWatch can add to the analog channel characterization function, the function of characterizing the bit error rate, bipolar violation rates, synch losses and slip and several other parameters of digital T-carrier facilities.

Several telemarketing organizations have found that ownership of the NetWatch product puts them on an equal level with their transmission vendors in negotiating problem fixes and refunds and in managing general transmission quality issues.

Although there are many good call accounting products on the market, there are only a few network monitoring products available. TelWatch offers both. Inquiries may be directed to them at (312) 961-3536.

TELEPHONE SALES REP MONITORING

Virtually all ACD's (automated call distributors) have monitoring or training capability. There is also peripheral monitoring equipment that can be added to virtually any telephone system.

The use of this equipment can be controversial and there are employee privacy issues that have spilled over into the legal and legislation arena, but it still remains a valuable tool to employers.

The reason is simple. Employers need the ability to effectively supervise their telephone sales reps on the phone in order to ensure that the job is being performed properly, that customers are being treated with respect and to ensure the quality of the product (which is the service they are performing).

The only alternative is cumbersome. That is physically walking around and hearing only one side of the conversation. That's where monitoring comes in.

Other than the ACD manufacturers, *Augat Melco* is one of the few companies that manufactures "service observing" (monitoring) systems. The company recently introduced a new product, RA-330 Remote Access Unit, which allows observers remote access to telemarketing phone lines or workstations. When used with Melco service observing systems, *a center's lines can be monitored from an off-site location.*

690

APPENDIX D: TELECOMMUNICATIONS (PERIPHERAL EQUIPMENT)

The RA-330 is joined via modular connectors to a local monitoring station within the telemarketing department. To access the system from off-site, the remote observer dials the number assigned to the RA-330, then an assignable security code.

If the local observer's station is already in use, a busy tone will be heard. Once connected to the line, the remote observer can listen on any station connected to the monitoring system.

This kind of product opens new opportunities for enhanced client services within telemarketing service bureaus (TSB's). A TSB can now be equipped so clients can access and monitor the representatives assigned to their accounts. . .facilitating more frequent monitoring to telemarketing projects without having to travel to the TSB.

Clients can thus provide TSB management with timely feedback and additional training information to achieve and maintain higher standards for telemarketing projects entrusted to service vendors.

This remote access unit is the latest addition to Augat Melco's line of service observing systems, which allow for observation of up to 90 lines or stations. Melco monitoring systems can be used with central office, PBX, Centrex or key systems lines.

One optional feature that may be of interest to telemarketing supervisor/managers is "Talk Assist." This option allows the supervisor to cut in on the conversation to offer immediate assistance.

Augat Melco can be reached at P.O. Box 6909, Bellevue, WA 98008.

AUTOMATED ATTENDANTS

Do you have an inbound telemarketing operation that is deluged with incoming calls? Are these calls answered by a live operator and then routed into the appropriate department or sub-group within an automatic call distributor (ACD)? How do you distribute calls if you do not have an ACD?

You may have already considered enhancing your live receptionists or telemarketers with an automated switchboard attendant. An automated attendant answers calls and invites the inbound caller to respond to a series of prompts in routing themselves to the appropriate department or individual.

A typical message may say:

"Thank you for calling CommuniTech. If you know your party's extension number, you may dial it any time during this message. If you are calling for headsets, dial 1; for power protection dial 2; and automated attendants, dial 3. If you need assistance, please stay on the line...an operator will be with you shortly."

Perhaps this brief script sounds familiar. While only a few years ago these systems were unusual, they have now become commonplace and are increasingly found in the telemarketing environment.

One of the newest developments is *Dytel Corporation's* (50 E. Commerce Drive, Schaumburg, IL 60173) introduction of what they call "Interactive Call Distribution" (ICD). This feature can enhance or in some cases even replace the ACD.

Typically an inbound telemarketing operation, agent group, or customer service group receives more calls than they can handle at one time. The ACD partially solves the problem by asking customers to remain on hold. ICD keeps customers fully informed of their status in queue (even telling them how long they will wait) and gives callers an alternative if they choose not to wait. Such alternatives may include dialing another extension or leaving a voice mail message by dialing a single digit prompt. Agents can retrieve messages and return calls when time permits.

Another valuable feature is Extended Messaging and Site Recording (EMSR). This feature offers an additional capability that allows users to record a greater number of personalized messages that can be changed or reprogrammed at any time to meet changing business circumstances.

EMSR is most helpful in situations where long messages or detailed verbal instructions are necessary; where voice messages require on-site updates; or when you need personalized routing using a large number of messages.

Advanced database capabilities and EMSR help make a good impression on a caller's first experience with the system--perhaps his or her first call to your company. Callers who dial extensions, rather than single-digit codes, can be differentiated and routed accordingly. First-time callers can be guided through the process, while frequent callers can move through the system more quickly.

Calls are handled based on the department extension, or informational service dialed by the caller. As the call processing requirements of the business change, the automated attendant system is simply reprogrammed to meet the need.

Last year Quill Corporation went shopping for an automated attendant to enhance their Rockwell ACD. Jerry Barber, the Customer Service Manager, had two important criteria:

1. *On-site messaging was an absolute necessity.*

2. *The ability to create different messages and routing instructions for different calls was mandatory.*

Since installing a Dytel Automated Attendant, callers calling during Quill's regular business hours are greeted by the pleasant voice of Roxie Davis, telephone orders supervisor. Customers who have had reason to deal with Roxie Davis in person have been pleasantly surprised to find out that she's a real person and a Quill employee.

"*I like to think that everything we do is personalized,*" notes Barber. "*We do things with the customer in mind; we didn't just automate for automation's sake and to save dollars.*"

Instead of three different phone numbers, for general information, telephone orders and customer service, Quill customers need only remember one number. The Automated Attendant answers within one or two rings--another important customer service consideration.

Automated Attendants such as the Dytel can support factory-recorded, studio-quality messages, or a combination of pre-recorded and user-recorded messages. Total capacity can be as much as up to 66 minutes of digitized message and 32 separate routing instructions or personalities.

Recording and reprogramming messages are relatively simple processes that can be learned in 15 to 20 minutes. Once recorded, a message can be cancelled or activated from any push-button phone by authorized personnel.

692

APPENDIX D: TELECOMMUNICATIONS (PERIPHERAL EQUIPMENT)

Figure D-1
Selecting Telephone Headsets

	HEADSETS			
	TYPE 1	TYPE 2	TYPE 3	TYPE 4

1. **COMFORT:** How comfortable is the headset over an extended period of time? (Should be tested over days, not hours.)

2. **CLARITY:** Can the user hear clearly?

3. **TRANSMISSION:** How does the headset sound to the party on the other end?

4. **COST:** Total cost should include after-sale customer support.

5. **FEATURES DESIRED:** Noise cancelling, binaural, monaural in-ear, monaural on-ear, mute switch, noise suppression, under chin.

6. **CUSTOMER SUPPORT:** Is vendor knowledgeable about headset compatibility with your phone system, have product and spare parts available within the time frame needed, offer trials and ability to provide after-sale support?

7. **COMPATIBILITY WITH EXISTING OR FUTURE PHONE SYSTEM:** Are the headsets compatible with the telephone equipment?

8. **WARRANTY PROCEDURES:** What are the procedures for headsets that may fail during the warranty period?

9. **EASE OF USE:** Is the headset easy to use?

10. **AVAILABILITY OF SPARE PARTS:** All headsets come with disposable items. Optimum headset performance depends on the parts being in good condition. What is cost and availability?

TOTAL POINTS to determine headset selection:

Rating Scale: Excellent -- 4
Good -- 3
Average -- 2
Fair -- 1
Poor -- 0

This chart may be reproduced for your own use.

693

A GLOSSARY OF TELEMARKETING TERMS

Richard L. Bencin
Donald J. Jonovic, Ph.D.
Eugene Kordahl
Judy Lanier
Lee Van Vechten

Abandoned Calls: Calls received in a telemarketing center but never reaching a TSR (usually hang-ups due to caller impatience).

Access Line: The serving central office line equipment and all outside plant facilities needed to connect the serving central office with the customer premises.

Account Qualification Matrix: The scientific method of measuring each case as it is completed as to potential to buy a product or service.

ACD (Automatic Call Distributor): The primary purpose of an ACD is to switch incoming calls electronically--answering the call, placing it on hold when necessary, playing a message or music, switching calls on a priority basis to the first available operator and identifying the trunk group.

Acoustic Coupler: A device that converts electrical signals into audio signals, enabling data to be transmitted over the public telephone network via a conventional telephone handset.

Additional Local Messages: The term refers to message rate telephone service, and designates the messages in excess of the number included in the minimum charge for the service.

ADRMP (Automated Dialing and Recorded Message Players): Used for announcement programs or for mass calling.

After Market: A market for parts and/or accessories that develops after a product sale (e.g., razor blade sales to a razor purchaser).

AMA: (See: *Automatic Message Accounting.*)

American Standard Code for Information Interchange (ASCII): A seven-bit plus parity code established by the American National Standards Institute (formerly American Standards Association) to achieve compatibility between data services. Also called USACII.

American Telemarketing Association (ATA): A trade association organized to serve telemarketing professionals. ATA provides an information exchange, publications and seminars to keep its members up to date on new technologies and telemarketing methods.

ANI: (See: *Automatic Number Identification.*)

Anticipative Dialing: (See: *Dial-Ahead Auto Dialing.*)

Area Code: Three-digit number associated with a geographic area for long-distance calling.

ARS: (See: *Automatic Route Selection.*)

ASCII: (See: *American Standard Code for Information Interchange.*)

Assumptive Close: A closing technique; offer of product or service with the assumption that the prospect/

694

customer has made the decision to buy. Minor details are the choice; ex., *"Shall we ship regular UPS or use the 2-day blue-label option?"*

Asterisk Bills: State laws or bills that require telephone companies to advise subscribers that they can have an asterisk placed in front of their name if they do not want telemarketing calls (or an extra line designating same).

ATA: (See: *American Telemarketing Association*.)

AT&T Advanced 800 Service: Enhanced 800 Service for business customers requiring greater management control of their toll-free networks.

AT&T Communications: Name of AT&T's regulated division, a new name for AT&T Long Lines.

AT&T 800 Call Allocator: A service that apportions calls to different call-answering locations by a subscriber-determined percentage allocation.

AT&T 800 Call Attempt Profile: A reporting feature providing a summary of call attempts by area codes, time of day and date for days the subscriber selects.

AT&T 800 Call Prompter: A service that prompts callers with recorded messages requesting that they dial digits to receive specific messages or reach specified departments.

AT&T 800 Command Routing: A service allowing a rerouting of 800 service to alternate routes in the event of emergencies or other sudden needs.

AT&T 800 Customized Call Routing: A service allowing specification of specific terminating points for calls originating in specific geographic locations.

AT&T 800 Day Manager: A service that routes calls differently depending on the day of the week.

AT&T 800 Routing Control Service: A service allowing a real-time change in Routing Service using on-site terminals.

AT&T 800 Service: Toll-free, inbound long-distance service which is paid for by the call recipient and requires no operator assistance.

AT&T 800 Service--Canada: A service allowing a subscriber in the U.S. to receive calls from services in exclusively Canadian area codes.

AT&T 800 Single Number Service: A service allowing one 800 number to access multiple locations and/or multiple lines at a single location, designed to simplify greatly, the use of national direct response advertising and publicity.

AT&T 800 Time Manager: A service allowing changes in call routing depending upon time of day. Time intervals are specified on the quarter hour and the service assumes a repeating 24-hour cycle.

AT&T Informations Systems (ATTIS): A division of AT&T Technologies that supplies and manufactures customer premises equipment.

AT&T Long Distance Service: AT&T Message Telecommunications Service (MTS).

AT&T Network Services: Name of AT&T Technologies' subdivision that manufactures and supplies equipment primarily to Bell operating companies, regional Bell operating companies and independent phone companies.

AT&T Technologies: Formerly Western Electric; name of AT&T's unregulated equipment manufacturing and supply division. Includes AT&T Information Systems and AT&T Network Services.

AT&T WATS Service: Lower-rate, large-volume outgoing service for long-distance calls to areas in and out of state.

Attempt: A dialing of the telephone, regardless of the results (e.g., wrong number disconnects, prospect unavailable). A category of call used to measure activity.

ATTIS: (See: *AT&T Information Systems.*)

Audiotex: An interactive computer allowing response callers to use touch-tone input in response to questions asked by the Central Processing Unit (CPU).

Auto Dialer: A machine can automatically dial telephone numbers either in a programmed mode or simply sequentily.

Automatic Call Distributor: (See: *ACD.*)

Automatic Dialing: Placing an outbound call by pressing a key which accesses a stored telephone number in the database.

Automated Dialing and Recorded Message Players: (See: *ADRMP.*)

Automatic Message Accounting (AMA): A set of features that provides billing information, i.e., the control of collections and recording of the calls charged, and any other pertinent information as a record for the calling and billing process.

Automatic Number Identification (ANI): A PBX management reporting capability breaking down a bill by the telephone extension originating the call.

Automatic Route Selection (ARS): A feature that allows for the automatic routing of calls over the most economical route.

Auto-Paced Dialing: After the TSR completes a call, the computer dials the next record after a programmed interval.

Back-End Computer Analysis: Computer analysis/reporting of telemarketing results. For example, closure rates by SIC/size, size of orders by SIC/size, script comparisons, part-time vs. full-time telemarketers, list comparisons, offer/response comparisons, etc.

Batch Processing: A type of data processing operation and data communication transmission where related transactions are grouped together and transmitted for processing, usually by the same computer and under the same application. Generally regarded as non-real-time data traffic, consisting of large files, where network response time is not critical.

Bellcore (Bell Communications Research): An organization established by the AT&T divestiture, representing and funded by the BOC's for the purpose of establishing telephone network standards and interfaces. Includes much of former Bell Labs.

Bell Operating Companies (BOC's): Regional phone companies (seven) formed as a result of the AT&T divestiture.

Benefits: What the features of a product do for the buyer. Benefits are what sell the product or service.

Binaural: Both-ears/channel headset.

Bingo Cards: Magazine reader service cards.

Blocked Calls: Inbound calls not connected due to busy signals.

BOC: (See: *Bell Operating Company.*)

Boiler Room/Bucket Shop: A term to describe outbound phone rooms that are very call intensive (40-50 calls per hour). The facilities are less than appropriate for the TSR and many times for the activity itself. High turnover of TSR's and low expense for the owners are trademarks.

BOS (Business Office Supervisor): At the telephone company, this is the person to whom the service representatives answer. A problem solver.

Bounce-Back Cards: Self-addressed, printed questionnaires that ask the prospects returning *bingo cards* to

696

further qualify themselves for the benefit of the vendor.

Buffer: A software program, storage space in random access memory (RAM) or a separate device used to compensate for differences in the speed of data transmission.

Bulletin Board System: A name for an electronic message system usually running on a microcomputer. Callers can leave and read messages.

Burnout: A phenomenon of excess TSR fatigue due to working a steady eight-hour shift. Burnout is usually associated with outbound calling to prospects. Rejection seems to be at the core of this particular malady.

Business Office (Telephone Company): The telephone company office whose number appears on your telephone bill. This office is only capable of handling simple requests about service.

Business-to-Business Telemarketing: Telemarketing to industry.

Business-to-Consumer Telemarketing: Telemarketing to individuals at their residences.

Busy Hour: The peak 60 minute period during a business day when the largest volume of communication traffic is handled.

Call: A concept that is unmeasurable as a management benchmark. Includes uncompleted and completed connections, busies, temporarily disconnected, disconnected-no referral, disconnected but referred, and no answers. Does not include status of results such as sale/no sale/follow-up.

Call Accounting: A record of calls placed, organized by extension, time of call, date of call, number dialed and length. Also refers to the equipment that provides such a record.

Call Anatomy: The layout of a presentation from beginning to end.

Call-Back: Any contact required to follow up any activity.

Call Card: Record of details on prospects or customers. Often arranged in chronological sequence.

Call Detail Recording (CDR): A feature of PBX and electronic key systems that records and lists all calls leaving the system, including relevant details such as duration, extension, etc.

Call Diverter: Equipment that forwards or transfers calls from one telephone to another, pre-arranged number.

Call Forcing: Automatic direction of an incoming call to an available agent, signalled by a tone and not requiring button pressing to receive the call.

Call Forwarding: A service feature that allows subscribers to pre-arrange a number for receiving calls directed to another number.

Call Guides: (See: *Prompts*.)

Call Load: The total number of inbound or outbound telephone calls which attempt to pass through a telemarketing center's equipment at any specific time.

Call Management: The process of managing the mix of equipment, services and labor to obtain the optimum productivity of a telemarketing center.

Call Management System: Equipment designed to produce management reports on phoning activity, costs, etc.

Call Objective: The clear reason for the call. The best calls are the ones that tend to have only one major objective.

Call Objective Guideline: A worksheet that allows preparation for the specific objective. The guideline is often used in training as well as for new product introductions.

Call Queuing: The process of ordering incoming calls in a waiting "line" for processing.

697

ENCYCLOPEDIA OF TELEMARKETING

Call Report: The daily record of tasks and/or sales work. This record often provides the data for call tracking.

Call Restriction: Setting limits and parameters on the ability of employees to use the phone system.

Call Sequencer: A device similar to an ACD which distributes and queues calls, as well as providing recorded announcements.

Call Tracking: The act of gathering statistics from the call report or electronic reporting devices for the purposes of management decisions. Used for forecasting both TSR defeats and victories.

Camp-On: A feature wherein an incoming call is allowed to wait on a line for automatic connection when the line becomes available.

Captive Unit: A telemarketing unit in which TSR's are employees of the company selling its own proprietary products.

Case: A complete and measurable telephone sales cycle from beginning to end (e.g., 100 names on a list equals 100 cases.)

Case in Progress: Initial contact has been made.

Cathode Ray Tube (CRT): A television-like picture tube used in visual display terminals.

CCR: (See: *Communicator Call Report*.)

CDR: (See: *Call Detail Recording*.)

Census Tract: A grouped area within a ZIP code containing households with uniform demographic characteristics.

Central Office (C.O.): The place where communications common carriers terminate customer lines and locate the equipment that interconnects those lines.

Central Processing Unit (CPU): The place where data is actually processed. The ''heart'' of the computer.

Centrex: A widely used telephone company switching service that uses central office switching equipment, to which customers connect via individual extension lines.

Change Masters: Organizations and people able to anticipate and implement needed change.

Chip: A minute square of thin, semiconducting material, such as silicone, processed to have specified electrical characteristics. Also called *microchip*.

Circuit: In communications the complete electrical path providing one- or two-way communication between two points comprising associated send and receive channels.

Close: Accomplishing a sale or call objective.

Closed Case: Any case that has completed the sales cycle and has ended in a sale, no sale or no potential.

Closed-Ended Probe: A question asked that has only one- or two-word answers.

Closed-Ended Question: A question seeking specific choice of specified answers, either ordered or unordered.

Clustering: Grouping names on a telemarketing list according to specific psychographic, demographic or geographic characteristics.

C.O.: Central Office.

COAM: Customer-owned and maintained equipment.

Cold Call: Call made to a number where no previous contact has been made from the caller's office.

Common Carrier: Utilities providing transmission facilities for communication by voice, data, video and/ or facsimile (e.g., AT&T, MCI, Sprint).

Communication Satellite: An earth satellite designed to act as a telecommunication radio relay. Most communication satellites are in geosynchronous orbit 22,300 miles above the equator so that they appear from the Earth to be stationary in space.

Communicator: A person skilled in the successful negotiation of either inbound or outbound cases. A trained telephone professional.

Communicator Call Report (CCR): The basic record for storage of all customer information and customer contact results.

Completed Contact: Any contact that finalizes a pre-planned portion of a sales cycle.

Computerized Top-Down Selling: (See: *Electronic Top-Down Selling*.)

Computer Network: An interconnection of assemblies of computer systems, terminals and communication facilities.

Configuration: A particular design or layout of a computer system and its peripherals to meet the specific requirements of the user.

Connect Time: A measure of system usage by a user, usually the time interval during which the user terminal was on-line during a session. Also the amount of time it takes a switching system to connect the calling party to the called party.

Connection: A contact that allows two-way communication and is billable by the telephone company.

Consultative Selling: The sales process of identifying customer needs, then selling products/services that fill that need.

Contact: Any conversation with a decision maker or one that advances a *case* toward completion.

Contact-to-Closed-Case Ratio: The number of completed contacts required to complete a case (e.g., contact-mail-contact would be a "two contacts to closed case" ratio).

Contained Choice Close: Closing technique that allows a selection for quantity, color, size, etc. Example: *"Would you prefer black or gray?"*

CPE: (See: *Customer Premises Equipment*.)

CPI: Cost per inquiry.

Cross-Selling: Promotion of similar items in addition to the product originally requested. Examples would be: indices for notebooks, supplies for copiers, a stand for a typewriter.

CRT: (See: *Cathode Ray Tube*.)

CSR: Confusing title meaning either "Customer Sales Representative" (non-management) or "Communications Systems Representative" (management).

CTMS: Computerized Telephone Management System (not to be confused with database management). This equipment handles and reports on telephone traffic.

Customer: A company or individual who purchases products or services.

Customer Cycling: Periodic, planned customer recontact.

Customer Premises Equipment (CPE): Equipment that interfaces with the telephone network and physically resides at the user's location. Includes most, but not all, of the gear referred to as network channel terminating equipment.

Customer Profile: A history on a customer which includes relevant information (e.g., buying history, credit information, job title) on potential buyers.

Customer Service Representative (CSR): Anyone whose job it is to handle customer questions, complaints and concerns.

Database: Either a manual or electronic information base, stored in file cabinets or the memory of a computer.

Database Definition: The clear understanding between telemarketing management and database management as to what will be captured and displayed from the database.

Data Processing: Data manipulation to record, classify, sort, summarize, disseminate and store data. Can be manual or electronic, although the term typically refers to electronic processing.

Delivery (Voice): The method of presentation used (e.g., business-like, informal, formal, etc.).

Demographics: Vital statistics describing a population. Most commonly refers to such characteristics as title, occupation, age, etc.

Detailed Station Message Accounting (DSMA): A listing of numbers called, areas most often reached, etc. Used to expose and manage system abuses and determine optimum configurations.

Dial-Ahead Auto Dialing: Computer dials ahead based on anticipated TSR availability. The system is loaded with a dialing program that balances a number of statistical issues (dialing algorithm).

DIAL-IT 900 Service: A polling or message delivery service paid for by the caller.

Direct Distance Dialing (DDD): Long-distance calls placed without operator assistance.

Direct Inward Dialing (DID): A system allowing individual employees to be assigned individual access numbers to outside trunks connected to the company. Access numbers are usually bought in lots of 100.

Direct Mail: Mail that will be sent prior to or after a contact with a prospect or customer.

Direct Marketing: The process of moving goods and services from seller to buyer utilizing a database for tracking customers, analyzing results of advertising, studying purchasing performance and serving as a vehicle to continuing direct communication by mail or phone.

Direct Marketing Association (DMA): Trade association whose members are in the business of direct marketing.

Direct Response: Response to advertised messages. Also refers to advertising designed to elicit response.

Disk: A storage medium for digital data. Can be hard or floppy. Disks store information as magnetic pulses which are created by short bursts of voltage. Disk storage capacity is the amount of information usually measured in thousands or millions of characters.

Distributor: Any business that takes title to goods, warehouses them, and sells to other businesses.

DMA: (See: *Direct Marketing Association.*)

DMA, TMC: Direct Marketing Association, Telephone Marketing Council.

DOS: Acronym for Disk Operating System. A set of programs that instruct a disk-based computing system to schedule or supervise work, manage computer resources and operate or control peripheral devices.

Dot Matrix: A method used by some printers to transfer images to paper. Characters are made up of small dots.

Dumb Terminal: A CRT terminal that can receive and transmit data only. Does not have processing capabilities.

800 Service: Toll-free inbound long-distance service paid for by the call recipient.

Electronic Cloning: Ability to "clone" an organization's brightest sales people by using programmable sales dialogue. Customized CRT telephone scripts can handle complex branching, appropriate responses to questions/objections and time the closing as well. Electronic cloning combines the best of the sales reps with the "memory" of the computer.

Electronic Mail: Transmission and receipt of messages electronically, usually computer to computer or terminal to terminal.

Electronic Marketing: Goes beyond telemarketing to use more sophisticated database, market segmentation, reporting and selling techniques--all computer assisted. Among its support elements are high-speed data and facsimile transmission, word processing, on-line computers with CRT's, advanced telecommunications, remote display/printers and attendant software. Electronic marketing helps to determine the most appropriate distribution channels in terms of price, product and market.

Electronic Telephone Sales Center: Uses database management fully.

Electronic Top-Down Selling: After calling a test batch of various types and sizes of businesses, each market segment is categorized and ranked by sales potential. Qualification rate, sale rate and average order size are the determinants. After ranking assisted by a computer, sales reps begin selling from the "top down," calling on the most productive and profitable prospects first in a scientifically determined tier pattern.

Ergonomics: The science of matching the human form and psyche to the work habitat. Ergonomic chairs, equipment and work areas are considered essential in a professional telemarketing operation.

ESS: Electronic Switching Systems. Computerized central office equipment owned by the telephone company.

Exchange: All numbers within a given three-digit (prefix) area. Also known as an "NNX." Example: Randolph, New Jersey = 361-XXXX.

Facsimile (FAX): Transmission of pictures, maps, diagrams, etc., via the phone lines. The image is scanned at the transmitter, reconstructed at the receiving station and duplicated on paper.

FCC: (See: *Federal Communications Commission.*)

Feature: An inherent characteristic of a product or service, e.g., rapid release feature. Customers buy benefits, which are supported by features.

Federal Communications Commission (FCC): Board of commissioners appointed by the President under the Communications Act of 1934 with the authority to regulate all interstate telecommunications originating in the United States.

Fiber Optic Cable: Thin filaments of glass or other transparent materials sheathed in an insulator through which a light beam may be transmitted for long distances by means of multiple internal reflections. Used principally to transmit digital information.

Field Sales: A primary face-to-face sales strategy involving staff typically assigned to territories or sales areas. Compensation is usually, but not always, based on sales within the territory (commission).

File: A collection of specific information relating to a subject stored on a computer system's disk. Similar to manual file systems used in any office.

File Server: A device containing files which are shared by everyone connected to the local area network. File servers can offer anything from simple data storage to gateways and protocol conversion. A file server usually has software rules for allowing LAN users to get into and out of the files and databases on the server.

Follow-Up Contact: Any contact required to finalize a previous commitment or to close a case.

Foreign Central Office: A central office in the same exchange area but other than the office from which the customer is ordinarily provided telephone exchange service.

Foreign Exchange: Any other exchange than that in which the customer is located.

Foreign Exchange Service (FX): A long-distance service that allows the placing or receiving of calls in a

701

given area outside of the central office area for a flat monthly rate.

Formal Script: A verbatim presentation of a written script.

Fulfillment: The response by a business to a prospect. Includes letters, literature, samples or the product itself.

Guided Scripting: Using prompts or key words instead of word-for-word scripts.

Hardware: Physical equipment, as opposed to a computer program or software, e.g., mechanical, electrical, magnetic or electronic devices.

High-Potential/Immediate Need: Any case that requires immediate contact by the outside sales force.

Holding Time: The length of time a communication channel is in use for each transmission. Includes both message time and operating time.

Host: A computer system that provides computer service for a number of users, usually a mainframe.

Hotline: A specific inbound customer-service number dedicated to customer questions or concerns.

Hunt Group: An arrangement of a group of telephone lines such that a single telephone number is listed in the directories. A person dialing that listed number is automatically connected by the telephone switching equipment to an available line in that group. Only if all lines in the group are busy does the caller get a busy signal.

ICSMA: International Customer Service Manager's Association.

Inbound: Phone calls received by a telemarketing center.

Inbound Telemarketing: The handling of incoming telephone sales calls. Generally requires less sophistication on the part of the telephone sales rep than outbound telemarketing, because the interest already has been generated by broadcast advertising, direct mail or catalog.

Inbound Telesales: A department within a telemarketing operation devoted to the handling of incoming calls.

Incoming Specialist: A trained professional telephone specialist skilled at handling incoming order request and cross-selling or up-selling to close a case.

Independent Telephone Company: A telephone company not associated with AT&T, GTE, etc. There are 1,400 in the United States.

Informal Script: A device used to train TSR's in the art of the phone presentation. It is written out at first, and later the TSR's convert it to their own language.

In-House Telemarketing: Telemarketing carried out by a unit of the organization or corporation rather than some outside service bureau.

Inside Sales: A unit or function that is involved with handling inbound calls from customers to handle inquiries, expedite orders, provide quotes, process returned merchandise and take orders.

Intelligent Dialing: (See: *Dial-Ahead Auto Dialing.*)

Interconnect Vendor: A supplier of telephone equipment.

Interest-Gathering Statement: Follows the introduction and usually states the reason for the call. Often includes a benefit with a supporting feature.

Interface: A demarcation between two devices where the electrical signals, connectors, timing and handshaking meet.

International 800 Service: Allows person in one country to call toll-free to another country.

Introductory Statement: The first part of the call during which the TSR introduces him or herself and the organization.

A GLOSSARY OF TELEMARKETING TERMS

I/O: Abbreviation for Input/Output. Refers to the data transfer from the computer to peripheral devices.

Junk Phone Calls: Cold incoming sales calls, usually those received by consumers. Often symptoms of poorly targeted marketing, these calls are among the primary causes of the clamor for "asterisk" laws and other legal restrictions on telemarketing.

K: A standard quantity of measurement of computer storage. A "K" is loosely defined as 1,000 bytes. In actuality, it is 1,024 bytes (2^{10}).

Key System: A phone system with "keys" corresponding to outside lines. Pressing these keys gives access to the outside lines.

LAN: (See: *Local Area Network*.)

Language: A symbolic system for coding instructions to computers.

LATA: (See: *Local Access Transport Area*.)

LCR: (See: *Least-Cost Routing*.)

Lead: Someone who has expressed interest in, or inquired about a product or service.

Lead Communicator: A person designated by management as responsible for any kind of "special project" in a telephone sales operation. Usually considered a temporary supervisor for the special project only. Can also mean a communicator with on-going, part-time management responsibility. Often is the "substitute supervisor" when the regular supervisor is not available.

Lead Generation: The deliberate stimulation of leads.

Lead Qualification: The act of discerning, through probing, whether a target is a prospect. A call objective or function of an outbound or inbound call.

Lead TSR: (See: *Lead Communicator*.)

Leased Line: A line reserved for the exclusive use of a leasing customer without switching arrangements. Also called a private line.

Least-Cost Routing (LCR): A system that routes outgoing calls through the most cost-effective lines available.

Letter Quality: A type of computer printer output that approximates the print quality of a typewriter; a printer capable of producing such quality.

Line: A wire connected to the phone system or the circuit that connects the subscriber to the Central Office.

Line Capacity: The number of telephones a switch can handle.

List Acquisition: Either lease or purchase of lists from external services or the use of internal corporate lists.

List Management System: A database system that manages customer and prospect lists by merging/purging duplicates, allowing entry and editing of information and sorting/selecting data on the list.

Local Access Transport Area (LATA): One of 161 local telephone serving areas in the United States, generally encompassing the largest standard statistical metropolitan area. They are subdivisions established as a result of the Bell divestiture that now distinguishes local from long distance service. Circuits with both end points within the LATA (intra-LATA) are generally the sole responsibility of the local telephone company, while circuits that cross outside the LATA (inter-LATA) are passed on to an interexchange carrier.

Local Area Network (LAN): A data communications network spanning a limited geographical area (a few miles distance, at most). It provides communication between computers and peripherals, some switching to direct messages.

Local Calling Area: The area in which customers may call a local exchange without the payment of message toll charges.

Look-Up Service: A service specializing in adding telephone numbers to lists.

Loop: A local channel.

Mainframe: A large computer normally supplied complete with peripherals and software by a single large vendor, often with a closed architecture. Mainframes almost always use dumb terminals, connected in star configurations.

Management Information System (MIS): Automated or manual system providing management information and sales support information to TSR's and management.

Manual Telephone Sales Center: Completely paper-driven telephone sales center.

Marginal Account: Customer who, because of low volume or remote location, is uneconomical for calls by the field sales force.

Market: The collection of potential buyers for a particular product or service.

Market Identification: The establishment of criteria to predetermine specific markets that will be a primary target of a telemarketing project.

Marketing Mix: The collection of marketing strategies and techniques.

Marketing Strategy: The coordinated plan for selecting target markets, marketing mix, expenditures in order to reach a marketing objective.

Megabyte: The basic unit of mass storage and data transfer rate (1,048,576 bytes).

Merge-Purge: The process of combining lists while eliminating duplication.

Message Rate Service: Monthly service that provides a specified number of local calls before an additional charge is added for calls in excess of that number.

Message Unit: A unit of time used to measure a length of a local toll call. Or, it could be that the unit equals *one* call.

Microcomputer: A computer which uses a microprocessor for its CPU. (See: *Central Processing Unit.*)

Minicomputer: A small or medium-sized computer accessed by dumb terminals. A minicomputer is larger and more powerful than personal computers, and is usually used by more than one person.

Modem: A device that converts (*MOdulates*) serial digital data from a transmitting terminal to a signal suitable for transmission over a telephone (analog) channel. At the other end another modem reconverts (*DEModulates*) the analog for use by the computer.

Monaural: Single-ear/channel headset.

Monitoring: The practice of supervisory monitoring of TSR conversations, usually done as part of TSR training and/or quality control. Also known as *Service Observing.*

Multiple Contact Case: More than one contact with a prospect or customer is needed to complete or close a case.

Multiple Tasking: A computer's ability to perform multiple tasks at once without interrupting the use of the system.

New Case: Telephone contact yet to be made.

NNX Number: Three-digit Central Office or exchange number.

Objections(s): Reason(s) given by the prospect to the TSR as to why he/she is not interested in the product or service presented.

OCC: (See: *Other Common Carrier.*)

On-Line: Direct connection to a computer, working in real time.

A GLOSSARY OF TELEMARKETING TERMS

Open-Ended Question: Eliciting responses in the respondent's own words.

Open Territories: Those not assigned to a specific field sales representative.

Operations Manager: Person responsible for the day-to-day management of a telephone sales center. Includes guidance, motivation, and coaching of supervisors, lead communicators, communicators and incoming specialists.

Operations Review: An annual or semi-annual review of the entire telephone sales center and strategic plan of a company.

Order Processing: The simple process of recording and processing orders. Can be combined with more complex telemarketing techniques such as cross- and up-selling.

Original Equipment Manufacturer (OEM): Supplier of components to a final assembler. Final assembler usually attaches the name to the product and does the marketing/distribution (e.g., a supplier of disk drive components to a computer manufacturer is an OEM supplier).

Other Common Carrier (OCC): Usually applied to companies offering long-distance service in competition with AT&T.

Outbound: Calls placed by the telemarketing center.

Outbound Telemarketing: The initiation of outgoing telephone sales calls. Usually requires more sophistication than an incoming call program because more "selling" is required, greater sales rep frustration is involved and there is a greater risk of telephone sales burnout.

Outbound Telesales: A pro-active approach to a given market by a planned program to develop leads and/ or sales.

PABX: (See: *Private Automatic Branch Exchange.*)

Paraphrase: Basically, a restatement by the TSR. A rewording of the prospect/customer's previous statements.

Partial Electronic Telephone Sales Center: A combination of both manual and electronic telephone sales center operation.

PBX: (See: *Private Branch Exchange.*)

Pending Case: A case where an initial contact has been made and the communicator is awaiting response of someone else, either intra-company or by the called party.

Performance Evaluation: The periodic review of a telephone sales person's performance by first-line supervisors, usually done weekly and monthly.

Peripheral: Equipment which is outside and additional to the main computer (e.g., printer, modem).

Phonathon: A fund raiser done via telephone.

Phone Power: Concepts of phone usage designed to increase efficiency and/or reduce operating costs. Usually includes a low-cost sales and management training offered by AT&T.

Phonophobia: Fear of the telephone or its use.

Pilot: A test program used to demonstrate the feasibility of a full-scale telemarketing program.

Power Dialing: (See: *Dial-Ahead Auto Dialing.*)

Pre-Call Planning: Call preparation for maximum effectiveness.

Predictive Dialing: (See: *Dial-Ahead Auto Dialing.*)

Pre-Recorded Message: Any message recorded prior to a call and played back during an inbound or outbound call.

Presentation: Talking to a qualified decision maker about the call objective.

Preview Dialing: (See: *Self-Paced Auto Dialing*.)

Printer: A device used to print data output from a computer.

Private Automatic Branch Exchange (PABX): An automatic switch connecting a number of telephone sets with a public network (automated switchboard).

Private Branch Exchange (PBX): A switch connecting a number of telephone sets with a public network, commonly known as a switchboard.

Private Line: A leased line, a non-switched circuit.

Pro-Active: Causing an activity to happen by plan (opposed to "reactive").

Probing Sequence: The art of using open- and closed-ended questions to qualify and determine a prospect/customer's needs.

Program: A series of instructions which tell a computer how to perform a particular task.

Prompts: Outline format to provide a progressive linear track for the telephone sales rep to follow. Key statements and responses to repetitive questions/objections should be pre-planned and well-rehearsed.

Prospect: A potential customer, client, contributor or member.

Psychographics: Life style and attitude statistics.

PUC/BPU: Public Utilities Commission or Board of Public Utilities. Both are state regulatory activities.

Qualified Lead: Prospects known to want/need a specific product or service, and able to purchase same.

Queue: The collection of inbound calls held by an ACD in the order in which they arrive, pending the next available TSR.

RAM (Random Access Memory): A chip or collection of chips where data can be entered, read and erased. RAM loses its contents when the power supply is interrupted.

Rate of Speech: Words spoken per unit of time.

Ratios: The comparison of numbers in telemarketing (e.g., attempts to presentations, attempts to closes, presentations to closes).

RCF: (See: *Remote Call Forwarding*.)

Reactive: Responding to events (e.g., inbound calls) without prior planning or procedures.

Reactive Telemarketing: Buying initiated by the customer.

Referral: Using the credentials of others, with their permission, to create confidence between callers on the first call.

Remote Call Forwarding (RCF): Toll-free calling that reroutes a call from one city to a city designated without the caller's awareness of the process.

Request for Proposal (RFP): A document defining specific purchase requirements and soliciting responses from vendors.

Response: Incoming telephone contact generated by media advertising or promotion.

Response Curve: Anticipated incoming contact volume, including peaks and declines, covering hours, days, weeks or months.

Response Rate: A ratio of responses to the estimated audience of the promotion/advertisement. Percentage of return.

RFP: (See: *Request for Proposal*.)

Rifle Cataloging: Sending catalogs only to prospects qualified previously by phone. Often includes phone follow up.

A GLOSSARY OF TELEMARKETING TERMS

RMP (Recorded Message Player): Often used with an auto-dialer.

Roll Out: Full-blown telemarketing effort after initial testing and program modifications are made.

Sale: A formal agreement to buy, make an appointment or any other definition of a sale as determined by the objective of a case.

Sales Conversion Rate: Ratio of sales to calls (inbound or outbound).

Sales Message: The structure of stating features and benefits.

Sales Presentation: Structured anatomy of an offer describing how the product or service works.

Sales Techniques: Specific ways and methods used by telephone sales representatives to overcome the lack of face-to-face contact with prospects/customers (e.g., tone, volume, rate of speech, etc.).

Scientific Marketing: Uses many of the sophisticated elements of direct mail, telemarketing, electronic marketing, electronic cloning and computerized top-down selling. At its heart, provides marketing control, measurability and analysis.

Screening: The process of managing incoming calls to a given executive or contact, usually carried out by a secretary.

Script: A prepared textual presentation that is closely followed by TSR's as a tool to convey their telephone sales message.

Sectional Center Facility (SCF): Area designated by the first three ZIP code digits.

Seeding: The process of inserting dummy names in a rented list to check for unauthorized usage.

Segmentation: Breaking a market into coherent groups.

Self-Paced Auto Dialing: The cursor on a video display terminal can be moved to the telephone number field and, with a single key stroke, the identified number is called.

Server: A computer providing a service to LAN users such as shared access to a file system, a printer or an electronic mail system. Usually a combination of hardware and software.

Service Observing: (See: *Monitoring*.)

Service Representative: Person who takes orders for telephone service and explains the accompanying other charges and credits (OCC). Trained to deal with basic telephone questions.

SIC (Standard Industrial Classification): A seven-digit code system defined by the U.S. Department of Commerce and used to identify line of business activity.

SMDR (Station Message Detail Recorder): Add-on equipment that measures telephone activities by station.

Soft-Referral: Encouraging a contact to respond, when needed, to answer questions that may arise concerning a presentation, but only if needed.

Software: The intangible set of instructions used to operate a computer, including the operating system, utilities, languages and applications.

Software Analysis: The process of determining exactly what the software requirements are in a telesales operation.

Source Identification: Feature of ACD systems presenting TSR's with an audible indication of the origin location of incoming calls.

Speed Dial: A phone network feature allowing the access of frequently dialed numbers through one- or two-button dialing.

Standard Industrial Classification: (See: *SIC*.)

Start-Up Program: A telemarketing venture just beginning.

ENCYCLOPEDIA OF TELEMARKETING

Station: A telephone.

Station Message Detail Recording: (See: *SMDR.*)

Suspect: Someone who has potential to become a prospect.

System Administrator: A person who has full responsibility for taking care of a computer system.

Taping: The act of recording the call between prospect/customer and TSR, usually pre-announced and performed by the TSR.

Target: The person to whom the call is directed.

Target Market: A market group or segment selected with respect to its high potential for buying a product or service.

Tariff: The policies and laws governing telephone as set down by the FCC and the PUC/BPU.

Telco: An acronym for "telephone company."

Teleadvertising: Making calls to various market areas in an attempt to qualify and sell. As this selling attempt occurs, a residual product or service awareness is created for prospects. Even after the initial efforts are made, prospect call-ins noticeably increase. A doubling of the prior call-in rates often occurs six to 12 months after the initial outbound calling.

Telecommunication: Any process that permits the passage from a sender to one or more receivers of information of any nature delivered in any usable form (printed copy, fixed or moving pictures, visible or audible signals, etc.) by means of any electromagnetic system (electrical transmission by wire, radio, optical transmission, guided waves, etc.). Includes telegraphy, telephony, video-telephony, data transmission, etc.

Telecommuter: A TSR working at home.

Telecommuting: Linking home-based TSR's to the office by telephone and computer.

Telecomputer: A term sometimes applied to ADRMP's machines which will dial numbers automatically, play pre-recorded messages and record responses.

Telefocus Marketing: An integrated process that combines telemarketing, direct mail and video brochures. It uses the inherent strengths of each direct marketing discipline, while leveraging each other for maximum marketing efficiency.

Telemarketing: A controllable and measurable method of professional marketing using telecommunications and computers. Its basic objective is to increase bottom-line profitability while reducing the cost of selling and improving market share.

Telemarketing Insensitive: Any medium used to advertise a product or service that does not properly highlight a telephone number.

Telemarketing Project: A telesales program designed to accomplish a specific part of management's strategic plan.

Telemarketing Service Vendor: Another name for a telemarketing service bureau or agency, someone who sells telemarketing as a service to clients.

Telemod: The formalized communicator work area that includes desk, chair, storage, files and all work-related tools.

Telephone Bucket Shop: An unsophisticated telephone selling operation. Often characterized by noisy offices, unskilled personnel and questionable sales practices.

Telephone List Appending: The process of adding phone numbers to mailing lists.

Telephone Marketing Council: A special interest industry group within the Direct Marketing Association, formed to develop ethical guidelines for telephone marketing practices and to give members a forum for staying on top of rates, tariffs and other key issues.

Telephone Preference Service (TPS): A Direct Marketing Association program which allows consumers to remove their names from a majority of telemarketing lists at a single request.

Telephone Sales: The implementation of the telemarketing plan.

Telephone Sales Representative (TSR): Agents who market and sell by telephone. Could also be referred to as "telemarketers."

Telephone Sales Supervisor (TSS): A person who oversees TSR's.

Telephone Sales Techniques: Formalized methods that structure the entire sales process through the use of proven telesales experience.

Telephone Service Center: (See: *TSC.*)

Telephony: Generic term describing voice telecommunication.

Telesales: A function dedicated to receiving or making outgoing contact by telephone. A non-management task.

Terminal: A device used by an operator to communicate with a computer. Usually consists of a video screen and a keyboard.

Test: A period of time during which a minimum of 100 cases are completed for analysis and management decision as to whether or not a particular project or program is appropriate.

Test Market: A market in which a new product or service is tested and where offers are evaluated.

Third-Party Telemarketing: (See: *TSB.*)

Third Party Unit: A service bureau that makes calls for hire, also known as a contract unit.

Tie Line: A private line communication channel of the type provided by communications common carriers for linking two or more PBX's or systems together.

Tight Leads: High-quality leads demonstrating significant motivation by responding.

Time Zone Sequencing: Organizing outgoing call lists by time zones for efficiency and greatest call productivity.

Toll-Free 800 Service: Inbound WATS service paid for by the recipient.

Traffic: The number of calls made or received per hour, day, etc., on a single line or trunk of a telephone system.

Transition Period: Generally referred to when a telephone sales center is migrating from a manual operation to an electronic operation.

Trunk: A telephone circuit terminated only in a PBX or ACD.

Trunk Capacity: The number of trunks connected at a given site.

Trunk Queue: The first-come, first-served line-up of incoming calls awaiting an available line.

TSB: A Telemarketing Service Bureau, a firm that offers incoming or outgoing (or both) telesales support to another organization.

TSC: Telephone Sales Center. A department responsible for making and receiving phone sales contacts.

TSR: (See: *Telephone Sales Representative.*)

Turnkey System: A term referring to provision of a complete system/operation. In telemarketing, a "turnkey system" would be a packaged operation, complete from design to implementation.

Turnover: The rate at which employees enter and leave an organization, usually expressed as the ratio of new replacements to total employment per unit of time.

ENCYCLOPEDIA OF TELEMARKETING

Two-Pass Program: Includes both a telephone qualification call and a follow-up contact. The first pass is a survey, which helps to obtain qualifying data on products and/or services marketed by a company. A second-pass call is then made to only those prospects who meet minimum prospect parameters.

Uniform Call Distributor (UCD): A routing system which assures calls are distributed to agents on a basis other than simple availability.

Up-Selling: Attempt to sell more appropriate, a more feature- or benefit-laden, or more expensive product than the one originally requested by the customer. Also, up-selling can be simply increasing the quantity ordered.

User: A firm that uses telemarketing in its overall marketing program, whether it is executed in-house or by a TSB.

Value-Added Services: Usually services offered by distributors to users (e.g., preventive maintenance, assembly, repair, etc.).

Video Display Terminal (VDT): A computer's display or the display on a terminal.

Videologs: Full-motion video catalogs used as either a complement to or an extension of print catalogs.

Videotex: An interactive data communication application designed to allow unsophisticated users to converse with a remote database, enter data for transactions and retrieve textual and graphics information for display on subscriber television sets or (typically) low-cost terminals.

Voice Mail: Hardware and software which allows voice interaction between the caller and the device, thence allowing retrieval of digitized voice messages by another caller or the organization.

Voice Recognition: Recognition of meaning and acting upon words of a human voice by a computer.

Voice Response Technology (VRT): (See: *Audiotex*.)

Walking Marketing Survey: Continuous monitoring of telephone and coordinated activities via computer reporting. The evolution of customer and prospect database creation can be tracked continuously, thereby providing an ongoing marketing survey.

Wide Area Telecommunication Service (WATS): Specially discounted long-distance service based on call volume.

Word Processing: An application program that enables the user automatically to create, edit and output text files.

Work Station: Input/output device at which an operator works. Usually a personal computer, sometimes a terminal. A device used to send data to or receive data from a computer.

ZIP Code: A five to nine-digit code identifying more than 40,000 postal regions in the United States. The term is a registered trademark of the U.S. Postal Service.

Index

711

INDEX